www.routledgesw.com

Alice A. Lieberman, The University of Kansas, Series Editor

An authentic breakthrough in social work education . . .

New Directions in Social Work is an innovative, integrated series of texts, website, and interactive case studies for generalist courses in the Social Work curriculum at both undergraduate and graduate levels. Instructors will find everything they need to build a comprehensive course that allows students to meet course outcomes, with these unique features:

- All texts, interactive cases, and test materials are **linked to the 2015 CSWE Policy and Accreditation Standards (EPAS).**
- **One Web portal with easy access** for instructors and students from any computer—no codes, no CDs, no restrictions. Go to www. routledgesw.com and discover.
- **The series is flexible and can be easily adapted for use in online distance-learning courses as well as hybrid and bricks-and-mortar courses.**
- Each text and the website can be used **individually** or as an **entire series** to meet the needs of any social work program.

TITLES IN THE SERIES

Social Work and Social Welfare: An Invitation, Fourth Edition by Marla Berg-Weger

Human Behavior in the Social Environment, Fourth Edition by Anissa Taun Rogers

Research for Effective Social Work Practice, Third Edition by Judy L. Krysik and Jerry Finn

Social Policy for Effective Practice: A Strengths Approach, Third Edition by Rosemary K. Chapin

The Practice of Generalist Social Work, Third Edition by Julie Birkenmaier, Marla Berg-Weger, and Martha P. Dewees

Human Behavior in the Social Environment

Fourth Edition
by Anissa Taun Rogers, University of Portland

In this book and companion custom website you will find:

- A comprehensive overview of the issues related to human behavior and the social environment that are important to understand for practice, updated with current and relevant information on important topics in social work practice and expanded to clarify complex issues. Additional relevant content, contemporary theories, and intervention modalities have been added and incorporated throughout the text to keep students up to date with what is happening in the field.

- Careful organization of chapters to first present foundational theoretical perspectives on the human condition, and then provide information on basic facets of human development, encouraging students to use conceptual lenses to inform their practice with individuals at different stages of life. The organization of the chapters also helps students better understand how contemporary theories and approaches to issues stem from foundational theories and how they can be used to inform work with clients.

- Particular emphasis on the ways in which poverty, diversity, and strengths affect human development and behavior.

- The opportunity to see how the concepts fit into social work practice using case examples that open each chapter and are referred to throughout the chapter.

- Interactive case studies at www.routledgesw.com/cases: Six easy-to-access fictional cases with dynamic characters and situations that students can easily reach from any computer and that provide a "learning by doing" format unavailable with any other text. Your students will have an advantage unlike any other they will experience in their social work training.

- A wealth of instructor-only resources at www.routledgesw.com/hbse that provide full-text readings that link to the concepts presented in each of the chapters; a complete bank of objective and essay-type test items, all linked to current CSWE EPAS (Council on Social Work Education Educational Policy and Accreditation Standards); PowerPoint presentations to help students master key concepts; annotated links to a treasure trove of social work assets on the Internet; and a forum inviting all instructors using books in the series to communicate with each other and share ideas to improve teaching and learning.

- Ideal for use in *online* as well as *hybrid* course instruction—in addition to traditional "bricks and mortar" classes.

Human Behavior in the Social Environment

The fourth edition of *Human Behavior in the Social Environment* takes a life course perspective to give a concise, compact treatment of human behavior. The text also comes with a companion set of readings and five unique cases that encourage your students to learn by doing and to apply their knowledge of human behavior to best practices.

Go to www.routledgesw.com to explore the cases and additional resources.

Anissa Taun Rogers, PhD, MSW, MA, LCSW is Professor of Social Work at the University of Portland in Portland, Oregon, where she serves as Director of the Social Work Program and Co-Director of the Gender and Women's Studies Minor. She teaches courses across the social work curriculum as well as courses on gender, gerontology, sexuality, and international social work. She also is registered, with her dog, Sookie, as a pet therapy team, working primarily with older adults and hospice patients.

Human Behavior in the Social Environment

Perspectives on Development and the Life Course

Fourth Edition

Anissa Taun Rogers
University of Portland, Oregon

Routledge
Taylor & Francis Group

NEW YORK AND LONDON

First edition published 2013 by Routledge
This edition published 2016
by Routledge
711 Third Avenue, New York, NY 10017

and by Routledge
2 Park Square, Milton Park, Abingdon, Oxon OX14 4RN

Routledge is an imprint of the Taylor & Francis Group, an informa business

British Library Cataloguing in Publication Data
A catalogue record for this book is available from the British Library

Library of Congress Cataloging-in-Publication Data
Rogers, Anissa, author.
Human behavior in the social environment / by Anissa Rogers. -- Fourth edition.
pages cm. -- (New directions in social work)
Includes bibliographical references and index.
ISBN 978-1-138-81950-4 (hardback : alk. paper) -- ISBN 978-1-138-81951-1 (pbk. : alk. paper) -- ISBN 978-1-315-74439-1 (ebook) 1. Social service--Psychological aspects. 2. Human behavior. 3. Developmental psychology. 4. Social psychology. I. Title.
HV40.R664 2015
302--dc23
2015029615

ISBN: 978-1-138-81950-4 (hbk)
ISBN: 978-1-138-81951-1 (pbk)
ISBN: 978-1-315-74439-1 (ebk)

Typeset in ITC Stone Serif by
Servis Filmsetting Ltd, Stockport, Cheshire

Printed in Canada

To all social workers, both students and those in the field, who helped to shape my ideas and inspired me personally and professionally.

BRIEF CONTENTS

DETAILED CONTENTS

PREFACE

MAJOR CHANGES TO THE FOURTH EDITION

Like the last three editions of *Human Behavior in the Social Environment,* this latest edition provides students with an overview of the issues related to human behavior and the social environment that are important to understand for practice. This information has been updated to offer students current and relevant information on important topics in social work practice and expanded to help students understand the complexity of the issues they will face in the field, including how poverty, diversity, and strengths affect human development and behavior.

Additional important and relevant issues, theories, and treatment modalities have been added and incorporated into the chapters to help students understand how foundational theoretical and empirical knowledge have shaped contemporary knowledge in, and approaches to, social work and to give students up-to-date information on work being done in the field. For example, additional research and content have been added to explore how issues at all stages of life affect different populations, and new evidence-based research on many issues has been added throughout. Several new theories and perspectives have been added throughout the book such as critical practice theory and person-centered, participant directed models. Content has been updated to reflect changes in many areas including the DSM; PTSD; grandparenting; discipline approaches; HIV, AIDS, and STIs; caregiving issues for different populations; the effects of poverty and stress on the brain; changing views on death, anxiety, schizophrenia, intelligence, and disabilities; health disparities for different groups including transgender individuals; and expanded definitions and views on privilege, racism, and microaggressions. A new, final chapter has been added that explores the future of social work and some of the emerging issues the profession will face.

For the new editions of all five books in the New Directions in Social Work series, each addressing a foundational course in the social work curriculum, the publisher offers a uniquely distinctive teaching strategy that revolves around the print book but offers much more than the traditional text experience. The series website www.routledgesw.com leads to custom websites coordinated with each text and offering a variety of features to support instructors as you integrate the many facets of an education in social work.

At www.routledgesw.com/hbse, you will find a wealth of resources to help you create a dynamic, experiential introduction to social work for your students. The website houses companion readings linked to key concepts in each chapter, along with questions to encourage further thought and discussion; six interactive fictional cases with accompanying exercises that bring to life the concepts covered in the book, readings, and classroom discussions; a bank of exam questions (both objective and open-ended) and PowerPoint presentations; annotated links to a treasure trove of articles, videos, and Internet sites; and an online forum inviting all instructors using texts in the series to share ideas to improve teaching and learning.

The fourth edition contains a set of Quick Guides, which are meant to be useful for students engaged in field work. They appear in the book as well as at the website for the book. They can be printed out and carried along for reference.

You may find most useful a set of sample syllabi showing how *Human Behavior in the Social Environment,* fourth edition, can be used in a variety of course structures. A master syllabus demonstrates how the text and website used together through the course satisfy the 2015 CSWE EPAS.

The interactive cases offer students rich and detailed examples of complex situations they will face in their work as well as additional opportunities to apply theory and concepts to real-world situations. Other cases provide students opportunities to apply concepts to mezzo- and macro-level situations and to better understand how individual issues are interconnected to and impacted by larger, more macro issues.

The organization and content of this book and companion website are such that students at the bachelor's and master's levels of their social work education can utilize the knowledge gained from studying the material; specifically, this knowledge can be applied to both generalist and specialized practice. The fourth edition, along with the new supplemental chapters, can be used throughout a two-semester sequence as well as a one-semester course, and the integrated supplements and resources on the Web make the text especially amenable for online distance-learning and hybrid courses.

For example, a supplemental online chapter on the autism spectrum can be used to help students learn more about the disorder, spark in-depth discussions about the causes and treatments for autism, and help students understand the ways in which it might impact their practice. Readings (and accompanying questions) have been specifically added to offer more breadth and depth to selected topics, giving students and instructors options about which topics to explore more thoroughly and to provide opportunities to explore the diversity and complexity that are associated with the social issues with which social workers grapple. These readings can also be used to help students with more self-directed learning in areas about which they are particularly interested and may want to explore further beyond the scope of the material that is normally covered in the course.

ORGANIZATION OF THE BOOK

The chapters of this book are arranged first to give students an overview of the content, next to offer brief discussions of theoretical perspectives on the human condition, and then to provide information on basic facets of human development. Chapters 1 through 5 expose students to theoretical thinking and why it is important in social work as well as how it can help them to organize their thinking about clients and the issues they present in practice. Chapters 6 through 12 introduce students to important developmental, social, and cultural issues related to specific phases of life that are often relevant to practice. These chapters present developmental information extending from before conception into old age and encourage students to consider how development on biological, psychological, social, and cultural levels can impact individuals, families, communities, and social institutions. Exploring the various dynamic interactions that occur between the individual and the environment will help students to understand these interactions from theoretical and practice perspectives. Additionally, Chapters 6 through 12 offer discussions on relevant theoretical models and treatment modalities, grounded in theoretical perspectives introduced in Chapters 1 through 5, that are often used to better understand and work with specific issues and tasks faced by people in different developmental time frames. Chapter 13 explores broad, contemporary and future issues that will pose challenges and opportunities for social workers and their clients such as climate change, demographic shifts, and health and economic disparities.

The following paragraphs briefly introduce each of the chapters included in this book, with emphasis on the updated content.

Chapter 1

Human Behavior and the Social Work Profession offers a detailed discussion about why thinking about human behavior within the social environment is so important to social work education and to the profession. It will give students a sense of why they were asked to learn all those theories that were presented to them in other classes as well as all the other information that did not seem relevant to their major. The goal of the first chapter is to answer for students the questions, How does all this fit together, and why is it relevant to my work with clients? It also helps students understand how this knowledge base fits with CSWE's education policies. Finally, the first chapter will set the context for the rest of the book and help students to think about how to approach the information.

The next four chapters give students an overview of the theoretical concepts often used by social workers to help them make sense of the interactions between human behavior and the social environment.

Chapter 2

Lenses for Conceptualizing Problems and Interventions: The Person in the Environment presents broadly based, comprehensive theoretical models—for example, the biopsychosocial approach, systems theory, and the strengths perspective—that tend to be used frequently in generalist practice. These theories, though often borrowed from other disciplines, lend themselves well to social work because they address constructs of problem conceptualization and intervention that are unique to the profession. Chapter 2 is designed to give students a base on which to incorporate more specific theories discussed in the following chapters.

Chapter 3

Lenses for Conceptualizing Problems and Interventions: Biopsychosocial Dimensions provides an overview of some specific theories that come out of psychology and related fields. These theories help students to think about how and why we become the people we are. Students will encounter theories related to physical, emotional, and cognitive development as well as ways to think about how we learn in both individual and social contexts. Students will also learn how the brain, genetics, neurobiological processes, and the endocrine systems shape and affect behavior.

Chapter 4

Lenses for Conceptualizing Problems and Interventions: Sociocultural Dimensions takes a look at how societies function and how individuals are affected by the order and purpose of various social institutions. Each of the theories discussed in this chapter has a distinctive "slant" on the way in which it attempts to explain society, which in turn affects the way the social worker explains personal problems. Learning about the theories covered in Chapter 4 will give students an opportunity to think about the larger society and the ways in which its structure affects the work done in the profession. Additional material on theories and related issues was added to this chapter to expand students' thinking in these realms.

Chapter 5

Lenses for Conceptualizing Problems and Interventions: Social Change Dimensions continues the discussion on the broader context of human lives and problems. It explores theories that address the social context in which we live and ways in which we can effect change to better our lives. Chapter 5 explores the problems of social injustice that affect people individually but that are often rooted in larger social contexts. These theories help students to think about how personal issues are often intertwined with social and political issues, and why addressing them often requires social action to change lives on the individual level.

The remaining chapters address particular stages in life.

Chapter 6

Pre-Pregnancy and Prenatal Issues offers information on fetal development and some of the issues that clients may present with during a pregnancy and after birth. For example, students explore topics of low birth weight, planned and unplanned pregnancies, and hazards to fetal development. Students also explore familial and environmental issues such as access to health care, workplace policies, and international issues affecting family planning, with a focus on some of the ethical dilemmas posed by prenatal testing and other related health care situations. Students will find updated research on various topics and a discussion on abortion.

Chapter 7

Development in Infancy and Early Childhood exposes students to physical, psychological, and emotional developmental issues in early childhood and some of the issues that can affect clients and their families during this stage of development. It discusses theoretical perspectives on attachment that are pertinent to this stage of life as well as recent research in areas such as autism, parenting, child abuse, child care, and policies affecting children and families.

Chapter 8

Development in Middle Childhood exposes students to developmental processes of children in this age range and presents pertinent information on related individual, familial, and social issues. Debates and updated information on areas such as intelligence and intelligence testing, learning disabilities, parental discipline, gay and lesbian parenting, divorce and remarriage, and the effects of media are included. Students are also introduced to theory on play in this chapter.

Chapter 9

Development in Adolescence covers developmental considerations of this life stage and the various issues that clients are likely to deal with at this age. Issues such as eating disorders, self-esteem, pregnancy, sexual identity development, substance abuse, and suicide are discussed, as are issues around sex education, violence, and heterosexism and homophobia. Students are introduced to theories on moral and sexual identity development, which are likely to be pertinent to their work with clients at this age.

Chapter 10

Development in Early Adulthood covers the continued physical and cognitive development into adulthood and issues that people at this life stage are likely to face, such as mental illness, disability, and problems with spirituality. Theory around spirituality development and an expanded discussion on spirituality are included in this chapter. Domestic violence, sexism, sexual harassment, and related social policies are also discussed.

Chapter 11

Development in Middle Adulthood explores continued development as we age and explores in depth some of the physical and cognitive changes that can occur, as well as issues these changes may raise. Topics such as immigration, menopause and the male climacteric, health care and chronic illness, and marriage and love are explored. A section on health disparities highlights problems that some minority groups face with regard to chronic illness. Retirement and theories surrounding retirement are discussed, as are issues around ageism.

Chapter 12

Development in Late Adulthood discusses developmental issues in older age and continued physical and cognitive changes that take place as we age. In this chapter, students are exposed to various theories of aging and how they can be used to conceptualize work with older clients. Discussions on spirituality, depression, sexuality, grief and loss, and issues for gay and lesbian elders are included, as are topics surrounding grandparenting, caregiving, living situations, end-of-life care, and social policy issues impacting older adults.

Chapter 13

Looking Forward: Challenges and Opportunities for the Social Work Profession explores emerging trends and issues that are affecting or will affect social workers and their clients. This chapter helps students think about current and further challenges that will change the shape of problems clients face and the ways in which the profession approaches these problems. The chapter also explores the opportunities that will be created in the wake of these trends. Issues that are discussed in this chapter include climate change, growing health and economic disparities, demographic shifts, technological advances, global violence, and shifting cultural views on social issues.

INTERACTIVE CASES

The website www.routledgesw.com/cases presents six unique, in-depth, interactive, fictional cases with dynamic characters and real-life situations that students can easily access from any computer. They provide a "learning by doing" format unavailable with any other text. Your students will have an advantage unlike any other they will experience in their social work training. Each of the interactive cases uses text, graphics, and video to help students learn about engagement, assessment, intervention, and evaluation and termination at multiple levels of social work practice. The "My Notebook" feature allows students to take and save notes, type in written responses to tasks, and share their work with classmates and instructors by email. These interactive cases allow you to integrate the readings and classroom discussions:

The Sanchez Family: Systems, Strengths, and Stressors The 10 individuals in this extended Latino family have numerous strengths but are faced with a variety of challenges. Students will have the opportunity to experience the phases of the social work intervention, grapple with ethical dilemmas, and identify strategies for addressing issues of diversity.

Riverton: A Community Conundrum Riverton is a small Midwest city in which the social worker lives and works. The social worker identifies an issue that presents her community with a challenge. Students and instructors can work together to develop strategies for engaging, assessing, and intervening with the citizens of the social worker's neighborhood.

Carla Washburn: Loss, Aging, and Social Support Students will get to know Carla Washburn, an older African–American woman who finds herself living alone after the loss of her grandson and in considerable pain from a recent accident. In this case, less complex than the Sanchez Family, students will apply their growing knowledge of gerontology and exercise the skills of culturally competent practice.

RAINN: Rape Abuse and Incest National Network The RAINN Online Hotline links callers to local Rape Crisis Centers and hospitals, as well as other services. In addition, rape crisis telephone hotlines have played an important role in extending services to those in communities in which services are not available. Students will learn how and why this national hotline was developed; they will evaluate both qualitative and quantitative data to assess how the program can better achieve its goals.

Hudson City: An Urban Community Affected by Disaster Hudson City has just been devastated by Hurricane Diane, a category four hurricane with wind speeds of 140 miles per hour. Students will take up the role of a social worker who also resides in the community, who has been tasked with finding workable solutions to a variety of problems with diverse clients systems. Students will learn about disaster response and how to focus on many clients at once.

Brickville: Families and Communities Consider Transitions Brickville is a low-income community faced with a development proposal that would dramatically change the community. Students will take the role of a social worker who lives in the community and works for a community development corporation. Students will learn about community development and approaches that can be used to empower community members.

This book takes full advantage of the interactive element as a unique learning opportunity by including exercises that require students to go to the Web and use the cases. To maximize the learning experience, you may want to start the course by asking your students to explore each case by activating each button. The more the students are familiar with the presentation of information and the locations of the individual case files, the Case Study Tools, and the questions and tasks contained within each phase of the case, the better they will be able to integrate the text with the online practice component.

IN SUM

When presented as separate issues, all of the aforementioned developmental topics can seem overwhelming to students, particularly when they realize they have to keep at hand all their knowledge when working with clients. However, all of these topics, as well as other topics that are discussed, are set in a framework that will help students to think about the types of problems their clients might be likely to face at different phases in life. Students will also learn that organizing their knowledge about these areas into a theoretical context that "makes sense" to them will help them to manage the seemingly endless stream of information at their disposal. Ultimately, then, students will become more and more proficient at applying concepts to client problems. Meanwhile, students can enjoy the process of learning about them.

Being an effective social worker means being able to understand the complexities of human behavior, the societies and cultures in which we live, and the interplay between them. Being an effective social worker also means having a solid grounding in various disciplines, such as psychology, sociology, and human biology. It means possessing a well-rounded education and an ability to apply this knowledge to the myriad client problems and situations that students will face in the profession. This edition is intended to help students understand this complexity in the field and to help them gain the knowledge and critical thinking skills they will need to practice social work.

ACKNOWLEDGMENTS

I owe my gratitude to all the social work students I have known since the beginning of my career, for their questions, musings, and insights, and for pushing me to think about what it means to be a social worker. They are the inspiration for this book. I would like to extend my thanks to Tara Benavente and Patricia Stein, graduates of the Social Work Program at the University of Portland, who gave a great deal of their time and energy to help me with revisions of this book. Similarly, Rayne Funk, administrative assistant to the Social Work Program, was extremely helpful in the production of this book. Without her, most of my work would be impossible. I would also like to give a heartfelt thank you to Dr Joseph Gallegos, my former colleague at the University of Portland, for all his support and mentorship. And for his support, I would like to thank Michael Andrews, Dean of the College of Arts and Sciences.

A big thank you goes to Samantha Barbaro and Elsa Peterson for their time, energy, and insights as well as their editorial and writing assistance. The project coordinator, Alice Lieberman, and the other authors of the book series, Rosemary Chapin, Marla Berg-Weger, Jerry Finn, and Judy Krysik have been great sources of inspiration and motivation. I have appreciated their feedback and insights throughout the process of writing this book. I am grateful to the editors and staff at Routledge, whose input was invaluable in helping me to move the book forward in a meaningful way, and to the reviewers of the book:

Patricia O'Brien, University of Illinois at Chicago

Pamela Saulsberry, University of Louisiana at Monroe

Belinda Bruster, Florida Gulf Coast University

Martha Sheridan, Gallaudet University

Hazel Arthur, Lipscomb University

Sandra Naeger, Saint Louis University

Teri Kennedy, Arizona State University

Barbara Palantone, Eastern New Mexico University

Danilea Werner, Auburn University

Bill Loewen, University of Sioux Falls

Valerie Borum, University of Illinois at Chicago

Luanne Hirsch, Sul Ross State University

Johanna Thomas, University of Arkansas at Little Rock

Gail Horton, Florida Atlantic University

Peg Whalen, Wheelock College

Jessica Whilen, Washington University in St. Louis

Deborah Ketcham, Community College of Vermont

Sean Place, University of South Carolina

Laurie Lawson, Mississippi College

Guillermo Ernest Gonzales, Boston University

Debra Norris, University of South Dakota

Cynthia Hudley, University of California, Santa Barbara

Jean Toner, Central Michigan University

Leslie Hasche, University of Denver

Guangqing Chi, Mississippi State University

Deborah Louis, Eastern Kentucky University

Anna Escamilla, St. Edward's University

Finally, I want to thank Tammy Rogers for her unwavering show of enthusiasm and encouragement for my work, and my family, Jim Koch, Olivia, and Grady, for their support, patience, and tolerance for my endeavors.

ABOUT THE AUTHOR

Anissa Taun Rogers, PhD, MSW, MA, LCSW, is Professor of Social Work at the University of Portland in Portland, Oregon, where she serves as the Director of the Social Work Program and Co-Director of the Gender and Women's Studies Minor. She teaches courses across the social work curriculum as well as courses on the body, gender, human sexuality, international social work, and suffering and death. She is also registered, with her dog, Sookie, as a pet therapy team, working primarily with older adults and hospice patients.

Before finding her way to social work, Dr Rogers studied psychology, in which she earned undergraduate and graduate degrees. After receiving her MSW and PhD in social work, Dr Rogers began her career in undergraduate social work education and clinical practice. In addition to teaching, her main clinical and research interests are gender, sexuality, gerontology, mental health, and end-of-life care.

CHAPTER 1

Human Behavior and the Social Work Profession

Janice is a single, 25-year-old veteran who just returned from serving for one year in Afghanistan. Janice is having trouble finding a job, and she is struggling to support herself. Although Janice wants to work, she finds it difficult because of the depressed economy in her town, her lack of job skills, and several health problems. Among other symptoms, Janice suffers from severe migraine headaches and symptoms of PTSD, and she has trouble sleeping and concentrating. The stress caused by unemployment, by health problems, and by the experiences she had while serving in the army has caused Janice to wish sometimes that she could find a way out and not feel so bad all the time.

JANICE'S STORY EXEMPLIFIES THE COMPLEXITY OF HUMAN problems. When you carefully examine her situation, you will probably identify several major issues: health problems, potential mental health issues, developmental issues associated with Janice's age, program policies (such as those established through the Veteran's Administration that dictate which services veterans can access), cultural expectations of self-sufficiency, access to affordable housing, and employment availability and policies.

Rarely in social work will you find yourself working with people whose problems are straightforward. Regardless of the type of agency in which you work or the population with which you work, you will find people's problems to be multifaceted and interconnected on many different levels. Because the human condition is so complex, social workers need to seek a solid, knowledge-based understanding of human behavior in the context of the social environment.

DEFINING "HUMAN BEHAVIOR IN THE SOCIAL ENVIRONMENT"

No single definition for "human behavior in the social environment" exists. Nevertheless, the social work profession agrees on the importance of understanding how individuals interact both with other people and with their environment, as well as understanding how individuals are affected by these interactions.

The Council on Social Work Education (CSWE), the body that accredits undergraduate and graduate social work programs, requires that programs prepare students to apply knowledge of human behavior and the social environment. This is how the CSWE (2008, p. 6) articulates its policy:

> Social workers are knowledgeable about human behavior across the life course; the range of social systems in which people live; and the ways social systems promote or deter people in maintaining or achieving health and well-being. Social workers apply theories and knowledge from the liberal arts to understand biological, social, cultural, psychological, and spiritual development.

Social workers use this knowledge in their work with clients—from assessments to evaluations of intervention—and this knowledge is based in and supports the core value system of the profession. Thus social workers must have the ability to critique knowledge that is applied to practice (Council on Social Work Education, 2008). Students of accredited social work programs must learn about the interrelationships between individual behavior and the larger social environments.

Exhibit 1.1 illustrates the concept of human behavior in the social environment. Each circle represents a level of practice on which social workers might focus. This visualization also shows you how the different areas of people's lives and environments can intersect. The intersections are those areas in which social workers generally focus their assessments and interventions.

Depending on the agency or population, though, social workers sometimes move outside the overlapping areas to focus on issues related to a specific circle or realm. For example, a social worker might be employed to conduct mental health

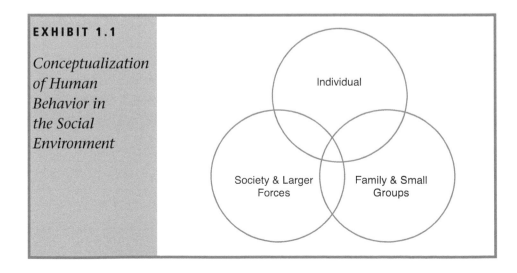

EXHIBIT 1.1

Conceptualization of Human Behavior in the Social Environment

Individual

Society & Larger Forces

Family & Small Groups

assessments for children. Her main focus thus would be on the individual level, specifically each child's mental health issues. Nevertheless, she would probably still consider issues in the realm of family and small groups and the realm of society and larger forces. For instance, she may attend to issues relating to the child's family, peers, school, economic status, cultural background, and so on. Moreover, she might consider other factors on the individual level besides mental health, such as the child's coping skills and physical health. The complexities and intricacies of this conceptualization should become clearer to you as you move through this chapter and the remainder of the book.

Learning about human behavior in the social environment will help you to place your knowledge into a meaningful and coherent context as you work with clients, organizations, and communities. It will challenge you to use your existing knowledge of human behavior and social environments while incorporating it into new ideas and perspectives on the human condition. It will give you more complex ways to think about assessment and intervention, which in turn will help you to become a more creative and effective social worker.

UNDERSTANDING HOW KNOWLEDGE AND THEORY INFORM SOCIAL WORK

As a profession, social work tends to generate, draw from, and apply knowledge based in strengths, empowerment, and social justice tenets. At the same time, though, it is also inclined to incorporate knowledge from many different disciplines that may not explicitly adhere to these tenets. *Knowledge* in this context refers to a wide range of information such as theories, empirical research, and practical experience that might be generated from different disciplines.

Given the complexity of individuals' lives and the multifaceted nature of the problems that clients bring to the working relationship, social workers need to have a broad knowledge base in many different areas—such as politics, biology, psychology, sociology, and economics—and they need to understand how aspects from these different realms interact with and influence one another in ways that affect the well-being of individuals, families, and communities. In other words, social workers must be able both to think comprehensively and creatively and to access their knowledge and "pull it all together" to assess and intervene with client problems.

Further, because social work is concerned with social justice and the dignity and worth of people, among other values, social workers must also understand how to incorporate strength-based and empowerment concepts into their work. This is why a strong liberal arts base in your education is so helpful. The more you know about different areas such as history, government, and philosophy, for example, the better the foundation you will have for conceptualizing and intervening with client problems.

You can also be more helpful when working with a client if you are familiar with some basic facts or updated research on the particular problem with which the client is struggling. Other times, you can use your knowledge to offer a client a different viewpoint on a particular problem, no matter how technical or philosophical, to give the client a new way to think about the problem. These are situations in which your familiarity with different theories of human behavior will be useful.

To see the benefits of drawing on a broad knowledge base, let us consider how practitioners from other disciplines might approach Janice's situation:

- *A physician might be concerned only with identifying and alleviating Janice's physical symptoms.*
- *A psychologist might attend only to the individualistic or psychological aspects of Janice's case. These might include her symptoms of PTSD, her potential for developing depression or other mental illness, her emotional and cognitive development, her issues of self-esteem and self-efficacy, and her ability to adjust to civilian life. After pinpointing these problems, the psychologist might focus on improving Janice's functioning in these areas.*
- *An economist or politician might concentrate on employment prospects, economic conditions of the community, and the costs of supporting Janice through social services. Economic interventions would include activities to improve employment conditions in the community and to curb costs by reducing the amount of time that Janice might need to rely on veterans' or other services.*
- *A sociologist might be interested in examining the larger social and cultural dynamics that contribute to unemployment and other problems for returning soldiers. Interventions might include helping Janice adapt to cultural expectations of employment or working to change societal attitudes toward poverty and returning service members.*

Although all of these perspectives are important, considering them in isolation contributes little to understanding the scope and complexity of Janice's problems and, consequently, to the effectiveness of the interventions.

The Role of Theory

Given the deeply human issues that are addressed by social workers, and the profession's roots in charity societies, "theory" and "empirical knowledge" may sound overly scientific and out of place. However, social workers need theory to help pull sources of information together into a meaningful perspective when working with clients. They need to understand basic theories in different areas, how theories can be applied to problems, and how theories' limitations can affect their explanations of problems. And then they need to back up those theories with knowledge based in research.

A **theory** is a set of ideas or concepts that, when considered together, help to explain certain phenomena and allow people to predict behavior and other events. Theories differ from other types of knowledge in that they allow you to organize knowledge on a particular issue or topic. If theories are well developed, they provide a blueprint for testing hypotheses or hunches about behavior and other phenomena, predicting certain events, and validating assumptions and knowledge about certain issues.

Without theories, knowledge about human behavior and social issues would remain unwieldy; you would not be able to make connections among related facts and information to form ideas that could help you advance your knowledge about human behavior and social issues. A variety of theories can help social workers organize information and make sense of certain problems.

Theories can offer social workers contexts from which to approach problems with the confidence that interventions are sound. Of course, some theories are more valid than others, but part of being a skilled social worker is knowing how to evaluate theories for their strengths and limitations and how to apply them responsibly.

It is important to keep in mind that the terms *theory, model, approach,* and *perspective* often are used interchangeably. Like theories, these other terms refer to ideas, structures, and conceptualizations that help social workers organize information. They provide ways to visualize and think about problems and issues. However, unlike theories, they lack some of the necessary elements that allow for empirical testing of hypotheses and constructs. Those elements will be discussed later in the chapter.

Theoretical Lenses Because social work touches on so many aspects of human behavior, its practitioners have a large variety of theories to draw on—both its own and theories developed in other disciplines. Thus, you will find it helpful to think about theories in broad categories based on which aspects of human behavior they address. For example, does a theory explain personality development or economic development? Does it explain causes of racism or causes of obsessive-compulsive behavior?

You will see by looking at this book's table of contents that Chapters 2 through 5 are organized in categories, or by "theoretical lenses," to help you focus on various aspects of human behavior. Chapter 2 discusses broad organizing theories used in social work, while Chapters 3, 4, and 5 focus on theories that are more specific to three aspects of the human experience. Each set of theories offers a different theoretical lens through which to view problems.

This is just one way to organize the many theories with which social workers are likely to come in contact. Another way would be to group theories in terms of whether they address individual, familial, or larger social issues or some combination of these. Alternatively, theories can be grouped into subcategories according to the specific area or problem that they address. For instance, some theories explain personality development, while others address social development. Some theories explain how social change occurs, while others explain why social dysfunction is resistant to change. As you read the next few chapters, keep in mind that theories of human behavior can be organized in many different ways, depending on your purpose and perspective.

Interactions of Theories   As you can see in Exhibit 1.2, sometimes concepts from different theoretical frameworks overlap; theories can explain aspects of problems in different realms. For example, theories that address how children and their caregivers establish attachments to one another might be informed by theories that explain how individuals in a relationship interact with one another, how they perceive these interactions, and how attachments impact these interactions. Attachments and interactions can also be explained by broader family system dynamics. Social workers' understanding of learning processes can be augmented by an understanding of how family systems may impact the development of individual members. Similarly, understanding of family systems might be improved by

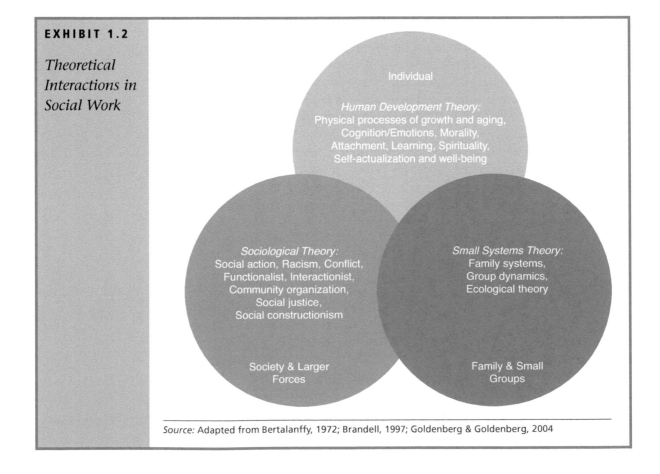

EXHIBIT 1.2

Theoretical Interactions in Social Work

Individual

Human Development Theory:
Physical processes of growth and aging,
Cognition/Emotions, Morality,
Attachment, Learning, Spirituality,
Self-actualization and well-being

Sociological Theory:
Social action, Racism, Conflict,
Functionalist, Interactionist,
Community organization,
Social justice,
Social constructionism

Small Systems Theory:
Family systems,
Group dynamics,
Ecological theory

Society & Larger
Forces

Family & Small
Groups

Source: Adapted from Bertalanffy, 1972; Brandell, 1997; Goldenberg & Goldenberg, 2004

theories addressing social justice (for example, to improve access to resources that support families), which can indirectly impact the nature and quality of attachments, interactions, and learning that take place within families. Of course, these are only a few of the many ways in which theories might be used in combination to help explain various problems that occur at individual, familial, and social levels.

As another example of how theories might overlap, a social worker who works with Janice could rely on various theories that explain not only individual development and functioning but also social problems and change. Because some of Janice's problems surrounding unemployment are interrelated with problems such as physical health, experiences in combat, and larger social forces such as the economy, the social worker can incorporate theoretical concepts from all of these areas to better explain how problems on different levels contribute to Janice's situation, as well as to develop interventions that will help to alleviate these problems.

For many social workers, the sheer amount of knowledge that is available for use with clients can seem overwhelming at times. Keep in mind that many disciplines have established and well-known theories whose concepts tend to be used more than others. One approach is to learn these theories well and then expand your knowledge of other theories depending on the type of agency and problem with which you will be working. To augment theoretical knowledge, social workers also acquire a lot of knowledge about problems (such as facts, statistics, new research findings) from their experience, education, and other sources that can inform their thinking. Thus, problem conceptualization and intervention in social work are part of a dynamic process. Social workers' thinking needs to be flexible as they work with clients because there can be many different ways to work toward problem solving. As you read about theories in the next several chapters, think about different aspects of social work for which these theories might be useful. You might come up with better ways to group or conceptualize theories that are more meaningful to you and that you can use in practice.

The Debate About Empirical Knowledge and Practical Knowledge

There are many ways to gain knowledge and develop theories in the social work discipline, and there has been considerable debate over the years about which methods are best. One way is through practical knowledge, or practice-based wisdom, which is knowledge generated from experience and informal observations. The experience that we gain as we go through life contributes to this knowledge. How we construct our reality and perceptions of things is often based on the types of experiences we have. These experiences allow us to feel that we "know" things. Historically, social work was rooted in charity and volunteerism, so social workers (or their predecessors) relied almost exclusively on experiential or practical knowledge.

Only recently did social work practice become more rationalized and scientific, with an emphasis on **empirical knowledge**, or knowledge based in observable fact (Fischer, 1981). As the disease model emerged in the medical field, other disciplines, such as psychology, sociology, and economics, also began using more scientific methods to advance knowledge and theory. Similarly, the new standard in social work became **science-based knowledge,** which is developed over time through the process of research and investigation, using objective methods to test hypotheses.

The scientific approach allows practitioners, with some degree of reliability and accuracy, to generalize their knowledge beyond single-client cases. It also allows social work theorists to modify existing theories and develop new ones that might explain issues more accurately. The movement among social workers to use more scientific approaches has also been driven by a trend toward **evidence-based practice,** or social workers' increased responsibility to document that their interventions are effective.

Despite the trend toward science-based knowledge, there is considerable debate about how much the social work profession can and should rely on empirical and theory-based knowledge given the complexity of human behavior (Osmond & O'Connor, 2006; Parton, 2000; Sheppard, 1998). On one end of the continuum is the idea that social workers must have some kind of guiding conceptualization of client problems, which can support empirical testing of interventions, which can lead to the modification of theoretical conceptions and ideas and, ultimately, to better and more effective interventions (Simon & Thyer, 1994).

On the other end is the tradition of practice-based argument. One argument against it, however, is that it tends to be anecdotal and ambiguous and cannot always be generalized to new situations. In addition, although practice-based knowledge can be based on theoretical foundations, it often is not subjected to controlled tests to verify how valid and reliable it may be for work with clients outside of a particular practice context.

However, practice-based knowledge certainly has value. Throughout practitioners' careers, they might work with thousands of people, giving them rich insights into various issues and problems. And, practice-based knowledge can lead to hunches, questions, and curiosity about various problems, which can lead to scientific exploration—which in turn can generate science-based knowledge and the development of theories.

Another approach that lies on the practice-based knowledge end of the continuum is social work based in "unknowing." While "knowing" is aligned with science-based knowledge and evidence-based practice (for example, we know, from empirical evidence, what interventions are best for certain problems), approaching work with clients from an "unknowing" stance suggests that people's problems and behaviors are inherently unpredictable and the contexts in which people live are complex and diverse. Further, interactions we have with clients are dynamic and continually changing, shaping future interactions and the therapeutic relationship.

Thus, social workers must remain open to the unpredictable and realize that knowledge of a client and various issues is only general at best. For example, we can't possibly know, for certain, what the outcomes will be for individual clients based on preconceived notions from established knowledge (Blom, 2009).

From this standpoint, social workers must remain deliberately unknowing in their work; they need to be reflective about what they think they know and willing to set it aside. The practice of unknowing doesn't imply that we forget all we know or never employ theoretical models and evidence-based practices. Rather, it suggests that while knowledge can help guide our work and should be utilized when warranted, practicing unknowing is a way to assess situations comprehensively and not exclude any possibilities as we work with people. If we adhere to a predefined way of viewing situations based on our knowledge, our work is at risk of becoming routinized, and we miss the richness and diversity of human lives and behavior. We operate from a false sense of surety that all decisions can be made logically and predictably. Proponents of this viewpoint would argue that good social work practice should maintain a balance between knowing and unknowing to challenge rigid assumptions about what we think we know based on science and embrace new possibilities for our work and outcomes with people (Blom, 2009; Håkansson, 1982; Morén, 1994).

You will see similarities between this approach and some of the other theories we'll cover in this book and methods you'll find employed in social work practice, such as Carl Rogers' idea of "starting where the client is" in person-centered therapy; principles in feminist theory that challenge established knowledge and promote different ways of knowing; and techniques in interviewing that require taking an unknowing stance in our work with people to avoid making assumptions and working off of bias and stereotypes.

The Quality of Knowledge and Theory

To make matters more complicated, there are yet more debates within the social work discipline about what kinds of knowledge are appropriate for practice. Should you rely on practical or experiential knowledge, even if its effectiveness cannot be proved? Alternatively, should you rely on experts, even if what they say does not seem to fit with the problems of your clients?

Everyone, not just social workers, faces the issue of the validity of her or his knowledge. For instance, how do you know you can rely on information given to you by those you know? Who is an expert? Do you consider celebrities, athletes, and the media to be experts? How might your culture influence various facts and ideas? How do your own values and beliefs bias the knowledge that you seek or the way in which you interpret it?

Social workers confront many other questions about the quality of knowledge and theory as well. Some researchers argue that many of the theories taught in social work curricula and from which social work borrows are outdated and ineffective for social work practice. They point out that many constructs or concepts in these theories have not been (and probably cannot be) supported through empirical research. They point to various limitations in the development of many theories, making them biased and inappropriate for use with people who come from diverse situations. For instance, Freud's theory of psychosexual development and Piaget's theory on cognitive development were developed in specific times and cultural contexts. At best, such theories need additional testing to understand how well they help to explain problems of contemporary clients who come from contexts other than the typical Eurocentric ones in which these theories were developed and often are employed.

Then there is the question of social work values, which are difficult to measure and observe. What role should they play in applying knowledge to your work? If some of the knowledge used in practice is potentially biased or suffers from other problems, is it ethical to use it in work with clients? All of these questions have implications for the effectiveness of social work and the policies and funding that support it.

Given the myriad theories from which to learn and choose when practicing social work as well as the ongoing debates about the utility of learning one or more theories (or even learning any theory at all), where do you go from here? One place to begin to tackle these issues is to think about how to arm yourself with skills to understand what knowledge is valid and what is not. An understanding of the characteristics of a useful theory—and well-designed empirical research that assists in theory development—can help you to wade through the flood of knowledge that you will encounter as you move through your career.

There are a lot of ways to judge the accuracy and applicability of knowledge, particularly theoretical and empirically based knowledge. And there are a lot of ideas about what makes knowledge "good," or valid for practice. Quick Guide 1 displays some basic guidelines for evaluating theoretical knowledge. These guidelines are generally accepted in many disciplines as the standards by which to determine the quality, usefulness, and applicability of theories in explaining certain phenomena (Homans, 1967; Lenski, 1988; Popper, 1959). A theory that meets these criteria is likely to offer information that allows you to reasonably predict and explain behavior in a way that will help you develop appropriate and effective interventions for your clients.

You should also be aware that people make all kinds of judgments when they conduct research to develop theories and generate knowledge about social and other issues. Consequently, there is a lot of room for bias, error, and misinterpretation, which can affect the quality of research and its outcomes. When you evaluate research, you need to be clear about factors such as which variables are being manipulated and controlled and which have not been accounted for. You also need to recognize how researchers' biases, values, methods, and motives for doing research can influence outcomes. A number of human errors can affect the way research is developed, carried out, interpreted, and applied to human situations. Here are some of the more common ones:

QUICK GUIDE 1   **Evaluative Criteria for Theory**

When judging the usefulness of a theory, think about the following criteria:

- *Is it functional?* Does it clearly explain how concepts are related to one another and to the phenomenon it is trying to explain?
- *Is it strong?* Is it able to make certain predictions about behavior that can be confirmed through empirical observation?
- *Is it parsimonious?* Do the theory's concepts explain a lot about the phenomenon in clear, simple, and straightforward terms?
- *Is it falsifiable?* Can it be tested and refuted by empirical observation?
- *Does it make practical sense?* Does it inform your work with clients and relate to what you already know about various phenomena?
- *What are the philosophical underpinnings of the theory?* Does it fit with and promote social work values and ethics?

Source: Adapted from Bertalanffy, 1972; Brandell, 1997; Goldenberg & Goldenberg, 2004

- *Problems with observations:* Human beings have notoriously faulty memories, and our own experiences of events can be very unreliable. Moreover, we tend to look for evidence to support our assumptions about certain phenomena, ignoring evidence that contradicts what we think we know.

- *Overgeneralizations:* We tend to assume that what we experience can be generalized to other people and circumstances.

- *Biases and value judgments:* We often impose our own values, inclinations, expectations, and experiences onto an event to help make sense of it.

- *Lack of inquiry:* We stop asking questions about an event because we think we understand it or have pursued it sufficiently.

Any of these pitfalls can result in the development of faulty knowledge, which in turn can lead to problems with accurately assessing and intervening with clients. For instance, many feminist scholars and others working in minority research argue that, historically, a great deal of empirical and theoretical knowledge that has been generated in social and other sciences has focused on the concerns of white males. However, knowledge and theoretical developments coming from this research is often applied to minority groups (such as women and ethnic and sexual minorities). This does not take into consideration their biological, cultural, economic, and other differences from white males, which might invalidate the use of this knowledge with diverse groups (Reinharz, 1992; Solomon, 1976). Many classic theories and empirical research on human behavior have been criticized because of these pitfalls.

When evaluating empirical research that is being used to support or discredit a theory or that might be used for practice, there are other questions to ask

---

QUICK GUIDE 2   Evaluative Criteria for Research

Some criteria to consider when evaluating research:

- *How current is the information?* If it is not current, is it likely to still be valid? Is there a good reason why it has not been updated?
- *Who is the intended audience?* Is the research conducted for the purposes of a particular interest group? Are the results biased to serve the needs of a particular group?
- *Who is the author?* What is the author's expertise and affiliation?
- *Are original sources of information listed?* Can you locate original works cited by the author? Are you given other sources where you can check facts and statements or do further research?
- *Is the information peer reviewed?* Have other experts in the field reviewed the information?
- *Is the information biased?* Does the language seem biased or slanted to suit particular purposes?
- *What is the purpose of the information?* Is it to inform, teach, entertain, enlighten, sell, persuade?

---

yourself; Quick Guide 2 outlines some of them. Keeping these criteria in mind and posing some well-thought-out questions as you read through the mounds of information you will find in newspapers, on the Internet, in agency and government reports, and even in scholarly journals will help you to make some educated decisions about which information is appropriate to use in your practice. The complexity of information about human behavior and social issues makes this sort of scrutiny essential.

In considering how this information might be useful in Janice's case, the social worker might want to think about whether the theories and other knowledge used to work with Janice's problems are appropriate. For instance, some theories and other knowledge regarding PTSD might be biased toward male soldiers. Or theories and other knowledge regarding unemployment might focus solely on individual responsibility while overlooking social contributions to the problem. Practice experience could play a role as well. If the social worker has extensive training in mental illness, she or he might focus more on Janice's physical and mental issues and not attend as much to broader issues, such as a poor economy, which are outside of Janice's control but still may add to her problems.

Theoretical Eclecticism

Social work is naturally informed by multidisciplinary knowledge. For example, social work with children and families might borrow from psychological theory that deals with aspects of development and behavior change. Social work with communities might rely on sociological theory that addresses group dynamics and social change. Administrative social work might be heavily informed by economic or organizational theory.

Nevertheless, some social workers adhere to a particular theory. For instance, some social workers might describe themselves as behaviorists, psychoanalysts, or family system theorists. These theoretical preferences tend to be influenced by the political and philosophical climate in which social workers received their training (Saltman & Greene, 1993) as well as the contexts in which they work. Social workers' tendencies to use some theories more than others influence the ways they conceptualize clients' problems, the ways in which they move through assessment, and the types of interventions they choose.

There is considerable debate about whether social workers can be more effective when working with clients if they are "pure theorists" who tend to rely on a single theory or if they are **eclectic practitioners** who borrow ideas and constructs from several theories. Because of the scope of problems with which social workers grapple, multiple theories do come in handy.

The Single Theory Argument   Proponents of adhering to a particular theory maintain that the sheer number of potentially useful theories cannot be taught in sufficient depth for students to understand them adequately and to apply them correctly in practice (Simon & Thyer, 1994). To thoroughly understand the essence of a theory and to apply its constructs effectively and appropriately, social workers must study and adhere to only that particular theory when working with clients. For example, a social worker who uses behavioral theory to assess children's behavior problems needs to have a deep understanding of the underlying tenets of behaviorism (its history, developers, applications, constructs, and limitations).

Proponents of using a single theory also argue that in order to remain valid, theories must be used as a whole; they become invalid when only parts of them are used in isolation. Using just one behavioral technique—for example, such as time-outs in work with children—should not be done without using other related techniques supported by behavioral theory. Using isolated parts of a theory is especially inadvisable if the person using the technique does not adequately understand the underlying assumptions of behavior as explained through behavioral theory.

Other arguments along this line of thinking include the following (Payne, 1997):

• Social workers get their training early in their careers and are likely to stick to the ways of thinking and practice that they learned in school. Thus, they are unlikely to be familiar with new knowledge across a range of theories and therefore cannot integrate this knowledge into their practice.

• There are no guidelines or rules about how to choose concepts from one theory or another, making the use of different theories rather haphazard and unsystematic.

• Social workers are unlikely to get needed supervision on using multiple theories and techniques, so relying on multiple techniques in practice can be risky.

• The underlying philosophies about human behavior tend to differ from one theory to the next; trying to integrate their concepts may lead to disjointed practice or even contradictory applications.

The Argument for Eclecticism   The other side of the argument is that social work should not adhere to a "one theory fits all" policy. The proponents of eclecticism state that because social work is concerned with people and problems on many different levels, the need to be flexible and comprehensive is inherent in the work. If social workers try to use one theory for all types of populations and problems, they will inevitably be ineffective. Some might even argue that rigidly adhering to only one perspective can be oppressive to clients, forcing the unique characteristics of clients and the human condition into a uniform mold.

Further, because uncertainty is a constant in the social sciences, particularly when it comes to human behavior and social issues, relying on a single theory to explain all problems will cause social workers to miss the bigger picture. Consequently, they will be more likely to misinterpret problems and apply inappropriate interventions, potentially doing more harm than good for clients. Being eclectic, flexible, and comprehensive allows social workers to be creative and resourceful in finding solutions to their clients' myriad problems. Indeed, some social workers argue that doubt, ambiguity, and uncertainty are hallmarks of the profession. Thus, social workers should be equipped with a broad "toolbox" of theoretical knowledge to work effectively with clients.

This line of thinking supports the idea that clients should benefit from all of the theoretical knowledge available to social workers. And because every theory has its limitations, social workers need a wide array of resources when working with clients. Social work processes such as intake (initial client interviews and information gathering), relationship building, assessment, planning, intervention, evaluation, and follow-up are commonplace in many agency settings and working relationships. Relying on one approach from one particular theoretical orientation might not be all that social workers need in certain circumstances or at different places in the working relationship (Payne, 1997).

One recent study took a closer look at the single theory versus eclecticism controversy. The researcher examined the ways in which social workers' theoretical biases might play out in practice (Saltman, 2002). The researcher surveyed 175 social workers in Jewish Family and Children's Agencies in the United States and Canada. She administered questionnaires and case vignettes to explore workers' theoretical orientations and interventions in practice. The respondents reported that they did not necessarily choose interventions whose theoretical underpinnings were the same as their stated orientation. A majority (87.5 percent) of respondents reported having a psychosocial orientation, for example, but they applied a family systems intervention to the case in the vignette. According to the researcher, it may be that respondents were using theories that best "fit" clients' problems rather than forcing the problems to fit respondents' favored theories. In other words, respondents probably were relying on practice knowledge, empirical knowledge, or both, rather than their personal preferences, to guide their decisions about which theoretical approaches to use in their interventions.

Although results from studies like this one cannot tell us whether all social workers would respond to client situations in the same way, they do help us to understand that social workers often rely on multiple theories when working with clients. The results also suggest that other forces, such as the client, the agency, the political sphere, and even popular opinion, might influence the theories that social workers use in their interventions with clients. For example, a social worker might use a particular theory for a specific problem because of recent empirical research that supports its effectiveness in explaining that problem. Similarly, an agency or funding source may only pay for the use of treatments based on a particular theory or set of theories. In these cases, social workers may be dealing with outside pressures to pick one theory over another, or even to use certain constructs from multiple theories, regardless of their personal orientations or biases.

Regardless of which perspective you take on this debate, it is obvious that to be an effective social worker, you must have at least a working knowledge of various theories that explain human development and behavior. Without this knowledge, you will not be able to make informed decisions about how to use theory, whether that means taking the eclectic approach or the single theory approach. Keep in mind, however, that the educational and work settings in which you find yourself will dictate, to some extent, how theories get used in practice. For example, some treatment programs for children with behavioral problems only use behavioral theory in their interventions, while some social workers in private practice may only use Freudian psychoanalysis. To be adaptable, as well as to serve clients ethically and responsibly, you need to understand multiple theories as well as how to use them in the appropriate context.

The Application of Theory and Knowledge in Social Work Practice

There are numerous approaches to social work practice that help to guide how social workers actually work with people and systems in addressing their issues. Regardless of the approach employed, social workers need to have a well-grounded knowledge base, know how to evaluate the effectiveness and validity of knowledge and theory, and understand how knowledge and theory can potentially affect the helping process (both positively and negatively). Often, the knowledge base and theoretical orientation of the social worker influence the way in which the social worker engages with the client, focuses questions in assessment, develops interventions for problems, and terminates and evaluates the process.

Let us look at the case of Janice to explore how this might work with two different social workers:

- *One social worker might focus his assessment on the resources and abilities Janice has to help her cope with her situation. He may then help Janice develop a plan to use these resources and abilities more effectively to lighten her stress level and address her health, mental health, and job-related problems. For example, he might point out that Janice is motivated to seek out help (she keeps appointments with him) and has shown a great deal of strength, bravery, and resiliency in her role as a member of the military. The social worker might help Janice transfer these skills to the task of seeking out health and mental health care and job training. The social worker would also bring in knowledge, research, and methods that inform this perspective (the strengths perspective, described more thoroughly in Chapter 2).*
- *Another social worker might focus her assessment on the physical problems that Janice is having—the insomnia, the headaches, the symptoms of PTSD— to determine how they are impacting her ability to follow through on finding employment and other responsibilities she has. The social worker may focus an intervention on assisting Janice to get the health care she needs, which from this perspective (the disease model, discussed in Chapter 3), would help Janice solve her other problems.*

Both social workers would keep in mind the goals of empowering Janice and working toward supporting her integrity, dignity, and self worth—regardless of the way in which they would go about working with her.

Let us look at another example. This one shows how multiple knowledge bases and theoretical perspectives can be combined to serve a client. In an agency serving a population of adults with developmental disabilities and diagnosed mental illnesses, staff members have many different ways of understanding and working with clients. One staff member helps her clients work on their family of origin issues. She favors the concepts in Freud's psychoanalytic theory and bases her work with clients on that theory. Another worker who uses systems theory and the ecological approach to guide his work thinks it is important for clients to learn to understand and work with the rules, roles, and boundaries of the social systems with which they interact. Still another worker who prefers the behavioral approach helps clients learn new skills by using modeling and rewards. All three staff members are guided by the strengths-based approach. They all assess client strengths and use existing supports in interventions they develop. The focus is on empowering clients and not just focusing on problems.

As you move through the book and read about different theories and perspectives and the research on different issues, take note of the theories that seem to resonate with you. What explanations for human behavior seem to make sense for you? When you think about working with people and systems, do you have a particular approach that seems to come to mind more often than another? What evidence are you using to support your perspectives? Being aware of your own preferences and ways of looking at human behavior is extremely important, as they influence how you go about your work.

MAINTAINING SOCIAL WORK VALUES

The social work profession is unique and in many ways different from other helping professions, such as psychology. One key difference involves the core values on which the social work profession is based. This idea has been alluded to in previous sections of the chapter, but it is now time to state it explicitly. Regardless of the knowledge base or theoretical perspective being applied, the social work profession strives to uphold values of service, integrity, competency, social justice, the importance of human relationships, and the dignity and worth of people in its approaches to individual and social problems. Ethical guidelines in the Code of Ethics are grounded in these values and also guide the work that social workers do (National Association of Social Workers, approved 1996, revised 2008).

Because of these unique values, social workers are particularly concerned with ensuring that interventions and approaches to work with people and systems are culturally appropriate. Each person and system functions in a cultural context and is influenced by unique cultural characteristics that help to define who that person or system is and how problems and solutions might play out. Therefore, social workers are cognizant of cultural aspects that contribute to environmental contexts of people and systems and that contribute to how problems and solutions are perceived.

Social workers also focus more than most helping professions on the strengths that all people and systems naturally possess. In social work, it is not sufficient to only look at problems when working with people and systems. In addition, social work values dictate that it should be recognized that people and systems are

CORE SOCIAL WORK VALUES	SOCIAL WORK ETHICAL PRINCIPLES	**EXHIBIT 1.3**
Service	Help people in need and address social conditions and concerns.	*Ethical Principles of Social Work Based on Core Values*
Social justice	Challenge social injustice.	
Dignity and worth of the person	Respect the inherent dignity and worth of the person.	
Importance of human relationships	Recognize the central importance of human relationships.	
Integrity	Behave in a trustworthy manner.	
Competence	Practice within areas of competence, and develop and enhance professional expertise.	

inherently resilient and that they possess skills and capabilities that allow them to persevere—despite problems that might exist. Social workers actively look for, promote, and support the natural strengths within people and systems to empower them to grow and thrive.

Whenever social workers incorporate knowledge or theory in their work, they are careful to ensure that the core social work values and ethics are reflected. Throughout this book, core values and ethical guidelines (see Exhibit 1.3) are discussed as they pertain to different concepts.

LEARNING ABOUT HUMAN BEHAVIOR AND SOCIAL WORK PRACTICE

You can see how having a broad knowledge base in human behavior and the social environment can be useful for social work practice. Social workers can never know enough about the many facets of human life. Fortunately, courses in social work offer a foundation on which to apply knowledge of human behavior and to build new knowledge that is more specifically related to various aspects of your work. This book has been organized to fulfill that goal as well.

Relating Knowledge of Human Behavior to Other Social Work Courses

The overall objective of all social work courses is to help you develop competencies that are grounded in a knowledge base that promotes best practices, cultural competency, and ethical practice. That knowledge base relies heavily on the subject of this book: human behavior. The following are a few of the courses you will encounter in the social work curriculum, with an indication of how they relate to the study of human behavior:

- *Policy courses* prepare you to develop, interpret, analyze, and apply social policies, which in turn influence the well-being of individuals, families, and communities. You need to understand the interrelationships between policy and human behavior and how to apply perspectives on social policy to client problems.

- *Research courses* are an important facet of social work education because they teach you how to evaluate practice as well as how to incorporate research into practice for more effective results. Research skills are the key to building theory and to ensuring that the approaches and outcomes built on theory are effective. Moreover, social workers need to keep themselves up to date on research in various fields that relate to their practice. New data or research on certain disorders or programs, for example, are constantly being produced, and social workers must be able to evaluate this research to ensure that it is sound and to understand how it can be used to inform practice.

- *Practice courses* rely heavily on theory to teach you empirically based practice methods for working with clients. Depending on the level of the program (undergraduate or graduate), you will learn either generalist theories or specific theories to help guide your assessments, planning, and interventions with clients, agencies, and communities. Often, these courses are paired with your field experiences and related seminars, which give you opportunities to apply your knowledge of human behavior and various theoretical approaches to your work and to integrate your knowledge with your practical experiences.

In addition to the core courses in the curriculum, social work programs also must incorporate certain content into courses throughout the curriculum. These areas deal with diversity, populations at risk, and values and ethics. All of these areas are crucial components of human behavior and the social environment because, when you consider human development and social problems that affect development, you run into ethical issues, questions of how diversity influences people and their surroundings, and how people can be marginalized by personal and social problems and situations.

Framing the Study of Human Behavior through this Book's Organization

This book is organized to help you think about how theory and other knowledge relate to human development and social problems that affect people. It presents information sequentially, discussing theory first as a base on which you can build your knowledge about specific issues relating to human development. This chapter sets the stage for thinking about knowledge and how it is applied to social work practice. Keep in mind the debates about how knowledge of human behavior in the social environment should be evaluated and used in practice applications.

Chapters 2 through 5 present some of the many theories that are commonly used in practice or whose concepts serve as a foundation for interventions. The discussions in these chapters review popular theories that can inform practice and describe some of the limitations to using these theories. Once you have gained an understanding of these theoretical foundations, you will be better prepared to read the remainder of the book.

Chapters 6 through 12 take you through common human developmental processes across the life span. Along with developmental information, these chapters introduce issues that tend to present themselves during various life stages and discuss specific theories that help explain these issues. To help you conceptualize the issues within the practice context, they are presented as they relate to different levels—individual, families and small groups, and society and large groups. These chapters will also improve your understanding of how theory, research, and practice inform one another. The goal is to learn to think critically about the debates discussed in this chapter and to develop your own opinions regarding the role of theory and other knowledge in practice.

CONCLUSION

Understanding human behavior in an environmental context is a crucial aspect of good social work. To be an effective social worker, you need a broad knowledge base that incorporates information on theories of human behavior, basic human development, and social issues that affect people in various stages of life.

There are many debates in the social work discipline about what kind of knowledge is needed to be an effective practitioner. Most social work scholars would agree, however, that social workers should be able to evaluate the quality of the knowledge they encounter and to determine how appropriate it is to use in practice.

As a social worker, you also need to be aware of how your own values, experiences, and training have influenced your perceptions of people and social problems. These biases and preferences for certain ways of perceiving social issues affect the work you undertake and how you interpret and use information. Having a solid and broad knowledge base as well as consistently questioning and evaluating knowledge and motivations for pursuing certain avenues when working with clients will help to ensure that you are doing all you can to be an effective social worker.

MAIN POINTS

• Human behavior in the social environment is a core area in the social work curriculum that includes content on human development and various theories that explain interactions between behavior and social dynamics.

• More so than other disciplines, social work requires a broad knowledge base in many different areas such as politics, biology, psychology, sociology, and economics. Moreover, social workers need to understand how aspects from these different disciplines affect the well-being of individuals, families, and communities.

• Knowledge can be empirical or practical; it comes from many sources, including experience, tradition, and authority.

• Theories should allow you to reasonably predict and explain behavior in terms that are as clear and straightforward as possible. They should also be testable through empirical observation, and they should make practical sense.

- There are many pitfalls to logical thinking, including problems with observations, overgeneralizations, biases and value judgments, and lack of inquiry.

- Elements for judging the validity of knowledge include the currency of the information, the intended audience, the expertise and affiliation of the author, the availability of original sources and other related information, agreement by other experts on the validity of the information, and the purpose of relaying the information.

- There is debate among social workers regarding whether practitioners should adhere to one theory when working with clients or whether they should take an eclectic approach that uses components of several theories.

- The social work profession is unique in its adherence to core values and a code of ethics based on universal human dignity and worth of the person.

- Policy courses, research courses, and practice courses within the core curriculum in social work offer a foundation of knowledge that informs the conceptualization of human behavior in the social environment.

EXERCISES

1. *Sanchez Family interactive case at* www.routledgesw.com/cases. Thoroughly review the major issues involving the Sanchez family. Then answer the following questions:
   a. What would you say are the three most crucial problems facing the family? Briefly justify your choices.
   b. In what ways might the way you have attained your knowledge affect your choices? For example, has your culture influenced the way you think about certain problems, and thus the importance you place on them?
   c. In what ways might theory help you in conceptualizing the family's situation?
2. *Riverton interactive case at* www.routledgesw.com/cases. Review the situation and the issues presented in the case and answer the following:
   a. What would you say are the three most pressing problems facing this community?
   b. How do you think you could use theory to help you conceptualize the situation in this case?
3. *Riverton and Sanchez Family interactive cases at* www.routledgesw.com/cases. In what ways do the two cases differ with regard to the problems the client systems face, the complexity of the situations, and the ways in which you might approach intervention with the problems?

4. *RAINN interactive case at* www.routledgesw.com/cases. Review the case and then answer the following:
   a. How would having multiple perspectives, referred to in this chapter as eclecticism, help RAINN serve the needs of both Sarah and Alan?
   b. What are the human development processes, family relationships, and societal forces that are impacted by Sarah and Alan's experiences with sexual assault?
5. *Hudson City interactive case at* www.routledgesw.com/cases. Thoroughly review the major issues involving this case. Then answer the following questions:
   a. What are some of the most crucial issues facing this community?
   b. In what ways might knowledge, including theory, help you to organize the ways in which you think about these issues and how to work with them?

CHAPTER 2

Lenses for Conceptualizing Problems and Interventions: The Person in the Environment

Juan is a 16-year-old Latino whose parents migrated to the United States from Mexico before he was born. Recently, Juan has been struggling in school. His grades have been dropping over the past two years, his attendance has been poor, he often falls asleep or gets bored in class, and he fights frequently with other students. Juan does not have many friends, but he does get along with several of his teachers. Juan's home life has also been in turmoil over the past several years. His father was laid off from his job at a manufacturing plant and has not been able to find a new job. His mother was diagnosed with cancer about a year ago. Because the family lost their health care and other benefits when Juan's father lost his job, his mother has been unable to receive proper treatment. Since her diagnosis, Juan's father has been drinking heavily, and when he is drunk, he gets violent with Juan.

Juan stays away from home as much as possible, mostly wandering the neighborhood or spending time at his church. Juan has a good relationship with the priest at his church, and he likes to volunteer when he is not in school. Juan has been referred to the school social worker regarding his academic problems.

EVEN IN THIS BRIEF SCENARIO, YOU CAN PROBABLY SEE THAT a lot is happening in Juan's life. If you were to explore his situation further, you would probably uncover more information that would potentially help you in your work with Juan. Where should you begin? How could you conceptualize Juan's situation to make some decisions about the way to approach his problems? This is the sort of situation in which theories can be applied, and in this chapter, we explore some of the most common theories and perspectives used in social work. In Chapter 1, the discussion focused on understanding what theories are. This and following chapters introduce theories as well as various models, approaches, and perspectives that help social workers conceptualize and work with client problems.

The theories and perspectives discussed in this chapter adopt a comprehensive approach to describing human behavior and problems in relation to their interaction with the environment—what social workers often refer to as the **person-in-environment approach.** This approach views client problems within the environmental context in which they occur, and it is the cornerstone of social work practice (Gordon, 1969; Richmond, 1920). These theories and perspectives tend to be broad, dynamic ways of conceptualizing work with people.

Theories and perspectives within the person-in-environment approach also tend to focus on client **systems,** which are the interrelated aspects of clients' lives which, when considered together, function as an integrated whole. To think of it another way, your body and the physiological processes that support it can be considered a system. The body is made up of parts that work together to allow it to function. Families and communities are also systems; they each have members who contribute to those systems through the relationships they share and the various roles they play. Similarly, a workplace, a school, and a church also function as systems. Each consists of individuals, processes, and interrelationships that keep it organized and running and that contribute, in turn, to the lives of the individuals who are part of it.

The theories and perspectives presented in this chapter address how different

QUICK GUIDE 3	The Person in the Environment Lens: Theories, Approaches, and Perspectives	
	MICRO-MEZZO-MACRO	**BIOPSYCHOSOCIAL**
Type	Approach	Approach
Focus	Individual & environment	Individual & immediate environment
Assumptions	People are active in their environment	Some emphasis is placed on people's active involvement in their immediate environment
Strengths	• Comprehensive approach to problems • Useful in assessment of client problems • Considers dynamic interaction between person and environment • Looks for causes of problems at individual and environmental levels	• Some focus on biological aspects of behavior and problems • Helpful in guiding assessment and intervention process
Limitations	• Too broad to easily predict behavior • Difficult to define and test constructs empirically • No consistent set of concepts that can be applied to client situations	• Too focused on immediate environment • Difficult to test constructs empirically and predict behavior • Too problem-oriented

systems in clients' lives operate independently and interdependently and how this affects clients' well-being. Quick Guide 3 summarizes all of the theories and perspectives discussed in this chapter for purposes of review and comparison.

MICRO, MEZZO, AND MACRO LEVELS OF CONCEPTUALIZATION

Social work education and literature often use the terms *micro, mezzo,* and *macro* when describing the different levels at which people can experience problems. Rather than focusing solely on the individual, the **micro-mezzo-macro approach** helps social workers to view people as active agents whose lives, relationships, and environments are interdependent. Thus the micro-mezzo-macro approach exemplifies the person-in-environment idea.

Although it does not provide testable constructs that help to predict behavior, it does offer a visual framework that is useful when organizing a great deal of information about a client and thinking about how various aspects of a person's life and environment can interact with one another:

SYSTEMS	ECOLOGICAL	STRENGTHS
Theory	Theory	Perspective
Individual & environment as part of various systems	Individual & environment	Individual & environment
Systems are interactive	People are active in their environmental settings	People are active agents in the change process
• Comprehensive approach to problems • Easy to apply concepts in practice • Considers dynamic interaction among systems	• Comprehensive approach to problems • Easy to apply concepts in practice • Considers dynamic interaction between person and environment	• Positive, empowering approach to working with clients • Easy to apply concepts in practice
• Too broad to easily predict behavior • Difficult to test constructs empirically and predict behavior • Not enough focus on biological aspects of behavior and problems • Too problem-oriented	• Too broad to easily predict behavior • Difficult to test constructs empirically and predict behavior • Not enough focus on biological aspects of behavior and problems	• Too focused on individual responsibility and autonomy • Difficult to test constructs empirically and predict behavior • Too present-oriented for use in some agency settings

- The **micro level** incorporates facets of the individual such as biological, psychological, developmental, spiritual, emotional, cognitive, recreational, and financial aspects of personality and individual functioning considered vital to a person's well-being. This level also includes factors such as age, gender, income, and ethnic background.

- The **mezzo level** consists of elements in a person's immediate environment. Family, friends, co-workers, neighborhood, work environment, church activities, local resources and services, and transportation could all fall into the mezzo level.

- The **macro level** includes larger social forces that might affect an individual, such as governmental policy, discrimination, oppression, social policy, economic conditions, societal values, and even historical events.

Exhibit 2.1 illustrates this approach and the different aspects that make up each level.

When assessing and developing an intervention with a client, social workers would consider these and many other aspects on all three levels that seem relevant to the client's particular problem and situation. Further, the micro-mezzo-macro approach can be used to explore how past issues on different levels have affected

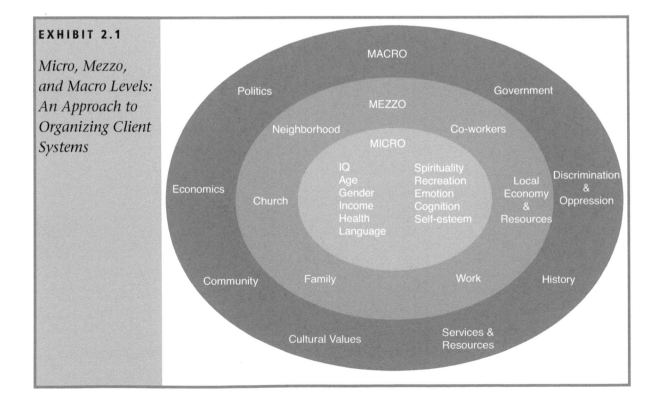

EXHIBIT 2.1

Micro, Mezzo, and Macro Levels: An Approach to Organizing Client Systems

MACRO

MEZZO

MICRO

Politics

Government

Neighborhood

Co-workers

IQ
Age
Gender
Income
Health
Language

Spirituality
Recreation
Emotion
Cognition
Self-esteem

Local Economy & Resources

Discrimination & Oppression

Economics

Church

Community

Family

Work

History

Cultural Values

Services & Resources

clients as well as how they are affecting clients' current functioning. Often social workers use this conceptualization as a jumping-off point to explore other facets of their clients' behavior and environment.

In many ways, this approach is similar to the other approaches and theories described in this chapter, and as you will see, they are often used interchangeably in social work practice. Indeed, Chapters 6 through 12 of this book organize issues based on the micro-mezzo-macro conceptualization.

Applying the Micro, Mezzo, and Macro Levels of Conceptualization

Let us look at how the micro-mezzo-macro conceptualization could be applied to Juan's situation.

As the social worker in his case, you would pay attention to Juan's situation on all three levels:

- *Micro: You would explore facets of Juan's individual, or micro, system, such as his spirituality, impulse control, progress in school, ethnic identity, physical and mental health, and cognitive and emotional development.*
- *Mezzo: At the mezzo level, you would consider small groups and aspects of the immediate environment that impact Juan's functioning, such as family dynamics, relationships with peers and teachers, his connection with his church, and resources in his neighborhood.*
- *Macro: You would assess how components of the larger social environment impact Juan's situation. You might look at school policies, issues of discrimination, cultural factors that may be impeding the efforts of Juan and his family to fit into the community, and lack of access to resources such as health care and employment opportunities.*

Based on this assessment, you would identify the major problems affecting Juan's behavior and then design interventions to address them.

Given that all three levels of analysis work together to define a person's situation, intervention on one level should impact Juan's functioning on other levels. For example, you might find that, based on a physical exam, Juan has some health problems that need to be addressed. Theoretically, improving Juan's health would likely enhance his performance in school, which in turn might improve his feelings of social and academic competence. Specifically, as his health and academic performance improve, he is likely to feel more motivated and self-assured, which may give him more confidence in his interactions with peers. These improvements may also help him cope more effectively with the problems he faces at home. If Juan has areas in his life in which he feels successful, he may be less likely to blame himself for problems such as his father's violence or his mother's illness. In essence, his feelings of competence at school and with his peers will act as a buffer against other problems over which he has little or no control.

Similarly, you could intervene on the mezzo and macro levels by helping the family to access resources such as unemployment and health benefits and resources such as Medicaid or health services in the Latino community. As the family's situation improves, the members' relationships with one another are likely to improve as well. For instance, Juan's father may become more motivated to control his drinking and his violent behavior, which in turn will have a positive impact on Juan's physical and mental well-being. You might also look at factors in the community, such as hostile attitudes against ethnic minority groups or discriminatory policies that might have detrimental effects on Juan and his family. You could work to improve the larger environment and its impacts on Juan's well-being. Improvements in these areas may help Juan to improve his academic performance, and he may feel more confident in his interactions with his peers. Increasing these feelings ultimately might help him to address his problems at school and at home. Because the micro-mezzo-macro levels are interrelated, there is a ripple effect when intervention takes place at one level in one particular area.

Another example of how this conceptualization could be used in practice is in the medical realm. A social worker who is assigned to work with a Native American woman who has been diagnosed with diabetes may conclude that the woman will not only need to change her diet and take certain medications (the primary focus for the physician) but also address other issues in order to successfully manage her diabetes:

- *Micro:* The social worker may explore with this client factors such as the stresses in her environment; her family history of illness; ways she can successfully make changes to her daily life to help improve her health; and her ability to afford care and lifestyle changes.

- *Mezzo:* The social worker may need to take into account the woman's family's attitude toward health, disease, and health care providers; health care providers' attitudes and potential biases toward members of ethnic minority groups; the family's access to affordable fresh produce and methods to prepare them; and the woman's access to safe, affordable, and accessible means of exercise. Prescribing a low-salt diet with plenty of fiber and fresh produce is not reasonable for a family that is living on a low, fixed income where the only grocery store within an hour's drive is a convenience store that sells only preserved foods high in sodium.

- *Macro:* Broader factors that may help or hinder the woman's efforts to control her diabetes may include cultural attitudes toward food, health, and wellness; community, health, and financial resources; and institutional discrimination, which might contribute to health disparities and inequitable access to care. For example, the family may have strong generational memories of discriminatory behavior by churches, schools, governments, and the health care system. Because of this, the woman may prefer to consult with an alternative practitioner, such as a shaman or healer, as this person may be a more trusted source for health care advice or treatment than a physician or social worker.

Critiquing the Micro, Mezzo, and Macro Levels of Conceptualization

Obviously, the micro-mezzo-macro approach enables a social worker to obtain vast amounts of information about a client. This is actually one of several criticisms of this approach:

- There is an endless list of things that social workers could explore with their clients, and gathering too much information may paralyze clients as well as their social workers. Specifically, social workers and clients may have difficulty identifying and prioritizing problems in a way that will make client goals seem achievable. Indeed, social workers want to help clients feel that problems are not insurmountable. If the micro-mezzo-macro approach is not used skillfully, clients (and their social workers) may get a sense that they are facing too many problems, which may leave them feeling defeated before any work gets started.

- Many social workers will probably not have time to fully explore the range of issues that may be impacting clients. This is especially true if social workers wish to obtain an extensive history of these issues.

- As discussed earlier, because the micro-mezzo-macro approach is not a theory, it cannot be empirically tested. Ideas about which concepts should be assessed at each level may vary from one social worker to another; so interventions based on this approach can vary a great deal.

- This approach does not have a consistent set of constructs that can be applied to client situations, which means that there is really no valid or reliable way to measure how effective it is when used with clients.

Nevertheless, the micro-mezzo-macro approach is useful when thinking about the complexities of clients' lives, and it helps social workers to consider the myriad factors that can affect clients, particularly on the sociocultural level. For this reason, this approach tends to take the focus and "blame" off the client and instead looks for causes of problems in the client's environment. Though social workers are likely to assess individual problems, they tend to consider these problems along with problems on other levels. Thus, they do not consider individuals to be the sole "cause" of problems. Consequently, they frequently target their interventions at larger forces such as unresponsive governmental institutions that fail to provide adequate support for clients.

THE BIOPSYCHOSOCIAL APPROACH

Several disciplines, including social work, conceptualize human behavior from a **biopsychosocial approach,** which breaks down human behavior into several components that involve a person's biological, psychological, and social functioning. Unlike the micro-mezzo-macro model, the level of functioning in these areas is usually assessed on the individual level; that is, each area is assessed as it relates to the client or person with the presenting problem. Clearly the biological and psychological facets of this model are inherently individualistic. However, the social realm, which some people might interpret as very broad influences, also tends to be defined rather narrowly as those issues that affect the individual directly. In fact, it is usually limited to the immediate social environment, particularly friends, family, and workplace.

These are some of the areas on each level that a social worker might consider:

- *Biological level:* The client's diet, health (both past and present), exercise patterns, sexual functioning, medication and substance use, and family health and genetic history—in fact, any factor that relates to the client's biological functioning and affects the client's well-being.

- *Psychological level:* The client's self-esteem, coping skills, mental health (both past and present), personality characteristics, family history of mental illness, spiritual development, and cognitive and emotional development.

- *Social level:* The client's work stability, engagement with social activities and recreation, and relationships with family, friends, and co-workers.

In essence, all of the levels included in the biopsychosocial approach are encompassed in the micro and mezzo levels of the micro-mezzo-macro model discussed previously. This is one reason why the latter approach is considered more comprehensive than the biopsychosocial approach.

Many social service agencies use the biopsychosocial model to assess client problems, particularly in their intake processes. Governmental programs, hospitals and health care clinics, community mental health care agencies, and nonprofit organizations often rely on this approach when collecting information on clients and developing interventions. Even when social workers and other practitioners use other perspectives in their work, the biopsychosocial approach can often be found as part of their agency's infrastructure. Some social workers use only this information to begin work with clients, whereas others use it as one part of a more comprehensive approach to assessment and intervention.

Applying the Biopsychosocial Approach

Despite its seemingly limited scope, especially when compared to the micro-mezzo-macro approach, the biopsychosocial perspective can be incorporated into social work practice in many ways. Again, let us look at how Juan's situation might be viewed from this perspective.

Some of Juan's problems involve absenteeism, falling grades, sleepiness in the daytime, lack of interest in school activities, and fighting with peers. He also seems to be having problems with his relationships with his parents, which directly and indirectly could affect him physically, emotionally, and financially. His father's drinking, violence, and unemployment as well as his mother's illness all have potential ramifications for Juan's overall functioning.

Here are some of the issues in Juan's situation, broken down by level:

- Biological level: *You might look at Juan's physical health and functioning. You might examine his nutrition and general health habits, assess his overall physical development in comparison to his peers, and refer him to a doctor for a physical exam. It could be that poor nutrition, lack of sleep, or hormonal imbalances are contributing to some of Juan's symptoms such as aggression and poor concentration. You might also want to assess whether Juan is getting enough exercise or is using drugs or other substances, as these issues can exacerbate some of his problems.*
- Psychological level: *You might assess Juan's emotional and cognitive development. You could refer him to a psychologist for intelligence (IQ) and other tests to determine whether he has any learning disabilities or related problems that might account for his low academic performance. You can assess various emotional and psychological realms to determine whether his problems with academics or peers might be caused by problems in functioning in these areas. For instance, you might look for signs of depression that could be impacting all aspects of his life or assess factors such as impulse control that could be causing his aggressive behavior.*
- Social level: *You might focus on family issues and dynamics, the quality of Juan's peer relations, and his interactions and relationships with others, such as his teachers and his priest.*

In addition, you would rely on information from theories that address specific developmental processes to help assess Juan's level of psychosocial development. Many of these theories are discussed in the following chapters. Depending on the outcomes of these assessments, you would prioritize Juan's problems and choose interventions that best target them.

Critiquing the Biopsychosocial Approach

Although biopsychosocial information is vital in working with clients, there are some criticisms of this particular conceptualization of problems:

- Some social workers argue that the focus of this approach, when used by itself, is too narrow. That is, conceptualizing clients' functioning from these three realms fails to acknowledge both the complexity of clients' lives and clients' interactions with larger social forces. For example, social workers run the risk of overlooking economic, political, and cultural influences as well as problems of racism and discrimination. By missing out on some pertinent information, social workers are at risk of implementing only partial interventions; there could be many other problems that, if not addressed, could undermine any potential gains made in working with clients.

- The biopsychosocial approach is too problem oriented and not sufficiently focused on people's strengths. It tends to define a person's problems as "limitations" or even failings.

- A related criticism is the idea that the biopsychosocial perspective focuses entirely on the individual who is experiencing problems. It views the individual having the problems as being responsible for causing them. Therefore, the individual is also responsible for fixing them.

- This treatment of individuals can be too short-sighted and can perpetuate an individual's problems by ignoring larger social issues that can contribute to individual problems and make them more difficult to overcome. For instance, a person may begin drinking after experiencing difficulties in finding a job, particularly when the economy is weak. An intervention focused on the drinking behavior may be ineffective, or its gains might be short-lived. Further, the social worker would miss the opportunity to target and address the root of the person's problem—the lack of jobs and the poor economy. Although the social worker may not be able to do much, at least immediately, about the availability of jobs, she or he could facilitate access to training or unemployment benefits, which may, indirectly, alleviate the person's destructive drinking behavior. The social worker could also become involved politically, or otherwise, to help improve the economy or bring more jobs to the community.

- There is some debate in the social work discipline about whether social workers know enough about biological aspects of human behavior to effectively assess various problems and to incorporate alternative interventions into their work. One group of researchers (Johnson *et al.*, 1990) has argued that social workers need more knowledge and training in the biological bases of behavior to work effectively with other practitioners such as health care professionals and to meet the challenges in working with various populations such as older adults and individuals with mental illnesses. Because many people in these populations are experiencing problems and illnesses that are based at least in part in biology—for example, schizophrenia, substance abuse, and Alzheimer's disease—social workers need to be well versed in biological processes that can contribute to symptoms and disease progression.

On the other hand, the biopsychosocial approach can help social workers focus on biological issues that may be affecting clients' lives. Using this approach may encourage social workers to acquire and incorporate biological knowledge into their work with clients.

By using the biopsychosocial approach, social workers can also obtain a lot of information about their clients. Aspects involving biological, psychological, and social functioning are crucial building blocks to clients' health and well-being, and being knowledgeable about these aspects will affect social workers' approaches to their clients' situations.

SYSTEMS THEORY

Although systems theory has been heavily influenced by many disciplines, particularly sociology, it is discussed in this chapter because of its utility in social work and its comprehensive approach to human behavior. Systems theory is widely used in social work as a way to understand human interactions within the environment; it is also popular in social work with families.

The term "general systems theory" was first used in 1949 by biologist Ludwig von Bertalanffy (Bertalanffy, 1972). However, many other scientists in disciplines such as physics, mathematics, psychology, and engineering were also exploring ideas of interactions within systems.

Social workers became more interested in systems theory in the 1960s during a movement away from a psychiatric focus toward greater inclusion of environmental factors. Systems theory fit well with this new, broader focus. Social workers tended to rely heavily on the influence of scholars such as Talcott Parsons, Kurt Lewin, Urie Bronfenbrenner, and of course, Ludwig von Bertalanffy. The use of systems theory in family therapy was also influenced by these scholars, but social workers and other family therapists relied heavily on other theorists (see Bateson, 1972; Hoffman, 1981; Jackson, 1957; S. Minuchin, 1974).

Systems theory views human behavior as the result of active interactions between people and their social systems. The idea of "systems," then, is central to this theory. Recall that systems consist of interdependent parts that, when combined, make up an organized whole (Goldenberg & Goldenberg, 2004; P. Minuchin, 1985). To describe this process, systems theory uses several key concepts, which are listed in Exhibit 2.2.

Systems can include any formal or informal grouping of people or facets of organizations, including couples, families, schools, communities, governments, and social service agencies. All of these systems are made up of smaller, interdependent

EXHIBIT 2.2

Key Concepts in Systems Theory

- *Boundaries:* Patterns of behavior that define relationships within systems and give systems their identity.
- *Differentiation:* A system's movement from a simple existence toward a more complex form of functioning, while still maintaining its unique characteristics.
- *Entropy:* A system's movement toward disorganization and death. Negative entropy is a system's movement toward growth and development.
- *Equifinality:* The tendency for the same end state or outcome in a system to be achieved through many different paths or trajectories.
- *Feedback:* A form of input, which informs a system about its performance. Feedback can be positive or negative; this tells a system what it is doing correctly or incorrectly with regard to functioning.
- *Homeostasis:* The tendency that systems have to work toward and maintain stability and equilibrium.
- *Input/Output:* Input is the information, communication, or resources coming into a system from other systems. Output is what happens to this information, communication, or resource after it has been received by a system.
- *Multifinality:* The possibility that similar circumstances or conditions in a system will lead to different results or outcomes.
- *Reciprocity:* The necessity for a change in one part of the system to impact other parts of the system.
- *Roles:* Socially or culturally sanctioned patterns of behaviors expected of individuals within a system.
- *Subsystem:* Secondary, smaller systems within a larger system.
- *Synergy:* The energy that systems create to maintain themselves.
- *System:* Set of parts that are interdependent and make up an organized whole.

Source: Adapted from Bertalanffy, 1972; Brandell, 1997; Goldenberg & Goldenberg, 2004

parts that contribute to the entire system. For example, a school is made up of administrators, teachers, and students. Each contributes to the functioning of the school system as a whole. Each of these parts could also be considered a *subsystem.* Administrators make up a smaller, organized system within the school, and they often have their own way of functioning within the larger system. This is true of teachers and students as well.

For each subsystem, and for the system itself, there are *boundaries* that define its roles, rules, and identity; these boundaries inform those outside the system or subsystem as to how open or closed it is to interaction, communication, relationships, and the like. A subsystem of teachers might have boundaries that let students know how and when to approach teachers for help or personal matters and what to expect from teachers in the school setting. Furthermore, teachers' boundaries also inform the boundaries of the students. Based on how they perceive the roles of the teachers, students quickly learn their own roles. For instance, students learn when they are permitted to talk in class, how they should behave around teachers, and what is expected of them academically.

Systems are always striving to maintain status quo with regard to their functioning, whether this functioning is seen as positive or negative. That is, systems hum along in their daily routine, and members of systems usually know what to expect and how to behave to keep them running as usual. Members assume *roles,* such as teacher or student, that ensure that systems run smoothly. Sometimes a subsystem or a member of a system does something different that upsets the status quo. According to the concept of *homeostasis,* others within the system will adjust their behavior or try to influence the wayward member to restore the system to its original state of functioning. **Synergy**, or energy that systems create to help maintain themselves—to maintain homeostasis—is part of this process.

An example of this process is a family system in which one member has an alcohol problem. If the problem has been present for many years, each member of the family has probably learned how to behave during different situations so as not to "rock the boat." That is, each member has become adept at reading verbal and nonverbal cues in the environment and can therefore alter her or his behavior to ensure stability in the family. Now, suppose that the member with the alcohol problem decides to get help. Even though this decision can be viewed as positive, the system will still be upset, because this member is changing her or his behavior. Other family members will need to adjust to this new behavior and find other ways of interacting with one another. Some family members might need to work on communicating openly with one another, or they may need to alter their own drinking behaviors to support the member who is getting help. Making such adjustments is often challenging, especially if the system has been functioning in a particular way for a long time. However, once members of the family learn and become used to new ways of interaction, they can establish a new, and hopefully better, level of homeostasis. This is an example of **reciprocity**, where a change in one part of the system impacts other parts of the system.

Systems are continually receiving information about how they are performing. *Input,* also referred to as energy, information, communication, or resources, comes to a system from sources outside of itself. For example, schools receive input about educational goals and standards from parents, students, and communities. Based on the nature of the input, schools develop curricula and programs to serve students. These latter actions constitute a form of *output* by the schools. That is, output refers to the ways in which a system responds to input. A special form of input is *feedback,* which informs the system about its performance. A school could receive positive feedback on programs and policies from these same sources, causing the school to believe that it is functioning as it should be. Conversely, negative feedback on a particular aspect of the school might cause the school to undertake an evaluation to determine effectiveness of a program, or to change a policy that does not seem to be working for parents or students or that treats different groups of students unfairly.

Over time, systems tend to become more and more complicated. Interrelationships within systems develop and change; roles and rules become more complex as people and ways of doing things change; and subsystems, boundaries, and homeostasis all shift. This tendency toward greater complexity is referred to as *differentiation,* and it is a natural part of a system's life. For example, as children in a family grow older and gain experience, they change as individuals. As a result, relationships within the family change, as does the way the family system itself functions.

Similarly, systems have a tendency to move toward disorganization, or *entropy.* In a school, for example, teachers leave, administration changes hands, programs are cut, and funding dries up. However, schools can also improve and become better organized. A school can recruit better-qualified teachers, develop improved and equitable programs, and secure a constant, stable source of income. This movement toward growth and development is referred to as *negative entropy.*

Also, when thinking about systems and the individual parts that make up a system, it is important to keep in mind the concept of **equifinality**; that is, systems and parts of a system can take many different paths to end up with the same outcome. In other words, many different situations or circumstances may occur in a system to change it, but the same outcome might still occur for the systems or its parts. A related concept is *multifinality,* in which systems could experience similar situations or circumstances that produce very different outcomes for these systems or their parts.

Diagramming Family Systems

When assessing and working with families from a systems perspective, it can be useful to have a visual image of the family, which can help you and the families with which you work sort out and keep track of complex family structures. There are a variety of tools you can use to do this; two are discussed here.

Genograms **Genograms** provide a visual representation of a family system—similar to a family tree, but more complex. They offer a visual guide for families and social workers, allowing both to see how the family is structured and how various dynamics might be playing out in a family system. These "pictograms" use symbols to denote key events, characteristics, relationships, health and mental health issues, and communication patterns that might persist across generations. These are some of the categories of information that are often depicted in genograms:

- demographic information for each family member: gender; dates of birth, death, marriage, and divorce; significant health or mental health related issues such as drug or alcohol use and hereditary diseases such as cystic fibrosis;

- relationships and communication shared among family members;

- types of boundaries between family members;

- subsystems that might exist in a family system.

Genograms allow families and social workers to see how issues may impact individual family members, intergenerational relationships, and the family system as a whole. They also allow families and social workers to identify strengths within the family system that can be used to help solve problems.

Here is an example of how a genogram might be used. The parental rights of Tina Faye Hampton were terminated after years of her not complying with substance abuse recommendations mandated by the state human services agency. The decision was made to plan for the adoption of Tina's two oldest daughters, Lily and Daisy Todd. As part of the adoption process, Tina answered questions about her family history, which became part of the children's case file. She revealed three generations of substance abuse and clinical depression in her maternal family. She also revealed a history of early deaths for the women in her family. Both her mother and grandmother had died in their twenties from a ruptured appendix. The social worker realized that Tina had recently had her appendix removed while she was hospitalized for substance abuse treatment. Seeing this pattern on paper allowed the social worker to alert prospective adoptive parents to the high risk of appendix problems for the two little girls. The genogram created a lasting picture of the biological family that could be given to the children to under-stand their biological and social history. Exhibit 2.3 is what Tina's genogram might look like. Notice the disrupted lines indicating broken or problematic relationships.

Ecomaps   Ecomaps are similar to genograms, but they go beyond genograms by demonstrating visually how family members are affected by, and react to, their broader ecological context:

- In the center of the ecomap, basic genogram information is incorporated.

- Using symbols similar to those used in a genogram, an ecomap diagrams a family's relationship with its social environment by identifying various systems with which a family is involved such as schools, churches, medical clinics, extended family, work and economic activities, political and legal organizations, and media exposure.

- An ecomap may also diagram the energy flow between the family and external systems. Ecomaps can highlight strong connections to outside systems as well as weak or stressful ones, and they can provide a visual representation of support systems for the family as well as sources of strain on the family system. Ecomaps can be extremely useful in assessing resources for the family, uncovering hidden strengths, and determining places where services are needed or duplicated.

EXHIBIT 2.3

Sample Genogram: Tina Faye Hampton, for Lily and Daisy Todd

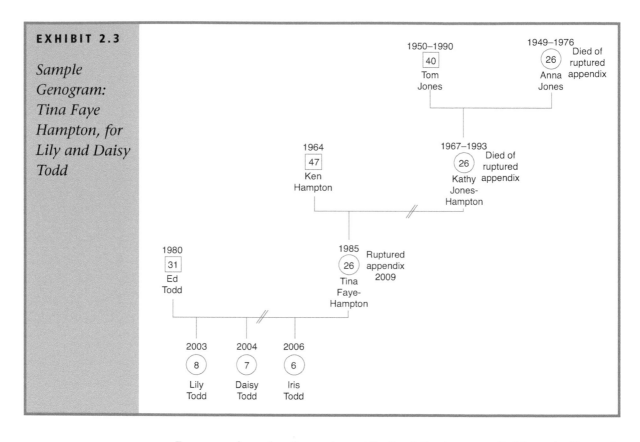

For example, a family coping with the father's recent Parkinson's diagnosis worked with a social worker to identify various supportive resources and systems accessible to the family as well as aspects of their ecosystem that created barriers and stressors for the family in getting care and support for their situation. By using an ecomap, the family was able to identify their church as an existing positive support system while they identified their relationship with the medical community as weak and stressful because of cost and communication issues. Once the visual image of the ecomap was created, the family and the social worker identified ways to increase support from the church and developed a plan to identify new funding sources and improve communication with the father's doctors.

In the case of Tina Hampton and her daughters, the ecomap might look like Exhibit 2.4. As you can see, the girls' strongest links are to each other and to the educational system, which might provide some stability in their lives as they enter the adoption system. Adoptive parents would certainly want to know about Daisy's learning disability and perhaps work with the teacher to help Daisy feel less frustrated with school. Tina's links are all weak or stressful—mostly stressful—which indicates that she will need a great deal of help in building supportive relationships. The best options for her, according to the ecomap, are probably joining a church and obtaining her high school diploma.

EXHIBIT 2.4

*Sample Ecomap
Todd/Hampton
Family*

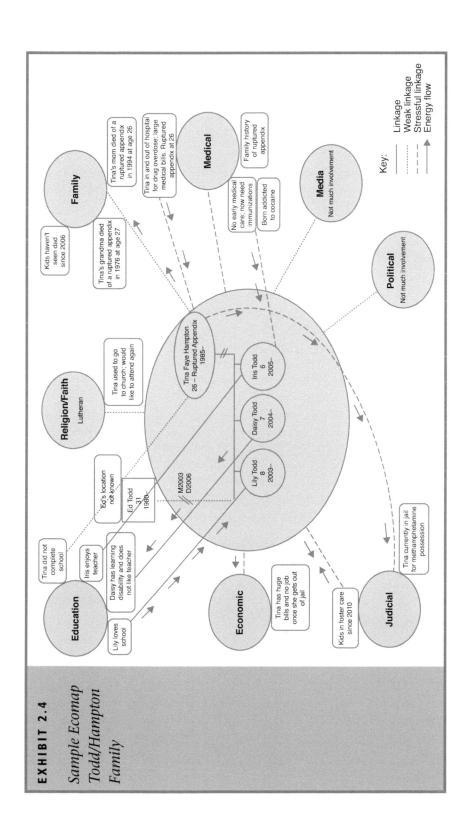

Key:

——— Linkage
·········· Weak linkage
----- Stressful linkage
→ Energy flow

Family

Kids haven't seen dad since 2006

Tina's grandma died of a ruptured appendix in 1976 at age 27

Tina's mom died of a ruptured appendix in 1994 at age 26

Tina in and out of hospital for drug overdose; large medical bills. Ruptured appendix at 26

Medical

Family history of ruptured appendix

No early medical care; now need immunizations

Born addicted to cocaine

Media
Not much involvement

Political
Not much involvement

Religion/Faith
Lutheran

Tina used to go to church; would like to attend again

Tina Faye Hampton
26 – Ruptured Appendix
1985–

Iris Todd
6
2005–

Daisy Todd
7
2004–

Lily Todd
8
2003–

M2003
D2006

Ed Todd
31
1980–

Ed's location not known

Tina did not complete school

Iris enjoys teacher

Daisy has learning disability and does not like teacher

Lily loves school

Education

Economic

Tina has huge bills and no job once she gets out of jail

Kids in foster care since 2010

Judicial

Tina currently in jail for methamphetamine possession

Applying Systems Theory

Imagine that you are the school social worker using systems theory to make sense of Juan's situation. First, you would want to define Juan's systems. You could look at his family system, his school system, and his church system. Within each of these systems, Juan will belong to various subsystems; have different roles, relationships, and boundaries; and receive different forms of input and feedback. For the sake of space, let us focus on Juan's family system because he seems to be experiencing many problems at home that are probably impacting other aspects of his life.

Family Subsystems and Boundaries   *Juan's family system consists of Juan and his parents. The main subsystem in Juan's family consists of his parents, although it is possible that Juan is in a subsystem with one parent as well. You would need to assess the boundaries of the family system as well as boundaries of the subsystem of the parents and each individual within the system. For the family system, you would want to know how open the family is to outside help, support, and feedback; how private the family keeps its affairs; and how rigid or flexible the family seems to be about allowing interaction with other systems. You would determine whether the family's boundaries seem flexible enough to allow for outside interaction yet firm enough to give the family a sense of identity.*

In addition, you would consider whether there could be cultural differences that dictate boundaries that might not seem appropriate in terms of U.S. culture but that are very appropriate in the context of Juan's parents' culture. For instance, Juan's parents may insist that the family's problems be solved within the family unit. In some Hispanic or Latino cultures, family problems are viewed as private matters; thus, taking private concerns to a stranger, such as a social worker, is not viewed as appropriate. Further, it may be that systems with which Juan's family interacts are discriminatory in their policies and practices, affecting the type of feedback and resources his family receives. Conversely, in mainstream U.S. culture, many families deem it appropriate to seek outside help when they experience problems. If you do not take issues such as this into consideration, you may incorrectly assume that Juan's family is not open to help or is denying their problems.

As mentioned previously, you would also need to assess boundaries for Juan's parents as a subsystem of a couple. For example, Juan's father might have some trouble with boundaries, as indicated by his violence and drinking. When he is drunk, Juan's father appears to have trouble maintaining not only his father and husband roles but also his personal space, both physically and emotionally.

This blurring of boundaries will likely affect Juan: His father's behavior seems inconsistent, and Juan lacks a good role model for appropriate behavior. Juan also may be learning that violence is an appropriate response to personal troubles.

You would also want to find out how Juan's mother is responding to her illness. It could be that she is shutting herself off from her family and friends, choosing to handle her illness on her own. Further, Juan may be taking sole responsibility for caring for his mother, assuming more than his share of the mental and emotional burden for her illness.

Looking at Juan's personal boundaries, you can see that Juan seems to pull away from his peers, and he often responds with violence when he has problems. However, Juan seems to maintain positive boundaries with some of his teachers, his priest, and the social worker. Further, you need to explore the patterns of Juan's interactions with his parents to determine whether the boundaries between Juan and his parents are appropriate for a teenage boy and his parents. Here again, you would want to take into consideration what appropriate boundaries are for parents and children in Juan's and his parents' particular cultural context.

Roles and Homeostasis   In addition to exploring boundaries, you would want to assess the roles that each family member assumes. Given Juan's age, you could expect him to perform certain developmental tasks that are normal for a teenage boy. Similarly, you would expect his parents to carry out certain roles and responsibilities, although these might differ slightly from those normally expected in North American society, given his parents' cultural background.

Assessing roles is particularly important in Juan's case because so much has happened to the family. For example, Juan might have assumed a parental role because of his father's drinking and his mother's illness. This disruption in the family system's homeostasis may be disrupting roles and responsibilities. Because the stability of the family has been shaken up considerably, you may even choose to begin intervention here, helping the family find ways to achieve a new level of stability given the circumstances.

Input and Output   Juan's family does not seem to be receiving much input, other than negative feedback from Juan's teachers. The family's income has dropped due to his father's unemployment and his mother's illness, and the family does not seem to be getting much emotional or other financial support.

The family also does not seem to be receiving much positive feedback. In fact, they are certainly receiving a great deal of negative feedback about their functioning, which may be eroding their sense of self-efficacy as a family. Further, this feedback may be based in biased or stereotypical views of Latino culture in general. On the positive side, Juan may be receiving input from his interactions with his church, which results in output through Juan's volunteer work. However, you might want to help Juan and his family find ways to receive more positive input and feedback, leading to positive outputs from the family.

Entropy   Under present circumstances, Juan's family seems to be moving toward entropy. Juan is continually doing worse in school, and his interactions with most people seem to be poor. Further, his father's drinking and his mother's illness seem to be moving the family toward depletion and death.

It also does not appear that anyone in the family is working toward growth, development, or differentiation; rather, all family members seem "stuck" in their personal development because of their circumstances. It may be that as you intervene in other areas of the family's life, the process of entropy will reverse itself, leading to negative entropy.

Equifinality and Multifinality *Even if Juan's family situation were improved—his mother were healthy, his father were employed, the family had needed resources, and the environment were nurturing—Juan could still be struggling with school and other issues. This is an example of equifinality: A different home life for Juan might not change Juan's struggle with academic and other problems.*

Conversely, even with Juan's current family situation, Juan could be immersing himself in sports, academics, and community work. He might have a reputation for being a high achiever in school and extracurricular activities. This is an example of multifinality; the same system could lead Juan to behave differently in each setting.

Critiquing Systems Theory

As with the micro-mezzo-macro approach, systems theory can be a little unwieldy to use when working with clients. The other criticisms of this theory include the following:

- Identifying the many systems in a client's life and assessing how these systems interact and impact a client's functioning is not an easy task. Systems theory is often more appropriate for working with family or other identifiable systems such as an organization or workplace. Applying the concepts from this theory can be more straightforward in those situations.

- As with the other approaches discussed so far, this broad focus on systems as well as concepts that seem somewhat abstract can make the theory difficult to articulate and test empirically, especially when attempting to predict behavior. However, many social workers and other professionals succeed in applying the theory consistently enough to support its validity and reliability across client situations.

- Some social workers also argue that this theory is too problem oriented, ignoring positive areas of functioning in clients' lives.

- The focus on family and other systems in this theory makes it less likely that social workers will attend to individual biological aspects that could be contributing to clients' problems. Thus, this information may be overlooked in assessment and intervention.

- Because this theory tends to concentrate on current functioning of clients and their systems, social workers may overlook important information about past functioning that could be relevant to current problems.

At the same time, systems theory provides a broad look at client problems, and it considers people as active, living beings who are an integral part of a dynamic environment. The concepts used in this theory are effective at explaining behavior and problems, and they go a long way to inform work with clients. For example, concepts such as boundaries or homeostasis can be easy to use for assessment and intervention, particularly when working with families or organizations. However, these concepts can be difficult to explain to clients.

A growing body of literature explores these concepts and uses of systems theory in social work. This research provides an empirical foundation for social workers who want to apply this theory to their work with clients and who want to better understand its effectiveness when used for intervention.

ECOLOGICAL THEORY

Originally developed by psychologist Urie Bronfenbrenner (1979), **ecological theory** explains human development by describing aspects of the individual, the environment, and the interaction between the two. Ecological theory argues that people are actively involved in their environments and their own development (versus some developmental theories that argue that people are passive—they do not play an active role in their development) and that both development and environments are always changing. People are born with both negative and positive tendencies, and they are influenced equally by nature and nurture. Development, then, is influenced by the actions of the individual, occurrences within the individual's environment, and the interactions between the two.

A fundamental tenet of ecological theory is that the way people *perceive* their environments and experiences significantly affects their well-being. Specifically, the meaning that people place on the events that happen to them and the way they interpret these events in the context of their environments have a major impact on how these events influence their well-being. For example, two people living in the same community may have different reactions to economic downturns that cause both of them to lose their jobs. One person may view unemployment as a crisis in which he will be unable to pay bills and support his family. This prospect may leave him feeling depressed and hopeless, which may mean that he needs mental health support to cope with the situation and to find the motivation to look for employment. Conversely, another person may view her unemployment as an opportunity to return to school or develop new skills, which will lead to a job that is more enjoyable or profitable. She may feel relieved, or even liberated, by being "forced" to take a new direction in her life.

Clearly this example oversimplifies the situation of unemployment and people's reactions to it. However, it does highlight the importance of people's perceptions of their circumstances, a key tenet of ecological theory. Indeed, this concept is central to social work and is discussed throughout this book: Regardless of how problems may appear to social workers, they need to explore how clients view their situations before assuming that certain situations are problematic.

The organization of ecological theory is very similar to the micro-mezzo-macro conceptualization. Exhibit 2.5 displays the four levels of the environment described by the theory:

- **Microsystem:** In ecological theory, it consists of all the roles and relationships that a person has in the immediate environment. This level contains physical places such as home, school, work, and the neighborhood; these are places where people have daily face-to-face contact with one another.

- **Mesosystem:** The focus at this level is the interactions among two or more environmental settings in which people live. To put it another way, the mesosystem comprises a system of microsystems. For example, the dynamics in a person's work and home lives often impact one another; this is exemplified when a person brings home the tensions from her work.

- **Exosystem:** All those social settings in which things happen that affect people (for example, child's school, parent's workplace, neighborhood community center) make up the exosystem. Although the person is not necessarily an active participant in these settings, what happens in them will impact the person directly or indirectly. An example is policy decisions about school closures in a community. Though residents of the community are not involved in making these decisions, their children and families are affected when a school closes. Some families may decide to move to another school district or bus their children to a school that is far away. Residents who do not have children will also experience the impact of community change created by the decisions.

- **Macrosystem:** It encompasses all the ways in which larger cultural factors affect the other levels of a person's environment and, consequently, how they affect a person's development. This includes aspects such as laws, political philosophy, and cultural beliefs. Societal attitudes against gay marriage, laws prohibiting it, and resulting discrimination in benefits (such as health care for a partner) are examples of how issues in the macrosystem can play out and affect individuals.

As with the micro-mezzo-macro approach, ecological theory contains several levels that describe factors within a person's environment that are significant in

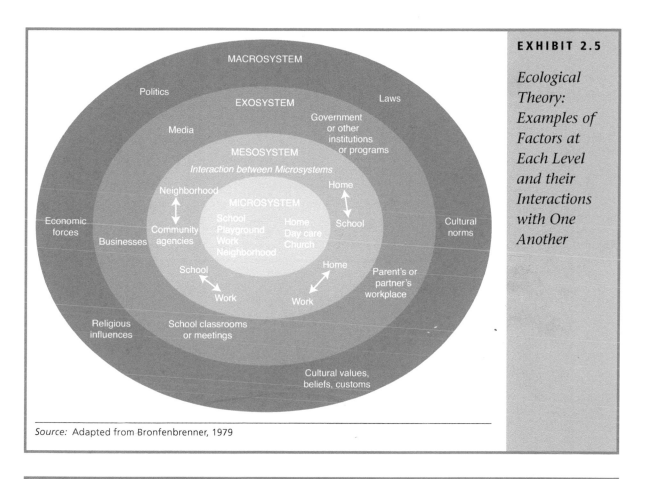

Source: Adapted from Bronfenbrenner, 1979

EXHIBIT 2.5

Ecological Theory: Examples of Factors at Each Level and their Interactions with One Another

Source: Scott Vandehey

PHOTO 2-A

One common mesosystem interaction is between home and work realms

EXHIBIT 2.6

Key Concepts in Ecological Theory

- *Adaptation:* The ability of individuals to adjust to their environments.
- *Coping:* The ways in which individuals deal with negative events and situations.
- *Energy:* The active engagement of people with their environments. Energy can take the form of input or output.
- *Interdependence:* The reciprocal and mutually reliant relationships that people have with one another and with their environments.
- *Social Environment:* The conditions, circumstances, and human interactions that encompass human beings.
- *Transactions:* Communication, interactions, or exchanges that occur between people and their environments. These can be positive or negative communications or exchanges.

Source: Adapted from Brandell, 1997; Bronfenbrenner, 1979

development. Ecological theory treats these levels a little differently from the micro-mezzo-macro approach, though, in that there is an additional level, and the dimensions of the environment that fall within each level are slightly different. Ecological theory also places more emphasis on the physical settings in which people live as well as on how two or more settings interact with one another to affect people and their experiences. The arrows in Exhibit 2.5 represent the dynamic interactions between different levels.

In addition to conceptualizing individuals and their environments based on different systems or levels, ecological theory employs several constructs to help describe how interactions among systems or levels take place and how individuals react to those interactions. Some terms used in ecological theory are similar to those in systems theory, but others that are specific to ecological theory are presented in Exhibit 2.6.

According to ecological theory, all people have *transactions,* or positive and negative exchanges, with others. For example, a positive transaction would occur when a person receives praise or money for doing good work. A negative transaction might occur when a child is scolded for not sharing toys.

Because people are actively engaged in their environments, they receive and expend *energy* in the form of *inputs* and *outputs.* Recall that these last two terms were introduced earlier in the chapter, in the discussion on systems theory. Another way to think about inputs and outputs, according to ecological theory, is to consider all aspects of information, communication, or resources that add something to or take away from an individual's life. Education, services, or health benefits are examples of inputs. Spending time or money on a family member's care or putting efforts into a neighborhood renewal project are examples of outputs. Keep in mind that even though outputs imply that energy is being spent, it can be spent on activities that are rewarding, which can be viewed as an input. In this sense, inputs and outputs have a dynamic relationship.

The ecological theory also instructs us that, to maintain health and well-being, people must be able to *adapt* to changes in their environments. Adaptation is a significant issue because, according to ecological theory, people and their environments are always changing. A key role for social workers is to help people adapt to changes that take place in their environments as well as to adapt environmental circumstances to the changing needs of individuals. For instance, people must adapt to events such as moves, marriages, and job promotions. Similarly, environmental issues such as housing, transportation, and social policies need to be adapted to meet the needs of individual members of society.

Social workers are also concerned with how well people cope with various situations. *Coping,* similar to adaptation, deals with how people adjust to the negative events that occur in their lives. For example, people have different ways of coping with death, stress, or crises. Coping styles can either add to or detract from people's ability to function.

Finally, ecological theory is concerned with the *interdependence* of people with others and their environments. In the context of their *social environments,* people have a mutually reliant relationship in which each depends on the other for growth and development. Similarly, people have dynamic relationships with their environments and vice versa; each maintains a balance with the other to sustain life and growth. When one is out of balance, so is the other. Many of these concepts are similar to those used in systems theory. These similarities are discussed in more detail later in the chapter.

Applying Ecological Theory

Now let us look at Juan's situation from the point of view of ecological theory. Looking at Juan's microsystem, *you could assess his developmental status as a teenager, all the settings in which Juan interacts, and the roles he plays in each. These areas might include his physical, emotional, and cognitive development; the physical environment of his home, school, church, and neighborhood; his interactions with his family, teachers, peers, social worker (you), and priest; and his roles of son, student, friend, and parishioner. You would also want to explore how Juan perceives his roles and interactions within each of these settings.*

In Juan's mesosystem, *you would want to consider how two or more of the systems within Juan's environment interact to influence his development as well as how Juan interacts with people and situations within these settings. For example, you could examine the interplay between Juan's home and school life and between his home and church life. You could also look at how Juan's neighborhood affects all the other settings in which he is involved.*

Juan's exosystem *would consist of facets such as the manufacturing plant where his father worked, his mother's physician and the health care system where she receives care, bars or other places where his father goes to drink (if his father leaves the home to drink), and community agencies that could provide support for Juan. You would assess various factors in Juan's environment that affect him indirectly but that could potentially impact his development.*

The macrosystem *would involve issues such as local, national, and international economic pressures; school policies regarding educational standards; societal attitudes about families, teenagers, and minority groups; tenets within the Hispanic or Latino culture and its interface with the majority culture; societal expectations about roles, norms, and expectations of individuals; and other factors such as laws and social policies that can affect individual lives.*

In addition to assessing the levels on which Juan is experiencing problems, you would need to assess the ways in which Juan is dealing with his problems and how his interactions with others and his environment are affecting his functioning and development. In doing this, you would assess how Juan's transactions with others and his environment are affecting his well-being, how well Juan seems to adapt and cope with problems and new situations, how energy is expended and replenished in his life, and how Juan's interdependence with others and his environment both supports and hinders his well-being.

Given all of this information, you would need to make some decisions about which factors in Juan's environment are exerting the greatest influence on his development and functioning. These factors would then serve as the point at which to develop interventions for improving Juan's situation. Because of the interactive nature of this theory—as with the micro-mezzo-macro approach—it is likely that as you intervene on one level or with a few facets of Juan's environment, this intervention will have a ripple effect. That is, intervention at one point will have an impact on other areas of Juan's environment to create change in his situation.

Critiquing Ecological Theory

Perceiving client problems from the ecological theory can be daunting, as you saw in the discussion of the micro-mezzo-macro perspective. There are some other criticisms of the theory as well:

- There are, potentially, an endless number of areas in each level that could be assessed, which can seem overwhelming. Two practitioners working with the same client and using the ecological theory could end up choosing two completely different realms on which to focus, making it seem as if the theory lacks validity and reliability.

- The broad scope of the theory makes it difficult to test empirically and to predict behavior. These weaknesses are especially true if social workers attempt to gather historical information on these levels in addition to current information.

- Ecological theory does not pay enough attention to biological aspects of clients. However, social workers could choose to incorporate biologically related information into an assessment and intervention. For example, social workers could request information from a client's physician about that client's health status, results of various tests, and medications that the client is using.

Nevertheless, the ecological theory also has some compelling strengths. First, it is comprehensive. It goes beyond the psychological and attends to the larger environment in which clients live. The theory takes a balanced approach to human nature (it considers the interaction between an individual and the environment); therefore, it is less likely to place "blame" for problems in functioning entirely on the individual or the environment. Rather, solutions to problems can be sought from both realms. Also, ecological theory attends to the interactions that occur within and between systems, which underscores the complex and important dynamics that exist in clients' lives.

Finally, the constructs that make up ecological theory, particularly coping and adaptation, can be relatively easy for social workers to apply to client situations and for clients to understand, which can facilitate the helping process. And it is possible to standardize definitions for many of these constructs, which means that they could be applied and evaluated in ways that add to their empirical value in social work practice.

THE ECOSYSTEMS APPROACH: COMBINING ECOLOGICAL AND SYSTEMS THEORIES

This chapter has pointed out similarities among concepts and ideas in the ecological and systems theories. Because these two theories share similar ideas relating to systems and the interactions between individuals and their environments, many scholars and practitioners combine them to create an even more comprehensive way to work with clients (Beckett & Johnson, 1995). Specifically:

- Both theories look at the interactions and interdependence between person and environment.
- Both view these interactions and relationships as dynamic, changing processes.
- Both focus on systems and how these systems maintain themselves, influence other systems, and work together to function as a whole system.

Alone, each theory provides a comprehensive way to view people in their environment. Each offers slightly different ways to think about how systems impact one another and how people adapt to their changing circumstances and surroundings. Taken together, however, these theories build on each other to explain more fully how various processes might affect individual functioning. For example, systems theory focuses on the roles that people assume to help bring order to their systems. Ecological theory takes a slightly broader view by looking at the settings in which people play out those roles and how aspects of these settings might interact to impact people's functioning. Systems theory offers ideas about how systems maintain homeostasis. Ecological theory contributes to this idea by considering how people adapt to their environments and cope with problems, which are ways to maintain homeostasis in their environments.

Keep in mind, however, that some critics argue that combining concepts from two theories undermines the validity and effectiveness of each. Recall from Chapter 1 that pure theorists or single-theory advocates would question the use of these two theories in combination because, although they share similar characteristics, they differ slightly with regard to definitions and approaches. Others would argue that the utility of combining the theories far outweighs any compromises in the theories' reliability and validity that might result from doing so.

THE STRENGTHS PERSPECTIVE

Another approach that is widely used in social work is the strengths perspective. The **strengths perspective** is based on the assumption that all human beings have the capacity for growth, change, and adaptation (Weick, Rapp, Sullivan, & Kisthardt, 1989). All people, regardless of the severity of their situation or problems, possess skills, capabilities, and strengths. To put it another way, people are much more than their problems. Using the strengths perspective in social work means examining clients' skills, goals, talents, abilities, and resources, as well as the strengths and resources found in their environments, and then incorporating these strengths into the processes of assessment and intervention.

In addition, the strengths perspective asserts that people are experts on their situations and problems, which means that they are naturally well positioned to develop solutions to those problems. People have usually survived both troubling and successful times in the past, so they have insight into which approaches to problems have worked and have not worked for them.

An important tenet of the strengths perspective is that people are resourceful and resilient, characteristics that should be used when clients seek help from social workers. Even so, social workers recognize that oppression, discrimination, and other forces beyond the individual's power also contribute to client problems. Therefore, social workers need to assess their clients' abilities while evaluating the environment for potential barriers that may be beyond the control of even the most resourceful client (Early & GlenMaye, 2000; Saleebey, 1992).

The strengths perspective requires that the client and the social worker be collaborators in the change process. Social workers begin "where the client is," relying on the client's interpretation of the situation and trusting the client to accurately state her or his needs and desires about how to make changes and which goals to achieve. The social worker is responsible for identifying opportunities for clients to use their strengths in the change process and to help clients learn new skills that will support them in achieving their goals. Social workers also may need to provide education about the larger environment if there are conditions that the client may be unable to change. This education process is viewed as *empowerment*: The social worker is arming clients with information that they can add to their set of skills (Early & GlenMaye, 2000; Saleebey, 1992).

When working with clients from the strengths perspective, social workers do not focus on labeling the problem or identifying its causes. Rather, they spend time assessing clients' strengths and resources to change their situations. The focus on strengths is a way to empower clients and divert attention from obstacles that might be impeding clients' progress. This does not mean that social workers ignore their clients' problems. Rather, they view these problems as catalysts for change. The fact that a client has a problem means that there is opportunity for her or him to do something differently and to learn or use skills that will help to achieve the established goals (Early & GlenMaye, 2000; Saleebey, 1992).

This idea of taking the focus off problems is central to the strengths perspective. Some social workers argue that typical social work assessment and intervention place too much emphasis on client problems. Focusing on the problem leads to several assumptions about the helping process (Weick *et al.*, 1989):

- The client is helpless and unable to resolve problems.

- The social worker is the expert, because only a professional with the right expertise can solve the client's problems.

- Finding the precise cause of the problem leads to a specific solution and focuses on the individual (she or he "has" a problem) rather than on socioenvironmental issues that contribute to problems.

The strengths perspective directs the social worker and client away from the problem to focus on the expertise of the client in understanding her or his situation. This focus enables the client to use skills to deal more effectively with the problem, which can improve feelings of competence in dealing with other problems.

Social workers often identify client strengths as part of an initial assessment. Many social service agencies include a section in client records where social workers can list client strengths. However, using the strengths perspective involves much more than writing a list (Early & GlenMaye, 2000). Rather, the social worker consistently focuses on the client's strengths and skills throughout her or his work with the client and helps the client mobilize resources to achieve goals. The social worker has to use these strengths in the helping process from beginning to end, with the main focus being on empowering clients to use their own resources to make changes. The social worker's job is to help the client reframe negative situations to find the skills and resources needed to move forward.

Applying the Strengths Perspective

As Juan's social worker, how would you apply the strengths perspective to his case? One of the first places to start is to identify his strengths, skills, and resources. Juan seems to have many resources, including his positive relationships with several teachers and his priest. The background information suggests that Juan might have some positive relationships with students at the school and in the neighborhood; so you could explore those resources. Also, it is possible that Juan has a good relationship with his mother and other family members, but more information on these relationships needs to be gathered. You can help Juan apply the positive aspects of these relationships to other relationships that may not be functioning as well.

Juan seems to have several interests and abilities that include his volunteer work and his involvement with his church. You could begin with these interests and build on them to find other activities in which Juan is interested. For example, you might want to find out if Juan enjoys sports, art, music, or writing. More involvement in activities that Juan enjoys may help to build his self-confidence, which could help improve his performance in other academic areas.

Related to academic performance, Juan's grades and attendance are described as worsening over the last couple of years. What were these areas like a few years earlier? It is possible that Juan was doing well academically before his family situation worsened.

You could also explore what Juan's relationships with his peers and parents were like before things started to deteriorate. For example, has Juan always had a problem with behaving violently? If Juan had performed well before his parents' problems developed, then you would only need to tap into his previous successes to help him find ways to deal with his current situation. For example, you could start with building his skills at school. Thus, Juan could work on his grades, behavior, and relationships and then use his skills to improve relationships at home.

You could also educate Juan and his family about resources in the community that could target his father's unemployment and his mother's health care needs. By focusing on education instead of the family's "lack of ability" to find work and health care, you take the focus off what seems like individual "problems" and put it onto the family's efforts to develop skills that will allow them to problem-solve effectively now and in the future. Similarly, rather than making Juan's problems the central focus for intervention—which could feel overwhelming to him—you would consider his strengths and skills as the starting point for intervention. By adopting this approach, you are likely to help Juan to feel more empowered and more hopeful that things can improve. Through this process, you would consistently identify the family's existing skills and strengths and use these as the basis on which to develop further skills and solve problems.

Critiquing the Strengths Perspective

The strengths perspective does come with criticisms, including the following:

- A major issue is that the tenets of the perspective can be linked with values of individual responsibility and personal autonomy, ignoring the impacts of class, race, and other sources of inequality on personal well-being and the responsibility that government has in addressing social problems that impact individuals.

- A focus on the individual is also criticized for promoting the idea that self-esteem in and of itself can promote well-being and solve social problems.

- A focus on strengths alone may undermine the legitimacy of recent empirical evidence pointing to biological and related causes for individual issues, such as neurological bases for certain mental health problems (Taylor, 2006).

- The strengths perspective assumes that communities and other resources on which people may draw for resources are inherently good, ignoring the possibility that communities and other organizations can sometimes perpetuate oppressive, self-serving agendas—again blaming individuals for problems that may be more related to discriminatory and inequitable social and economic structures (Gray, 2011; Jordan, 2008; Kristjansson, 2007).

- Many agencies probably would not be amenable to using only this approach. Because of governmental mandates and funding issues, many agencies rely on, and are required to collect, extensive background information on their clients. Further, many agencies operate from a problem-focused perspective, which naturally dictates that social workers delve deeply into the circumstances surrounding the client's problems. Social workers can incorporate elements of the strengths perspective to augment approaches based on other theories and perspectives, but this might not be sufficient to use the strengths perspective effectively.

- Although the strengths perspective seems straightforward and its concepts appear simple, different social workers will probably define the meaning of *strengths* very differently. Therefore, defining and measuring the concepts from this perspective could be difficult, making empirical testing difficult as well. That being said, some empirical evidence does exist on the effectiveness of strengths-based social work interventions, pointing to the feasibility of testing concepts from this perspective (e.g., Vanderplasschen, Wolf, Rapp, & Broekaert, 2007).

- Because of the current popularity of problem-focused models, social workers who want to use the strengths perspective may not be taken seriously by other professionals, and the methods that these social workers employ may not be considered as valid as other, more accepted methods—although, as empirical evidence increases on the effectiveness of this perspective, these attitudes and views may change.

An obvious benefit to the strengths perspective is that it is a very positive framework in which to conceptualize clients' issues. Working with client strengths can be empowering for the client and the social worker. This is congruent with the value of dignity and worth of the person outlined in the *Code of Ethics* (National Association of Social Workers, approved 1996, revised 2008). Specifically, the strengths perspective allows social workers to support the dignity and worth of clients by concentrating on their strengths; as clients' strengths develop, their problem-solving skills can be enhanced, which ultimately can lead to deeper feelings of dignity and self-worth.

Another benefit is that the strengths perspective diverts the focus from the client's problems, thereby removing sole responsibility for problems from the client. Also, because the social worker is not spending time identifying problems and looking for causes, she or he can spend more time identifying resources that the client already has to solve problems. This last point is related to the idea that the strengths perspective is "present oriented." Very little time is devoted to collecting client histories other than to identify skills that the client has used in the past to solve problems. A focus on the present can make working with the client easier than approaches that call for a lot of history taking and information gathering.

Finally, the concepts that underlie the strengths perspective are fairly straightforward and can be easily applied to work with clients.

CONCLUSION

Although social work relies on many theories, the theories and perspectives discussed in this chapter as part of the person-in-environment lens can be viewed as bases on which to conceptualize client problems in the context of client environments. Social workers often use these theories and perspectives as guiding concepts, while also incorporating knowledge from other areas to enhance their understanding of client situations. Using these comprehensive theories and perspectives helps to ensure that social workers consider different areas of a client's situation, not just the areas that are particular to the client's immediate environment.

The theories and perspectives presented in this chapter get at the essence of social work; that is, they help to view clients as dynamic, active beings who interact with their environment. Although these theories and perspectives have their limitations, they help to ensure that social workers consider a broad range of factors that could influence their clients' problems and well-being. These considerations include factors that might perpetuate problems of discrimination and oppression, which are key issues addressed by the social work profession. Indeed, these theories and perspectives serve as the foundation to which other theories, models, approaches, perspectives, and supporting knowledge can be added when working with clients.

All of the theories and approaches discussed in this chapter are similar, in that they move from the individual to the environment to explore complex characteristics that are part of a client's life. Although some are more inclusive and far-reaching than others, they all offer a template on which social workers can begin to assess and intervene with clients. Look back at Quick Guide 3 to review and compare the characteristics of the theories discussed in this chapter.

MAIN POINTS

- Social work tends to use a comprehensive approach to conceptualizing client problems, often referred to as the person-in-environment lens: Client problems are viewed within the environmental context in which they occur.

- The micro-mezzo-macro approach provides a helpful way to organize a great deal of information about a client and to think about the ways in which various aspects of a person's life can interact with one another. Rather than focusing solely on the individual, the micro-mezzo-macro approach views people as part of a system of individual, immediate social, and larger social systems with which they interact.

- The biopsychosocial approach is used by several helping professions and is useful in conceptualizing client problems from a multidimensional perspective. It tends to view the client's situation from an individualistic perspective; that is, it assesses the client's biological, psychological, and immediate social environment to identify problems and areas in need of intervention.

- Systems theory describes the active interactions between people and their social systems. It is used in social work as a way to comprehensively understand human interactions within the environment. It is also used to work with families when trying to understand family dynamics and interactions.

- Genograms provide visual maps or representations of families to help social workers and their clients see how the family is structured and how dynamics might be playing out in a family. Ecomaps are tools that social workers can use to help families see how their broader ecological context impacts their well-being.

- Ecological theory separates the factors within a person's environment that are important to development into four distinct levels. This theory emphasizes the physical settings in which people live as well as how two or more settings interact to affect people and their experiences.

- Many scholars and practitioners combine ecological theory with systems theories to create an even more comprehensive way to approach work with clients. However, some critics argue that combining concepts from more than one theory undermines the validity and effectiveness of each.

- The strengths perspective conceptualizes people as much more than their problems. It is based on the assumption that people have the capacity for growth, change, and adaptation, and that people possess skills, capabilities, and strengths to improve their situations. An important tenet in the strengths perspective is that people are resourceful and resilient, characteristics that should be used in the intervention process.

EXERCISES

1. *Carla Washburn interactive case at* www.routledgesw.com/cases. Study the situation presented in this case. After getting acquainted with Carla Washburn's situation, apply concepts from the biopsychosocial approach to assess it. Below are questions to guide your analysis:
   a. What are some of the biological issues you might want to attend to?
   b. What are some of the psychological issues you might want to attend to?
   c. What are some of the social issues you might want to attend to?
   d. How would the assessment of the three areas above help guide your intervention with Carla? In what ways?
   e. What are some of the limitations to using this approach in Carla's situation?
2. *RAINN interactive case at* www.routledgesw.com/cases. Use the information presented for this case to answer the following questions:
   a. What are some biological issues a social worker should address with Sarah?
   b. What are some psychological issues a social worker should address with Sarah?
   c. How do Alan's psychological and physiological issues overlap?
   d. Identify at least two social issues that affect Sarah and two that affect Alan. Both Sarah and Alan experienced sexual assault, but are their social issues similar or different? Explain.
3. *Sanchez Family interactive case at* www.routledgesw.com/cases. After getting acquainted with the family, apply concepts from systems theory to assess their situation; refer to Exhibit 2.2 to review concepts from the theory. Below are questions to guide your analysis:
   a. What are the subsystems in this family?
   b. What are the boundaries like between subsystems and for the family as a whole?

    c. In what ways does the family maintain homeostasis?

    d. What roles does each family member take? Would you say these are age and relationship appropriate?

    e. What inputs and feedback (positive and negative) are the family receiving? What are the family's outputs?

    f. Is the family moving toward differentiation, entropy, negative entropy? Why or why not?

    g. Given your assessment, are there areas that might be of concern with regard to the well-being and functioning of this family? At what points might you want to intervene?

    h. What are the strengths and limitations to using systems theory to assess and intervene with this family?

4. *Critical thinking*. Imagine that you are Juan's social worker, and you want to create a genogram and an ecomap to visualize his situation.

    a. Use the vignettes throughout this chapter to draw a genogram and an ecomap. Do not make up any information.

    b. List the information you would like to obtain from Juan to complete the genogram and the ecomap.

    c. Based on the information you do have, are you able to draw any conclusions about how to help him approach his problems? Please explain and elaborate, drawing on any of the theories in this chapter.

5. *Hudson City interactive case at* www.routledgesw.com/cases. Review the issues facing the community. Then, answer the following questions:

    a. How could the micro, mezzo, macro levels of conceptualization be applied to this case to help you better understand the issues facing the community?

    b. In what ways can you use the ecomap to help guide your work with the community?

    c. How might the biopsychosocial conceptualization or ecological theory help explain how environmental issues impact the citizens' well-being on the individual level?

    d. What are the potential strengths of this community, and how could they be used in your work with the community?

CHAPTER 3

Lenses for Conceptualizing Problems and Interventions: Biopsychosocial Dimensions

Carlos is a 61-year-old Cuban immigrant whose family came to the United States when he was 15. After 20 years of marriage, Carlos's wife died five years ago, and he has not been in a serious relationship since. Carlos retired from his job in sales two years ago after he noticed that he was having trouble remembering client names and orders. Shortly after noticing these symptoms, Carlos was diagnosed with Alzheimer's disease.

Carlos has three adult children, all of whom live at least 100 miles away. Carlos misses his children, and he has not been able to spend much time with his grandchildren because of the distance and his children's busy schedules. Carlos also has two siblings, both of whom moved back to Cuba 10 years ago, and he does not get to see them much, either. Carlos describes his relationships with his children and siblings as "close," and he feels lonely because of his lack of contact with them. He misses the strong family ties that characterized his life in Cuba. Carlos has a few close friends in his church and his neighborhood, but he is afraid that he will lose these connections if he moves into a care facility when his symptoms get worse.

When he thinks about having to move, Carlos gets depressed over losing his independence and his sharp intellect, which he has always prized. Moreover, Carlos is worried about how he will pay to live in a care facility, particularly if he is there for a long time. Lately, Carlos has been feeling depressed, and he finds himself struggling with the meaning of life. He is not sure what all his hard work was for, and he feels as though all that he has done for his family has been in vain, especially because he knows how he will "end up" in the final stages of the disease. Carlos has been referred to a social worker at the health clinic where he receives care.

CARLOS'S STORY, ALTHOUGH SEEMINGLY STRAIGHTFORWARD, can quickly become complicated due to the many factors that may be affecting his well-being. On the surface, it seems as if many of Carlos's problems are psychological. Indeed, many social workers might begin by exploring psychological or even biological issues that appear to be causing these problems.

Chapter 2 discussed how social workers could use a biopsychosocial conceptualization for client problems. In this chapter, we will explore specific biopsychosocial theories and models that social workers often use to explain client problems. The theories, models, and perspectives discussed in this chapter are summarized and their various characteristics compared in Quick Guide 4.

THE DISEASE MODEL

The disease model is rooted in physiological processes that affect behavior and development. It is concerned with individual illness and dysfunction, which contribute to its problem-oriented focus. The disease model maintains that there is a clear and identifiable relationship between "dis-ease" and people's functioning and behaviors and problems. Therefore, according to this model, if interventions are targeted toward dysfunctional behaviors or physiological processes, the resulting problems can be "cured."

The disease model tends to be popular among health care and other helping professionals, including social workers. Indeed, regardless of the setting, much of social work involves assessment and intervention related to biological processes. Although many social workers may use other types of theories or approaches when working with clients, aspects of physiological functioning or biological processes are often relevant to the problems that clients present in practice.

Moreover, social workers often collaborate with other health professionals in their work with clients. Thus, social workers need to understand how to assess and intervene with clients based on the disease model as well as how to communicate to other professionals about physiological and biological concerns related to their clients' issues.

As you will see as you move through this book, the disease model can be used not only to inform many aspects of assessment and intervention, but also to augment other theories and more effectively explain client problems.

The Medical Model

Probably one of the most fundamental disease-based models for conceptualizing problems and interventions in social work and other professions is the **medical model.** This model emerged from Freud's ideas about the roots of psychological problems as well as from advances in medicine and in our understanding of physiological processes. Indeed, Freud's work on psychosexual development (which is discussed in a later section) and increasing knowledge of disease processes had a profound effect on the way many disciplines conceptualized problems. After decades

QUICK GUIDE 4   The Biopsychosocial Lens: Theories, Models, and Perspectives

	MEDICAL MODEL	COGNITIVE DEVELOPMENT	PSYCHOSEXUAL DEVELOPMENT
Type	Model	Theory	Theory
Focus	Individual	Individual	Individual
Assumptions	People are passive agents in their development.	People are passive agents in their development.	People are passive agents in their development.
Strengths	• Places emphasis on biological issues that can cause problems, which often get overlooked in assessment. • Physiological problems and their interventions can be empirically tested. • Diagnostic criteria offer clinicians a common language to use when working with clients. • Pinpointing problems can offer clients hope for a cure.	• Many constructs can be tested empirically and used to predict behavior. • Many constructs are consistent with knowledge on biological aspects of cognitive development. • Practical for use with clients. • Behavior can be predicted in the context of stage development.	• Credited with bringing sexual issues to the forefront. • Constructs such as defense mechanisms are widely used in practice. • Used in practice with clients who want to explore psychosexual development. • Behavior can be predicted in the context of stage development.
Limitations	• Diagnostic information is contained in health records, so appropriate and ethical use of model is important. • Use of diagnostic criteria for mental illnesses can be unreliable among clinicians. • Reduces clients to a set of symptoms, which may leave them feeling powerless to change. • Not enough focus on how environmental issues affect client problems.	• Explanation of development stops at adolescence. • Theory was developed on a small, nonrepresentative sample. • Isn't very flexible to allow for individual variations in development. • Does not consider sociocultural influences on development.	• Use with clients may not be practical. • Constructs cannot be tested empirically. • Does not consider environmental influences on development. • Theory was developed on a nonrepresentative sample. • Some constructs such as penis envy are considered sexist and outdated.

*C = classical conditioning; O = operant conditioning; SLT = social learning theory.

of relying on interventions based on morality and charity, social work adopted this more "scientific" model.

The emergence of the medical model promoted doctors to the level of experts who could diagnose and cure the ills that plagued their patients. It also introduced a new language that influenced how social workers thought about problems.

PSYCHOSOCIAL DEVELOPMENT	LEARNING*	HUMANISTIC
Theory	Theories	Perspectives
Individual and limited focus on the environment	*C/O:* Individual *SLT:* Individual & environment	Individual & environment
People take an active role in their development.	*C/O:* People are passive agents in learning. *SLT:* People are active agents in learning.	People are active agents in their development.
• Places some emphasis on interactions between individuals and their environments. • Explains development across the life span. • "Normalizes" some developmental crises and struggles that might otherwise be considered dysfunctional. • Practical for use with clients. • Behavior can be predicted in the context of stage development.	• Concepts are useful and easy to apply to practice. • Constructs can be tested empirically and can be used to predict behavior. • SLT, and to a certain extent C/O, can be empowering for clients if they are taught or made aware of tenets behind behavior change. • SLT addresses people's active role in learning to influence behavior.	• Positive, empowering approach to work with clients. • Interventions are client focused, allowing clients to guide process. • Focuses on strengths rather than problems. • Some specific interventions based on these perspectives can be applied in a systematic manner, which lend themselves to empirical testing.
• Is not very flexible to allow for individual differences in development. • Constructs can be difficult to test empirically. • May lack relevance for different minority groups.	• C/O theories may give too little credit to people and their roles in learning. • C/O theories do not place emphasis on the environment and its influence on learning and behavior.	• Concepts are vague and difficult to define from person to person. • Broad constructs cannot be tested empirically or predict behavior.

For example, the medical model turned people into "patients," who were said to suffer from "disorder" and "disease." (Social workers often use "client," "consumer," or "participant" as opposed to "patient" to demedicalize the client–worker relationship.)

The medical model posits that:

QUICK GUIDE 5   DSM-5 Assessment

Section 1: DSM-5 Basics: Introductory section that outlines changes implemented in DSM-5 from DSM-IV-TR, use of the manual, and a cautionary statement.

Section 2: Diagnostic Criteria and Codes: Divides mental health disorders into topics with subtopics, diagnostic criteria, and separate notations for psychosocial and contextual factors impacting disorders. Major catagories for disorders include:

- Neurodevelopmental disorders.
- Schizophrenia spectrum and other psychotic disorders.
- Bipolar and related disorders.
- Depressive disorders.
- Anxiety disorders.
- Obsessive-compulsive and related disorders.
- Trauma- and stressor-related disorders.
- Dissociative disorders.
- Somatic symptom and related disorders.
- Feeding and eating disorders.
- Elimination disorders.
- Sleep-wake disorders.
- Sexual dysfunctions.
- Gender dysphoria.
- Disruptive, impulse-control, and conduct disorders.
- Substance-related and addictive disorders.
- Neurocognitive disorders.
- Personality disorders.
- Paraphilic disorders.
- Other mental disorders.
- Medication-induced movement disorders and other adverse effects of medication.
- Other conditions that may be a focus of clinical attention.

Section 3: Emerging Measures and Models: Includes assessment measures, cultural formulation, alternative DSM-5 model for personality disorders, and conditions for further study.

Source: Adapted from American Psychiatric Association, 2013.

- Diseases can be identified through a list of symptoms.
- These symptoms can be alleviated through logical and scientific examination of the patient.

Thus, problems and ills are viewed as being a part of the patient: Something about the person is causing the problem, and this cause can be treated.

A tool based on the medical model that is commonly used by social workers and other helping professionals is the *Diagnostic and Statistical Manual of Mental Disorders* (often called the *DSM*), currently in its fifth edition (American Psychiatric Association, 2013). This manual describes the symptoms, etiology (causes), prevalence, and other aspects of most major mental health problems. Quick Guide 5 describes how the DSM-5 is organized. Along with the DSM-5, practitioners use the World Health Organization's *International Classification of Diseases, Tenth Revision, Clinical Modification* (ICD-10-CM) (World Health Organization, 2011).

Before a diagnosis can be made, the client has to meet a certain number of criteria described under each disorder in the DSM-5. Most insurance companies and social service agencies require that clients presenting with mental health issues be assessed using the DSM-5 and ICD-10-CM. Further, this assessment often dictates how the social worker will intervene with the client.

The transition from the previous edition of the DSM (DSM-IV-TR) to the DSM-5 was not without controversy. Significant changes were made that sparked intense debates about constructs and research behind mental health disorders, as well as how the changes would affect consumers of services. Some of the controversies surrounded modifications made to diagnostic criteria for conditions such as autism, major depression, bipolar disorder, and attention-deficit hyperactivity disorder. For example, some experts asserted that the changes would result in fewer children qualifying for treatment for autism, while others accused the pharmaceutical industry of influencing DSM changes to increase profits. Still others charged that, according to DSM-5 criteria, "normal" reactions to grief, stress, and other life problems would become pathological and treatable through medication (Frances, 2013). Other criticisms of the DSM-5 and the medical model in general are discussed below.

Key Elements of Human Biology

Medical research has illuminated how important biological structures and processes are to wellness, illness, and disease. Social workers need some of this basic knowledge about the brain and neurological and genetic processes so they can help their clients better understand how these factors can contribute to disease and other issues.

For example, a client who wants to start a family and is a known carrier for a hereditary disease may want to know her chances of passing the disease on to her children. This information can help her with decisions about childbearing and planning for possible consequences if her child inherits the disease. Social workers can help clients better understand how hormones are implicated in disease processes and how to manage symptoms through diet or medication. Social workers can also assess the potential role of biological processes in the development of mental health issues. For example, dysfunction of the thyroid hormone can cause weight gain and symptoms of depression. A social worker who knows this fact might suggest that a client get a full medical checkup to ensure that no biological problems are complicating the client's symptoms. Furthermore, many social workers are part of interdisciplinary teams that include health professionals, so they need to be well versed in basic physiological systems to communicate with their colleagues about clients.

Here, we will look at the basic structure of the brain, neurons, neurotransmitters, hormones, and genes as well as their roles and functions in the human body. In future chapters, we will look at how these different structures and processes affect people at different stages of development and how the interaction of the environment and these structures and processes can affect the health and well-being of people as they grow and develop.

The Brain and the Nervous System The nervous system is a complex electrochemical communication system for the body. The central nervous system consists of the brain and the spinal cord, and the peripheral nervous system connects the brain and spinal cord to other parts of the body. On the cellular level, the nervous system sends the body information through a complex interaction of nerve cells, chemicals, and electrical impulses.

With advances in technology, we have been able to study and understand the brain in ways not possible in the past. We now have many ways to image the brain, such as positron emission tomography (PET) scans, functional magnetic resonance imaging (fMRI), and transcranial magnetic stimulation (TMS). These imaging techniques allow us to assess energy flow and mental processing in the brain, which in turn helps us to better understand the brain's role in emotional and behavioral dysfunction. They also help us understand our subjective experiences in interactions with others and the environment (Lepage & Theoret, 2010).

The structures of the brain are organized in a way that reflects their evolutionary development. The base of the brain is made up of the more primitive structures including the brainstem, which regulates physiological functions such as sleep, temperature, and heart rate. The **thalamus** sits at the top of the brainstem and serves as a relay station for sensory information. It sorts information and sends it to other parts of the brain for interpretation. It also seems to be involved in sleep and wakefulness (Hirata & Castro-Alamancos, 2010).

The more advanced structures of the brain, which are depicted in Exhibit 3.1, are newer from an evolutionary standpoint and thus make up the outer part of the brain. These are the main structures:

- **Cerebral cortex:** The principal outer structure is responsible for complex mental functions such as planning and thinking.

- **Neocortex:** The outermost part makes up about 80 percent of the cortex. It

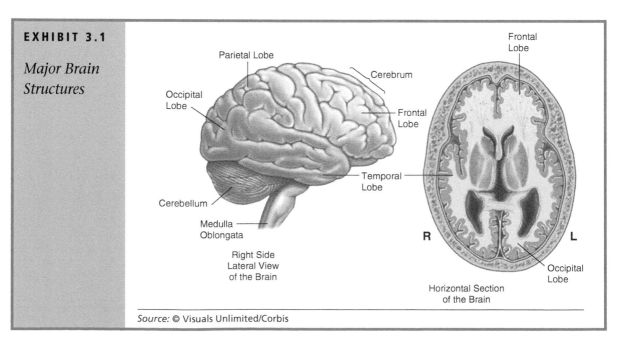

EXHIBIT 3.1

Major Brain Structures

Parietal Lobe

Cerebrum

Occipital Lobe

Frontal Lobe

Frontal Lobe

Temporal Lobe

Cerebellum

Medulla Oblongata

Right Side Lateral View of the Brain

R

L

Occipital Lobe

Horizontal Section of the Brain

Source: © Visuals Unlimited/Corbis

is thought that the neocortex developed to help human beings understand each other with regard to intentions, feelings, and thoughts (Adolphs, 2009).

- **Right hemisphere and left hemisphere:** The cerebral cortex is divided into two large hemispheres, each of which is divided into four lobes. The right hemisphere is responsible for helping us process emotion, nonverbal communication, and sensations such as touch and pressure. The left hemisphere helps us to process things like language and fine motor movements.

- **Broca's area and Wernicke's area:** These two areas are located in the left hemisphere and help us to control and understand language.

- **Corpus callosum:** This large bundle of axons connects the two hemispheres and relays information between the two (Gazzaniga, 2010).

- **Occipital lobes:** These two areas at the back of the cerebral cortex allow us to process information such as color, shape, and motion. An injury to this lobe can cause blindness or damage to part of a person's visual field (Swisher *et al.*, 2010).

- **Temporal lobes:** Two lobes at the sides of the cerebral cortex are responsible for hearing, language, and memory. Damage to these lobes can result in problems with long-term memory (Lambon Ralph, Ehsan, Baker, & Rogers, 2012).

- **Frontal lobes:** Large areas at the front of the cerebral cortex are responsible for personality, intelligence, and voluntary control of muscles. Damage to these lobes can create changes in personality among other problems. You may be familiar with the famous example of the 25-year-old Phineas Gage. In 1848 he was a victim of a work-related explosion, which resulted in an iron rod being driven through the left side of his face and out the top of his head. Before the accident, he was described as calm, mild-mannered, and well-liked. After the accident, he was described as aggressive, unreliable, and hot-headed.

- **Prefrontal cortex:** This part of the frontal lobes is responsible for planning, reasoning, and self-control (Rahnev, Lau, & de Lange, 2011).

- **Parietal lobes:** These lobes on the top of the head are responsible for attention, spatial location, and motor control (Arcizet, Mirpour, & Bisley, 2011).

- **Limbic system:** Between the brainstem and the cerebral cortex are two important structures. The **amygdala** helps us to recognize and discriminate things necessary to our survival, such as mates, food, and social rivals. The **hippocampus** helps us determine what information to store as memories and which information to recall (Wang & Morris, 2010).

Research is helping us to better understand these structures and their functions and the role they play in behavior and mental health problems such as stress, trauma, and depression.

Some of the recent research focused on the brain relates to traumatic brain injuries (TBI). TBI is in the headlines because of growing awareness of the long-term impacts of concussions from sports and military injuries. Most TBIs result from closed-head injuries such as concussion (as opposed to penetrating injuries like that of Phineas Gage). The leading causes of TBI are falls, violence (like those that can occur with explosives and firearms), and motor vehicle accidents (National Institutes of Health, 2012). Sports injuries are another major cause of brain injury. Professional athletes such as football players and wrestlers experience TBI, but young athletes are a special concern, particularly since TBI is a leading cause of death and disability in the United States. The National Center for Injury Prevention and Control (2010) estimates that 5.3 million Americans (2 percent of the population) live with a disability resulting from TBI. We will discuss some of these issues in later chapters.

Neurons   As brain researchers have discovered, the brain's ability to function depends in large part on **neurons**, which are the cells that process information. There are about 100 billion neurons in the human brain. Most neurons develop early in life, but their shape, size, and connections constantly change and are greatly affected by environmental factors, such as stimulation from a parent or exposure to alcohol or other substances.

Exhibit 3.2 is a diagram of a neuron. As the diagram shows, neurons consist of the following key structures:

- cell body with the **nucleus**;

- **dendrites** that allow neurons to receive input from other neurons;

- **axon**, which carries information away from the cell body to other neurons;

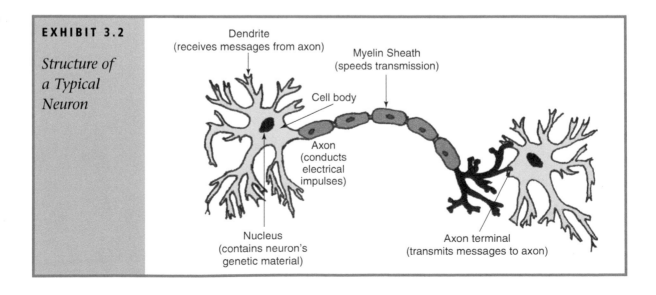

EXHIBIT 3.2

Structure of a Typical Neuron

Dendrite (receives messages from axon)

Myelin Sheath (speeds transmission)

Cell body

Axon (conducts electrical impulses)

Nucleus (contains neuron's genetic material)

Axon terminal (transmits messages to axon)

PHOTO 3-A

"Brainbow"

To see a "brainbow," a color image showing how neurons interact with one another, go to http://cbs.fas.harvard.edu/ science/ connectome-project/ brainbow.

This "brainbow" was created by staining brain tissue with different colors to illuminate the extensive connections among the neurons. The colors allow us to follow each neuron as it connects to other neurons to better understand the circuitry of the brain and nervous system.

Source: Lichtman, Livet, & Sanes, 2008

- **myelin sheath**, a layer of fat covering the axon that facilitates the nerve impulses that allow neurons to communicate. Disorders involving the myelin sheath can cause numerous problems. For example, multiple sclerosis is caused when the myelin sheath hardens and is replaced by scar tissue (Haines, Inglese, & Casaccia, 2011).

Neurons play an important role in the brain's plasticity, or ability to change and adapt. Children's brains demonstrate the most plasticity, but as we grow older, our brains can still recover from injury or damage. How well we recover depends a great deal on whether neurons have been damaged or destroyed (Huang & Chang, 2009). If neurons have not been destroyed, there are three main ways in which repair can happen:

- **Collateral sprouting:** The axons of healthy neurons adjacent to damaged ones grow new branches.

- **Substitution of function:** A damaged region of the brain is taken over by another, healthier area of the brain.

- **Neurogenesis:** New neurons are generated. Neurogenesis has been demonstrated in mammals such as mice. In humans, it has been documented in the hippocampus (Hagg, 2009).

The complexity of neural networks is continually being realized, as is the way in which neurons develop, make connections to one another, and are affected by environmental influences (Hashimoto-Torii, Kawasawa, Kuhn, & Rakic, 2011).

Neurotransmitters   One of the questions that once confounded brain researchers was how the electrical impulses from the axon of one neuron are transmitted to the dendrites of another neuron. The answer is **neurotransmitters,** which are chemicals that can activate electrical impulses in the nervous system. Exhibit 3.3 gives a close-up view of the complex mechanism by which neurons communicate with one another:

- **Synapse,** or synaptic gap. Since neurons do not directly touch one another, they must use chemicals to carry messages across the space between them, which is called a synapse. These gaps mostly lie between the axon of one neuron and the dendrite of another.

- **Terminal buttons.** Electrical impulses of a neuron are converted in the terminal buttons at the end of an axon into a chemical signal that can communicate with another neuron across the synapse. The terminal

EXHIBIT 3.3

Structure of a Synapse Between Neurons

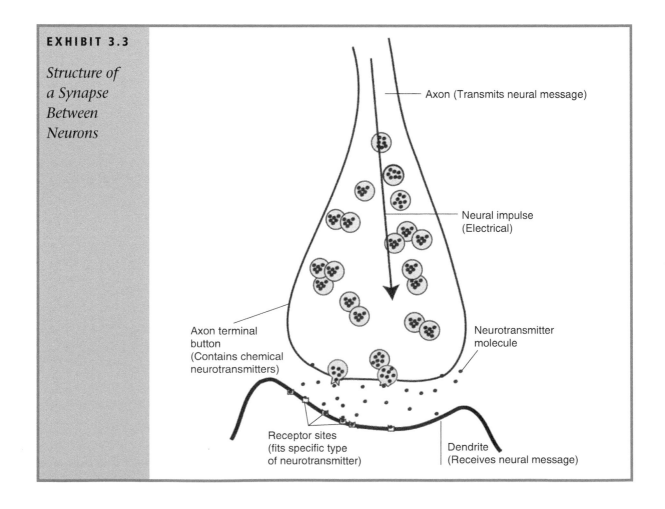

Axon (Transmits neural message)

Neural impulse (Electrical)

Axon terminal button (Contains chemical neurotransmitters)

Neurotransmitter molecule

Receptor sites (fits specific type of neurotransmitter)

Dendrite (Receives neural message)

buttons are little sacs containing neurotransmitters. When an electrical impulse travels down the axon of a neuron, it triggers the release of a neurotransmitter, which enters into the synaptic gap.

- **Receptor sites.** The dendrites of the receiving neuron have a variety of receptor sites, each of which accommodates a specific neurotransmitter. If there is a fit between the receptor and the neurotransmitter, the receiving neuron will accept the signal.

Once the transmission of a neural impulse is complete, some of the neurotransmitter molecules that have not fit into receptor sites are reabsorbed into the axon. This process is called reuptake. These neurotransmitter molecules are then available for the next neural impulse.

As you can see, neurotransmitters play a crucial role in facilitating communication between neurons. Some neurotransmitters stimulate neurons to fire while others inhibit neurons from firing—some do both. Generally, neurons secrete only one type of neurotransmitter, but the synapse between two neurons can simultaneously contain several different neurotransmitters from different neurons trying to communicate with nearby neurons. Exhibit 3.4 lists the major categories of neurotransmitters that have the largest effects on behavior.

Neural processes are important to understand because neurotransmitters and the process through which messages are sent and received are implicated in certain behavioral and mental health disorders, such as posttraumatic stress disorder (PTSD)

NEUROTRANSMITTER	ROLE	EXAMPLES OF HOW IT WORKS	**EXHIBIT 3.4**
Acetylcholine (ACh)	Stimulates neurons to fire; involved in muscle movements, learning, and memory.	Botox, made from botulin, destroys ACh, paralyzing facial muscles that cause wrinkling. People with Alzheimer's disease have a deficiency of ACh.	*Key Neurotransmitters and Their Effects on Behavior*
Dopamine	Controls voluntary movements; affects sleep, mood, learning, and attention.	Activation of dopamine receptors can cause excitement, alertness, and elevated mood. Too little dopamine is implicated in Parkinson's disease.	
Endorphin	Stimulates neurons to fire and depresses nervous system activity.	An increase in endorphins helps to reduce pain and increase feelings of pleasure.	
GABA	Inhibits neurons from firing.	Low levels of GABA are associated with fear, anxiety, and depression.	

EXHIBIT 3.4	NEUROTRANSMITTER	ROLE	EXAMPLES OF HOW IT WORKS
Continued	Glutamate	Stimulates neurons to fire; involved in learning and memory.	Too much glutamate can cause migraine headaches and seizures. It has been implicated in anxiety, phobias, depression, schizophrenia, and Alzheimer's and Parkinson's diseases.
	Norepinephrine	Inhibits firing of neurons in the central nervous system; stimulates neurons to fire in the heart, muscles, intestines, and urogenital tract; controls alertness.	Too little norepinephrine can cause depressed mood; too much can cause agitation.
	Oxytocin	Associated with love and bonding.	An increase in oxytocin happens with vaginal birth, facilitating bonding, lactation, and breastfeeding. Oxytocin also increases during orgasm, facilitating emotional attachment.
	Serotonin	Regulates sleep, mood, attention, and learning.	Too little serotonin can cause depressed mood.

Source: Adapted from Adlard *et al.*, 2010; H. D. Anderson *et al.*, 2012; Bertram *et al.*, 2010; Eriksen, Jorgensen, & Gether, 2010; Kuan, 2009; Möhler, 2012; Penner *et al.*, 2010; Plaitakis, Latsoudis, & Spanaki, 2011; Rajkumar & Mahesh, 2010; Riaza Bermudo-Soriano *et al.*, 2012; Tarhan *et al.*, 2011; Tarkan, 2011; Tokita, Yamaji, & Hashimoto, 2012

and attachment issues. Many psychotropic drugs and other therapies are designed to alter this process. We will discuss some examples in later chapters.

The Endocrine System   The **endocrine system** consists of a set of glands that work in concert with the nervous system. By releasing chemicals called hormones into the bloodstream, these glands regulate different organs and functions in our body. Cells in our body contain receptors for different hormones, similar to the way that neurons contain receptors for different neurotransmitters.

Exhibit 3.5 lists the endocrine glands and their locations and functions in the body.

Genetics   Our genetic makeup impacts all of the processes of our bodies and thus also has consequences for behavior, wellness, and disease. Inside the nucleus of each of our cells are 23 pairs of chromosomes. One of these pairs contains the

EXHIBIT 3.5	ENDOCRINE GLANDS (AND LOCATION)	HORMONES RELEASED	FUNCTIONS AND DYSFUNCTIONS
Endocrine Glands and Their Functions	Adrenal glands (above both kidneys)	Epinephrine (adrenaline); norepinephrine (noradrenaline)	Regulate mood, energy level, and stress reaction. Chronic stress can lead to persistent release of hormones, causing damage to immune system.
	Ovaries (in pelvis on sides of uterus in women)	Estrogen	Regulate female sexual development and reproduction. Decrease of estrogen in menopause can contribute to osteoporosis and sexual dysfunction.
	Pancreas (under stomach)	Insulin	Controls glucose (blood sugar); regulates metabolism and weight. Insulin regulation problems can cause diabetes and obesity.
	Pituitary gland (just under hypothalamus)	Anterior lobe: Adrenocorticotropic hormone (stimulates the adrenal glands to produce hormones); follicle-stimulating hormone (ensures functioning of the ovaries and testes); growth hormone (facilitates healthy growth, bone and muscle mass, and fat distribution); luteinizing hormone (ensures functioning of the ovaries and testes); prolactin (stimulates breast milk production); thyroid-stimulating hormone (stimulates thyroid to produce hormones). Posterior lobe: Anti-diuretic hormone (prompts kidneys to increase water absorption); oxytocin (stimulates breast milk production and contractions during childbirth).	Known as master gland because it controls growth and regulates other glands. Hypothalamus sends signals to anterior lobe of pituitary gland to release hormones or inhibit hormone production. Posterior lobe of pituitary gland receives hormones directly from hypothalamus and releases them. Tumors and other problems with pituitary gland can disrupt its ability to release hormones, such as causing release of too much or not enough of specific hormones.

EXHIBIT 3.5 *Continued*	Testes (in scrotum in men)	Testosterone	Regulates sexual development and reproduction. Low levels of testosterone are implicated in cardiovascular disease, sexual dysfunction, and diabetes.

Source: Adapted from Davidovici, Orion, & Wolf, 2008; Lee, 2010; Lewiecki, 2009; Simon, 2011; Skipworth *et al.*, 2011; Yassin, Akhras, El-Sakka, & Saad, 2011

sex chromosomes, which determine whether we are male (XY) or female (XX). In each pair of chromosomes, one comes from the egg and one from the sperm. The chromosomes contain deoxyribonucleic acid (DNA), which carries our genetic information.

When chromosomes from the egg and sperm pair, genes for specific traits also pair. **Genes** are units of hereditary information composed of segments of DNA that direct and regulate the production of proteins, or amino acids, which are the basis of all of our bodily functions. Genes work with one another, with different hormones, and with the environment to shape who we are. Examples of these interactions will be discussed in future chapters.

Genes in a pair of chromosomes can be dominant or recessive, which contributes to the differences among children of particular biological parents. If a pair of chromosomes consists of two dominant or two recessive genes, it is called *homozygous*. If a pair consists of a dominant and a recessive gene, it is called *heterozygous*. In a heterozygous pairing, a dominant gene dominates over the recessive one, overriding the expression of the recessive gene. Recessive genes can only express themselves if there are two recessive genes in a homozygous pair.

For example, people with traits such as brown eyes, curly hair, farsightedness, and an ability to curl the tongue possess dominant genes for those traits (it does not matter if the other gene in the pair for that trait is dominant or recessive). Traits such as blue eyes, straight hair, nearsightedness, and freckles are carried on recessive genes, so people who have those traits must possess two recessive genes to allow those traits to be expressed.

It is important to keep in mind that the ways in which genes contribute to the expression of our characteristics are complex. All of the traits we possess from hair color to intelligence to the development of certain diseases are usually the result of the interaction of multiple genes (and sometimes the interaction with the environment).

The genes that we inherit and carry—that we possess in our chromosomes—are called the **genotype**. The way in which these genes are expressed—that are actually observable, such as blue eyes—are called the **phenotype.** Exhibits 3.6, 3.7, and 3.8 display Punnett squares, or diagrams of gene pairings, for three genetic disorders that are inherited through different combinations of dominant and recessive genes:

- Dominant single-gene disorder: Huntington's disease. The first example, in Exhibit 3.6, is for Huntington's disease, which causes nerve cell degeneration in the brain, leading to movement problems, mood disturbances, and dementia. In this example, one parent carries one dominant gene and one recessive gene (the genotype) and thus develops Huntington's disease (the phenotype). The odds are that 50 percent of the children will have the genotype for Huntington's as well (Hh). They will develop the disease (phenotype) because it is carried on the dominant gene. They can also pass it on to their children. The other 50 percent of the children do not have the genotype (they are hh) or phenotype for Huntington's and cannot pass it on to their children.

- Recessive single-gene disorder: Cystic Fibrosis. Exhibit 3.7 is the Punnett square for cystic fibrosis, which causes mucus build-up in the lungs and digestive tract. In this example, both parents are carriers of the recessive gene for Cystic Fibrosis (they have the genotype), but they do not have the disease (the phenotype). One out of four (25 percent) of the children (CC) will not be carriers of the disease, will not develop it, and cannot pass it on to their children. Half (50 percent) of the children are carriers for the disease (Cc), but because it is a recessive disease, they are protected by the dominant gene; they will not develop the disease, but they can pass it on to their children. The other fourth (25 percent) of the children (cc) will develop the disease because it is carried on the recessive gene and they do not have a dominant gene to protect them from expression. They would pass the gene on to their children.

- X-linked single-gene disorder: Hemophilia. In this example, hemophilia, which creates blood-clotting problems, is related to a single gene carried on the X sex chromosome. As you can see in Exhibit 3.8, the mother, who has XX sex chromosomes, is a carrier of hemophilia (genotype), which is expressed by the recessive X_p gene. But she does not have the disease (phenotype) because she is protected by a dominant X_n gene that does not carry the disease. The father, who has XY sex chromosomes, is not a carrier of the disease (genotype) and does not have the disease (phenotype). One fourth (25 percent) of the children (X_nX_n) are females who are not carriers of the disease, will not develop it, and cannot pass it on to their children. One fourth (25 percent) are females (X_pX_n) who are carriers of hemophilia; they will not develop the disease because they are protected by a second X chromosome, but they can pass it on to their children. One

EXHIBIT 3.6

Dominant Single-Gene Disorder: Huntington's Disease

H = dominant gene for Huntington's Disease
h = recessive gene that does not carry Huntington's Disease

	Parent without Huntington's	
Parent with Huntington's	h	h
H	Hh	Hh
h	hh	hh

EXHIBIT 3.7

Recessive Single-Gene Disorder: Cystic Fibrosis

c = recessive gene for Cystic Fibrosis
C = dominant gene that protects against Cystic Fibrosis

	Parent is a carrier for Cystic Fibrosis	
Parent is a carrier for Cystic Fibrosis	C	c
C	CC	Cc
c	cC	cc

fourth (25 percent) of the children are males ($X_n Y$) who are not carriers of the disease, will not develop it, and cannot pass it on to their children. The remaining 25 percent of the children are males who carry the gene for hemophilia. Since they do not have another X chromosome to potentially protect them, they will develop the disease and will pass it on to their children.

p = recessive gene for hemophilia
n = dominant gene that does not carry hemophilia

EXHIBIT 3.8

X-Linked Single-Gene Disorder: Hemophilia

	Male parent who is a carrier for hemophilia	
Female parent who is a carrier for hemophilia	X_n	Y
X_p	$X_p X_n$	$X_p Y$
X_n	$X_n X_n$	$X_n Y$

These examples show how genotypes and phenotypes work and how our inheritance of certain genes can cause or protect us from disease.

Applying the Medical Model

As Carlos's social worker, if you were using the medical model you would focus on the biological and disease-based issues impacting Carlos's problems and affecting his well-being. Because of Carlos's age and his diagnosis of Alzheimer's disease, you would concentrate your efforts on how these factors may be causing problems as well as how to prevent further problems from developing as Carlos ages and his disease progresses.

To do a thorough job, you would need to spend some time asking Carlos about his symptoms and other problems affecting his functioning. You could begin by assessing Carlos's symptoms using diagnostic criteria in the DSM-5:

- *Because Carlos has already been diagnosed with Alzheimer's disease, this fact would likely be noted as an area for attention.*
- *You could request medical information from Carlos's physician to ascertain whether health issues are complicating the Alzheimer's disease or vice versa. You could also request information from other professionals, such as a psychiatrist, who might have treated Carlos in the past. This additional information would offer a historical view of his problems and help to inform the current diagnoses.*
- *Several psychosocial and environmental problems might be noted, such as problems with Carlos's primary support group, social environment, and potentially with housing, as his disease progresses.*

*   *You would want to determine to what degree Carlos's problems interfere with his daily functioning.*

    After making an assessment, you would develop an intervention based on Carlos's diagnoses. The intervention would most likely focus mainly on his Alzheimer's disease and the problems associated with it. Carlos might want to consider trying new medications that target various neurotransmitters in the brain in an attempt to slow the development of Alzheimer's symptoms.

    In addition to problems related to Alzheimer's disease, you may choose to examine Carlos's physical health to determine whether he has any problems associated with his age or general health status, such as diabetes, heart disease, or high blood pressure. For example, he could be referred to a physician to check for testosterone levels and medication side-effects that could contribute to or exacerbate his symptoms. Ensuring that he is as healthy as possible can help prevent or minimize some of the complications that may result from Alzheimer's disease. Moreover, improving or maintaining Carlos's physical health will add to his overall well-being and functioning as he ages.

Critiquing the Medical Model

Limitations of the medical model center on the difficulties in using medical information and its narrow focus:

*   Because DSM-5 criteria are so widely used and are often a part of clients' permanent health care records, any use of the manual needs to be taken seriously. Professionals need extensive training and supervision before using the manual in clinical settings to ensure its ethical and appropriate use.

*   Even though criteria for the disorders are generally based on research, there is still much room for speculation and error. Keep in mind that the process of diagnosis is not an exact science and that diagnoses can lack reliability from clinician to clinician.

*   Besides being subject to error, the research that supports the diagnostic criteria in the DSM-5 is open to criticism. Although this research is empirically based, it still suffers from weaknesses associated with the inability to control and account for all of the possible biopsychosocial factors that could influence symptoms of mental illness. Even with the increasing knowledge about the biological etiology of some mental disorders, the question of how much these disorders are influenced by environmental and other factors remains. This question is the reason why conducting empirically based research in this area can be

so difficult, much more so than research that is conducted on purely biological processes, where variables can be identified and controlled. Regardless of how well developed the studies are that support the diagnostic criteria in the DSM-5, there will probably always be some doubt surrounding the validity, reliability, and applicability of diagnoses in some circumstances.

• If clients learn of their diagnosis, the symptoms or disorder might become a self-fulfilling prophecy. That is, clients may come to believe that because they have been labeled with a disorder, they have no control over the symptoms or its "cure." For this reason, the DSM-5 and the medical model in general have been criticized for reducing clients to nothing more than a set of symptoms, a process that ignores larger issues and undermines clients' power to solve their own problems (Katz, 1983). Specifically, some professionals argue that this approach may give clients an excuse not to attempt to solve their problems.

• The medical model tends to focus exclusively on the individual. This focus views the problem as coming from inside the individual, which minimizes ways in which the person's environment might contribute to or exacerbate problems. Information on psychosocial and environmental problems is generally limited in scope to clients' immediate environment, and it is usually not the primary consideration in assessment and intervention.

• The medical model focuses on clients' problems, ignoring their strengths and resources. This problem-focused approach can be discouraging to clients, particularly those clients who have multifaceted problems that seem overwhelming and impossible to solve.

These criticisms notwithstanding, the medical model does have certain strengths. A major strength is that it emphasizes the physiological processes that can cause problems. Decades of research and medical advances have revealed a great deal about the etiology of many diseases that can interfere with daily living. Every day, we learn more about how the brain and neurological systems play an integral part in our health and behavior, so incorporating this knowledge into our practice is an essential part of ethical, competent practice. Many symptoms can be controlled through diet, medication, and behavior modification, and many diseases and disorders can be cured and even prevented. Further, there are usually a finite number of variables associated with physical diseases and processes, which means that they can be easily controlled and tested, making it easier to develop theories and hypotheses that can predict outcomes of interventions.

Another benefit of the medical model is that the use of diagnostic criteria, whether in the form of DSM-5 or a set of symptoms that make up a physical disease, gives clinicians across disciplines a common language to describe problems. This uniform basic understanding increases the likelihood that interventions originating from different clinicians will complement each other.

Finally, some clients who suffer from physical or mental health problems may experience relief just by receiving a diagnosis. Putting a name to a problem can help some people by validating the fact that the problem exists and by offering hope that it can be treated.

THEORIES OF COGNITIVE DEVELOPMENT

Several theories focus on the development of **cognition** (or mental processes) and how this development can impact behavior. The next section covers one well-known approach to explaining cognitive development and some of the ways it can be applied when working with clients. Chapters 6 through 12 present more specific information on cognitive development as it relates to different stages and growth processes across the life span.

Piaget's Theory of Cognitive Development

One of the best-known theories of cognitive development was introduced by the Swiss psychologist Jean Piaget in the 1950s. Piaget's theory describes how people develop their capacities to think, learn, and process information from birth through their teenage years. Piaget proposed that people actively develop their cognitive skills in relatively fixed and universal stages that are qualitatively different from one another.

Cognitive development from birth to about the late teen years is characterized by increasing cognitive complexity and flexibility. Development begins with children's use of basic reflexes to get needs met and progresses to their being capable of thinking abstractly and examining multifaceted relationships among many variables. According to Piaget, by the age of 16 or 17, young people should possess the skills necessary to operate in the adult world (Piaget & Inhelder, 1969).

Piaget's theory consists of several substages, each of which includes its own key concepts or cognitive skills. Though all the substages are not presented here, we will look at the main developmental tasks that occur in each stage (Piaget, 1952).

In the **sensorimotor stage** (birth to age two years), the major accomplishment is *object permanence*. This is when children learn that even if objects and events are out of the range of their senses, they continue to exist (for example, when Mom leaves the room, she has not disappeared). Children begin to coordinate their actions through reflexes such as sucking and rooting, and they learn that they can get pleasurable results by performing certain actions, such as crying when they are hungry or want to be held. Additionally, a child's preoccupation moves away from the self toward the outside world. Eventually, children learn to combine and coordinate actions and to manipulate objects to get novel results. By the end of this stage, children have attained primitive symbolic capacities that allow them to hold rudimentary pictures of objects, or words for objects, in their minds.

In the **preoperational stage** (two to seven years), children continue to exhibit many limitations in their cognitive abilities. A major characteristic of this stage is *egocentrism,* which means that children cannot take into account the perspectives of others when thinking about objects or events. Children also tend to show characteristics of *animism,* the belief that inanimate objects have lifelike qualities. They also display a tendency known as *centration,* which means that they can focus on only one aspect of an object at a time. Children at this stage also lack a sense of *conservation,* meaning that they cannot understand that an object remains the same even if its characteristics change, such as its shape or the way it is contained. For example, if a child were shown a cup of juice, she would think that the amount of juice was different if it were poured into a different-shaped container. Finally, children demonstrate *irreversibility,* or the inability to think about events in reverse order. For example, a child might understand that John is his cousin but not that he is, therefore, John's cousin.

At the same time, however, children in the preoperational stage undergo a great deal of development. Two major examples of this development are classification and seriation. Clas*sification* means that children can differentiate between two objects based on their differences and unique properties. By the end of this stage, children should be able to separate blocks into groups based on their color and shape, for example. Children should also be able to differentiate among objects based on their size, weight, or length, which is known as *seriation*. This means, for instance, that a child can put pebbles in order from smallest to largest or from lightest to heaviest.

During the **concrete operations stage** (7 to 11 years), children develop the cognitive skills that were lacking in the previous stage. Children become adept at understanding events from the perspective of others and appreciating the more complex relationships among variables. In addition, they master all of the skills associated with classification, conservation, and seriation. Finally, they learn to use symbols effectively to represent objects and events in the real world. This skill improves children's performances at certain activities, such as math and the use of language.

Finally, in the **formal operations stage** (11 to 16 years), children learn to use *hypothetical-deductive reasoning*. They can engage in abstract thinking, consider multiple aspects of an object or event at one time, formulate hypotheses about what might happen if certain variables were manipulated, and analyze the properties of an object or event to derive conclusions about its nature or behavior. It is at this stage that children develop the ability to use logic and to systematically work through a problem to come to viable solutions.

For cognitive development to take place, we need to organize new information and adapt it to our existing knowledge. We also have to be able to adapt our thinking to new information and ideas. Central to Piaget's theory, then, are these three concepts:

- **Schemas** are the internal ideas and representations we hold about the world. They result from our efforts to systematically process and store information to make sense of what happens around us. According to Piaget, this happens in two ways: accommodation and assimilation.

- **Accommodation** is when we *change* our schema about something because new information we receive about it does not fit our preexisting ideas about how that something should be. In other words, sometimes we have to change our ideas about something because we learn something new about it that is contrary to, or different from, what we originally thought.

- **Assimilation** occurs when we bring in new information about something to *fit* our existing schema. In this case, we incorporate or integrate new information into what we already know about something without altering our schema (Piaget, 1952).

Applying Piaget's Theory

As Carlos's social worker, you would probably only be able to use Piaget's theory in a limited way to help understand what is happening in his situation. This is one of the criticisms of Piaget's theory: It does not explain continued development into adulthood. In contrast, many psychologists and other professionals argue that development progresses well into older age. You could try, however, to ascertain whether Carlos successfully moved through the formal operational stage and how that development has affected him since. You could assess how his level of cognitive development may be affected by Alzheimer's disease and come up with interventions to maximize his functioning as the disease progresses.

It would probably be more useful, though, for you to look at Carlos's schemas for older age and Alzheimer's disease. What thoughts and attitudes about aging does he hold? Does he define Alzheimer's disease, isolation, and loneliness as "normal" components of aging? It may be that Carlos's schema of aging and disease is not helping him to cope well with the inevitable changes that he will experience.

One approach to altering Carlos's schema is to look at how he assimilates and accommodates information about aging and disease. For example, let us say that Carlos has a schema about aging that includes characteristics of misery, disability, and isolation. He is familiar only with older people who have these characteristics, so these observations get assimilated into his existing schema about aging, thus reinforcing his negative views. One of your goals might be to get him to alter his schema to include other ideas of aging. To accomplish this you need to show Carlos different examples of aging, perhaps by exposing him to elderly people who are active, happy, and functioning well. According to Piaget, this last experience would be an example of accommodation: Carlos would have to change his schema about aging to incorporate new ideas, which in turn might improve his attitude about the possible outcomes of his own aging process.

Critiquing Piaget's Theory

We have already encountered one major limitation of Piaget's theory, but there are others as well:

- Piaget's model of the development process stops in adolescence.

- Piaget developed his ideas based on observations of his own children. Some critics therefore contend that his methods biased his work and did not offer a large enough sample from which to generalize his results to other children.

- His theory tends to focus on what is "normal" or "average" for development, leaving little room for individual deviations in development that may also be "normal."

- The stage-like progression of development tends to underestimate the variations that take place in development: Does everyone really follow these stages in precise order and in the time frames proscribed? Many critics would argue that development is too individualistic to fit into neat stages.

- Piaget does not pay enough attention to sociocultural factors that affect cognitive development. He does not offer much explanation for how personality, stimulation, social interaction, cultural context, and other related factors promote or detract from development, although he attempted to incorporate these ideas into his theory later on (Piaget, 1972).

- Research based on Piaget's theory suggests that he may have underestimated children's abilities, lending credence to the idea that children may develop skills earlier than Piaget originally thought possible. For example, some researchers argue that if you alter the methods used to test skills, the test results demonstrate that children are capable of understanding and performing various skills at earlier ages than those proposed by Piaget (Baillargeon, 1987).

- Research has also found that skills that Piaget assumed to be mastered in the formal operations stage, which takes place during adolescence, do not develop predictably or universally at any specific time. Rather, it is likely that there are many individual differences related to formal operations that are influenced by neurological changes based on individualistic experiences (Kuhn, 2008).

On the positive side, Piaget's theory provides relatively sound and usable guidelines for thinking about children's cognitive development. Many of the theory's concepts are, indeed, consistent with current knowledge concerning various aspects of biological development, such as neuron growth and synapse connections. For example, we now know that it takes time for children to fully develop neuron connections to perform certain mental tasks, which corresponds with many of Piaget's ideas on how skill development occurs. This fact can help explain the occurrence of separation anxiety among young children, which fits well with the idea of object permanence. What child would not be frightened when his mother leaves the room if he does not have the physiological capability to keep a mental picture of her in his mind? It takes time for young children to develop neural pathways and mental capabilities that allow them to retain these mental pictures. There is also substantial evidence to support the idea that a great deal of cognitive development takes place in the teen years, leading to skills articulated in formal operations (Kuhn & Pease, 2006).

Finally, many of the constructs in Piaget's theory are testable. Thus, the theory has been subject to replication and modification based on research since it was first proposed.

PSYCHODYNAMIC THEORIES

This section discusses two theories of personality development that are psychodynamic in nature and have been influential in social work and other helping professions. Sigmund Freud and his ideas on psychosexual development are well known, as is Erik Erikson's theory of psychosocial development. Though some of the ideas from these theories, particularly Freud's, are considered outdated or controversial, concepts originating from these theories still contribute to many facets of social work practice.

Freud's Theory of Psychosexual Development

Sigmund Freud, a physician, was a leader in developing psychoanalytic theory. This philosophy underscores the importance of unconsciousness and early experiences in shaping personality. His stage theory of psychosexual development is based on the psychoanalytic tradition, and it describes three concepts or mental structures thought to be at the crux of personality:

- **Id:** An element of our unconscious, which is made up of our basic needs and drives such as sex, thirst, and hunger. The **pleasure principle** governs the id to ensure that needs are satisfied. When needs are not met, the id creates tension until the drive or need is satisfied. For example, many infant behaviors such as sucking and crying are driven by the id; these behaviors help to ensure that the need for food is met.

- **Ego:** The rational aspect of the mind. When children gain experience, their ego develops, which helps keep the id in check. Thus, a child learns to decide rationally how to meet the id's needs in ways that are socially acceptable. The **reality principle** governs the ego by ensuring that actions are evaluated according to their consequences. Neither the id nor the ego has moral components. They are not concerned with what is right or wrong, just with what is needed (in the case of the id) or what is reasonable (in the case of the ego).

- **Superego:** The conscience. It is based on society's morals and values, which Freud believed are incorporated into the superego between the ages of three and five. The superego tells the person what is right and wrong. So, if the id wants something that the superego does not approve of, the superego creates anxiety or guilt, forcing the ego to suppress the drive. The ego would then find a way to meet the need that is in accordance with the superego (or with societal values). In this sense, the ego is the mediator between the id and the superego, ensuring that neither dominates (Freud, 1920a).

In addition to these ideas, Freud delineated five stages through which personality develops, which are summarized in Exhibit 3.9. Freud believed that within each stage, a person must resolve a conflict to successfully move on to the next. That is, a person must deal with the tensions between satisfying needs or seeking pleasure and the reality or morality of satisfying those needs or achieving pleasure. If this does not happen, the person can become fixated at a particular stage, leaving the person's development halted or incomplete.

ORAL STAGE (BIRTH TO 18 MONTHS)
Pleasure centers on activities of the mouth, including feeding, sucking, chewing, and biting. Child focuses on receiving and taking.

ANAL STAGE (18 MONTHS TO 3 YEARS)
Pleasure centers on anal activities such as toileting. Child focuses on giving and withholding.

PHALLIC STAGE (3 TO 6 YEARS)
Pleasure centers on the genitals and self-manipulation. In this stage, children experience the Oedipus and Electra complexes, resulting in castration anxiety.

LATENCY STAGE (6 YEARS TO PUBERTY)
Sexual instincts are unaroused, and the child focuses on play, learning, and socialization.

GENITAL STAGE (PUBERTY ON)
Pleasure centers on love, work, and maturing sexually.

Source: Adapted from Freud, 1920a

EXHIBIT 3.9

Freud's Stages in Psychosexual Development

A person who is fixated would either resolve the conflict or construct a defense mechanism to deal with the conflict. **Defense mechanisms** are unconscious attempts to hide, suppress, or otherwise control the conflict. Some common defense mechanisms are described in Exhibit 3.10. Defense mechanisms have many forms, some more productive and sophisticated than others. For instance, sublimation is considered to be a more highly developed and constructive defense mechanism than **projection** or denial because it allows a person to satisfy needs through productive and socially accepted activities instead of avoiding them. One goal of psychoanalysis is to bring a conflict to the person's conscience, break down defense mechanisms that are maintaining or perpetuating it, and help the person resolve the conflict that is keeping her or him fixated in a particular stage (Freud, 1909, 1914, 1920b; Rickman, 1957).

To exemplify how conflicts and defense mechanisms work, let us turn our attention to the phallic stage, where Freud argued that boys and girls deal with Oedipus complex and the feminine Oedipus attitude, respectively. Freud described the *Oedipus complex* as a dilemma or conflict in which boys fall in love with their

---

EXHIBIT 3.10

Common Defense Mechanisms in Psychoanalytic Theory

- *Denial:* Avoidance of unpleasant realities by ignoring or refusing to acknowledge them; probably the simplest and most primitive defense mechanism.
- *Identification with the aggressor:* Increasing feelings of worth by taking on the attributes of people or institutions of greater power, strength, or importance.
- *Intellectualization:* Creating emotional distance through rationalizing or using logic.
- *Projection:* Blaming others for one's own shortcomings and mistakes; unconsciously ascribing to others one's own unacceptable impulses and desires (for example, a person with a tendency to be lazy criticizes others for laziness).
- *Reaction formation:* Developing attitudes and behaviors that are the opposite of repressed and unconscious dangerous or unpleasant impulses and desires (for example, expressing abhorrence of homosexuality when one has repressed homosexual feelings).
- *Regression:* Retreating to behaviors that were appropriate in earlier stages of development (for example, temper tantrums) that bring easy satisfaction of desires or needs.
- *Repression:* Unconscious process whereby painful or dangerous thoughts and desires are excluded from consciousness. These can be revealed through dreams, jokes, or slips of the tongue.
- *Sublimation:* Consciously satisfying socially unacceptable needs and desires through socially acceptable activities (for example, playing football to satisfy aggressive impulses); probably the most advanced defense mechanism.
- *Withdrawal:* Retreating into solitude to avoid painful emotions and situations.

Source: Adapted from Freud, 1909, 1914, 1920a

mothers. At the same time, boys feel antagonistic toward their fathers because of the rivalry for their mother's attention. Boys fear that their fathers will find out about this attraction, which leads boys to have castration anxiety, or the fear that their father will remove their genitals. To successfully resolve this conflict, boys must repress their sexual feelings for their mother, develop a reaction formation in which they have positive feelings for their father, and eventually identify with their father by taking on their father's behaviors. In essence, this is how boys learn to become men and take on gender-specific roles.

The female equivalent of the Oedipus complex, according to Freud, is the *feminine Oedipus attitude*, later renamed the *Electra complex* by his contemporary, Carl Jung (Jung, 1961). Girls' love for their fathers also results in castration anxiety, but this anxiety is different from that experienced by boys. Specifically, this anxiety forces girls to realize that they do not have penises, so they conclude that they were castrated in infancy by their mother. Consequently, because they "lack" penises, girls feel inferior to boys, which is the foundation for girls' submissiveness and other gender roles later in life. Like the process for boys, Freud posited that girls must resolve their hostility toward their mothers or risk losing their mothers' love. This allows girls to internalize their identification with their mothers and move on to the next stage in development. As with boys, defense mechanisms are used to help girls successfully resolve conflicts so that they can move on to the latency stage, without being fixated in the phallic stage (Freud, 1955; 1961).

Many theorists who subscribed to Freud's ideas broke away to form their own theories on development. Most neo-Freudians believed that Freud placed too much emphasis on sexual drives, so they constructed theories that incorporated many of Freud's ideas but moved away from the sexual focus. Some of the better-known neo-Freudians are Carl Jung, Alfred Adler, Karen Horney, Erich Fromm, and Harry Stack Sullivan.

Applying Freudian Theory

If you wanted to apply Freud's theory to Carlos's case, you would need a lot of time! Psychoanalysis can take several years. But putting time issues aside, you could delve into Carlos's past, examining his relationships with his parents and the process of his psychosexual development. You may find areas in which he has become fixated, and you would help him resolve conflicts he may have at various stages.

One way to find areas for work is to explore Carlos's defense mechanisms, such as denial, to ascertain whether he is avoiding issues by blocking them out of his consciousness. For example, he may be denying the painful reality of the losses he has faced (for example, his wife's death and the loss of family ties) and will face in the future (the loss of his health, independence, and social networks, for example). This may be hindering his free expression of feelings such as grief. Through the expression of his feelings, Carlos may be able to come to terms with his situation and find productive ways of dealing with it. Carlos's cultural background may dictate that it is unacceptable for a man to express his feelings, which could be contributing to denial about his situation. Perhaps his superego, which has been shaped by the values, norms, and mores of his culture, is successfully repressing his id's need to express his grief about his situation.

If Carlos finds it unacceptable to express his feelings about his situation, a better approach might be to help him find more productive ways to satisfy his needs, such as through the use of sublimation. You could help Carlos find more culturally relevant ways to work through his feelings, such as through art, music, or writing. In essence, you would help Carlos replace one defense mechanism that may be destructive to his well-being with another, more industrious one. Because you don't know how quickly his cognitive capacities will diminish, trying to rid Carlos of his defense mechanisms altogether may not be useful. Rather, the more prudent approach is to find ways to work with defense mechanisms that will maximize his well-being.

In addition to helping Carlos get rid of, or work with, his defense mechanisms, you may also explore with him how and why his defense mechanisms were constructed in the first place. For instance, perhaps in the phallic stage, rather than resolving the Oedipus complex through the defense of reaction formation, Carlos denied his feelings toward his parents. Thus, as he moved through later stages and into adulthood, he employed denial in his romantic and intimate relationships to protect himself from unwanted feelings.

You would have to spend a great deal of time exploring Carlos's past and current issues to arrive at some conclusions about how his problems may relate to defenses or fixated development. Given the reality of Carlos's disease, he may not be able to participate cognitively in this kind of exploration, and depending on how quickly his disease is progressing, he may not have the luxury of time to do so. You may be more successful if you were to focus on problematic defense mechanisms and attempt to begin an intervention at that point.

Critiquing Freudian Theory

Despite the frequent use of Freudian terms in everyday life ("she's in denial" or "he's fixated on that new phone"), the underlying theory is often criticized as impractical:

- It frequently does not seem applicable to client situations. Sometimes it can be a stretch to relate problems of daily living to psychosexual development.

- Psychoanalysis can take a lot of time, which is not practical in many social service agencies given their budget constraints.

- The constructs in this theory are almost impossible to define, measure, and test, which makes it even more unlikely to be used in many agencies that insist on outcomes that can be quantified and proven to be effective.

- Like the medical model, it focuses solely on the individual, ignoring the impact of outside forces on client problems, such as economics or discriminatory or problematic social policies. Thus, interventions based on this theory may be irrelevant for many clients who are facing environmental barriers.

- Freud based his ideas on the experiences of his patients, who were almost exclusively wealthy Caucasian women seeking therapy during the Victorian age, when sexual repression was the norm. Application of his ideas to diverse groups of people from varying sociocultural contexts and experiences could be limiting and problematic.

- Freud's ideas surrounding the Oedipus complex and castration anxiety, which supposedly occur in the phallic stage, have been criticized for being male centered and sexist. Specifically, some critics argue that this theory places too much emphasis on the importance of male genitalia and women's supposed envy of them.

On the positive side, Freud can be credited with bringing sexual issues to the forefront of psychological thinking. Application of this theory to client problems may be desirable if the client is open to exploring relationships and psychosexual developmental processes.

Many of Freud's concepts are still widely used today as many social workers refer in a clinical way to clients' use of defense mechanisms such as denial, projection, and repression. For example, terror management theory (Greenberg, Pyszczynski, & Solomon, 1986), discussed later in the book, explains how we use defense mechanisms to deal with thoughts of death. Work with defense mechanisms can be useful (for example, focusing on a client's denial of various problems or withdrawal from painful situations), and this type of work does not necessarily require a lot of time. Thus many agencies may be amenable to incorporating such interventions into work with clients.

Erikson's Theory of Psychosocial Development

Erik Erikson's theory of psychosocial development incorporates many of the basic tenets of Freudian theory, though it places greater emphasis on social versus sexual influences on development. Erikson's theory proposes that a person progresses through eight stages of psychosocial development, which extend throughout the life span. Exhibit 3.11 describes these stages.

Erikson (1950) argued that we move through each stage in a consistent manner, dealing with developmental tasks and resolving crises unique to each stage. Developmental tasks are healthy, normal activities that help promote growth. Within each stage, there are periods in which people are highly susceptible to learning age-appropriate tasks that help them adapt to, and gain mastery over, their

EXHIBIT 3.11

*Erikson's Stages
of Psychosocial
Development*

STAGE ONE: TRUST VS. MISTRUST (BIRTH TO 18 MONTHS)

In this stage, children learn to trust others, particularly their caregivers. Infants learn that they can count on their caregivers to give them food, shelter, and love, and to meet their needs. If their needs are not met, infants learn to mistrust others.

STAGE TWO: AUTONOMY VS. SHAME AND DOUBT (18 MONTHS TO 3 YEARS)

Children learn to do things, such as eat and dress, independently. Through accomplishing various tasks, children gain a sense of self-confidence. If children's independence is not encouraged, or if they are punished for acting on things independently, they can develop a sense of self-doubt.

STAGE THREE: INITIATIVE VS. GUILT (3 TO 6 YEARS)

Children are active in their environment. They need to take initiative to learn, explore, and manipulate their surroundings. Children who are encouraged to do so will develop skills that allow them to pursue goals and interests in the future. Children who are discouraged will lack confidence to act on their interests and will not take the initiative to shape their lives.

STAGE FOUR: INDUSTRY VS. INFERIORITY (6 TO 12 YEARS)

Children need to be productive and have successful experiences. Children are busy playing and learning, giving them opportunities to master various tasks. Children who are able to find ways to succeed will learn to be industrious. Those who experience repeated failures will develop feelings of inferiority, hampering their chances of success in the future.

STAGE FIVE: IDENTITY VS. IDENTITY CONFUSION (ADOLESCENCE)

Adolescents are exploring who they are and developing their sense of identity. They try out roles for the future and integrate these into their sense of self. Adolescents who have difficulty integrating their roles into their identity will experience confusion about who they are.

STAGE SIX: INTIMACY VS. ISOLATION (YOUNG ADULTHOOD)

Young adults are looking for intimacy and closeness in their relationships. They learn to give and take with a significant other without sacrificing their identities. If they are unable to establish intimacy, they are at risk for isolation as they move into adulthood.

STAGE SEVEN: GENERATIVITY VS. STAGNATION (ADULTHOOD)

Adults are involved in investing in their work, families, communities, and future generations. They begin to look past their own lives to the well-being of those around them. Adults who are unable to do this never move past investing in themselves and are self-absorbed. They become stagnated and are unable to be productive for the sake of others.

STAGE EIGHT: INTEGRITY VS. DESPAIR (OLD AGE) People in older age reflect on their lives and take inventory of their successes. People who are satisfied with what they have accomplished have a sense of well-being and peace. Those who are not satisfied have a sense of despair, and they mourn for lost opportunities.	**EXHIBIT 3.11** *Continued*
Source: Adapted from Erikson, 1950	

environments. *Crises* are psychological efforts to adjust to the demands of the social environment. These are "normal" stressors that can be anticipated at each stage to help people develop (versus rare, extraordinary events or trauma that are unanticipated). The goal at each stage is to resolve crises by developing positive qualities that allow for growth and that support the exploration of self and the environment.

If people successfully negotiate the tasks and crises in each stage, they gain and process new information that helps them maintain control over their emotional states and their environments. Even if particular tasks and crises at a stage are not learned or resolved, people still move on to the next stage, but they will probably face problems due to the unresolved crises experienced at earlier stages. According to Erikson, we can reach the end of our lives without having fully resolved crises from earlier stages of development.

Erikson's theory focuses on the continual interaction between the individual and the social environment. Erikson based his theory on the **epigenetic principle**, which states that people have a biological blueprint that dictates how they grow and reach maturity. Although people's growth and development are guided by this biological blueprint, social forces and expectations also influence growth and development and help to determine how well people adapt and adjust to their environments.

Applying Erikson's Theory

There are several ways in which you could apply Erikson's theory to Carlos's situation. You could begin by exploring the tasks Carlos faces given the stage he is in, which, based on his age, is integrity versus despair. According to Erikson, Carlos will be reflecting on his life and determining whether he has accomplished all that he has wanted. Indeed, in many ways, Carlos seems to be doing just that. It is a normal developmental task for Carlos to question the value of his past activities and the course that his life is taking. Not only may Carlos be reflecting on the quality of his relationships with his wife, children, and friends, but he may also be reviewing the contributions he has made through his work. He may be contemplating how the progression of Alzheimer's disease will impact his relationships and contributions to society in the future.

You may want to help Carlos explore other areas, such as his identification with his culture, his investment in his community, and his perceptions of his own growth and development. You could also help him to articulate how his perceptions of himself and his relationships with others might change as his health deteriorates.

The crisis with which Carlos must contend relates to his contemplation of these issues. Specifically, if Carlos concludes that his work, relationships, and personal development have been wasted, then he will likely feel despair. Helping him to gain a sense of integrity despite his current challenges might be one goal in your work. For instance, you might encourage him to reflect on the successes of his life and identify the ways in which these successes have been fulfilling. You could also help him find positive ways of coping with his disease and his changing environment. Doing so might relieve Carlos of some of the stress he feels because of his deteriorating health and the uncertain future that it represents.

If Carlos takes steps to secure comfortable housing and assistance as his disease progresses, he may feel that he has some control over his environment, which can lead to a sense of integrity. Likewise, he may want to find ways to work through his grief over the loss of relationships in his life, or he could explore how to reconnect with his cultural roots, if he feels this is an issue. If Carlos is successful, he will avoid feeling despair and will be able to face his disease and other problems with a renewed sense of hope.

Other possibilities are that Carlos has some unresolved conflicts or that he did not successfully complete certain developmental tasks from earlier stages. For example, he may feel that during the previous stage (generativity versus stagnation) he did not contribute enough to the well-being of his children or that he was not a significant part of his community. Consequently, he would be experiencing a sense of stagnation rather than generativity. You would want to explore these areas as well to identify barriers to Carlos's current developmental tasks that could be hindering his growth, making his disease and aging more troublesome.

Integrating Erikson's Theory with Piaget's Theory

Often a particular situation calls for the application of multiple theories. Before moving on, let's take a look at one such situation. A social worker at a job training and case management center may find both Erikson's and Piaget's theories useful in helping clients seeking new jobs.

At the center, a social worker is working with Tim, a 35 year old who has recently returned to his hometown after serving for 17 years in the army and completing his second tour of duty in Afghanistan. Tim joined the army the day after he graduated from high school and is now at a loss to determine what he wants "to do with his life" post-army. In addition to having trouble finding stable employment, he states he has had a series of unsuccessful relationships. He also does not seem able to focus on "cause and effect" consequences for his actions, which he admits got him into a number of disciplinary situations with his unit commanders.

After conducting an assessment, the social worker might conclude that Tim does not seem to have, in Piaget's terms, fully developed formal operational thinking skills. In working with Tim, the social worker might want to break down job seeking and training tasks into small steps that focus on specific, concrete outcomes rather than on hypothetical thinking or abstract planning.

In addition, Tim may never have successfully completed the developmental tasks in Erikson's fifth stage, Identity vs. Identity Confusion. Although he did choose a career in the army, Tim may never have made conscious choices and explored his options for his identity. Without understanding his own sense of self, Tim will likely be unable to commit to serious relationships or fully commit himself to anything that may threaten his own sense of self.

Using knowledge from Erikson's and Piaget's theories can help this social worker start with Tim "where he is." That is a far better approach than blaming Tim for failure when he is faced with tasks he cannot successfully complete, given his stage of development. Further, this approach is more likely to support Tim in his continued cognitive and social development, increasing the likelihood that he will experience successes as he works on his goals, and keeping him motivated to learn, grow, and move forward in his life.

Critiquing Erikson's Theory

This theory has limitations in common with many of the other theories discussed in this chapter:

- Erikson's emphasis on stages of development can be limiting. Because there are so many individual differences in development, trying to place people in a particular stage based on their age can be problematic.

- The constructs of this theory are quite abstract and therefore difficult to measure and test. For instance, practitioners and clients may have different interpretations of constructs such as "integrity" or "inferiority," making a common definition of them difficult.

- Societal norms and expectations about the developmental processes that should occur at various ages are always changing. You can see an example of this in the traditional activities of marriage and having children, which seem to characterize Erikson's stages of intimacy versus isolation and generativity versus stagnation. Because of economic conditions, technological advances, expanding employment opportunities for women, and changing attitudes about marriage, many young people may put these activities off until later years. Further, different ethnic and cultural groups may hold views about the importance and timing of developmental milestones that are different from Erikson's. Similarly, people may find alternative ways to achieve intimacy or generativity that do not include traditionally accepted activities.

- This theory may lack relevance for some ethnic and other minority groups. It does not account for how developmental tasks may be different for gay and lesbian youth, for example, or how people develop ethnic identity.

Nevertheless, Erikson contributed a great deal to the understanding of development because he placed more emphasis on the social dynamics of human behavior than many other early theorists did. Also, unlike other theorists such as Piaget and Freud, Erikson described development into old age, which assists practitioners' work with clients of all ages.

Erikson's theory also provides a useful developmental guide for social workers and other professionals when working with clients. By helping people understand some of the struggles that are a "normal" part of development, it can promote tolerance and patience with certain behaviors. For example, parents may be more patient and willing to work with their children's temper tantrums if they can view these behaviors as a normal way that children develop autonomy and test limits and boundaries. In essence, this theory views some seemingly problematic behaviors and stressors as necessary in the process of development and growth.

It also highlights the resilient nature of people and the capabilities they have to adapt to their social environment. Although this theory emphasizes individual development more than the influences that the social environment has on that development, it still considers the interaction between the two and acknowledges the importance of that interaction on human development. Indeed, researchers are increasingly realizing just how much our environment shapes our biological development—what Erikson and neurobehaviorists call the epigenetic principle. Recent research validates the notion that individual experiences influence the development and shaping of brain and neural circuits, which impact our behavior (Hammock & Levitt, 2006).

BEHAVIORAL AND LEARNING THEORIES

Now that we have considered a number of theories related to development, we shift our focus to several ideas relating to learning that have been incorporated into many social work interventions. Concepts from these theories describe, among other things, how people learn and modify their behaviors.

"Pure" behaviorists argue that personality development occurs through learning and shaping behaviors. Social workers tend not to take a pure behaviorist stance on personality development, but many concepts associated with behaviorism and learning lend themselves well to interventions that involve behavior change.

We look at three behavior and learning theories here: classical conditioning, operant conditioning, and social learning theory. Because so many of the tenets in behavioral and learning theories are similar, their applications and strengths and weaknesses are discussed under the general heading of "learning theory."

Classical Conditioning

Ivan Pavlov (1927) is the theorist most commonly associated with **classical conditioning**, which focuses on how people respond to stimuli in their environment. In his classic experiment, Pavlov noted that dogs naturally salivate at the sight of food. Pavlov thus labeled the food an **unconditioned stimulus** and the salivation an **unconditioned response** because the dogs learned this behavior "naturally"; that is, the dogs did not need any training or conditioning to salivate at the sight of food.

When Pavlov subsequently paired the food with another stimulus—in this case, he sounded a musical tone when the food was presented—he was able to train the dogs to salivate at the sound of the tone. The tone thus became the **conditioned stimulus**, and the salivation to the tone became the **conditioned response**. Thus, Pavlov concluded that the dogs' natural salivation response could be elicited through training simply by presenting an alternative stimulus with their food.

John B. Watson (1925) generalized this work to humans. He conducted an experiment with a little boy called Albert, conditioning him to fear white rats. Before the experiment, Albert showed no fear (unconditioned response) of white rats (unconditioned stimulus). Watson then created a loud noise (conditioned stimulus) while Albert played with a white rat, startling Albert (conditioned response). After a while, Albert associated the loud noise with the white rat, and when Watson showed Albert the rat, Albert became startled. Thus, Albert's fear of white rats was conditioned. Though this type of experiment is considered unethical now (who knows what kind of psychological consequences this experiment had on Albert!), it is a powerful example of how behavior can be learned.

Operant Conditioning

Building on the ideas of classical conditioning, B. F. Skinner (1938) developed the concepts underlying operant conditioning. In **operant conditioning**, it is the consequences of behavior that result in behavior change (either an increase or decrease in behavior). So, if a child scribbles on the wall with a crayon (the behavior) and is punished (the consequence), the child's behavior of scribbling on the wall will decrease. Conversely, if the behavior is rewarded, the behavior will increase. Skinner argued that behavior could be shaped through this type of interaction.

Reinforcement, a primary component of operant conditioning, refers to a consequence that occurs immediately after a behavior that increases the strength of that behavior. Reinforcements can be positive or negative:

- **Positive reinforcement:** Adding something positive to strengthen a behavior. For example, after a child cleans her room, she may receive praise or get to watch her favorite movie. These positive consequences strengthen the behavior of cleaning.

- **Negative reinforcement:** Taking away something negative to strengthen a behavior. An example of negative reinforcement is when you get into your car and hear a buzzer. That buzzer is annoying, and the only way to get it to stop is by latching your seat belt. Once you do that, the buzzing sound stops. The annoying buzzer stops, or is taken away, every time you put on your seat belt. The desired behavior, wearing your seat belt, is negatively reinforced, or strengthened, by the buzzer turning off.

The important thing to remember is that positive and negative reinforcement both strengthen a behavior, they just do so in different ways—by adding something (positive reinforcement) or taking away something (negative reinforcement).

Let us take a look at how positive and negative reinforcement work together. A mother has taken her son to the grocery store. While they are shopping, the child begins to cry because he wants chocolate. At first the mother refuses to give him the candy, and the child continues to scream while they move through the store. Finally, the mother, becoming really annoyed at his screaming, breaks down and gives him the chocolate, which quiets him down. In this scenario, the crying behavior of the child and the chocolate-giving behavior of the mother both have been reinforced. The mother's behavior is negatively reinforced because the child's screaming stops as soon as she gives him chocolate. The child's crying behavior is positively reinforced because he learns that he will be given chocolate when he cries.

Another component of operant conditioning is punishment:

- **Punishment:** Weakening or reducing the frequency of a behavior by adding something negative or removing something positive. An example of punishment is when a child misbehaves and her mother tells her that she must take time out in a quiet room, without her toys, for 15 minutes. Placing the child in this situation removes something positive: The child loses the stimulation of being with others, and she loses her toys. Hopefully, the removal of these positive things will decrease the frequency of the child's misbehaving. In another scenario, the mother could scold the child for misbehaving, which is adding something negative, or unpleasant (in this case, scolding), to decrease the frequency of the inappropriate behavior.

Punishment is thus quite different from negative reinforcement. Punishment aims to weaken or reduce a behavior, and negative reinforcement aims to strengthen a behavior.

Social Learning Theory

A theory related to classical and operant conditioning is **social learning theory,** or social cognitive theory. Albert Bandura (1977), a leading proponent of social learning theory, posits that people are active agents in their learning. His theory supports the ideas put forth by other learning theorists but goes further by maintaining that people use cognition and social interactions in learning. People do not simply respond automatically to stimuli. Rather, they are able to think about processes in learning, and they actively interact with their surroundings, which often results in learning. Specifically, people think about the ramifications of their actions and make decisions about whether to act based on the outcomes of those actions.

Social learning theory suggests that people can learn vicariously, or through watching others. This type of learning is called **modeling.** That is, we can learn behaviors by watching how others do things and then imitating those behaviors. Moreover, we often watch what others do to see what the consequences will be for their behavior. If we observe someone being punished for a particular behavior, we are less likely to engage in that behavior ourselves. Conversely, if we observe someone being rewarded for a behavior, we are more likely to imitate that behavior to receive the same rewards. Therefore, according to social learning theory, people do not actually have to perform a behavior themselves to learn from it. Rather, people learn by others' successes or failures (Bandura, 1965).

Bandura identified one important aspect of learning as **self-efficacy**, which he defined as people's expectations that they can perform a task successfully. According to social learning theory, successful experiences are necessary to build self-efficacy. When people have high levels of self-efficacy, they are more likely to perform well in school, work, and other areas of their lives, which helps to build and reinforce their feelings of competence (Bandura, 1997). In essence, the development and maintenance of self-efficacy is a cyclical process: The more successful experiences that people have, the more likely they are to seek other opportunities that lend themselves to successful outcomes, which helps to further build a sense of competence.

Applying Learning Theory

In Carlos's situation, you could use concepts from social learning theory or combine them with concepts from classical and operant conditioning to help him deal with his current situation. For example, let us say that Carlos has a fear of care facilities. Every time he sees one, he becomes anxious and cannot step inside. To help him overcome this anxiety, you could use **systematic desensitization***, which builds on the concepts of positive reinforcement and self-efficacy. You could begin by talking to Carlos about care facilities while teaching him relaxation techniques. Eventually, you would show Carlos pictures of facilities, then take him on a drive or walk past one, and then finally help him to physically walk into one. The idea is to expose Carlos to these facilities gradually while helping him to calm his anxiety. Simultaneously, Carlos will gain intrinsic rewards through feeling pride in his successes, which will reinforce his behaviors of approaching facilities. After some work, he should be able to enter a facility without any fear or anxiety.*

PHOTO 3-B

Modeling is an important way for children to learn behaviors

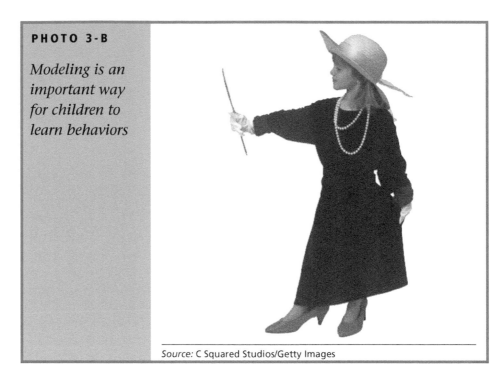

Source: C Squared Studios/Getty Images

You could also use the concept of modeling by introducing Carlos to other people who have Alzheimer's disease but who are coping well with the symptoms. Carlos may be able to learn new ways of coping and functioning. This exposure may also help to reduce some of his fears about having the disease.

You could also use his past successes and high level of functioning to tap into his sense of self-efficacy. Carlos seems to have performed well in the past: He was successful at his work, he has close relationships, and he has shown that he can cope with adversity. Carlos may need to be reminded of his successes to help him transfer this self-efficacy to his current situation and to future challenges.

You may also find it useful to explore with Carlos how learning has shaped his perceptions of certain behaviors such as intimacy, independence, and display of emotion. Because these issues seem to be relevant in his current situation (and they are likely to be relevant in the future), you may want to explore whether behaviors that could be beneficial to Carlos, such as expressing feelings, have been punished or not reinforced. For example, because of gender role stereotypes or cultural context, Carlos may have been punished for crying or talking about feelings. Or, he could have been positively reinforced for stereotypical masculine behavior such as holding in feelings. You could help Carlos by extinguishing behaviors that are detrimental to his well-being. For instance, you could help him "relearn" that expressing feelings is acceptable by positively reinforcing any efforts on his part to talk openly about his fears, regrets, or other feelings associated with his situation.

Critiquing Learning Theory

Social workers have found many ideas from learning theories to be effective for a wide range of client problems. Nevertheless, there have been criticisms:

- Some of the tenets behind classical and operant conditioning theories treat people as passive agents who sit back and allow things to "happen" to them. These theories fail to address innate cognitive processes that may be motivating people's behaviors. However, there is some debate about how much these theories do acknowledge the influence of active cognitive process in the individual (Jensen & Burgess, 1997; Swann, 2009). Also, social learning theory recognizes that people can gain insights into their behavior and ultimately can take an active role in changing behavior based on these insights.

- Classical and operant conditioning do not consider the ways in which the environment influences people's decisions and behaviors. Conversely, social learning theory takes into account the interactions between people and their environment. Although social learning theory incorporates some of the basic learning concepts, it augments these ideas with more complex processes that affect how people learn and behave.

One reason for the continuing relevance of learning theories is that the concepts underlying them are fairly easy to define, measure, and evaluate. Thus, they can be applied to interventions, and the outcomes can be tested empirically. Many of these interventions can also be applied quickly, making them popular in settings that mandate short-term work with clients. Further, the ideas about learning incorporated in these theories can be empowering for clients. They offer a straightforward approach to changing behavior that, with some guidance from social workers, helps to put control into the hands of clients. Specifically, social workers can help clients understand how to change undesirable behaviors, which can be generalized to other situations in which clients wish to change behaviors.

HUMANISTIC AND EXISTENTIAL PERSPECTIVES

There are many other biopsychosocial theories that could influence your work with clients. The last type that we will look at in this chapter are humanistic and existential theories, which deal with the effects of people's worldviews or the meanings they place on life and on their behavior. These theories have a strong base in philosophy and are tied to Eastern beliefs of Zen Buddhism, Hinduism, and Islam (Payne, 1997). Existentialist and humanistic perspectives assert that people are capable of developing their spiritual selves, although aspects of spirituality may be defined differently by social workers than they are within an organized religion.

Existentialism focuses on the meaning of life and people's views on existence. It teaches that people have control over their lives. People are cognitive beings who can think critically about who they are and who they would like to be. However, society also influences these thinking processes by "selling" stereotypes and images of success and happiness. Although people often understand that these are stereotypes, they have a tendency to allow these images to dictate how they view themselves as well as how they perceive happiness and well-being. Existentialism thus addresses the human motivation to live lives that can sometimes be painful and unrewarding. Because the relationship between people and their environments is dynamic, existentialism acknowledges that predicting human behavior is difficult. People are constantly growing and making choices that can change their lives, and these choices are influenced by their social surroundings (Payne, 1997).

Like existentialism, the **humanistic perspective** focuses on the ways people view life and being. This perspective emphasizes people's role in shaping their own experiences. Essentially, it posits that each person has the potential for healthy and creative growth. There is no predetermined pattern to personality development; rather, people's subjective views on life help to shape their personality and experiences. These experiences, along with the feelings, values, and perceptions surrounding them, are important factors in shaping development. The humanistic perspective is rooted in the belief that people are active agents in their lives; people have the ability to reason, make choices, form their experiences, and control their destiny (Payne, 1997). Humans are resourceful, purposeful, and independent beings who are motivated to achieve love, growth, success, and acceptance.

These two perspectives are very similar with regard to their underlying tenets and view of human development and behavior. In social work, they tend to be grouped under the humanistic model. To better articulate their views on human development, we will look at specific therapeutic interventions that have been developed based on these perspectives.

Person-Centered Therapy and Transactional Analysis

One of the most famous humanistic theorists is Carl Rogers. Rogers is best known for client-centered or **person-centered therapy**, which is based on a person's self-concept. Rogers agrees that people are the product of their experiences and how they perceive those experiences. His theory states that people have a natural inclination toward self-actualization: We strive to develop our ideal self or the person we would like to be. We achieve self-actualization when

- our self-concept is congruent with our experiences;

- we experience positive regard (respect, esteem) from others; and

- we have positive self-regard (we value ourselves).

Similarly, a lack of well-being results from an incongruence between our self-concept and experiences. Rogers proposed that psychological maladjustment occurs when a person denies or distorts her or his experiences and is unable to deal with incongruence. From this perspective, the crux of social work with clients is to establish warmth, respect, empathy, genuineness, and positive regard in the working relationship. According to Rogers, these factors must be present for change to occur (1951).

Other theorists who fall into the humanistic category are Fritz Perls, who developed gestalt therapy, and Eric Berne, who founded transactional analysis. **Gestalt therapy** is based on psychodynamic theory. It posits that people go through life with "unfinished business" (for example, unresolved feelings or conflicts with others) that affects behavior and relationships. People naturally attempt to avoid this unfinished business because they erroneously believe that experiencing it will bring catastrophe. As people avoid the powerful feelings associated with unfinished business, they disown essential parts of themselves and do not fully experience life. Gestalt therapy is geared toward helping people work through this unfinished business and fully "own" the self. People work toward making the past and hidden aspects of themselves fully known, and they are encouraged to live in the present (Perls, Hefferline, & Goodman, 1973).

Transactional analysis is also based on psychodynamic theory, and it shares the notion that maladaptive behavioral patterns established in childhood often get in the way of well-being in later life. However, unlike psychodynamic theory, transactional analysis states that people are active, responsible beings who have the capacity to solve problems. This theory posits that in infancy, people have a need for physical contact. As people age, they satisfy this need through conversation and verbal contact with others. Transactional analysis focuses on people's transactions with others, especially on the problems that occur in these transactions that can hinder positive behavior and development. This therapy uses different types of analyses to work with clients in promoting well-being. One technique used in this therapy is *structural analysis*. It looks at people's ego states, or the structures that make up personality. These ego states are thought to be associated with people's behavioral patterns. Structural analysis examines the interactions of ego states among two or more people. Another technique, *game analysis,* examines specific patterns of interactions and behaviors among two or more people (Berne, 1961).

Person-Centered and Participant-Directed Service Models

Based in humanistic and strengths perspectives as well as the social work value of self-determinism are *person-centered* and *participant-directed* service models. These service models grew out of the self-determination, disabilities rights, and independent living movements of the 1990s. Sometimes referred to as self- or consumer-directed services, the goals of these models are to help people of all ages and ability levels remain independent as long as possible and determine what services best fit their needs. These models view the participant as expert and strive to give control to the consumer in all service decisions (The National Center for Participant-Directed Services, 2013).

Over the past few decades, person-centered and participant-directed service models have been incorporated in many programs like Medicaid and long-term care programs as well as implemented for people with various health and mental health needs like Alzheimer's disease and physical disabilities. For example, people receiving Medicaid assistance guided by this service model have the ability to recruit, hire, train, supervise, and fire caregivers and have control over how funds they receive from Medicaid are spent. Medicaid workers provide support, training, assistance, and oversight to help consumers make decisions and manage their services and to serve as a liaison between the consumer and program. Another example of this service model is options counseling offered through aging and disabilities programs. Counselors in these programs assist consumers and their family members and significant others to develop plans for long-term care services and supports that are consistent with consumers' needs, values, preferences, and strengths.

Research conducted on the efficacy of these types of service models suggest that they provide a cost-effective alternative to other traditional care models such as long-term care facilities and agency-based service provision, even among consumers who have severe cognitive disabilities such as dementia. Further, research suggests that consumers want to have choices and control over care decisions and delivery, and these service models are resulting in a great deal of life and service satisfaction for consumers (Polivka, 2000; Polivka & Salmon, 2001). Some of the criticisms of these service models include fears about fraud, abuse, and safety; unsustainable reimbursement to caregivers; consumer reluctance to use services; and resistance by service providers to change existing service delivery models (Polivka & Salmon, 2001; The National Center for Participant-Directed Services, 2013).

Applying Humanistic and Existential Perspectives

Given the broad philosophies found in humanistic and existential perspectives, there are many ways in which you could approach your work with Carlos. However, the basic approach would be to better understand how Carlos perceives his situation. You would want to know how his subjective views of the world and of the meaning of life are shaping his experiences. While acknowledging the need to recognize that Carlos has the capacity to shape his future experiences and to control his own destiny, you will want to keep in mind that these considerations might not apply to Carlos in a literal sense since his physical problems will take much control out of his hands. You could still help Carlos find meaning in what is happening to him or at least help him come to some sense of peace with his situation.

Working from person-centered therapy, you would strive to establish a working environment with Carlos that promoted warmth, empathy, genuineness, and positive regard. You would then work with him to explore his views of his self-concept and his ideal self. Your goal would be to ensure that Carlos experiences congruency between his self-concept and his experiences, which may be a problem given his diagnosis and impending loss of independence. Carlos might be in denial about his situation, which means that he could be distorting his experiences and maintaining a state of incongruence. His diagnosis is also likely to be in conflict with his view of his ideal self.

Taking a person-centered, participant-directed approach, you might focus on Carlos's uniqueness and work to understand his perspective on the world and provide a social environment that supports his needs. This would include supporting his personhood, preserving his autonomy, creating a sense of normality in his environment, honoring his dignity and sense of meaning in life, empowering him to guide his caregiving plans, and cultivating positive interactions and communication.

Critiquing Humanistic and Existential Perspectives

Critics voice a couple of concerns about using humanistic and existential perspectives in social work:

- One of the main limitations is that these approaches are not based on a coherent theory of personality. Rather, they espouse vague ideas and concepts that are not easily defined. Thus, evaluating whether these approaches are effective in creating change with clients is difficult.

- Depending on the philosophy of the social worker, these ideas can be applied very differently by different workers.

Proponents of these theories assert that they are positive and strengths based (as opposed to problem-based theories) and can help to empower clients. Some social workers favor these approaches because they put the client at the center of the working relationship, allowing the client to guide the process. Indeed, concepts in Rogers' theory such as respect, empathy, and positive regard are seen as crucial components in the working relationship regardless of the theory used to guide the process. Moreover, the use of these skills has been empirically shown to be more effective in producing positive client outcomes than the use of any specific theory (Gurman, 1977; Orlinsky and Howard, 1986; Patterson, 1984). These approaches also allow social workers to explore how the larger social environment has impacted clients' identity and self-concept. For example, years of discrimination, oppression, and devaluing of one's culture can have significant impacts on development of self-concept and regard and ability to achieve self-actualization.

Finally, some approaches, such as transactional analysis, can be applied to work with clients in a somewhat systematic manner. Many agencies have developed therapeutic programs that use these concepts as guiding principles. For example, social workers can employ structural or game analysis in their interventions. Social workers can be trained in the use of transactional analysis, which helps to ensure that it is used consistently and accurately across clients and agencies.

CONCLUSION

The theories, models, and perspectives discussed in this chapter tend to focus on the individual and how various problems and processes affect development and behavior on an individual level. To review their main characteristics, look back at Quick Guide 4. Although some of the theories and approaches discussed here do take into account environmental influences, these influences tend to be limited to those within a person's immediate environment. Many social workers argue that these types of considerations are too limited, and that larger environmental forces outside of clients' control must be considered in assessment and intervention.

Still, the ideas presented in this chapter influence social work in general, and they contribute a great deal to clinical social work practice. The underlying tenets of these theories, models, and perspectives also need to be understood in order for social workers to communicate and work with other helping professionals.

As discussed in Chapter 1, these theories and approaches can be used in combination with other theories and approaches that address larger social forces to offer a more comprehensive view of client problems. Moreover, tenets of the theories and models discussed in this chapter, particularly some of the constructs used in disease-based models, can be used to inform person-in-environment conceptualizations of client problems. Keep in mind that with technological advances and an increasing need for social workers to stay abreast of biological knowledge, disease-based and other micro-focused theories and models are an integral part of social workers' knowledge base.

MAIN POINTS

- One of the lenses for conceptualizing client problems and considering interventions is the biopsychosocial lens. Social workers may use several models, theories, and perspectives within this dimension, including the medical model, theory of cognitive development, psychodynamic theories, learning theory, and the humanistic perspective.

- The medical model is a disease-based model that focuses on the symptoms of problems, which can be cured by an expert. When applying this model, social workers may begin by assessing the client's problems using the DSM-5.

- Social workers need to have a basic understanding of brain structures and how the brain works, along with neural processes, because of their strong influence on behavior.

- There are many neurotransmitters, hormones, and genetic processes that influence human development and behavior and that are the root of many mental health and other issues.

- Piaget's theory of cognitive development consists of four main stages that describe cognitive development from birth to about age 16 as becoming more complex, flexible, and capable of abstract reasoning.

- Freud's theory of psychosexual development, based on the concepts of the id, the ego, and the superego, consists of five stages that explain personality development. People can become fixated in any stage, and they use defense mechanisms to suppress conflicts that may occur at each stage.

- Erikson's theory of psychosocial development consists of eight stages that describe development across the life span. He proposed that people face crises in each stage that must be resolved; otherwise, they take unresolved crises into the next stage, which affects development and the ability to face new crises.

- Learning theories focus on how people respond to stimuli in their environment. Some theories, such as classical conditioning, view people as passive learners, while others, such as social learning theory, view people as actively involved in their environments, which means that they are actively involved in learning.

- Humanistic and existential perspectives, which focus on how people view life and meaning, emphasize the abilities of people to make decisions and shape their own experiences; this is even truer of person-centered and participant-directed service models. Although critics argue that the ideas in these perspectives are vague and outcomes difficult to evaluate, person-centered therapy and transactional analysis are two well-used concepts in social work.

EXERCISES

1. *Sanchez Family interactive case at* www.routledgesw.com/cases. Review the issues facing each member of the Sanchez family. Pick a family member or two on whom you would like to focus for this exercise. You will also need to choose three different theoretical perspectives discussed in this chapter to apply to the problems of the family member(s). When you have chosen your clients and perspectives, answer the following questions:

    a. Briefly describe the problems you see with the family member(s) you have chosen.

    b. Describe how you would perceive the family member(s) and their problems through the lens of each theory you chose. Make sure you are being detailed enough to capture the essence of the theory.

    c. Briefly discuss how you would develop an intervention that is based on each theory.

    d. Discuss how the family member, problems, and interventions differ from one another from the perspective of each theory.

    e. Discuss some of the strengths and limitations to working with the family member from each perspective.

    f. Based on your discussion thus far, which approach would you take with the family member and why?

2. *Riverton interactive case at* www.routledgesw.com/cases. Review the situation described in this case and the problems faced by that community. Based on your assessment of the situation, could you use any of the theories discussed in this chapter to help you conceptualize the problems faced by this community and to help guide your intervention? Why or why not? Be specific and give examples to justify your thoughts.

3. *RAINN interactive case at* www.routledgesw.com/cases. Referring to the case, answer these questions:

    a. How does Social Learning Theory apply to Alan's case? What macro-level systems have influenced how Alan reacted to his trauma?

    b. How would you use Erikson's theory to explain Sarah's behavior? How would Piaget's theory explain Sarah's behavior differently?

    c. If you only had the medical model as your theoretical lens, how would your interactions with Sarah and Alan be different than if you also had behavioral, learning, and cognitive theories incorporated into your lens for understanding human behavior?

4. *Hudson City interactive case at* www.routledgesw.com/cases. Review the issues facing the community and answer the following questions:

    a. If you were using the medical model to work with residents of this community, what areas or problems might be the focus of your work?

    b. If you were working with a three-year-old child who lived in this community, using Erikson's theory as a conceptual guide to your work, what developmental issues might you be concerned with, and how might larger environmental and other events impact this development?

    c. How might a Humanistic approach be used with residents of this community?

Lenses for Conceptualizing Problems and Interventions: Sociocultural Dimensions

The Smith family has just adopted Aisha, a 10-year-old African–American girl who has been in the foster care system for three years. Aisha was placed in foster care after her mother was convicted of theft; Aisha's father has not been involved with her since she was two years old, and her other family members were unable to care for her. Before Aisha was placed in foster care, she lived in poverty with her mother and two siblings. However, despite these difficulties, she seemed to be thriving in her environment, and her mother was able to provide the necessities for her family. After her mother's arrest, Aisha was placed briefly with an African–American family and had been adjusting well to school, peers, and her new family.

Aisha's new adoptive family are devout Roman Catholic, upper-class Caucasians with three other children who are all older than Aisha. For the past several weeks, Aisha has experienced trouble adjusting to her new family. She will not talk or eat, and she has encountered problems in school. Aisha told the social worker at the foster care agency that she misses her foster family, church (her family of origin is Baptist), friends, and neighborhood. She feels out of place with her new family and school, and she is not sure how she will fit into her new environment.

AISHA'S SITUATION RAISES MANY ETHICAL, PRACTICAL, and philosophical questions for a social worker. Some of these questions relate to Aisha's adjustment and well-being as a new family member. Others involve the adjustment of the adoptive family as they attempt to accommodate a new member. Still other questions focus on the utility of institutions such as family, religion, adoption, and foster care and how these institutions support or undermine individual functioning and the integrity of cultural diversity and ethnic differences. To look for answers to some of these broad philosophical questions, social workers often turn to sociological, feminist, and cultural theories to conceptualize larger social issues.

As in Chapters 2 and 3, the theories and perspectives discussed in this chapter are presented in Quick Guide 6 for purposes of comparison and review.

	QUICK GUIDE 6 The Sociocultural Lens: Theories, Models, and Perspectives	
	CONFLICT	**FUNCTIONALISM**
Type	Theory	Theory
Focus	Social groups	Social groups
Assumptions	Tensions among groups shape social structures.	Aspects, or functions, of a society work together to maintain stability.
Strengths	• Can be used to conceptualize interventions in community-based practice. • Helps social workers understand the complexity of client problems. • Focuses on how power can be misused to create inequality and to disenfranchise clients.	• Offers clients an alternative viewpoint to problems. • Understanding manifest and latent functions of social institutions can help social workers target interventions. • Tenets of theory fit well with ideas from systems and ecological theories. • Focusing on changing dysfunction within a system could be an empowering approach for clients.
Limitations	• Focus is limited to the macro level. • Interventions based on conflict can be difficult to carry out. • Can be difficult to define and empirically test constructs.	• Little attention given to the complexity of interactions that take place among systems. • Does not address the inequity that may result from a system's manifest and latent functions. • Can be difficult to use for developing interventions. • Can be difficult to define and empirically test constructs.

SOCIOLOGICAL THEORIES

The discipline of sociology focuses on the study of social behavior and groups. Sociologists develop theories to explain how social forces affect people on a large scale. For example, sociological theory might explain how unemployment affects a community or why a group of people would follow a leader of a religious sect to the point of committing suicide.

Most sociological theories reflect the **sociological imagination,** a term coined by C. Wright Mills (1959) to describe the relationship between the individual and the wider society. According to Mills, this awareness allows us to better understand the connection between our personal lives and larger social forces that influence us. An important component of the sociological imagination is the need to view outside social forces from an objective perspective and not just from our own culturally biased point of view.

SYMBOLIC INTERACTIONISM/SOCIAL CONSTRUCTIONISM Theory	FEMINISM Theory	CULTURALISM Perspective
Society and the individual	Society and the individual	Society and the individual
Ways in which people and systems interact, and the meaning that people attach to those interactions, shape individual experiences and society.	Interactions of individuals and social forces affect development, oppression and discrimination, and institutional structure and functioning.	Individual experiences help give structure to experiences and shape society.
• Provides a useful way to assess problems. • Focus on the meanings clients place on their experiences can be empowering. • Approach to assessment fits well with humanistic perspectives and can be combined with other theories. • Tenets have been useful in postmodern research.	• Focuses on equality and the role of the dominant structure in causing and perpetuating client problems. • Tenets have helped guide postmodern research. • Has raised awareness of multiple points of view on issues.	• Offers ways to articulate, organize, and understand cultural elements of clients' lives. • Helps social workers to be more culturally competent in practice.
• Does not offer a clear way in which to intervene with clients. • Too micro focused. • Lacks a solid, consistent theoretical base from which to examine relationships. • Can be difficult to define and empirically test constructs. • Difficult to predict behavior.	• Focuses on women at the expense of other minority groups. • Can be difficult to define and empirically test constructs. • Cannot predict behavior.	• There is no single, coherent theory of culture. • Concepts may be difficult to define, apply, and test empirically. • Cannot predict behavior.

Based on the topics discussed in the previous chapters, you can see how well sociology fits with social work. Many of the theories, models, and perspectives that we have reviewed are rooted in the idea that social workers need to understand individuals within their environmental context. The first part of the chapter discusses some fundamental theories in sociology and how they can be applied to social work practice.

Conflict Theory

One of sociology's first theoretical orientations was **conflict theory**, an approach that views social behavior from the perspective of conflict or tension among two or more groups. This theory provides a framework from which conflict between superordinate and subordinate groups in society can be systematically analyzed (Turner, 1998).

Karl Marx and Conflict Theory   Conflict theory can be traced to the writings of Karl Marx, who believed that struggle or conflict among classes was an inevitable feature of capitalism (Marx, 1987; Marx & Engels, 1977). Marx argued that various groups in society, or social classes, are perpetually fighting and competing for resources and power—he viewed resources primarily in terms of economics—and that groups remain polarized against one another. As resources become scarcer and are more unequally distributed—with the upper classes accumulating an increasing portion of them—this conflict increases. In addition, as subordinate groups become aware that they are being treated unfairly, they are more likely to question and fight against the status quo. Finally, as groups become increasingly polarized, the conflict becomes more intense and ultimately leads to change in the status quo (Marx, 1994; Turner, 1998).

Significantly, Marx argued that conflict is not necessarily violent. Rather, it can take the form of struggle within business or political negotiations, religious or philosophical ideologies, or personal attitudes and beliefs (Lefebvre, 1968; Marx, 1973; Mills, 1994; Sayer, 1989; Turner, 1998). For instance, conflict can be represented in differing opinions between two religious groups or in the competition for resources between two political parties.

Conflict Theories since Marx   Marx's views sparked a great deal of thought and debate. Numerous sociologists, including Max Weber, Georg Simmel, W. E. B. Du Bois, and various feminist thinkers, developed and modified Marx's views. Their efforts contributed to the development of sociological research and conflict-based theory.

- *Max Weber:* An economist, he was one of the biggest critics of Marx's ideas (1958, 1968). Weber agreed with Marx that conflicts among groups can emerge and that they can lead to structural change and a more equal distribution of resources. However, Weber argued that Marx's theory was too focused on the inevitability of conflict in society. Weber also maintained that groups need a leader to spur the conflict. These leaders must be able to incite resentment and anger in subordinate groups. Weber also disagreed with Marx's views of absolute polarization among groups. Weber argued that groups possess a great deal of variation with regard to class, politics, philosophies, and so on (Turner, 1998; Weber, 1957, 1994). Thus, Weber maintained that groups could be defined by class, status, and party rather than just by social class, as Marx had posited. He further argued that membership or identification with a particular group did not automatically assure power.

- *Georg Simmel:* Many aspects of his ideas were similar to those of Marx and Weber. Simmel generally concurred with Weber regarding the origins of conflict in society. Specifically, he argued that as the levels of emotional involvement and solidarity increase among group members, the level of violence also increases. He further argued that conflict serves to centralize power, establish clear boundaries between groups, and restrict deviance among group members. Simmel also proposed that conflict can be beneficial for society if it is not too intense or violent. If the ground rules can be agreed on, conflict can encourage coalition building and discussion between groups (Turner, 1998).

- *W. E. B. Du Bois:* He focused primarily on racial and ethnic inequality (1911, 1970), arguing that sociologists should pursue scientific knowledge to help overcome bias and prejudice in society. To pursue this objective he supported various social groups and organizations that questioned the status quo. For example, he helped found the National Association for the Advancement of Colored People (NAACP) in 1909. Du Bois' push for more concentrated research on conflict and its effects on minority groups helped to increase sociological knowledge of racial and social inequality, much of which has benefited the African–American community.

Many other theorists have developed ideas that have been integrated into conflict theory. In addition, various movements and events of the 1960s and 1970s— the women's and civil rights movements as well as riots, demonstrations, and confrontations over such issues as the Vietnam War and governmental scandals— increased the support for conflict theory. In the past few years, class has become an increasing source of conflict and concern for many Americans. In 2012 the Pew Research Center found that 66 percent of the public believed that we were experiencing significant conflicts between the rich and the poor; in 2009, that number was only 47 percent (Pew Research Center, 2012). This sense of an increasing divide between the wealthy and the middle class and poor, as well as a sense of dwindling economic and other opportunities for the majority of Americans, prompted thousands of people across the country to "occupy" various public spaces such as Wall Street and government buildings.

Sociologists have expanded conflict theory to include not just societal conflict but also struggles that occur in many different aspects of social and personal life. These later theories examine which groups either benefit or suffer from the established order and the distribution of resources. They focus on who has power and how this power is used to perpetuate inequality. These perspectives explore conflicts among gender, ethnic, religious, and cultural groups as well as conflicts that occur within social institutions such as the media, family, and government. In addition, these approaches examine how power and resources can be distributed among groups more equitably to benefit everyone instead of just a few (Dahrendorf, 1958). Some argue that conflict approaches encourage sociologists to examine issues from the perspective of people who enjoy fewer privileges and influence than others in society.

Applying Conflict Theory

This section offers some additional examples of how conflict theory can be applied to a couple of common institutions: family and health care. These examples take a contemporary look at conflict theory and its relevance to social issues. We will also consider the relevance of conflict theory to social work in general and to Aisha's situation in particular.

Family The conflict perspective views families as institutions that both reflect and perpetuate the unequal distribution of power and resources within the larger society. In other words, families serve as the means through which wealth, power, poverty, privilege, and inequality are passed from one generation to another, thereby contributing to economic injustice. For example, children inherit the poverty or privilege of their parents. Children born to wealthy, educated, well-connected parents benefit from quality housing, education, health care, and access to opportunity. These children are at an advantage as they grow older due to their inherited resources. Conversely, children born to poor and uneducated parents are exposed to debt, limited growth experiences and opportunities, and inferior education and health care, all of which can hinder their ability to get ahead in life.

Families also pass on to their children other characteristics besides economic and related opportunities. The social class and economic status of families influence the ways in which children are socialized, which impacts the children's views, values, beliefs, attitudes, and behaviors. Children carry these values and perspectives into their adult lives, which in turn influences the ways they vote, make policy, and believe that society should distribute resources.

In addition, according to conflict theory, the family legitimizes male power and dominance, which in turn validates and perpetuates the lower status of women and children. This unequal power distribution affects women and children in realms outside the immediate family such as education, economics, child care, workplace policy, health care, reproductive choices, and freedom to move about and express themselves. For example, women are still more likely than men to leave their jobs and relocate when they get married, when the man receives a promotion, or when child or elder care is needed. Women are also more likely to postpone their education or career goals after marriage. In addition, domestic violence remains a serious problem. Though the feminist movement has helped women and children to achieve broader rights, men are still viewed as dominant within the family unit.

Health Care Another example of how conflict theory can be applied to a sociological issue is health care. From the perspective of conflict theory, medicine and medical professionals hold a great deal of status in U.S. society. The medical institution has the power to define wellness and illness as well as acceptable treatments for people who are ill. This power enables the medical establishment to exert a certain amount of social control in many areas, not just health care, and to define and reinforce many social values.

Sociologists have coined the term **medicalization of society** to describe the influence of the health profession. As the range of expertise in medicine has grown over the decades, the medical profession has acquired the power to influence knowledge, attitudes, opinions, and even social policy. For example, the opinions of physicians and other medical professionals increasingly influence and shape public opinion and policies regarding such issues as old age, obesity, sexuality, and addiction. Conflict theory argues that the enhanced power of the medical establishment reflects the perception among the lay public that medical professionals possess special knowledge and expertise that make them uniquely qualified to evaluate health-related issues. As a result, the medical profession has achieved unchecked jurisdiction over policies and procedures that would otherwise be open to public scrutiny, such as those related to childbirth, child care, drug costs, and national health care.

One prominent example of the medicalization of society is childbirth. Formerly the realm of female midwives, in the early 20th century childbirth was turned over to a mostly male medical profession which foisted largely unnatural childbirth practices onto women. Physicians undermined the credibility of midwives by creating a perception that their practices were "unscientific." It took nearly a century for midwives to begin to recapture their reputation and their influence over childbirth practices (Schoen, 2000). The resulting increase in use of midwives, home birth, and birth centers as an alternative to maternity wards within hospitals helps to restore women's control over the birth process and to decrease the medicalization of birth (Parry, 2008). Similarly, since the 1960s and 1970s, women (and physicians) have rediscovered the benefits of breastfeeding. A generation earlier, the experts had recommended scientifically engineered formula over breast milk.

Conflict Theory and Social Work   Because conflict theory fits so well with the underlying values and ethics of social work, including empowerment and social justice, social workers can find many uses for it. Social workers who work with victims of domestic violence, for example, can use conflict theory to conceptualize the power differential that exists between men and women and the ways in which patriarchal society supports and maintains this inequality. This conceptualization, in turn, can help social workers to understand the obstacles that discourage or prevent many women from leaving their situations. Many of these obstacles are embedded in the fabric of societal values, which makes leaving for some women extremely difficult. For example, the expense of child care, women's struggle to earn wages that will support themselves and their families, and the court system's slow and often ineffective response to domestic violence can all create barriers to women's successful exit from violent situations. Further, some social workers may choose to intervene against domestic violence on a larger societal level by dealing with policies and value systems that perpetuate current thinking about the unequal roles of men and women in society.

With regard to health care, social workers can use conflict theory to better understand how medicine as an institution affects clients. If the medical establishment possesses the ability to influence people's lives, as posited by conflict theory, then social workers need to be educated about how organized medicine uses this power to determine policies and services that directly affect clients. In addition, social workers frequently intervene with clients whose values conflict with those of the medical establishment. For example, what if a client's beliefs dictate that she seek alternative medicine or refuse all medical treatments? Conflict theory can help social workers to understand how hospitals can exert pressures that might conflict with patients' personal values and beliefs. Social workers must act as mediators between hospitals and clients to ensure that clients' rights are not undermined by the policies and mandates of hospitals.

As another example, the health care institutions in the United States—which include privatized and managed care, soaring health care costs, and ever-advancing technology—have created a two-tiered health care system. One tier is for the wealthy and gainfully employed, who can afford private health insurance or receive it as an employment benefit; the other is for people who are poor, unemployed, and underemployed. The Affordable Care Act of 2010 was designed to help people in this second group, who were being forced out of the system and left without quality care. However, considerable social and judicial conflict continued to surround this legislation years after it was signed into law. For example, as of 2015, 22 of the 50 U.S. states were refusing to enact the expansion of Medicaid, the federal health care program for low-income citizens, provided for in the law (White House, 2015). It may be some time before all the provisions of the legislation are implemented, even if they survive court challenges.

Another sign of conflict in the health care system is that many qualified physicians are abandoning their communities and practices for safer and more lucrative positions, leaving many poor people, particularly in rural areas, without care. This phenomenon is occurring worldwide. In the United States, infant mortality rates are higher than in many other countries, reflecting unequal access to health care (World Bank, 2012). In 2012 there were 42 other countries with a lower infant mortality rate than the United States (World Bank, 2012).

Conflict theory offers one perspective from which to view these problems, which can be used as a springboard for devising interventions that will lead to system change. Indeed, it is often social workers who bring attention to ethical, cultural, and other issues that may clash with the predominant medical model, thereby helping to initiate changes that can benefit clients.

In fact, conflict theory offers social workers a perspective from which to better understand why any social movement begins and gains momentum. Conflict theory also points the way for social workers to advocate for socioeconomic equity and opportunity for lower income families. Conflict theory suggests to social workers that as long as the public perceives "very strong conflicts" between poor people and rich people, there is a strong likelihood that the tension between groups will force change. This forced change could either hamper efforts to create more equitable opportunities for everyone or it could result in positive change that benefits the majority of people in society. Social workers can use these ideas to help shape the outcomes of conflict and to promote positive change that supports the well-being of society as a whole.

> **Aisha's Case and Conflict Theory**   *Let us look at how Aisha's early life might be viewed from the perspective of conflict theory. As the social worker, you might be inclined to focus on the broad issues that forced Aisha into this situation in the first place, which can then help you focus on specific areas appropriate for intervention.*
>
> *One place to begin would be to look at the poverty in which Aisha's birth family was living. You might question why Aisha's mother was unable to secure employment that paid enough to support the family. Based on conflict theory, you might argue that unequal distribution of resources and access to opportunities are causing poverty for Aisha's family. Further, this inequality is being maintained by societal values and a status quo that keep families like Aisha's in poverty.*
>
> *For Aisha's mother, discrimination in the workplace is a likely barrier as are more insidious factors such as unequal access to quality education that provides employment skills; lack of a livable wage (being African–American and female probably contributes to low wages as well); lack of opportunities to "network" with those who might provide opportunities; lack of access to resources such as child and health care that could free up time for work; and lack of access to reliable and affordable transportation to get to work.*
>
> *You could also assess other areas of Aisha's background in a similar vein, such as institutional policies in education, foster care, and criminal justice. They too seem to have a disenfranchising impact on Aisha and her family of origin.*

Critiquing Conflict Theory

Though you might find many areas to assess from the conflict perspective in Aisha's situation, it has limitations:

- The main limitation of conflict theory is that it tends to lend itself only to the macro level of conceptualization of problems. Developing interventions based on this theory at the micro level—especially within the realm of practice with individuals—is problematic.

- Carrying out conflict-based interventions after they are developed is also problematic. Issues of inequality are often firmly institutionalized and embedded in the fabric of societal values. Of course, this assertion does not suggest that you should not focus your attention on social issues that create problems for your clients or try to address these issues on a global level. It does recognize, however, that some social workers are not in a position to devise interventions on this level.

* Conflict theory does not often help social workers identify time- and cost-effective strategies for dealing with their clients' institutional problems, though these can be developed over time. Because many agencies, including foster care agencies, must focus on efficient interventions, unfortunately they usually do not have the luxury of pondering issues involving social change.

Social workers who focus on community- or organizational-based interventions, especially community action and change, will find perspectives like conflict theory useful. Their work can then inform work done on the micro level. The conflict perspective also allows social workers and clients to analyze societal problems that contribute to clients' situations.

Conflict theory is also useful for understanding the different levels of social work and of the environment that may be the source of many client problems. It can help you grasp the complex and varied relationships that occur within and among groups at these levels and the ways in which power can be used and misused to create inequality. Finally, the focus on how individuals and groups can become disenfranchised by unequal power distribution is congruent with the values and ethics of the profession, which serves as a reminder that the causes of problems are often out of the hands of the individuals facing them.

Critical Practice Theory

A social work theory that is similar to conflict theory in its ideas is critical practice theory. Critical practice theory borrows from several different theoretical perspectives including Marxism, feminism, postmodernism, critical theory, anti-oppressive theory, and the social model of disability. Critical practice theory emerged from radical perspectives in social work from the 1930s and the 1970s and takes a social change view of social work and its practices.

Critical practice theory views social problems as caused by oppressive societal structures and the cultural and moral assumptions generated and maintained by dominant groups. Goals of this theoretical perspective in social work are to help clients overcome limits and the oppressive nature of the existing social order and to help clients, especially those who are marginalized, find and use their voices to create social change.

According to critical practice theory, social workers can be viewed as contributing to the oppressive social order because they often work in social structures that have considerable power, control, and influence over clients' lives. However, because social workers are embedded in these structures, they can also change and disrupt oppressive and discriminatory systems that keep clients powerless. Further, traditional social work practices, like those that rely on psychological theories or individual explanations of social problems, take for granted the powerful influence of the social order that often causes individual problems. Even theories that take a more comprehensive view of problems, like ecological theory, espouse concepts of coping and adaptation, which suggest that people must adjust to the social order rather than fight against and change it. Thus, traditional social work practices tend to blame the victim, privatize problems (for example, through practices that endorse client confidentiality), and even strengthen the exploitative structures that disenfranchise people.

Practice terms used in critical practice theory include *praxis*, a term used by Paulo Freire and others (Freire, 1972; Held, 1980; McKerrow, 1989), which employs clients' experiences of injustice to better understand how society functions and strengthens people's capacity to pursue social change. In this sense, clients must gain knowledge about their current reality and then act upon their environment to further reflect on their situations and create further change. *Conscientization*, a term credited to Paulo Freire (Freire, 1972), is a practice to help raise people's awareness of oppressive social structures and strengthen clients' abilities to critically think about how these structures contribute to inequity. Finally, *dialogic practice* involves exchanging views of social structures through egalitarian relationships with clients.

Applying Critical Practice Theory

How might Aisha's situation be viewed through critical practice theory? Similar to the application of conflict theory, you might examine the oppressive social structures that have contributed to the discrimination Aisha's birth family has experienced in education, employment, transportation, health and childcare, and other areas, and that have contributed to poverty and the family's disintegration. From this viewpoint, it would be important to explain to Aisha that her years in foster care and her separation from her birth mother is not her fault; it doesn't stem from individual failings or weaknesses. The focus would be on macro causes of her situation.

In addition, you might engage with Aisha in an egalitarian relationship to discuss her experiences, her views on her current situation in her adoptive family, and her ideas about how she wants things to change. Particularly because Aisha is expressing unhappiness in her current situation, it is important to explore what her views are on what is happening and how she feels in her interactions with different social structures. This dialogue may help Aisha develop critical thinking skills around how social structures contribute to individual problems and how she can take control over her life and change things in the future.

Some aspects you might want to focus on with Aisha include discussing how different systems are structured and function (like the foster care system), and the role they may play in her problems, as well as those of her birth mother. At this point, you and Aisha could discuss how she might operate within these systems to find better outcomes. It's worth explaining to Aisha that although these systems cannot be changed immediately, working to find better options for Aisha, and advocating her position within these systems, is a good way to begin to change the systems that keep her and so many others oppressed.

Critiquing Critical Practice Theory

Critical practice theory shares many of the same weaknesses as conflict theory. Other limitations to this theory include:

- Traditional social work practice is often viewed as a means by which to help people who are suffering from individual or personal effects of oppressive structures. Thus, social service agencies are set up to target individual problems to help relieve individual distress, not to focus on large-scale social change, which could take considerable time to achieve. The view is that it is more ethical and timely to give priority to people's immediate needs.

- Social workers who work in traditional social service agencies are often bound by policies and laws that mandate the use of interventions focused on individual problems, not social change as espoused by critical practice theory.

- Many individual problems, such as health and mental health problems, are caused by biological factors—or at least some combination of biological and environmental factors. Critical practice theory alone does not lend itself well to intervening with these types of problems. However, social workers can still use critical practice theory to better understand clients' situations more fully, such as discriminatory practices that create barriers to accessing health care systems and treatments.

Functionalist Theory

Another of sociology's original theories is functionalist theory. In contrast to conflict theory and critical practice theory, **functionalist theory** attempts to explain how various aspects, or functions, of a society work together to maintain stability. Specifically, functionalist theory is concerned with the ways in which values, norms, institutions, and organizations contribute to the overall good of society. Like the systems and ecological theories discussed in Chapter 2, the functionalist approach views society as a living organism that consists of parts functioning as a whole. All systems coexist and are dependent on one another; and they work together to ensure the smooth functioning of the whole. Aspects of society that are functional and contribute to society will be maintained and passed on from one generation to the next. In contrast, dysfunctional systems will be changed or thrown out altogether.

Emile Durkheim   Emile Durkheim (1933, 1938), a pioneer in the field of sociology, made many contributions to functionalism through his work on biological processes and their application to social systems. He also promoted the idea that behavior must be considered within its social context. He concluded that society must be considered as a functioning whole; its parts cannot be viewed separately. He posited that these parts serve a function, purpose, or role that contributes to the whole. Through his analyses and ideas, Durkheim influenced other sociologists who were developing functionalist theory.

One of Durkheim's observations was that, for society to function well and to maintain homeostasis, it must meet various needs (such as social, physical, emotional, and economical) of its members and institutions (Turner, 1998). Durkheim was particularly interested in how industrialization affected people, especially the workers, who were increasingly exposed to specialized labor, isolation from the institutions that employed them, and other changes that accompanied this process.

Durkheim became convinced that when society undergoes dramatic change such as industrialization, people lose their sense of meaning in life and feel directionless in their activities. He coined the term **anomie** to describe this process. Ultimately, if anomie goes unchecked, society as a whole loses its sense of purpose and becomes unable to control individual behavior (Durkheim, 1933, 1938).

Robert K. Merton   Functionalist theory proposes that various functions of society work together to ensure the well-being of society as a whole. These functions can express themselves in different ways, some of which are more observable and obvious than others. Theorist Robert K. Merton (1968) was the first to articulate these key concepts within social science:

- **Manifest functions** are those whose purposes are readily discernible. For instance, many students would agree that the purpose of course grades is to give students feedback on their performance and to provide a report to outsiders (such as parents, employers, and graduate schools) that reflects the student's abilities. The purpose of giving grades, then, seems apparent and straightforward.

- **Latent functions** are those whose purpose is not necessarily what it seems to be on the surface. Again using grades as an example, although grades do offer students feedback, they can perform a number of less obvious functions as well. For example, they can discourage students, they can misrepresent a student's true capability, they can be given arbitrarily without a fair or uniform standard, and they can be used to discriminate against students. In other words, whether intended or not, latent functions can either promote or undermine an institution or an aspect of society, depending on the viewpoint of the person experiencing them.

- **Dysfunctions** are those parts of society that do not contribute to the well-being of the larger system. Dysfunctions may actually add to instability and chaos in a system, sometimes causing the system to disintegrate. For example, most people perceive crime as dysfunctional. Criminal acts such as fraud, theft, arson, and murder all disrupt the order of the personal lives affected by such acts, and they can create chaos for communities and society. Depending on the crime, they can cause physical, financial, emotional, and psychological instability. Sometimes criminal acts can cause total disintegration of systems; for example, a person may commit suicide in the wake of losing all her money due to fraud, or riots may break out in a community because of a murder.

Talcott Parsons   Talcott Parsons, another prominent functionalist theorist, was influenced by the work of Weber and Durkheim. Parsons (1951, 1994) supported the ideas behind functionalism throughout much of the 20th century, and he helped shape the field during this time. Parsons agreed with Durkheim that society is the sum of its parts. If a particular part is not contributing to the operation of society, it will "die off" or become obsolete. Parsons offered an in-depth and scholarly analysis of society through the lens of functionalist theory, and this analysis helped to place emphasis on larger social systems and their effect on individual behavior.

Applying Functionalist Theory

As with conflict theory, functionalist theory can be applied to many social realms. This section offers specific examples of how functionalist theory can be applied to problems and issues and looks at the relevance of functionalist theory to social work.

Education and Language   The functionalist perspective looks for ways in which cultural elements contribute to the homeostasis of society. For example, how does the education institution contribute to social stability?

- Education contributes to society by imparting knowledge to children. Schools teach children many skills, from reading and writing to understanding complex mathematical equations. This is a manifest function of education.

- Schools impart social status to children, depending on the school that children attend (for example, well-funded or poorly funded, private or public, focused on academics or on practical skills). The students become a reflection of the type, quality, and reputation of the school's instruction. This, too, is a manifest function of education.

- Schools also serve many latent functions. They intentionally or unintentionally pass along social norms, values, beliefs, and philosophies, and they "train" children to control their behavior and obey authority.

Functionalist theory can also be applied to language. Manifest functions of language include the transmission of wants, desires, needs, and ideas from one person to another. We need language to communicate and to ensure that things run smoothly. Latent functions of language include reinforcing social status and roles, transmitting and perpetuating values and beliefs, and instigating social change. For instance, aspects of language such as nuances in vocabulary, nonverbal communication, and vernacular can be used to reinforce social class, to isolate or solidify groups, and to incite rage or encourage pride among group members.

Functionalist Theory and Social Work   Social workers who adopt a functionalist perspective might look at the ways in which various social institutions help to maintain order in clients' lives. For instance, as a school social worker, you might focus on the ways in which the educational system benefits society through educating and socializing children. You may want to work toward improving these functions to ensure that all children benefit from them. You may also see the value of certain latent functions (for example, providing social control), in which case you might encourage teachers and parents to support this aspect of education.

Of course, conflicts can arise between social workers who support functionalist theory and those who do not "buy into" the functions of various institutions such as education. For example, how might you intervene with parents who choose to educate their children at home? Does home schooling undermine the functions of established educational systems? As another example, what should you do when parents or a community disagree with the school's curriculum? These questions pose challenges for social workers who attempt to view client issues through the functionalist lens.

Aisha's Case and Functionalist Theory   *How might you view Aisha's problems from the functionalist perspective? There are actually many angles from which this situation can be analyzed. From this perspective, you would want to ensure the functionality of Aisha's placement with an adoptive family. Accomplishing this objective might involve assessing where dysfunction in Aisha's system is occurring.*

One place to start is by looking at the foster care and adoption systems in which Aisha has been involved. You might see these systems as a way to provide stability for children whose biological families have broken up. They act as substitutes for families to provide basic needs, love, socialization, and so on. You might try to find out the extent to which Aisha's family seemed to be fulfilling her needs before her mother was arrested and she entered the foster care system. Another area of investigation might be to identify ways in which Aisha's foster homes fell short of fulfilling these needs for her.

Aisha's adoption by a Caucasian family could be viewed in several different ways. On the one hand, the family is able to provide for Aisha's needs, which is functional. On the other hand, the family may not be providing for her other needs such as a feeling of belonging to an ethnic and cultural group. And, because this family practices Roman Catholicism, it would be providing manifest functions through organized religion (for example, transmission of morals, beliefs, and ideology), but the latent functions of this particular religion might be different from those provided by Aisha's Baptist religion. You might think in terms of what types of role models this particular church would provide for her, and what beliefs about herself and her heritage she might develop in this environment. Because Aisha is not doing well in school or at home since her placement with the Caucasian family, this placement could be dysfunctional; that is, it may not be effectively performing the functions of a family that Aisha needs. One solution would be helping the family to make adjustments to better suit Aisha's needs. An alternative solution would be removing Aisha from the home and placing her in one that is a better fit.

In that light, placement with an African–American family might seem to be the most functional way to meet Aisha's developmental needs. Not only could this family meet her basic needs, but they could also help to socialize her into a specific ethnic and cultural environment. Based on this functionalist analysis, you could advocate Aisha's return to an African–American foster or adoptive family.

Critiquing Functionalist Theory

Given the examples we have looked at thus far using the functionalist approach, you might see some obvious strengths and limitations to relying on this theory in practice. These are some of the limitations:

- One main limitation is that functionalist theory views the interactions among systems as closed; that is, it does not take into account the complex interactions that take place among systems, which can create a great deal of conflict.

- Functionalist theory does not address the possible inequity within a system, which is an important ethical consideration. It treats social functions as rather benign and one-dimensional: As long as they help a system run smoothly, the problems that they can cause for individuals and groups are not addressed. For example, although Aisha's needs seem to be met according to the functionalist theory, she is not doing well in her new placement. What accounts for the underlying problems that seem to be creating stress for Aisha? What if Aisha were placed with an African–American family and she still had problems? What would account for those problems? The functionalist theory does not necessarily explain these issues.

- Like conflict theory, functionalism does not lend itself well to developing interventions for clients. For example, although you could proceed by finding ways to make Aisha's current situation more functional, this intervention may not be the most culturally appropriate for Aisha. Indeed, anything short of returning Aisha to her biological mother may not be a functional approach to her situation.

On the positive side, using functionalist theory to explain issues to a client may offer the client an alternative way to think about problems and provide insight into why social institutions function in the ways they do. If clients and social workers understand the manifest and latent functions of social institutions, they can work toward eliminating those functions that are contributing to clients' problems as well as to broader societal inequity and disempowerment. Focusing on changing dysfunction within a system could be an empowering approach for clients. Overall, the functionalist theory fits well with ideas from systems and ecological theories, so it could be used in conjunction with these approaches in work with clients.

Symbolic Interaction Theory and Social Constructionism

Symbolic interaction theory refers to the unique ways in which people and systems interact and communicate with one another as well as the essence and characteristics of that interaction and communication. An important tenet of symbolic interaction theory is that we all attach meaning to our communications with others within the context in which the interaction takes place. So, even though several of us might experience an interaction in the same place and time, we might interpret that interaction very differently, depending on the meaning we place on it. Symbolic interaction theory maintains that we are not just passive receivers of information. Rather, we filter and interpret the information based on our culture, cognitions, experiences, and so on, and we respond to this information based on how we interpret it (Blumer, 1969).

There are three main premises to symbolic interaction theory:

- We act on our world based on the meanings that we attach to our experiences.

- The meanings we attach to our experiences stem from our interactions with others.

- These meanings are affected by our interpretations of our interactions.

Thus, our experiences, interactions, and interpretations of our experiences and interactions constitute an ongoing, dynamic process. People make meaning of their experiences and the nature of society as they interact with others, which in turn shapes how society develops and is structured (Blumer, 1969).

Symbolic interaction theory is similar to **social constructionism,** which asserts that we construct our reality based on our experiences. Social constructionism argues that there is not a single reality, but rather, multiple realities, because each of us perceives the world around us differently. We are active in our world, and how we perceive our interactions is a reflection of our culture, history, language, and experiences as well as how these things have impacted our interpretations of the world. Social constructionism thus focuses on the process of how we go about constructing our own reality. In other words, this perspective is not so much concerned with the results of interactions as with what happens within and among people during interactions. The emphasis is on people as actors and how they make sense of interactions to form their individual realities.

Once a group's reality becomes accepted by a majority, it acquires the power to shape subsequent beliefs, policies, behaviors, and other aspects of society. That reality becomes the "right" way to do things. One example of this process involves patriarchy and the norms, beliefs, and values about women's roles that it espouses. In a patriarchal society, men have most of the power and money to make decisions. They can decide, for example, what types of stories and images are depicted in music videos. Many music videos portray women as sex objects, with men manipulating women for their own pleasure. These images perpetuate gender role stereotypes. Even when women overcome the obstacles and generate the type of money and power needed to control music videos, they tend to perpetuate patriarchal gender stereotypes and still present women as sex objects.

The term *social constructionism* is probably used more than *symbolic interaction* in social work; though again, they espouse the same ideas, and we will use the two terms interchangeably for the remainder of this discussion. However, *social constructionism* better reflects the ideas of diversity that social workers support, and it fits well with recent discussions on postmodern theory and practice. It also provides a basis for **deconstruction**—the analysis of how one group's construction of reality has become the accepted reality, justifying and reinforcing that group's power over social values, beliefs, and institutions. The literature often exhorts social workers to "deconstruct" the prevailing realities in social institutions and client thinking in order to initiate change.

Social constructionism also offers social workers a framework in which to view humans as active beings who interact in a world full of meaningful objects. These objects—things, people, behaviors, animate or inanimate symbols, and so on—help members of a society find common ground. These objects bind people together, help them make sense of the world, and help society to run more smoothly. Understanding how people make sense of their world helps social workers better understand how society's laws, norms, values, and social institutions are developed and maintained (Schaefer, 2001).

These approaches are similar to the humanistic and existential approaches discussed in Chapter 3 in that they focus on clients and their interpretations of their situation. Clients are the experts on their situation and must articulate how they view their problems, a belief that is congruent with social work values and ethics.

George Herbert Mead   One of the founders of the interactionist perspective was George Herbert Mead. Mead's contribution to this perspective was the focus on the self, which he saw as an active player in society. The self maintains the process of shaping experiences and is not merely a structure that is acted upon, as we saw in Freud's and others' theories (for example, self as ego).

Because people are active, they can act toward themselves as well as toward others, which affects the ways in which they deal with the world. For example, people can use introspection to help guide their actions, make decisions, and place meaning on the outside world. In other words, people do not simply respond to their environment; rather, their "self" is constantly changing as it encounters new experiences and attaches meaning to them (Blumer, 1969; Mead, 1934, 1956).

Mead identified two types of interaction:

- **Nonsymbolic interaction:** How people respond directly to the actions of others. For example, we respond to cues such as tone of voice, language, and hand gestures while we interact with others.

- **Symbolic interaction:** The ways in which we interpret the actions of others. For example, we can interpret another person's tone of voice as threatening or sarcastic, depending on the context in which the interaction takes place and the meaning that we assign to it. Similarly, we can perceive a pointing hand gesture as either informational or challenging.

Both symbolic and nonsymbolic interactions play a part in the ongoing process of developing meaning and reality (Blumer, 1969; Mead, 1934, 1956).

Charles Horton Cooley   The concept of the **looking-glass self**, coined by Charles Cooley (1902), is closely related to the ideas behind symbolic interactionism and social constructionism. The looking-glass self refers to the idea that we learn who we are through our interactions with others. We develop our sense of self through our social interactions and our impressions of how others view and perceive us. So our views of ourselves stem from our perceptions of what others think of us—which are not necessarily based in reality or fact.

The process of developing a self-identity generally takes place in three phases:

1. We have a perception of how we present ourselves to others around us.

2. We then have a perception of how others evaluate us based on this presentation.

3. We develop feelings about ourselves based on these perceived evaluations.

For example, a young child may think she is a good big sister because she helps feed and bathe her little brother. But perhaps her parents have a negative response to her "helpfulness"—for instance, they comment about how she is getting in the way. Thus she develops a self-perception that she is not a good big sister. However, this self-perception can change if she overhears her parents telling others that she is, indeed, helpful with her little brother.

Erving Goffman   Another major player in the development of the interactionist perspective, Erving Goffman, espoused an interactionist method known as the **dramaturgical approach,** which likens everyday life to the drama of theater and stage. According to this approach, we go through our lives acting and projecting images that we want others to see. We have rules, rituals, and props, and we create settings to ensure that our interactions project an image that is important to us.

All of these things help to define our environment and guarantee that behavior is predictable and that social order is maintained. Without them, we might not know how to react or interact with others in given situations (Goffman, 1959).

Applying Symbolic Interaction Theory

As with the previous sections on applying conflict and functionalist theories, this section provides a discussion on the application of symbolic interaction theory and its relevance to social work practice.

Body Piercing   In previous decades, Western society generally defined piercing and tattooing as deviant (and in some contexts and groups, they still are). Therefore, in most contexts it was rare to see someone with a nose ring or tattoo. If someone with a tattoo were seen at an expensive, elite restaurant, for example, he would be viewed as going against social norms and might be asked to leave—at the very least, people would stare at him. However, if this same person were observed on a navy ship, he would be seen as fitting into the dominant culture of those who serve in the navy.

This situation demonstrates how our interpretation of certain events, the contexts in which they occur, and the meanings we place on them influence our views of what is appropriate. Over time, as more and more people have been tattooed and pierced different body parts, we have been increasingly exposed to these practices and have come to accept them in more settings. Our interpretations of these behaviors change as we see that people other than sailors engage in them.

Symbolic interaction theory and social constructionism help us see that the meanings behind such practices change, our experiences and interactions with people who engage in these behaviors change, and the contexts for such behaviors change. This ongoing process continually shapes the norms, meanings, and acceptance level for such behavior in larger society.

Aisha's Case and Symbolic Interaction Theory   *How might you view Aisha's case from this perspective? You would most likely focus on how Aisha perceives her situation and how her daily experiences help her to construct her reality. Her reality would include her relationships with her birth mother and family of origin, as well as her foster and adoptive families; her experiences in the Baptist and Catholic churches; and her perceptions of her new school and peers. You would pay particular attention to the meanings Aisha places on all of these elements and how these meanings might be contributing to her problems.*

Although symbolic interaction theory does not guide you in developing an intervention, assessing Aisha's situation from this perspective would give you some indication as to where Aisha believes her problems lie. This insight would then give you a place to begin intervention.

Critiquing Symbolic Interaction Theory

The application of symbolic interaction theory in Aisha's situation suggests the first in this list of the limitations of the theory:

- This perspective can help you assess and examine a client's situation, but it does not offer a clear intervention strategy.

- Symbolic interaction theory is micro focused, emphasizing individual experiences. The conflict and functionalist approaches, in contrast, tend to be more macro focused and emphasize broader social factors that affect people. An interactionist focus might therefore fail to take into account larger social forces that are impacting clients. Specifically, it ignores the power of majority group members to impose their construction of reality on the broader society. This criticism is highly relevant to social work because any intervention that disregards the realities of the larger society might be ineffective.

- The interactionist perspective lacks a solid, consistent theoretical base from which to examine relationships. In other words, the constructs that make up this approach can be vague and difficult to define, apply, and measure consistently across different contexts.

However, many social workers and other professionals have used the philosophy behind interactionism to guide research methodology and to empower participants in research studies. In fact, social work researchers have increasingly conducted studies that employ deconstructive methods to explore perspectives of those on whom the research is focused. That is, they aim to better understand the worldview of the participants, which guides the analysis and the application of the results. The research process includes deconstruction of the dominant view of reality by exploring the perspectives of the research participants and reconstructing reality from different viewpoints. Symbolic interaction theory thus focuses attention on individualistic thinking, which can be useful when trying to move beyond the majority mind-set.

Another major strength of symbolic interaction theory is that it provides an empowering way to examine clients' problems. More specifically, it empowers the client to guide the working relationship (versus the social worker guiding the process), and it focuses on the meanings that clients place on their experiences, lending validity to their points of view. Social workers who use the symbolic approach might think that the meanings that clients place on forces are more important than the forces themselves. Thus, it is also an ethical approach to working with clients.

Moreover, this approach to assessment fits well with humanistic perspectives on working with clients, and it can easily be combined with other theories in practice.

FEMINIST THEORY

Feminist theories are helpful in analyzing societal processes. They can be applied to many different levels of social assessment, including psychological development, oppression and discrimination, and institutional structure and functioning.

As its name suggests, feminist theory is based on the ideas of **feminism,** which can be defined as the advocacy of social, economic, and political equality between men and women. Many social workers take this definition a step further by applying it to all minority groups, advocating for equal rights in all arenas. Feminist theory provides an avenue for examining various personal and social issues as they relate to inequality, oppression, and disenfranchisement.

In reality, there is not a single feminist theory or founder (indeed, feminists can differ considerably on certain ideas), and feminist thinking is influenced by many different disciplines and theorists. During the Enlightenment period of the 18th century, women such as Mary Wollstonecraft, Judith Sargent Murray, and Abigail Adams played key roles in espousing the idea, which was radical for its time, that women are equal to men. Later, other women including Sarah Grimké, Margaret Fuller, Harriet Taylor Mill, and Simone de Beauvoir contributed to the analysis of social inequality and promoted views that laid the foundation for more recent feminist thinkers. Simone de Beauvoir's book *The Second Sex* (1949) articulated theoretical views that closely resembled those discussed in symbolic interactionism but reflected a very different and pointedly female perspective. For example, she asserted that the ideas of "self" have been written and exemplified by males and that historically males did the acting, thereby creating the majority reality (Donovan, 1994). As another example, you will see in Chapter 9 that Carol Gilligan responded to Lawrence Kohlberg's male-oriented theory of moral development by constructing her own theory concerning different—yet equally valid—patterns of moral development. There is a rich history behind the development of feminism, and feminist thought has encouraged many lines of thinking and theories that continue to influence social work.

Branches of Feminist Theory

Several branches of feminist thought exist. The three perspectives described below differ primarily in their views on equality and social change, which affect social work in different ways.

- **Liberal feminism** was the first to support the ideas of equal rights and equal treatment for women. Liberal feminism developed during the 18th century, when women such as Mary Wollstonecraft demanded that such Enlightenment principles as equality and self-determination be applied to women as well as men. Like their historical counterparts, contemporary liberal feminists believe that biological differences between men and women are not important, and they fight to achieve equal rights for women in all social realms, including politics, economics, and education. Social workers who support this ideology can pursue equality on a macro level by advocating for policies and laws designed to change the structure of society. On a micro level, they can educate or empower clients to fight for their rights.

- **Socialist feminism** charges conservative viewpoints with undermining social change and supporting the unequal status quo, and it criticizes liberalism as being too focused on politics. The socialist perspective views economic equality as paramount to true equality and freedom for women. Truly promoting equality requires more than perpetuating traditional societal values, and securing women's right to vote is not sufficient to truly promote equality. Social workers who support socialist feminism focus on economic justice and equality. For example, they may work with international agencies to help communities establish self-sustaining economic systems.

- **Radical feminism** argues that oppression and inequality are supported through male hierarchy and domination. A basic tenet of radical feminism is that men construct reality for all of society. Not surprisingly, this reality includes the notion that men are superior, forceful, aggressive, and intellectual, whereas women are weak, emotional, and irrational. To challenge these stereotypes, radical feminism espouses the idea that dominant values should be reestablished to include the realities of women (Hunter College Women's Studies Collective, 1995). A social worker using a radical feminist perspective might help clients to gain insight into traditional values and social systems, thereby empowering them to reframe their reality and change their situation.

Despite these differences, all feminist theories share certain basic tenets, which are listed in Exhibit 4.1. Many of these tenets are similar to the philosophy behind social constructionism, and they question reality as it is generally accepted in U.S. culture. As you review the tenets in the exhibit, consider how you could apply them to social work practice.

Applying Feminist Theory

As Aisha's social worker, there are several different ways that you could conceptualize her situation from the feminist perspective. The particular strategy that you adopt will depend, of course, on which branch of feminism you choose to apply. In general, though, you would begin by analyzing how systems (family, foster care, adoption, education, and religion) are perpetuating inequality, and therefore problems, for Aisha. You may want to deconstruct dominant social values regarding what is "appropriate" for Aisha in order to gain a better understanding of what Aisha wants in her life.

Going further, you might need to advocate for Aisha in negotiating various systems to ensure that her welfare, as she sees it, is addressed. Even though Aisha is young, respecting her wishes is essential. Finally, as Aisha matures and becomes independent, you may help her to become her own advocate as a female and ethnic minority.

Critiquing Feminist Theory

Feminist theory has a number of strengths, but there have been two serious criticisms:

• Feminist theory focuses exclusively on women and thereby ignores the plight of other minority groups.

• The exclusive focus on women actually perpetuates their oppression by highlighting their special circumstances, thereby making them "separate" from men and suggesting that they require special treatment.

- *Challenge false dichotomies:* The social practice of creating mutually exclusive categories (dichotomies) to describe various behaviors and characteristics creates expectations. For example, Western society places much emphasis on the differences between men and women, rich and poor, and young and old. These categories prescribe behaviors for those who fit into a particular category.

- *Rethink established knowledge:* Reevaluate and critically analyze what we know, how we know it, and where this knowledge comes from. As an illustration of this point, consider that until recently, research topics and methods excluded issues that are particularly important and beneficial to women and ethnic minorities.

- *Examine different patterns of socialization:* Examine the differences between men and women based on differing socialization and experiences. Men and women adhere to different gender roles and expectations, which ultimately influence behaviors and development.

- *Deconstruct patriarchal hierarchies:* Examine patriarchy as it exists in society and influences the experiences of people. This strategy challenges the power of and domination by men over women in all social institutions.

- *Increase opportunities for empowerment:* Specifically, empower women to instigate social change. For instance, women's active involvement in policy concerning reproductive rights gives women more control over their own bodies. This involvement ultimately gives women more control over health care procedures such as birth control and childbirth, which can directly affect women's and children's physical, economic, and emotional well-being.

- *Value process orientation:* Feminism often focuses on the different ways in which men and women work and think. Women tend to be more process oriented, which refers to the ways in which people interact and relate to one another when they work on and solve problems. Conversely, men tend to be more product oriented, which places emphasis on the end result of the problem-solving process. In Western society, product is often valued more than the process through which the product is made.

- *Understand that the personal is political:* All personal behaviors are influenced by political actions; what we might traditionally classify as the personal realm can also be political. For example, a woman's decision to become pregnant is influenced by health care and other policies that will affect her during and after her pregnancy.

- *Respect diversity:* Maintain solidarity with others in an oppressed group such as women while simultaneously respecting individual differences. Women, especially, need to find common ground to effect change without losing individual diversity in the process.

- *Promote awareness of interactions between the individual and social forces:* Once women become aware of the larger social forces that affect them and their personal and social lives, change can take place.

EXHIBIT 4.1

Fundamental Tenets of Feminist Theory

Source: Adapted from Van Den Bergh and Cooper, 1986

Both of these criticisms have been rebutted along similar lines. Although feminist theories focus primarily on inequality between the sexes, many social workers use these theories to examine inequality for members of other groups. In addition, more recent research using feminist perspectives has applied its tenets to the general study of oppression for many disenfranchised groups. Feminist theory has played a major role in raising awareness of multiple points of view on issues.

As with symbolic interactionism, feminist theory teaches that people construct their own realities. In the case of women and other minority groups, this reality is often based on history and past experiences of discrimination and oppression. Thus among the obvious strengths of feminist theory are its focus on equality and its questioning of the dominant structure. These strengths uphold the basic ethical tenets of the social work profession.

Regardless of a person's standpoint on the appropriate focus for feminist theory, this perspective clearly has drawn attention not only to predominant cultural values and structures but also to the ways in which we generate knowledge. Many social workers and scholars in other disciplines have relied on feminist theory to guide their research. One result of this process has been the creation of a body of literature that is qualitatively different from past work. Feminist theory has also validated the use of alternative research methods such as inductive reasoning, qualitative methods, the equal treatment of research participants (for example, they are often called "co-investigators" in this type of research), and the ways in which results are interpreted and applied.

CULTURAL PERSPECTIVES

Although no single theory explains culture and its effects on human behavior, we need to consider cultural theories, particularly in the context of social work. Ideas, concepts, and applications of culture are inextricably linked with social aspects that affect clients. Of all the disciplines, social work is probably the most concerned with understanding the complexities of culture, especially when working with people.

There is no universally accepted definition of culture; culture can mean different things to different people. In fact, definitions vary depending on the discipline and theory from which they originate. Even within the field of social work, the meaning of culture will differ depending on the context, problem, client, and social worker. From a sociological standpoint, **culture** is the result of all human endeavors. Culture can be viewed as including all things human such as norms, values, customs, symbols, thoughts, traditions, politics, religions, languages, philosophies, and material objects (Barker, 2003; Turner, 1998). Culture consists of both external and internal components. External components are things that can be observed or quantified, such as behaviors, products, artifacts, and other tangible objects. In contrast, internal components are not readily observable. Examples are ideas, interpretations, perceptions, and the meanings that people attach to the external components.

PHOTO 4-A

Cultural Perspectives Are Important to Effective Social Work Practice

Culture is created through experiences, but it also helps to give structure to the experiences. This is a dynamic process that continually develops and changes as the experiences of people in a society change. Even the meaning of the word *culture* changes over time.

Over the years, social work has developed theories and models of culture and its effects on behavior and has incorporated many ideas and terms from models coming out of related disciplines. The terms in Exhibit 4.2 are important to social work practice. They all help to define the essence of culture and the various ways in which culture affects people in their environment.

Some of these terms, such as ethnicity and social class, can help social workers understand how society perceives clients, however biased this view might be. Other concepts, including ideology, ethnic identity, and worldview, can provide insight into how clients view themselves relative to their culture. These terms refer to the cultural construction of a client's reality. Without this knowledge, it would be difficult for a social worker to understand a client's experience in the context of her or his immediate and larger community environment. Consequently, any intervention that the social worker develops will be ill-informed at best and harmful at worst.

The concept of *ethnocentrism* helps to explain how a dominant ideology can perpetuate cultural values that help or hinder clients. Understanding the effects of ethnocentrism can help social workers to grasp how clients may view their own culture as superior, which can create problems for clients in interfacing with other cultures, particularly if their culture is not the dominant one. Maintaining a sense of cultural relativism can assist social workers in their assessment of all of the potential cultural variables that come into play when working with clients. Beyond simply recognizing that different cultures cannot be ranked as superior or inferior to other cultures, social workers can better understand that each client will bring her or his own reality to the working relationship, which will contribute to the qualities of the client, the client's problems, and her or his approach to solutions.

All of these ideas come into play when you actually work with clients. They are also critical to understanding the issues of racism, discrimination, and oppression, which are discussed in Chapter 5.

Cultural Perspectives and Social Work

To be effective practitioners, social workers must understand how a client's culture affects the client's behavior, perceptions, and life. To achieve this understanding, social workers must recognize how values, beliefs, philosophies, experiences, and social structures vary from one society to another. They should be able to separate stereotypes that define cultures and the people who live within them from

EXHIBIT 4.2 *Cultural Concepts in Social Work Practice*	• *Cultural relativism:* The idea that different cultures should be treated equally; cultures cannot be ranked based on which is better or superior. • *Ethnic identity:* How people form their identity in relation to their ethnicity. • *Ethnicity:* How people associate themselves with a group through the use of aspects such as values, traditions, customs, language, and religion. • *Ethnocentrism:* The belief that one culture is superior to others and that culture serves as the norm by which others should be judged. • *Ethos:* The moral, ethical, and aesthetic tone of a person's life; the emotional aspect of the worldview. • *Ideology:* One's dominant ideas about what is correct and how things should be. • *Social class:* A category for groups of people who share similar economic stratification. • *Worldview:* The way in which people perceive their world that gives them a frame of reference; a personal philosophy about how things are and the way things should be.

individual client realities. Clients are more than the culture with which they identify. Thus, social workers need to be skilled at identifying how people function as active agents within their culture. They must realize that clients are both recipients and shapers of culture and that both of these roles impact their clients' behaviors.

Culture and the NASW Code of Ethics   The National Association of Social Workers (NASW) *Code of Ethics* (approved 1996; revised, 2008) strongly supports the idea of cultural competence. It states that social workers should

> understand culture and its function in human behavior and society, recognizing the strengths that exist in all cultures, … demonstrate competence in the provision of services that are sensitive to clients' culture and to differences among people and cultural groups, [and] obtain education about and seek to understand the nature of social diversity and oppression with respect to race, ethnicity, national origin, color, sex, sexual orientation, gender identity or expression, age, marital status, political belief, religion, immigrant status, and mental or physical disability.
>
> (p. 9)

Further, in 2001, NASW approved the standards for culturally competent social work shown in Exhibit 4.3. These standards define social workers' responsibilities to become culturally competent with clients and familiar with the broad, complex definition of *culture* held by the profession.

Minorities' Dual Perspective   In addition to cultural concepts and terms that social workers use in practice, several perspectives help social workers think about cultural diversity in the context of human development. For example, the **dual perspective** (Norton, 1978) gives context to the ways in which people from minority groups experience different systems throughout development and how these experiences

---

- Recognize how personal and professional values impact work with culturally diverse clients
- Continually develop knowledge around cultural diversity
- Use culturally appropriate methods in work with clients
- Be knowledgeable about culturally appropriate services for clients
- Understand how policies and programs affect culturally diverse clients
- Support efforts that advocate for professional diversity in social work education and practice
- Work toward eliminating service barriers for culturally diverse clients
- Provide leadership in cultural competence for the profession

Source: Adapted from NASW, 2001

EXHIBIT 4.3

NASW Standards for Culturally Competent Social Work Practice

impact development. This perspective acknowledges that minority group members, figuratively, have their feet in two worlds:

- *Nurturing system:* This is the primary system, and it consists of people and circumstances close to an individual—for example, immediate and extended family and local environments with which the individual is connected (e.g., church, the neighborhood, etc.).

- *Sustaining system:* This is the world of the dominant culture, consisting of the larger systems that impact an individual, such as political and economic dynamics and educational and social service systems.

According to the dual perspective, culturally relevant values, beliefs, customs, and behaviors are instilled in individuals within the nurturing system. As individuals grow and increasingly interact with sustaining systems, they may find that the values of their nurturing system clash with those of the sustaining system and are devalued by the sustaining system. This is when members of minority groups may experience racism, prejudice, and discrimination. Further, conflicts in values between the two systems may cause developmental problems, such as low self-esteem, for members of minority groups.

Multiculturalism   To capture this cultural complexity, social workers often use the term **multiculturalism,** which refers to the idea that all cultures should be recognized, respected, and treated equally. Similarly, **cultural pluralism** refers to the recognition and accommodation of a variety of cultures that have different values and norms. Often social workers focus on multiculturalism as it applies to groups who are at risk of marginalization and oppression (Fellin, 2000). This last reference probably best defines how the concepts of culture and multiculturalism are currently used in social work.

Other perspectives and models also help social workers conceptualize how members of minority groups may experience development differently from the majority group. For example, the concept of *bicultural socialization* refers to the idea that members of minority groups not only receive extensive enculturation and socialization from their cultural group (e.g., through language, customs, and traditions), but they also receive socialization from the majority culture. Models of bicultural socialization help to explain developmental tasks such as formation of self-esteem and identity for minority group members. These models also draw attention to some of the bicultural tensions that may exist between two cultures of which a person is a member (Chau, 1991; de Anda, 1984; Lum, 1995; Nguyen & Brown, 2010; Robbins, 1984; Uttal & Han, 2011). Within the process of bicultural socialization, some people may develop coping skills that allow them to effectively function in the context of two cultures. However, others may experience problems that negatively affect their development.

Viewing development from these perspectives helps social workers conceptualize issues from a more culturally competent standpoint. For instance, these perspectives make it less likely that social workers will view client problems from a dominant group ideology, blaming clients for "lacking" the ability to adapt to the majority culture or for somehow being "deficient" because they have not adopted larger cultural values. Social workers who use these perspectives to conceptualize development within a cultural context are able to choose assessment and intervention techniques that are more effective and culturally appropriate with minority clients.

Applying Cultural Perspectives

In Aisha's case, there are many cultural factors that you will need to consider. Recall from Chapter 2 that cultural factors can be placed into macro, mezzo, and micro levels. These are how some of the issues in Aisha's case can be conceptualized in terms of those levels:

- *Macro level: The ideology and ethos of the social institutions with which Aisha is involved, which are reflected in the policies and procedures of the foster care and adoption agencies working with Aisha and her family of origin, as well as her foster and adoptive families.*
- *Mezzo level: Aisha's school and church as well as her peers and her two family structures.*
- *Micro level: Aisha's worldview and her construction of her cultural reality.*

All of these cultural factors interact to create the dynamics unique to Aisha's situation. You also need to be aware of ethnocentrism and other cultural dynamics that could be creating problems for Aisha. For example, the adoption agency could be operating from the value that family is crucial to the well-being of children, regardless of whether or not that family is ethnically similar to the child being placed. From Aisha's perspective, similar ethnic background may be more important to her well-being than belonging to an intact family.

As another example, Western society tends to view poverty as a culture, which places responsibility onto the people who are living in poverty. The so-called **culture of poverty** is perceived to be a worldview and ethos contributing to poor people staying in poverty. They develop an identity that is congruent with those who live in poverty, which makes it difficult for them to move up the economic ladder. For example, a cultural view on poverty posits that poor people are characterized by laziness and a poor work ethic, which validates the reliance on public assistance, from generation to generation. Children learn from their parents that laziness is a way of life, as is receiving public assistance; children never gain the motivation to work their way out of poverty. However, in attributing poverty to people's cultural values, the culture of poverty perspective denies that societal forces and dominant culture play a significant role in perpetuating poverty.

As Aisha's social worker, you need to assess many cultural factors on many levels. The outcomes of these assessments will help guide you in developing an intervention that addresses cultural issues that are creating problems for Aisha.

Critiquing Cultural Perspectives

Developing methods to articulate, organize, and understand cultural elements is important to social work. However, there is a negative side to cultural perspectives:

- Instead of a single, coherent theory of culture, there is a collection of ideas and definitions of culture from many disciplines. As a result, the application of cultural perspectives to social work is difficult to define, apply, and measure. Determining whether interventions are as effective as they could be, as well as whether social workers are including all relevant aspects of culture, is difficult. There is still much work to be done to further develop and define culture and its place within the social work profession.

- Even a social worker who embraces multiculturalism and cultural competency will be hard-pressed to truly understand their clients' world views if the clients grew up in a culture different from the social worker's. How do social workers know if they are applying cultural relativism to their clients? Can they be sure they are not responding ethnocentrically to certain situations?

A natural strength of cultural conceptualization is that it offers tools to help social workers incorporate the conceptualizations into the assessment process, which enhances their understanding of clients and clients' situations. Viewing clients in the context of their culture ensures that social workers will grasp some, if not all, of the complexities in their clients' lives and reduces the risk of working with clients from an ethnocentric perspective. Culturally competent social workers will be better able to empower clients and advocate for larger social change. Though cultural perspectives do not necessarily inform intervention directly, when they are combined with other theories, they contribute to more powerful and effective interventions.

CONCLUSION

In this chapter, we have looked at many sociological theories and perspectives that relate to social work practice. To review and compare them, look back at

Quick Guide 6. Sociological theory focuses on broad aspects of society and how these affect human behavior. Many of these theories and perspectives help social workers to think about clients' problems from a broad perspective and to develop interventions that will target issues on a macro level. As you have seen in previous chapters, this macro focus can be helpful because it takes the focus off the individual, which tends to be the emphasis of biopsychosocial approaches. In essence, sociological theories and perspectives offer social workers a balanced approach to their work.

All of the theories, models, approaches, and perspectives discussed thus far in this book have applications to issues of social and economic justice, but sociological theories and perspectives are especially useful for supporting the ideas espoused in the NASW *Code of Ethics*. For instance, societal causes of oppression and discrimination are more fully explained by sociological models than by micro or mezzo approaches, and these models help guide social work interventions on a macro level where problems of oppression and discrimination can be eradicated. Moreover, sociological models allow social workers to think more comprehensively, including in their assessments and interventions cultural and ethnic issues that can affect and perpetuate client problems.

MAIN POINTS

- The sociological imagination is a term coined by C. Wright Mills to describe the relationship between the individual and wider society.

- Conflict theory, which can be traced to Karl Marx but has had many more contributions since his time, views social behavior from the perspective of conflict or tension among two or more groups. Although it fits well with the underlying values and ethics of social work, it often does not offer practical interventions.

- A somewhat more applied approach is critical practice theory. Using this approach, social workers aim to help clients overcome the oppressive nature of the existing social order and to use their voices to create social change.

- Functionalist theory explains how aspects of society work together to maintain stability. Social workers can use functionalist theory to explain how social institutions maintain order in clients' lives.

- Symbolic interaction theory, which is similar to social constructionism, describes the unique ways in which people and systems interact and communicate with one another as well as the essence and characteristics of that interaction and communication. Social constructionism reflects the ideas of diversity that social workers espouse and helps explain how one group's construction of reality can become the dominant reality.

- Feminist theory is based on the ideas of feminism and provides an avenue for examining various personal and social issues as they relate to inequality, oppression, and disenfranchisement. Several branches of feminism guide social work in different ways with regard to how equality and social change are viewed.

- Culture involves the "complex pattern of living that directs human social life, the things each new generation must learn and to which eventually they may add" (Stark, 1998, p. 36). According to the NASW *Code of Ethics,* social workers should strive to be culturally competent practitioners.

EXERCISES

1. *Hudson City interactive case at* www.routledgesw.com/cases. Review the case, and answer the following questions:
   a. In what ways might critical theory be used to help explain some of the issues the residents of the city are dealing with?
   b. Using functionalist theory, what are some of the dysfunctions the city and its residents are facing?
   c. In what ways might symbolic interaction theory help explain the ways in which the city's systems and residents interact to perpetuate the problems and issues?
2. *RAINN interactive case at* www.routledgesw.com/cases. Review the case, and answer the following questions:
   a. How would the tenets of feminist theory apply to both Sarah and Alan's situations?
   b. Explain how a social worker who used the feminist theoretical lens could begin to help Sarah and Alan regain a sense of control over their lives.
3. *Carla Washburn interactive case at* www.routledgesw.com/cases. Reacquaint yourself with Carla's situation. Review the cultural concepts discussed in this chapter and then answer the following questions:
   a. What elements presented in Exhibit 4.2 might be important to consider in Carla's case and why?
   b. In what ways might Carla's culture help or hinder her situation?
   c. How could you use Carla's culture to help guide your assessment and intervention with her problems?
4. *Sanchez Family interactive case at* www.routledgesw.com/cases. Review the case and the issues facing each member and the family as a whole. Using the theories presented in this chapter, answer the following questions:
   a. How might the Sanchez family's problems be explained through conflict theory? Give specific examples.

b. How might some of the problems experienced by the family and individual members be explained through symbolic interaction theory?

c. How might culture be defined for the Sanchez family? What aspects might you want to take into consideration when trying to understand this family's culture?

d. In what ways might a cultural perspective be applied when working with this family?

CHAPTER 5

Lenses for Conceptualizing Problems and Interventions: Social Change Dimensions

In a western state there is a small, rural town we can call Crow Crossing, with a population of about 200. It is surrounded by larger cities that offer some variety in banks, grocery stores, clothes shops, entertainment, and other services, but the closest city is 20 miles away. Crow Crossing itself does not have a bank, school, or large grocery store. Instead, it has only a small post office and a very small conven-ience store where items are limited and expensive. The town's population consists mostly of Hispanic/Latino elderly individuals and young families who work at nearby farms or mills or who commute at least 50 miles to cities with more industry. Public transportation is nonexistent.

The school that the Crow Crossing children attend lacks money, qualified teach-ers, good programs, and a competitive curriculum that will help its students get into college or land well-paying jobs. In addition, the children must take a bus into the next town to go to school, a trip that usually takes more than an hour each way because the bus picks up students whose homes are spread out geographically. The high school has a graduation rate of 70 percent. Many students drop out of high school to help their families run the farms, so they never escape the poverty that has charac-terized past generations. There are few recreational opportunities or paying jobs for teens in Crow Crossing, and many teens in this town have problems with unintended pregnancy, alcohol and drug abuse, and vandalism and other petty offenses. The suicide rate among the young people is higher than the state and national average.

Crow Crossing also lacks social services, including those that address domestic violence, which is a problem for many families. The town has been unable to secure resources or services, primarily because of a lack of leadership. Residents are not well represented in the state legislature, and they struggle to get their concerns heard by policy-makers. Sheriff Bidarte, who is also the Crow Crossing mayor, has tried a few times to rally the townspeople to confront their problems, but he has been unsuccess-ful. Sheriff Bidarte lacks the necessary knowledge and skills to help people with their problems or to initiate change for the community. He has been referred to a social worker in a nearby town to express his concerns and to enlist her help in solving the town's problems.

THIS SCENARIO IS A COMMON ONE AND COULD REPRESENT MANY rural towns in the United States. Many social workers are interested primarily in working with individuals, but as this situation brings to light, many individual problems are the result of, or are aggravated by, larger social problems. If a social worker were to intervene with an individual or family from this small town, she or he would quickly find that skills in macro assessment and intervention would be necessary.

This chapter discusses some of the models used in social work to conceptualize and address macro-oriented issues that affect clients. Although not an exhaustive discussion, it examines several fundamental perspectives that are frequently used in the field and that can be combined with other theoretical approaches. These perspectives deal with such broad categories as ethnicity, oppression, social change, community organization, and social and economic justice. As you will see, many of the concepts discussed in this chapter are interrelated. For example, when social workers speak of justice, they are also frequently referring to social change and the instigation of some kind of action that will lead to social and economic justice. Social change and action are also closely related to community development. Despite such overlaps, we will look at each concept separately to focus on its unique attributes. Keep in mind, though, that in many ways these concepts are inextricably linked in social work practice.

We begin by examining prominent theories that focus on the macro-level forces of race, discrimination, and oppression. As in previous chapters, all the chapter's theories and perspectives are compared and contrasted, in Quick Guide 7.

THEORIES OF RACISM, DISCRIMINATION, AND OPPRESSION

Race, as a contemporary term, refers to biological differences among groups of people. The term was developed in the 18th century to describe blood lineage and then to differentiate among people and groups based on skin color and other visible, physical characteristics. With the growth of biology and science in the 19th century, race became associated with biological factors and evolution. Race as a biological construct became the basis on which to judge people's social status and to classify members of certain races as superior to other races. Members of one group of people who deemed certain racial characteristics objectionable used these characteristics to justify separating themselves from those groups who possessed them (Payne, 1997).

Currently, there is ongoing debate regarding the question of whether race is a

QUICK GUIDE 7   The Social Change Lens: Theories and Perspectives

	RACISM, DISCRIMINATION, AND OPPRESSION	SOCIAL & ECONOMIC JUSTICE	SOCIAL CHANGE & ACTION	COMMUNITY ORGANIZATION
Type	Theories	Perspectives	Perspectives	Theories
Focus	Individual and environment, depending on the theory	Society	Society and the individual	Society and community members
Assumptions	Varied: Some view behavior as influenced by psychological factors; others view behavior as influenced by external forces.	Varied: Some view society as "owing" its members; others view social institutions as having limited roles in providing resources to members.	Varied: Some view interactions among people as important instigators of change; others view external sources as important factors in change.	Varied: Some view community members as key change agents; others view "experts" outside of community realms as key change agents.
Strengths	• Concepts are useful for effective and ethical practice. • Considering factors of diversity, such as race, as socially constructed concepts can be useful in understanding and working toward ending oppression.	• Concepts are powerful tools for social change, which is a central charge of the social work profession. • Concepts fit well with other theories used in social work.	• Can provide a useful way to assess problems and guide intervention. • Constructs are amenable to empirical testing. • Can be combined with other theoretical approaches.	• Can provide useful tools for assessing and intervening with community problems. • Constructs are amenable to development and empirical testing. • Can help to predict behavior of communities.
Limitations	• No single theory on racism, discrimination, or oppression exists, making clear explanations of problems difficult. • Because there are a wide range of constructs behind theories, and many theories are not well developed, it is difficult to empirically test constructs and predict behavior.	• No clear organization of concepts, which makes articulating common definitions among practitioners difficult. • Lack of clear definitions in and among perspectives makes empirical testing of perspectives difficult. • Cannot predict behavior.	• Because theories are used in different disciplines and contexts, a consensus on the definition of constructs is difficult.	• Increased numbers of theoretical perspectives have created problems with definitions and applications of constructs. • Number of theories can make comparison of approaches difficult.

socially constructed, rather than a biological, category (Goodman, 2000; Harris & Sim, 2002; Kim, 2004; Shih & Sanchez, 2009):

- Traditional thinkers argue that race defines groups of people who, after many generations of living together or in close proximity, have developed a common gene pool. Over time, these people breed and pass on to their children unique genetic patterns that identify them as a race.

- Contemporary thinkers posit that true biological differences among groups do not exist. Though groups of people often live together and breed among themselves, creating generations of people who share biological characteristics, this does not mean that they have created a unique race that is quantitatively and qualitatively different from others who do not live in the same area. This line of thinking supports the notion that groups of people, even those who have been geographically separated from others over time, still share a basic genetic composition that makes all groups more similar to one another than different.

Some critics of biological theories of race go even further, arguing that historically, groups of people have intermixed more than they have remained separate, creating an even more complex and diverse genetic lineage. To them, race as a biological phenomenon is an idea that has been constructed by society to justify separating and treating groups differently based on certain characteristics. More specifically, the concept of race as a biological category is reinforced by societal institutions through ideologies and policies that segregate people based on skin color and other distinguishing physical characteristics (Fong, Spickard, & Ewalt, 1995; Montague, 1964). As one example, census forms ask people to designate their race, and this information is used to make funding and program decisions.

Regardless of whether true biological distinctions among groups exist, there are many political and social ramifications associated with race. We still use race in many social contexts: It holds personal meaning for us, we base assumptions about people on it, and we rely on it to make social policy and other decisions. Though it can mean different things to different people, and different groups use it for different purposes, it is still a powerful concept in U.S. society. For this reason, understanding the origins of the term as well as its implications for individuals and for society as a whole is particularly important for social workers.

Racism

One reason why understanding race is so important is because it leads to the potential for racism. **Racism** involves stereotyping people based on their race. Stereotypes tend to be negative (though sometimes they can be positive), and they are generalized to all people in a racial category (Barker, 2003). More specifically, racism refers to sociological and other ideological processes that promote differential treatment of racial and ethnic groups in interpersonal and institutional interactions (Payne, 1997). For example, **biological racism**, rooted in the medical model, promotes the notion that white people are genetically superior to non-white people. Related to this is the concept of **colorism**, which is the idea that within racial or ethnic groups, lighter skin color is superior to darker skin color. Colorism can result in lighter-skinned individuals within racial or ethnic groups enjoying economic, educational, and other advantages over their darker-skinned counterparts, leading to what's known as a **pigmentocracy** (Bonilla-Silva & Dietrich, 2009), where different racial or ethnic groups have different social statuses based on their skin color.

When applying the concept to social work practice, you can think of racism as it occurs on different levels:

- **Individual racism,** a micro-level concept, refers to personal or one-on-one actions between two or more people. It involves the negative attitudes and beliefs that people hold about persons from other groups that usually result in actions such as name-calling, ostracizing, or even the violence played out in hate crimes. Because individual racism occurs on a personal level, it is often overt, which makes intervention relatively straightforward. For example, a social worker who hears one child call another child a derogatory name can step in and talk with them about the ramifications of such actions. In more extreme cases, such as in hate crimes, individuals committing the crimes are often caught and brought to trial. Even though racism on this level can be devastating, it is often easier to deal with than more subtle types of racism, which are described next.

- **Institutional racism,** which exists on a broader, macro level, involves actions that occur in social institutions (for example, legal, economic, political, and educational realms) and, more generally, attitudes that are reflected in the larger society. Examples of institutional racism are policies, programs, and procedures that systematically benefit members of certain racial groups more than others. These acts and policies tend to be embedded in social systems. They are pervasive and persistent ways of functioning in institutions, which can make them difficult to identify and to change, even when they are illegal (Barker, 2003).

- **Cultural racism** also exists on the macro level. This type of racism views the disadvantages faced by ethnic minority groups as caused by the behaviors, philosophies, and ways of living that are rooted in their particular cultures. Instead of examining structural or institutional factors that inhibit a group's success, the group's cultural context is blamed. An example of cultural racism is the widely held belief that the pervasive poverty experienced by the black community is caused by the fragmentation of the black family, the absence of black fathers in these families, and inferior parenting practices. From this viewpoint, the solution to poverty in the black community is to restore men as fathers and breadwinners in the family and to improve parenting behaviors. However, this viewpoint fails to recognize the institutional discrimination prevalent in employment, the judicial system, and other arenas that perpetuate poverty for this group as a whole.

- **Environmental racism**, also a macro level construct, stems from institutional and structural policies and practices that differentially impact the health and living conditions of racial and ethnic groups. Environmental racism can be seen in communities primarily populated by different minority groups. For example, many factories and hazardous waste facilities are located in non-white communities, and these communities continue to experience substandard living conditions such as a lack of plumbing, exposure to lead paint, and polluted air, soil, and water. Consequently, many minority groups suffer from devastating health disparities that cause chronic illness, high mortality rates, and shortened life spans.

One example of institutional racism involves the ways in which African–Americans are consistently treated differently by the criminal justice system. Because of stereotyping and poor training, racial profiling by police is an issue in many communities. Some police officers are more likely to stop and arrest African–Americans than people from other ethnic groups. Consequently, African–Americans tend to be overrepresented in the criminal justice system, including everything from the county jail to death row, and are therefore more likely to have criminal records. Because a criminal background can restrict people's employment and other opportunities, this process can contribute to higher rates of unemployment and, ultimately, poverty. Further, many African–Americans cannot afford good legal representation, which perpetuates their overrepresentation in the criminal justice system. It is this pervasive, consistent process of bias that characterizes institutional racism.

Institutional discrimination is often tied with (and often causes or leads to) cultural and environmental racism. Discriminatory policies, practices, and stereotypes facilitate decision-making by dominant groups about such questions as where to place facilities housing toxic waste, funding of programs to help build community infrastructure, and providing health care resources to improve community health.

In general, cases of institutional, cultural, and environmental racism present greater challenges for social work intervention than individual acts because transforming an entire system is more difficult than modifying individual behavior. Moreover, as mentioned earlier, institutional forms of racism are often covert and difficult to expose, making them difficult to eradicate.

Discrimination, Prejudice, and Privilege

Three issues with which social workers are concerned that are closely related to racism are discrimination, prejudice, and privilege:

- **Discrimination** is the "prejudgment and negative treatment of people based on identifiable characteristics such as race, gender, religion, or ethnicity" (Barker, 2003, p. 123). Discrimination thus involves treating individuals or groups differently based on preconceived notions about them. This treatment is usually intended to create some type of disadvantage for that individual or group (Newman, 1973).

- **Prejudice** tends to be more of a cognitive process than a behavioral one. That is, prejudice refers to the attitudes, beliefs, and stereotypes that a person holds about others. It involves making prejudgments about people based on preconceived ideas about characteristics of certain groups. Although prejudice can be positive or negative (for example, we can hold positive stereotypes about our own group and negative stereotypes about dissimilar groups), prejudice is usually discussed in terms of negative views that we hold about others who have characteristics different from our own. These prejudices tend to be reinforced by the belief that groups who possess different characteristics also possess different values, morals, skills, and so on (Newman, 1973). For example, a Caucasian person may believe that a person who looks Mexican is lazy and one who looks Asian is industrious. Moreover, if the Caucasian person identifies with industriousness, she is also more likely to see the Asian person in a positive light because she perceives the value of industriousness to be similar to her own, whether or not it actually is.

- **Privilege** refers to the advantages that a dominant group in society has. For example, **white privilege** refers to the advantages enjoyed by individuals categorized as white. The work of sociologist W. E. B. Du Bois, discussed in Chapter 4, led to the concept of white privilege. He observed poor white workers in the United States increasingly identify with their white supervisors, the dominant group, and distance themselves from recently freed black slaves. By doing so, white workers received economic and other advantages. This phenomenon could also be seen among immigrant workers who "learned to be white" to gain these advantages in the workplace (Roediger, 1999). The concept of white privilege has been expanded by Peggy McIntosh (2008) and others to refer to whiteness as an unmarked identity that reaps benefits associated with whiteness. Specifically, ethnic minority groups—blacks, Asians, Latinos, Native Americans and others—are always being reminded of their race or ethnicity through interactions with others and through our social structures and practices. While being white is also belonging to a certain race or ethnicity, it has become normalized so that people categorized as white often do not notice the unearned privileges they enjoy every day. For example, most white people take for granted that they are not followed around in stores, asked for identification when using credit cards, or profiled by police when driving or walking down the street.

Once you understand the concepts of discrimination, prejudice, and privilege, you can examine the interplay among them. For example, if an individual is prejudiced toward another person, will these attitudes lead to a discriminatory act? The answer is maybe, but maybe not. Not everyone deliberately acts upon her or his thoughts or beliefs, especially because many discriminatory acts are illegal; but these beliefs may still be evident in subtle ways. Therefore, it is possible for prejudice to exist in the absence of discrimination. However, some people argue that the opposite condition cannot exist; that is, an act of discrimination means that prejudice must be present. Why, they ask, would an individual discriminate if he did not hold preconceived ideas about the person or group against whom he is discriminating? In this sense, then, prejudice constitutes the thought and discrimination constitutes the act. And does white privilege help to perpetuate prejudiced beliefs and discriminatory acts? Is it possible for white privilege to exist alongside efforts to eradicate prejudice and discrimination?

Regardless of your views on the relationships among prejudice, discrimination, and privilege, you need to understand these concepts. Not only do social workers concern themselves with these issues, but they must also be aware of how these issues are related to other *isms* such as racism, sexism, ageism, and others that will be discussed in later chapters. Discrimination and prejudice are at the heart of all the isms that social workers encounter.

Theories of Prejudice

As with other phenomena that social workers confront, there is not a single explanation for prejudice. Rather, several theories attempt to explain where prejudice comes from, how it is generated, and how and why it occurs; most of these theories are borrowed and adapted from different disciplinary theories and perspectives. These are some of the theoretical concepts used to explain prejudice and discrimination:

- **Authoritarian personality:** The tendency to be highly sensitive to totalitarian and antidemocratic ideas and therefore prone to prejudice. Theodor Adorno (Adorno, Frenkel-Brunswik, Levinson, & Sanford, 1950) argued that those with an authoritarian personality tend to be hostile to those who are of perceived inferior status, but obedient to people with perceived high status. Adorno posited that people with authoritarian personalities are likely to categorize people into groups of "us" and "them," seeing their own group as superior (Mcleod, 2009). An authoritarian personality may result in being rigid, inflexible, conformist, and loyal to authority figures, which is more likely to lead to discrimination and oppression of others.

- **Displaced aggression:** Attacks by a dominant group on a weaker group when the cause of the frustration cannot be attacked because it is viewed as too powerful (Healey, 1997). For example, members of a majority group might be frustrated in their day-to-day lives and may use members in a minority group as scapegoats. Prejudice in this case serves to diffuse and provide an outlet for personal or social frustration.

- **Projection:** A defense mechanism described by Sigmund Freud (1914) that allows people to deny owning uncomfortable feelings or perceived negative characteristics by pointing out these same negative characteristics in others. We "project" onto others our own undesirable personal characteristics or feelings to reduce our own tension and anxiety. Placing blame on another person or group is a form of prejudice.

- **Vicious cycle:** The process of creating and perpetuating a condition merely by assuming it to be true. For example, a dominant group may use its power to put another group into an inferior position. To justify the discriminatory behavior, prejudices are created and accepted by the group holding the power. Further discrimination reinforces the lack of opportunities for the group in the inferior position, thus reinforcing the beliefs of the group with power (Healey, 1997). Simply put, prejudice limits opportunities for the group in the inferior position and leads to support for the creation of that prejudice in the first place.

In addition, several theories have offered insights into the origins and mechanisms of prejudice and discrimination:

- **Attribution theory:** This theory attempts to explain how we perceive and make judgments about others. Attributions are the inferences people make about their own and others' behavior. *Internal* or ***dispositional attributions*** suggest that people's behaviors are caused by something inherent in individuals such as their personality, motives, or qualities. For example, if you came across someone who was homeless and you thought that the person must just be lazy, you would be attributing her homelessness to something inherent in her personality. In contrast, ***situational attributions*** suggest that behaviors are caused by situational factors, often outside of one's control. In the case of the person who was homeless, you might think that the person is homeless because of an external situation, such as a poor economy and lack of jobs (Heider, 1958). Attribution theory suggests that we maintain positive thoughts about people like us and place blame on groups different from our own (Pettigrew, 1980). For example, if the person who is homeless is of the same ethnic background as you, you are more likely to assume that a lack of jobs is to blame. If she is of a different ethnic background than you, you are more likely to think that she is homeless because she is lazy or lacks motivation to find a job.

- **Social Learning Theory:** People are socialized to think and behave in certain ways. **Socialization** is the process through which we learn to value some characteristics, ideas, and behaviors more than others. This process leads to a bias in favor of what we have learned and against the unfamiliar. That bias may become what we are referring to as prejudice, according to Social Learning Theory. People of influence such as parents and teachers model behaviors for children, which the children tend to adopt. Those behaviors are then further reinforced by actions observed in society. Children learn to treat people the way they see their parents, teachers, and pastors, for example, treating people. If respect is modeled, children will tend to respect others. If prejudice and negative treatment of others is modeled, children will tend to be socialized toward prejudiced behaviors toward others.

- **Conflict theory:** Karl Marx theorized that a competitive society creates conditions in which some groups perceive themselves to be superior, leading to the exploitation of perceived inferior groups (Marx, 1994). Prejudice is thus seen as a side issue in the struggle to control or expand the dominant group's share of resources (Healey, 1997). As an example, in the early 1800s in the American South, the elite plantation owners needed cheap labor, adopted the use of enslaved Africans to serve those purposes, and then developed anti-black prejudices to justify their exploitation of slaves. Going a step further, Marx wrote that elites use ideology, including religion, to attempt to control the thought processes of the exploited groups.

A few other explanations for prejudice have been given, which include religion and history:

- *Religion:* In some cases, believing that a particular religion is "correct" can lead to feelings of superiority and the condemnation of others who believe otherwise.

- *History:* Historical oppression has consequences for the way in which members of oppressed groups are viewed. For example, African–Americans have at times been viewed as inferior because of their ancestors' enslavement.

As you can see, prejudice can be explained from different standpoints. These concepts focus on the ways in which individuals learn to value certain characteristics more than others, to develop stereotypes about groups whose characteristics are different from theirs, and, ultimately, to discriminate against others based on prejudgments about them. Often more than one theoretical concept or standpoint is involved.

For example, projection and socialization can help to explain why a self-identified heterosexual man might possess prejudiced attitudes toward homosexual men. U.S. society tends to instill in young boys the characteristics of being male (for example, toughness, aggressiveness, controlled expressions of emotion). Boys who subscribe to these characteristics may learn to view those who do not possess these characteristics as "unmanly," inferior, and "gay," which in and of itself could lead to discrimination. However, at some point in his life, the heterosexual man may discover that he possesses some of the very characteristics that he has been socialized to despise (for example, femininity, emotionality). This realization can lead to anxiety, which may cause him to "project" the unwanted characteristics he sees in himself onto others who are perceived to display them (that is, gay men and heterosexual men who have feminine characteristics). In an extreme case, the heterosexual man may lash out at a man who has feminine characteristics, thereby relieving his anxiety and confirming his "manliness" because he has physically assaulted (a socially acceptable manly expression) a man who does not possess traditional masculine characteristics. Although men, regardless of their sexuality, display a range of feminine and masculine traits, in this scenario those who display feminine characteristics are likely to be targets of discrimination or abuse and be called "gay" because they deviate from the traditional norm of masculine behavior.

Frustration and displaced aggression may work in similar ways, although the motivation is usually more external to the self than projection is. As an example, when economic times become difficult, some groups (those who have some power and status) blame other groups (those who do not have much power or status), such as immigrants, for "taking all the jobs," even though those jobs are probably minimum-wage jobs that the more powerful groups would not take under normal (or even extreme) circumstances. However, the more powerful group uses the less powerful one as a scapegoat for their economic woes. The less powerful group is often unable to fight back when accused of stealing jobs, so it constitutes an easy target. The more powerful group is less likely to blame an even more powerful group, such as the government or wealthy corporations, for their problems because they are not likely to get very far, even though the government or corporations are probably more responsible for the poor economy and lack of jobs than the less powerful group.

Oppression

A concept related to prejudice, **oppression** can be difficult to define. Its root word, *press,* means to mold, flatten, reduce, or immobilize something (Frye, 1983, as cited in Brittan & Maynard, 1984). Oppression has also been described as "the social act of placing severe restrictions on an individual, group or institution" (Barker, 2003, p. 306). People living under oppressive conditions usually have a deep understanding of these processes because they encounter them on a daily basis.

One widely accepted model defines oppression in terms of who is facilitating the oppression and why (Hanna, Talley, & Guindon, 2000):

- **Primary oppression:** Perpetrated by the dominant group directly against an oppressed group. An example is any policy, regulation, or law that discriminates against immigrants on the assumption that they are inherently inferior to native-born Americans.

- **Secondary oppression:** Perpetrated by people who remain silent in the face of, and benefit from, oppression by others. For example, a person from the dominant group who accepts a job opportunity that has not been extended to a minority-group member who is equally qualified is benefiting from secondary oppression.

- **Tertiary oppression:** Perpetrated by members of an oppressed group when they seek acceptance by supporting the dominant group's oppressive acts. For example, a minority-group member might discriminate against fellow group members to curry favor with dominant-group members.

Another approach to oppression commonly used in social work is the **anti-oppression model,** or anti-oppression practice, which explores the ways in which oppression is integrated in social and other systems that impact the lives of clients. The goal of this model is to eliminate all oppression by transforming society and all its social structures, creating equity, inclusion, and social justice for everyone, regardless of individual situations. So, rather than just focusing on the micro level, on the experience of oppression for individual clients, social workers using this model would assess how oppression plays out for clients in broader, more pervasive ways, in an effort to identify and eliminate it at the mezzo and macro levels as well (Bishop, 1994; Campbell, 2003; Dominelli, 2002; Mullaly, 1997).

These conceptualizations of oppression are important because too often oppression is analyzed from a primary perspective. However, this reductionistic approach tends to isolate oppressive actions from the complex nature and various sources from which it can stem. In social work, this complexity is crucial to understand if social workers are to truly help clients and work toward eliminating oppression in different social realms.

Applying Theories of Racism, Discrimination, and Oppression

In what ways might information on race, discrimination, and oppression be applied to the case of Crow Crossing introduced at the beginning of the chapter? One of the best ways to use this information is to consider which diversity factors are affecting the community. On a large scale, the town lacks resources, which directly or indirectly may be contributing to its oppressed situation. Given the lack of effective representation in the state's legislature and access to power that will help community members obtain resources they need to improve their situation, there seems little that can be done to improve their situations. Thus, poverty, domestic violence, low-quality education, teen pregnancy and suicide, and other problems are perpetuated.

With regard to race, prejudice, and discrimination, you could assess the situation in Crow Crossing and intervene on many different levels:

- Macro level: *You might identify some biases at the policy level. For example, some powerful state officials might hold prejudices and stereotypes about rural areas that lead to discrimination in allocating budgets and resources.*
- Mezzo level: *Members of the community will need to explore their visions for the community as well as the ways in which their values, beliefs, and culture affect their interactions with one another and help or hinder their growth as individuals and as a community.*
- Micro level: *Preconceived notions about older adults and Hispanics/Latinos may be affecting the people in the community, the ways in which the children are reared, the ways that older citizens are perceived, the resources to which community members have access, and the culture and environment to which they are exposed. Moreover, growing up in a rural area with a lack of quality education and other social services, the children will likely encounter stereotypes held by others outside their community as well as those that they might develop about themselves. In turn, these stereotypes will affect their socialization and their long-term chances of improving their situation.*

In general, prejudice and discrimination on different levels seem to be interacting in ways that are contributing to the oppression of many members of this community. You must decide at which level you would help Sheriff Bidarte intervene to begin to solve the community's problems.

Because of the complex origins of prejudice and discrimination, social workers should approach them from several different perspectives. For example, some clients may exhibit personality traits that leave them susceptible to projection or authoritarianism, which can contribute to prejudicial attitudes about others. However, social workers need to explore these possibilities in some detail before concluding that the client's personality is to "blame" for prejudicial attitudes. Other clients may be a "product" of their social environment, unquestioningly subscribing to the values and beliefs of those around them. For still other clients, a combination of personal and social factors might interact in such a way that they develop prejudicial attitudes toward certain groups. In other words, even though you have some ways of explaining how prejudice develops, there is no single, certain explanation, which means that you must use caution when designing interventions to deal with prejudice.

Critiquing Theories of Racism, Discrimination, and Oppression

There is reason for caution when bringing these concepts into play:

- There is no coherent theory to organize the information that exists on race, discrimination, oppression, and issues of diversity.

- Social workers cannot distinctly or consistently define factors of diversity, nor can they empirically test these factors.

Yet these concepts remain highly relevant to social work. Probably one of the most important reasons to consider theories or perspectives on race, discrimination, and oppression is that many facets of assessment rely on information about diversity and need to be considered when developing interventions. Being cognizant of diversity factors as well as having ways to organize diversity information when working with clients is paramount to ethical and effective social work. Because social workers are concerned with pursuing justice and equality, being aware of how issues related to difference can create and maintain oppression is a primary skill they must develop. In fact, any successful efforts toward social change rely on a combination of knowledge and skill that can contribute to ending oppression.

Finally, considering race as a socially constructed concept can be helpful in understanding how society may use it to maintain oppression. This understanding can be advantageous in developing interventions and instigating social change. It can also help social workers to educate clients about how socially constructed concepts are influencing their lives and well-being. The best that social workers can do is to be knowledgeable about the many facets of diversity that might influence their clients' lives and to keep up to date on issues and information concerning diversity.

Manifestations of Racism, Discrimination, and Prejudice: Microaggressions

We have explored some of the theories around why racism, discrimination, and prejudice occur. Here we will look at ways they often are manifested in everyday life. These concepts are helpful for social workers because they can be used to better understand how racism, discrimination, and oppression play out in subtle ways, as well as to develop interventions to disrupt the perpetuation of these destructive behaviors.

Microaggressions are intentional and unintentional derogatory insults and slights that are communicated verbally, behaviorally, or through the environment to people of target groups. Target groups often include women, people with disabilities, and people identifying with racial, ethnic, sexual, religious or nonreligious minorities, and other disenfranchised groups such as older adults, people viewed as underweight or overweight, and so forth (Sue *et al.*, 2007).

Microaggressions are particularly insidious ways to harm those in target groups and perpetuate biased, stereotypical, and destructive views and beliefs about individuals and groups of people. They maintain prejudice, discrimination, and oppression through subtle, negative messages given to others that often serve to deflect blame from the person sending the message.

Microaggressions can be divided into several major categories (Sue, 2010; Sue & Capodilupo, 2008; Sue *et al.*, 2007):

- Microassaults: Similar to individual racism discussed earlier, microassaults are deliberate, conscious, biased, derogatory messages sent to target groups, either interpersonally or through the environment. These messages can be subtle or explicit such as name-calling, acts of violence, avoidant behaviors, telling or laughing at jokes, or discriminatory practices meant to harm those in the target group.

- Microinsults: Microinsults are subtle, unconscious slights that take place interpersonally or through the environment. These convey hidden messages meant to insult and demean the target person or group. An example of a microinsult might be ascribing irrelevant descriptors to someone such as "the intelligent female doctor" or "the intelligent African–American lawyer" when a Caucasian male may be introduced simply as "a doctor" or "a lawyer." Adding these descriptors implies they need to be pointed out because these attributes are not common or expected among people in these groups (e.g, women and African Americans). Another example might be assuming that a Hispanic young man seen running down a street has just committed a crime. Yet another example would be an agency worker commenting that the agency she works for does not track the race/ethnicity of its consumers, but she knows they serve Asian Americans because she recognizes accents over the phone. And, some would argue that certain sports mascot names, like the Washington Redskins, are microinsults.

- Microinvalidations: Microinvaldiations are often unconscious messages that are meant to exclude or negate the feelings, thoughts, and experiences of the target group. Examples might be a co-worker telling a female colleague to "stop being so emotional" when she's angry over an injustice that occurred in the workplace. Another example would be a potential employer telling a female or Hispanic job applicant that he is "color blind" and that "everyone has an equal chance of being hired." Yet another example would be college students commenting on female faculty members' clothing and appearance on teaching and course evaluations.

- Environmental Microaggressions: Similar to the ideas behind institutional racism discussed earlier, environmental microaggressions are the demeaning and threatening messages that are communicated to marginalized groups through our environment. These messages often are not communicated through interpersonal interaction, but they are embedded in our policies, institutions, and culture. Examples include gay, lesbian, bisexual and transgendered (GLBT) students who experience a hostile campus climate; government and workplace policies that do not offer partner benefits; corporate leadership that is made up of all white males; and public spaces that are not easily accessible to people with disabilities.

Using these constructs along with the theories on racism, discrimination, and oppression presented earlier, social workers can work to define, recognize, deconstruct, disrupt, and transform the meanings and messages behind microaggressions. To do this, social workers must be willing to examine the ways in which they participate in and are affected by microaggressive behaviors and commit to helping others, including clients and colleagues, do the same.

SOCIAL AND ECONOMIC JUSTICE PERSPECTIVES

A central tenet of social work is social and economic justice. The basic premise of **social justice** is that all humans have a right to live fulfilling lives, which requires access to appropriate resources (economic and otherwise), decision-making opportunities, and freedom from fear of persecution (Prigoff, 2003).

Promoting social justice is a core value and ethical principle of the NASW *Code of Ethics.* This principle calls for social workers to "pursue social change, particularly with and on behalf of vulnerable and oppressed individuals and groups of people. Social workers strive to ensure access to needed information, services, and resources; equality of opportunity; and meaningful participation in decision making for all people" (NASW, approved 1996, revised 2008, p. 5).

This sentiment is also reflected in the Educational Policy and Accreditation Standards (EPAS) set forth by the Council on Social Work Education (CSWE). In its educational policy, CSWE states that "social work's purpose is actualized through its quest for social and economic justice, the prevention of conditions that limit human rights, the elimination of poverty, and the enhancement of the quality of life for all persons" (CSWE, 2008, p. 1). Further, Educational Policy 2.1.5 articulates basic human rights, such as freedom, privacy, and education that social workers should strive to protect, and it stresses the need for social workers to incorporate knowledge and practices related to economic and social justice in their work (CSWE, 2008).

Much of the impetus in the development of social and economic justice perspectives has been rooted in efforts to overcome discrimination and oppression.

PHOTO 5-A

Promoting social and economic justice is a central tenet of social work

Source: Getty (Digital Vision)

There is a long history of writers and activists from diverse disciplines who have contributed to the development of these perspectives. For example, movements that include voting rights, settlement houses, labor organization, abolition of slavery, and civil and women's rights have all brought heightened awareness to injustices suffered by different groups at the hands of individuals and social institutions. Important figures in this history include Jane Addams, Martin Luther King, Jr., Cesar Chavez, Simone de Beauvoir, Paolo Freire, Nelson Mandela, Frances Fox Piven, and bell hooks, to name a few (Prigoff, 2003).

Well-known scholars have grappled with the issue of how to achieve justice in society. For example, **distributive justice** is concerned with what a society "owes" its members (Van Soest, 1995). It is thought that communities should support their members in social, economic, and other important ways that promote their well-being. Distributive justice is thus the essence of equality: Every person is considered to be deserving, and no one is required to suffer for the "good" of the whole of society (Rawls, 1971). For a society to be just, everyone must have equal rights and access to equal opportunities. Keep in mind that social workers are interested in distributive justice not only as it relates to economic equality, but as it relates to all realms of life—social, sexual, political, educational, spiritual, and so on—that might promote the full development and well-being of people. This philosophy contrasts sharply with other schools of thought regarding justice (Van Soest, 1994, p. 714):

- **Libertarian perspective:** Government and other dominant institutions should have only a limited role in human affairs. They should not be involved in securing people's rights to liberty, property, and personal protection.

- **Utilitarian approach:** Justice is made up of beliefs and policies that support the "greatest good for the greatest number of people."

Though there are some useful aspects to these last two approaches, they tend not to be as widely used in social work as the distributive justice perspective, mostly because tenets of distributive justice seem to fit well with social work values.

Based on justice perspectives, the social work profession has identified several practice activities that promote the goal of equality, listed in Exhibit 5.1. This might appear to be a daunting list of tasks, but they reflect fundamental ideas that are at the heart of social work values. Though these activities tend to be macro focused, they have compelling implications for the lives of individuals. For instance, supporting affirmative action within institutional settings not only has ramifications for entire groups, but also has far-reaching consequences for individuals within those groups. As individuals who benefit from these policies gain status and power within various institutions, they can improve access to these institutions for others.

ECONOMIC JUSTICE	POLITICAL JUSTICE	MULTICULTURAL JUSTICE	**EXHIBIT 5.1**
PROMOTE:	ADVOCATE FOR:	SUPPORT:	*Social Work Activities for Social Justice and Equality*
• Local and cooperative economic development	• Campaign finance reform	• Diverse perspectives in assessment and intervention	
• Regulated and deprivatized public and other services	• Inclusive participation in political processes	• Affirmative action efforts	
Source: Adapted from NASW, 2001			

Applying Social and Economic Justice Perspectives

Let us return to the opening case study and consider how you could assist Sheriff Bidarte in conceptualizing the town's problems from the perspective of economic and social injustice. Issues surrounding lack of resources, inadequate representation at the state level, lack of quality education, and a lack of social services to improve the situation of its members are all major issues that contribute to the injustice facing this community.

From a distributive justice standpoint, you could help Sheriff Bidarte conceptualize how the community might benefit each member, considering each member to be valuable and deserving of equal rights and opportunities afforded to other members in the community and members of other communities. Using activities listed in Exhibit 5.1, you might help the sheriff assess the needs, problems, and strengths of the community and its members, focusing on the unique ethnic and cultural aspects of each. You and the sheriff could work toward finding ways to include each member in political processes to ensure fair representation in budgetary and other issues that affect the community. Moreover, you could help the sheriff and community members to develop the town's employment, education, and other resources to help the community become more self-sustaining. Community members could also strive toward developing coalitions within the community and with other communities to gain more power and representation in government and other entities where decisions about resource allocation are made. Finally, you and the sheriff might want to think about how issues of racism, discrimination, and oppression, as discussed earlier, might be impacting community members' efforts toward change and growth. For example, it may be that state legislators have prejudices about Hispanic/Latino Americans that are causing them to discriminate against community members, leading to their underrepresentation in the state legislature.

Critiquing Social and Economic Justice Perspectives

As with issues surrounding diversity and oppression, perspectives on social and economic justice have some drawbacks:

- They are not well conceptualized, at least insofar as an organized theory has been developed to help guide actions toward achieving justice. In reality, defining and testing concepts related to justice can be difficult.

- They have yet to make a significant, long-lasting impact at the macro level or to affect social policy in a concrete way.

However, a great deal has been written on social and economic justice by social workers and theorists from related disciplines, which has helped the profession to make significant inroads with regard to social change. This work has been and will continue to be a powerful resource for social workers and the clients and communities with whom they work.

Although these conceptualizations have great potential for larger social change, other theories and perspectives, discussed in the following sections, have been more successful. On a smaller scale, however, they have heightened awareness of the impact that larger social and international issues have on individual clients and communities. For example, the social work literature contains an extensive discussion about transnational policies and organizations, such as the North American Free Trade Agreement (NAFTA), the International Monetary Fund (IMF), and the World Bank, and how these entities impact workers and communities in the United States and other countries.

In addition, justice perspectives obviously fit very well with the core values of social work practice. They also complement theoretical and other models such as the strengths perspective, multicultural approaches, feminist theories, and humanistic perspectives.

SOCIAL CHANGE AND SOCIAL ACTION PERSPECTIVES

Much of social work deals with change, whether it occurs on the individual, community, or larger social level. It is change on a social level that often sets social work apart from other related disciplines. As you may have noticed, a great deal of our discussion of theories in this chapter has focused on how they can be used to create some kind of positive change on a broad scale.

Significantly, when social workers talk about social change, they are often also referring to social action, which can lead to change geared toward social and economic justice. Within the social work profession, **social action** is defined as efforts to modify societal institutions to meet needs, resolve issues, achieve social and economic justice, and provide for the well-being of society's members. Generally, social action refers to coordinating activities intended to meet these goals, and it can be used to describe change efforts in the policy, community, or legislative realms. Social action usually involves **advocacy**, which entails representing or defending the rights of clients or those who lack skills or resources to represent themselves. **Social movement,** a term that social workers often use interchangeably with social change, consists of efforts conducted on a large scale to produce changes that affect people's lives (Barker, 2003).

The roots of social change efforts in the United States can be traced back to many great social movements, including abolitionism, women's equality, and the Progressive Era, when great changes were occurring within the country:

- Beginning in the late 1800s and early 1900s, industrialization and its subsequent social dislocations spurred efforts at reform. This period saw a shift away from charity work toward advocacy to abolish poverty and other social problems. Many reformers viewed settlement houses as the best way to accomplish these goals. Located within communities that needed help, **settlement houses** provided organized programs that addressed nutrition, literacy, day care, and other needs. In addition, they enabled workers to learn about social problems directly from the people who suffered from them. This knowledge was used to change social policy at the legislative level, which affected the lives of millions of people. During this time, social workers began to use scientific research methods (for example, data collection and dissemination) to increase knowledge about social problems. Social workers also learned more effective methods of public relations and use of the media in trying to influence the legislative process (National Association of Social Workers, 1987).

• During the Great Depression, another round of social action efforts was undertaken. Severe social and economic problems in the 1930s forced millions of Americans to turn to the federal government for help. President Franklin Delano Roosevelt initiated the New Deal, which created many social programs such as Social Security and Aid to Families with Dependent Children. Many social workers were employed to administer these programs. In addition, communist ideology fueled the fires for labor movements and discussion of revolution.

• The 1960s witnessed social change efforts in the form of civil rights and other movements that championed entitlements, racial equality, and local control of community institutions. The Great Society agenda of Lyndon Johnson's administration, especially its War on Poverty, created many new social programs and provided funds that enabled social workers to legitimize their efforts toward social change. Some of the professional skills that were developed during these times were methods for confronting racism and sexism; perfecting fund raising and intragroup processes (for example, meeting and working with organized groups with many agendas); using political skills while working with coalitions (for example, working with the disparate political ideologies of different groups); and understanding political structures and the power that stems from them.

• During the conservative era of the 1980s and into the 21st century, public funds began to dissipate, which spurred movements toward community organization, development, and leadership. Because money and resources were scarce, social workers shifted their focus onto one issue at a time, allowing them to raise awareness of the issue and gather information that could be persuasive to constituents and policy-makers. During this time, many social workers became more politically active to effect change at legislative levels (National Association of Social Workers, 1987).

Contemporary Social Action Perspectives

Several perspectives guide contemporary social action and change efforts, though we will look at only a few of them here. As you read the following descriptions, ask yourself how these perspectives can contribute to the social work profession:

- **Political opportunities perspective:** Views political structures as benefiting only the elites, who have access to power and resources that are needed to maintain or change social institutions. This arrangement disenfranchises other groups with less power, which makes it difficult for them to instigate changes that will benefit them. However, institutions can be vulnerable and unstable at times, which affords "outsiders" the opportunity to gain access to them (Tarrow, 1994). If these outsiders are able to change one aspect of an institution, this success can lead to further changes in other realms.

- **Mobilizing structures perspective:** Promotes the idea that disenfranchised groups can organize and use existing resources (for example, power, money, people, and information) to initiate change. This process can occur through informal channels, as when people gather in a community to take on tasks, or through formal channels, as when they enlist the help of professionals who are in positions of power. For change to continue, though, groups must be able to continually recruit members to keep energy flowing into their efforts. Coordination of change efforts can take place through **social movement organizations (SMOs)**, which rely on professionals who possess social change skills (Zald & McCarthy, 1987). Social movement agencies are often set up under the auspices of these organizations to tackle specific issues through the delivery of direct services. For example, feminist health clinics and domestic violence shelters are social movement agencies. In addition to providing services, these agencies strive for social change through educating, advocating, and raising awareness of the issues they represent.

- **Cultural framing perspective:** Suggests that social movements are successful only when those in a group striving toward change agree on the purpose or issue behind the movement (McAdam, McCarthy, & Zald, 1996). Like the interactionist theory discussed in Chapter 4, this perspective emphasizes that people's interactions are crucial in defining the issue and in raising awareness of the problems associated with the issue. It further posits that people must feel a sense of solidarity and commitment to working on the issue.

Applying Social Change and Social Action Perspectives

With regard to Crow Crossing, you may want to help Sheriff Bidarte assess the community's situation and then choose a model from which to work based on the outcome of the assessment. To accomplish this task you would need to consider several factors:

- *Can community members agree on the definition of change and the need for it? Some residents may be content with the status quo, making them reluctant to support any efforts toward change.*
- *Will community members agree on the need for advocacy, which the sheriff is already pursuing? Will they be open to continued advocacy?*
- *Which model of social change and action best addresses the community's needs?*

The political opportunities perspective might be useful in this case, because state power seems to be concentrated in the hands of officials who represent the interests of larger communities. Opportunities may arise for the community to access this power when the existing power structure is vulnerable and unstable—for instance, when election campaigns are under way. Indeed, because this community rarely makes itself known, it is in a position to "sneak up on" legislators when they least expect it. If community members are able to access existing power structures, they are likely to bring about some modest but permanent changes in policy and budget decisions that will benefit the community.

The mobilizing structures perspective may not be as feasible for this community. Because the community lacks resources such as money and political power, it might not have the local support in place to take advantage of organized efforts.

However, the cultural framing perspective may be useful. Given the multitude of problems facing the community, it may be advantageous to get a better understanding of how community members view the situation. As we have seen, it is possible that not everyone agrees that problems exist or define them in quite the same way. If any efforts are to be successful, everyone must be willing to support the change efforts.

Finally, you can assist the sheriff in identifying and developing local leadership to help guide the change process.

Critiquing Social Change and Social Action Perspectives

These perspectives have many of the same limitations as other social change theories and concepts we have looked at:

- Many of the concepts related to social action and change can be difficult to articulate.

- Because these concepts are being discussed in so many different contexts and disciplines, consensus on meanings can be difficult to achieve.

Though difficult to define and measure, ideas surrounding social change and action may be amenable to empirical testing with further development and articulation of the models discussed previously. In fact, the social work profession could probably achieve a consensus on both the definitions of *social change* and *social action* and strategies for defining and measuring the basic concepts contained in these models. Certainly, practitioners could determine whether change actually took place, although they would have to agree on what constitutes change.

These problems notwithstanding, the perspectives discussed in this section offer social workers a framework on which to base macro practice, which is a vital part of the discipline's charge. Until recently, social workers had little by way of a foundation on which to build their work. However, with continued additions to the knowledge base, social workers can build on this framework by implementing strategies that are time-tested and that are being formed into increasingly sound theoretical concepts. Moreover, these models, in combination with other theoretical approaches, can offer social workers a broad range of strategies and skills from which to choose when developing social change interventions.

COMMUNITY ORGANIZATION THEORY

Many concepts associated with justice and social change can be applied to community organizing. Indeed, community organization is closely related to these concepts and, in large part, has developed alongside of them. However, we still want to take a closer look at some of the theories and strategies that social workers use in their practice with communities.

The development of community organizing as a practice reflects the development of social action strategies. Because community organizing is frequently the crux of social change activities, its development has tended to occur simultaneously with events that call for social change.

Community practice began in the late 1800s with charity organizations and the settlement house movement. Many private organizations provided social services, and the Charity Organization Society (COS) was created to coordinate service efforts and to plan for how best to meet community needs. However, the COS focused on individual casework that sought to "morally uplift" the poor, whereas settlement houses were concerned with self-help and social and political action. Settlement house workers successfully negotiated legislative channels to create social change and recruited community members to join community development efforts. Thus community organization brought with it a set of defined skills and strategies that could be organized within a theoretical context.

How Social Work Defines and Perceives Community

The term *community* can have many definitions depending on the discipline and the context in which it is being used. For our purposes, though, a **community** is a group of people who are bound together through geography (**territorial community**) or common ties such as values, beliefs, and culture (**relational community**). As you can see, people do not necessarily have to live within close proximity to consider themselves a community. Often, communities develop when common ideas, issues, causes, and struggles bring people together, regardless of whether they live next door to one another or across the globe. Examples of relational communities include the Hispanic/Latino community, the gay and lesbian community, and the social work community (Garreau, 1992).

Generally, in macro-level social work practice, there are three contexts in which to view community (Homan, 1999):

- *Community as the milieu in which practice actually occurs:* This view focuses on the community as a unique, living entity. The dynamics of the community are central to the change strategies that are chosen. This context defines the problems that communities face, and it helps to determine the types of services that will be provided and the interventions that can be used based on those problems.

- *Community as the change target:* This perspective views communities from a more objective stance. Social workers devise standardized strategies and interventions to create change within communities. Assessment and intervention are typically conducted by social workers and others from outside the community rather than by the community members themselves.

- *Community as a mechanism for change:* This perspective sees the community itself as responsible for solving its own problems and for using the skills and talents of its members toward the goal of change. Social workers help to support those change efforts by guiding members through the assessment and intervention process.

In addition to the contexts in which community practice can take place, several perspectives describe the ways in which social workers can view communities and the ways they can approach their work with them:

- Physical and other properties such as the community's geographical location, population distribution, and rules and regulations.

- Level of commitment shown by community members and the relationships that members have with their community.

- Systems with unique norms, symbols, cultures, and interactions among community members (similar to systems theory).

- Power structures in communities and the ways in which community members control assets and compete for resources.

All of these perspectives can be used to analyze problems and strengths of communities within the different contexts. These ways of viewing communities give social workers a place to begin in assessing and intervening with community issues.

Community and Social Work Practice

The ways in which social workers define and perceive communities obviously influence the interventions they develop in macro practice. Over time, different theoretical approaches and strategies have been developed to better define the activities involved in community change. For the most part, all community approaches are based on planned change. But how this change is implemented differs from one approach to another. Some approaches emphasize working with traditional institutions and power structures within a community, using gradual and deliberate methods, usually through service delivery, to bring about change. Others emphasize challenging traditional institutions and power structures.

Using these methods, social workers attempt to confront issues and mediate change efforts. They also strive to turn control over to community members and to find alternative ways of functioning for communities that will benefit and improve the lives of their members. Social workers may also emphasize strengthening the skills and resources of community members through the use of lobbying, legal maneuvers, and coalition building.

Three main models for community work are based on these ideas:

- **Locality development model** (also known as community development): Uses the skills of community members to approach problems from the local level. Community members who possess a wide range of talents are recruited to find relevant, broad-ranged solutions to issues. In this model, social workers are not the main change agents. Rather, they support community members and leaders by offering education, information, and guidance. In this way they become participants in the change process, using their skills to support the efforts of community members.

- **Social planning model:** Relies on social workers to act as experts who take the lead in developing change strategies. This model tends to focus on the process of problem solving, assuming that only social workers or other professionals have the expertise to guide this process. In other words, the social planning model relies on specialized skills and methods to develop interventions, and community members "contract" with outside professionals to plan and intervene on the community's behalf.

- **Social action model:** Maintains that community members must be empowered to initiate changes for themselves and their communities. Social workers seek to organize community members, who in turn challenge existing power structures to increase the equitable distribution of resources, create more just institutions, and instigate social reform. Community members are active agents in the change process. Social workers are activists, agitators, and protestors, who work in concert with community members to create tension that will lead to change. They can also use their knowledge and skills to engage in activism, lobbying, boycotting, and publicity to help communities achieve their goals (Rothman, 1995).

A well-known person associated with the social action model is Saul Alinsky. Alinsky was concerned with how community members become oppressed and disconnected from the functions of their communities. He focused on how institutional and other social structures maintain oppression and alienation among community members as well as how institutions determine the distribution of resources. Alinsky argued that these dynamics create learned helplessness and apathy among community members, particularly those who are disenfranchised.

Thus, Alinsky insisted that the disenfranchised persons themselves must instigate social and institutional change, with a goal of creating justice and equal distribution of resources. Disenfranchised people can become empowered, develop their capabilities, and strengthen their connections with one another to increase cooperation and collaboration. Thus, he focused on methods and strategies to organize community members and to develop effective change strategies.

To summarize, Alinsky argued that community change occurs through the following strategies (Pruger & Specht, 1969):

- Build power among community members.

- Generate methods that are representative of the needs of the group.

- Contribute to positive conflict resolution.

Applying Community Organization Theory

Once more, let us return to Crow Crossing and see how you might help Sheriff Bidarte develop a plan for community organization. Probably the best place to begin is to assess how invested the community members are in solving problems. If it seems unlikely that the sheriff will be able to mobilize community members in working toward change, you would not want to use the locality development model. Because this model relies on the skills of community members, it may not be the best approach if people lack the skill or desire to organize.

The social planning model may be a good approach if community members are willing to accept advocacy from a social worker who is an outsider. In this case, the community might need someone with the expertise to effectively plan for change and to negotiate the various systems that might offer viable resources.

Ultimately, however, given the longevity of the problems that confront this community, the best approach might be to empower the community members to solve their own problems. Using, the social action model, you might be able to instill in the community members a sense of self-efficacy from which they could create permanent change. Of course, this approach would require community members to organize and work toward change, but it may be the approach that would best lead to lasting and positive change for the community.

Critiquing Community Organization Theory

As the use of community organization strategies in social work has increased, so has awareness of its limitations:

- The increase in the number of theories and perspectives dealing with this aspect of macro practice has produced increased inconsistency within and among approaches.

- Inconsistency within and among the various approaches has led to problems in fairly and effectively comparing them as well as in evaluating their outcomes.

Nevertheless, regardless of the particular approach you adopt in working toward change, you can easily use different aspects of these models in concert with other theoretical approaches in developing community interventions.

As with social change and action models, community organization approaches have the potential to develop into coherent theories that can be tested empirically. In addition, over time, the definition of community organization and the ideas behind the practice have been shaped and structured in such a way that they are useful tools for macro practice.

CONCLUSION

Dealing with macro-oriented issues has long been a common activity in social work, although social workers' interest in these types of activities tends to ebb and flow depending on the political and economic climate. Yet overcoming oppression, along with the racism, prejudice, and discrimination that usually lie at the heart of oppression, is a core social work value. Social workers must not only be knowledgeable about the history of oppression as well as contemporary issues surrounding it to effectively serve their clients and communities, they must also be willing to advocate for their clients and communities.

Although there are many theories, perspectives, and ideas about how to achieve social and economic justice and social change and to organize communities, social work relies increasingly on coherent, organized perspectives to guide practice. Look back at Quick Guide 7 to see how the theories and perspectives presented in this chapter compare. No discipline can lay claim to a fully developed theory that includes all of the constituents of oppression, but having some strong emerging theories helps to guide assessment and intervention in macro-level practice.

MAIN POINTS

- Race, as a contemporary term, is defined as biological differences among groups of people. Although the debate over its precise meaning and use goes on, social workers need to understand its origins and implications for individuals and U.S. society as a whole.

- Racism, which involves stereotyping people based on their race, occurs on different levels. Individual racism refers to personal actions such as name-calling or hate crimes; institutional racism refers to practices in social institutions, such as racial profiling, that systematically treat one race differently from another; cultural racism refers to the notion that disadvantages faced by those in ethnic minority groups are caused by aspects of the groups' culture; and environmental racism refers to policies and practices that differentially affect the health and living conditions of ethnic groups.

- Discrimination generally refers to behavior, whereas prejudice refers to the attitudes, beliefs, and stereotypes that a person holds about others. Privilege refers to the advantages enjoyed by a dominant group in society.

- Oppression can be defined as severely restrictive social acts that affect individuals, groups, and institutions.

- Microaggressions are conscious and unconscious behaviors and practices that manifest racism, discrimination, and prejudice.

- Although theories of racism, discrimination, and prejudice help to inform social workers' interventions with clients and help to guide social change to end oppression, no specific, coherent theory exists that can be empirically tested.

- A core value and ethical principle in the NASW *Code of Ethics* involves promoting social justice, and it is also a core educational policy set forth by the CSWE. Social workers often look to social action strategies to work toward social and economic justice for their clients.

- Social change and social action efforts (often used interchangeably with the term *social movement*) concentrate on changing societal institutions to meet needs, resolve issues, achieve social and economic justice, and provide for the well-being of society's members.

- A community can be defined as a group of people who are linked geographically (territorial community) or through common ties such as values, beliefs, and culture (relational community). Three main models for community work are the locality development model (community development), the social planning model, and the social action model.

EXERCISES

1. *Sanchez Family interactive case at* www.routledgesw.com/cases. Review the issues facing each family member and the family as a whole. Using theories presented in this chapter, answer the following questions:
   a. In what ways might racism, discrimination, and oppression be contributing to the family's problems?
   b. How could social and economic justice perspectives be applied to this family's situation?
   c. How could social change and action perspectives be applied to this family's situation?
   d. In what ways could community organization theories be used to intervene with this family?
2. *Hudson City interactive case at* www.routledgesw.com/cases. Review the facts of the case and answer the following questions:
   a. Describe the ways in which racism, prejudice, discrimination, and privilege are affecting the residents of Hudson City. What are some examples of institutional racism? Of individual racism?
   b. Which theories of prejudice might help explain some of the issues facing the community? In what ways do the theories you chose help inform the situation?
   c. How might you apply a perspective of social and economic justice to the situation to help improve conditions of the city's residents?
   d. How could you apply a social change or social action perspective to work with the community?
3. *RAINN interactive case at* www.routledgesw.com/cases. Review the case and then answer these questions:

    a. How does a belief in social justice guide RAINN's services to clients like Sarah and Alan?

    b. Explain multiple ways that sexual assault is both socially and economically unjust.

    c. In addition to meeting the immediate needs of clients, how can RAINN also be an agent of social change and social action?

    d. Can RAINN provide direct services to Sarah and Alan as well as serve as an SMO (Social Movement Organization)? Explain.

4. *Riverton interactive case at* www.routledgesw.com/cases. Reacquaint yourself with the different facets of the community, then answer the following questions:

    a. Which social action perspective might you want to use to help guide your change efforts with this community and why? What might be some of the limitations to using the perspective you chose?

    b. Describe the territorial community and relational community involved in this case.

    c. Which community practice approach would you pick for your work with this community and why? What might be some of the limitations to using the model you chose?

CHAPTER 6

Pre-Pregnancy and Prenatal Issues

Josie is a 15-year-old Japanese–American who has just found out that she is two months pregnant. The father of the baby is Josie's 17-year-old boyfriend of one year. They both are in high school, have a lot of friends, and are doing well in their classes. Josie's parents are first-generation Americans and hold conservative views on family, dating, marriage, religion, and roles for family members. For this reason, Josie is afraid of how her parents will react if they find out she is pregnant. In fact, her parents do not even know she has been dating.

At the insistence of her friends, Josie went to a local Planned Parenthood when she did not seem to be recovering from flulike symptoms. The social worker at Planned Parenthood was not required to get parental permission to run a pregnancy test, but she wants to work with Josie to include her parents in Josie's decisions about how to proceed. Josie is reluctant to tell her parents: She is afraid her parents will disown her, and she is not sure if her extended family will offer any support, regardless of whether she decides to keep the baby. Josie's boyfriend has told her that he will not help her if she chooses to keep the baby. Josie also does not want to drop out of school, so she is trying to explore all of her options with the social worker.

THIS SCENARIO RAISES MANY ETHICAL AND PRACTICE ISSUES ON several different levels. Imagine that you are the social worker who is helping Josie. You and Josie have many decisions to make, and you must possess not only sound practice skills but also solid knowledge about human development; sensitivity to cultural issues; awareness of your own values and beliefs concerning teen pregnancy, adoption, and abortion; and up-to-date information on legal and ethical issues surrounding working with minors.

This chapter explores human development from conception to birth, along with some of the issues, such as those just stated, that may present themselves when working with clients who are pregnant or who have recently given birth. For the purposes of this chapter, the birth parent will be referred to as "she" and "birth mother," even though it is important to acknowledge the possibility that the person may identify as male.

DEVELOPMENTAL MILESTONES IN THE FETUS

Given the extraordinary process of fetal development as well as the many psychosocial factors related to being pregnant, social workers need a thorough, accurate, and broad knowledge base about pregnancy, childbirth, and postnatal considerations. Clients often rely on social workers for decision-making support and basic knowledge on pregnancy, because social workers are often the first professionals with whom some clients come into contact after discovering they are pregnant. Social workers can provide a great deal of support and education to clients during this crucial time.

Although most of the developmental information presented here is couched in medical and biopsychosocial models, social workers often incorporate information from other theories in their interventions to help understand how pregnancy and fetal development can affect clients on individual, interpersonal, and social levels.

Growth Processes from Conception through Birth

The fetal growth and development that takes place during the short months of pregnancy is both vast and complex. Although many women experience pregnancies without complications or problems, equipping clients with as much information as possible about fetal development can help to prevent some otherwise devastating problems with their babies. Some of these problems are discussed in more detail in a later section. However, because these problems can occur, social workers must have a basic understanding of "normal" fetal development. This knowledge includes the milestones of development as well as maternal behaviors that should be promoted or discouraged at each stage.

Quick Guide 8 displays a timeline of fetal development along with the major milestones in growth that take place during each stage. Fetal development is broken into trimesters, each of which lasts about 13 weeks. Social workers should become familiar with the developments that occur in each trimester so that they can assist their clients in tracking the progress of their babies' growth.

Keep in mind that medical professionals often track fetal growth not by the date of actual conception, but rather by **gestational age,** which means that the age of the fetus is based on the start of a woman's last menstrual period, or LMP. Assuming a regular cycle, the LMP date is about 14 days before the time of ovulation, when conception would have taken place. Calculated fetal age based on the date of conception is the **fertilization or conception age.** Because the actual date of conception often cannot be determined, using LMP to determine the age of the fetus tends to be more reliable if the woman's menstrual cycle is regular. It is

QUICK GUIDE 8   Milestones in Fetal Development

FIRST TRIMESTER

Weeks 0 through 13 (up to week 10 based on fertilization age) are considered the most critical with regard to prenatal care and fetal exposure to maternal and environmental toxins.

Month One
- Primitive brain, heart, lungs, and digestive and nervous system development by end of month one
- Beginnings of arms and legs

Month Two
- Internal organs become more complex
- Eyes, nose, mouth become identifiable
- Heartbeat is detectable
- Up until eight weeks, the baby is referred to as an embryo, after which it is called a fetus

Month Three
- Formation of arms, hands, legs, feet, fingernails, hair, eyelids
- Fingerprints are established
- Gender is distinguishable (though it may not be seen via ultrasound until around 16 weeks)
- Bone development
- Can smile, frown, suck, swallow
- End of first trimester, baby is about three inches long and weighs about one ounce

SECOND TRIMESTER

Weeks 14 through 27 (up to week 25 based on fertilization age) are marked by continued development and growth.

- All development continues; differentiation of organs and systems proceeds
- Toes and fingers separate
- Fingernails and toenails form
- Has coordinated movement
- Hair, eyelashes, eyebrows are present
- Regular heartbeat is established
- Wake and sleep cycle is established
- End of second trimester, baby is 11 to 14 inches long and weighs 1–1½ pounds

THIRD TRIMESTER

Weeks 28 through 40 (up to week 38 based on fertilization age) mark the final stages of development.

- Completed development, organs become functional
- Fatty tissue develops under skin
- Fetus is very active until time of delivery
- Responds to sound
- End of third trimester, baby is 19 inches long and weighs about 6+ pounds

Source: Adapted from Curtis & Schuler, 2004

important to recognize, however, that many women experience variance in their cycles from month to month (Murkoff & Mazel, 2008).

Often, when the gestational age is used to determine fetal age, the fetus is said to be about two weeks older than it actually is (based on when it was likely to be conceived due to ovulation patterns). In Josie's case, her physician has told her that her baby is eight weeks old, which means that the developing embryo is actually around six weeks old, based on conception. Social workers who understand these systems of dating can help explain them to confused and anxious clients who are not privy to the methods used by physicians.

Referring back to Quick Guide 8, you can see that the most complex and crucial development in the fetus occurs during the first trimester. For this reason, the first trimester is considered the most critical for prenatal care and fetal exposure to maternal and environmental toxins. Throughout pregnancy, the fetus is vulnerable to the mother's behavior and environment. However, because critical organs and systems such as the heart, eyes, limbs, ears, teeth, and central nervous system develop during the first nine weeks, major structural and physiological damage to these systems can occur during this period.

As development progresses past nine weeks, harm to the fetus can still occur, but it tends to be less severe. The type and extent of damage depend on the type of substances to which the baby is exposed and the timing and amount of exposure (Moore & Persaud, 1998). These issues will be addressed in more detail in a later section.

Low Birth Weight

Generally, a full-term pregnancy lasts between 38 and 40 weeks' gestational age. Babies born three weeks or more before the pregnancy reaches full term (35 weeks or less) are called **preterm**. The age of viability (age at which babies are able to survive) for preterm babies is about 25 to 26 weeks. Babies born as early as 21 weeks have also survived, but babies born this early tend to have many short- and long-term problems. According to the March of Dimes (2010; 2013), one out of nine babies in the U.S. are born prematurely. About 10 percent of infants delivered before 39 weeks experience complications, and the risk of death is nearly twice as high among infants born at 37 weeks compared with those born at 40 weeks.

One critical issue surrounding preterm babies is **low birth weight**, which refers to babies who weigh less than 5½ pounds at birth. **Very low birth weight** babies weigh less than 3 pounds, and **extremely low birth weight** babies weigh less than 2 pounds (Klaus & Fanaroff, 2001).

Low birth weight and premature birth can be caused by a variety of factors, including smoking, disease, maternal age (both young and old mothers are at risk), drug abuse, malnutrition, and excessive stress (Murkoff & Mazel, 2008).

In Josie's case, she is very young, which puts her at higher risk for having a preterm, low-birth-weight baby. However, with early intervention that includes good prenatal care, you can help Josie with education and other supportive resources to increase the chances that she will have a healthy baby, should she choose to continue with the pregnancy.

Approximately 1 in 12 babies born in the United States is categorized as low birth weight. Rates for ethnic minority groups tend to be higher than both the rate for Caucasians and the national average. For instance, African–American babies are twice as likely as Caucasian or Hispanic babies to suffer from low birth weight (Children's Defense Fund, 2012) due to factors associated with unequal access to health care and other health-related disparities explored later in the chapter and in Chapter 11. Significantly, the United States in general does not fare well in rates of low birth weight compared to other developed countries such as Spain, Canada, Norway, France, and Italy. All of them have lower annual rates of low-birth-weight babies than the United States. Estimates based on 145 countries suggest that about 16 percent of all babies born each year (more than 19 million) are low birth weight. Southeast Asia has the highest rate: More than half of the low birth weight babies born each year are from this region. Low-birth-weight babies are also common in sub-Saharan Africa and the Caribbean. Approximately 16.5 percent of all babies born in developing countries are considered low birth weight compared to 7 percent in developed regions (UNICEF, 2007).

In industrialized countries, low-birth-weight babies tend to survive and eventually thrive. However, as birth weight decreases, the number and severity of short- and long-term problems increase. Low-birth-weight babies are 20 times more likely to die in infancy than babies born with higher birth weights. Those who survive may be more susceptible to infectious diseases, inhibited growth, and problems with cognitive development. Although industrialized nations have access to technology that enables babies who are born at 25 weeks to survive, increased survival increases the chances that these babies will develop problems such as brain damage and cerebral palsy. Low-birth-weight babies are also more likely to suffer from chronic illnesses in later life. Long-term effects of low birth weight include higher risk of death, stroke, asthma, diabetes, hypertension, malnourishment, heart disease, learning problems, social impairments, impaired immune function, attention deficit hyperactivity disorder, and reduced muscle strength (Barker, 2008; Klaus & Fanaroff, 2001; Moster, Lie, & Markestad, 2008; UNICEF, 2004).

Of course, all of these problems have other ramifications for children and their families. For example, depending on the circumstances, low-birth-weight children and their families can face economic problems, increased stress, lack of support, inadequate access to health care, and educational issues throughout life. Moreover, the cost of caring for low-birth-weight babies is one of the contributors to rising health care costs. This is not to say that there are no positive outcomes to situations involving preterm births. Nevertheless, social workers must be aware of the potential problems, for clients and society, that tend to be correlated with preterm and low-birth-weight babies in order to provide appropriate, responsible, and effective services.

Much of the knowledge surrounding fetal development is couched in the medical model, and social workers usually rely on this approach when working with clients who are pregnant or planning to become pregnant. Certainly, information on development is a crucial part of biopsychosocial assessment, which can include other factors that might affect a mother and her unborn baby, such as economics, social support, cultural considerations, and spiritual issues surrounding pregnancy. In Josie's situation, you must have this basic knowledge to help her come to some conclusions about how to proceed in her situation, particularly with regard to prenatal care should she choose to continue with the pregnancy.

PREGNANCY, BIRTH, AND THE INDIVIDUAL

Many social workers have the daunting task of being knowledgeable about and staying current with the many issues surrounding pregnancy, birthing, and postnatal situations. Clients often bring myriad issues and questions to the working relationship. To work effectively with clients, social workers need to feel confident in their understanding both of contemporary issues and of rapidly expanding knowledge created by advances in technology. Given all of the potential scenarios with which clients might be faced, social workers must be ready to take on a variety of helping roles, including advocate, educator, facilitator, and mediator.

Planned and Unplanned Pregnancy

Social workers frequently encounter clients who are dealing with unintended, unwanted, or unplanned pregnancies. These pregnancies often raise a host of questions, dilemmas, and issues for the clients and their families. Clients confronted with an unplanned pregnancy face decision-making prospects on many different levels, many of which we will consider in later sections. On the individual level, clients must work through personal decisions about the pregnancy, which often involves, among other things, exploring their spiritual and religious beliefs.

An important part of a client's decision-making process relates to the client's right to self-determination. According to the NASW *Code of Ethics* (NASW, approved 1996, revised 2008), social workers have a responsibility to promote clients' desire to set and pursue their own goals unless the social worker determines that those goals may pose an imminent threat to clients or others. This consideration has particular relevance to issues that may arise when working with clients who are faced with an unplanned pregnancy. For example, the prospect that a client may want to pursue an abortion can pose an ethical dilemma for some social workers. Based on personal beliefs, some social workers may feel that this option should not be available to clients, even though it is legal. Social workers in this situation often find themselves attempting to balance their own beliefs about abortion with the ethical responsibility of client self-determination. Even if social workers support clients' rights to abortion, an ethical dilemma arises if they question the ability of some clients to make reasonable, well-informed decisions about continuing or ending a pregnancy.

Even when a pregnancy is planned or desired, working with pregnant clients may not be any easier or more straightforward than working with clients whose pregnancies are not planned. Clients experiencing pregnancies face similar challenges, ranging from personal feelings about pregnancy to accessing resources throughout pregnancy, particularly for women in ethnic minority groups, and child rearing. Making matters more complex, many women cannot articulate whether their pregnancy was planned or unplanned. That is, many pregnancies fall somewhere in between being planned and unplanned, leaving women with conflicted feelings about their pregnancies.

Researchers have investigated the question of whether planning affects the outcomes of pregnancy and childbirth. So far the results have been inconclusive. Some studies suggest that planning has no effect on the use of prenatal and postnatal care services and is not related to rates of spontaneous abortion or other negative outcomes (Bitto & Gray, 1997; Winterbottom, Smyth, Jacoby, & Baker, 2009). Other studies conclude that lack of planning places infants at risk for health and mental health disadvantages such as abuse, premature birth, developmental delays, delayed or inadequate prenatal care, and insecure attachments to their mothers (Blake, Kiely, Gard, El-Mohandes, & El-Khorazaty, 2007; Dott, Rasmussen, Hogue, & Reefhuis, 2010; Hulsey, Laken, Miller, & Ager, 2000; Joyce & Kaestner, 2000; Joyce, Kaestner, & Korenman, 2000; Kost, Landry, & Darroch, 1998; Waller & Bitler, 2008). Still other studies suggest that some women who are faced with unplanned or unwanted pregnancies suffer from higher rates of stress, depression, pregnancy complications, and mortality and morbidity, as well as lower rates of paternal support (Maxson & Miranda, 2011). This is particularly true for women belonging to ethnic minority and low socioeconomic groups who experience higher rates of adverse family planning outcomes (e.g., unintended pregnancies, unintended births, abortion, teen pregnancies) than women from non-ethnic minority and higher socioeconomic groups (Dehlendorf, Rodriguez, Levy, Borerro, & Steinauer, 2010). For example, data from the National Survey of Family Growth indicates that approximately 69 percent of pregnancies among black women and 54 percent of pregnancies among Hispanic women are unintended, resulting in higher unintended births and abortions than for women in other ethnic groups (Finer & Henshaw, 2006).

Circumstances surrounding the pregnancy may also impact outcomes. For instance, the highest rates of unintended pregnancies occur among women between the ages of 20 and 24 who were cohabiting with the father of the child (Finer & Zolna, 2011). It may be that unintended pregnancies for younger women, many of whom, because of their age, are also experiencing less stability in work, education, finances, and relationships, put them at higher risk for negative outcomes. However, outcomes often depend on the use of family planning methods and on the woman's philosophy regarding abortion, childbearing, and so on. Differences in knowledge and attitudes toward and trust in contraceptives contribute to disparities in unintended pregnancies and births, as do unequal access to safe and affordable family planning services and discriminatory treatment by health care providers toward ethnic minority women (Dehlendorf, Rodriguez, Levy, Borerro, & Steinauer, 2010). Thus, social workers need to be cognizant of the diverse variables that may influence pregnancy outcomes and not focus solely on whether the pregnancy was planned.

Perhaps the main thing social workers need to consider is that for many clients, there are many complex emotions and circumstances surrounding pregnancy, whether it is planned or unplanned. Social workers must understand their own beliefs as well as the scientific literature around these issues if they are to effectively help clients fully explore their circumstances and feelings and support them in the decision-making process. Focusing on the needs of clients instead of the clients' ultimate decision or how the pregnancy is resolved is one way that social workers can help support their clients who might be dealing with these difficult issues.

Abortion Abortion rates in the U.S. have been declining for decades. Rates (post *Roe v. Wade* in 1973) went from a high of 29.3 per 1,000 women in 1981 to a low of 16.9 per 1,000 women in 2011. The decline in rates is likely primarily due to long-acting contractive methods aiding in the decline of unintended pregnancies (Jones & Jerman, 2014). While abortion rates have been falling for all women, black women have the highest rate at 37 percent, followed by Caucasian women at 34 percent, and Hispanic women at 22 percent. The higher rates of abortion for some ethnic minority women are largely due to the issues discussed in the previous section on unintended pregnancy (Cohen, 2008).

Because issues such as these can be so personal, emotional, and value-laden, social workers must be prepared in advance to deal with them. They must explore their own feelings and values about such issues before working with clients; this exercise will decrease the likelihood that the worker's own biases will hinder the working relationship. For example, after engaging in self-exploration, some social workers might choose not to work with clients seeking abortions. Alternatively, some social workers may work toward increasing the options that are available for clients who choose not to keep their babies but who do not want to abort. Social workers also may work toward making social policies more family oriented so that some women do not feel compelled to choose abortion, or they may work toward changing the laws surrounding abortion options on a legislative level. Regardless of the outcome, self-exploration is a necessary part of effective social work practice that helps to ensure that clients are not harmed through the working relationship.

Another important way that social workers can prepare themselves to deal with issues around abortion is to be knowledgeable about the research around pregnancy issues in general including abortion, pregnancy, adoption, and prospective parenting and their potential effects on women and their partners. For example, there is a great deal of research examining effects of abortion and unwanted and unplanned pregnancies on women. In general, this research cannot say, definitively, whether or not choosing abortion or continuing with a pregnancy has negative, positive, or neutral effects on women. Rather, the effects of these decisions depends a great deal on the individual circumstances of the woman such as her attitudes toward parenting and adoption, emotional and mental health state, religious and other beliefs and values, and available support systems.

Meta-analyses on research in this area indicate that some women who have abortions report a great deal of psychic and emotional relief and experience reduced risk for mental health problems. Distress around unwanted pregnancies can put some women at risk for emotional and other problems. The meta-analyses also indicate that some women who undergo abortions may suffer negative consequences such as grief and remorse (Kendall, Bird, Cantwell, & Taylor, 2012). In reality, many women experience both positive and negative emotions and reactions, regardless of whether they choose abortion or to continue with the pregnancy.

Pregnancy in Later Life   Increasingly, social workers are working with clients who are waiting until later life to become parents, which again raises many issues. For example, advancing technology is allowing women to wait until their forties, fifties, and even sixties to begin families. Although on the surface this development might seem liberating for women, social workers must deal with the ramifications of such issues as infertility, emotional aspects of later parenthood, economic challenges to the health care system, potential birth defects and other problems for the baby, and changing societal roles as older people begin raising infants. People who choose to become parents in later life may also face ethical dilemmas about genetic testing and terminating pregnancies if the testing identifies problems. And, because prenatal care is so crucial, social workers can play a role in helping clients obtain care as early as possible.

On a more positive note, women who wait until later life to become parents may have many advantages, such as maturity and economic and emotional stability, and social workers can take advantage of these strengths when working with these clients.

Fertility Issues   Social workers also intervene with clients who would like to become pregnant but cannot because of fertility problems. Approximately 10 to 15 percent of couples in the United States have problems involving conception (National Institute of Child Health and Human Development, 2013). Infertility can be caused by many conditions, including fibroid tumors, low sperm count, hormonal problems, and structural problems involving male or female reproductive organs (National Women's Health Information Center, 2013).

Increasingly, people are taking advantage of technology that can alleviate fertility problems. Some of the methods now being used are surgery, medication, sperm donation, embryo adoption, hormone therapy, in vitro fertilization, artificial insemination, and the use of surrogate mothers (National Women's Health Information Center, 2013). Technology is even making it possible for egg cells to be extracted, frozen, and stored when a woman is young so that they can be used later in her life. As another example, not only can we deliberately choose the physical characteristics of babies such as eye color and athletic abilities through "designer baby companies," but we can also create embryos from the genetic material of *three* parents. New techniques allow the mitochondrial DNA from one woman who is healthy to be inserted into the egg of another woman who has mitochondrial disease, after the defective mitochondria have been removed. Sperm from a man—the third parent—can then fertilize the egg.

All of these methods have their supporters and critics, and there are many legal, ethical, and economic considerations associated with each method. For example, what are the financial and social ramifications of a 50-year-old woman carrying an embryo that was frozen when she was in her twenties? What are the biological and social ramifications of multiple families using sperm from one donor who could have 150 offspring? (However, because of increased odds of accidental incest between half-siblings and potential negative genetic consequences, such as rare diseases being spread through the population, many fertility clinics have regulations restricting the number of families in specific geographical areas that can use sperm donated from one person.) Should all people have access to fertility treatments, regardless of their ability to pay? Are children who are born in vitro from the harvested sperm of fathers who died before conception entitled to survivor's benefits? Are we headed down the road of "designer babies"? And what are the long-term health and social implications of such procedures?

These are just some of the ethical questions with which social workers must grapple in clinical work and in their work on the legislative level. Because of these issues, social workers need to remain current on technological advances in reproductive technology to help clients wrestle with the complexity of the situations with which they may be dealing.

Parents' Biological, Psychological, and Emotional Health

Social workers are likely to confront many biopsychosocial issues when intervening with pregnant clients. They will face various issues regardless of whether the pregnancy was planned or unplanned.

First and foremost, some clients must work through the decision of whether to continue with the pregnancy. To assist in working through this decision, social workers can help the client explore her religious and spiritual beliefs, the emotional ramifications to different decisions, and practical considerations in parenting, adoption, or ending a pregnancy.

If the client decides to continue with the pregnancy, the social worker must assess both parents' biological health to help determine the likelihood that the mother will have a relatively healthy and uneventful pregnancy and that postnatal problems can be avoided. This process involves exploring factors such as nutrition, disease, stress, exercise, and substance use with clients. Further, some clients may have family histories of disease or genetic problems that can be assessed through genetic testing. Both the mother and father should be assessed, because paternal factors such as substance abuse and exposure to environmental toxins can affect the baby. Social workers can offer a great deal of support to clients by educating them about expected growth throughout pregnancy and client behaviors that can optimize the health of the mother and the baby.

Other factors that social workers need to consider with prospective mothers and fathers are their strengths, developmental and emotional levels, cognitive functioning, mental readiness for parenting, spiritual and religious beliefs, economic situation, relationship issues (particularly if domestic violence has been a problem), access to quality supports and other resources, problems stemming from discrimination, and postnatal and parenting preparation.

Let us consider Josie's case as an example.

There are many factors that you will want to address that can increase Josie's chances of having a healthy baby, if that is what she chooses to do. To begin with, you can assess Josie's physical health and psychosocial status. Further, at this point you might decide to use a theoretical perspective (or perspectives) to help guide your assessment and intervention. For example, just by examining the individual factors affecting Josie, you are using both the biopsychosocial and micro levels of conceptualization. Further down the road, you can consider mezzo- and macro-level factors such as family functioning and economic and cultural issues. Ecological theory might also be useful in organizing all of the individual and environmental factors impacting Josie and her situation.

Erikson's theory of psychosocial development could also be very helpful. Josie is likely in stage five, Identity vs. Identity Confusion. She will have to make decisions about issues such as her health, her role as a mother, and all of the emotional, financial, and logistical circumstances surrounding having a child at this point in her development. The ramifications could be serious, not only for the way in which Josie approaches these decisions at this point in her development but also for the way in which her identity ultimately develops based on the decisions she makes. The developmental tasks of this stage and how she deals with them impact how she sees herself both now and in the future and in relation to her peers. Her decisions will have consequences for her tasks and development in future stages, such as her intimate relationships (both with her child and others), her productivity, and her overall well-being later in life.

At the same time that you are looking at individual factors, you may want to employ narrower psychosocial theories for ideas about how Josie might cope with her situation. For instance, components of the medical model will come into play as you consider Josie's physical health. In assessing Josie's cognitive and emotional status, you can apply concepts of Piaget's theory to determine how far along Josie is in her cognitive development; this determination will be important in assessing how well Josie will cope with her situation. Perspectives on temperament may also be useful (these are discussed in Chapter 7), particularly if Josie decides to parent her child. Determining the "fit" between Josie and her baby could help Josie deal with potential problems with her baby such as fussiness and excessive crying. Erikson's theory might also be useful to help you think through which developmental tasks Josie might be facing and how a new role of parent might affect Josie's growth in the future. Bringing in aspects of the strengths perspective will help to empower Josie, as will exploring relevant cultural and religious issues. Finally, you may want to consider Josie's current stage of moral development (discussed in Chapter 9), which may affect her decisions about proceeding with her pregnancy.

All of these approaches, whether used in isolation or in combination with other theories, will offer suggestions for how to conduct the intervention with Josie. Depending on the outcome of the assessment, the theories and perspectives used, and Josie's wishes, you can choose from several intervention strategies.

Birth Defects and Hazards to Fetal Development

Approximately 120,000 babies are born with birth defects each year in the United States. Worldwide, approximately 8 million babies are born with birth defects each year. A **birth defect** can be defined as a structural or physiological abnormality present at birth that causes disability or death (March of Dimes, 2006; 2014). Many birth defects vary by ethnic group. For example, infants of non-Hispanic black mothers tend to have higher rates of trisomy 18 and lower rates of Down syndrome than infants of non-Hispanic white mothers. Infants of Hispanic mothers tend to have higher rates of spina bifida and lower rates of cleft palate than non-Hispanic white mothers (Centers for Disease Control and Prevention, 2013b). One study of birth defects among over 110,000 infants found that many birth defects were more prevalent among non-Hispanic white children than non-Hispanic black children (Ibrahim, Tran, Pierce, Johnston, Richmond, & Berry, 2014).

Exhibit 6.1 lists some common hazards to prenatal development. Hazards that are not naturally occurring are often referred to as **teratogens**; these are substances that can cause birth defects. The timing and amount of exposure to a teratogen, the type of teratogen, and the manner in which the mother's body handles the teratogen greatly influence the kinds of problems these substances might pose for the fetus. Further, genetic abnormalities in the mother or father can also cause problems in fetal development.

Because of the many problems that can occur with fetal development, prenatal care and maternal health are of primary importance in working with pregnant clients. We have already looked at issues surrounding preterm and low-birthweight babies. However, many other problems can occur, and social workers—in

PSYCHOACTIVE DRUGS • Alcohol • Nicotine • Illegal drugs (for example, cocaine, marijuana, heroin) **INCOMPATIBLE BLOOD TYPES** • Rh positive/Rh negative **ENVIRONMENTAL TOXINS** • Radiation • Pesticides • Chemicals • Emissions **MATERNAL AND PATERNAL FACTORS** • Disease (for example, rubella, syphilis, herpes, AIDS, toxoplasmosis) • Nutrition • Stress • Age • Genetic abnormalities	**EXHIBIT 6.1** *Common Hazards to Prenatal Development*

combination with clients' physicians—are often the primary source of information about fetal development. Social workers can help clients prevent problems and can support clients who are already expecting problems with their babies.

In general, the earlier clients access prenatal care, the better the chances that they will avoid problems. Unfortunately, many clients do not receive adequate prenatal care in a timely manner. This deficiency is often due to lack of knowledge as well as a lack of resources, a topic we will explore later in the chapter. Social workers can be invaluable in helping clients to access quality and timely care.

Alcohol, Tobacco, and Drugs   Maternal substance use can cause serious birth defects. One of the most common is **fetal alcohol syndrome (FAS)**, a cluster of characteristics that occur in some infants who have been exposed to alcohol prenatally. FAS is one among many disorders categorized under fetal alcohol spectrum disorders.

No evidence currently exists to suggest exactly how much alcohol might be considered safe to consume during different stages of pregnancy. It is difficult to develop "safe" guidelines on drinking while pregnant for many reasons: Each woman metabolizes alcohol differently; the amount and timing of alcohol consumption can affect the fetus differently; and not every baby exposed to prenatal alcohol exhibits adverse symptoms (Centers for Disease Control and Prevention, 2014c). Therefore, physicians and other health care professionals recommend that pregnant women and women thinking about becoming pregnant should not drink alcohol at all.

EXHIBIT 6-A

Alcohol consumption and cigarette smoking are teratogens that can negatively impact fetal development

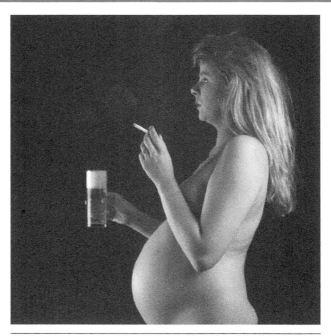

Source: S. Pearce/PhotoLink/Getty Images

Characteristics of children born with FAS include a small head for body size; facial characteristics such as widely spaced eyes, flat nose, and thin upper lip; heart defects; defective joints; low IQ; behavioral problems; poor mental capabilities; and a shortened attention span (Barr & Streissguth, 2001; Centers for Disease Control and Prevention, 2014c; Jacobsen, Jacobson, Sokol, Martier, & Ager, 1993; Thackray & Tifft, 2001). It is estimated that as many as 40,000 children with symptoms of prenatal alcohol exposure are born each year in the United States. However, this estimate may be low because many children who are affected by prenatal alcohol exposure do not show these outward characteristics, although they experience related problems later in life (Lupton, 2003; Stratton, Howe, & Battaglia, 1996).

Smoking is another hazard to the prenatal environment. Fetal and postnatal problems such as premature birth, low birth weight, respiratory difficulties, high risk of death and sudden infant death syndrome (SIDS), and poor language and cognitive skills have been associated with the mother's nicotine use during pregnancy (Fried & Watkinson, 1990; National Institute of Environmental Health, 2008; Schoendorf & Kiely, 1992). Exposure to secondhand smoke in childhood has also been associated with behavioral problems among children (National Institute on Drug Abuse, 2008; Weitzman, Gortmaker, & Sobol, 1992). Maternal smoking during pregnancy accounts for an estimated 20 to 30 percent of low-birth-weight babies, up to 14 percent of preterm deliveries, and approximately 10 percent of all infant deaths (U.S. Department of Health and Human Services, 2001). The trend for maternal smoking during pregnancy is going down. In 2005, 10.7 percent of all women smoked during pregnancy, down almost 45 percent from 1990 (Centers for Disease Control and Prevention, 2005).

Maternal use of cocaine and other illicit drugs can cause severe problems for the fetus. Many babies whose mothers use cocaine or heroin during pregnancy are born addicted and experience long-term problems. For example, babies exposed to cocaine are at risk for low birth weight and impaired motor development and cognitive abilities (Arendt, Angelopoulos, Salvator, & Singer, 1999; Bauer *et al.*, 2005; Chiriboga, Burst, Bateman, & Hauser, 1999; Frank, Augustyn, Knight, Pell, & Zuckerman, 2001). Babies exposed to heroin are at risk for withdrawal symptoms upon birth (for example, tremors, irritability, and disturbed sleep) as well as behavioral and concentration problems (Chiriboga, 2003; Smith *et al.*, 2003; Weinstein, 2000). Prenatal exposure to methamphetamines has been indicated in long-term behavioral and mental health problems among children such as anxiety, depression, and attention deficit hyperactivity disorder (LaGasse *et al.*, 2012). Effects of prenatal exposure to marijuana are not as clear. There is a lack of research on the topic, although some studies indicate that exposed babies are at risk for low birth weight and poor attention skills (Fried & Smith, 2001; National Institute on Drug Abuse, 2001; Richardson, Ryan, Willford, Day, & Goldschmidt, 2002).

Rh Incompatibility   Another hazard to fetal development involves the presence or absence of a blood protein known as the Rh factor. Specifically, when a mother has an Rh negative blood factor—that is, her blood does not contain the protein—and the father is Rh positive, the fetus can also be Rh positive. In these cases, the mother's body may produce antibodies that attack the fetus, which can result in anemia, jaundice, miscarriage, stillbirth, heart defects, or brain damage.

Fortunately, blood transfusions and vaccines can prevent problems for the fetus as well as for the mother's future babies (Narang & Jain, 2001).

Environmental Toxins   Radiation, pesticides, chemicals, emissions, and other environmental toxins have been associated with birth defects and long-term developmental problems. Prenatal exposure to X-rays, mercury, and other chemicals and pesticides can affect the development of the fetus. It can also cause problems such as miscarriage, fetal disfigurement, low birth weight, and slow cognitive processing. Keep in mind that paternal exposure to environmental toxins can affect the genetic makeup of sperm as well, causing chromosomal and other abnormalities that can be passed on to the fetus (Gardella & Hill, 2000; Lanphear, Vorhees, & Bellinger, 2005; Timins, 2001).

Lead poisoning is another serious hazard. In 2012, approximately 100,000 children younger than 72 months had blood lead levels greater than 5 micrograms per deciliter of blood (5µg/dl), the level at which the CDC recommends that public health actions be initiated (Centers for Disease Control and Prevention, 2012b; 2012c). Lead poisoning can affect nearly every system in the body. Recent studies suggest that even children with blood lead levels well below the federal standard can suffer from diminished IQ and behavioral problems (U.S. Environmental Protection Agency, 2008). Because lead poisoning often occurs with no obvious symptoms, it frequently goes undetected (Centers for Disease Control and Prevention, 2011b).

Some communities are seeing the deleterious effects of environmental toxins on birth patterns. For example, a community of the Aamjiwnaang First Nation in Canada has seen the number of male babies being born decline dramatically since the 1990s. This decline is being blamed on environmental toxins and stress due to economic hardships (Ecojustice, 2008; Global Community Monitor, 2007).

Research on the effects of environmental toxins has shown that the financial costs are high. For example, a study conducted in 2008 found that the financial costs of lead poisoning, methylmercury exposure, childhood cancer, asthma, mental disability, autism, and attention deficit hyperactivity disorder estimated to $76.6 billion in the United States (Trasande & Liu, 2011).

Paternal Age   The mother is not the only parent whose age may affect pregnancy and birth. Sperm can also be affected; the chances for chromosomal damage that can be passed on to the baby increase with the father's age (LaRochebrochard & Thonneau, 2002; Schrag & Dixon, 1985). Children of older fathers are at increased risk for problems such as autism, dyslexia, epilepsy, schizophrenia, and lower IQ (Nybo Andersen, Hansen, Andersen, & Smith, 2004; Saha *et al.*, 2009; Vestergaard, Mork, Madsen, & Olsen, 2005).

One large study indicated that the risk of having a child with autism increased with paternal age, but only if the child's mother was under 30. These findings suggest that the mother's age may mediate or interact with the father's age when it comes to risk of autism (Shelton, Tancredi, & Hertz-Picciotto, 2010).

Maternal Health   Research clearly indicates that the overall physical health of the mother, both before she becomes pregnant and during pregnancy, impacts the development of the fetus as well as the lifelong physical, cognitive, and behavioral development of the child. These are the primary factors in maternal health:

- *Disease.* One example is rubella—also known as German measles—which can cause infant death and structural malformations. Similarly, syphilis can damage organs later in fetal development and, if present at birth, can cause problems with the central nervous system and gastrointestinal tract. Herpes, which babies can contract as they move through the birth canal, can cause death or brain damage. Toxoplasmosis, a parasitic disease that the mother can contract through eating raw meat or coming into contact with animal feces, can cause brain damage and premature birth (Westheimer & Lopater, 2004). Another hazard is HIV, which can be transmitted to the fetus from the mother through the placenta, bodily fluids during birth, and breast milk. Not only do HIV infection and AIDS have ramifications for the baby's quality of life, but mothers who learn of HIV infection during pregnancy may be at risk for developing disorders such as anxiety and depression, which can further threaten the health of the fetus (Kwalombota, 2002).

- *Nutrition.* Research suggests that fetal development (e.g., fetal insulin, hormones, metabolism) responds to the mother's nutritional environment (often referred to as "fetal programming"). In addition, fetal undernourishment can promote the development of diseases in the child, many of which are not manifested until later in life (Osmani & Sen, 2003). Diseases and problems such as stroke, cancer, diabetes, obesity, hypertension, and coronary heart disease have been associated with poor maternal nutrition (Barker, 2001, 2008; Vogt *et al.*, 2014). For example, one study suggests that women who had a history of being fetally malnourished were less able to nourish their own babies during pregnancy (Barker, 2008).

- *Metabolic problems.* Another study indicates that women who are obese or who suffer from diabetes or hypertension during pregnancy are at higher risk of having a child with autism than women without these problems. The researchers hypothesize that obesity and related problems create an environment in which the fetus is deprived of optimal oxygen, damaging the development of the brain (Krakowiak *et al.*, 2012). Women who are overweight also tend to have high-birth-weight babies (exceeding 9 pounds, 15 ounces), which puts children at risk for stroke, diabetes, and high blood pressure later in life (Barker, 2008).

- *Stress.* Research suggests that high maternal stress creates hormone changes in the fetus, leaving the child less prepared to handle stress later on in life (Radtke *et al.*, 2011).

- *Maternal mental illness:* Issues with mental health, particularly depression, can have severe adverse effects on the mother and the baby. The focus on *postpartum depression* is giving way to a more comprehensive view on depressive and other disorders that can occur at any point in pregnancy, from preconception to postpartum. Approximately 19 percent of all women in developed and low- and lower-middle income nations experience depression at some point during or after pregnancy (Fisher *et al.*, 2012). Various psycho-socio-economic factors including stress, previous mental health issues, low social support, and low marital satisfaction increase the likelihood of women developing mental health issues during and after pregnancy, particularly for black and Hispanic women (Liu & Tronick, 2013; O'Hara, 2009; Robertson, Grace, Wallington, & Stewart, 2004). Maternal mental illness can negatively impact the relationship between the mother and her partner as well as bonding between the mother and her baby (Parfitt & Ayers, 2009), which can result in social, cognitive, emotional, and behavioral developmental deficits for the child (Grace, Evindar, & Stewart,

2003; Hay *et al.*, 2003). More on mother–child bonding and attachment will be discussed in Chapter 7.

Genetic Disorders Various genetic disorders can have severe consequences for the fetus. Chromosomal abnormalities are caused by errors that occur as the egg or sperm cell develops or as cells divide in a developing embryo. Down syndrome is one of the most frequently occurring chromosomal abnormalities that occur in a developing fetus. **Down syndrome** occurs when a fetus has an extra chromosome attached to chromosome pair number 21; hence, Down syndrome is also known as trisomy 21. Down syndrome causes a combination of problems, ranging from mild to severe, including mental retardation, identifiable facial characteristics, heart defects, and problems with hearing and eyesight. The average life expectancy of a child with Down syndrome is 55 years, with some people living into their sixties, depending on the severity of the symptoms (Hassold & Patterson, 1998; National Association for Down Syndrome, 2012). The risks of having a baby with Down syndrome increase with maternal age. Women 25 years old have a 1 in 1,200 chance of having a baby with Down syndrome. These odds increase to about 1 in 100 for women 40 years old. Some evidence suggests that women who have had a Down syndrome baby also have had an abnormality in how their bodies metabolized folic acid, one of the B vitamins (National Down Syndrome Society, 2009; Santos-Reboucas *et al.*, 2009). Other chromosomal abnormalities include trisomy 18, Turner's syndrome, Triple X syndrome, and Klinefelter's syndrome.

Spina bifida, also known as *open spine,* is a defect that affects the backbone and sometimes the spinal cord. It occurs when the neural tube—the embryonic structure that forms into the brain and spinal cord—does not close completely during development. Spina bifida is one of the most common severe birth defects. Each day, about eight babies are born with spina bifida or a similar birth defect in the United States, an average of 2,900 babies per year. It occurs more frequently among Hispanics and whites of European descent than among African Americans or Asians. Affected babies can exhibit no problems, or they can experience spinal fluid leakage, high risk of infections, bladder and bowel control problems, and paralysis. There is no known cause of spina bifida, although women who have diabetes or seizure disorders seem to be at higher risk. Also, although 95 percent of babies born with spina bifida come from families with no history of the disorder, chances of recurrence of the disorder increase with subsequent births (Menkes & Till, 1995; Spina Bifida Association, 2014).

Many genetic problems can be diagnosed prenatally, and the use of genetic testing on embryos has soared recently as methods have been improved and more disease-causing genes have been identified. Increasingly, pregnant women aged 35 and over are being referred for tests that can detect many fetal problems if conducted at certain stages of pregnancy. These are the most common tests:

- **Ultrasound** uses sound waves to capture images of the fetus and can offer views of basic anatomy. Although regular ultrasound exams are limited in terms of the types of defects they can detect, more technologically advanced ultrasounds are available that can aid in detecting Down syndrome, spina bifida, and other abnormalities.

- **Amniocentesis,** a test that uses a small amount of amniotic fluid, is used to discover birth defects.

- **Chorionic villus sampling (CVS)** is an exam that uses tissue samples from the placenta, also to determine whether birth defects are present.

- Blood tests can detect fetal proteins that indicate the likelihood of defects (American College of Obstetricians and Gynecologists, 1996; Centers for Disease Control and Prevention, 1995; Hobbins, 1997; Spencer, Spencer, Power, Dawson, & Nicolaides, 2003).

Other, less invasive tests are being developed to help identify fetal problems early in the pregnancy. For example, a test that analyzes fetal DNA in the mother's blood can identify the sex of the fetus as early as seven weeks, which can help to identify gender-linked diseases (Devaney, Palomaki, Scott, & Bianchi, 2011).

Some women may not have health insurance coverage for these tests, which can be cost prohibitive. In addition, many of these tests carry some risks. Many women decide against testing, choosing to avoid the anxiety that it can create.

Increasingly, advocacy groups are pushing states to require newborn screenings for an increasing array of diseases, including ones that have no easy diagnosis or have no treatment, which can create a great deal of anxiety and emotional anguish for families. In addition, none of the tests can offer results that are 100 percent accurate. Nevertheless, families are suing hospitals and physicians for "wrongful birth" related to prenatal testing. Some families seek damages when prenatal tests fail to catch birth defects or when birth control procedures such as tubal ligation fail to prevent pregnancy. They claim that they deserve to recoup the lifelong medical and other costs of raising an unexpected or special needs child. Some states have barred these types of lawsuits, but other states allow them.

Issues around costs, access, and information gleaned from prenatal testing create interesting ethical dilemmas for social workers and the families they work with. How do social workers help ensure that all families have accurate information about and access to prenatal testing? How do social workers help families decide whether or not to test? How do social workers work with families who find out they will have a child with a disability or a terminal illness? What rights do families have if prenatal testing is inaccurate, particularly if faulty information restricts the options and decisions a family can make about the pregnancy? At what point do we decide a birth defect is severe enough to warrant terminating the pregnancy? Should we blame parents for wanting to terminate such pregnancies? Should we consider the quality of life for the child and the family? And should individuals be responsible for all of the costs related to raising a child with disabilities, or should society help support these families?

Ethical dilemmas aside, social workers can provide a great deal of support and information about birth defects and genetic testing to clients, which can be very empowering. They can educate clients on these issues, provide basic information, help clients access health care resources, and counsel clients about their options in cases where defects are an issue.

In Josie's case, you can provide her with information about prevention measures that she can take to avoid some of the serious problems just discussed. Particularly because of Josie's age and current situation, your help in terms of education, information, referrals, and emotional support will be crucial.

PREGNANCY, BIRTH, AND THE FAMILY AND IMMEDIATE ENVIRONMENT

Working with individuals requires social workers to assess their clients' problems and strengths from multiple levels. This rule clearly applies when working with clients like Josie, who present with multilayered yet interconnected issues. This section discusses some aspects of pregnancy that need to be considered in clients' immediate environmental context.

Access to Health Care

Access to affordable and quality health care is an issue for many people in the United States. Though health care, in general, can be considered a macro issue, we discuss it here because of its strong links with income and employment. Health care, of course, is a particularly pertinent topic for pregnant women or women who are planning to become pregnant. Indeed, two of the most fundamental roles for practitioners who work with women and children are advocating for health care and assisting clients in receiving care.

Receiving good care early in pregnancy can prevent many long-term problems that are likely to result in high personal, economic, and social costs later on. However, even with the high level of awareness of the benefits of prenatal and postnatal care, many women still do not receive timely or adequate care. What are the barriers to receiving this care? Three major, interrelated barriers are poverty, lack of health insurance, and spiraling health care costs.

Two big issues for many clients are poverty and lack of health insurance. Many people are unemployed or underemployed; thus, they either do not receive health benefits from their employers or cannot afford to purchase health insurance on their own. In 2012, 48 million people (15.4 percent) in the United States were uninsured (DeNavas-Walt, Proctor, & Smith, 2013). Many of the uninsured do not qualify for government programs such as Medicaid that cover health care costs, including prenatal care.

The lack of health insurance and access to affordable and culturally appropriate care disproportionately affects members of minority groups. The resulting health disparities include higher rates of untreated chronic illness and mortality for these groups (Centers for Disease Control and Prevention, 2013d; U.S. Department of Health and Human Services, 2011). Though some advances have been made in decreasing health inequalities for minority groups, many issues still persist. For example, health disparities worsened for infants and African–American men aged 35 and over between the years 1960 and 2000. Using data from 2002, researchers estimate that over 83,000 deaths each year in the U.S. could be prevented if disparities could be adequately addressed (Satcher *et al.*, 2005).

Women also experience health care inequities. Traditionally, women were often charged disproportionately more for health insurance than men (National Women's Law Center, 2012). This practice, known as gender rating, was one of many that were deemed inequitable in the Patient Protection and Affordable Care Act of 2010, which required many of these practices to change.

A related issue is the high cost of health care. Rising health care costs can be attributed to three developments:

* *Technological advances:* Although high-tech facilities and procedures have their advantages, they are also expensive. For example, in the United States the technology used to treat newborns with disabilities costs over $2.5 billion annually (Robbins *et al.*, 2007). Wealthy people or persons with insurance are generally those who have access to advanced technology—or the costs are passed on through higher prices for health care and higher insurance premiums.

* *Decreasing access to health insurance:* Allowing people to remain uninsured also contributes to the problem because uninsured patients often postpone treatment until their health problems become severe. Serious problems are more costly to treat in both the short and long terms, which in turn raises the overall costs of health care. The Affordable Care Act was meant to address this problem upon full implementation.

* *Increasing numbers of malpractice suits:* As the number of malpractice suits increases, doctors' malpractice insurance fees rise, which they pass on to consumers. This point is related to the ethical dilemma posed by prenatal testing. The more prenatal tests that are conducted, the more expense that is incurred. Increased testing leads to more lawsuits due to incorrect results, leading to higher health care costs. But the increase in lawsuits promotes more use of prenatal testing to avoid lawsuits. As this scenario illustrates, testing has its advantages, but it also brings with it a whole host of ethical and cost-related dilemmas.

In response to some of these health care access and costs issues, the Affordable Care Act of 2010 attempts to increase access to health care and reduce health disparities created by barriers to care. The Act requires most U.S. citizens and legal residents to have health insurance, which is subsidized for low-income individuals and families; increases access to many preventive and other services; and ends many health insurance practices like pre-existing condition exclusions and withdrawal of coverage. For women, 22 preventive and other services have become accessible under this Act, many targeted to support pregnant women and the health of their babies. These include various screenings for illnesses and genetic issues; support for breastfeeding; well-women visits before, during, and after pregnancy; and screenings for issues like mental illness, including maternal mental illnesses and postpartum depression, and domestic violence (U.S. Department of Health and Human Services, 2012).

Social workers who intervene with women and children need to be aware of these issues and to stay current on laws and policies that affect clients' access to health care and their eligibility. In addition to changes in federal health care law, many states are passing laws that require pre- and postnatal and maternal screenings and treatment for genetic disorders and various health and mental health issues. This responsibility becomes particularly important when clients need services but are not eligible for them because of restrictive policy criteria or rigid service boundaries, or when clients aren't aware of existing services or services for which they are eligible under state or federal laws.

Let us look at some considerations you might take into account while developing an intervention in Josie's case.

One way to approach Josie's situation is to explore the programs available that will help Josie with prenatal and postnatal care should she decide to keep and parent her baby. This step will become crucial if Josie's parents decide not to support her, if Josie decides to continue with school rather than work, and if her boyfriend also refuses to participate in the process. Another approach is to rely on community organization or social action approaches to ensure that appropriate services are made available to people like Josie. For example, you may need to examine school policies to ensure that Josie has the support necessary for her to continue with her education should she decide to parent her child. You also need to work with the communities in which Josie lives and interacts to secure support for Josie in her decision-making processes.

The Relationship between the Birth Mother and Her Care Providers

Another consideration for social workers is the support that clients receive from their health care providers. Many pregnant women lack health insurance or depend on Medicaid to cover health care costs. Finding physicians who either accept Medicaid payments or charge fees on a sliding scale and who are geographically accessible can be difficult for many pregnant women.

These observations also apply to many women whose private health insurance does not allow them to "shop around" for a physician who will be a good fit for their physical and emotional needs. These women frequently must use doctors who do not share their philosophies toward childbirth and child rearing, who do not have the time to spend with them to discuss their problems or anxieties regarding pregnancy and childbirth, or who may hold biases and stereotypes about their patients that can lead to discriminatory treatment or mistrust on the part of the patient. As a result, these women sometimes postpone or reduce the number of prenatal visits they make to their doctor.

Control over the Childbirth Environment

Pregnancy and childbirth in the United States have tended to be treated as an illness and disability rather than a natural event. Control over the process has tended to be given to the health professionals and not the women who are experiencing pregnancy. For many women, becoming educated about the childbirth process and asserting control over decisions about childbirth are a necessary part of the experience. The degree to which women achieve education and control depends a great deal on their access to literature on childbirth and to facilities with staff who will support their decisions. Women who can afford expensive care generally have much greater access to these choices than women living in or close to poverty.

Over the past few decades, physicians and health care facilities have responded to research that encourages them to allow women to birth in more natural settings. Many health care professionals argue (based on empirical evidence) that women benefit when they are free to physically move around during labor and are given control over choosing the types of delivery procedures that are performed. Some women seek even greater control over the environment by choosing to give birth at home, bypassing medical facilities altogether.

Social workers can be strong advocates for women and their partners during pregnancy and childbirth, particularly for women who have trouble accessing care or who face difficult and confusing decisions about their care.

Returning to the case of Josie, should Josie decide to carry out her pregnancy, she will need assistance in locating and securing a good physician. Given Josie's age and familial status, she will probably need to secure extra support, most likely from community sources, because her family may not help provide for her needs. A doula or midwife might be useful for her later in her pregnancy. This person can provide knowledge on positive health practices that will increase Josie's chances of experiencing a healthy pregnancy and birth. Moreover, along with the physician and a midwife or other practitioner, you can help Josie identify her strengths and needs to better cope with the many decisions she will have to make. Ultimately, you can help

*empower Josie to become her own advocate throughout the process and into par-
enthood. In this case, systems theory is one approach that you can use to organize
all of this information and develop interventions that will benefit Josie. The following
sections describe some of the decisions that will face Josie.*

Birthing Classes   Most communities and health care facilities offer birthing classes
that help prepare women and their partners for the processes of labor, breastfeeding,
and caring for the newborn. In these classes the woman and her partner compose
a birth plan that specifies which procedures she wishes to undergo and which ones
she wishes to avoid.

There are several different approaches to birthing, and most communities offer
courses that provide training on these different methods. Exhibit 6.2 lists several of
the more popular birthing methods and options currently available.

C-Sections   There has been a great deal of debate over the need for **Cesarean sections (C-sections),** which involve an incision in the abdomen to deliver the baby.
Research has suggested that the rate of C-sections in the United States—32.7 percent
in 2013—is much higher than that in other developed countries (Hamilton, Martin,
Osterman, & Curtin, 2014).

Indeed, C-sections are the most commonly performed surgical procedure in
the U.S., though one study of 593 hospitals in the U.S. found that rates vary significantly from hospital to hospital (from 2.4 to 36.5 percent), even after controlling
for high-risk pregnancies (Kozhimannil, Law, & Virnig, 2013). Further, evidence
suggests that non-Hispanic black, Hispanic/Latina, and Native American women
are more likely to have a C-section than non-Hispanic white women as are women
from higher SES groups (Roth & Henley, 2012). Significantly, the World Health
Organization (2003) suggests that rates over 15 percent indicate inappropriate use
of the procedure. Reasons for high C-section rates include a trend toward hospital
births and technological advances related to childbirth.

Because technology has increased the control that physicians have over the
birthing process, women are now more likely to initiate a malpractice suit in the
event that problems arise during childbirth. As we already observed, malpractice insurance for doctors is skyrocketing because the overall number of suits is
escalating. Moreover, these suits often result in astronomical awards being given
to the plaintiffs. Indeed, obstetrics is one of the medical specialties whose malpractice costs are spiraling out of control. Consequently, many doctors are abandoning the specialty and leaving many areas, particularly rural areas, without their
services. In some rural areas, women must travel more than 100 miles to find an
obstetrician.

To avoid being sued, many doctors now take all possible precautions, including
performing a C-section at the slightest sign of trouble during the birthing process.

LOCATIONS AND PROCEDURES

- *Hospitals:* Options for hospital births can vary a great deal by facility. Some popular options are labor and recovery rooms, homelike "suites," and birthing centers. Hospitals also vary in the types of methods used for birth. Some offer tubs, Jacuzzis, birthing bars and balls, and rooms that accommodate movement and encourage massage, snacking, and listening to music. All of these settings allow doulas, midwives, and physicians to attend births, and they all provide access to pain relief and other medical procedures if needed. Some hospitals allow rooming-in, which is when the baby stays in the room with the mother for the entire hospital stay.

- *Freestanding birthing centers:* These centers provide an environment that is more homelike than many hospitals. Birthing centers encourage medication-free birthing techniques such as tubs, massage, and relaxation techniques. Births may be attended by doulas or midwives. However, most birthing centers are not equipped to perform C-sections or other medical procedures.

- *Home births:* Most people who choose home births have an assistant such as a doula or midwife. Many physicians will agree to serve as a backup to a home birth should complications arise. Tubs can be rented for use in the home. Many professionals do not recommend home births for women with high-risk pregnancies.

EDUCATION

- *Hospital classes:* Most facilities offer classes taught by doulas, midwives, or other childbirth specialists. These classes vary, but most incorporate information on nutrition, processes of labor, pain management, breastfeeding, and infant care.

- *Bradley method:* Many communities offer classes on natural methods of childbirth. They focus on techniques that do not require medication and that promote the participation of the husband or partner. Relaxation and breathing techniques are used that focus on "tuning into" the body.

- *Lamaze method:* Most communities, and many hospital programs, offer classes in the Lamaze method. This method advocates for natural childbirth techniques and active support by others during the labor process. It teaches relaxation and breathing techniques that train women to control pain by focusing outward to minimize pain.

- *Hypnosis/hypnobirthing:* Classes explain that pain is not a necessary part of labor. They instruct women in the physiology of childbirth to reduce fear and anxiety and to help women control the process of labor. They also teach relaxation and focus techniques to allow the body to use its own source of pain relief.

EXHIBIT 6.2

Birthing Methods, Options, and Classes

Finally, some women prefer C-sections because this procedure enables them to select a date and time of birth that fits into their busy schedules.

Regardless of the reason, compared to vaginal births, C-sections tend to be riskier and more expensive, and they require a much longer healing time (AbouZahr

& Wardlaw, 2001; Anderson, 2004). Further, research indicates that C-sections contribute to higher maternal mortality rates, particularly for poor women, women who had prior C-sections, and African–American women (California Department of Public Health, 2011). Research also suggests that C-sections contribute to poor infant outcomes such as obesity in later life and respiratory problems, particularly among premature babies (Darmasseelane, Hyde, Santhakumaran, Gale, & Modi, 2014; Werner *et al.*, 2012).

Episiotomies   Although C-sections are still common, one example of women's exercising greater control over the birthing process is the decision by many to avoid having an episiotomy. An **episiotomy** is a procedure in which the doctor makes an incision in the perineum (the area of skin between the vaginal opening and the anus) to avoid tearing during childbirth.

Although episiotomies were popular throughout much of the 20th century, recent research suggests that they are painful, and that women who undergo this procedure often require longer healing time than women who tear naturally. In fact, research suggests that few women tear anyway, making these procedures largely unnecessary. Critics of the procedure contend that some doctors who perform episiotomies do so because stitching up the incision after birth is easier than stitching up a tear.

Episiotomy rates tend to differ based on country, culture, practices, beliefs, ethnic group, and training philosophies. Thus, social workers who advocate for women in health care facilities need to be aware of the history, rationale, benefits, and risks behind the procedure (Carroli & Mignini, 2009; Goldberg, Holtz, Hyslop, & Tolosa, 2002).

Doulas and Midwives   With the movement toward more natural childbirth and against such traditional practices as C-sections and episiotomies, more women are turning to doulas and midwives to assist in childbirth. **Doulas** are assistants who provide physical, emotional, and informational support to women during the pre- and post-labor process. They specialize in nonmedical skills and do not perform clinical tasks such as exams. Women sometimes rely on doulas for assistance with healing, breastfeeding, and other aspects of caring for the newborn. Generally, doulas are not regulated except within the profession itself, which has various organizations that offer training, oversee certification, and maintain a code of ethics.

In contrast, **certified midwives** are registered nurses who have completed graduate-level programs in midwifery. Midwives offer an alternative to physicians for women who want extra attention and plan on a low-risk, natural childbirth.

Increasingly, medical facilities are supporting the services of doulas and midwives, who often work side by side with the physician in the birthing process. Further, many women who opt for home birth use these services as well.

Breastfeeding   Breastfeeding is actually becoming more popular after years of reliance on scientifically developed formula. With the rise of the medical model, many companies developed formulas that were touted as superior to breast milk. However, recent research indicates that the components in breast milk cannot be duplicated through formulas, mostly because researchers still cannot identify all of the constituents that make up breast milk (Gokcay, 2009; Oddy, 2002). Women and physicians now acknowledge the benefits of breastfeeding for both mothers and babies. However, like many other aspects of maternal and infant care, research indicates there are racial differences among rates of breastfeeding. The Centers for Disease Control and Prevention (2014g) suggest that non-Hispanic black mothers are less likely than non-Hispanic white mothers to breastfeed, perhaps because the hospitals black mothers utilize during childbirth are less likely to promote it.

Research further suggests that children who are breastfed from birth are generally healthier than children reared on formula. They suffer from fewer infections over their lifetime, are better able to maintain their weight, handle stress better later in life, have slightly higher IQs, and develop fewer behavioral problems than children given formula. The benefits of breast milk are so numerous and important that some hospitals and organizations are offering donor milk programs for mothers who are unable to breastfeed or who need supplementation to their own milk supply. While these programs exist for premature babies, more of them are also being established for mothers of full-term babies.

Mothers also benefit from breastfeeding. They return to their pre-pregnancy weights much faster, exhibit lower rates of cervical and breast cancer, and recover from childbirth more quickly than women who do not breastfeed. Specifically, breastfeeding helps the uterus to return to its pre-pregnancy shape, and it helps to stop bleeding after delivering the placenta (Gokcay, 2009; Habicht, Davanzo, & Butz, 1986; Heikkiia, Sacker, Kelly, Renfrew, & Quigley, 2011; Howie *et al.*, 1990; Montgomery, Ehlin, & Sacker, 2006). Among a multitude of other benefits, research also suggests that women who breastfeed are at lower risk of developing Alzheimer's

EXHIBIT 6-B

Breastfeeding carries many benefits for the child and mother

Source: PhotoDisc/Getty Images

disease than women who do not breastfeed. This risk decreases as the length of breastfeeding time increases (Fox, Berzuini, & Knapp, 2013).

Social workers can certainly help to educate clients on the benefits of breast-feeding and help support clients who choose to do so. However, many women, for a variety of reasons, choose to breastfeed for a short time or not at all. Often, these women face criticism from physicians, family members, and other mothers for their decision. Social workers can provide a great deal of emotional and other support to these women, helping to ensure the best possible outcomes for them and their babies.

Adoption

Social workers can help mothers and their partners make decisions about whether to give their child up for adoption. They not only assist both the birth and adoptive parents in adjusting to the adoption, but they also work with the children to ensure that they are adjusting well to their new situation.

In addition, social workers often play a pivotal role in national and international adoption agencies, helping birth mothers and prospective adoptive parents navigate their way through the process of making decisions, filling out paperwork, meeting agency requirements, and working through the emotional aspects of adoption. Social workers also have been key players in securing rights for gay couples to adopt.

If Josie decides to give her baby up for adoption, you will need to understand state and federal laws, agency procedures, and Josie's own feelings on open adoption and interracial adoption.

Open Adoption   One trend that is becoming more common is **open adoption**, a policy that permits the biological parents, in collaboration with the adoptive family, to visit and communicate with their children. Usually, agencies help devise ground rules that guide the number and types of visits, and at times they also help facilitate the initial meetings between the two parties. Social workers can facilitate these processes while helping clients work through the emotions that open adoptions can generate.

Although problems with this approach do exist, research indicates that open adoptions tend to have emotional advantages for both the adoptive children and their biological parents (Gross, 1993). Still other research suggests that openness in adoption has little impact on families' adjustment to adoption (Berry, Cavazos Dylla, Barth, & Needell, 1998). Many adoptive families feel that these contacts offer continuity in their children's lives and help the children adjust to the adoptive situation.

Interracial Adoption   One controversial issue that can confront social workers is interracial adoption. Some people argue that children need to be placed in loving homes, regardless of racial or ethnic background. Indeed, some research (e.g., Hamilton, Cheng, & Powell, 2007) suggests that adoptive parents, regardless of ethnic background, invest more time and financial resources into their adoptive children than do biological parents. This argument suggests that there are not enough families from all racial and ethnic groups to adopt the number of children from these groups who are waiting for homes, and children who are adopted are better off in general than children who are not.

Critics of this approach contend that children should be placed only with families who share common ethnic origins, culture, and traditions. They further argue that ethnic groups experience discrimination when trying to adopt children and that Caucasian families receive preference for placement (Glazer, 1993; Samuels, 2009).

Social workers need to be well informed on this debate so they can work effectively with their clients. Race and ethnicity are, by law, not allowed to be considerations for adoption. The Multi-Ethnic and Inter-Ethnic Placement acts of 1994 and 1996 denied consideration of race in adoption placements, with a goal of speeding children's movement into homes (Quiroz, 2007). Social workers also need to make educated decisions about how to affect social policies on these issues. We will examine adoption in greater detail in Chapter 7.

Workplace Policies on Pregnancy and Birth

Social workers often play an important role in assisting women with issues concerning employment policies when they are thinking of becoming pregnant, when they are going through pregnancy, after they have given birth, and while they are raising their children. Historically, and maybe even more so today, employment policies in the United States have not been supportive of family responsibilities. Many businesses lack maternity policies that clearly identify the rights of mothers, fathers, and other caregivers during pregnancy and afterward. In addition, many employers still do not allow women time or sterile facilities in which to breastfeed or pump and store breastmilk, nor do they provide quality day care resources. To address these problems, some states have enacted laws to force businesses and public places to allow women to breastfeed without harassment.

Unfortunately, having a baby can have short- and long-term effects on the woman's (and the family's) economic well-being. When businesses allow women to take time off for maternity leave, breastfeeding, and other family responsibilities, it is unpaid time. Thus, women often find that they must choose between having children and receiving a paycheck. Also, many women lose time and seniority when they take time off to have a child, which affects the amount of money that they earn for Social Security and pensions.

Yet many women choose to leave their jobs because they want to stay home to raise their children, because they cannot afford day care, or for some other reason. Social workers can advocate for equitable workplace policies as well as broader social policies that will support all mothers and other caregivers regardless of their choice to remain employed or to stay at home.

PREGNANCY, BIRTH, AND THE LARGER SOCIAL ENVIRONMENT

When working with clients, social workers need to be able to negotiate the complex social and economic issues that can affect individual lives. This section examines some of the issues that social workers are likely to encounter in their work with pregnant mothers and their partners, particularly poverty, social policies, and environmental issues.

Effects of Poverty on Pregnancy and Birth

Poverty can have devastating effects on new mothers, their babies, and their families. You have already seen how issues of health insurance and health care are related to poverty. In addition, many families face challenges regarding food, safety, shelter, clothing, and transportation, all of which are affected by income. Also related are issues of substance abuse, domestic violence, and other familial and relational problems that can be aggravated by poverty. One study found that poor women who are victims of domestic violence are less likely than non-abused women to use prenatal care and childbirth classes (Martin *et al.*, 2001).

Poor women also face discrimination that can affect their treatment or medical care during pregnancy. For instance, poor women who use or abuse substances while they are pregnant are more likely to be prosecuted or lose custody of their children than are wealthy women who use or abuse substances. This differential treatment may be due to many factors, including lack of legal representation or access to services that can support their attempts at recovery; but it may also be due to stigmas attached to poor, pregnant women who are addicted to substances. Specifically, these women are often viewed as immoral, incompetent, and undeserving of their children or support services. These attitudes, which are often held by health care and other workers, can make it less likely that these women will receive appropriate or equitable care (Carter, 2002).

Maslow's Hierarchy of Needs   One way to view poverty and its effects on pregnant women is through the **hierarchy of needs** model developed by psychologist Abraham Maslow (1954). Maslow developed his model primarily through his clinical experiences. Maslow viewed humans as active players in their development, and he believed that people are naturally motivated to promote their well-being.

Maslow's theory is based on the ideas that humans have multiple needs and that they will actively work toward meeting their needs to maintain stability in their level of functioning. Exhibit 6.3 displays the needs that Maslow felt are common to all humans. This list is presented in hierarchical order of importance. As you can see, Maslow considered basic physiological needs to be more fundamental than needs of safety, love, and self-esteem. At the top of the hierarchy is **self-actualization**, Maslow's term for the desire of each individual to achieve her or his fullest potential. Theoretically, people need to meet fundamental needs before they can move up in the hierarchy to address higher needs. For example, our need for food is more critical to our survival than our need for love.

However, Maslow conceded that not all individuals satisfy needs in this order. In some cases, people might satisfy needs indirectly by meeting other needs. For example, a person might be able to satisfy the need for belonging and love through satisfying the need for esteem. That is, feelings of esteem, respect, and acceptance may be sufficient for a person to feel love and belonging, which ultimately can lead to feelings of self-actualization.

Although Maslow recognized that people can satisfy their needs in diverse ways, he nevertheless maintained that movement toward self-actualization is universal. According to Maslow, self-actualized people are self-accepting and respectful of others. They seek order and justice; appreciate truth and beauty; can effectively solve problems; are involved in satisfying relationships; show creativity,

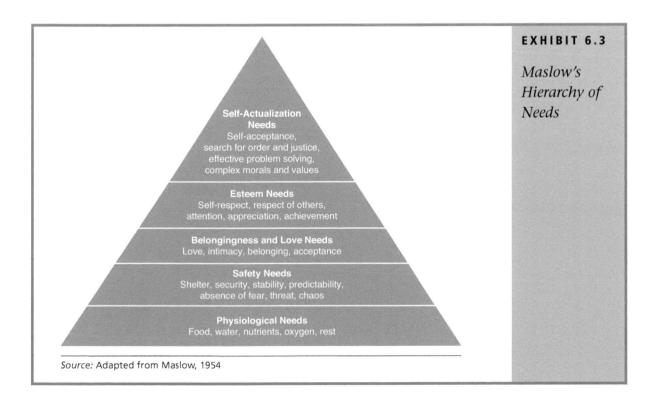

EXHIBIT 6.3

Maslow's Hierarchy of Needs

Self-Actualization Needs
Self-acceptance,
search for order and justice,
effective problem solving,
complex morals and values

Esteem Needs
Self-respect, respect of others,
attention, appreciation, achievement

Belongingness and Love Needs
Love, intimacy, belonging, acceptance

Safety Needs
Shelter, security, stability, predictability,
absence of fear, threat, chaos

Physiological Needs
Food, water, nutrients, oxygen, rest

Source: Adapted from Maslow, 1954

stability, and variety in emotional response; and have developed complex morals and values. However, although all people seek self-actualization, many people never achieve it. Rather, they spend their lives simply trying to fulfill lower-priority needs.

Poverty, Pregnancy, and the Hierarchy of Needs Maslow's hierarchy of needs can be used to better understand the roadblocks that many pregnant low-income women have to overcome to achieve self-actualization and satisfy other needs. For instance, many pregnant women who are living in poverty struggle to secure food and shelter for themselves and their families. Most of their energy and motivation is directed toward these activities, leaving them with little energy or motivation to satisfy other needs such as belonging and achievement.

In Josie's case, she might be more worried about her physical well-being than her need for love or other higher-order needs. In addition, she might need to focus on her baby's health and on securing adequate nutrition, shelter, and clothing for her baby as well as for herself. Consequently, she will likely postpone any efforts at addressing higher-order needs until she can meet her more basic needs. This kind of conceptualization can help you prioritize her needs and guide interventions so that Josie can move toward self-actualization.

To a certain extent, Maslow's theory promotes a positive conceptualization of human behavior. Its view of humans as active and dynamic players in their development can be empowering for clients. Moreover, this theory can provide much-needed structure and direction in work with clients who have many problems. It offers social workers and clients a way to prioritize problems and interventions, helping to keep both parties from feeling overwhelmed. Further, many of the lower-level needs are more concrete and "easier" for clients to satisfy than, say, working toward feeling a sense of peace and well-being in their life. In other words, locating housing can be a realistic place to begin and can help clients feel in control of their lives more quickly than working on abstract ideas of happiness, which may seem out of reach to clients.

At the same time, moving through a hierarchy with clients can seem rigid and may go against the idea of "starting where the client is," which is a central tenet in social work practice. For example, a homeless, unemployed pregnant woman may want to begin by exploring her fears about being a parent. Or she may insist on talking about her desire to avoid the parenting mistakes that her parents made instead of focusing on good nutrition, prenatal care, and secure housing. Sometimes clients might not be amenable to adhering to the structure imposed by a hierarchical model, so social workers need to be flexible in their applications of such models.

Social Policies Related to Pregnancy and Birth

The United States has been criticized by many citizens and by other countries for its lack of attention to issues involving children and families. Some of this criticism is based on the relative lack of social policy that ensures equitable rights and services, including health care, employment leave, and assistance for stay-at-home parents, to various groups such as women, children, and underemployed and unemployed people. Of the numerous social policy considerations relating to children and families, we will consider two critical issues: laws regarding medical leave, and policies affecting international family planning.

Medical Leave Laws   The **Family and Medical Leave Act (FMLA)** of 1993 allows employees to take up to 12 weeks of unpaid time off from work within a 12-month period for the following reasons: (1) the birth or adoption of a child, (2) to care for a sick family member, or (3) serious health problems. This policy ensures that workers will not lose their job if they take time off. The FMLA applies only to businesses that employ more than 50 people and to employees who have been employed at the same business for at least 12 months (U.S. Office of Personnel Management, 1993).

In 1997, the FMLA was expanded to allow employees unpaid leave up to 24 hours in a 12-month period for school activities, medical purposes, or elderly relatives' health care (U.S. Office of Personnel Management, 1997). In 2009, new military family leave entitlements within FMLA became effective. These additions allow family members to take time away from work to care for military personnel and to attend to matters that arise when military personnel are deployed, such as participating in military-sponsored functions or arranging for child care in the absence of a parent who is on active duty (U.S. Department of Labor, 2014b).

Unfortunately, many of the people covered by this law either do not know that it exists or do not know how to use it. Social workers can assist these workers by ensuring that they are treated fairly with regard to this policy. Moreover, although the FMLA is a step in the direction of helping individuals balance work with family life, it does not go far enough with regard to securing wages when workers need time off for family matters. Simply put, many workers cannot afford to take this time without pay. While employers can voluntarily provide pay for leave time, only 11 percent of workers employed in private industry and 16 percent of state government employees in the U.S. have access to paid family leave. The U.S. federal government offers no paid family leave. Indeed, the United States is the only developed nation in the world that does not offer paid family leave (the U.S. is joined only by Suriname and Papua New Guinea in offering no paid family leave) (United States Department of Labor, 2013). Therefore, social workers must continue to campaign for policies that include compensation for time spent on family responsibilities.

International Family Planning   An important but sometimes controversial issue has emerged in the past few years. **International family planning** refers to support for policies in foreign—and usually less-developed—countries that provide funds for abortions, birth control, reproductive health, and other family services. Depending on the administration in power, the U.S. government tends to shift its philosophy on how international family planning should be conducted and for which activities it will pay. For example, conservative administrations tend to withhold funding from agencies that provide abortion services, regardless of the other services they provide; liberal administrations generally support such agencies. There is ongoing debate about how U.S. policy should be applied to international family planning and what role family planning should play with regard to population control and women's health. Within the social work discipline, the philosophy toward family planning and women's rights globally tends to be congruent with feminist perspectives.

A good example of how family planning might be viewed through a feminist lens comes from a symposium held in 1997 by the International Women's Health Coalition. Central to the ideas generated at this symposium is that women's rights globally, particularly those involving access to health and reproductive care, are not sufficiently supported by U.S. foreign policy or funding. Indeed, according to symposium participants, many U.S. policies that support foreign economic trade encourage the abuse of women's rights. The Coalition further charged that the goal behind family planning abroad historically has been to provide women with contraception or sterilization to avoid future pregnancies. Instead of providing services that encourage healthy pregnancies and ensure healthy children who can contribute to the community, current policies focus exclusively on contraception and thus undermine women's abilities to contribute to the growth and well-being of their communities. This approach ignores the other problems that women face in achieving optimal health, such as poverty, illness, discrimination, and high maternal and infant mortality rates. It also undermines women's self-determination (International Women's Health Coalition, 1997).

Reflecting ideas similar to those espoused by the International Women's Health Coalition, social workers tend to support funding and strategies for family planning that offer a wide range of services and maximize individuals' right to self-determination. Although some social workers may disagree with offering certain services, such as abortion, they can still work within a feminist framework that advocates for human rights and lifestyle choices (for example, allowing women to remain at home with the child or securing quality day care that enables women to work full time) without compromising their own values. For example, they can advocate for policies that enhance the safety and effectiveness of contraceptive methods, widen the range of family planning methods available to men and women, and improve the quality of family planning service delivery. They can also work to eliminate violence toward women, including genital mutilation, and retaliation against women who become pregnant outside of wedlock. Abortion services, including counseling to avoid abortions or repeat abortions, are just one aspect of a complex array of services that social workers can provide to help improve the lives of women (World Health Organization, 2003).

Research clearly shows that family planning saves the lives of millions of women and children in developing countries. Family planning efforts promote the healthy spacing of births, prevent the spread of sexually transmitted infections such as AIDS/HIV, reduce the number of low-birth-weight babies, allow for longer breastfeeding, prevent unsafe or repeated abortions, and decrease the mortality rates of mothers and babies (Ahmad, 2000; Krisberg, 2003; Smith, Ashford, Gribble, & Clifton, 2009; Women's International Network, 1998).

Further, research indicates that women are just as likely to seek abortions in countries where such procedures are illegal as they are in locations where abortions are legal. Restrictive abortion laws are not associated with lower abortion rates. In fact, lower abortion rates are found in areas with more liberal abortion laws. Unfortunately, women who receive abortions in locations where they are illegal are at higher risk for mortality due to unsafe procedures (Sedgh, Henshaw, Singh, Ahman, & Shah, 2007; Sedgh *et al.*, 2012). Research indicates that the proportion of unsafe abortions has increased over the past few decades (Sedgh *et al.*, 2012). Ultimately, healthy women and children contribute to the economic base and overall development of their communities. This is very much in keeping with social work goals.

Environmental Issues Related to Pregnancy and Birth

The environment clearly plays a significant role in the health and well-being of pregnant women and their children. Environmental racism and environmentally based problems such as violence, disease, famine, pollution, and overcrowding severely affect millions of children and pregnant women around the world, particularly in less-developed countries.

Social workers have been criticized by other helping professionals and by some within the social work profession for not paying enough attention to global issues that affect human health and well-being. Though social workers cannot be expected to solve the world's environmental problems singlehandedly, they can act locally, nationally, and globally to alleviate these problems. For example, they can advocate for stricter regulation of immigrant workers' exposure to pesticides in the fields in which they work. These pesticides can cause irreparable damage to sperm and egg cells, which in turn can harm the fetus, causing birth defects. Social workers can also lobby for higher wages for these workers and for access to better health care services that provide prenatal and postnatal care for their children.

Social workers who provide services in foreign countries can campaign for improved and safer working conditions in factories. This strategy would include advocating for the rights of workers not to be exposed to harmful chemicals and to receive equitable benefits that allow them to tend to family responsibilities. Social workers can also assist communities in developing sustainable farms and economic structures that enable people to maintain self-sufficiency and support their families. Understanding social action and community organization theories and approaches helps social workers to become effective practitioners and social change agents on this level.

CONCLUSION

Prenatal development is an important concept that social workers need to understand in the course of their work. They often have frequent contact with pregnant clients and their partners, which means that they can have great impact on clients' decisions and behaviors regarding prenatal and other issues. Many clients will approach social workers with issues surrounding pregnancy, pregnancy planning, health care, parenting issues, and similar concerns.

While much of the focus of this chapter has been on biological issues affecting the fetus, many of the theories discussed in previous chapters can help guide social workers' assessment and intervention with clients who are pregnant. For instance, you can use systems and ecological theories to help ascertain the various factors, besides biological ones, that might impact a pregnant woman and her decisions and overall well-being. You can use Erikson's theory of psychosocial development to better understand the developmental stages of clients and the ways that pregnancy may impact the tasks that clients must complete to successfully move on to subsequent stages. You may find conflict and other sociological theories helpful in considering how social factors help or hinder clients' access to support services. Finally, community organization theories may help you to ensure that services such as abortion, adoption, and pre- and postnatal care are available in all communities.

MAIN POINTS

- The first trimester involves the most complex and crucial development in the fetus; thus, it is considered the most critical with regard to prenatal care and fetal exposure to maternal and environmental toxins. Social workers need to be aware of factors that can cause low birth weight and premature birth and consider interventions that can help prevent them or alleviate their consequences.

- Client self-determination, a core ethical standard in social work, is particularly relevant when working with women who are pregnant or considering becoming pregnant. Social workers must be prepared in advance to deal with personal, value-laden issues surrounding pregnancy, both planned and unplanned.

- The many hazards to fetal development include birth defects; exposure to teratogens, toxins, and other substances; Rh incompatibility; paternal age; maternal diseases; and genetic disorders.

- Poverty, lack of health insurance, and lack of access to quality health care are major problems for many clients. Employers' policies on family leave also have considerable impact on clients.

- Social workers need to attend to the relationship between pregnant clients and their health care providers because it is important to clients' well-being and many clients do not get to choose their health care providers.

- Maslow's hierarchy of needs views people as active agents who strive to meet physiological, safety, belongingness, esteem, and self-actualization needs. Although it is a positive and useful conceptualization, it is not always amenable to "starting where the client is."

- The Family and Medical Leave Act is an attempt to address issues of workers needing to take care of their family responsibilities. International family planning is a controversial policy issue in the United States that tends to reflect the philosophy of the federal administration about women's and family health issues.

- Environmental issues such as pollution, violence against women, and trade policies present opportunities for advocacy by the social work profession, especially as they relate to women who are pregnant. Parents often face environmental threats that influence the health of their children and that dictate the nature of the care that parents provide to their children.

EXERCISES

1. *RAINN interactive case at* www.routledgesw.com/cases. Referring to the case, answer these questions:
   a. If Sarah had become pregnant and wanted to have the baby, what "common hazards" would she need to be aware of?
   b. If Sarah had become pregnant and her mother refused to believe the pregnancy was the result of sexual assault, Sarah may find herself pregnant and homeless. If you were the first social worker Sarah contacted for help in finding housing and medical care, how would you use Maslow's hierarchy of needs to address Sarah's problems? How would Maslow's theory help you point out strengths in Sarah's situation?
2. *Hudson City interactive case at* www.routledgesw.com/cases. Review the issues in the case and answer the following questions:
   a. In what ways might the issues facing the community impact the development and well-being of expectant mothers and fathers?
   b. How might these issues impact the development of a fetus? Be sure to consider issues on the micro, mezzo, and macro levels.
3. *Sanchez Family interactive case at* www.routledgesw.com/cases. Review the major

issues involving the Sanchez family, particularly those involving Emilia, who is experiencing an unplanned pregnancy. After thoroughly reviewing this information, answer the following questions:

a. What problems, either existing or potential, do you see in the Sanchez family that are related to the topics discussed in this chapter? What strengths can you identify?

b. In what ways might these problems affect individual family members and the family as a whole? (Remember to include aspects related to individual, family, and larger social levels.)

c. As a social worker who intervenes with the family, how would you prioritize these problems and why?

d. What types of interventions might you develop for the individual members and the family as a whole?

e. What ethical issues might you face in working with the family?

Development in Infancy and Early Childhood

Sam is a four-year-old Native American boy who has been attending Head Start classes in his community, an urban town located several hundred miles from the reservation where he was born. Sam's parents moved to this town shortly after Sam was born to look for better employment. Sam's teacher asked a social worker from a mental health agency to come and observe Sam because she noticed that his cognitive and social development seemed to lag behind that of the other children. For example, Sam has trouble remembering when to use the bathroom, has not developed a very large vocabulary, and seems overly withdrawn when other children try to engage him in play.

The teacher has discussed her concerns with Sam's parents, who state that they notice nothing unusual in his behavior at home. Sam's mother states that Sam has no problem with toileting at home and is able to express his needs well to his parents. Sam has no siblings, but his mother states that Sam frequently plays with neighborhood children. Sam's parents see no need for concern and are upset that the Head Start teacher would ask a social worker to observe Sam.

DEVELOPMENT IN EARLY CHILDHOOD TAKES PLACE VERY rapidly. In fact, it happens so quickly that many parents and caregivers are taken by surprise at how their children seem to change overnight. These rapid developments can also be a source of stress for parents and caregivers if they think that their children are not developing "normally" or keeping pace with other children in the same age range.

This chapter explores just some of the developmental milestones that occur in infants and young children up until five or six years of age. Though the pace at which infants and children develop varies greatly, this discussion offers some basic guidelines to follow that will help you in your work with clients. For social workers in situations like Sam's, understanding basic developmental milestones in infants and young children will help them make an accurate biopsychosocial assessment, which will then help to inform them whether or not some kind of intervention is, indeed, necessary.

DEVELOPMENTAL MILESTONES IN INFANTS AND YOUNG CHILDREN

Many parents and caregivers are amazed (and sometimes disheartened!) to see how quickly their children develop motor, language, cognitive, and other skills. Young children rapidly become assertive individuals who verbalize their needs and wishes. Developments in the following areas are perhaps best understood through medical and similar models.

Language Acquisition

For most parents, hearing a child's first words can be one of the most exciting events of parenthood. From the day their child is born, most parents spout a near-constant stream of words, sounds, and phrases in hopes that the child will offer a verbal response. After all, language is a crucial aspect of human interactions. It is the way we communicate, whether that communication takes place in written, verbal, or nonverbal form. Even though infants cannot communicate through spoken language, they can communicate in other ways that ensure that their needs will be met until they are able to articulate their needs through spoken words.

Right after birth, infants interact by using vocalizations that convey different messages to their caregivers. Generally, these vocalizations develop beginning with basic sounds and progress to more complex verbalizations (Sigelman & Rider, 2005). Exhibit 7.1 lists these vocalizations in order of development and complexity.

EXHIBIT 7.1	VOCALIZATION	AGE EXHIBITED	DESCRIPTION
Early Vocalizations in Language Development of the Infant	Crying	Beginning from birth	Can signal fear, anger, pain, and hunger.
	Cooing	Approximately three weeks to two months	Repeated vowel-like sounds such as "ooh" or "aah." Cooing is often associated with contented states.
	Babbling	Approximately four to six months	Repeated consonant and vowel combinations that sound like words but have no outward meaning such as "baba."
	Gestures	Approximately 8 to 12 months	Behaviors that include pointing and showing, such as waving, nodding, and pointing out objects.

Source: Adapted from Hopper & Naremore, 1978; Snow, 1999

Evidence suggests that infants recognize meaningful spoken sounds before they understand words. For instance, infants can distinguish the 150 sounds that make up speech, and by six months of age, they can specialize in the sounds that make up their native language. The clearer caregivers' articulation is in making those sounds, the more infants can discriminate among them (Kuhl, 1993; Liu, Kuhl, & Tsao, 2003). They show signs of comprehending words at around eight months of age (Sigelman & Rider, 2005).

On average, spoken language skills develop rapidly between 10 and 36 months:

- 10 to 15 months of age: On average, children speak their first words, after which their vocabulary increases at a rapid rate.

- 18 to 24 months of age: Children begin this phase with a vocabulary of 50 words, and by the end of it their vocabulary has expanded to include around 200 words. Usually, children will begin using words that have meaning to them, such as *dada, mama, doggie, juice, bye-bye,* and so on. Children use two-word combinations to express thoughts such as "more juice" and "want ball."

- 24 to 36 months of age: By the end of this phase most children have a vocabulary of approximately 1,000 words and can speak in full sentences.

Some evidence suggests that there are separate and unique tasks that must be mastered in speech production. For example, researchers found that children between the ages of four and six are better at recognizing print forms of letters and words and the sounds that different letters make before they are able to recall or reproduce those letters and sounds or understand the rules of grammar (Dodd & Carr, 2003).

Moreover, children who came from groups of lower socioeconomic status (SES) had more difficulty in developing all of these tasks than children from higher-income groups (Dodd & Carr, 2003). This suggests that the environmental context may influence the rate of speech development. The effects of SES on language development have been articulated in other studies (e.g., Hoff, 2003; Pungello, Iruka, Dotterer, Mills-Koonce, & Reznick, 2009), which have suggested that children from higher-SES families develop larger vocabularies than children from lower-SES families. Other studies have indicated that ethnic background (controlling for SES) and parenting behaviors also influence language acquisition. For example, one study of young children found that African–American children scored lower than European American children on receptive language skills and showed slower development of expressive skills. Children exposed to parenting behaviors such as negative mother–infant interactions and negative intrusive parenting (e.g., consistently disrupting or controlling play) also showed slower language acquisition than children whose parents were more positively engaged. With regard to race and SES, stress and anxiety stemming from poverty, discrimination, and prejudice may play a role in these differences, affecting parents' verbal interactions with children, which in turn impact the rate and quality of children's language development (Pungello, Iruka, Dotterer, Mills-Koonce, & Reznick, 2009).

Biological vs. Behavioral Perspectives on Language Development   A comprehensive discussion of language acquisition must address a fundamental question: Are language development and proficiency genetically preprogrammed, or do environmental factors influence these skills? Specifically, are we born with language skills, or is language development solely a product of our environment and learning?

Language development is universal, meaning that children across the globe tend to reach various milestones at roughly the same time. For this reason, many psychologists argue that there is a biological basis of language. Indeed, mounting evidence suggests that biological factors do influence speech and speech development. For example, two specific areas of the brain have been identified in speech production and comprehension. Broca's area, associated with speech production, is located in the left frontal lobe, and Wernicke's area, associated with speech comprehension, is located in the left hemisphere. Injuries to these areas can lead to significant impairment in language skills (Brown, 1977).

Noam Chomsky (1975), a well-known linguist, has argued that humans are prewired to develop language skills at certain times. According to his theory, children are born with a **language acquisition device (LAD)**, a built-in mechanism for acquiring language that allows them to make sense of language and eventually master it.

In contrast, B. F. Skinner and other behaviorists posit that children learn language through listening to others in their environment and repeating the sounds, words, and phrases that they hear. Parents and those around them reinforce children for appropriate speech patterns, which in turn helps children learn language. As children grow older, they continue to be corrected when they make mistakes in speech, which helps them to learn correct forms of grammar.

A Balance of Biological and Behavioral Influences on Language   A more balanced view of language development can be found somewhere between biologically and behaviorally centered views. Evidence suggests that although the capacity to develop language skills is genetic, children must be exposed to various environmental stimulants, such as interaction with others, to master these skills (Berwick, 2009; Harkness, 1990; Hopper & Naremore, 1978; Snow, 1999). There has been no specific evidence to suggest that language development is strictly based on either genetic or behavioral and environmental influences.

Several studies examining behavioral influences have found that although parents offer praise and reinforcement for their children's vocalizations, they tend to reinforce incorrect verbalizations along with correct ones. However, children are able to correct themselves without appropriate models. Further, many children in societies or conditions where little interaction or reinforcement is given still manage to develop skills comparable to children reared in more interactive contexts (Clark,

2000). These studies suggest that factors other than behavioral influences affect language acquisition skills. However, at the same time, some evidence indicates that children reared in environments in which interaction is limited exhibit smaller vocabularies and less-developed language skills than children who have more exposure to regular discourse (Hart & Risley, 1995; Hoff, 2003). In sum, then, genetic and environmental factors appear to work together to influence language development.

In what ways might information on language development be helpful in Sam's situation?

If you were Sam's social worker, you might want to assess the degree to which his limited vocabulary is a product of genetic issues, learning challenges, or environmental context—so you could assess this situation from a biopsychosocial or ecological approach. Based on the research, you might want to pay attention to all of these aspects, including cultural factors that could be impacting his use of language. Given his mother's lack of concern for Sam's developmental level, it may be that his performance is "normal" for his culture.

Emotional Development

Emotion, as a concept, is difficult to define because it encompasses so many facets of the human experience. Generally, **emotion** constitutes affect, or a feeling that causes some kind of physiological, behavioral, or cognitive response. Emotion has also been defined as a "feeling that motivates, organizes, and guides perception, thought and action" (Izard, 1991, p. 14). In infants and toddlers, you can generally sense what kind of emotion they are experiencing through their use of language (for example, cries or coos). As children grow older, they can verbalize their emotions, making it clearer how they feel.

Research suggests that infants express interest, distress, and disgust from birth. Indeed, studies indicate that young children can exhibit symptoms of emotional disorders such as major depression, social anxiety disorder, prolonged bereavement, and posttraumatic stress disorder. Using functional magnetic resonance, studies suggest that the amygdalae of children can be negatively impacted by environmental conditions such as social isolation and prolonged stress, which can affect their emotional health and emotional-regulation skills (Tottenham *et al.*, 2011).

As with language, emotions become increasingly complex as children grow. These are some typical developments (Denham, 1998; Izard, 1982):

- four to six weeks: Infants exhibit social smiling—that is, smiling in response to external stimuli.

- three to four months: They will show anger, sadness, and surprise.

- five to seven months: Children express fear.

- six to eight months: Children exhibit shame and shyness.

- 24 months: By this age, children typically can express guilt and contempt.

- two to three years old: Children can use language to describe their emotions, and they have a better understanding of the causes and consequences of emotions.

- four to five years old: Children begin to understand how events bring about emotions in themselves and others, and they become aware of the importance of controlling emotions.

There are two other common forms of emotional response among infants and young children:

- **Stranger anxiety,** or intense fear of unfamiliar people, tends to develop around six months of age. Infants vary widely in the ways they display this reaction, if they demonstrate it at all. Infants' reactions tend to depend on the stranger and the situation in which infants encounter the stranger.

- **Separation anxiety** is a fear that many children have of being separated from their caregivers. It can manifest itself as early as eight to nine months of age, but it more typically appears at around 12 to 18 months and then gradually decreases after 18 months. The intensity and frequency with which children show separation anxiety tend to vary a great deal. Childrens' reactions may depend on the situation as well as personality characteristics such as their temperaments, discussed later in the chapter (Partamian, 2009; Rende, 2000; Scher & Mayseless, 2000).

Another emotional development milestone in infants and young children is **social referencing,** in which children can detect emotional cues in others and respond to them appropriately. Beginning in early infancy, children look to their caregivers for cues. While facial cues are important in social referencing, studies suggest that infants react more strongly to caregivers' vocal cues. One study using functional magnetic resonance to examine the brains of 21 infants indicated that these infants, some as young as three months old, processed and responded to human voice and negative emotions (Blasi *et al.*, 2011). Another study suggested that, in dangerous situations, infants tended to react more strongly to caregivers' verbal warnings than to their facial expressions (Vaish & Striano, 2004). As infants get older, they become more adept at reading and responding to these cues (Mumme, Fernald, & Herrera, 1996).

When observing Sam, you might want to pay attention to "normal" emotional devel-
opmental milestones such as those relating to separation anxiety and regulation of
emotion. However, because emotion is such a complex construct, you might also
want to explore how cultural, biological, behavioral, and environmental factors might

be affecting Sam's emotional development, which is why assessing his situation from a biopsychosocial perspective might be useful. For example, it would be useful to know what cultural expectations Sam's parents may have with regard to how they express emotions toward Sam or how they expect him to react to them. You might also want to consider the type of attachment that Sam has with his parents, as well as the developmental tasks with which Sam is grappling (for example, from Erikson's or Piaget's point of view).

These perspectives may help you organize the information that is gathered in observation and assessment. For example, these constructs may help you answer such questions as, "Cognitively, how might Sam be able to control his emotions?" or "Which emotions might be 'normal' for Sam at this particular psychosocial stage?" Moreover, you may want to attend to the strengths that Sam and his family exhibit, using these as a starting point from which to develop an intervention, if one is warranted. For example, perhaps Sam's family encourages emotional expression; this might be viewed as a strength upon which you can build an intervention to help Sam work through emotional issues, if present.

Motor Development

Many motor skills develop during infancy and early childhood. As with other areas of development, these behaviors begin as simple reflex actions and develop into more complex and deliberate movements as the child grows.

Motor skill development can be considered in two main categories:

- **Gross motor skills:** Movements that use large muscles, such as walking or pushing an object. During the first year, infants develop gross motor skills very rapidly. Some of the major tasks that children master in this first year are controlling their heads, controlling their balance, and stabilizing their arm and leg muscles for walking and manipulating their environments. Preschoolers are more coordinated in their gross motor skills than infants, and by three years of age children can easily perform actions such as jumping, skipping, and running. By ages four and five, children become even more adept at these skills and can become very adventurous in their play. Quick Guide 9 lists the ages at which infants and young children generally reach some of the major milestones for gross motor skills.

- **Fine motor skills:** Small movements made by small muscle groups such as those found in the fingers and toes. By two months of age, infants can hold objects, albeit only briefly. By four months, they can hold onto objects, and by six months they are able to manipulate objects by banging them against other objects. At eight months, infants can lift objects with all fingers, and by one year they can grasp small objects such as handles and cords.

QUICK GUIDE 9	Major Milestones in Gross Motor Development
AGE	**SKILL**
0–1 month	Infants can stabilize the head and neck.
2–4 months	Infants can lift their chest and use arms for stabilization.
2–5 months	Infants can roll over.
3–6 months	Infants can use their legs to support weight.
5–8 months	Infants can sit up unaided.
5–10 months	Infants can stand with some support.
6–10 months	Infants can use their arms to pull themselves to standing position.
7–13 months	Infants can walk using supports.
10–14 months	Infants can stand without support.
11–14 months	Infants can walk without support.

Source: Adapted from Sigelman & Rider, 2005

(This means, of course, that they can now get into drawers, cupboards, and other places that parents need to secure!) By 18 months children can manipulate objects by pushing and pulling, and by age two, children can manipulate even smaller objects such as pages in a book. At age three, most children can manipulate small objects, but they are still clumsy at it. By age four, children become much more coordinated, and their movements are more precise. At age five, children's eye–hand coordination improves significantly, making movements even more precise (Sigelman & Rider, 2005).

The developmental progression of both types of motor skills tends to follow an orderly, predictable pattern. There are two aspects to this pattern:

- **Cephalocaudal development:** Development occurs from head to toe. Infants learn to control their necks, heads, and arms before they learn to crawl or walk.

- **Proximodistal development:** The trunk area tends to develop before the extremities do. For example, infants learn to sit up and move their trunks before they are able to use two fingers to grasp an object.

Having a basic understanding of these milestones can be useful to you, as Sam's social worker, in determining how well he is progressing in developing his motor skills. Although there are no apparent problems in this area for Sam, with some

observation, you may find some problems that could offer insight into other devel-
opmental issues, such as toileting and shyness in play. Because the pace and order of
motor skill development tend to be universal, with some variability, Sam should be
exhibiting certain skills based on his age. However, keep in mind that cultural differ-
ences in expectations of certain skills could exist for Sam's family. Further, because
Sam seemingly shows no troubles with skills at home, something about the classroom
environment could be causing Sam trouble. You could also rely on Piaget's theory of
cognitive development to help guide your assessment of various motor skills, keeping
in mind the limitations of this theory, as discussed in Chapter 3.

THE INDIVIDUAL IN INFANCY AND EARLY CHILDHOOD

In addition to the cognitive, emotional, and physical changes that occur in infants
and young children, social workers need to consider other significant areas in development. Many of the areas discussed next are best viewed from psychological, sociological, or person-in-environment perspectives.

Attachment

Many theorists and practitioners maintain that attachment is a critical facet of infant
development. **Attachment,** as discussed here, refers to the bond or relationship
between an infant and her or his caregivers, particularly the mother. Though there
have been many famous studies on attachment in infancy (for example, J. Bowlby,
1969; Harlow & Zimmerman, 1959; Lorenz, 1965), perhaps the most popular theory
of attachment was developed by Mary Ainsworth. Through her research, Ainsworth
(1979) described four different types of attachment styles between infants and their
mothers, which are listed in Exhibit 7.2.

   Ainsworth proposed that the quality of attachment in early infancy affects subsequent social behavior and development. However, studies on attachment show
mixed results. Some studies suggest that secure attachments lead to better friendships and positive relationships in late childhood and adolescence (for example,
McElwain, Booth-LaForce, Lansford, Wu, & Dyer, 2008; Salter, 1940; Schneider,
Atkinson, & Tardif, 2001; Zimmerman, 2004). Others suggest that the relationship between attachment and the development of later peer relationships may be
more complex, with other psychosocial factors also influencing the development of
friendships (for example, Coleman, 2002; Polenski, 2002; Thompson, 2000).

   Attachment theory can be useful for social workers who work with children and
families, particularly those who focus on parenting skills and child–parent relationships. However, social workers should keep in mind that research findings on the
consequences of attachment are inconclusive.

EXHIBIT 7.2

*Ainsworth's
Styles of
Attachment*

- *Secure:* The caregiver serves as a safe base from which an infant can explore the outside environment. The infant seems confident in exploring her world but will return to the caregiver if unsure or afraid.

- *Insecure avoidant:* Infants show little interaction with the caregiver but will cry when the caregiver leaves. The infant shows reluctance in interacting with the caregiver when that person returns.

- *Insecure resistant:* The infant may be clingy with the caregiver and refuse to explore but try to push away when being comforted.

- *Insecure disorganized:* Infants appear confused and fearful. They may show fear, anxiety, or resistance around the caregiver.

Source: Adapted from Ainsworth, 1979

Secure Attachment: The Debates   For many researchers and practitioners, positive attachment between infants and their caregivers is viewed as the primary foundation of stable and healthy development in later life. Recall that Erikson espoused this view in his first stage of psychosocial development. Based on Ainsworth's and subsequent research, caregivers who are consistently responsive to their infants' needs and who serve as a secure base to which infants can turn when needed will provide a secure attachment for their infants.

Infants possess many innate and early developed emotional processes, but interactions with caregivers and the environment help to refine these processes and dictate how well children develop emotional regulation and attachment to others. So, early interactions, whether they are qualitatively and quantitatively positive or negative, form the psychobiological foundation for attachment for infants (Schore, 2000). This "dance" between infant and caregiver may play out in different ways. For example, one study (McElwain & Booth-LaForce, 2006) found that mothers' responses to their infants' distress were more important for secure attachments than attention given when infants were content. Other researchers (McElwain *et al.*, 2008; Zimmerman, 2004) argue that infants whose mothers respond to their distress are, in turn, more likely than infants and mothers who display other attachment styles to develop secure and healthy relationships with others in the future.

This view on attachment has raised many questions and sparked many debates, including the following:

- How does the relationship between the infant and the father (or partner) affect attachment?

- How does the relationship between caregivers affect attachment between caregivers and the infant? Does a child who has a secure attachment to any caregiver fare just as well as one who has a secure attachment only to her or his mother? What effect does a marital or similar relationship have on the quality and type of an infant's attachment to her or his caregivers?

- How does day care affect an infant's attachment?

The question of the influence of day care on attachment is a volatile one. Some researchers contend that day care, particularly in the early months of an infant's life, negatively affects the attachment between the infant and her or his primary caregiver (for example, Belsky & Braungart, 1991; Brandtjen & Thomas, 2001). Other studies have challenged this negative assessment of day care. Some evidence suggests that infants placed in quality day care settings do not show any problems in attachment (for example, R. Bowlby, 2007; Owen, 2002). Moreover, when studying the effects of day care on infant attachment, researchers have difficulty controlling for other variables that might contribute to secure or insecure attachments. For example, stress, poverty, poor relationships, and other problems occurring outside the day care setting may compound other problems that caregivers encounter in responding to infants' needs.

These questions and debates are particularly important in light of research that suggests a strong neurobiological connection to the development of attachment. This research indicates that infants simply need another caring individual with whom to engage in meaningful interactions, regardless of gender or relationship, to allow neurons and the brain to develop in ways that promote strong emotional regulation and attachments.

Insecure Attachments: The Causes   Often, clinicians and others are too quick to blame caregivers, particularly mothers, for insecure attachments between the mothers and their infants. Many caregivers who are experiencing multifaceted problems brought on by unemployment and lack of resources, for example, may be less likely or able to respond to their infants in a secure and loving way. Caregivers who have adequate social supports and resources and are not investing all their energy in survival are more likely to be able to focus attention on their infants.

Substance abuse also needs to be considered when examining relationships between infants and their caregivers. As an example, one study found that infants exposed prenatally to alcohol were more likely than those not exposed to exhibit insecure attachments with their mothers (O'Connor, Kogan, & Findlay, 2002). However, attachments became more secure if mothers showed support to their infants after birth. Though this study focuses on some of the possible biological mediators that can influence attachment (such as developmental problems caused by alcohol that can interfere with attachment), it also exemplifies the complex nature of attachment and environment. Specifically, mothers who drink alcohol during pregnancy may also be dealing with a variety of problems such as stress and poverty.

In cases of extreme problems with attachment, a child may be diagnosed with **reactive attachment disorder.** This disorder is characterized by strange and developmentally inappropriate social interactions that are present before the age of five, such as ambivalence toward a caregiver or unusual trust toward a stranger. Some cases of reactive attachment disorder occur in situations in which the children's emotional or physical needs were often unmet (Encyclopedia of Mental Disorders, 2014). Most of these children have had severe problems or disruptions in their early relationships. Many have been physically or emotionally abused or neglected. Some have experienced inadequate care in an institutional setting or other out-of-home placement such as an orphanage, hospital, residential program, or foster care placement (American Academy of Child and Adolescent Psychiatry, 2011a). These issues further speak to the strong relationship between positive early interactions between infants and caregivers and infant brain development to support positive attachment and emotional regulation.

Determining which variables, and in which combinations, are affecting attachment styles is a difficult task. Using multiple theories and perspectives helps to ensure that important influences on attachment receive attention.

In Sam's case, although no evidence suggests that his attachment to his caregivers is anything but secure, assessing these relationships might be useful, particularly if you are using a theoretical perspective such as Erikson's or Ainsworth's to assess Sam's level of development. Specifically, the quality of Sam's attachments, in combination with developmental milestones, may tell you a great deal about Sam's developmental level. They might also suggest the kinds of problems that Sam might face in later development if intervention does not take place. If Sam is dealing with problems related to physical development or trust, for example, and these issues are not addressed, he could experience more serious problems as he moves into the next stage (in Erikson's theory) and is expected to perform at levels that are more physically and emotionally complex.

Gender Identity

A complex interplay of biological and environmental factors creates our **gender identity,** our perception of ourselves as male or female (or both or neither, or some combination of these). Gender identity is a product of innate characteristics that are shaped by and interact with our social experiences. Usually, children have a strong sense of gender identification early in childhood. Children as young as two can accurately identify men and women based on physical characteristics (Newman & Newman, 2009).

Keep in mind that a person's gender identity does not say anything about the gender or other characteristics of the people that she or he might be sexually attracted to. For example, many people who identify as transgender also identify as heterosexual (for example, a biological male who identifies as female may be sexually attracted to men). As social workers, it is important to keep this distinction in mind when working with people, particularly around gender issues, and not make assumptions or operate on stereotypes about their sexual identity. In Chapter 9, the chapter on development in adolescence, we discuss sexual identity development and sexual orientation.

Sex Characteristics and Gender Identity   Upon conception, the sex chromosomes determine whether we will be female (XX) or male (XY) or some combination of the two. We all begin with a set of undifferentiated or "sexless" gonads and two sets of ducts (the Wolffian and Mullerian) that will later transform into the genitals. The differentiation into male and female is a complex process:

- Development of male genitals. If the Y chromosome is present, typically an SRY gene will activate. It prompts the development of testes, which produce testosterone. The testes also inhibit the growth of the Mullerian ducts and stimulate growth of the Wolffian ducts, which will develop into the male genitals. A substance called dihydrotestosterone (DHT) also contributes to the development of the male genitals. Testosterone and other hormones play a role in "masculinizing" the brain.

- Development of female genitals. Without the SRY gene and DHT, the Mullerian ducts will develop into the female genitals and the Wolffian ducts will deteriorate (Blakemore, Berenbaum, & Liben, 2009; Bostwick & Martin, 2007).

Like all processes in fetal development, the complex hormonal process that plays out in this aspect of development is susceptible to internal and outside forces that can result in variations on the sex chromosomes. For example, some babies may have genotypes such as XXY or XO. Or some babies may be born as **intersex**, which is a term used to describe babies born with some combination of reproductive or sexual anatomy that is not congruent with their gender appearance. For instance, a baby might appear to be male (the baby has a penis and testicles), but the baby also has a uterus. Or, a baby might be born with some combination of external genitalia such as a large clitoris and no vaginal opening (Intersex Society of North America, 2012). In the vast majority of cases, however, the presence of the XX chromosome will produce genotypical and phenotypical females, and the XY chromosome will produce males, with the typical physical characteristics.

Often, once the parents or caregivers know the sex of the fetus, they begin behaving in gender normative ways that are congruent with the child's assigned gender. They may paint the nursery pink and buy dolls for a girl, or paint the nursery blue and buy "action figure" toys for a boy. In this situation, parents are acting on **gender roles,** or a set of culturally accepted activities, expectations, and behaviors assigned to males and females (Gender Spectrum, 2014). Once the child is born, parents often behave toward the child in gender normative ways that are congruent with cultural expectations for girls and boys. They may talk a lot to girls and be more physical with boys, for instance.

In addition, the child has a sense of his or her gender based on physiological characteristics, which intersects with social experiences and reinforcement the child receives from the environment. Our **gender expression** involves the ways in which we communicate our gender identity to others (Gender Spectrum, 2014). Generally most children do tend to develop behavioral characteristics that are socially acceptable for their gender (for example, boys playing with trucks and in more physical ways). This gender-congruent behavior is further encouraged and reinforced by caregivers. This process is a complex interplay between hormonal influences on the brain and the feedback given from the environment.

Transgender Children   Usually a child's gender identity and gender expression are congruent with the sex they were assigned at birth. This congruency is often referred to as **gender normative** or **cisgender** (Gender Spectrum, 2014). Gender normative behaviors are further reinforced through the child's social environment, validating the child's gendered experience and strengthening identity.

But sometimes this experience is not congruent, or the child's experience may not fall clearly into the rather restrictive range of acceptable gender behaviors for his or her sexual phenotype. Children whose gender identity is not congruent with their assigned sex at birth may be referred to as **transgender** (Gender Spectrum, 2014). This term is generally used to describe anyone whose gender identity or behavior does not fall within culturally stereotypical gender norms.

Another term that is commonly used to describe this incongruency is **gender dysphoria.** The DSM-IV-TR (American Psychiatric Association, 2000) defined gender dysphoria as incongruence between one's experienced gender and assigned gender, and the diagnosis could apply to children, adolescents, and adults. However, in preparing the DSM-5, published in 2013, there was a great deal of debate about whether this incongruence is really a problem worthy of a label or diagnosis. Indeed, the DSM-5 states that once someone undergoes sex reassignment surgery or otherwise feels congruency between identity and assigned sex, the diagnosis of gender dysphoria no longer applies. Even with this debate, a diagnosis of gender dysphoria is still required before a person can seek sex reassignment surgery, a requirement with which many transgender individuals disagree. They believe that it implies they have a mental illness and takes focus off of the problematic and narrow ways in which society defines gender (Malpas, 2011).

Increasingly, researchers and other professionals are acknowledging that gender identity may not exist in a strict male/female binary form. Rather, gender variance or **gender fluidity** is being seen as a normal part of human expression. These terms refer to the idea that there is a wider, more flexible range of gender experiences that people can have, that these experiences may or may not be congruent with socially acceptable binary definitions of gender, and that people's identities and experiences may change with time (possibly even on a daily basis). Sometimes this idea is also referred to as **gender queer.**

Gender Reassignment   Not so long ago, parents of babies who were born intersex were advised to surgically alter the baby at birth to "make" the baby male or female. Parents of children demonstrating transgender behavior were advised to "socialize" their children into gender conformity. We now know, from some unfortunate examples and more recent research on gender identity development, that these types of interventions are not only unlikely to be effective; they can have seriously negative consequences on gender nonconforming children.

One famous example from the 1960s and 1970s is the case of David Reimer, who experienced a botched circumcision as an infant. A famous researcher by the name of John Money, a proponent of the idea that gender identity was a product of socialization, convinced David's parents to raise him as a girl. They changed David's name to Joan, dressed him in feminine clothes, and put David through sex reassignment surgery. After the publication of John Colapinto's story, "As Nature Made Him" in 2000, David told his story to the public. David described lifelong depression and feeling like he was in the wrong body. David later reclaimed his male identity and married but never fully recovered from the issues caused by this event and committed suicide in 2004 (AASECT, 2004).

Increasingly, physicians, social workers, and other helping professionals are advising parents of intersex babies to wait until the child is older and able to express his or her gender identity before undergoing treatments such as hormone therapy and sex reassignment surgery. More controversially, some professionals advocate the use of hormone blockers for transgender children as well, to temporarily block the permanent effects of puberty. Blocking puberty is particularly relevant for biological males who identify as female or for some intersex children, since surgery and hormones are not completely effective in reducing masculine characteristics such as large hands, fingers, foreheads, and Adam's apples. Altering these features takes numerous, costly surgeries. Hormone blockers temporarily halt this development, and if a child decides not to move forward with sex reassignment, the hormones can be discontinued and puberty will progress normally. Some professionals see this as a humane and viable option for transgender and intersex children, while others disagree with this type of intervention and feel it is too extreme (Malpas, 2011).

Temperament

The complex concept of **temperament** can be thought of as the consistent ways in which we respond, behaviorally and emotionally, to our environment. Significantly, temperament is generally thought to be present at birth and is considered to be a fairly stable trait throughout life, although it can be shaped by later experiences. Research suggests that temperament in infancy is associated with heredity; however, this association tends to lessen as infants grow older, further supporting the notion that environmental influences may play a part in temperament (Barry, Kochanska, & Philibert, 2008; Goldsmith, Buss, & Lemery, 1997; Goldsmith, Lemery, Buss, & Campos, 1999; Lemery, Goldsmith, Klinnert, & Mrazek, 1999). Indeed, many developmental researchers spend a great deal of time and effort studying infant temperament and how it impacts and interacts with the infant's environment.

Social scientists have created a variety of ways of classifying temperament. One classification scheme developed by Stella Chess and Alexander Thomas (1977), based on their research, conceptualizes three main temperament styles:

- *Easy child:* These children generally display happy, positive moods and adapt easily to their environment.

- *Difficult child:* These children are fussy, cry frequently, and have trouble adapting to changes in the environment.

- *Slow-to-warm-up child:* These children tend to show low levels of activity, emotion, and adaptability and tend to be somewhat negative.

Temperament theories have generated a lot of discussion and controversy. One of the biggest issues is whether the current classifications accurately capture the complete range of temperaments. This issue can be resolved only through further study. In the meantime, using these classifications as guidelines for understanding emotions and their effects on relationships can be useful in practice.

More recently, research has suggested that much of the importance of temperament has to do with "goodness of fit" (e.g., Daniel, Grzywacz, Leerkes, Tucker, & Han, 2009; Pluess & Belsky, 2009). This concept relates to how well infants' temperaments fit with their environmental context and what consequences might occur because of this fit. For example, an easy child exposed to a strange and intimidating situation may react by taking things in her stride and adapting readily to the context, limiting the amount of stress experienced by the infant and those in her environment. Conversely, a difficult child who is exposed to the same strange situation may react by crying and fussing and not adapting to the situation. This behavior will create stress not only for the infant but for those around her, as they will probably fail to console her and may blame themselves for her distress.

This interaction between an infant's temperament and the environment becomes an issue for parenting, which many social workers tackle in their work with clients. Specifically, social workers can help parents or caregivers better understand their infants' temperament and possible reactions to their environment, which in turn can help parents alter their own reactions to their children when problems occur. Social workers can help parents become more flexible and adaptable to the unique characteristics of their children, which may help parents avoid unfairly or prematurely labeling their children in negative ways and responding to them based on these labels. Parents who understand temperament issues of their children are

PHOTO 7-A

At birth, babies already display individual temperaments

Source: Jack Star/PhotoLink/Getty Images

more likely to adapt their own parenting style and their environmental context to better fit the temperament of the child, which may alleviate some of the problems that the parents experience in dealing with their children. Some health care clinics offer computerized assessments of children's temperaments that parents can use to learn more about their children's behavior. These computer programs also offer suggestions about how to use certain parenting skills to adjust to particular temperament styles.

In Sam's case, you might want to assess his temperament style to ascertain whether some of the behaviors labeled as problematic by the teacher might be due to a problematic fit between his temperament and the school environment. It may be that Sam has trouble adjusting to the classroom, which may cause him to withdraw and display other behaviors that might not seem age-appropriate.

Autism

Autism is a developmental disability characterized by impaired social interaction and communication (American Psychiatric Association, 2000; National Institute of Child Health and Human Development, 2008). Autism falls under a larger umbrella of autism spectrum disorders, which include Childhood Disintegrative Disorder (CDD) and Rhett's Disorder, Asperger Syndrome, and Pervasive Developmental Disorder Not Otherwise Specified (PDD). All of these disorders share characteristics of problematic communication, social interaction, and repetitive or restricted patterns of behaviors, but it is important to remember that individuals diagnosed with these disorders, particularly autism and Asperger Syndrome, often display a set of unique symptoms that vary in how disabling the symptoms are for psychosocial functioning (National Institute of Child Health and Human Development, 2008).

The exact prevalence of autism is difficult to ascertain, but recent estimates suggest that as many as one in every 68 children in the United States is autistic, with some communities seeing higher rates than others. Over the past several decades, rates of autism have been increasing, but this may be due to improved diagnostic tools as well as the fact that more behaviors and symptoms are now included under the autistic spectrum disorder umbrella (Centers for Disease Control and Prevention, 2014a).

Autism affects children from all ethnic and SES groups. However, boys are almost five times more likely to be diagnosed as autistic than girls, and siblings of those who have the disorder as well as children with other developmental disorders are also more likely to be diagnosed with autism (Centers for Disease Control and Prevention, 2014a; National Institute of Child Health and Human Development, 2008). Further, white children are more likely to be diagnosed with autism spectrum disorder than black and Hispanic children, though it may be a lack of access to health care and assessment resources that contributes to that ethnic difference in diagnosis rates (Centers for Disease Control and Prevention, 2014a).

By the age of 18 months, many signs of autism are evident. For example, children may exhibit problems with eye contact, nonverbal communication, age-appropriate play, and response to directions or to their own name. Some signs are detectable at even earlier ages; for example, infants may not coo or make other verbalizations or they may not point, wave, or grasp objects. One study of over 100 infants found that children diagnosed with autism later in childhood showed diminished eye contact between the ages of two and six months (Jones & Klin, 2013). However, many parents do not notice symptoms until around two or three years of age, when children have noticeable problems with verbal communication or when they drastically lose skills they had mastered. Increasingly, physicians, educators, and even parents are better equipped to look for early signs of autism as research indicates that early diagnosis and treatment, which can include a whole host of behavioral, educational, and medication therapies, may lead to an improved lifelong prognosis, minimizing the symptoms that a child may exhibit (National Autism Association, 2009; National Institute of Child Health and Human Development, 2008). Indeed, a small pilot study focusing on enhanced parental interaction with infants showing signs of autism indicated that by age three, none of the seven children who participated in the study showed continuing evidence of autism or developmental delays (Rogers, Vismara, Wagner, McCormick, Young, & Ozonoff, 2014).

Research into the cause of autism is ongoing and ever growing. It is likely that autism is caused by a combination of biopsychosocial factors, and research is probing into these areas. Studies on autism to date have found links to many potential causes including mutated genes, viruses, immunological diseases, and environmental triggers. These are some of the studies:

- A consortium of researchers is working on identifying genes associated with autism (Autism Consortium, 2009).

- Other researchers (Auyeung *et al.*, 2009; Auyeung, Lombardo, & Baron-Cohen, 2013; Korvatska, Van de Water, Anders, & Gershwin, 2002) have identified increased fetal testosterone levels and immune abnormalities in children with autism.

- One study found that low-birth-weight babies were five times as likely to develop autism as babies born near normal weight (Pinto-Martin *et al.*, 2011).

- One study found that children born after shorter intervals between pregnancies (particularly less than a year after their siblings were born) were at higher risk of developing autism than children born after longer intervals between pregnancies (Cheslack-Postava, Liu, & Bearman, 2011).

- A meta-analysis of past studies found a link between autism and the mother's age at birth (Sandin *et al.*, 2012), especially for mothers over the age of 35. Mothers under 20 years of age had a lower risk of bearing autistic children.

- Still others have found links between rates of autism and environmental factors. One study found that children in areas with high precipitation such as Washington and Oregon had higher rates of autism, suggesting that children in these areas stay indoors more often, leading to increased Vitamin D deficiency and exposure to household chemicals, which might trigger the disorder (Waldman, Nicholson, Adilov, & Williams, 2008).

- Another study examining autism among twins found that susceptibility to autism spectrum disorders was moderately linked to genetic factors and strongly associated with shared environment (Hallmayer *et al.*, 2011).

To date, studies have found no clear connection between autism and childhood vaccines (National Institute of Child Health and Human Development, 2008), which was a claim, now discredited, in a 1998 medical journal.

Nevertheless, because of increasing rates of diagnosed autism, parents are justifiably anxious about the health and well-being of their children. Social workers can help parents by remaining current on autism research, treatment, and debates over causes. There are many resources available to help parents make informed decisions about health care issues for their children, including vaccination and autism diagnosis and treatment.

Effects of Low Socioeconomic Status on Individual Development

Although a family's SES could be considered a mezzo issue, it is an important influence on physical development in infants and young children. In an extensive literature review, many links between SES and developmental problems were found (Bradley & Corwyn, 2002). With regard to health, children from low-SES groups are more likely to die and suffer from injuries, illnesses, infections, low IQ, tooth decay, lead poisoning, sensory delays, cognitive delays, and neurological problems than children from high-SES groups. Perhaps as a result, children from low-SES groups have also been found to have lower rates of attendance and achievement at school and higher school dropout rates than children from high-SES groups. And these effects are likely to persist into adulthood, affecting abilities and success in areas like education, parenting, employment, and relationships (Kim *et al.*, 2013). Many of these findings have been replicated across cultural contexts.

Low-SES children also exhibit more symptoms of maladaptive social functioning and psychiatric problems than children from high-SES groups, though these findings must be interpreted with caution (Bradley & Corwyn, 2002). Specifically, those living in poverty are often diagnosed with mental illness more frequently than wealthier individuals, even when displaying similar symptoms. Also, there is no evidence to suggest a causal relationship between low SES and mental illness, only an association between the two. Often, people with mental illness move into low-SES categories because of loss of family, employment, benefits, and other resources.

The consequences of low SES on development can be explained in many different ways. Some of the effects could be due, in part, to genetics, biology, and problems in development. For example, research suggests that poverty and resulting stressors like exposure to food insecurity, family violence, and crowded housing has long-term and chronic effects on brain development and functioning. One study demonstrated that as young adults, impoverished children showed greater activity in the amygdala and less activity in the prefrontal cortex when asked to regulate emotions than young adults who were not impoverished as children (Kim *et al.*, 2013). Other studies have linked poverty and stress to dendrite shrinkage in the brain, causing problems with learning, attention, memory, creativity, and concentration (Christian, Miracle, Wellman, & Nakazawa, 2011; Martin & Wellman, 2011). Still other effects can be attributed to a lack of resources, opportunities, and exposure to a nurturing environment. Environmental factors as well as issues around discrimination may disproportionately impact members of minority groups. Research in this area is inspiring evidenced-based interventions targeting brain development and interpersonal interactions, such as *trauma-focused cognitive behavioral therapy*, which incorporates concepts from cognitive-behavioral, attachment, humanistic, empowerment, and family systems models (Child Sexual Abuse Task Force and Research & Practice Core, National Child Traumatic Stress Network, 2004).

> *When working with children and families from low-SES groups, social workers may want to assess potential problems from a person-in-environment framework to capture the many facets of the child's life that may be contributing to problems in development. For example, although you do not know the specifics of Sam's SES, because he is attending Head Start, it is likely that he comes from a low-income family. This factor should be considered in your assessment, as it could be contributing to Sam's problems at school. However, given Sam's seemingly "normal" behavior at home, SES may not be an issue in his case. Be careful not to let research on the effects of SES on behavior bias your assessment and subsequent intervention.*

THE FAMILY AND IMMEDIATE ENVIRONMENT IN INFANCY AND EARLY CHILDHOOD

Because infants and young children are so dependent on their caregivers for their well-being, social workers must assess many different aspects of the environment when working with children and families. Many families bring their children to social workers in an attempt to "fix" the children. However, as you learned from systems theory, only rarely is a problem isolated to one individual. More frequently, social workers must assess and intervene with the family and larger systems to help people overcome problems that seem to be stemming from an individual's behavior. This section discusses some of the more common topics that social workers face when working with children and families.

Parenting

Earlier, we examined parenting issues related to children's temperaments, but many other facets of parenting are important for social workers to understand when working with children and families. Many of these are related to parenting styles, feelings of competency, and skills that can be used to improve parenting.

Unfortunately, parenting is not an innate skill; many new and even seasoned parents express anxiety over the daunting task of rearing a child. Part of this anxiety can be traced to the inundation of advice, much of which is contradictory, that is available in the popular media. Many parents become overwhelmed with information and find it difficult to make decisions about their parenting. This is particularly true for parents of children who are disabled or who have other special challenges. Moreover, new research is perpetually being produced, adding to the confusion about what constitutes a "good parent." But what are the characteristics of a good parent? Which skills are needed to be successful? How much of a child's healthy development and ultimate success in life can be attributed to nurture? None of these questions is straightforward or easy to answer. However, there is some basic knowledge that social workers can use in their work with parents.

Through her research, Diana Baumrind (1968, 1971) identified different styles of parenting that help describe patterns that parents consistently use in child rearing. These are described in Exhibit 7.3. Some evidence suggests that in Western culture, authoritative parenting is the most effective style for rearing well-adjusted children (Bronstein & Clauson, 1993; Eisenberg, Chang, Ma, & Huang, 2009; Slicker, 1998). Researchers argue that this style helps to teach children skills of compromise, negotiation, and decision making while helping them to value independence. However, this conclusion may not hold true for parents in other cultures. Not all cultures hold the same values with regard to child rearing, and parenting styles vary widely to reflect what characteristics are valued and thus instilled in children. Evidence suggests that what is important and most effective in parenting, maybe even more so than a particular style, is consistency and caring (Luxton, 2008; Whiting & Edwards, 1988).

Another factor that tends to be associated with positive parenting and child-rearing environment is parental self-efficacy. Recall the discussion on Albert Bandura's social learning theory in Chapter 3. A central tenet of his theory is self-efficacy—our expectation that we can successfully perform a task. Research suggests that parental feelings of self-efficacy are associated with certain positive child behaviors such

---

EXHIBIT 7.3

Baumrind's Parenting Styles

- *Authoritarian:* Parent is controlling and insists on conformity; establishes rules and ideas about how child should behave. This style is associated with children who are unhappy, fearful, and anxious and who lack initiative and communication skills.

- *Authoritative:* Parent offers some control, consistent support, and compromise; encourages independence with limits and negotiation. This style is associated with children who are cheerful, motivated, and self-directed and who demonstrate social competence in communication and cooperation.

- *Neglectful:* Parent is uninvolved with the child; offers little structure for or control over the child. This style is associated with children who have low self-esteem and poor self-control and who are immature and socially incompetent.

- *Indulgent:* Parent is highly involved with child; does not offer much structure for or control over the child; makes few demands of the child. This style is associated with children who show poor self-control and a lack of respect for others.

Source: Adapted from Baumrind, 1968, 1971

as compliance, enthusiasm, persistence, and affection toward the caregiver as well as with positive cognitive performance by the child (Coleman & Karraker, 2003; T. Jones, 2007). It may be that parents who feel efficacious in their parenting also feel empowered to manage their responsibilities and to find intrinsic interest in parenting and their children.

Keeping in mind the limitations to this research (for example, no causal relationship has been established between self-efficacy and positive child outcomes), social workers who work with children and families can apply these ideas using Bandura's theory as well as concepts from other frameworks such as the strengths perspective. Identifying parent strengths and building on those will help increase parents' feelings of self-efficacy and empowerment, which may in turn help promote their children's positive development.

As Sam's social worker, you may want to assess how his parents' parenting styles may be affecting his behavior at school, keeping in mind that cultural variations in patterns and expectations may exist. Perhaps helping Sam's parents to feel more effective would improve their parenting skills, which may influence his behavior at school. To begin, you might identify strengths that Sam's parents have in their parenting skills, building on these to increase their feelings of self-efficacy.

Grandparenting

Because people are living longer, they have more opportunities than previous generations to interact with their grandchildren and great-grandchildren. Today many older adults are also caring for their grandchildren because their own children have problems such as unemployment, substance abuse, chronic illness or disability, and issues related to criminal behavior. According to the United States Census (2010a), 7.5 million children, approximately 10 percent of all children in the United States, lived with a grandparent in 2010. Even when grandparents do not act as primary caregivers, they can fulfill vital roles in the lives of their grandchildren. Generally, grandparents can provide stable and loving environments for their grandchildren. Moreover, in cases of parental abuse or neglect, grandparents can provide some consistency in their grandchildren's lives that may improve the children's chances of becoming well-adjusted adults despite an inhospitable environment.

Exhibit 7.4 describes the different categories of grandparenting styles that tend to characterize Western society (Neugarten & Weinstein, 1964). Whether or not they want to, grandparents are increasingly assuming the surrogate parent role. And, because more generations are living simultaneously, grandparents have more opportunity to assume other roles as well, such as the fun seeker. However, geographic boundaries also create situations where grandparents find themselves in the distant figure role.

Research indicates that many factors can influence the quality of the

PHOTO 7-B

Grandparents often play significant roles in their grandchildren's lives

Source: Scott T. Baxter/Getty Images

EXHIBIT 7.4

Grandparenting Styles

- *Fun seeker:* Grandparent acts as a playmate to grandchild; both achieve mutual enjoyment out of the relationship.

- *Distant figure:* Grandparent has only occasional contact with grandchild; grandparent has little involvement in grandchild's life.

- *Surrogate parent:* Grandparent assumes much of the caregiving responsibility for the grandchild.

- *Formal figure:* Grandparent is involved only to provide babysitting services occasionally or to give special treats to the grandchild; all child rearing is left to the parents.

- *Reservoir of family wisdom:* Grandparent takes on the authoritarian role and acts as sage to pass on skills, traditions, stories, and so on.

Source: Adapted from Neugarten & Weinstein, 1964

grandparent–grandchild relationship. The role of grandparents in grandchildren's lives can vary according to factors such as age of the grandparent and grandchild (e.g., grandparents are often caregivers to younger children and confidants to older grandchildren, and older grandparents may have health or mobility problems that limit their interactions with grandchildren) (Crosnoe & Elder, 2002; Dunifon & Bajracharya, 2012). Ethnic background and gender may also affect the grand-parent–grandchild relationship. For example, some research indicates that black grandparents take on more parent-like roles than white grandparents, and that granddaughters tend to have closer relationships with grandparents than grandsons, particularly with maternal grandmothers (Hirsch, Mickus, & Boerger, 2002). Finally, family structure may play a role in the grandparent–grandchild relationship, with grandchildren from divorced families having less contact with paternal grandparents (Creasey, 1993).

Many grandparents benefit emotionally and psychologically from interacting with their grandchildren. For example, grandparenting may be a useful develop-mental task for older adults in Erikson's integrity versus despair stage. If older adults can remain active and feel useful to younger generations, they may be more likely to feel a sense of accomplishment. More on grandparenting is presented in Chapter 12.

> *The case scenario does not say whether Sam has grandparents. If he does, and if the relationship between Sam's immediate family and his grandparents is positive, this relationship could be considered a strength in Sam's case. You could discuss with the family the roles that Sam's grandparents could take in his life to support his develop-ment, keeping in mind the cultural expectations of immediate and extended family in child-rearing practices.*

Siblings

Sibling interaction has been a topic of much research and debate. In the United States, more than 80 percent of children have at least one sibling, and the influences that siblings have on one another are factors to consider in social work. The role that siblings play in one another's lives is probably even more important than that of parents. Siblings take on many roles in the socialization process for one another, including mentor, teacher, playmate, adversary, and supporter; these roles usually last a lifetime (Cicirelli, 1994; Tucker & Updegraff, 2010).

Personality Traits and Birth Order   One area of study that has brought with it a great deal of interest is personality traits and birth order. Some evidence supports the idea that characteristics of first-born children differ from those of later-born children, though much of the difference can be accounted for by the different ways in which parents interact with first-born and later-born children as well as other factors such as the spacing of children and the resources available to the family.

Generally, first-born children tend to have more access to parental time and energy than later-born children, and parents show more engagement in first-born children's lives (Steelman, Powell, Werum, & Carter, 2002). A literature review on birth order found that first-born children tend to be higher achievers with higher

IQs and self-esteem (Eckstein, 2000). One study conducted on over 240,000 men and controlling for numerous psychosocial factors found that the eldest children scored about 3 percent higher on IQ tests than second children and 4 percent higher than third-born children (Bjerkedal, Kristensen, Skjeret, & Brevik, 2007). In addition, first-born children have greater academic success, mature earlier socially and sexually, are more easily influenced by authority, are more conformist to parents' values and dependent on approval, and are more likely to be leaders, responsible, and self-disciplined than later-born children. Conversely, later-born children tend to be more empathic, popular, and "spoiled" than first-born children.

Finally, children without siblings ("only" children) showed similar characteristics as first-born children (Eckstein, 2000). They are more likely to have a high need for achievement, go to college, and be selfish, trusting, and cooperative.

Social workers need to consider how birth order might affect a family and its individual members. Some researchers argue that as a society, North Americans tend to "buy into" birth order differences without thinking about the limitations to the research on birth order issues or how mediating variables might affect birth order differences. People may behave in ways that are expected of children born in a certain order, or they may not (Herrera, Zajonc, Wieczorkowska, & Cichomski, 2003; Steelman *et al.*, 2002).

Family Size and Access to Resources   Some evidence suggests that later-born children are more likely than earlier-born children to be the beneficiaries of their parents' economic resources (for example, financial assistance in college) because their parents are older and more financially stable. Their parents are also more likely to have renewed energy to focus on them, particularly if the first-born is older, independent, and lives away from home (Steelman *et al.*, 2002).

Another consideration that social workers should keep in mind when working with children and families is the size of the family. In addition to many other challenges, large families are more likely to live in poverty, and their children are more likely to have lower levels of educational achievement than smaller families. One explanation for this is the **resource dilution model.** This model posits that the larger the family, the fewer the resources available to give to each member (Steelman *et al.*, 2002).

Social and reproductive policies are often based on stereotypes about family size (Herrera *et al.*, 2003; Steelman *et al.*, 2002). For example, family planning and other services may be more accessible to families with more than one child on the assumption that single-child families do not need extra support. Specifically, these services may target families with multiple children to prevent or intervene with problems associated with birth order such as rebelliousness or acting out that might be expected of later-born children. Families with only one child may be viewed as not being at risk for such problems. Social workers can help educate clients and policy-makers about the strengths and limitations surrounding knowledge on birth order and family size to ensure that issues related to it are viewed more realistically.

Since Sam is an only child, you may expect certain behaviors from him based on the resources his parents are able to give him. However, cultural dynamics may make these behaviors more or less pronounced, depending on Sam's parents' expectations of him as an only child. You will need to better understand Sam's parents' beliefs about the role of children to accurately assess how being an only child in this family may affect Sam's behavior. Using multiple perspectives, such as person-in-environment and biopsychosocial perspectives, while bringing in information discussed here may help you to more accurately and comprehensively assess Sam's situation.

Day Care

Given the importance of early caregiving on child development, it is not surprising that there is so much debate about the strengths and limitations of day care. Currently, approximately 2 million children in the United States, many of whom are from low-income families, receive formal care. The rate of day care use is directly related to the number of single parent households, the number of women in the workforce (particularly women who are receiving welfare), and the recognition of the impact of early educational experiences on child development.

The cost for day care varies a great deal; unfortunately, many low-income families cannot afford quality day care. For many working parents, wages provided through service-sector jobs are not adequate to pay for quality child care (Magnuson, Meyers, & Waldfogel, 2007). The cost of child care for some families is greater than costs for housing or car payments and can exceed the cost of sending a child through college (Moodie-Dyer, 2011).

Day care facilities in the United States vary greatly in the type and quality of care that they provide. Arrangements can range from large centers providing care for large numbers of children, to small nonprofit facilities run by religious organizations, to care given in private homes. Further, given the increase in nonstandard work schedules (approximately 40 percent of the U.S. labor force works nonstandard hours), some day care providers are offering night time and weekend care in addition to traditional daytime care (Presser & Ward, 2011).

Data from a longitudinal study on day care experiences suggests that quality day care in which caregivers are responsive to children shows no adverse effects on child behavior (Owen, 2002). More recent research suggests that aggressive behavior might be an exception to this generalization; that is, the more time children spend in non-parental care, the more likely they are to exhibit disruptive behavior. However, this research also suggests that behavioral problems tend to dissipate after the sixth grade and that children in non-parental care also tend to exhibit higher vocabulary scores than children who do not spend time in non-parental care (Belsky, 2009). Other research supports this idea that the higher the quality of care, the more advanced the children's verbal and cognitive abilities. This research also concludes that children from low-income families are more likely to receive low-quality care (Owen, 2002), which disproportionately affects those from some minority groups.

Other studies have indicated that parental knowledge about the quality of day care facilities is lacking. For instance, many parents are not familiar with center policies on hiring, firing, and training, what licensure requirements the center meets (or does not meet), or how their children spend the day (Shpancer *et al.*, 2002). Social workers can be a source of education for parents as they seek day care facilities for their children, and they can help parents, particularly those with low incomes, to advocate for more quality care. Simply by making parents more aware of what constitutes quality care, social workers can help empower parents to secure the best possible care for their children. In addition to designing interventions on the individual level, social workers may need to rely on community organization theory to guide interventions that will increase the availability of affordable, quality day care.

Social policy has not kept pace with the funding or developing of quality day care for children (Shapiro & Applegate, 2002). Social workers can help to educate policy-makers about the role of day care for families. Using theories and perspectives such as family systems, person-in-environment, or even Erikson's or Piaget's theories, social workers can articulate the influence of day care on the developmental needs of children as well as the short- and long-term ramifications that care has on children, families, and larger society. Those who are making decisions about the structure of day care should be knowledgeable about how care affects children and families on multiple levels, particularly low-income families.

As Sam's social worker, you may want to find out what child care arrangements his parents used when Sam was younger. It may be that Sam's parents had to rely on low-quality day care, which could have impacted his development when he was an infant. Problems with early development could be affecting his current development and behavior.

Child Abuse and Neglect

Child maltreatment is a widespread problem in the United States. The term **maltreatment** is a broad one that encompasses both abuse and neglect. **Abuse** refers to specific and repeated acts of sexual, physical, and emotional mistreatment; whereas **neglect** refers to an ongoing pattern in which caregivers fail to meet their children's basic needs. Quick Guide 10 lists common signs of various forms of child maltreatment.

According to the U.S. Department of Health and Human Services (2013), approximately 865,478 children were abused or neglected in 2012. Over three-quarters of these (78 percent) were neglect cases; 29.7 percent of the cases were children

QUICK GUIDE 10	Common Signs of Child Maltreatment		
PHYSICAL ABUSE	**SEXUAL ABUSE**	**EMOTIONAL ABUSE**	**NEGLECT**
• Frequently occurring cuts, scrapes, or scratches • Multiple fractures • Head injuries • Internal injuries (for example, spleen, kidney) • Burns, especially those that take the shape of common objects (for example, cigarettes) or that occur in unlikely places (for example, bottom, stomach)	• Sexually transmitted diseases • Throat or mouth problems • Pregnancy • Bruising in the genital area • Genital discharge or problems urinating • Low self-esteem • Anger, fear, anxiety, depression • Withdrawal or aggression • Inappropriate sexual behavior	• Low self-esteem • Anxiety, depression • Poor outlook on life • Suicidal behavior • Emotional instability and poor impulse control • Substance abuse and eating disorders • Relationship problems • Violent or criminal behavior • Poor school performance	• Failure to thrive syndrome • Psychosocial dwarfism • Lack of supervision • Poor hygiene • Lack of appropriate health and mental health care • Exposure to hazards • Poor household sanitation

Source: Adapted from Mather & Lager, 2000

younger than 12 months; and about half were Caucasian, while 22 percent were African American and 21 percent were Hispanic. An estimated 1,315 children died due to maltreatment, with nearly 44 percent of child fatalities being younger than four years old. More than 80 percent of perpetrators of maltreatment were parents, and women were more than half (54 percent) of all perpetrators (U.S. Department of Health and Human Services, 2011). Keep in mind that these are likely to be underestimates of the occurrence of maltreatment since these numbers represent reported cases. No estimates exist for how many cases of maltreatment go unreported each year.

Consequences of maltreatment extend to children's physical, cognitive, emotional, psychological, and behavioral development. Some of the effects of abuse and neglect include physical injuries, brain damage, low self-esteem, substance abuse, teen pregnancy, relational problems, low academic achievement, and aggressive and criminal behavior (Child Welfare Information Gateway, 2008; Hildyard & Wolfe, 2002; Kelley, Thornberry, & Smith, 1997). Maltreatment is also a risk factor for issues such as anxiety, mood disorders, personality disorders, and reduced volume of the hippocampus in adulthood, further validating the role that stress plays in brain development (Teicher, Anderson, & Polcari, 2012).

There are also social costs to maltreatment. The judicial, health care, child welfare, mental health care, and law enforcement systems respond directly to cases of child maltreatment. Moreover, costs are incurred in areas such as special education, teen pregnancy support, domestic violence services, and welfare payments, which are indirectly related to child maltreatment (U.S. Department of Health and Human Services, 2003, 2007b).

The causes of child maltreatment must be viewed from a person-in-environment or ecological perspective because they are multifaceted and complex. In assessing cases of maltreatment, social workers will find issues contributing to maltreatment on many different levels, from the individual and familial levels to the social, economic, and cultural levels. Indeed, research points to the multifaceted nature of maltreatment. For example, research suggests that factors such as poverty, economic and other stressors, poor parenting skills, familial strife, lack of support systems, parental youth and inexperience, and characteristics common among special needs children (for example, disabilities and behavioral problems) increase the likelihood of maltreatment (Baumrind, 1994; Cicchetti & Toth, 2005; Martin & Lindsey, 2003).

Within child welfare services, social workers and other professionals and paraprofessionals work with children and families in maltreatment cases. Much of this work is reactive; that is, it takes place after maltreatment has occurred. There is certainly much that can be done for families who have entered the system due to maltreatment. However, there are many other roles that social workers can play to prevent maltreatment. Activities on the micro, mezzo, and macro levels are useful in the prevention of potential abuse and neglect problems. These might include making support resources accessible for new parents, particularly teen parents; providing quality and affordable day care, health care, and other professional services; and working toward more flexible legislation that supports and empowers women in the welfare system. Unfortunately in U.S. society, dollars tend to be spent on reactionary services, even though preventive services are ultimately cheaper in both economic and human costs.

THE LARGER SOCIAL ENVIRONMENT IN INFANCY AND EARLY CHILDHOOD

In this section, we will take a look at some of the macro issues that affect children and families. Although we touch on just a few topics that you will work with in your practice, they are important to consider, as they have far-reaching implications for the well-being of your clients. These topics include child protection, permanency planning, health care, and educational policy.

Child Protection

Child maltreatment remains a major problem in the United States, despite federal and state attempts to prevent it. Across the country, a complex network of child welfare services has been developed to work with the issue. For the most part, states have much control of these services and have a great deal of power in developing policies and guidelines for child protective services, though federal guidelines and mandates as well as local forces have some influence on policy development at the state level (Webb & Harden, 2003). Among the many policies that directly or indirectly address maltreatment issues, these two federal laws impact social work with children and families:

- Child Abuse Prevention and Treatment Act of 1974: Was established to provide support to states in developing and delivering child protective services. It also mandated that professionals, including social workers, report suspected abuse. This act also provides some funds for research and pilot programs on maltreatment.

- Adoption and Safe Families Act of 1997: Among other things, places a higher priority on the safety and well-being of the child than on family preservation (Waldfogel, 2001; Webb & Harden, 2003). This policy represents a shift in focus from previous decades, when family preservation was viewed as paramount, regardless of the family situation.

Generally, children who have been reported as abused or neglected are referred to a local child protective services (CPS) office. The role of CPS is to investigate reports of abuse and neglect and to assess the risks posed for the child. CPS also has the authority to remove the child from the home and make placements in the foster care system. CPS workers, many of whom are social workers, work in concert with court and family systems to develop plans that will best meet the needs of the maltreated child and her or his family (Waldfogel, 2001).

Many of the policies dealing with child maltreatment are the crux of social workers' work with children and families. These policies dictate the scope and nature of their work, which means that social workers, particularly those in government agencies, must be familiar with policy guidelines and laws.

In Sam's case, you do not know if there is any reason to suspect maltreatment, but both the Head Start teacher and you would be responsible for observing Sam and his behavior and reporting any suspicions about potential maltreatment. Social workers use guidelines such as those presented in Quick Guide 10 to assess whether certain children are at risk for abuse or neglect.

Permanency Planning: Foster Care, Adoption, and Family Support

Child protective services workers often work in conjunction with others to develop service objectives for families in the CPS system, which include permanency planning. **Permanency planning** focuses on long-term planning for children and families, either to prevent out-of-home placements or to make foster or adoptive placements as quickly as possible. The goal is to achieve stability for the child and her or his family without lengthy delays (Waldfogel, 2001).

Legislation associated with permanency planning includes the following:

- Indian Child Welfare Act of 1978: Gave tribes the right to intervene in child welfare issues, including the right to assume legal jurisdiction over children and their care.

- Adoption Assistance and Child Welfare Act of 1980: Required CPS to make reasonable efforts to prevent adoptive placements and provide service plans to avoid them.

- Child Welfare Services, Foster Care, and Adoption Assistance Reforms of 1993: Created the Family Preservation and Support Services Program. This law was enacted to provide funding for family preservation and support and prevention services that are delivered by CPS and community agencies.

- Multi-ethnic Placement Act of 1994: Developed to address issues of interracial adoptions. This legislation prevents agencies from discriminating against prospective foster or adoptive parents based on ethnic or national origin, although it does require that children's cultural needs be considered in placements.

- Adoption and Safe Families Act of 1997: Revisited and revised the Adoption Assistance and Child Welfare Act of 1980, specifying when adoption placements should not be made, pushing for permanency planning, and reducing the amount of time for placement from 18 to 12 months (Waldfogel, 2001).

As discussed earlier, social workers need to keep abreast of current legislation that influences permanency planning. These policies have direct consequences for the services that social workers can provide, but they also make statements about the current philosophy on issues such as abuse, neglect, the role of the family, and governmental and social responsibility for family support.

Often, social workers find that they either disagree with current federal philosophy on such issues or that the mandates coming from these philosophies are difficult to carry out in practice. Because clients' problems are usually multifaceted, a policy that seems reasonable on paper may be troublesome or even counterproductive to clients' goals in practice. For example, while permanency planning may seem like a noble goal, often social workers and families find that other barriers such as unemployment, mental illness, and lack of housing stand in the way of achieving this goal in the time frame mandated by law.

Further, processes that take place during permanency planning can create unintended problems. One study (Haight, Kagle, & Black, 2003) describes how developmental and attachment needs of children can be undermined by parent visits when their children are in foster care if they are not planned carefully and deliberately, using theoretical and other knowledge to guide the visits.

This issue helps to exemplify the need for social workers to have a broad knowledge base of theoretical and developmental information to help inform policy and practice guidelines. Social workers' knowledge of social action and legislative and policy development is also useful, as social workers are often the professionals who shape and interpret these policies and advocate for services for their clients.

Health Care

Throughout the book we have touched on the importance of health care for children. Much of this discussion has centered on problems that poverty and lack of access to care can cause in the short and long terms for the development of children. Access to health care is crucial for healthy prenatal development; however, once a child is born, the importance of access to regular, quality health care does not diminish.

Not surprisingly, lack of access to quality health care tends to be more common among children living in poverty than among children from wealthier families (DeVoe, Graham, Angier, Baez, & Krois, 2008; Huang, Yu, Liu, Young, & Wong, 2009; Scott & Ni, 2004). However, one large study of 1,536 children in 12 metropolitan areas indicated that children, regardless of socioeconomic status, received appropriate medical care only 47 percent of the time. These results suggest that all children are at risk for more long-term health problems due to the lack of proper medical attention when they are younger (Mangione-Smith *et al.*, 2007).

One role that social workers perform in their work with children and families is to facilitate access to federal, state, and local programs such as Medicaid and the State Children's Health Insurance Program (SCHIP). Medicaid, created in 1965 under the Social Security Act, is a joint federal and state program that provides medical care to low-income people. Many Medicaid recipients are children. SCHIP is a health insurance program created in 1997, and reauthorized in 2009, also under the Social Security Act. SCHIP expands health care benefits to uninsured children. Social workers can educate low-income families about programs like these as well as help them navigate the systems so they can gain access to these and similar programs.

Access to health care alone does not necessarily dictate positive developmental outcomes; many other factors such as income, housing, safety, and education also come into play (Roberts, 2002). Social workers who work with children may be able to mediate some of the problems caused by lack of health care by ensuring that other facets contributing to healthy development are in place while also working to ensure access to quality health care.

As part of a comprehensive assessment of Sam, you would want to make certain that he has access to quality health care. Because so much of Sam's development and

behavior depends on good health, this would be a primary element of the interven-
tion. Although there is no indication from the case scenario that Sam has any health
problems or that he does not receive regular care, you could discuss with his family
the importance of timely preventive services and treatment to ward off any future
problems.

Early Childhood Education

Provision of and access to quality education for young children have been long-standing issues for social workers. Because educational opportunities are vital for the short- and long-term development of children, ensuring that quality programs exist for children from all backgrounds is an important charge of the profession.

Head Start   One controversial area regarding education has to do with Head Start programs. Initiated in 1964 under the Lyndon Johnson administration as part of his Great Society, Head Start programs were developed to serve low-income children and families. These programs aspired to end the cycle of poverty by providing services that met children's social, nutritional, emotional, educational, and psychological needs.

Currently, more than 1,130,000 children attend Head Start programs nationwide. Ninety-eight percent of these children are four years old or younger, and approximately 60 percent are from ethnic minority groups (Administration for Children and Families, 2013). Generally, research indicates that Head Start programs can have some positive effects for low-income children. For example, several studies have suggested that children who attend Head Start show short-term cognitive gains and over time exhibit fewer personal and social problems, including dropping out of school and being unemployed. However, many studies have reported mixed results in Head Start's ability to break the cycle of poverty for families and to help African–American children maintain cognitive gains over time (Caputo, 2003).

Many social workers, legislators, and families agree that Head Start is beneficial to low-income children. However, they disagree as to how these programs should be funded, who should have control over their services and curricula, and how beneficial they truly are with regard to preventing future problems for children and allowing them to begin their elementary years on equal footing with other, more advantaged children. The conservative philosophy about entitlement programs that characterized the 1996 welfare reform measures during the Bill Clinton administration brought the debate over Head Start's value back to the forefront. Attempts to make the program more efficient and accountable continued through the George W. Bush and Barack Obama administrations. Though the political tone changes from administration to administration, the debate over Head Start and similar programs will likely continue.

One current debate revolves around who should administer the program. Some people argue that states should control the funding and development of programs so that they can be integrated with local preschool programs. Advocates of state control also propose that states become more accountable for raising the quality of Head Start curricula and focusing on literacy and math skills. Critics respond that the shift to state control would dismantle the program as it has been established, making its administration and evaluation disparate across states. That would make "proving" that such programs help low-income children even more difficult (Jacobson, 2003).

An Ecological Perspective on Educational Policy Despite the unclear consequences of Head Start programs on the long-term development and adjustment of low-income children, recent developmental research has underscored the importance of the environmental context in which low-income children are reared and educated. Specifically, this body of literature suggests that the ecological model is an appropriate and effective way in which to view the problems of low-income children and from which to build interventions (Anderson *et al.*, 2002; Berlin, 2001; Evans, 2001). Because Head Start programs approach problems from a framework that closely parallels the ecological model, they may prove to be an effective way to promote optimal development of young, low-income children.

> *In Sam's case, you might be able to make some useful progress by conceptualizing his situation from the ecological model. Many factors influence Sam's development besides biological processes and elements of Sam's immediate environment. Recognizing that many ethnic minorities may not reap long-term benefits from Head Start and that the program may not be addressing cultural needs important to Sam and his family, you may be able to suggest other ways in which you can help Sam and his family meet those needs. Moreover, you may be able to help the local Head Start program itself modify some of its practices to better fit the emotional, cognitive, cultural, and social needs of Sam and his family.*

One mandate within NASW's *Code of Ethics* (approved 1996, revised 2008) states that "social workers should monitor and evaluate policies, the implementation of programs, and practice interventions" (p. 25). You can help the local program review its evaluation processes to ensure that reliable data is collected on program effectiveness. Results in outcome research on Head Start programs have tended to be mixed, which is in part why they continue to be controversial. Social workers can use their research skills to help Head Start programs to design and implement research methods that can add reliable and valid information to the debate.

CONCLUSION

Infancy and early childhood is a time of rapid growth and development. Some of the hallmark developmental activities that take place during this time include language acquisition and emotional and motor development. In addition to physical changes, infants and young children experience other changes on individual and social levels that affect their long-term development.

When problems with development occur, social workers need to be able to comprehensively assess issues on different levels to develop effective interventions that will bring about permanent, positive change. Moreover, because of the great variability that exists in development, including variability in cultural definitions of what "normal" development is, social workers must be aware of their own viewpoints on developmental issues. This awareness will help to ensure that social workers provide ethical and culturally appropriate services that promote children's optimal development.

When dealing with developmental issues, social workers can easily become entrenched in medical and similar models to guide assessment and intervention. Viewing these issues from the strengths perspective as well as other perspectives that incorporate environmental factors will help social workers move beyond physical considerations. Given all of the emphasis on "normal" development during infancy and early childhood, social workers need to consider the strengths that clients and their families and communities possess.

MAIN POINTS

- Major developmental milestones in infancy and early childhood include language acquisition, emotional development, and fine and gross motor skill development. Understanding the debates over biological versus behavioral sources of language acquisition helps social workers to assess and intervene with their clients effectively.

- Attachment theory suggests that the quality of attachment to caregivers affects the infant's development. Ainsworth developed four infant attachment styles: secure, insecure avoidant, insecure resistant, and insecure disorganized.

- Gender identity develops in early childhood and is thought to be a complex interaction between innate processes and the social environment. Gender expression involves the ways we communicate our gender identity to others.

- Temperament is the consistent ways in which individuals respond to their environment and is thought to be present at birth. Chess and Thomas identified three main temperament types in infants: the easy child, difficult child, and slow-to-warm-up child.

* Research indicates that children from families with low SES are more likely to suffer from poor health, lack of access to quality day care, and long-term developmental outcomes than children from high-SES groups.

* Interactions with parents, grandparents, and family size and birth order have a lasting effect on children, and those interactions are, in turn, influenced by the children's characteristics.

* Social workers often work directly with children who have been abused or neglected and thus must be familiar with federal and state protective policies and services. Along with protective services, social workers are often involved in permanency planning for children and families who have abuse and neglect issues.

* Lack of access to quality health care is a major problem for many children, and it can have long-term consequences for children's development. Programs such as SCHIP and Medicaid are designed to provide health care services for these children.

* Head Start is a federal program geared toward enhancing the social, psychological, and educational needs of low-income children. It is often the subject of debates over funding, administration, and effectiveness.

EXERCISES

1. *RAINN interactive case at* www.routledgesw.com/cases. Alan is concerned about his relationship with his one-year-old son. He has heard about attachment problems and worries that his experience with sexual assault makes it hard for him to feel close to his son.
   a. How would you explain attachment to Alan, and what questions could you ask to help him assess if he has cause to worry about attachment issues with his young son?
   b. What theoretical lens (or lenses) from previous chapters would you use to help you understand the needs of Alan's son? How could those theories help you to explain to Alan the needs of his son?
2. *Sanchez Family interactive case at* www.routledgesw.com/cases. Review the major issues involving the Sanchez family, paying particular attention to the description of Joey, the grandson. Then answer the following questions:
   a. Given Joey's age, what developmental milestones might you expect him to be experiencing?

b. In what ways might his environment (for example, exposure to cocaine, placement in foster and kinship care, eligibility for services) affect his physical and emotional development (for example, developmental milestones, attachments)?

c. If you were to work with Joey, what ethical and cultural issues might you want to consider?

d. What strengths might Joey or the family possess that could be used in working with Joey?

3. *Riverton interactive case at* www.routledgesw.com/cases. Review the situation of Felipe and Maria Gonzales, and then answer the following questions:

a. How might the information presented in this chapter be relevant to the problems faced by Felipe and Maria Gonzales? Be specific.

b. How could you use this information to work with Felipe and Maria?

4. *Riverton interactive case at* www.routledgesw.com/cases. Review the situation of Mary Stark and then answer the following questions:

a. What issues presented in this chapter might be relevant to Mary's situation and why?

b. Do you think there might be any information presented in Chapter 6, on prenatal development, that might be relevant to Mary's case? In what ways?

c. What theoretical perspective might be useful to you in conceptualizing Mary's situation and why?

d. Using the theory you chose in the last question and the information in this chapter and Chapter 6, how could you proceed with an intervention for Mary and her family?

5. *Hudson City interactive case at* www.routledgesw.com/cases. Review the issues in the case and answer the following questions:

a. In what ways could the issues facing the community affect development of infants and those in early childhood?

b. How could these issues impact parents and the ways they interact with their children?

6. *RAINN interactive case at* www.routledgesw.com/cases. If Sarah decided to raise her baby, what are some programs that you could refer her to that will help both her and her baby?

CHAPTER 8

Development in Middle Childhood

Eric is an eight-year-old boy being reared by gay parents who adopted him when he was an infant. Eric's biological mother is of Chinese descent, and his biological father is Caucasian. One of Eric's adoptive fathers is of Chinese descent and one is Caucasian. Eric's parents have brought him to a social worker because of "behavioral problems." Eric's parents complain that he refuses to do what he is told, has trouble keeping up with his school work, and does not get along with other children his age. In fact, Eric's parents claim that he does not have any close friends and spends a lot of his time playing by himself. Eric shows little interest in age-appropriate activities, and he frequently appears withdrawn and incapable of attending to school or other activities. Eric's parents are concerned that he will fall behind developmentally and will be held back a grade in school if his performance does not improve.

MIDDLE CHILDHOOD IS A TIME OF CONTINUED BIOPSYCHOSOCIAL DEVELOPMENT and, as such, can be characterized by problems and worries for parents and caregivers. In the case scenario, we see Eric struggling with issues in many areas, and, naturally, his parents are worried that he will be "left behind" in his physical, emotional, and social development.

In this chapter, we explore some developmental milestones that occur in middle childhood as well as common issues surrounding education, family, the media, and peer relations that social workers face when working with children in this age range and their families.

DEVELOPMENTAL MILESTONES IN OLDER CHILDREN

Middle childhood, or the age range of five or six to approximately 11 years old, is a time when growth and development continue at a steady, consistent pace, particularly in the area of physical, cognitive, and motor skills. During this time, children are increasingly exposed to the outside world of their peers, and they become more focused on achievement and self-control.

- *Physical development.* Middle childhood is characterized by increases in height, weight, muscle mass, and coordination skills. Children's skeletal structure is taking its adult shape as permanent teeth are established and bones become harder. These last changes are important to note because children's dental hygiene and other nutritional habits can have a great impact on their health later in life. During middle childhood, children continue to develop and refine their motor skills such as hitting, running, jumping, climbing, and other activities that require fine motor skills with the fingers and hands. Though children are able to sit still and attend to tasks, they need to be physically active to continue to develop their motor skills (Nuba, Searson, & Sheiman, 1994). Unfortunately, with computers, television, and other electronic media competing for their time and attention, many children do not get the exercise they need to refine their skills, which often leads to childhood obesity and other problems in adolescence and adulthood. From the medical model, middle childhood is a crucial time for physical development in which children need a balance of physical and intellectual stimulation as well as proper nutrition and other positive habits to promote lifelong health.

- *Cognitive development.* Children continue to develop critical thinking skills and the ability to think with more flexibility and complexity than before. Children show gains in memory, attention, and the ability to think about details of tasks. Long-term memory tends to increase during this time, as does their ability to link new information with existing knowledge. According to Jean Piaget, children at this age develop schemas, or frameworks for organizing information, as they grow older, which helps them incorporate increasing amounts of information. In turn, acquiring more information helps children to improve their memories and further develop schemas for other things. Along with improving memory, children also become better at critical thinking skills, which means that they are better able to understand things on a deeper level, taking into consideration different points of view to evaluate perspectives and information. This latter point also relates to Piaget's cognitive development theory. Children who are in the concrete operational stage can think flexibly, which allows them to compare and contrast information and use abstract skills to consider information (Piaget, 1952).

- *Emotional and personality development.* Middle childhood is a time for developing greater abilities to define self and emotions. In younger years, children tend to define themselves based on external characteristics such as age and eye and hair color. In middle childhood, children tend to use more internal characteristics to define themselves. For example, children can describe themselves as kind, intelligent, generous, or popular (Harter, 1999). Middle childhood is also characterized by an increased ability to understand and express complex emotions such as pride, guilt, and jealousy. Moreover, these emotional states tend to become more integrated into children's sense of self and sense of personal responsibility. Children can better understand how emotions are related to various events and actions, and they become more adept at concealing certain emotions and finding alternative or more socially acceptable ways of expressing certain emotions (Wintre & Vallance, 1994). Children with secure attachments to caregivers tend to be more adept at expressing and processing negative emotions than children who do not have secure attachments (Waters *et al.*, 2010). Further, self-control related to impulse control, delayed gratification, and modulated emotional expression in childhood has been shown to predict factors such as physical health, personal finances, criminal behavior, and various mental health and substance abuse problems in adulthood (Moffitt *et al.*, 2011).

Quick Guide 11 summarizes the developmental milestones for middle childhood.

QUICK GUIDE 11	**Developmental Milestones in Middle Childhood**	
PHYSICAL	COGNITIVE	PERSONALITY AND EMOTION
• Increases in height, weight, muscle mass, and coordination skills.	• Continued development of critical thinking skills and the ability to think with more flexibility and complexity than before.	• Increased ability to define self through internal and social characteristics.
• Skeletal structure is taking its adult shape as permanent teeth are established and bones become harder.	• Gains in memory, attention, and the ability to think about details of tasks.	• Increased ability to understand complex emotions.
• Continued development and refinement of motor skills such as hitting, running, jumping, climbing, and other activities that require fine motor skills with the fingers and hands.	• Long-term memory tends to increase during this time as does children's ability to link new information with existing knowledge.	• Improvements in the ability to control and redirect emotions.

Let us look at the kinds of developmental issues that might be occurring with Eric. You are not given much information about his physical and cognitive development, but you could collect this information through a biopsychosocial assessment.

Eric's parents are complaining about his lack of interest in "age-appropriate" activities; you might want to know what kinds of activities Eric's parents consider age-appropriate. Because children develop at different rates and because parents are often misinformed about what is "normal," it is possible that Eric is not experiencing any problems in this area. Rather, his parents may have expectations for Eric that are not necessarily appropriate. However, they have reported that Eric does not spend much time interacting with peers or engaging in schoolwork, which may be a sign that he is struggling, because children at this age tend to be focused in these areas. In general, you will need to conduct an in-depth and detailed assessment of particular behaviors, which may include a referral to a physician or psychologist for additional testing, to ascertain the level of Eric's development and whether he may be experiencing some developmental problems that need attention.

THE INDIVIDUAL IN MIDDLE CHILDHOOD

Developmental processes that take place in middle childhood can impact individual children and their families in many ways. Some children move through middle childhood smoothly, with no remarkable events that cause concern. Others may have some trouble developmentally that can cause problems academically, socially, or otherwise. This section focuses on some of the issues on an individual level that may come to the attention of social workers who work with clients in this age range and their families.

Intelligence and Intelligence Testing

Traditional definitions of intelligence, which rely on standardized intelligence tests and IQ (which is discussed later in this section), play a significant role in society. Many social institutions, including schools, use standardized definitions and assessments to categorize people into groups based on their intellectual abilities. These groupings often form the basis for receiving certain services, being placed in certain programs, and being labeled as competent to perform certain tasks.

While standardized definitions of intelligence have their uses, a great deal of controversy surrounds the degree to which society relies on these definitions. In fact, there is not one agreed-upon definition of traditional intelligence, so the concept can mean very different things to different people. In addition, theorists have developed models that try to account for the different ways that people can be considered intelligent.

Theories of Diverse Intelligences In contrast to the traditional ways in which we think about intelligence, Robert J. Sternberg's **triarchic theory of intelligence** emphasizes what people encounter in their environment as well as how they adapt to their environment. This theory focuses on how people think and solve problems (Sternberg, 1977, 1985).

- *Componential intelligence:* This is akin to the usual way we think about intelligence. It describes intelligence that is based in the way people process and analyze information. This component focuses on the way people formulate ideas, argue points, and evaluate results. People who are high in componential intelligence perform well on standardized IQ tests.

- *Experiential intelligence:* This component focuses on how people perform tasks. It describes how people bring in new information and incorporate it into what they already know to solve problems. People who are high in experiential intelligence can master knowledge and tasks to perform them as if on automatic pilot, which frees them to learn new things. This is also known as "insightful" intelligence.

- *Contextual intelligence:* This component stresses the practical side of a person's intelligence. It emphasizes a person's ability to adapt to new situations and to successfully navigate in different environments. Another way to describe this component is "street smarts." People who are high in contextual intelligence are good at "working the system" or "jumping through the hoops."

Source: Adapted from Sternberg, 1977, 1985

EXHIBIT 8.1

Sternberg's Triarchic Theory of Intelligence

Sternberg's theory has three main components (hence the name "triarchic") that explain a range of ways in which intelligence can be expressed. These components—componential intelligence, experiential intelligence, and contextual intelligence—are described in Exhibit 8.1. As you can see, this combination of components allows for individual differences in the way people approach problems.

Many professionals view Sternberg's approach to intelligence as a more positive and strengths-based way to think about people who score below average on standardized intelligence tests. This theory can help to explain why some people who do not seem to possess high levels of typical intelligence are able to succeed in life, despite barriers that appear insurmountable to others. Some social workers would argue that a theory such as this one is invaluable in their work with clients. It also speaks to the need to revisit the ways in which cognitive skills of children and adults are evaluated, given that these evaluations are often used as criteria for access to services and programs.

Sternberg's theory has limitations:

- It describes only one of many factors that can impact human behavior. After all, how useful can a theory be to social workers that describes whether someone is more likely to be good at crunching numbers or "jumping through the hoops" at her or his workplace?

- The underlying concepts can be difficult to define, measure, and evaluate. How do social workers define "street smarts," for example?

- Finding ways to validate and justify the use of alternative forms of intelligence can be daunting, given the widespread use of standardized intelligence testing. How can social workers prove to policy-makers the value of investing in people who have skills that differ from those included in traditional definitions of intelligence?

Other theorists have also debated the idea that intelligence encompasses a singular characteristic. For example, Howard Gardner (1983) proposed the theory of **multiple intelligences,** which states that individuals can possess competencies in many areas, including the linguistic, spatial, interpersonal, and natural. Daniel Goleman (2006) proposed the notion that people can possess emotional intelligence, which involves characteristics such as empathy, motivation, and self-awareness. Some leaders and educators have touted fostering emotional intelligence and the regulation of emotion as ways in which to stem bullying and increase collaboration and cooperation. However, some research suggests there is a dark side to emotional intelligence. Kilduff, Chiaburu, & Menges (2010) posit that some who are skilled at emotional regulation may use their skills to advance their own interests, even at the expense of others. People can become masters at manipulating situations and the emotions of others, while disguising their true emotions and motives. For example, Adolf Hitler manipulated the masses through carefully regulated and strategically expressed emotions, which motivated others to do things without reasoning or critically thinking about the consequences. Thus, emotional intelligence can be used for both prosocial and deviant purposes (Côté, DeCelles, McCarthy, VanKleef, & Hideg, 2011).

Standardized Intelligence Tests   Social work with children and their families frequently involves some use of standardized intelligence tests. For example, social workers often use test scores to help develop interventions because many school-based and other programs rely on these scores to determine individual needs. Understanding the structure of intelligence tests, their uses, and their strengths and limitations can help social workers to ensure that these tests are applied as fairly and appropriately as possible and that they do not end up harming clients in the long run.

Common standardized intelligence tests include these two:

- *Stanford-Binet intelligence test:* First developed by French psychologist Alfred Binet in 1905 to identify children with learning problems. Binet developed the concept of mental age, which compares a person's mental development with that of others. Mental age was used by William Stern to devise the **intelligence quotient (IQ)** that we are familiar with today. The IQ score is calculated by dividing a person's mental age by her or his chronological age and then multiplying the quotient by 100. Thus, a person whose mental and chronological ages are the same will have an IQ of 100, which is considered to be an average score on standardized tests. Over time, the Stanford-Binet test has been revised and used with large and diverse samples. The test, which can be administered to persons aged two years and older, consists of questions that tap into verbal, quantitative, and abstract/visual reasoning as well as short-term memory.

- *Wechsler scales:* Developed by David Wechsler to test three different age groups: 4 to 6½ years of age, 6 to 16 years of age, and adults 17+. These scales provide an overall IQ score as well as two separate scores on verbal and performance IQ.

The way intelligence is assessed or tested has a great deal to do with policies and programs designed to meet the needs of people whose intelligence scores are considered either above or below average. Both those giving standardized intelligence tests and those taking them often believe that they are tests of ability or capability in specific areas. Many people view traditional intelligence as a genetic characteristic, represented by a numerical value, that can predetermine a person's limits with regard to her or his capabilities (Nash, 2001). This belief can have long-term consequences for those who take the tests.

Another serious criticism of standardized IQ tests is that they are Eurocentric, meaning that they test for people's abilities to perform in ways that follow standards of the white majority, which are deemed the only valid standards. Minority group members are often faced with questions that are foreign to them and do not represent their experiences (Craig & Beishuizen, 2002; Freedle, 2006; Gould, 2008). For example, in the early 20th century when the United States began to experience high numbers of European immigrants, particularly from southern and eastern regions, intelligence testing was used to validate claims of intellectual superiority among certain groups of Europeans and justify their discriminatory treatment. These tests were often given to arriving immigrants, many of whom did not speak English or had never experienced North American culture, so they could not understand the test items, nor did they have the context from which to draw correct answers. Ultimately, these immigrants would score poorly on the tests and be labeled "feeble minded" and "inferior," fueling arguments against immigrants (Gould, 1996). Professionals and researchers also considered earlier versions of these standardized tests to be culturally biased against nonwhites living in rural areas and in low-socioeconomic groups. Even though someone not living in the dominant environment might offer a perfectly sound, rational answer to a question given that person's environment and experience, it would be marked incorrect because it was not the answer thought to be rational by those constructing the test. Moreover, historically, minority groups have scored lower on these tests than majority groups because of inherent bias that was built into the tests as a result of majority-culture assumptions and viewpoints held by test developers. However, as minority groups gain in socioeconomic and social status and as test developers make efforts to avoid bias, minority groups' scores become more comparable to those in majority groups.

Thus, there seems to be some evidence that intelligence is connected to factors beyond just the biological (Neisser *et al.*, 1996). Because IQ testing and scores still have the potential to be biased, and because scores can have so many individual and social ramifications, particularly for children, social workers need to be aware of the ethical dilemmas that standardized testing can pose.

> *In Eric's case, regardless of your perspective on intelligence and the value of testing, you will probably want to refer Eric for IQ testing. Because he is exhibiting so many problems at school, an IQ test is a logical step. It may be that he is having trouble with verbal or comprehension skills, for example, that keep him from understanding what is happening in the classroom. If he is not following along in the classroom, he may respond with behaviors similar to boredom or withdrawal. Similarly, if his skills are more developed than his peers', he may need a more advanced and challenging learning experience. IQ testing may also help to identify any potential learning disabilities that he might have. Despite the outcome of the IQ test, you will need to keep in mind the strengths and limitations of testing, to ensure that factors such as culture, definitions of intelligence, and other issues do not negatively impact Eric's situation.*

Learning Disabilities

Often, standardized intelligence tests as well as other assessments are used to determine whether children have learning disabilities that might necessitate additional services or special accommodations to ensure an adequate education. **Learning disabilities** are generally defined as problems among children who demonstrate normal or above normal intelligence and who show no signs of developmental disability, but who struggle in some area of their academic performance.

The numbers of children diagnosed with learning disabilities have been increasing. Boys tend to be diagnosed with learning disabilities more frequently than girls; however, it is difficult to determine whether there is a higher occurrence of disabilities among boys than girls. Specifically, boys tend to be referred for help more often than girls because of the behaviors caused by their disabilities, such as aggression and acting out on their emotions. Boys do tend to be more biologically susceptible to learning disabilities than girls, however (Hallahan & Kauffman, 2000; Hibel, Farkas, & Morgan, 2010). Research on the prevalence of learning disabilities between ethnic groups is mixed. Some research has not demonstrated significant differences in rates of learning disabilities among children from different ethnic groups (Child Trends Databank, 2014), while other research indicates that prevalence of issues such as attention deficit hyperactivity disorder is lower for children from Hispanic and African–American groups compared to white groups (Pastor & Reuben, 2005). However, research indicates that ethnic minority children with learning disabilities are treated for their symptoms less frequently than children from majority groups (Child Trends Databank, 2014; Pastor & Reuben, 2005).

Learning disabilities tend to be manifested through problems with listening, speaking, thinking, and concentration, which often result in performance problems in academic subjects such as math, reading, spelling, and composition. One of the most common types of learning disability is **dyslexia**, which results in severe reading and spelling impairments (Grigorenko, 2001; Ziegler & Goswami, 2005).

Children diagnosed with learning disabilities usually progress successfully through the public school system, generally with the assistance of special support services. However, there has been much debate about how best to educate children with special needs associated with learning disabilities (Kauffman & Hallahan, 2005). This debate generally centers on whether to keep these children in the classroom with others who do not demonstrate disabilities or to separate them and offer them specialized services tailored to their particular needs.

Adding to this debate is the issue that diagnosing learning disabilities can be challenging. Because many other problems can occur along with learning disabilities, social workers and other professionals need to be careful about how assessments are conducted and used with children who might have learning disabilities. Indeed, many psychosocial variables associated with learning problems (such as stress, abuse, poverty, and illness) come into play when labeling children with learning disabilities. We will examine services for children with learning disabilities and roles of social workers later in the chapter.

As Eric's social worker, you might want to assess him for possible learning disabilities that may or may not be related to his intellectual functioning. For example, Eric might be experiencing trouble reading or writing, which could be creating a whole host of problems with regard to his ability to maintain progress in the classroom. Since there is a wide range of potential problems related to learning that Eric could be experiencing, from the biological and developmental to the social, you need to undertake a thorough assessment to develop appropriate interventions, if necessary.

Attention Deficit Hyperactivity Disorder

One condition often associated with learning disabilities is **attention deficit hyperactivity disorder (ADHD)**. This disorder is characterized by consistent displays of inattention, hyperactivity, and impulsivity. Children with symptoms of ADHD seem easily bored, have trouble focusing on tasks and activities, demonstrate high levels of activity, show an unwillingness or inability to think before acting, and exhibit low levels of impulse control. Symptoms can present themselves in various combinations. For example, some children may exhibit inattention with little hyperactivity, or hyperactivity with an ability to focus their attention (American Psychiatric Association, 2000). Attention difficulties have become the most common reason why children are referred to mental health specialists, and over half of those children who receive special education are diagnosed with ADHD (Forness & Kavale, 2001; MMWR, 2005; Pastor & Reuben, 2008). For the most part, many children diagnosed with ADHD can benefit from medical and academic interventions.

Diagnoses of ADHD among children have been increasing over the past few decades. According to the Centers for Disease Control and Prevention (2013e) approximately 6.4 million children in the U.S. between the ages of four and 17 have received a diagnosis of ADHD, which represents a 16 percent increase since 2007 and a 41 percent increase in the past decade. Caucasian males are more frequently diagnosed with ADHD than any other gender or ethnic group. Some professionals speculate that increases in diagnoses are caused, in part, by increased knowledge of the disorder and better recognition of the symptoms. Further, many children diagnosed with ADHD have frequent contact with those who might make the diagnosis, such as primary care physicians. Diagnoses tend to be much lower among children who do not have health insurance, for example.

Social workers who work with children must also remain aware of other variables associated with an ADHD diagnosis. For example, a study of 23 preteen boys suggested that the fidgety behavior seen among children with ADHD may actually help them maintain alertness and focus on tasks; so asking kids with ADHD symptoms to "sit still" may actually be detrimental to their learning (Rapport *et al.*, 2009). These researchers hypothesize that kids with ADHD may be under-aroused—their brains do not produce sufficient amounts of dopamine to keep them alert, so they need to move around to keep their brains and bodies aroused, which is essential for learning to take place.

Children who exhibit undesirable or uncontrollable behavior in the classroom may be unfairly labeled with the disorder, regardless of whether their symptoms actually warrant it. Problems in the education system such as lack of funding, support, and overcrowding may contribute to increases in ADHD diagnoses simply because teachers and other staff do not have the resources to accurately identify or deal with problem behavior when it occurs. Moreover, some professionals speculate that otherwise "normal" behavior such as high activity levels may be labeled as maladaptive and abnormal in the context of contemporary settings such as the controlled, formal classroom (Brewis, Meyer, & Schmidt, 2002). Consequently, some children may be misdiagnosed and inappropriately referred to physicians, psychologists, social workers, and special education programs.

Conversely, given the potential ramifications of ADHD on learning and development, accurate identification and assessment of symptoms as well as appropriate intervention are important when working with children. Reflecting on developmental tasks that children undergo during this time, problems associated with ADHD can interfere with successful biopsychosocial development.

Social workers can be integral to ensuring optimal development of children who exhibit issues surrounding ADHD. Indeed, medications, while controversial, have shown promising results in managing symptoms of ADHD as have other psychosocial interventions such as parent training and behavior modification (Barkley, 2002; Olfson, Gameroff, Marcus, & Jensen, 2003). Social workers can be instrumental in developing and implementing such interventions in the home and academic settings.

Emerging research and debate is focused on a related condition coined *sluggish cognitive tempo*, characterized by lethargy, daydreaming, and slow mental processing. Although this condition is not included in the DSM-5, many mental health and other professionals are calling for more serious study of it. Conversely, others argue that there is no consensus on the symptoms that make up this condition, nor is there rigorous scientific evidence that it exists. This argument includes concerns that many children will be exposed to unwarranted diagnoses and medication (Becker, Marshall, & McBurnett, 2014).

Assessing Eric for ADHD, in addition to learning disabilities, could be worthwhile, particularly because the two problems frequently occur together. Although you cannot ascertain from the description how likely it is that Eric has symptoms of the disorder, you should not rule this out as a possibility.

Anxiety Disorders

Increasingly, young children are being recognized as having anxiety issues. A large national study indicated that symptoms of generalized anxiety disorder emerge as early as six years of age (National Institute of Mental Health, 2014), and an estimated 3 to 4 percent of children have a general anxiety disorder (Massachusetts General Hospital, 2010); this estimate increases to approximately 8 percent as children become teenagers (National Institute of Mental Health, 2011). While anxiety is a normal part of childhood, and children may go through phases when they are more anxious than usual, ongoing anxiety can impair learning and negatively affect how children interact with their environment.

Children may experience one or more specific types of anxiety problems (Anxiety Disorders Association of America, 2010):

- **Social anxiety disorder:** Fear of meeting new people or of embarrassing oneself in social situations.

- **Separation anxiety disorder:** Unreasonable fear of separating from home or primary caregivers.

- **Panic disorder:** Unpredictable and repeated panic attacks, marked by hyperventilating and increased heart rate.

- **Posttraumatic stress disorder:** Generalized panic or anxiety due to witnessing or experiencing a traumatic event.
- **Phobia:** Unreasonable fear of specific triggers such as dogs, spiders, air travel, or large crowds.

Looking at Eric's situation, his behavioral problems could be a result of an anxiety disorder. If, for example, Eric is found to be suffering from a panic disorder that interrupts his ability to concentrate at school, he and his parents can work with a therapist using techniques based in cognitive, behavioral, and learning theories. The goal would be to help Eric learn to identify and replace negative thinking patterns and behaviors with positive ones. The therapist might also work with Eric's family to teach them all how to best manage Eric's symptoms (Anxiety Disorders Association of America, 2010). If Eric's symptoms cause him a great deal of distress or interfere with his daily functioning, the therapist might recommend medication until he can learn techniques to control the anxiety symptoms.

THE FAMILY AND IMMEDIATE ENVIRONMENT IN MIDDLE CHILDHOOD

Of course, much of what happens to a child on an individual level also affects the child's family and vice versa. The previous section focused on individual problems that tend to be individual phenomena; in this section, we move to issues that tend to originate outside of the individual but impact the individual through her or his interaction with the immediate environment.

Peer Groups in Middle Childhood

Although families fulfill an important function in middle childhood with regard to socialization and providing feedback about the world and children's behavior, the role of peer groups in this process is equally important if not more so. **Peer groups,** which consist of children of roughly the same age, are a part of children's immediate environment that can have lasting effects on their development. Because of their similarity in age and experience, peers can offer one another valuable information about their abilities and their relation to the outside world.

Various theories touch on the importance of peer relationships in childhood. For example, Albert Bandura refers to modeling and social learning, and Erik Erikson's theory, as well as ecological and sociological theories, emphasize interaction with the environment as a factor in development. All of these theories highlight the need for children to have peers as reference points as they explore their environments, express their opinions, try on new roles, and test their social, physical, and academic capabilities. Indeed, some theorists argue that it is through peer relationships that children learn to develop intimate, sensitive relationships in which compromise and empathy are a part (Buhrmester & Furman, 1987; Parker, Rubin, Erath, Wojslawowicz, & Buskirk, 2006).

Conversely, peer relationships can have negative effects on childhood development. All children experience negative relationships and problems with friends. However, some children experience constant rejection and negative interactions with their peers, which can have lasting consequences on development. Feelings of rejection, hostility, loneliness, and depression can result from poor interactions with peers, which can impact later relationships with others (Hodges & Card, 2003).

In Eric's case, you may want to explore how he has been getting along with his peers. For instance, Eric's peers may be rejecting him because he has two fathers or because of his ethnic background. Eric's family history is unusual enough that he may be unable to relate to the other children his age and their family backgrounds and thus may be experiencing loneliness and confusion. From a strengths perspective, you could help Eric focus on the positive aspects of his ethnic background and family situation as well as the ways in which his situation is similar to that of his peers. In doing so, Eric may find new and more positive ways to interact and relate with his peers.

Play

The peer interaction of play serves many functions in childhood development. Apart from the obvious goal of having fun, play affords children opportunities to exercise their imagination, interact with others, practice social and other roles, develop cognitive and physical skills, and find natural ways to release tension and frustration. As with peer relationships, many theorists support the functional aspects of play in childhood development.

Much research has been conducted on play and its role in development. One of the first attempts to classify play comes from Mildred Parten (1932). Through her research, she developed categories of play, which are listed in Exhibit 8.2. These classifications help to identify different situations in which children engage in play and what that play might look like. More current research has focused on other types of play and various goals or purposes that play might have in development. One type is play that helps children practice a multitude of skills such as those involved in sensorimotor activities, coordination, symbolism, imagination, social interaction, and self-regulation (Bergin, 1988).

The skill-building goals of play relate well to various theoretical conceptualizations of childhood development. For example, Jean Piaget focused on issues of

PHOTO 8-A

Play is an important part of childhood development

Source: Ryan McVay/Getty Images

sensorimotor and cognitive development. Infants engage in play that stimulates visual and motor skills, and as they grow, they become better able to manipulate their environment in play, which stimulates development of coordination and other skills. Older children use their imaginations to manipulate objects in their play, and they have the ability to take the perspectives of others in role playing. Older children also gain the ability to understand rules and to organize their play, resulting in games that involve competition and negotiation.

According to Eric's parents, Eric spends a great deal of time by himself and seldom engages in play with peers. You might want to assess Eric's play to better understand what purposes his activities might have in his development and whether his play seems age or developmentally appropriate. For example, Eric may be engaging in frequent stationary play involving random movements and no apparent purpose, which could appear odd to his parents. Alternatively, Eric may not be engaging in other types of play that include interaction and that build on various motor skills, which may have ramifications for his future development. A detailed assessment of Eric's activities would help you understand potential issues in Eric's play that could impact other areas of his well-being.

CATEGORY OF PLAY	DESCRIPTION	
Unoccupied	Type of play that is uncharacteristic of typical play. Child often appears to be standing around, not doing anything, or engaging in movements or activities that seem to lack a goal or purpose. Child is often watching events happening around him or her.	**EXHIBIT 8.2** *Parten's Categories of Play*
Solitary	Play that involves solitary or independent activities. Child is often unconcerned with what others are doing. Common among children two to three years old.	
Onlooker	Type of play in which child observes the play of others. The child might ask questions or seem interested in others' play but does not participate.	
Parallel	Play that occurs simultaneously but separately from play of other children. Child may play with similar toys or in similar manner as other children. As children age, they are less likely to engage in this type of play.	
Associative	Type of play that involves a great deal of social interaction with other children, but play is still very individualistic. Though children play together, there is no real organization of, or attention being paid to, the play that is occurring. For example, children may talk together or share toys, but they are focused on their own activities.	
Cooperative	Play that includes social interaction with organized activity and a sense of group identity. Children share a purpose in play and work toward a common goal.	

Source: Adapted from Parten, 1932

Parental Discipline

As children grow older, parents find themselves struggling with many new issues surrounding discipline and parenting. Physically, cognitively, and emotionally, children are becoming capable of performing new tasks and taking on new challenges. According to Jean Piaget, they are developing the ability to better understand reason and to think concretely about their actions and those of others. Erik Erikson suggests that children at five or six years old and later are working on becoming industrious; they are curious, enthusiastic, and focused on mastering their environment. Systems, ecological, social learning, and similar theories emphasize the importance to the individual's development of interaction between the individual and her or his environment. All of these developing abilities, which are taking place within complex environmental contexts, pose myriad parenting challenges.

Discipline in Middle Childhood Many discipline issues that present themselves during this time involve school, self-regulation of behavior, responsibilities at home, and balance between time spent in and outside the home. Yet discipline during this time of childhood may be easier for parents than it was earlier in the child's development: Children's developing cognitive abilities allow for greater understanding and reasoning about rules and consequences. Discipline at this stage in development may also be easier than it will be during adolescence when teens begin to assert their independence and may resist discipline.

Middle childhood, then, is the period when children can understand the reasons behind their parents' actions, although they still do not possess the capabilities to act completely independently. Thus, major tasks in parental discipline at this point include helping children to develop the skills needed to act responsibly and independently while providing structured guidance to support them and ward against dangerous situations that they may not foresee.

Parents and professionals often disagree about the best way to provide parental discipline. Parents are often overwhelmed by the vast amounts of information available on disciplinary techniques, much of which is contradictory. In addition, they frequently worry about the long-term effects of using one method over another, as if their child will be scarred for life should some well-meaning technique be found harmful later. To make matters more complicated, advice about what is "best" for children is constantly changing. Moreover, parenting styles and child temperament (discussed in Chapter 7), among many other factors, influence how discipline actually plays out. It is a wonder that parents feel capable of providing any discipline at all!

How to discipline also has a lot to do with how we view behavior issues, which is often driven by different theoretical perspectives. For example, one approach to discipline issues is called *collaborative and proactive solutions* (CPS), formerly known as collaborative problem solving; this is an evidenced-based approach informed by Adlerian, medical, and cognitive-behavioral concepts (Greene & Ablon, 2006; Greene & Doyle, 1999; Pollastri, Epstein, Heath, & Ablon, 2013). The idea behind CPS is that children inherently want to feel belonging and competency in their environment, concepts from Adlerian and transactional psychology. Children inherently want to behave and do well, but sometimes they lack the cognitive and other developmental skills to meet the demands of their environment—concepts from the medical model. In other words, children do well if they can.

Behavioral problems occur, then, when environmental demands exceed children's competencies, and not from children's lack of motivation, attention seeking, being manipulative, or testing limits, for example—traditional ways in which we view behavioral problems. In this way, CPS views behavioral issues as learning disabilities. Rather than characterizing children as suffering from deficiencies in academic and related skills, CPS sees children as needing support in areas like maturity, flexibility, adaptation, tolerance, and problem-solving skills. These are skills that can be learned and often will come with further physical and cognitive development.

From this viewpoint, educators and parents can help teach children the skills they need to be successful and to feel competent and socially included. Children need to be collaborators in this process so they feel invested. Greene and Ablon (2006) as well as other researchers (e.g., Pollastri, Epstein, Heath, & Ablon, 2013) argue that CPS is more efficacious than traditional approaches that use punishment, reinforcement, consequences, and operant methods discussed in Chapter 3, which do not teach skills or recognize the cognitive and other developmental limitations of children. Traditional approaches operate on the assumption that children do well if they want to, so behavioral interventions are aimed at increasing children's motivation to behave. According to Greene and others, these are misguided attempts to coerce children into demonstrating desirable behaviors.

Because of the debates and conflicting information on discipline, as Eric's social worker, you might want to explore discipline issues with his parents. Eric's parents could benefit from discussion of the topic, and they might be relieved to know that many parents are confused about conflicting and changing knowledge about discipline. You may be able to provide some guidance to Eric's parents on how to evaluate knowledge and research to make some educated decisions about how to proceed with disciplining Eric.

Physical Punishment   One ongoing debate on discipline revolves around **corporal punishment**—the use of physical punishment, particularly spanking, on children. Spanking as a disciplinary technique has probably been around since people have been having children. In the United States, spanking as punishment is relatively prevalent; however, attitudes about its use have shifted over time. For example, data indicate that during the 1960s, 94 percent of parents perceived spanking as a legitimate form of discipline. By 1999, that number had declined to 55 percent (Children's Institute International, 1999; Gallup Organization, 1995). Indeed, many U.S. states and other nations have banned its use in public education settings, and many states include excessive corporal punishment in their definitions of child maltreatment (Davidson, 1997; Gaten, 2009; Straus, 2008). However, a vast majority—over 90 percent—of parents still report using corporal punishment at least once (Straus, 2001).

Attitudes about spanking specifically and corporal punishment generally are deeply embedded in the fabric of social, cultural, religious, and political life. Thus debates about the utility of spanking are usually heated, and middle ground on disciplinary techniques is difficult to establish, even among professionals. For example, several states have passed laws to secure parental rights to spank, which has refueled the debate about where parents should draw the line with regard to discipline. Research has attempted to offer some scientific insight into the pros and cons of spanking, but even these attempts are limited and are often met with much criticism.

In general, the main debates among scholars, parents, and professionals tend to center around whether spanking (or other forms of corporal punishment) promotes violent behavior among children who are spanked and whether spanking helps to reinforce other modes of discipline such as time-outs (Benjet & Kazdin, 2003). Those who support the notion that spanking reinforces violent behavior in children often reflect Albert Bandura's view of social learning. Children model behaviors of others, and spanking shows them that an effective way to get someone to comply with a demand is through physical violence. Conversely, others might argue, again using Bandura's theory, that spanking is an effective disciplinary technique because children who witness another child being spanked for undesirable behavior will be more likely to behave in desirable ways to avoid the same punishment.

Still others might argue that cognitively, young children are unable to understand the consequences of misbehavior, so techniques such as explanation and time-outs are unlikely to work to correct behavior until children reach a more mature age. Thus, spanking is a more effective approach, particularly when it is paired with other techniques such as the use of rewards.

Research on spanking dates back several decades, but only a few consistent findings across studies exist. The majority of findings agree that spanking is positively correlated with aggression, misconduct, and similar behaviors among children, even in cultures where it is socially acceptable and normative (Gershoff, 2002; Lansford & Dodge, 2008; Straus, 2008). At the same time, the studies also confirm that spanking does succeed at getting children to comply with parents' demands (Harvard Mental Health Letter, 2002). However, this association cannot establish causation, which tends to be at the heart of the spanking debate. The question remains: Does spanking cause increased aggression in children, or are children spanked more because they show aggressive behavior? Moreover, studies cannot possibly account for the many individual, familial, social, cultural, and other contextual variables that might be associated with relationships between spanking and aggressive behavior among children.

Separation and Divorce

Many parents experiencing separation and divorce worry about how their actions will affect their children. Parents often question whether they should remain together for the sake of the children.

In general, research indicates that many children who experience divorce do have trouble with adjustment, but the type and extent of this difficulty depend on many factors and vary a great deal from child to child (Sun & Li, 2002, 2009). While some research indicates that relatively few children face these types of problems and that the extent of these problems is rather small, other research indicates that the extent of problems associated with divorce is significant (Amato, 2000, 2001; Bing, Nelson, & Wesolowski, 2009; Hetherington, 2000).

Some of the major issues facing children who have experienced divorce include low self-esteem and academic, attachment, behavioral (for example, acting out, delinquency, promiscuity in teen years), and emotional problems (for example, anxiety, depression) (Hetherington, 2000; Leon, 2003; Pelkonen, Marttunen, Kaprio, Huurre, & Aro, 2008; Shansky, 2002).

What factors seem to place children at risk for experiencing adjustment problems with separation and divorce? Though it is impossible to account for all variables that might impact a child's ability to cope with separation and divorce, research has focused on several factors that seem to make a difference in children's adjustment:

- *Coping ability:* How children cope with problems, including pre-divorce stress, is a good predictor of how they will cope with the divorce and its aftermath (Amato, 2000; Eldar-Avidan, Haj-Yahia, & Greenbaum, 2009).

- *Level of development:* Children who are able to cognitively process the divorce as well as understand the complex nuances behind the reasons for the divorce will probably fare better than their younger counterparts, who are less likely to grasp why the divorce is occurring (Ängarne-Lindberg & Wadsby, 2009; Zill, Morrison, & Coiro, 1993).

- *Gender:* Earlier research has indicated that boys adjust better to divorce than girls. However, more current research suggests that these differences may be less significant than originally thought. Though girls may still struggle slightly more than their male counterparts, trends toward increasing participation by fathers after divorce and varying custody arrangements may be easing the difficulties that female children experience throughout the divorce (Amato, 2000; Ruschena, Prior, Sanson, & Smart, 2005).

Parents cannot control some of these factors, such as a child's temperament and personality, but they can control others. These are some of the things that parents can do to help their children adjust (Hetherington, 2003; Moxnes, 2003):

- Maintain open and respectful communication with children.

- Ensure that children (especially young children) understand that they are not to blame for the divorce.

- Maintain a consistent daily routine.

- Remain realistic but hopeful about the situation.

- Be supportive of the children.

Sometimes when there is a great deal of conflict and strife in the home before divorce takes place, separation and divorce can actually improve children's coping and functioning, especially if a consistent routine and respectful communication and relations can be established and maintained (Waite & Gallagher, 2000).

Though many more post-divorce custody and living arrangements occur today than in the past, the reality is still that single mothers take on the majority of child care and custody responsibilities. Unfortunately, after divorce, the income of many women decreases dramatically, causing potential problems such as stress, poverty, job instability, increased workload, and frequent moves and disruption in the child's life (Amato, 2000; Wang & Amato, 2000). As you might imagine, factors such as these can make children's adjustment to divorce more difficult as well.

Alternative Family Forms

Definitions of families and the ways in which families form are changing. Increasing numbers of blended families, single parent and cohabiting partner household families, and gay and lesbian families are driving questions about how family structures affect child development.

Stepfamilies and Blended Families   Given the high rates of divorce in this country, it is common for people to remarry and to combine families. Increasingly, children are reared in families with a biological parent and a stepparent after remarriage. If the new couple bear children after they get together, the existing children will have half-siblings. Often, remarried parents bring together two sets of children, which results in **blended families**.

As with divorce, remarriage and blending of families can bring about difficulties in adjustment for the children. When families are blended, the children from each parent need time to get to know one another and build relationships (Bray & Kelly, 1998; Gonzales, 2009). In addition, each member needs to adjust to new roles and responsibilities and to relocation. Moreover, the newly wed couple often needs time to adjust to marriage and living together, which can create additional stress for the children.

Single Parent and Cohabiting Households   The number of children born to households with single or cohabiting parents is increasing dramatically. In 2012, approximately 41 percent of all births were to unmarried women (Centers for Disease Control and Prevention, 2013c), and approximately 42 percent of children have lived with cohabiting parents by the age of 12, which is almost double the percentage of children living with divorced parents (Popenoe, 2008).

A great deal of research has examined the effects of single and cohabiting parenting on children. Much of this research indicates that children from these homes tend to exhibit more frequent behavioral, learning, and other problems than children living in homes where parents are married (Choi, 2010). For example:

- Children living with cohabiting mothers or single-mother caregivers, even when these mothers are well-educated, are not as likely to attain a higher education as children in households with married caregivers (Martin, 2012; Popenoe, 2008).

- Single mothers have a higher probability of using paid day care and spend more on day care than women with other caregivers in the home (Haksoon, 2012).

- Children living with cohabiting parents tend to suffer from poorer mental health than their peers living with married caregivers (Popenoe, 2008).

- Single parents who perceive fewer social supports and financial resources report higher levels of stress and more behavioral problems with their children (Solem, Christophersen, & Martinussen, 2011).

- Cohabiting caregivers often experience relationship issues serious enough to prevent marriage or that are brought into marriage, leading to increased risk of discord and stress between couples that impact children (Popenoe, 2008).

Some of the research also indicates that single and cohabiting parenting does not necessarily lead to negative outcomes for children:

- The quality of single mothers' parenting and relationships with non-custodial fathers as well as the frequency of fathers' contact with children increase the positive impacts on children's behavior and cognitive development (Choi, 2010; Choi & Jackson, 2011).

- While there are no behavioral or other benefits for children who live with same-gender parents, girls who live with male caregivers demonstrate higher academic achievement than girls living with other parent–child gender combinations (Lee & Kushner, 2008).

- Girls living in single-parent households demonstrate more problematic behaviors such as aggression than girls living with two caregivers; however, two-parent households do not seem to be a protective factor for boys. Problematic behavior among boys is similar for boys living in single-parent and two-parent (married and cohabiting) households (Mokrue, Chen, & Elias, 2012).

To summarize, simply having only one parent or two parents who are not married may not cause problems for children. Many of the negative outcomes for children may be related to issues associated with parental stress, relationship problems, and situational factors in the household, such as poor financial and social supports.

Gay and Lesbian Parents Another hotly debated issue surrounding parenting involves the ability of gay and lesbian individuals to be fit parents. Millions of gays and lesbians are parents, many as a result of prior heterosexual relationships in which biological children were born. Often in these past relationships, the other partner is heterosexual, as are the judges and others who might become involved in custody battles when partners split. So, many gays and lesbians face discrimination when entering such battles. For example, at least six states automatically assume that gays and lesbians are unfit to parent, thus requiring gay and lesbian parents to prove that they can be appropriate parents to their children (Kendall, 2003).

Many gay and lesbian couples also face considerable discrimination when attempting to adopt or foster a child. Though the number of children needing homes is increasing and gay and lesbian individuals could help fill the need for prospective parents, the current system fails to tap into this viable resource because of prejudices. Thus, in addition to focusing on common issues surrounding parenting and normal childhood development, social workers working with gay and lesbian families may also need to focus on attitudes about homosexuality when dealing with adoption, foster care, or other parenting issues. This includes facing religious and moral biases that are often prevalent in the social institutions, particularly privately funded ones, that facilitate adoption and foster parenting. Biases may be found in the missions and policies of these agencies as well as in the beliefs of the workers. It should be noted here that advances in technology that allow both heterosexual and homosexual parents to conceive and bear children are similarly controversial.

Despite the belief by some that gays and lesbians are unfit to parent, empirical evidence suggests that children of gay and lesbian parents are as well adjusted as children reared by heterosexual parents (Anderssen, Amlie, & Ytteroy, 2002; Brooks & Goldberg, 2001; Tasker, 2005). Other research suggests that children reared in such households show similar levels of development in cognitive, emotional, social, and sexual functioning as children reared in households with heterosexual couples (Anderssen, Amlie, & Ytteroy, 2002; Brooks & Goldberg, 2001; Hagan, 2002; Perrin, 2002; Tasker, 2005). There is also no evidence that children raised by same-sex parents automatically consider a same-sex relationship for themselves. Knowing that children benefit from having two parents who are involved in a loving, stable relationship, the American Academy of Pediatrics supports the adoption of children by gay or lesbian couples (American Academy of Pediatrics, 2002).

However, some professionals have responded negatively to the position of the American Academy of Pediatrics. They cite a number of reasons for rethinking the support for homosexual couples who want to parent: high HIV/AIDS rate among homosexual males (and thus a relatively short life span for those who are parents); the moral and religious beliefs of many people who do not support exposing children to homosexual lifestyles; and the likelihood that children raised in same-sex couple households will consider a same-sex relationship for themselves in the future (Golombok, 2002; Guttery, Friday, Field, Riggs, & Hagan, 2002).

Parenting can be a difficult endeavor under the best of circumstances. Often, simply identifying as gay or lesbian can create additional barriers for people that can make becoming a parent and parenting itself even more challenging (Marriage Equality USA, 2004). Unfortunately, dealing with these latter issues may take precedence over positive parenting and development of the child and family. Any ill effects on childhood development may come from prejudicial and discriminatory attitudes from others rather than from actual parenting issues.

In this context, marriage equality (discussed in more detail in Chapter 11) is extremely important for gay and lesbian couples who want to parent. Marriage has legal importance in a multitude of parental rights, from adoption to financial support to custody issues. Thus the ability to marry can have a profound positive impact on not only the homosexual couple's relationship, which can affect their parenting, but also on their ability to become parents and care for their children. Gay and lesbian couples who are trying to become parents are pushing the limits of courts and legislation, which are also challenging the definition of the traditional family. Social workers will continue to be at the forefront of these challenges and debates, shaping the way in which social attitudes and policies affect parenthood and grappling with ethical dilemmas as issues surrounding technology and morality intersect.

You can see many of these factors coming together in Eric's situation as the adopted son of gay parents. Eric is probably facing much discrimination from his peers, and possibly from his teachers, because of his situation. Unfortunately, Eric's cognitive abilities at this point in his development will not be adequate to deal effectively with this discrimination without support. Many of the behavioral problems that Eric is allegedly having may be a result of his attempts to cope with an environment that is less than ideal. You may need to intervene on mezzo and macro levels as well as the micro level to help build resources that will maximize Eric's coping abilities. This means that you may need to focus on the school environment, the teachers' attitudes and behaviors toward Eric and his parents, Eric's interactions with his peers, Eric's parents' actions, and Eric's own self-concept. In addition, you need to assess Eric's strengths as well as those of his family when considering ways in which to intervene. Since it is likely that Eric is experiencing a great deal of negativity in his environment, discussing strengths is an important part of your work with him.

THE LARGER SOCIAL ENVIRONMENT IN MIDDLE CHILDHOOD

We have looked at many issues on the individual and immediate environmental levels affecting the development of children that social workers must consider when working with children and their families. Additionally, there are other issues on a larger environmental level that impact children and their families. These areas often involve policy and other social issues with which social workers must deal either directly or indirectly when working with clients. This section addresses some of these macro issues and how they relate to the development and well-being of children.

Children and Media

One question that most parents have is about the effects of media and technology usage on children's development and behavior. With technological advances speeding ahead of our ability to answer ethical and other questions regarding their effects on humans, many parents and professionals often find themselves debating the strengths, limitations, and positive and negative ramifications of such technology on our lives. Indeed, extensive research has been generated on the topic in an attempt to untangle the endless array of psychosocial variables associated with the use of technology and its effects on everyday life. However, rather than provide concrete answers about how media can affect our well-being, much of this research has only generated more questions about the use of technology and media.

Much of the discussion surrounding media and children's development focuses on exposure to violence and other unsuitable content for children on television, in video games, and on the Internet. In the United States, children watch an average of 28 hours of television per week, and by the time they reach their 18th birthday, they will have witnessed some 200,000 acts of violence (American Academy of Child & Adolescent Psychiatry, 2011b). The Kaiser Family Foundation (2010) reported that eight to 18 year olds spend an average of seven-and-a-half hours per day using media (e.g., TV, computers, video games, etc.)—or around 53 hours per week. Though advances in programming are helping to filter violent or otherwise

PHOTO 8-B

Media use can have a negative impact on development in childhood

Source: Escobar Studios

inappropriate content on the Internet, parents and educators often find themselves frustrated when these programs turn out to be less than perfect in policing the content to which children are exposed online.

A great deal of research has been conducted on the effects of media violence on children. Generally, this body of research has concluded that witnessing violent acts on television and through other media does have adverse effects on child behavior (Funk, Buchman, Jenks, & Bechtoldt, 2002; Huesmann, Moise-Titus, Podolski, & Eron, 2003; Strasburger & Grossman, 2001). For example, media violence has been associated with increased aggressive and antisocial behavior among children as well as increased feelings of fear and insecurity (American Academy of Pediatrics, 2001; Cantor, 2000; Christakis & Zimmerman, 2005; Huesmann *et al.*, 2003).

In a famous study by Albert Bandura (1965), children who had watched an adult perform aggressive actions against an inflatable "Bobo" doll and get rewarded for it tended to replicate this violent behavior toward the doll. Many parents and professionals are concerned that violence shown on television and portrayed in video games is set within a context in which the violence is not only modeled but also glamorized. Those perpetrating the violence are either rewarded, or at least not punished, leading children to believe that violence is not a serious issue.

Many of the concerns surrounding media violence revolve around the developmental capacities of the children who are exposed to it. Reflecting back on Jean Piaget's work on cognitive development, young children are not able to separate reality from fantasy until various cognitive processes are in place. Preschoolers, for example, still engage in magical thinking, which means that they are likely to take what they view on television at face value. They do not understand that people on television are simply playing roles. Thus, young children do not understand that much of the violence seen on television is for "entertainment value"; rather, they may interpret violent behavior as something that is commonplace and acceptable in society.

A related issue has to do with the amount of time that children spend watching television, playing video games, or surfing the Internet. Recently, attention has been given to the increasing rates of obesity and diabetes among U.S. children. Many professionals attribute these problems, in part, to decreased activity rates among children who are spending more and more time on sedentary activities such as television watching and interacting with other media (Clocksin, Watson, & Ransdell, 2002; Kaiser Family Foundation, 2010). One study indicated that every additional hour of children's television exposure corresponded to reductions in classroom engagement, math achievement, and physical activity and increases in body mass index and consumption of soft drinks and snacks (Pagani, Fitzpatrick, Barnett, & Dubow, 2010).

As various forms of media become more mainstream in the lives of many children, social workers will be working with educators, parents, and other professionals to help find solutions to the problems that technology may bring for children's development. Mediating the effects of violence to which children are exposed, helping families find a balance between media use and other forms of entertainment that allow for physical activity and peer interaction, and influencing public policies and legislation that help to maximize children's development are all issues with which social workers will continue to grapple.

In Eric's situation, you may want to assess the amount of exposure that Eric has to television and other media, which could be impacting his development. You could also discuss with Eric's parents their values about media use as well as what the research has to say about the positive and negative effects of various forms of media on childhood development.

Children in the Educational Context

Increasingly, academic issues and the learning environment have been centers of debate in the United States. With shrinking budgets, growing class sizes, and questions about which curricula to use for optimal learning and how to meet the needs of a diverse student body, knowing how to proceed with choosing schools and understanding the issues can be perplexing for parents and professionals.

Particularly problematic is the *achievement gap* that persists in our education system. Many factors contribute to learning outcome disparities experienced by ethnic minority children. These factors include students' socioeconomic backgrounds; inequitable funding of schools; discriminatory labeling and handling of students' problematic behavior; cultural experiences of ethnic minority children who feel they are expected to "act white" in school; tracking practices that keep schools internally segregated; resources, supports, mentors, and networks available to students; and latent functions of schools' curricula (e.g., to reinforce majority ideas and culture) (Golash-Boza, 2015). The achievement gap can have lasting and far-reaching detrimental effects on ethnic minority children's learning experiences, success in school and other arenas, and exposure to opportunities and resources, which impact their future opportunities.

Social workers often deal with these issues on a daily basis, particularly if they are working directly with children and their families. Social workers also often work with teachers and schools as well as with school board officials, legislators, and communities to help educate others on issues related to education, which usually directly affect the policies and funding that go into the education system.

Special Education   A few generations ago, children with physical and mental disabilities were unable to access fair and equitable education in the public school system. In the 1960s and 1970s, federal and state movements were undertaken to provide educational and other resources to children with disabilities and special needs. These movements culminated in the 1975 Education for All Handicapped Children Act (Public Law 94–142), which mandated that all children with disabilities have access to free and appropriate education. In 1990, the name of this law was changed to the **Individuals with Disabilities Education Act (IDEA)**.

Some of the main provisions of IDEA are that:

- eligibility criteria for services be clearly defined;

- evaluations for these criteria be readily accessible to children who need them;

- children who meet criteria receive individualized education plans, which offer students specialized services targeted to their specific needs;

- students with disabilities be offered educational services in the **least restrictive environment (LRE)**, which means that the setting in which education for students with disabilities takes place is as similar and equal to that of other students as possible. This last effort is to ensure that students with disabilities do not end up in facilities that are less equipped or somehow inferior to those offered to students without disabilities (Crockett & Kauffman, 1999; Kauffman & Hallahan, 2005).

The current philosophy on educating children with disabilities is that they should spend time in regular classrooms interacting with children who do not have disabilities; this process has been referred to as **mainstreaming**, or inclusion. For mainstreaming to be implemented successfully, teachers must receive specialized training to meet the needs of children with disabilities, and social workers must provide support services for teachers, children, and their families.

Often, teachers, schools, and social workers complain that funding is inadequate to truly provide for the needs mandated by IDEA. Moreover, some professionals argue that regardless of the efforts made to provide appropriate services to children with special needs—whether through mainstreaming or separate classrooms—recipients of these services often experience discrimination because of educational policies and services that lack clear goals and fiscal, cultural, and other support (Davis & Watson, 2001).

Social workers are often the professionals who interpret policies on special education, develop programs to meet policy mandates, evaluate students for eligibility for special programs, and support families whose children need such services. Therefore, they need to be familiar with the issues and problems surrounding education for children with disabilities to ensure that programs and policies are as equitable and effective as possible.

Although there is no indication that Eric needs any special education services, as his social worker, you could advocate for these should the situation warrant it. You could also educate Eric's parents about their rights to services in the education system if Eric were to have any kind of disability or special need.

School Choice and Vouchers   Other controversial issues with which social workers are often involved include experimental and changing methods of providing educational services to children and families. In recent decades, novel programs have been developed in an attempt to solve problems faced by failing public educational systems. Poor student achievement, shaky funding, and low academic standards are just a few of the issues that many experts argue are plaguing the public school system. In response to these issues, there has been an increase in the number of charter schools, school voucher programs, and student bussing initiatives that allow students to attend schools of their choice.

Although many parents, educators, professionals, and researchers agree that the public school system is in dire need of reform, there is less agreement about how to proceed. For example, **school vouchers**, or certificates that can be used to pay for schools of parents' choosing, have been touted as a solution to poorly performing schools. Vouchers allow students to attend a school of their parents' choice. Specifically, vouchers are given to parents in lieu of tax dollars that would otherwise be spent on public education. Consequently, poorly performing schools lose students and tax-based funding, forcing the schools to improve their standards or risk closure.

Critics of school vouchers argue that the money allotted is not sufficient to provide students, particularly poor students, with a real choice. Specifically, most vouchers provide each student with between $1,000 and $4,000 to pay for education. Most private schools cost more than this, and many students cannot find public schools that perform better and that are worth the transfer. Consequently, many students who take advantage of voucher programs transfer to private religious schools, which, critics argue, should not be funded by public tax dollars.

Research conducted on the effectiveness of voucher programs to increase student learning and academic performance has been largely inconclusive. Most research has not found a significant difference in academic performance between students using voucher programs and those not using the programs. Findings are also inconclusive with regard to whether voucher programs benefit minority students, who largely attend inadequately funded and poorly performing schools (Viadero, 2003).

Along with educators and other professionals, social workers grapple with the debates about education on the policy and service-delivery levels. Social workers help shape opinions and debates on education through research, program evaluation, and service development and provision. In the confusion that can easily ensue in debates over education, social workers must also ensure that ethical standards are upheld and that clients are not lost in the debates. Generally, social workers are responsible for ensuring that all clients have access to quality and equitable education.

CONCLUSION

Middle childhood is a time of continued physical, emotional, and cognitive growth, particularly as children are increasingly exposed to others in their environment. Interactions with peers, teachers, technology, and other aspects of the outside world have an impact on the development of children. Healthy and steady development in middle childhood relies on physical, mental, and emotional stimulation and positive relationships with others. Theories of development such as those of Jean Piaget and Erik Erikson can help social workers to conceptualize development of their young clients in this time of life.

Social workers can be of great benefit to families who have children in the age range of middle childhood. Often, problems regarding development, parenting, family issues, school performance, and relationships with peers bring families to social workers for help. Understanding the ways in which individual and social factors can influence children and their families is crucial to providing effective assessment and intervention that will enhance clients' individual, familial, and social functioning. Further, social workers need to understand debates surrounding issues such as intelligence testing and education so that they can advocate for and support the needs of clients in the most ethical and appropriate way possible.

MAIN POINTS

- Motor, emotional, cognitive, and physical development continues to progress during middle childhood, the ages of five or six to approximately 11.

- Sternberg's triarchic theory of intelligence describes three main modes of intellectual functioning. Though professionals acknowledge the benefits of recognizing concepts of multiple intelligence, standardized intelligence tests and traditional definitions of intelligence still predominate in policy and service delivery, particularly in relation to learning disabilities.

- There are debates over diagnosis of learning disabilities, including dyslexia and ADHD, as well as how best to educate children with special needs associated with learning disabilities.

- ADHD and anxiety disorders are increasingly being diagnosed in children.

- Peer relationships have a profound impact on children's motor, social, emotional, and cognitive development. Types of play children engage in as well as parental discipline are two additional factors in the immediate environment that impact development.

- Results of research into the effects of divorce and remarriage on children and their development show that some children experience problems in development and behavior, while others seemingly show no adverse effects. A combination of factors such as children's temperament, their level of development, their gender, and whether parents maintain open communication and support their children during the divorce contribute to how well children cope.

- Although much controversy remains, research indicates that children reared by gay or lesbian parents do just as well developmentally as children reared by heterosexual parents.

- Evidence suggests that exposure to violence on television and through other media is associated with aggressive behavior in children as well as with decreased time spent engaging in physical and social activity.

- Laws enacted in the 1970s and updated in the 1990s have contributed to mainstreaming children with disabilities and special needs.

- Though there is consensus that the current public education system needs reform, many alternatives to education such as voucher programs have mixed results in providing quality and equitable education.

EXERCISES

1. *RAINN interactive case at* www.routledgesw.com/cases. The director of RAINN noticed that an increasing number of referrals are about school-age children experiencing sexual assault, and wants to develop a training course to help social workers at RAINN understand the needs of children. What are important physical, cognitive, and emotional milestones that this training should address?

2. *Hudson City interactive case at* www.routledgesw.com/cases. Answer the following questions:
   a. What might be important middle childhood developmental milestones that could be impacted by the issues facing this community?
   b. How might children's peer and family networks be impacted by the problems facing the community?
   c. What theoretical or other models or perspectives might be useful in conceptualizing work with young residents of the Hudson community? Why?

3. *RAINN interactive case at* www.routledgesw.com/cases. RAINN is hosting a community meeting to talk about the impact the media have on violence and sexualization in young children. What are some specific issues the meeting's organizers need to be prepared to address at the meeting on both sides of the issue (media hurts children/media can help children)?

4. *Riverton interactive case at* www.routledgesw.com/cases. Review the case, paying particular attention to issues surrounding Felipe and Maria Gonzales, their family,

and the school in the community. Based on the information in this chapter, answer the following questions:

a. How might the information in this chapter be useful in your work with the Gonzales family and the community's school, if at all?

b. Could any of the information presented in this and the preceding chapters be used with the family or community to prevent future problems? In what ways?

c. What strengths do you see with the family and the community's school that could be used to help solve problems?

5. *Sanchez Family interactive case at* www.routledgesw.com/cases. Review the major issues involving the Sanchez family, and then answer the following questions:

a. Given the various issues discussed in this chapter, which ones might be of concern for the Sanchez family and why? Describe, in some detail, how individual members might be affected by these issues and how they might impact the family as a system.

b. How might these issues be affected by cultural factors? Offer a thorough exploration of the cultural context in which the family lives and how you, as a social worker, would take into consideration this context as you pinpoint issues.

c. Based on problems that you identify for this family and your ideas about how to work with these problems and the family, what ethical dilemmas, if any, could potentially emerge for this family?

d. What theories might you want to use to guide your interventions and why?

e. Briefly describe what type of interventions you would recommend for this family based on your assessment of problems. Justify your plans.

CHAPTER 9

Development in Adolescence

Alicia is a 14-year-old Caucasian teen who has been living part time with her single mother and part time at a friend's home. Alicia has been having trouble getting along with her mother and has threatened several times to run away. She has been doing poorly in school and spends a great deal of her time roaming the streets and hanging out with kids who are homeless.

Alicia's troubles began about one year ago when her mother discovered that Alicia was purposely vomiting immediately after eating dinner. When Alicia's mother confronted Alicia, she became angry and withdrew from her mother, turning more and more to her "street friends."

Alicia has come to your attention as a social worker at a community center with a program for homeless teens where Alicia spends some of her time. You are concerned about Alicia's weight loss, depressed mood, low self-esteem, and seemingly slow developmental progress for her age. Though you do not have proof, you are also concerned that Alicia has been engaging in sexual intercourse with some of her male friends; Alicia refuses to discuss sex, contraception, or sexually transmitted infections, telling you that she would never get pregnant or get an infection. You have tried to get Alicia to come to the center with her mother for counseling, but Alicia does not see the need for it.

A CHALLENGING TIME FOR THOSE EXPERIENCING IT AS WELL AS for their families, **adolescence** typically begins around ages 10 to 12 and lasts until ages 18 to 22. Because of the many biopsychosocial changes that take place during this time, problems can emerge for individuals and their families. Further, because adolescents are developing their identity and independence while still legally dependent on their parents and guardians, social workers can face many legal, ethical, and practical challenges when working with teen clients. In the sections to follow, we will explore some of the most prevalent issues that affect clients during this period of the life span.

DEVELOPMENTAL MILESTONES IN THE TEEN YEARS

The teen years are characterized by continued physical growth and significant changes that signal the onset of sexual maturity and development into adulthood. This section discusses some of these processes and their effects on teens. Quick Guide 12 summarizes the major developments.

QUICK GUIDE 12	Developmental Milestones in Adolescence	
PHYSICAL	**COGNITIVE**	**PERSONALITY AND EMOTION**
• Onset of puberty and the hormonal changes associated with it.	• Cognitive skills become more complex and sophisticated.	• Identity development continues with the integration of physical, cognitive, and emotional components to form a more mature identity.
• Development of primary and secondary sex characteristics.	• Thinking becomes more abstract, and teens can think hypothetically about situations.	• Movement toward autonomy.
	• Teens can use reason and logic and take the perspective of others when considering situations.	

Physical Development

With regard to physical development, a hallmark of adolescence is puberty and the hormonal changes associated with it. **Puberty** is characterized by rapid physical and sexual growth, and it is often accompanied by hormonal, emotional, and other changes. The hypothalamus and pituitary glands in the brain and the sex glands, or gonads (testes in males and ovaries in females), are the main structures involved in hormonal changes during adolescence. Androgen in males and estrogen in females are the main sex hormones that are involved in genital, sexual, and other physical development.

One basic component of puberty is the development of **primary sex characteristics,** or those aspects of the body directly related to reproduction. For girls, this includes the development of the uterus, ovaries, and vagina. For boys, it is the development of the prostate gland and growth of the penis. Puberty also brings with it the development of **secondary sex characteristics,** or those aspects related to gender but not directly related to reproduction. Secondary characteristics include changes such as hair growth, breast development, and voice and skin changes.

Studies have indicated a trend toward earlier onset of puberty in industrialized countries. Over the course of the 19th and 20th centuries, for example, the average age of menarche, or first menstrual cycle, in the United States decreased from 15 years of age to 12½ years of age (Chumlea *et al.*, 2003). This trend is likely due to improved sanitation, nutrition, and related factors. The trend toward earlier menarche slowed somewhat in the latter half of the 20th century (Martorell, Mendoza, & Castillo, 1988).

A central question surrounding hormonal and other changes during adolescence is whether these changes cause dramatic changes in behavior. For example, many parents and professionals wonder to what extent increases in testosterone cause aggressive behavior in males. Similarly, some people ask to what extent increases in estrogen in females contribute to increases in depressive symptoms. Recent research indicates that there is no clear cause-and-effect relationship between hormones and behavior. However, evidence suggests that the two are associated. For example, a growing body of literature indicates that increases in androgens are related to increases in aggression among boys (Dorn *et al.*, 2009; Pasterski *et al.*, 2007; Van Goozen, Matthys, Cohen-Kettenis, Thisjssen, & Van Engeland, 1998).

Keep in mind, though, that other physical, emotional, cognitive, and environmental factors also play a role in determining behavior:

- In girls, factors such as stress, peer pressure, heredity, and timing of puberty, along with hormonal changes, can impact the development of depressive symptoms (Angold, Costello, & Worthman, 1998; Brooks-Gunn & Warren, 1989; Neiss, Stevenson, Legrand, Iacono, & Sedikides, 2009).

- Binge drinking among teens, particularly girls, tends to adversely affect brain development related to memory and spatial awareness (Squeglia, Schweinsburg, Pulido, & Tapert, 2011).

- Hearing loss is becoming more common among children and teens in part because of loud music, headphones, ear buds, and other environmental factors. Indeed, in the past 15 years, the proportion of teens with slight hearing loss has increased 30 percent, and those with mild or worse hearing loss has increased 70 percent. Hearing impairments can have negative impacts on speech, self-esteem, language development, educational achievement, and social-emotional development (Shargorodsky, Curhan, Curhan, & Eavey, 2010).

- Teens' sleep cycle is different from adults', which helps to explain why teens enjoy staying up late and waking late—and why they might have difficulty concentrating at school. Teens also are not getting enough sleep in general, which is associated with poor grades and increased risk of illness and alcohol and drug abuse (Tarokh, Carskadon, & Achermann, 2011).

So, in addition to viewing puberty from the medical model, social workers need to assess issues using other models such as the ecological or systems perspective since a complex array of factors can influence behavior.

When considering Alicia's physical development, you would most likely view it from the medical model. The medical model does provide valuable information regarding "normal" physical development, hormonal changes, and issues associated with these changes. For instance, you may want to assess whether Alicia is developing at a rate that is similar to her same-age peers. The fact that Alicia's development seems "slow" may be of some concern, particularly because she has been vomiting and losing weight. These problems, though they may not be caused by physical factors, may exacerbate problems with her physical growth in the long run. For example, she may not get the adequate nutrition she needs to continue to grow.

However, it may be more useful to assess Alicia's situation from a biopsychosocial perspective, bringing in aspects of other theories such as ecological theory and Piaget's theory of cognitive development. These theories will help you assess many other areas in Alicia's life, beyond the physical, that may impact her physical development. For instance, you may want to examine how Alicia's environment at home or school impacts her eating patterns. Specifically, does Alicia's mother have enough money to afford nutritious foods? Has her family established nutritious eating patterns? Does Alicia have access to low-cost lunch programs at school if cost is an issue? Because Alicia spends a great deal of time in the "street," where is she getting her meals?

Cognitive, Personality, and Emotional Development

Though a great deal of important cognitive development has occurred by adolescence, the teen years are a time when cognitive skills become more complex and sophisticated. To examine the cognitive milestones achieved during adolescence, we can revisit Jean Piaget's theory. Recall from Piaget's theory that it is in adolescence that individuals enter the formal operations stage. As a result, teens are able to think more abstractly than younger children. Adolescents move away from concrete thinking to think hypothetically about situations. They use reason and logic and take the perspective of others when considering situations.

With formal operations also comes the ability for **meta-thought,** or the ability to think about thinking. Adolescents are also able to think about abstract ideas such as ideals, qualities, and characteristics that describe people and their personalities as well as concepts related to right and wrong (Piaget, 1972; Piaget & Inhelder, 1969). Because of the ability to think abstractly and logically, adolescents become capable of grappling with complex issues such as morality and spirituality.

Although Piaget's theory of cognitive development offers helpful ideas about cognitive development and abilities in adolescence, keep in mind that this theory has limitations. For example, the white matter and prefrontal cortex in teens' brains are still developing, axons are still making neural connections, and the myelin sheaths are still forming to help neurons communicate with one another. This aspect of brain development progresses into our early twenties, so it is not unusual for teens to have limited logic, judgment, reasoning, decision-making, and other higher-order thinking skills (Paus, 2010).

Further, there tends to be great variability in the achievement of complex cognitive skills; that is, not all people achieve certain skills at the same time. Some adults never exhibit the cognitive skills described in the formal operations stage. For example, this may be particularly true of some individuals in non-Western cultures. Skills pertaining to logic and abstract thinking may not be deemed valuable by people in different cultures, so they are not encouraged or considered to be higher-order skills.

Personality development continues into adolescence. Although identity development is really a lifetime process, identity reaches a more adult-like state by this point. By adolescence many of the physical, cognitive, and emotional changes that occur in childhood have stabilized to a point where adolescents can begin to think of themselves in mature terms. Many adolescents have established identities that will endure into adulthood, although these identities likely will be modified somewhat throughout adulthood and into old age.

With regard to emotional development, although teens are much more emotionally mature than younger children, they tend to process emotion a bit differently than adults. Teens tend to rely on the amygdala for emotional processing whereas adults use the frontal cortex. Thus, teens tend to be more impulsive and overreactive than adults and less able to accurately interpret others' emotions (Gogtay *et al.*, 2004).

Adolescence is a time when many decisions must be made, such as whom to date, whether to experiment with drugs and alcohol, and whether to have intercourse. But, as was discussed previously, adolescents' brains may not be quite ready developmentally to logically handle these types of decisions or to think through their consequences. Thus, according to their adult caregivers, teens often make "irrational" decisions or even dangerous decisions, such as texting while driving. Adolescents also begin to think about their values and beliefs in many areas (politically, religiously, and socially) and how to live their lives based on these values and beliefs. All of these questions and considerations help adolescents to establish their identities, which is the foundation for their adult experiences (Habermas & Bluck, 2000; Habermas, Ehlert-Lerche, & de Silveira, 2009).

You could assess Alicia's cognitive development based on Piaget's formal operations stage to ascertain whether she is cognitively able to understand the consequences of her behaviors for her physical health. It is possible that Alicia is unable to think logically about the need for proper nutrition at this point in her development. Her possible malnutrition could further decrease her cognitive abilities, making her symptoms of depression and eating disorder worse.

Moral Development

As mentioned earlier, the development of higher-order thinking skills in adolescence is a factor in the development of an individual's moral code. Theories of moral development focus on how people come to espouse certain values and beliefs about what is right, wrong, good, and bad. You can use these theories to conceptualize moral development in adolescence as well as at other stages in the life span.

Kohlberg's Theory of Moral Development   One of the best-known theorists on moral development is Lawrence Kohlberg, who developed his ideas through studying children. His theory defines moral development as a process that occurs in six stages, categorized in three levels. He conceptualizes the basis of an individual's morality as progressing from simple rewards and punishment to moral principles concerned with the common good (Kohlberg, 1976). Exhibit 9.1 describes these levels and stages.

LEVEL 1: PRECONVENTIONAL REASONING (CONVENTIONAL ROLE CONFORMITY)

At this level, people have not internalized moral values. Rather, moral thinking is ruled by rewards and punishments.

- *Stage 1: Punishment and obedience orientation.* People make decisions about what is good and bad to avoid punishment.
- *Stage 2: Naive instrumental hedonism.* People obey rules to get rewarded.

LEVEL 2: CONVENTIONAL REASONING (ROLE CONFORMITY)

At this level, people value the opinions of others. Behavior is guided by external social expectations.

- *Stage 3: Good boy/girl mentality.* People behave in ways that please others.
- *Stage 4: Authority-maintaining morality.* People strongly believe in law and order. Social order is paramount and people will defer to higher authority to guide behavior.

LEVEL 3: POSTCONVENTIONAL REASONING (SELF-ACCEPTED MORAL PRINCIPLES)

At this level, people have internalized moral values. Morality extends beyond laws and self-interest.

- *Stage 5: Morality of contract, of individual rights, and of democratically accepted law.* People view laws and social order as necessary; however, laws need to be questioned in light of the common good.
- *Stage 6: Morality of individual principles and conscience.* People's behavior is based in internal principles of what is right and wrong. People make decisions based on what is right for the common good, regardless of whether or not decisions go against law or higher authority.

Source: Adapted from Kohlberg, 1969, 1976, 1981

EXHIBIT 9.1

Kohlberg's Theory of Moral Development

According to Kohlberg's theory, people develop their moral thinking at different rates. Ideally, this development takes place during childhood. However, not everyone will develop to the third, or final, level. Rather, people may remain in different stages depending on their experiences and cognitive development.

Critics make three main points about Kohlberg's theory:

- It places too much emphasis on cognition. That is, the theory describes what people think is right, but that does not necessarily translate into what people actually do.

- We can understand what people are thinking only if they can verbalize their reasoning. Unfortunately, not everyone can do this in the same way. Consequently, some people might seem as though they are not as morally "advanced" as others because they cannot verbalize their thinking.

- Kohlberg's theory is biased in that it may not apply to women or people of other cultures. Specifically, Kohlberg's theory is based in individualistic thinking, which may not apply to people who are more concerned with the perspectives of others and who take those perspectives into consideration when making decisions (Kohlberg, 1978).

However, this theory does offer social workers a broad way to think about the moral development of their clients and how this development might affect clients' behaviors and responses to problems.

Gilligan's Theory of Moral Development In response to some of the criticisms of Kohlberg's theory, particularly its focus on men's development, Carol Gilligan devised her own theory of moral development. Gilligan's theory emphasizes the individual's development of an ability to focus on care, inclusion, and attention to others (Gilligan, 1982; Gilligan & Attanucci, 1988). Exhibit 9.2 displays the levels of this theory.

Gilligan's theory provides some balance to Kohlberg's by demonstrating how people may place more importance on cooperation and inclusiveness than on independence and self-interest. From Kohlberg's perspective, women may be viewed as morally inferior to men. By addressing the ways in which women tend to be socialized, Gilligan's theory better accounts for how women achieve the highest level of moral reasoning.

Both theories have strengths and limitations. However, they both offer useful frameworks from which to conceptualize moral thinking and development.

You might want to identify which stage of moral development Alicia seems to have reached to better determine how she might be viewing her situation. For example, Alicia might be only at level one in Gilligan's theory. She seems to be focused on

EXHIBIT 9.2

*Gilligan's
Theory
of Moral
Development*

LEVEL 1: ORIENTATION TO PERSONAL SURVIVAL

This level describes women's orientation to self-interest and survival. Consideration of others is not important.

Transition 1: Transition from personal selfishness to responsibility. Women begin to take the considerations of others into account in moral reasoning. Self is still important, but women realize that the well-being of others is also important.

LEVEL 2: GOODNESS AS SELF-SACRIFICE

Women see morality as sacrificing their own needs for the sake of others. Women become dependent on the perspectives of others, to the point that they may sacrifice their own needs and feelings.

Transition 2: From goodness to reality. Women are able to balance the needs of others with their own. They consider what is best for others as well as themselves and make decisions that will benefit both.

LEVEL 3: THE MORALITY OF NONVIOLENT RESPONSIBILITY

At this level, women think about the consequences of their moral decisions. Opinions of others are not as important as the integrity of their decisions and the impact those decisions will have on everyone's well-being.

Source: Adapted from Gilligan, 1982

survival and her own needs. However, it could also be that this kind of focus is "normal" for an adolescent Alicia's age.

Regardless, you could use this conceptualization as a base from which to proceed with an intervention for Alicia. If Alicia is primarily concerned with her own needs at this point, an intervention that uses her concern for others probably will not be effective. Further, interventions that use family members and peers as supports might not be immediately effective since Alicia will probably not be concerned with what they think. Nevertheless, this kind of approach could help Alicia move into transition 1 of Gilligan's theory. Specifically, through working with family and peers, Alicia may begin to understand how others feel, which may lead her to take responsibility for her actions and her situation.

THE INDIVIDUAL IN ADOLESCENCE

Though physical changes during puberty can be dramatic, many other changes and issues that teens experience during this time can wreak havoc for them. Often, it is these issues that bring adolescents and their families to seek the help of social workers. Here, we will look at some of the micro-level problems that may present themselves during this time in life.

Learning

Traditional learning is often described in linear terms. Information is presented, comprehended, and then learned. However, it is obvious from problems that many adolescents have with learning in school that this model does not describe all learning experiences. David A. Kolb conceptualized learning as a circular, ascending spiral of learning. His **theory of experiential learning**, which is partially derived from Piaget's theory of cognitive development, suggests that learning is a four-step process (Kolb, 1984):

1. Students engage in hands-on learning to gain experience.

2. Students spend time in subjective, personal reflection on the experience.

3. Students engage in abstract conceptualization by connecting their experiences with larger perspectives provided from theory, research, and other authoritative sources that enable students to reflect on their experiences from an objective perspective.

4. Students practice their previous learning in more complex learning environments, which is followed by more reflection, connection, conceptualization, and experience (Caldwell & Claxton, 2010).

Kolb's model begins with students actively engaging with information, and learning continues as they gain experiences that help them to reflect on information and incorporate it into their existing knowledge base. According to Kolb, knowledge is created through this transformation of experience (Healey & Jenkins, 2000).

One of Alicia's struggles is in the area of education. She is described as doing poorly in school, but it is possible that the standard classroom structure, where the teacher talks and the students listen, is not a good learning method for Alicia. She may perform better in school if she is able to find a learning environment that actively engages her in learning, as Kolb's model suggests. If Alicia is more of a hands-on learner, she may want to explore other schooling options such as a charter or alternative school that follows a more active model of learning.

Self-Esteem

Different aspects of physical, cognitive, emotional, and social development can have profound short- and long-term effects on how adolescents view and evaluate themselves. Similarly, their evaluation can influence how they view the world, which can affect further development and well-being. The overall evaluation of the self is what we call **self-esteem**.

Some research indicates that self-esteem is fairly stable, at least over short periods of time (Tesser, 2000). Other research suggests that self-esteem tends to fluctuate throughout adolescence; it is not a static characteristic that persists over time (Baldwin & Hoffmann, 2002). In some cases, problems with self-esteem during adolescence may be related to mental health issues later in life (Polce-Lynch, Myers, Kliewer, & Kilmartin, 2001).

Perhaps one reason why it is difficult to fully understand how patterns of self-esteem unfold during adolescence is because so many variables can influence it, including:

- timing of physical development and onset of puberty;
- peer and family relationships;
- social norms and expectations; and
- psychosocial factors such as resilience, personality, and coping skills.

For instance, research indicates that self-esteem is influenced by family relationships and various life events (Baldwin & Hoffmann, 2002). Strong, positive family relationships and successful, rewarding life events help to strengthen self-esteem, while negative relationships and experiences can erode it. However, much depends on when certain life events occur and how they are perceived by those experiencing them.

Research findings tend to be mixed with regard to gender differences in levels of self-esteem throughout adolescence. Some studies have found boys to have higher self-esteem than girls, particularly in later adolescence, while others have not found this pattern (for example, Kling, Hyde, Showers, & Buswell, 1999; Polce-Lynch *et al.*, 2001). The relationship between gender and self-esteem seems to be influenced by certain psychosocial factors such as body image and emotional expression.

Media messages that dictate social norms on appearance have considerable effect on boys' and girls' self-esteem. For example, the media glorify thinness and pre-adolescent-like bodies for girls. As girls grow older, their bodies deviate from this norm, which can have a negative effect on self-esteem for some girls. For boys, self-esteem seems to increase as they get older because they "fill out" and better fit the image of the "macho" male (Baldwin & Hoffmann, 2002; Polce-Lynch *et al.*, 2001; Tiggemann, 2001). Interestingly, some research has indicated that high levels of masculinity tend to be associated with high self-esteem and few mental health problems, specifically depression, for both boys and girls (Barrett & White, 2002). It could be that masculine traits are validated by social norms; those who possess and exhibit them are validated by society, thus strengthening self-esteem.

In Alicia's situation, you would certainly benefit from assessing her self-esteem at this point. Because Alicia's problems (possible eating disorder, early maturation, and familial support issues) could be related to low self-esteem, building an intervention around her self-concept might be a useful approach. Moreover, as a girl, she could be at higher risk for low self-esteem than if she were a boy. Media messages, issues at home, and relationships with her peers could put her at risk for poor self-image and subsequent depression later on.

According to Erik Erikson, Alicia, as an adolescent, would be in the stage of identity versus identity confusion. If you adhere to this theory, you would focus on ways in which Alicia's self-esteem are influencing her developing identity and vice versa. You might consider how cultural and social messages are affecting her sense of identity and how familial and peer relationships could be strengthened to buffer her from environmental pressures that may negatively impact her self-esteem.

The interactionist perspective would also be useful in conceptualizing Alicia's situation, as her point of view and the ways she interprets the messages that surround her in her environment will significantly affect her development. A feminist model would also be useful in this scenario, since society tends to set norms that are different for boys and girls. Socialization can affect self-esteem and mental health, but positive interactions with family, peers, and social institutions may help to mediate these effects; for example, education in all-girl schools has been shown to promote self-esteem (Polce-Lynch et al., 2001).

Eating Disorders

In the United States and other Western countries, eating disorders have become a major problem among teens and young adults. Though obesity, binge eating, and other issues surrounding eating patterns fall under the rubric of eating disorders, this section will focus on anorexia and bulimia nervosa, since these tend to be primary concerns for many clients who seek the help of social workers.

Stress, genetics, and family and peer dynamics seem to contribute to the development of eating disorders (Pauls & Daniels, 2000). More recent research has been focusing on brain differences between people with and without eating disorders. For example, researchers like Eric Stice at the Oregon Research Institute are using magnetic resonance imaging to examine differences in the impulse control areas of the brain among those with eating disorders. Others are examining the hereditary nature of eating disorders and the role hormones play in development of symptoms (Klump, Keel, Culbert, & Edler, 2008). The media have also been implicated. They have a powerful influence on body image, which in turn may impact self-esteem. A body of research indicates that women tend to evaluate their bodies negatively more often and place more emphasis on their looks than do men (Muth & Cash, 1997; Tiggemann, 2001; Tylka & Sabik, 2010). However, other studies have found that men attend to their bodies as much as women, which may account for the

QUICK GUIDE 13	Diagnostic Criteria for Anorexia and Bulimia Nervosa
DISORDER	**DESCRIPTION**
Anorexia nervosa	Refusal to maintain body weight that is appropriate for age and height. Intense fear of gaining weight. Disturbance in perceived body image. Loss of menstruation for at least three consecutive months.
Bulimia nervosa	Recurrent binge-eating episodes (must occur in discrete time periods and person must feel loss of control over eating). Behaviors to avoid weight gain such as use of laxatives, excessive exercise, or vomiting. Behaviors must occur at least twice a week for at least three months. Disturbance in perceived body image. Disturbance does not occur with an episode of anorexia.

Source: From the *Diagnostic and Statistical Manual of Mental Disorders, Fourth Edition, Text Revision*, in Psychopharmacology. Copyright © 2000. Reprinted with permission from the *Diagnostic and Statistical Manual of Mental Health Disorders*, Copyright 2000. American Psychiatric Association

increasing numbers of men suffering from eating disorders (Striegel-Moore *et al.*, 2009; Wilcox, 1997). Viewing media images that promote thin bodies has been found to be an important predictor for a person's drive toward thinness, distorted body image, and eating problems (Vartanian, Giant, & Passino, 2001).

Quick Guide 13 lists the diagnostic criteria for anorexia and bulimia nervosa.

Below we will examine the factors that contribute to these disorders in more detail and consider how these disorders can affect social work.

Anorexia Nervosa A disorder characterized by behaviors that lead to extreme thinness, **anorexia nervosa** tends to develop in the early and middle teen years. Typically, anorexia begins after dieting and experiencing some kind of stressor. Dieting turns into a severe restriction of food intake, excessive exercise, and sometimes vomiting or intake of laxatives. Although anorexia is clearly associated with environmental pressures, some studies indicate a genetic link to the disorder as well, as was mentioned earlier.

These are some of the symptoms of anorexia:

- *Psychological symptoms:* anxiety, depression, flat affect (or little expression of emotion), obsessive-compulsive behaviors.

- *Physical symptoms:* dry skin, stunted growth, reduced bone density, loss of menstruation, fine downy hair on the body and face, heightened sensitivity to cold, cardiac problems, and ultimately, death.

Although physical problems associated with eating disorders can affect fertility, women with anorexia may underestimate their ability to get pregnant (Easter, Treasure, & Micali, 2011).

The prevalence of anorexia among teens in the United States is approximately 0.9 percent (Hudson, Hiripi, Pope, & Kessler, 2007). The disorder generally affects white, middle- and upper-class girls who come from highly educated and achieving families (Striegel-Moore, Silberstein, & Rodin, 1993). Though boys also develop the disorder, it is much more common among girls, who are about 10 times more likely to suffer from the disorder (Fairburn & Harrison, 2003; Garner & Desai, 2001). Its incidence appears to have increased somewhat since the 1970s, particularly among girls between ages 15 and 24 (Hoek, 2006).

People with anorexia are generally unable to see the destructive nature of their behaviors. Their extreme dieting is reinforced by messages in the environment about the desirability of weight loss and by comments made by others about their appearance. If properly treated, many of these problems are reversible. The most effective treatment methods appear to be antidepressant medications and couples, family-based, and psychodynamic therapies (Bulik, Baucom, Kirby, & Pisetsky, 2011; Fairburn & Harrison, 2003).

Bulimia Nervosa Although similar in some ways to anorexia, **bulimia nervosa** is characterized by a consistent eating binge-and-purge pattern. The purging occurs through exercise, vomiting, or laxative use. Bulimia usually develops in late adolescence or early adulthood and can persist through later adulthood. Bulimia often begins in similar ways as anorexia, but it is more prevalent—it afflicts approximately 1 percent to 3 percent of teens in the United States—and is found across social classes (Newport Academy, 2014). Research indicates that bulimia and related binge disorders may be more prevalent among those in ethnic minority groups, especially Latino and black groups, than previously estimated (Alegria *et al.*, 2007).

Like people with anorexia, people with bulimia are obsessed with thinness and suffer from a distorted body image. However, unlike people with anorexia, those with bulimia generally are of average weight, are ashamed of their behaviors, and have some insight into the disordered nature of their habits (Fairburn & Harrison, 2003).

Because many people with bulimia go to great lengths to hide their behaviors and tend to maintain average or above-average weight, bulimia can be more difficult to detect than anorexia. These are some of the symptoms:

- *Psychological symptoms:* depression, obsessive-compulsive behaviors, and substance abuse (Zaider, Johnson, & Cockell, 2002).

- *Physical symptoms:* Dehydration, dizziness, cardiac problems, electrolyte imbalances, erosion of tooth enamel.

Like anorexia, bulimia can delay pregnancy, increase rates of unplanned pregnancy, and increase negative feelings about being pregnant. Also as with anorexia, the most effective treatments for bulimia appear to be antidepressant, cognitive-behavioral, and family-based therapies (Fairburn & Harrison, 2003). However,

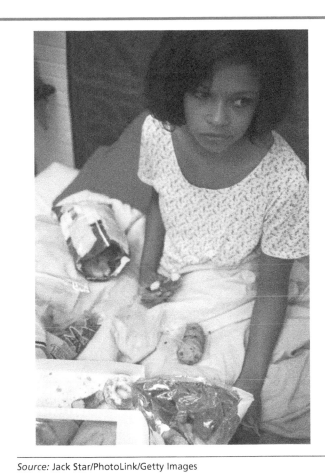

PHOTO 9-A

Bulimia is a serious eating disorder that can cause many physical and other problems for people who suffer from it

research suggests that eating disorders tend to be under-treated, particularly among men and ethnic minority groups (Striegel-Moore *et al.*, 2010).

From the information presented on Alicia, she appears to have several symptoms that are consistent with an eating disorder. Poor growth and development, depression, weight loss, family problems, and, of course, vomiting are all areas that you will want to assess. She may also be at risk for amenorrhea, or the absence of her period, which could put her at risk for future osteoporosis or other problems. Because there are many physical and psychological problems associated with an eating disorder that could be making Alicia's current situation worse, you will want to focus on these particular issues.

Though you could view the cause of her potential eating disorder from many different theories and perspectives, this is probably not as important as seeking treatments that have been shown to be effective through research. For example, rather than conceptualizing Alicia's eating problems through a biopsychosocial perspective, you might want to begin with a cognitive or behavioral intervention, since their effectiveness has been empirically supported in cases of eating disorders.

Early and Late Maturation

Even when eating disorders are not a factor, the timing and progress of physical development can have far-reaching emotional and other effects on teens. Since there is so much variability in the rate of development among teens as well as in the end result of that development (for example, differing body types), many professionals are interested in how developmental processes impact the emotional well-being and long-term adjustment of teens.

Generally, research has indicated that both early and late maturation patterns can have positive and negative effects for teens:

- *For boys:* Early maturation often means increased physical ability, which can bring respect and admiration from peers. Evidence from one longitudinal study suggests that early maturing boys are better adjusted and more confident than late maturing boys. Conversely, late maturing boys may be perceived as less physically desirable due to their small size. Thus, late maturing boys may engage in more attention-seeking behaviors that are viewed by others as immature and inappropriate (M. C. Jones, 1965; Jones & Bayley, 1950). However, some evidence suggests that early maturing boys may feel more social pressure than late maturing boys, since others may expect the former to behave responsibly and to act as positive role models for other boys (Papalia, Olds, & Feldman, 2001).

- *For girls:* The effects of early versus late maturation may be less clear. In one longitudinal study, researchers found that girls who matured early showed some problems in school but were more popular with boys and showed more independence than late maturing girls (Simmons & Blyth, 1987). More recent evidence suggests that early maturation among girls may place them at higher risk for anxiety, depression, substance use, early sexual exploration, dysfunctional responses to stress, and problems in school than their late maturing counterparts (Reardon, Leen-Feldner, & Hayward, 2009; Sarigiani & Petersen, 2000; Sontag, Graber, Brooks-Gunn, & Warren, 2008; Stattin & Magnusson, 1990).

Keep in mind that the research discussed here offers only a general idea of how maturation patterns can affect individuals. There is much variability among individuals, and responses to timing can also be affected by many other psychosocial factors such as peers, family, culture, personality, and cognitive and emotional development.

> *In Alicia's case, you may choose to assess her physical development to ascertain whether she may be at risk for some of the problems associated with early development among girls. For example, Alicia's possible sexual activity may be due to early development. However, you would also want to keep in mind that many other factors are probably influencing her sexual behaviors. Any intervention that targeted sexual issues would need to incorporate a comprehensive assessment of factors contributing to her behavior.*

Sexual Identity and Sexuality

During puberty, many physical changes take place that cause teens to think about and struggle with the person they are becoming. This can be a particularly tumultuous time for teens who are questioning their sexuality or who identify with being homosexual. **Sexual identity**, in general, refers to a person's sexual orientation as well as an array of beliefs, attitudes, and behaviors related to sexuality (Buzwell & Rosenthal, 1996). **Sexual orientation** refers to the gender with which a person prefers to have sex (men, women, or both) (Westheimer & Lopater, 2004). Forming a sexual identity also includes experiencing and managing sexual feelings and incorporating this identity into an overarching self-concept as a member of a larger societal context.

The development of a sexual identity is a complex process that is affected by many biopsychosocial factors. Because of the great diversity of individual experience, researchers find it difficult not only to articulate precisely what sexual identity is but also to study how identity develops in ways that describe the experiences of most people. Indeed, terminology used to describe sexual orientation is expanding to better capture the many different ways in which people experience sexual attraction. For example, terms such as **pansexual** are useful to describe the sexual orientation of people who describe themselves as having the capability of attraction to others regardless of gender identity or biological sex. Someone who identifies as pansexual may be attracted to a person who is male, female, transgender, intersex, or gender queer. In other words, the term pansexual is one way of defining sexual identity beyond the typical sexual binary of heterosexual/homosexual—and even beyond bisexuality.

Sexual Activity in Adolescence   For many people, the first sexual intercourse experience is associated with sexual maturity. They often see this as a "coming of age" event. Many adolescents decide to have sex because they feel they are in love, they want to be loved, they want to feel attractive, or they want to please their partners. Others do it to rebel against authority or because they are giving in to peer pressure (Westheimer & Lopater, 2004).

EXHIBIT 9.3	Ever Had Sexual Intercourse, High School Youth Risk Behavior Survey, 2011			
Experience with Sexual Intercourse Among High School Students	**RACE**	**TOTAL %**	**FEMALE %**	**MALE %**
	American Indian or Alaskan Native	69.0	69.2	68.7
	Asian	29.6	26.5	32.3
	Black	60.0	53.6	66.9
	Hispanic	48.6	43.9	53.0
	Native Hawaiian or Other Pacific Islander	53.6	N/A	N/A
	White	44.3	44.5	44.0
	Multiple Race	53.4	50.4	56.5
	TOTAL	47.4	45.6	49.2

Note: All youth who identify as Hispanic are included in Hispanic category; all other races include non-Hispanic youth only.
Source: Sexual Risk Behavior Data & Statistics 2011, Youth Risk Behavior Surveillance System. U.S. Centers for Disease Control and Prevention, 2012. Retrieved August 4, 2012, from http:// www.cdc.gov/ healthyyouth/sexualbehaviors/data.htm

Source: Adapted from Gilligan, 1982

Regardless of the reasons, one of the issues surrounding sexual intercourse among teens is the age and circumstance under which they have sex. As we will see later in this chapter, teen pregnancy and sexually transmitted infections (STIs) are serious issues that must be considered when working with sexually active teens. In addition, teens who are having sex at very young ages are at risk for other biopsychosocial problems such as low academic achievement and familial conflict.

In 2013, a large survey found that approximately 47 percent of all high school students have had sexual intercourse (Centers for Disease Control and Prevention, 2014m). This average tended to vary by ethnic group, as shown in Exhibit 9.3. Data from the Youth Risk Behavior Surveillance System show that about 60 percent of high school students used a condom the last time they had intercourse, and about 25 percent of students or their partners had used birth control pills, an IUD, or some other form of birth control (Centers for Disease Control and Prevention, 2014m). Although research cannot provide precise information about the sexual behaviors of teens, the information we do have is useful in understanding patterns of behaviors that can have lasting and profound effects on the health and well-being of teens.

If, as a social worker, you ascribe to Piaget's theory, you recognize that many adolescents who have not yet attained full formal operational thinking—that is, they cannot reliably think through consequences that may occur in the future—are making decisions about sexual activity. Indeed, as was discussed earlier, teens' brains are still developing, so the inability to rationally anticipate consequences of sex, particularly unprotected sex, is a real possibility. As a social worker, you can help teens in their decision-making process by talking with them about sexual activity and all of the physical, emotional, and social ramifications of engaging in sex.

Sexual Development in Heterosexual Teens   Dealing with the tasks of sexual development can be challenging. Many cognitive, emotional, and social factors influence "normal," heterosexual development. Various theories can be used to describe this process, all of which have something to offer:

- *Biopsychosocial lens:* Helps to conceptualize sexual development within teens' environment.

- *Medical model:* Offers a great deal of information about how hormones influence physical development and sexual preferences. Research is uncovering biological bases to hetero- and homosexuality through studies that involve genetics, hormones, and the brain (for example, studies on siblings, birth order, fingerprints, handedness). (See Westheimer & Lopater (2004) for a comprehensive discussion.)

- *Erikson's theory of psychosocial development:* Compares the stage of identity versus identity confusion to conceptualize how teens develop and articulate their sexual orientation.

- *Freud's theory of psychosexual development:* Explains how teens may have become fixated in previous stages, which may influence their sexuality as they age.

- *Feminist theory:* Shows how sex and gender roles, and even the idea of heterosexuality, are socially constructed and how these concepts might influence sexual identity.

- *Queer theory:* Examines socially constructed labels, categories, and relationships that are seemingly binary (as in male or female) in nature. It suggests that we should look at how definitions of "normal" are socially constructed and problematic for a large proportion of the population (Clark, 2011).

Although these theories can contribute to understanding sexuality and identity development, they are also limited with regard to explaining all aspects of sexuality and the complexities involved in its development.

Given Alicia's age and presenting problems, you may want to assess her sexual identity development. This may be helpful in better understanding how Alicia may or may not be dealing with developmental tasks and how her sexual activity may be impacting her physical, emotional, and psychological development. Peer pressure or loneliness, for example, may be driving Alicia to have sexual experiences before she is ready. These premature experiences could have further ramifications for her development as she ages. For instance, she could contract an STI that would affect her fertility.

Sexual Development in Gay, Lesbian, and Bisexual Teens   Sexual development for homosexual teens requires some of the tasks experienced by heterosexual teens, but many are in addition to the expected tasks associated with development. Many theories on which social workers rely do not address these variations. They view variations from the heterosexual "norm" as deviations ("normal" usually being defined from the Western cultural perspective). Negative connotations are generally attached to sexual deviations, which are viewed as problems that need intervention. Only recently have homosexuality, transgenderism, masturbation, and certain sexual fantasies and sex play been viewed as issues and behaviors that are not necessarily problematic. For example, it was in the 1970s that the American Psychiatric Association and the American Psychological Association took the stance that homosexuality was not a disorder (O'Donohue & Caselles, 1993).

In response to limitations to existing theoretical explanations of sexual development and behavior, various alternative models of sexual development for gay, lesbian, and bisexual teens have been presented (Appleby & Anastas, 1998; Johnson & Johnson, 2000). **Queer theory**, developed in the late 1980s and early 1990s, advocates for examining how a society's definition of "normal" effectively excludes, and even pathologizes, all that is not normal. With regard to homosexual identity development, queer theory would suggest that we reexamine the definition of heterosexuality and the binary of heterosexual/homosexual and articulate ways in which that definition is problematic and oppressive. By examining these labels, we can change the ways in which we perceive and approach human behavior. Another model in this tradition identifies the additional tasks that homosexual teens need to undertake to adapt within a culture that expects heterosexual development. These adaptive tasks are described in Exhibit 9.4.

Models such as these help to guide social workers in their work with gay, lesbian, bisexual, transgendered, and questioning teens as they grapple with their sexuality and other psychosocial issues associated with it. Social workers can provide a great deal of information and support to teens on all levels. They can help teens to explore their personal feelings and beliefs about sexuality, help teens explore how to involve family and friends in their work, and help them learn how to negotiate larger social issues such as heterosexism and negative attitudes toward homosexuality.

Although in general, helping professionals do not view homosexuality as a disorder, many issues associated with it (such as depression, isolation, violence, discrimination, relationship problems) are seen as problematic. Thus there are several ethical issues that may arise for social workers and their teen clients:

EXHIBIT 9.4

*Adaptive
Tasks for
Homosexual
Adolescents*

- **Expanding one's self-concept within the context of gender, family, and cultural group:** Many homosexual teens must come to terms with the discrepancies between how they think, feel, and behave and a world that assumes people are heterosexual. Teens must learn to develop positive feelings about themselves in an environment that rewards heterosexuality.
- **Changing one's relationships and establishing independence:** Adolescence is normally a time when people begin to question the values and beliefs of their parents. Many families hold heterosexist beliefs and may even openly condemn homosexuality as immoral. Homosexual teens must confront these beliefs and attempt to define themselves within the context of their relationships and social environment.
- **Building social supports:** Though peer groups can be helpful to teens in exploring identity, many homosexual teens may have trouble finding appropriate social supports in which to do this. Heterosexual peers may not be accepting of homosexuality and may aggravate homosexual teens' attempts to establish an identity and place within a social structure.
- **Exploring career, vocational, and educational goals:** Adolescence is a time to work on self-efficacy through achievement and success in academics, setting the stage for pursuing higher education and career-related goals. Homosexual teens must confront institutional discrimination and find ways to move toward their goals while fighting social barriers that may impede their success.
- **Establishing intimate relationships:** Dating, flirting, holding hands, falling in love, and other activities that occur during adolescence that help teens prepare for adult relationships are difficult for homosexual teens to do, at least in public. Homosexual teens must find other ways to "practice" relationship skills; often this is done through passing as heterosexual or lying about one's identity, which hinders the development of honest, trusting intimate relationships.

Source: From *Not Just a Passing Phase: Social Work with Gay, Lesbian and Bisexual People*, by G. A. Appleby and J. Anastas. Copyright © 1998 Columbia University Press. Reprinted by permission

- *Separation of homosexual teens:* To reduce the problems associated with non-normative teen sexuality, some communities have opened separate high schools for gay, lesbian, bisexual, and transgender teens. Although many teens enjoy the separation—they argue that in a separate facility they are free to learn rather than spend energy on fighting harassment—critics contend that this policy only perpetuates discrimination. One way to combat fear of homosexuality is through exposure to gay, lesbian, bisexual, and transgendered individuals.

- *Discrimination by authorities:* Even though gay, lesbian, and bisexual teens are not any more likely than their heterosexual peers to engage in criminal behaviors, they are more likely to be treated unfairly and harshly by police, school officials, and the court system. These teens are more likely to be stopped by police, expelled from school, and arrested than their straight peers, which can have many short- and long-term legal, educational, financial, and other ramifications (Himmelstein & Bruckner, 2011). Social workers must play a central role in thinking through these issues, educating those making such decisions about ethical and social considerations involved in their actions, and devising ways to eradicate the discrimination that propels people to take such actions in the first place.

• *Practitioners' own views on homosexuality:* Even within the helping professions, some believe that homosexuality is immoral. Ethically, practitioners have a responsibility to explore their own beliefs on the issue to better understand how these might interfere with their work with clients. This is particularly important since social workers are expected to support client self-determination (NASW, approved 1996, revised 2008). Social workers especially need to be cognizant of how their own prejudiced beliefs about sexuality might harm gay, lesbian, and bisexual clients.

• *Conversion of homosexual clients:* Practitioners also need to be aware of questionable interventions that are offered to "change" a client's orientation (often known as **conversion therapy**) from homosexual to heterosexual. Even if practitioners do not agree with a client's sexual orientation, suggesting interventions that are not empirically supported or that could be harmful to clients is unethical (indeed, California state recently banned the practice on minors). Given the amount of research that supports the biological and other underpinnings of homosexuality, simply changing an individual's orientation through therapy should be viewed with much skepticism (Behavioral Health Treatment, 1997; Cianciotto & Cahill, 2006; Shidlo & Schroeder, 2002). According to the *Code of Ethics* (NASW, approved 1996, revised 2008), practitioners have a responsibility to examine research on these and other interventions before suggesting them to clients. Examining this issue through the lens of Queer Theory, which views binary definitions of sexuality as the problem, would also speak to the harmful and oppressive practice of conversion therapy.

• *Client repression of homosexuality:* Social workers may work with clients who, because of religious beliefs or other reasons, wish to attempt to change their orientation or at least to live as a heterosexual while acknowledging homosexual feelings. Again, social workers need to understand how their own values in this area might affect their work with clients. Having sound, empirically based information to share with clients so that they can make educated decisions about how to approach their problems is an important step.

STIs, HIV, and AIDS   Social workers need to understand sexually transmitted infections, or STIs, especially if they work with adolescents. Many adolescents are having their first sexual experiences, some at very young ages, and these actions can impact their health and well-being, perhaps for the rest of their lives. It is usually when teens experience negative consequences of sexual behavior (for example, contracting an STI or becoming pregnant) that social workers are asked to intervene. Exhibit 9.5 lists common STIs as well as brief descriptions and treatments for each.

It is estimated that every year 20 million new cases of STIs develop, nearly half of them among those in the 15 to 24 age group (Centers for Disease Control and Prevention, 2014i). Teens only represent about a quarter of the population who

DISEASE	DESCRIPTION	TREATMENT	
Chlamydia	Caused by a bacteria. Most common STI in the United States. Often goes unrecognized and untreated in men and women. Can cause infertility in women and eye disease, prematurity, and pneumonia in infants. Can make contraction of HIV easier.	Antibiotics	**EXHIBIT 9.5** *Common Sexually Transmitted Infections*
Genital herpes	Caused by a virus. One of the most common STIs in the United States. Often goes unrecognized and can be fatal to a fetus. Can make contraction of HIV easier.	No cure; outbreaks can be controlled by antiviral medication	
Gonorrhea	Caused by a bacteria. Can cause pelvic inflammatory disease, infertility, and tubal pregnancy in women. Can make contraction of HIV easier.	Penicillin or other antibiotics	
Hepatitis B	Caused by a virus. May go away without treatment. Can cause chronic liver disease, liver cancer, and death. Can be passed to a fetus.	Vaccination or antiviral or other medications	
Syphilis	Caused by a bacteria. Progression takes place in stages, which if left untreated can cause cardiovascular and neurological problems and blindness. Can be transmitted to a fetus.	Penicillin	
HIV/AIDS	Caused by a virus. Destroys the body's immune system, which leads to a host of illnesses leading to death. Can be passed to a fetus.	No cure; "cocktails" consisting of various drugs can slow the progression of HIV to AIDS	

Source: Adapted from Centers for Disease Control and Prevention, 2000b

have sexual experience, but because they are more likely than people in other age groups to have multiple sex partners and engage in unprotected sex, they are more likely to contract an STI (Centers for Disease Control and Prevention, 2000a).

Further, psychosocial factors such as emotional and cognitive immaturity, peer pressure, and perceived invulnerability may make some teens more likely to engage in risky behaviors leading to the contraction of STIs.

Here are a few facts about STIs among teens:

- Chlamydia is by far the most commonly occurring STI. In 2012, for every 100,000 people in the U.S., approximately 457 reported being infected with chlamydia (Centers for Disease Control and Prevention, 2014i).

- Though many STIs are curable, teens who have contracted them often do not seek treatment because they are not aware that they have a disease. This failure to seek treatment can lead to severe and irreversible problems later in life such as pelvic inflammatory disease (PID) (Centers for Disease Control and Prevention, 2014i).

- Herpes, an incurable STI, has been estimated to infect about one out of every six people aged 14 to 49 (Centers for Disease Control and Prevention, 2014d).

- The Centers for Disease Control and Prevention (2014i) estimate that rates of chlamydia and syphilis are rising, and rates of gonorrhea are now also on the rise after having declined in the recent past.

- Although rates of herpes increased in the early 1990s, the percentage of people in the U.S. with herpes is declining (Centers for Disease Control and Prevention, 2014d).

- Rates of infection with the hepatitis B virus, which can damage the liver if not treated, are rising around the world but declining among youth in the U.S. due to a vigorous vaccination campaign for children (Nordqvist, 2011).

- Since the beginning of the HIV/AIDS epidemic, over 40,000 people in the U.S. aged 13 to 24 have been diagnosed. Many were likely infected in their teen or earlier years. African Americans represent 57 percent of all HIV infections in this age group (Centers for Disease Control and Prevention, 2014e). Approximately 15 percent of all new cases of HIV infection occur in people 13 to 24 years of age (American Social Health Association, 2010). Though there still is no cure for HIV, there have been advancements in prevention and treatment that have turned HIV/AIDS into a chronic disease. For example, antiretroviral drugs allow people to live with the disease for much longer periods of time, and other drugs are more than 99 percent effective at preventing infection if taken daily (Gilead Sciences, 2014). Further, researchers are developing gene therapies that turn the HIV protein against itself to stop it from replicating (Apolloni, Lin, Sivakumaran, Li, Kershaw, & Harrich, 2013).

Since teens are at high risk for contracting STIs (teens account for half of new STIs) and are the group most likely to have their STIs go untreated, many will undoubtedly have costly complications throughout their lives. For example, having an STI makes a person more susceptible to HIV. Many STIs can affect fertility or be transmitted to a fetus. Thus, in focusing on this issue when working with teens, social workers will not only be cost effective but may also save teens a great deal of physical and emotional grief over the course of their lifetimes. This is particularly important as recent studies indicate that condom use among teens is declining from a high of 60 percent a decade ago, and almost 50 percent of sexually active college students report not using condoms (Centers for Disease Control and Prevention, 2014i).

If Alicia is having sexual intercourse, you need to ascertain how much she knows about STIs and the things that she can do to protect herself. From a biopsychosocial standpoint, Alicia may be biologically and physically ready for sex, especially if she is an early developer, but she may not be cognitively or emotionally prepared for it and the ramifications it may bring. According to Piaget, Alicia is likely to be in the formal operations stage in which she should be able to reason and use logic. If, for some reason, she has not moved to or mastered this stage, she may not be able to cognitively understand the possible consequences of her actions. Or, from an ecological or systems perspective, you may consider that Alicia is experiencing a great deal of peer pressure, lack of familial support, and lack of educational and other services to help her learn about STIs and ways to protect herself if she is sexually active. All of these models, as well as many others, can provide useful ways in which to think about, assess, and work with Alicia's situation.

Substance Abuse

Unfortunately, the United States is the leader in adolescent drug use compared to other industrialized nations, with alcohol being the most commonly used substance (Johnston, O'Malley, & Bachman, 2001). The popularity of alcohol and other drugs tends to ebb and flow over time depending on factors such as the economy and the availability of various drugs; so social workers who may be concerned with such issues need to keep up to date on drug use trends in their local communities.

Teen drug use, including the use of nicotine, declined during the 1980s but increased during the 1990s. This trend hit its peak in the mid-1990s, after which the rates declined slightly until 2001 and have remained steady ever since. Some of the common drugs used by teens in the 1990s included LSD and other hallucinogens, inhalants, marijuana, and amphetamines. Since then, there has been an increase in the use of club drugs such as ecstasy, a methamphetamine, and Rohypnol, the so-called date rape drug. The latter drug is so named because it causes amnesia in users (Johnston, O'Malley, & Bachman, 2001; Moolchan & Mermelstein, 2002). Abuse of prescription medication, such as Hydrocodone and Oxycontin, is also a concern.

Alcohol and other substance use and abuse can cause myriad short- and long-term problems for adolescents and their families. For example, teens who abuse drugs exhibit higher rates of violence, accidents, early sexual intercourse, unintended pregnancies, and STIs than teens who do not have substance abuse problems (Bryan & Stallings, 2002). They are also at risk for disrupted development and low academic achievement, which can impact their long-term health and chances for financial and other success in adulthood (McCluskey, Krohn, Lizotte, & Rodriguez, 2002).

Factors Associated with Substance Abuse Extensive research has been conducted on the factors associated with substance abuse among teens. Results of this research indicate that stressful life events (such as illness and divorce) and conflicted relationships with peers and parents are consistent predictors for substance abuse among teens. Specifically, poor social supports from peers and parents, lack of quality relationships, and frequent conflict and arguments in relationships tend to place teens at risk for substance abuse. Conversely, close, supportive relationships with parents tend to buffer teens from substance abuse. This may be why alcohol use among teens tends to increase during high school years; this is a time, developmentally, when teens are attempting to assert their independence, which may cause conflict with their parents. When teens enter their twenties, these conflicts tend to decrease, as does alcohol use (Aseltine & Gore, 2000). So, while the cause-and-effect relationship between substance use and relationships may not be clear-cut, the two do seem to be associated.

Of course, many other situational and personality factors impact the association between relationships and substance use, which social workers need to explore with their teen clients. For example, exposure to family alcohol abuse in childhood also tends to be significantly associated with teenage substance abuse, particularly among males. A tendency to abuse or become dependent on alcohol may therefore be inherited, or teens may imitate the behaviors modeled by their parents or caregivers (Ritter, Stewart, Bernet, Coe, & Brown, 2002). Research also indicates that substance abuse and addiction are associated with abnormal brain structures responsible for self-control, suggesting that there are neurocognitive processes that contribute to addiction (Ersche *et al.*, 2012).

Many adult addictions are established in the teen years. Moreover, the health problems that result from these addictions do not manifest themselves until much later in life. Thus social workers often see adult clients who have significant health and addiction problems. Social workers who work with teens can play a significant role in preventing these addictions from developing in the first place.

As Alicia's social worker, you may be concerned about her possible substance use or abuse. The fact that she is having relationship problems—particularly with her mother—problems coping, and other acting out behaviors such as vomiting after meals, running away, and possible sexual involvement, means she is at risk for abusing drugs or alcohol. You may choose to conduct an in-depth assessment to determine which factors are present that increase her risk for substance abuse and develop an intervention that will target these areas. Since substance abuse could lead to many other serious and long-term problems for Alicia, this may be an area especially worth pursuing if you work with Alicia.

Research with Teens: An Ethical Dilemma   According to the *Code of Ethics* (NASW, approved 1996, revised 2008), social workers have an ethical responsibility to conduct research that will advance knowledge in the field and promote effective practice. Having current and accurate information on issues such as teen substance use as well as other issues such as sexuality, teen pregnancy, and sex education is crucial if social workers are to develop appropriate and effective interventions.

However, social workers and other professionals are often faced with dilemmas when conducting research that uses children or teens as participants. Although many sources of research grants such as the National Institutes of Health (NIH) now require that children and teens be included in research, there are many barriers that must be overcome in doing so. For example, parents or legal guardians are required to give consent for minors to participate in research projects. Researching touchy subjects such as drug use or sexual behaviors (some of which include illegal behaviors) may lead to inaccurate or biased results because of this consent issue. That is, participants who need consent from guardians to participate may not truthfully disclose the nature of their behaviors because they are afraid that their parents might have access to this information. Participants may also fear that they will be turned over to authorities if they disclose that they are participating in any illegal activity. Some parents may also volunteer their children for participation in a study even though, because of developmental limitations, their children may not fully understand the nature of the study or be able to weigh its risks and benefits (Moolchan & Mermelstein, 2002). Some researchers question if this situation can lead to true informed consent.

Even though social workers need to conduct research on these issues to gain knowledge, they can run into problems of whether or not they are producing valid and reliable knowledge and whether or not they are protecting the dignity and worth of the participants of this research. More than ever, it is crucial that social workers take an active role in dealing with and providing solutions for these dilemmas.

Suicide

Suicide among adolescents has been an increasing problem over the past several decades. Suicide is the third leading cause of death for young people aged 15 to 24, accounting for 20 percent of all suicidal deaths. One study found that female teens had significantly more suicidal thoughts and attempts than males. Also, white male and female adolescents had more suicidal thoughts than African–American male and female adolescents. However, males are more likely to die from suicide than females, with 79 percent of deaths being males. Further, Native American and Hispanic youth are more likely to die from suicide than young people from other ethnic groups (Centers for Disease Control and Prevention, 2014j).

Because of the complex relationship of biopsychosocial factors that contribute to suicidal thoughts and attempts, understanding which factors, by themselves or in combination, contribute to the problem is difficult. However, research on adolescent suicide has pointed to some consistent factors that seem to play a part in suicide (Bolognini *et al.*, 2002; National Center for Health Statistics, 2000; Perkins & Hartless, 2002):

- Stressful life events such as academic problems or unintended pregnancy.
- Strained relationships with peers, friends, parents, boyfriends, and girlfriends.
- Substance abuse.
- Feelings of hopelessness.
- Physical and sexual abuse.
- Previous suicidal thoughts and attempts.

Suicide is a particularly important issue among homosexual youths. Gay, lesbian, bisexual, and transgendered adolescents, as well as youths questioning their sexuality, are at even higher risk for suicide than heterosexual youths. Moreover, many teens may be victims of discrimination, violence, or family rejection because of their sexuality, which is an additional stressor that increases their risk for suicide (Almeida, Johnson, Corliss, Molnar, & Azrael, 2009; Plöderl & Fartacek, 2009; Ryan, Huebner, Diaz, & Sanchez, 2009). A variety of studies point out the suicide risk for this group:

- Approximately 15 percent of gay and lesbian teens said they had attempted suicide compared to only 7 percent of heterosexual teens (Russell & Joyner, 2001).
- Among almost 3,000 young gay men in one study, a significant percentage (21 percent) had made a suicide plan. Further, younger gay men were found to be at higher risk for planning and attempting suicide than older gay men, particularly those exposed to a hostile environment, defined as antigay harassment, parental abuse, and similar behaviors (Paul *et al.*, 2002).
- Gay and lesbian teens who perceive an unsupportive social environment (e.g., lack of gay–straight alliances or anti-bullying policies at school) are significantly more likely to attempt suicide than their gay and lesbian peers who feel they have more social supports in place (Hatzenbuehler, 2011).

The development of a homosexual identity in adolescence is difficult and can lead to problems such as depression, substance abuse, and feelings of isolation (Sullivan & Wodarski, 2002). These are factors that contribute to a higher suicide rate for sexual minority youth. Social workers need to be aware of these pressures so they can provide the added support that these young people often require.

A useful tool for assessing the possibility of suicide is the SAD PERSONS scale (Patterson, Dohn, Bird, & Patterson, 1983), which is shown in Quick Guide 14. The acronym makes it easy to remember, and the components to be assessed are empirically based predictors for suicide. The social worker gives one point to each component that is present for a client; the higher the score, the higher the risk for suicide for that particular client (Patterson *et al.*, 1983). For example, for a male client, the social worker would add one point. If the client is 20 years old, the social worker would add another point.

QUICK GUIDE 14   SAD PERSONS Suicide Assessment

Sex (Males are more likely to complete suicide.)
Age (Younger than 25 and older than 45 are more likely to complete suicide.)
Depression

Previous attempt
Ethanol abuse
Rational thinking loss
Social support loss
Organized plan
No spouse or partner
Sickness

Source: Adapted from Patterson, Dohn, Bird, & Patterson, 1983

Many of the behaviors that Alicia is exhibiting, particularly weight loss, depressed mood, low self-esteem, and problems with her mother, could indicate that she is at risk for suicide. You would need to do a more thorough assessment to determine whether or not this may be a problem that needs intervention. In Alicia's case, you would need to gain some additional information to use the SAD PERSONS assessment, but it would give you a fairly quick idea of whether or not suicide might be an issue for her.

THE FAMILY AND IMMEDIATE ENVIRONMENT IN ADOLESCENCE

Many of the issues discussed so far can have a profound impact on the adolescent's immediate environment. Families, peers, and other close social systems are areas that social workers must consider when they are working with adolescents. Because teens, developmentally, tend to be working toward independence but are still some-what dependent on their families for emotional, financial, and other support, this is a time when paying attention to the connections between the individual and the environmental realms is especially relevant for social workers.

Peer Groups in Adolescence

Just as in middle childhood, peer groups play a major role in the lives of adolescents. Most parents, professionals, and theorists (for example, Freud, Erikson, Bandura, interactionists) recognize this reality. In fact, peer pressure is one of the main con-cerns for parents of teenagers. Peers can exert a great deal of influence over an ado-lescent's behaviors, both in positive and negative ways. Thus, social workers need to understand the dynamics of peer relationships during adolescence and ways in which they can help their adolescent clients avoid and deal with negative conse-quences of these relationships.

The extent to which one teen influences the behavior of another teen can depend on many factors such as personality, coping skills, and other support systems. For example, a teenager may not be easily pressured into trying drugs if she has close, positive, and supportive relationships with her parents. Conversely, a teen who lacks positive parental relationships may benefit from imitating positive behaviors of close friends. An important consideration for social workers, then, is that peer pressure and peer relationships are not necessarily straightforward, making a thorough assessment of the situation necessary.

One helpful way to conceptualize peer relationships is through attachment theory. Some research suggests that the quality of attachments with parents influ-ences attachments with peers during adolescence and later in life. For instance, secure and supportive attachments with parents help teens form secure attachments with peers. Secure attachments with parents may also make teens more resilient to negative peer pressure.

Conversely, teens who have insecure attachments with their parents may be more vulnerable to negative peer pressure. They would tend to place more importance on peer relationships, feeling more pressure to conform to group norms and to please friends. However, one study showed higher levels of emo-tional problems among adolescents who lacked parental support but who had close relationships with peers (Helsen, Vollebergh, & Meeus, 2000). The explana-tion may be that, in addition to having negative relationships with their parents, these teens had not learned from their parents the basics of stable, positive rela-tionships. Thus, relationships with friends took on great importance, and when these relationships ran into problems, the teens had no skills to mend them or other support systems to help them. Thus, they may have been more likely to engage in negative behaviors just to please their friends rather than risk losing those relationships.

From an attachment point of view, Alicia may be vulnerable to negative peer pressure because of her strained relationship with her mother. In fact, her "street friends" might be her only source of support. You may want to assess Alicia's support systems to understand the extent to which she is, or may be, influenced by her peers.

Teen Pregnancy

You can view teen pregnancy as an individual issue, but we discuss it in this section because of its far-reaching effects on families and other social systems. Although the outcome of every teen pregnancy is not unfavorable, it frequently leads to a variety of individual, familial, and social problems in which social workers intervene.

The good news about the teen birth rate is that it declined by 36 percent between 2007 and 2013, reaching historic lows (Hamilton, Martin, Osterman, & Curtin, 2014). Among industrialized nations, however, the United States still has one of the highest teen pregnancy rates (Centers for Disease Control and Prevention, 2001). In 2010, teen birth rates in the U.S. (34 percent) were higher than in the United Kingdom (25 percent), Australia (15.5 percent), Canada (14 percent), France (12 percent), and Sweden (6 percent) (United Nations Millennium Development Goal Indicators, 2014); the United States still remains the leader in teen pregnancy, abortion, and STI rates (Centers for Disease Control and Prevention, 2009). Rates for Latinas in the United States continue to be high and of some concern (Centers for Disease Control and Prevention, 2001, 2009; Child Trends, 2001; Maynard, 1996).

Many types of problems are associated with teen pregnancy:

- Many health problems arise, particularly for the baby (as discussed in Chapter 6).

- Girls who become pregnant in their teen years are more likely to come from impoverished environments, drop out of high school, and spend much of their lifetime as single parents dependent on public assistance than teens who delay childbirth until adulthood.

- Children born to teens are more likely than children born to older parents to be incarcerated, to drop out of school or have low academic achievement, and to become teen parents themselves.

The financial costs of teen pregnancy are high. Preventing teen pregnancy and childbearing in the United States could save around $9 billion per year (Centers for Disease Control and Prevention, 2009; Hamilton, Martin, Osterman, & Curtin, 2014). Another estimate put the total costs of teen pregnancy at around $10.9 billion in 2008 (The National Campaign to Prevent Teen and Unplanned Pregnancy, 2012). These figures do not account for the psychological, social, and other costs of teen pregnancy that cannot be quantified.

Why do teens become pregnant? Piaget's theory indicates that teens may not have the cognitive capacity to understand the consequences of unprotected sex or the reality of parenting a child. However, some research suggests that this is not exactly true. One study suggests that, rather than viewing themselves as "invincible," which is a popular social conception of teens, many adolescents display "unrealistic optimism." They view themselves to be at low risk for certain problems such as STIs or teen pregnancy, so they are unlikely to take extra precautions to prevent them (Whaley, 2000). Other studies indicate that some teens seem overly optimistic about their capabilities to parent, to support a child financially, to obtain support from partners and family, and to continue with their education. Some teens may also have a strong need for stability and control and may view becoming pregnant as the only way to meet that need (Montgomery, 2001).

Regardless of the approach taken in conceptualizing teen pregnancy, social workers clearly need to be involved in providing services that either delay pregnancy among adolescents or that support teens who become young parents. Much of the focus of current programs is on the pregnancy itself, ignoring the many other psychosocial factors associated with pregnancy and parenting that ultimately influence the health and well-being of parents and their children.

Given the chances of poor outcomes for teen parents, Alicia's possible sexual activity is cause for concern. You will want to ascertain what kind of knowledge Alicia has about sexual intercourse and contraception as well as what her perceptions are about pregnancy and parenting. Since Alicia appears to be lacking support and stability, she may view becoming pregnant as the only way to gain a sense of control in her life. If Alicia needs a sense of self-efficacy, it may be particularly important for you to focus on her strengths in other areas of her life to help her build self-esteem and a sense of control that will allow her to make informed decisions about sex and parenting.

THE LARGER SOCIAL ENVIRONMENT IN ADOLESCENCE

Just as many physical changes take place during adolescence, many larger social issues affect the well-being of adolescents. This section explores some of these issues that social workers are likely to face when working with adolescent clients.

Sex Education

Earlier in this chapter, we explored sexuality and sexual identity development. With regard to these issues, there are many debates in the United States concerning how to deal with sexual issues and how to provide services for teens (if services are provided at all). Here, we will look at some of these debates and service issues that affect teens, families, and the social workers who work with them.

In addition, many programs and policies have been developed to curb teenage pregnancy. Many of these programs adopt a unilateral approach, focusing on specific aspects of sex education such as abstinence or responsible sexual behavior. In addition, many of the programs that address teen pregnancy are geared toward girls. Few programs offer comprehensive education that addresses the realities of sexual behavior among male and female teens and that provides information on the choices available to teens should they become sexually active.

The Debate over Sex Education Part of the problem behind a lack of appropriate and effective programs has to do with ongoing debates about whether sex education should be provided in schools and, if it is provided, what kinds of information should be presented. Some people argue that sex education is best provided by parents, and schools should not offer such programming. Other people maintain that programs should provide abstinence-only education. Still others feel that more comprehensive programs that provide information on abstinence as well as contraceptive options, life choices, and health care should be available in schools.

Conservative views on teen pregnancy and sex education in general tend to take the position that teens should wait until marriage to have sex; therefore, information on contraception choices and abortion should not be made available to them. Moreover, this viewpoint tends to support the notion that if information on sex is given in schools, it will pique teens' curiosity about sex, spurring more teens to have sex. A more liberal viewpoint insists that a lack of information on sex only puts teens at risk for pregnancy and STIs. Many teens will choose to have sex with or without information; so they should be armed with information intended to keep them as safe as possible.

A Critique of Sex Education Currently, many schools lean toward an abstinence perspective on sex. One study suggests that while nearly 90 percent of high schools teach abstinence, fewer than 60 percent teach about contraceptive methods (Guttmacher Institute, 2012). However, research on sex education has indicated that abstinence-only programs are not effective at reducing teen pregnancy rates or problems with STIs. Further, many professionals argue that abstinence-only programs fail those teens who are sexually active or who choose early parenthood (Rothenberg & Weissman, 2002; Women's International Network, 1997).

For example, one study of close to 3,500 teens found that those who made a "virginity pledge" to abstain from intercourse until marriage were just as likely as non-pledgers to have intercourse outside of marriage within five years of taking the pledge (81 percent of teens were no longer virgins five years after taking the pledge). There were no differences between teens who made the pledge and those who did not with regard to age at first intercourse, average number of sexual partners, types of sexual behaviors in which teens engaged, or sexual partners with STIs. Further, teens who made the pledge were less likely than non-pledgers to protect themselves against STIs, leaving them at higher risk for disease and pregnancy (Rosenbaum, 2009).

Based on research indicating that comprehensive sex education is more effective at reducing the rates of teen pregnancy and STIs, many of the George W. Bush administration's funding and other priorities favoring abstinence-only programs were reversed after he left office (Tanne, 2009). The Obama administration, while still funding abstinence-only programs, shifted more than $114 million to programs that could show they were effective in reducing STIs and unplanned pregnancy (Wilson, 2010).

That is not to say that comprehensive sex education programs are solving all problems related to teen pregnancy. Indeed, they have been criticized for being too limited and shortsighted. Some experts point out that even if accurate information is available at home or at school, teens are likely to turn to peers first for information. However, information from peer sources tends to be unreliable and even incorrect; it tends to be replete with myths, stereotypes, and misinformation about sex and contraception (Guthrie & Bates, 2003). Another problem is that even if teens have access to contraceptives through school or other programs, they may be made to feel guilty about using contraception (Westheimer & Lopater, 2004). Thus, comprehensive education programs need to consider these issues when developing and providing sex education curricula.

Effective sex education is probably best viewed from an ecological or systems approach. Comprehensive programs, even with their limitations, are the most effective in reducing rates of teen pregnancy and STIs. In general, reducing teen pregnancy relies on providing information on life options, access to contraceptive choices, sex education and family planning information, community involvement and support, and abstinence education for young teens (Omar, Fowler, & McClanahan, 2008; Potera, 2008; Zabin, Hirsch, Smith, & Hardy, 1986).

Evidence suggests that programs for reducing teen pregnancy need to be built around a comprehensive model that incorporates myriad components including, but not limited to, parenting education, job training, employment opportunities, academic support, health and mental health care, parental and familial support, developmentally and culturally appropriate sex and contraceptive education (including abstinence), and recreation (for example, sports, drama, and art activities) to promote self-esteem and appropriate emotional outlets. Supportive services for teens and their families also need to be provided after teens become parents.

Further, these programs need to use multidisciplinary staff (for example, social workers, health educators, nurses, physicians, educators, and community and business organizations). Programs need to be long term for staff and teens to develop trusting relationships and to engage teens in activities. Many studies have indicated that when teens and staff have sufficient time to build relationships, teens are more likely to participate fully in program activities. These studies also stress the importance of respecting teens' attitudes, beliefs, and decisions about sex and parenting, which helps to facilitate relationship building and engagement by teens (Morris, Ulmer, & Chimnani, 2003; Philliber, Kaye, Herrling, & West, 2002; Rothenberg & Weissman, 2002).

This latter point is also in keeping with NASW's *Code of Ethics* (approved 1996, revised 2008) relating to the value of respecting clients' self-determination. That is, even if social workers disagree with the opinions of clients and the choices that they make, social workers have an obligation to ensure that clients have access to information and to support clients based on informed decisions.

Heterosexism and Homophobia

As with other isms, such as ageism and sexism, heterosexism is a problem that is embedded in our social fabric. **Heterosexism** is the prejudice or discrimination in favor of those who are heterosexual (and against those who are homosexual). This type of prejudice and discrimination exists on various levels in society, some being more visible and overt than others. **Homophobia** is another type of prejudice based on sexual orientation, but it involves a fear of, or anger, disgust, or discomfort with, homosexuals and homosexuality. Studies indicate that people who are homophobic are generally men, often think that they do not know anyone who is homosexual, have a social network of people who are also homophobic, demonstrate rigidity in gender roles, and have a lower educational level than people who are not homophobic (Reinisch, 1990).

Many of the "causes" of prejudice discussed in Chapter 5 can help to explain how some people might develop homophobic and heterosexist characteristics. A couple of other explanations are useful as well:

- A combination of theories such as social interactionism and behaviorism also offers reasonable explanations for how some people come to hold prejudicial attitudes toward sexual minorities. For example, people who are reared with prejudicial beliefs about homosexuality tend to avoid having positive interactions with people they believe are gay or lesbian, which gives them fewer opportunities to question and analyze the beliefs on which they were reared. In other words, they have no opportunity to change their schema for homosexuality. Further, people with prejudicial beliefs tend to attend to the negative aspects of homosexuality, which reinforces the prejudices that they hold. By the time people are in their teen years, heterosexist beliefs and homophobia are well established.

- A more feminist-oriented explanation of homophobia is based on social constructionism. According to this view, homophobic behaviors are based on fear. Society values traditional, socially constructed masculine traits, which are reinforced at a very young age. Because society offers little flexibility for men in the way of gender roles, those who deviate from masculine norms or who might not "measure up" to these norms are made to feel inferior. These men become fearful of any thought, feeling, or situation that may call into question their masculinity (as defined by society). For such men, being "seduced" or "hit on" by a gay man would be the ultimate threat to their masculinity. When this occurs, they use violence (even though it is fear driven) to defend their masculinity because violence is a socially recognized masculine trait. The violent behavior proves their masculinity and conformance to social norms (Herek, 2001). Using violence against someone who is gay not only reinforces masculinity but also helps to alleviate the fear of being viewed as effeminate.

Individual prejudice and discrimination against people who are homosexual can be hurtful and damaging (even deadly), but institutional heterosexism is often the most problematic. Social and other policies that keep homosexual individuals from being employed, advancing in work, securing housing, adopting children, and marrying, among many other things, affect people in all facets of their lives. Moreover, this type of heterosexism is the most covert and difficult to change.

To reduce homophobia and heterosexism, social workers can maximize the client's positive interactions with sexual minorities to help challenge myths, stereotypes, and prejudicial beliefs about gays and lesbians. Further, as discussed earlier in the chapter, social workers need to be aware of how their own beliefs and values about homosexuality might affect their work with clients. For example, one study that examined prejudice against homosexuality among helping professionals found that social workers who had frequent contact with gay and lesbian clients had lower levels of homophobia than those with less frequent contact. However, social workers who held deep religious beliefs against homosexuality had higher levels of homophobia than social workers who did not have these beliefs (Berkman & Zinberg, 1997).

These conclusions do not suggest that working in a helping profession and having beliefs against homosexuality are incompatible. However, they do indicate that social workers and other professionals must be aware of their own personal values that might bias their work or harm their clients. They also raise myriad ethical questions for practitioners. Consider again, for example, how a social worker who believes that homosexuality is immoral would work with a teen client who thinks she is a lesbian and wants to discuss this in a session. On a broader level, how would social workers' personal beliefs affect their handling of issues such as communities that advocate separate high schools for gay, lesbian, and bisexual students?

Runaway and Homeless Teens

The problem of runaway and homeless teenagers has become increasingly serious over the past several decades. Although the exact number of homeless teens is impossible to pinpoint, estimates are that over 1.6 million youth are homeless, with the majority of them being between the ages of 15 and 17, and approximately 6 percent of homeless youth are gay, lesbian, bisexual, or transgender (Molino, 2007; National Coalition for the Homeless, 2008).

Adolescents who run away and who are homeless often come from chaotic and traumatic family circumstances. Problems at home include physical and sexual abuse, parental alcohol abuse and violence, and behavioral problems on the part of the teen, including drug abuse and discipline problems. Still other teens leave home or foster care situations because they lack self-esteem and strong attachments with caregivers (Kools, 1997; National Coalition for the Homeless, 2008).

Runaway and homeless teens face many challenges. Their situation places them at risk for many of the problems discussed in this chapter such as STIs, pregnancy, violence, substance abuse, and dropping out of school. In turn, these problems can lead to a whole host of developmental and social problems such as disease, mental illness, and relationship and employment difficulties.

Many of the shelters and other programs available to runaway and homeless youths provide only short-term services, such as beds, meals, clothes, counseling, and family mediation. Depending on their age, some older teens deciding not to return home can petition to become independent from their parents. Younger teens will likely enter the state foster system. Unfortunately, many of the programs and options available to runaway and homeless teens, because of their time limits, lack of funding, and overworked staff, do not address the underlying causes of home-lessness, such as low self-esteem and lack of trust and self-efficacy, which may only make the problem worse (Thompson, Bender, Windsor, Cook, & Williams, 2010; Williams, Lindsey, Kurtz, & Jarvis, 2001).

A study of five runaway teens who were considered to be resilient to many of the problems surrounding homelessness found that for a couple of them, establish-ing secure, trusting attachments with shelter and program workers was particularly helpful in increasing self-esteem, self-efficacy, and ultimately, resiliency (Thompson *et al.*, 2010; Williams *et al.*, 2001). Unfortunately, as we have seen, the short-term nature of many programs does not facilitate the building of such attachments. Although this study used a small sample, it still provides social workers with useful information that helps in conceptualizing problems related to teen runaways and barriers to solving these problems.

Looking at Alicia's case, she seems to lack secure attachments with adults; she spends most of her time with her peers on the streets. Nevertheless, the connections she has established with you and the community center, however tenuous they may be, may provide some needed support to build trust and self-efficacy.

Many theories and perspectives offer ways to work with Alicia, but building attachments and self-efficacy takes time. You can bring in the strengths perspective in Alicia's case, using her strengths as immediate examples of the positive aspects in her life. You may also choose to employ a community organization model or something similar to help change the service system for this population. Specifically, it would be useful to change the structure of these programs so they can provide more long-term, attachment-oriented services.

Deviance, Crime, and Violence

Violence and delinquency among adolescents are other problems of concern for teens, families, and social workers. For example, the national Youth Risk Behavior Survey (Centers for Disease Control and Prevention, 2014l) estimated that approximately 5 percent of high school students had carried a weapon to school (as opposed to 12 percent in 1993); about 7 percent had been threatened or injured by a weapon; 7 percent did not go to school because they felt unsafe; 20 percent had been bullied at school; and 8 percent had been in a physical fight at school (up from 4 percent in 2011). Unfortunately, social workers usually come into contact with teens who have problems with these issues after an act of violence has occurred.

Extensive research has been conducted on the causes of deviance, crime, and violence among adolescents (Kosterman, Graham, Hawkins, Catalano, & Herrenkohl, 2001; Walker, 1998). These are some of the factors that have been found to predict violence and delinquency in adolescence:

- *Micro level:* being male; substance use; low educational achievement; low impulse control; feelings of powerlessness; childhood aggression, hyperactivity, and withdrawal.

- *Mezzo level:* family conflict, lack of familial support and discipline, negative peer pressure.

- *Macro level:* poverty, living in high-crime urban neighborhoods, exposure to violence through the media and social environment.

Many of these factors are interrelated. For example, poverty can make it difficult for parents to provide adequate supervision of their children or to offer support. They may be working several jobs or be experiencing extreme stress, making it difficult to engage or spend adequate time with children. Moreover, many poor urban communities have high crime rates, exposing children to violence. They often lack adequate schools, which can contribute to poor academic performance among students.

Interventions geared toward preventing or stopping delinquent behaviors therefore need to focus on the interactive dynamics of the many psychosocial factors involved. For instance, social workers can work toward establishing sufficient funding for better schools and can help to support parents in their child-rearing efforts, particularly those parents who are living in poverty. Social workers can also help to promote self-efficacy and hopefulness in children and teens who are exposed to chaotic, violent, and poverty-stricken environments. Several other theories can also help guide social work interventions in this area.

In Alicia's case, symbolic interaction or social learning theory may be applicable. Alicia's negative interactions with her mother as well as her interactions with friends on the street may be shaping her view on which behaviors are acceptable and useful to meet her needs. Specifically, her friends may engage in some delinquent behaviors, such as stealing, to survive. In Alicia's interactions with these people, she may learn to justify certain delinquent behaviors.

This view intersects with aspects of social learning theory as well. Alicia may see people get rewarded, or at least go without punishment, for various delinquent behaviors. She may also learn how to engage in crimes without getting caught and receive praise from her friends when she is successful, which further reinforces her delinquency.

Using these theories, you could expose Alicia to other individuals (such as yourself or other peers who do not engage in delinquent behaviors) who can show Alicia that some people value nondelinquent behaviors. They can model other, more appropriate ways for her to meet her needs.

CONCLUSION

Adolescence is a time of rapid development and many biopsychosocial changes. Many social workers see teens and their families in their practice because of the issues that can arise. For many teens, self-exploration, identity development, and increasing independence are priorities. These activities are vital to development and can lead to positive experiences, but they can also bring with them problems and issues that need to be addressed to assure optimal health and well-being later in life.

Social work with adolescents often consists of a balance between promoting and supporting growth, development, and independence while acknowledging the interdependence between individual, familial, and societal factors. Many forces are helping to shape the emerging identity of teens, and sometimes these forces create tension and problems for individuals. Social workers play a valuable role in helping teens to work through these issues to help them become healthy, well-adjusted, and successful adults.

MAIN POINTS

- One of the hallmarks of adolescent development is puberty and the hormonal changes associated with it. Patterns in development can impact well-being depending on the timing of maturation and the gender of the individual.

- Cognitive development in adolescence allows the abstract thinking behind the development of moral reasoning.

- Self-esteem can be influenced by a number of factors, from an individual's immediate and larger social environments such as timing of the onset of puberty, family relationships, and the media. It is a protective factor for a number of risks to adolescent well-being.

- Developing a sexual identity includes experiencing and managing sexual feelings and incorporating this identity into an overarching self-concept as a member of a larger society. Teens of all sexual orientations grapple with the tasks of sexual development, but gay, lesbian, and bisexual teens have additional tasks related to discrimination and heterosexism.

- Learning styles, self-esteem, eating disorders, early and late maturation, sexual identity and sexuality, substance abuse, and suicide are major problems for adolescents in the United States, and they have many short- and long-term consequences for adolescents' overall health and well-being. Social workers need to educate themselves, and even advance the knowledge, about these issues and understand the interrelated factors that put youth at risk.

- Peer pressure can have both positive and negative effects on teens. The extent to which one teen influences the behavior of another can depend on many factors such as personality, coping skills, and the presence of other support systems, particularly parents.

- There are many debates in the United States about how to deal with sexual issues and how to provide services for teens, including teen parents. Generally, these debates center on whether to provide sex education in the schools and, if education is provided, what should be included in the curriculum.

- Heterosexism and homophobia exist at both the individual and institutional levels, and they greatly affect the well-being of gay and lesbian people. Social workers can use interventions that maximize positive interactions with sexual minorities, but they need to be aware of how their own beliefs and values might affect this work.

EXERCISES

1. *Sanchez Family interactive case at* www.routledgesw.com/cases. Review the major issues involving the Sanchez family, paying particular attention to Carmen's situation. Then answer the following questions:
   a. In Carmen's case, are there any developmental issues that might need attention? Explain.
   b. Do any of these issues put Carmen at risk for problems as she moves into adulthood?

    c. What interventions might you develop for Carmen to help her avoid potential problems as she matures?

    d. Is there evidence that older family members might now be struggling with issues that relate to developmental issues in adolescence? What might these be?

2. *Riverton interactive case at* www.routledgesw.com/cases. Are there ways in which the theory of moral development could be applied to any particular situation to help you conceptualize or work with problems in this community?

3. *RAINN interactive case at* www.routledgesw.com/cases. Review the case information for Alan and Sarah and then answer these questions:

    a. How would Kohlberg's theory of moral development explain why Alan never told anyone about being raped?

    b. Sarah told a counselor at RAINN that her mother was always bugging her about her weight, saying that Sarah is "too thin." What questions should the social worker ask to assess if Sarah may have a form of an eating disorder?

    c. When Alan was in high school he drank a lot of alcohol, getting drunk almost daily. He once took a case of beer and sat on train tracks to get drunk. His friends found him passed out and got him home before the train came through town. How would the SAD PERSONS scale assess his risk for suicide at that point?

4. *Hudson City interactive case at* www.routledgesw.com/cases. Review the case, and answer the following questions:

    a. How might you, as a social worker working with the Hudson community, apply Kohlberg's and Gilligan's theories of moral development to the Hudson case and those living in the community? How do these theories help to explain some of the issues facing the residents or how residents handle them?

    b. How might the Hudson community situation affect the developing self-esteem of its adolescent residents?

    c. In what ways could problems in the community impact or contribute to problems such as crime, violence, suicide, homelessness, teen pregnancy, substance abuse, and eating disorders?

CHAPTER 10

Development in Early Adulthood

Gudrun is a 25-year-old German American woman who has been admitted into the psychiatric unit of a local hospital. She was brought to the hospital emergency room by the police for "harassing" customers at a downtown business: She yelled at people as they walked by, accusing them of following her and attempting to control her thoughts.

As the social worker in the unit, you have discovered that Gudrun lives alone in a small apartment and is employed part time as a salesclerk. Gudrun's parents, who came to the United States from Germany 20 years ago, live near her apartment. However, Gudrun states that her parents frequently have violent fights, so she does not like to spend much time with them. Gudrun has a boyfriend, but she says that he recently told her that he wanted to break off the relationship. Over the past year, Gudrun has been disciplined twice by her employer for excessive absenteeism. During your interview, Gudrun admitted that recently she has been hearing voices, and she believes that the government and her employer have been monitoring her movements through her television set.

EARLY ADULTHOOD, GENERALLY REFERRED TO AS THE TIME between late adolescence and the early forties, is a time when a majority of individuals experience continued and enhanced growth in many areas such as the sexual, cognitive, emotional, and interpersonal realms. Many young adults are testing out their newfound independence by going to college, securing a job that can support them financially, and moving out on their own. In this chapter, we will explore some issues that tend to highlight this particular time in life and the ways in which social workers can help young adults who face problems.

DEVELOPMENTAL MILESTONES IN YOUNG ADULTS

With the conclusion of puberty, physical development tends to stabilize, and many individuals enjoy peak physical performance during young adulthood. Many young adults enjoy optimal physical health and find themselves relatively free of pain, disease, and illness. However, young adulthood is also a time when the negative consequences of lifestyle factors such as stress, smoking, overeating, substance abuse, lack of exercise, and poor sleep habits can begin to accumulate, causing illness and disease later in life.

Many of the processes of cognitive development that occur earlier in life begin to stabilize during young adulthood. According to Jean Piaget (1972), most people reach the formal operations stage in their early teens, when they become capable of qualitative thought, using logic and reason to guide their thinking. Specifically, then, teenagers have the cognitive abilities to "think like" adults. However, other theorists and researchers argue that cognitively, young adults are slightly different from their younger counterparts. Specifically, young adults may be more sophisticated in the ways that they proceed through formal operational thought than they were in their teen years. Some researchers further argue that young adults become more reflective and realistic as they gain experience, and they become more adept at applying knowledge to real-world situations. The development of these skills is very individualistic, however, meaning that not all people develop these skills fully or at the same time. There is evidence to suggest that the development of these advanced skills is not necessarily as predictable or universal as Piaget asserted (for example, Keating, 1990; Kuhn, 2008; Schaie & Willis, 2000).

In addition, young adults continue to develop intellectually and interpersonally while learning to master their emotions and deal with independence. Young adulthood is a time when most individuals in Western societies become autonomous, self-sufficient, and responsible for their actions. They also learn how to balance interdependence with independence in intimate relationships. Individuals continue to develop their self-identity and form their own opinions, values, and beliefs about the world. Although these concepts have been partially shaped over time by their peers, families, and other outside forces, young adults learn not to be easily swayed by the opinions of others (Chickering & Reisser, 1993). Quick Guide 15 summarizes the highlights of development in early adulthood.

QUICK GUIDE 15   Developmental Milestones in Early Adulthood

PHYSICAL	COGNITIVE	PERSONALITY AND EMOTION
• Stabilization of physical growth.	• Thought becomes more reflective, sophisticated.	• Stabilization of emotional growth; master emotions.
• Optimal physical performance, with declines beginning in the latter part of early adulthood.	• Capable of using reason and logic in thinking processes.	• Development of interpersonal, intimate relationships.
• Bad health habits are established.	• Begin to connect new information to past experiences to enhance learning.	• In Western culture, establishment of independence.
		• Established self-identity.

Social workers can play an instrumental role in the lives of young adults who are experiencing problems with development. For example, according to Erik Erikson, young adulthood is a time when individuals work toward closeness in their relationships. Young adults learn to sacrifice in their relationships with others without losing a sense of their identity. Some young adults may find that they are unable to relate to others in an intimate way, or they may experience difficulties in maintaining a stable sense of self when they are involved in close relationships. Social workers might assist clients who experience these types of problems by working with them to build self-identity, healthy boundaries, and relationship skills.

As Gudrun's social worker, you can assist her with relationship issues after her symptoms have been stabilized. Because of her mental health issues, Gudrun will likely need extra support in working on relationships with friends, family members, co-workers, and others with whom she has contact. The social worker can also assess Gudrun's physical, cognitive, and emotional functioning to help minimize any symptoms of mental illness and ensure that symptoms do not seriously impact her health and well-being.

THE INDIVIDUAL IN EARLY ADULTHOOD

Though physical development has slowed down somewhat by early adulthood, many changes still take place in other areas that, although generally positive, can create problems for some young adults. Just a few of the issues that young adults may bring to social workers involve mental illness, disability, and questions around spirituality. But before discussing them, let us look at a relatively new lens through which to view developmental tasks for people in this stage of life.

Emerging Adulthood

In recent decades, young people have been engaging in roles associated with adulthood much later than they did in previous generations. This shift led Jeffrey Arnett (2000) to conceptualize a new life stage called **emerging adulthood**, which addresses the development process of people between adolescence and the mid-twenties in industrialized countries. Arnett's purpose was to help explain the shifts in timing for moving into adult roles and the activities in which people in this age range are engaged.

Postponing adult roles is a central feature of this new stage of life. Some of the ways in which people in this age range now are different from their counterparts even just 50 years ago include a higher percentage of people pursuing higher education, more job instability and frequent job changes, increased engagement in risky behaviors, and postponement of marriage and parenthood (Arnett, 2000; Arnett, 2011).

Several features distinguish the stage of emerging adulthood from adolescence and young adulthood:

- *Age of identity explorations:* Young adults are exploring their interests and considering their choices in work and relationships. This age is marked by *instability* as young adults make frequent changes in jobs, partners, living arrangements, and educational goals.

- *Age of self-focus:* Young adults experience a great deal of independence without obligations. This age is marked by a feeling of being *"in-between"* adolescence and adulthood—people in this stage may feel they are neither.

- *Age of possibilities:* Young adults have a great deal of hope that one day they will reach adulthood and achieve the goals they envision for themselves. They may not worry about the instability of emerging adulthood because they feel that things will change for the better (Arnett, 2011).

This theory may help social workers working with young adults to reframe the developmental tasks at this stage of life and help them successfully move into adulthood and work toward their goals. Further, social workers can help parents to better understand their children's seemingly negative behaviors. Many parents of young adults struggle to understand why their children at this age cannot keep a steady job or relationship, take longer than usual to graduate from college, or want to move back home. These issues can cause a great deal of strain on the parent–child relationship (Arnett, 2010). Often just helping parents to see these behaviors as necessary for their children to successfully transition into adult roles can encourage parents to find ways to support their children and help their children set and achieve goals for adulthood.

Mental Illness

Though mental illness and problems associated with poor mental health can arise at any point in the life span, we discuss this issue in this chapter because many individuals with serious mental illnesses tend to exhibit initial symptoms in early adulthood. Symptoms of mental illness can begin to cause problems with functioning as young adults attempt to establish independence.

Schizophrenia Schizophrenia is an example of a mental illness whose symptoms tend to exhibit themselves in late adolescence or early adulthood. Symptoms include some or all of the following: delusions, hallucinations, flat affect, and disorganized and meaningless speech and behavior (American Psychiatric Association, 2000).

The exact cause of schizophrenia is unknown; however, there is a great deal of evidence, particularly through twin studies, to suggest that genetic and biological factors contribute to the disorder (Andreasen, 2001; Maier *et al.*, 2000). For example, research shows that more men than women have the disorder, which may indicate that estrogen serves as a protective factor against the disease (Faraone, Brown, Glatt, & Ming, 2002). Recent studies have also located specific gene mutations in at least half of schizophrenia cases. These are cases in which individuals who develop symptoms do not have a family history of the disease (Xu *et al.*, 2011).

Studies also indicate that a combination of genetic predisposition and environmental stressors tends to place people at risk for developing schizophrenia. Some studies indicate that for people who possess a genetic predisposition to schizophrenia, problems such as familial patterns of hostility, criticism, negativity, and dysfunctional communication make the symptoms and course of the disorder more severe (Bateson, 1978; Boye, Bentsen, & Malt, 2002; Schiffman *et al.*, 2001, 2002). Other studies point to the role of reinforcement and cognitive process in the development of symptoms among people with a genetic predisposition to the disorder. For example, researchers argue that some people with schizophrenia have not been positively reinforced for attending to "normal" social cues. Thus, these people attend to irrelevant cues in their environment, which results in seemingly odd behavior. Moreover, these researchers argue that people who experience abnormal cognitive processes resulting from biological problems attempt to "make sense" of these processes, which ultimately results in illogical thinking patterns and odd behavior (Garety, 1991; Murphy, 2007). More recent research suggests that schizophrenia is the result of several different genes interacting with one another in distinct ways that cause different sets of symptoms, depending on how the genes combine and interact. So rather than being caused by individual genes, schizophrenia is likely caused by clustering of genes that put people at risk for the disorder, and the specific symptoms people experience are the result of how genes interact (Arnedo *et al.*, 2014).

Schizophrenia is more common among people who were born prematurely or born with low birth weight, and those who experienced other complications with their prenatal development or birth, than it is among people who were born at full term, normal weight, and without complications. Some researchers suspect that fetal and birth conditions may play a part in activating genes associated with schizophrenia. Similarly, people with schizophrenia tend to be born in the late winter and early spring months, leading some experts to speculate that viruses common in these months interact with a genetic predisposition to the disorder, creating conditions that lead to the development of symptoms (Faraone *et al.*, 2002).

An interesting approach to thinking about and working with hallucinations and other symptoms of schizophrenia is called Hearing Voices (The International Hearing Voices Network, 2014). The philosophy of this approach is that hearing voices is not abnormal or deviant. Rather, it is a normal, albeit unusual, variation in our behavior, and it does not have to be a negative experience. Indeed, hearing voices can be a positive experience, but the meaning that society puts on it shapes our responses and attitudes to it. So in Western culture, with our medical model, we tend to view hearing voices as pathological—something to be medicated and fixed. A related view is that hallucinations themselves tend to be shaped by culture and not by the disease process itself. For example, the U.S. tends to place value on violence—we're exposed to it everywhere; thus, hallucinations for people in the U.S. will likely have violent themes. Contrast this with other cultures that might place emphasis on nonviolent behaviors. Hallucinations for people in these cultures might tend to have nonviolent themes centered on religion or group behavior, for example. From this viewpoint, then, hallucinations do not necessarily need to be frightening or negative, but the influence culture has on their content and the value judgments we make about them can turn them into negative experiences (Luhrmann, 2007). The Hearing Voices approach posits that people need to accept that the voices they hear belong to them and are based on life experiences. In this way, people can learn to cope with their voices in a way that does not medicalize or pathologize their symptoms, which may make them worse, and allows them to integrate their voices into their everyday experiences. This approach also aims to educate society about the nature of voices to reduce stigma and anxiety, which affects those who experience voices. Research on this approach is beginning to accumulate, indicating this can be an effective way for people to manage voices (e.g., Beavan & Read, 2010; Corstens, Longden, & May, 2012; Stainsby, Sapochnik, Bledin, & Mason, 2010).

Trauma and Posttraumatic Stress Disorder   **Trauma** can be defined as any experience that is emotionally distressing enough to overwhelm an individual's ability to cope, often leaving the individual feeling powerless (Van der Kolk, 2005). Traumatic events such as family violence, natural disasters, military combat, or victimization through war or criminal activity can have severe and profound effects on people's biopsychosocial functioning.

Exposure to trauma in childhood and adolescence is particularly serious since it can significantly impact brain development (Rich *et al.*, 2009; Williams, 2006). Research indicates that trauma, particularly trauma that is chronic and persistent (e.g., trauma caused by child abuse and neglect), can alter neural pathways in the brain that affect emotion, cognition, behavior, and attachments. Exposure to trauma is also strongly correlated with poor health outcomes and early death (Felitti, 1998).

Trauma theory has emerged over the past several decades, mostly in response to the experiences of war veterans (Vietnam, Iraq, Afghanistan), Holocaust and other genocide survivors, sexual assault victims, victims of mass violence (such as the shootings in Aurora, Colorado, in 2012, at Virginia Tech in 2007, and at Columbine High School in 1999), and other survivor groups. In general, this work has helped us to better understand how trauma affects people and to shift the focus off the victim as "sick" or flawed. Recently, many new approaches have also been developed to work with people affected by trauma. Interventions such as neural-strategic therapy and neurolinguistic programming help "remap" neural connections that have been altered by trauma. They help people develop connectedness, healthy relationships, and strong attachments to others and their communities (Rich *et al.*, 2009).

Most people have some stress reactions after a trauma; however, reactions that do not go away over time may signal a problem. When in danger, it is natural to feel afraid. This fear triggers many split-second changes in the body to prepare to defend against the danger or to avoid it. This "fight-or-flight" response is a healthy reaction meant to protect a person from harm. But sometimes this reaction is changed or damaged, and people may feel stressed or frightened even when they are no longer in danger, leading to Post Traumatic Stress Disorder (National Institutes of Health, 2009b). **Posttraumatic Stress Disorder (PTSD)** is characterized by several intrusive and distressing symptoms (American Psychiatric Association, 2000):

- recurring dreams, memories, or flashbacks;

- persistent avoidance of stimuli associated with the traumatic event;

- problems with cognition or mood associated with the event;

- changes in behavior such as increased aggression or exaggerated startle response.

This disorder has become a particularly serious issue for soldiers who have served in Iraq or Afghanistan in recent years. Indeed, PTSD is the most commonly occurring mental health problem for these service members. Estimates of the prevalence of PTSD for service members who experienced combat range from 5 to 24.5 percent (Litz & Schlenger, 2009; Ramchand *et al.*, 2010; Swanson, Favorite, Horin, & Arnedt, 2009). The prevalence of PTSD for all service members ranges from 6 to 18 percent but rises to nearly 50 percent for those seeking mental health services (Ramchand *et al.*, 2010). Sleep disorders such as insomnia and nightmares are the most common symptoms seen in service members (Swanson *et al.*, 2009). Further, research suggests that ethnic minority groups may be at higher risk for PTSD symptoms because of health care and service delivery disparities as well as exposure to a lifetime of discrimination, oppression, and other traumas that can tax people's coping abilities. For example, studies on racial disparities among breast and other cancer survivors indicate risk of PTSD symptoms after diagnosis is often higher among blacks and Asian Americans than whites (Ashing-Giwa, & Lim, 2011; Roberts, Gilman, Breslau, Breslau, & Koenen, 2011; Vin-Raviv *et al.*, 2013).

Treatments for PTSD range from medications to talk therapy as well as the interventions mentioned above for trauma. Some forms of therapy are based in behavioral theory and the medical model. For example, cognitive behavioral therapy (CBT), prolonged exposure therapy, and eye movement desensitization and reprocessing are effective interventions for PTSD.

One form of CBT that is gaining in popularity is behavioral activation, which empowers the person with PTSD symptoms to reengage in her or his environment through creative problem-solving (Jakupcak, Wagner, Paulson, Varra, & McFall, 2010). Behavioral activation incorporates elements of the strengths perspective in that it uses active problem-solving to navigate barriers and promote engagement in activities that increase pleasure and mastery. In contrast, other CBT therapies focus on exposing the client to activities that cause them fear or anxiety (Jakupcak *et al.*, 2010, p. 492).

Shawn, 27, returned to his home in Iowa after serving for 18 months with his Army Reserve unit in Afghanistan. He had decided that he wanted to make a career as a military chaplain and took an interim job as a youth pastor. After being home for six months, Shawn sought help from his VA center because he said he could not concentrate on his job, could not sleep, and felt like he had lost his motivation for his career goal. Shawn described his feelings of panic whenever he attended church, tried to go on a date, or tried to go to a restaurant or movie. He was especially upset by a panic attack he experienced during his younger sibling's track meet when the starter's gun sounded.

Shawn said he was having an average of eight major nightmares each week involving a suicide bombing he witnessed in a crowded city market that killed two of his unit members. He said he drank to the point of being drunk five of seven nights a week to try to avoid the nightmares. Shawn said he had been unable to sit through a church service, movie, or restaurant meal since he had returned home. The one spot in Shawn's life where he felt moderately comfortable was working with the youth at the small church near his home. However, this job was in jeopardy, according to Shawn, because he had arrived at church hungover on several occasions.

Following diagnoses of depression, PTSD, and active substance abuse, Shawn participated in behavior activation therapy for eight sessions, once a week, for approximately one hour each session. The therapist, holding a Master's of Social Work degree, educated Shawn regarding PTSD and depression, helped him analyze avoidance behaviors to identify the barriers to activity, and instituted weekly goal-setting and problem-solving activities to help Shawn reactivate his former life. The therapist worked with Shawn to develop his own, unique goals and to learn to develop creative problem-solving strategies to cope with stressful situations, such as being in crowds that he perceived as threatening.

At the completion of the eight sessions, the therapist and Shawn noted his progress toward three major goals. Shawn reported that he was having fewer than one nightmare per week. The reduction in nightmares had relieved his need to drink. He had not been intoxicated in four weeks nor had he had more than two drinks on any one occasion in those four weeks. Shawn said that he felt his major accomplishment was learning to identify triggers for his panic. Although he was still uncomfortable in large crowds, he had identified alternative coping strategies such as attending small group Bible study and engaging in daily prayer and text readings.

Mental Illness and Social Work Strategies Many young adults are entering the workforce, establishing intimate relationships, and attempting to become financially and physically independent from their parents. Problems with any of these transitions that are caused by mental illness are likely to come to the attention of social workers.

Any unresolved problems with mental health that individuals experienced in childhood will likely become more severe in young adulthood as individuals experience changing roles and new stressors. That is one reason why social workers need to attend to abuse and neglect issues in families with young children. For example, abuse and neglect are correlated with mental health problems (Bifulco *et al.*, 2002) as well as with a variety of social and relational problems in adulthood (Malinosky-Rummell & Hansen, 1993).

In addition, many young adults who experience their parents' divorce, separation, or marital problems tend to demonstrate more psychological problems than young adults whose parents did not have severe marital problems. Marital conflict is often accompanied by other problems, such as strain in relationships with their children, that can affect children's well-being as they move into adulthood (Amato & Sobolewski, 2001). Some children from homes with severe marital problems tend to have ongoing relationship troubles with their parents. This is just one of the issues with which these children must contend as they grow older.

The research on schizophrenia, PTSD, depression, and other serious mental health issues underscores the importance of using a variety of theories and models when working with clients:

- *Biopsychosocial approach and ecological model:* Concentrated on prevention efforts for children of parents who have been diagnosed with certain mental illnesses. For example, early warning signs of schizophrenia include social impairments, poor motor skills, and attention deficits. If a thorough assessment indicates that children are at risk for developing a mental illness, social workers can assist in eliminating some of the environmental risk factors such as stress and poor coping and communication skills (Faraone *et al.*, 2002).

- *Systems theory and ecological model:* Focus on the ways that family conflict affects children and their development into young adults. For example, when the homeostasis of the family system is disrupted through conflict, children must adjust to the new circumstances. Sometimes, this adjustment is negative and has long-lasting effects on the children's future relationships with peers, family members, and significant others. Other factors that are often part of marital strife, such as economic and legal issues, can also adversely affect children. Social workers can help families find resolutions to marital troubles that will not undermine their children's development, or that at least will minimize the amount of emotional, psychological, and physical harm generated by that conflict.

- *Medical model and other biopsychosocial approaches:* Useful when working with clients who have serious and persistent mental illnesses such as schizophrenia. Social workers need a comprehensive knowledge base to work effectively with these clients, because interventions often call for a combination of methods such as drug therapy and case management to help optimize clients' biopsychosocial and economic well-being.

- *Strengths perspective:* Sees individuals as resourceful and resilient beings who have many skills and abilities that transcend their problems. Thus, in the case of mental illness, social workers can examine clients' unique strengths and resources that can help them to work through problems caused by symptoms of mental illness. Focusing on client strengths can help social workers and clients with symptoms of mental illness draw on existing supports.

Social workers also need to be well versed in current research on physiological and medical advances in treatments for mental illness so they can offer the best, most effective evidence-based treatments to clients. Knowledge in this area is expanding rapidly. For example, new research on depression indicates that ketamines (found in the street drug Special K and in over-the-counter anti-nausea medications) may be more effective on depressive symptoms and suicide ideation than standard antidepressants (Larkin & Beautrais, 2011).

Newer treatments such as mindfulness training have also been used to effectively treat depression as well as other issues like anxiety, addictions, eating disorders, and PTSD. **Mindfulness**, a central tenet in Buddhist meditation, advocates actively and non-judgmentally paying attention to the present moment (Kabat-Zinn, 1994). The building blocks of mindfulness include a person's intentional goals, attention to the present moment, and attitude of openness and acceptance (Turner, 2009). Mindfulness has been shown to be a powerful tool in alleviating symptoms of mental illness and other problems and for bringing richness and meaning into life. Mindful meditation and practice, even in short sessions of 10 to 20 minutes a day, can profoundly change brain structures and functioning, which are implicated in improved physical and mental health, memory, empathy, stress levels, and sense of self (Holzel *et al.*, 2011; Siegel, 2007). Research also suggests that meditation can suppress genes associated with inflammation in the body (Kaliman *et al.*, 2014).

Given Gudrun's symptoms, it is likely that she is dealing with a mental illness. And given her age, it is also likely that this is the first time she has experienced such symptoms. She has not been able to maintain housing, employment, or relationships lately, so if she has experienced symptoms before, they were probably mild. You will want to conduct a thorough biopsychosocial and strengths assessment to ascertain the resources available to Gudrun as well as the issues that might intensify her mental illness in the future. Her past ability to function will be a strength that you can use when working with her; she clearly has many other strengths and resources upon which to draw. With the appropriate medications and case management, Gudrun may be able to continue to live and function independently.

Disability

Like mental illness, disability can occur at any age. Worldwide, more than one billion people live with a disability, which is approximately 15 percent of the world's population (World Health Organization, 2013). More than 90 percent of individuals with disabilities survive into adulthood. We discuss disability here because of its implications for the well-being of young adults. Young adults with a disability may find working toward independence and self-sufficiency difficult, depending on the type of disability, the psychosocial circumstances surrounding it, and the resources available in the community.

Prior to the passage of President Barack Obama's Patient Protection and Affordable Care Act of 2010, children with disabilities were often covered under their parents' insurance; however, when they reached young adulthood, they were often dropped from those policies, leaving them uninsured. Those covered by the State Children's Health Insurance Program (SCHIP) were also dropped at age 18. The many unemployed young adults with a disability could not secure private health insurance through an employer, and many had difficulty securing private insurance on their own because of preexisting condition clauses, limits to coverage, and expenses (White, 2002). Thus the majority of people with disabilities have relied on Medicaid for health insurance. However, the Affordable Care Act allows children, including those with disabilities and chronic conditions, to remain on their parents' insurance plan until the age of 26. Further, insurance companies are no longer allowed to consider preexisting conditions in insurance applications (Affordable Care Act for Americans with Disabilities, 2012).

Because many disabilities need medical attention and intervention, social workers and other helping professionals frequently use the medical model to help guide assessment and intervention when working with people with disabilities. However, they also need to consider other factors on the micro, mezzo, and macro levels that influence the health and functioning of people with disabilities. For example, coping skills and personal resources as well as community resources and policies can play an important role in determining the quality of life for people with disabilities.

Policies such as the Americans with Disabilities Act (ADA) of 1990 (amended 2008) is also important to the well-being of individuals with a disability. The ADA prohibits discrimination and encourages inclusion in most aspects of public life. The ADA covers four major areas (U.S. Justice Department, 2005):

- Title I: Requires employers with 15 or more employees to provide qualified individuals with disabilities an equal opportunity to benefit from the full range of employment-related opportunities available to others.

- Title II: Requires state and local governments to give people with disabilities an equal opportunity to benefit from all of their programs, services, and activities (e.g., courts, voting, employment, transportation, recreation, health care, public education, social services, and town meetings).

- Title III (Public Accommodations): Prohibits exclusion, segregation, and unequal treatment and provides architectural standards for new and altered buildings.

- Title IV: Requires telecommunications relay services (TRS) to be available to disabled persons 24 hours a day, seven days a week.

Given the power of language and its impact on shaping laws, policies, attitudes, and beliefs about any issue, it is important to discuss the debate on language usage in disability culture. During the last three decades of the twentieth century, person-first language emerged as the preferential way to refer to "people with disabilities," an example of person-first language. This stance suggests that aspects of a disability are a part of the person but do not define the person.

However, more recently, there has been a movement among many scholars and others in the blind and deaf community, for example, to shift to disability-first language, using terms like blindness, blind person, "Deaf person" to refer to someone identifying with deaf culture, and "deaf person" to refer to someone with an auditory condition. The reasoning behind this shift is that person-first language is rooted in a medical or pathology model, and it focuses on impairments. Further, many people in disability culture find terms such as "hard of seeing," "visually impaired," and "people with blindness" unacceptable because they avoid straightforward reference to the disability. Some people argue that being elusive about a disability through language only pathologizes it and disrespects the person with the disability. The disability-first argument posits that living life with a disability is simply different, and does not make people deficient, as person-first language seems to imply.

Many countries like New Zealand are changing to disability-first language in their laws, policies, and services. Even with such changes, the debate over language in disability culture is ongoing. For social workers, it is imperative that we remain mindful of debates over language usage with any issue we might encounter such as age, race, ethnicity, sexual orientation, gender identification, and so on. Language usage is constantly changing, and it has a powerful impact on how we view issues and the ways we approach our work with people, services, policies, and social change (Mackelprang & Salsgiver, 2009).

Gudrun, depending on her symptoms and how well she responds to intervention, may find herself disabled due to mental illness. Though she may be eligible for various governmental programs to help support herself financially and to cover her health care costs, she will likely need help in navigating through the paperwork and bureaucracy to secure these resources. She will also need assistance with maintaining these resources, as some programs require proof of continuing eligibility. Through case management, you will be able to ensure that Gudrun has access to programs that will help her to maintain a maximum level of independence and well-being.

Spirituality

In recent years, social workers have devoted greater attention to their clients' spiritual development. Within social work, spirituality tends to be seen as one aspect within the biopsychosocial view of an individual. One prominent researcher in social work and spirituality, Edward R. Canda, refers to spirituality as

> the human search for a sense of meaning, purpose, and morally fulfilling relations with oneself, other people, the universe, and the ground of being, however that's understood . . . Spirituality . . . involves centrally important life-orienting beliefs, values, and practices that may be expressed in religious and/or nonreligious ways.
>
> (2008, p. 27)

With the growing interest in spirituality has come an increasing body of literature examining how spirituality develops and how people use spirituality to

PHOTO 10-A

Spiritual development is an important consideration in social work practice

Source: M. Freeman/PhotoLink/Getty Images

enhance their well-being. Of course, opinions vary concerning the importance of religion and spirituality throughout the life span. This is particularly true of studies conducted with young adults, who are experiencing many changes that can influence their definition and perception of spirituality as well as their level of religious activity.

Some researchers have found that individuals who actively participated in religious activities during their younger years tend to spend less time in these activities in young adulthood. However, these individuals tend to increase their participation later in life, particularly if they were very active in youth and other programs offered by their religious institution. Further, when these young adults return to participating in their church, synagogue, mosque, or temple, they generally adopt the religious affiliation of their childhood (O'Connor, Hoge, & Alexander, 2002).

Other researchers have found that while religious beliefs tend to decline over time, religious participation tends to increase as individuals enter young adulthood and beyond. Their work indicates that religious participation seems to be related to traditional roles expected in adulthood such as marriage and child rearing. That is, some young adults perceive religious participation as an expected role that accompanies starting a family. Further, older adults may find social support in religious gatherings (Bengtson, Horlacher, Putney, & Silverstein, 2008; Stolzenberg, Blair-Loy, & Waite, 1995).

Spirituality and faith, though tied to religion for some young adults, can be totally different constructs from religion for others. For instance, some people may consider themselves to be very spiritual even though they do not participate in religious activities or identify with specific religious institutions. Others may perceive themselves to be spiritual because they participate in religious activities. Because spirituality, faith, and religion have different meanings for different individuals, they can be difficult to define, study, and apply to client situations.

Thus social workers may find it difficult to interpret research on the subject or to make sense of clients' particular faith issues. Moreover, various theories attempt to explain faith and beliefs, and in doing so, offer disparate views on how people engage in religious activities throughout the life span:

- *Social learning theory:* From this perspective you might view religiosity and spirituality as learned; that is, they are socialized into us as we imitate the beliefs and behaviors of people who are close to us. Thus, if our parents attend church regularly, we will likely carry on the activity as we grow older. Though we may question our parents' activity as well as their beliefs as we move into adolescence, we are likely to carry with us into young adulthood the same tendencies and beliefs as our parents.

- *Erikson's theory of psychosocial development:* From this perspective, you might view faith and religious participation as dependent on the particular developmental tasks and crises with which people must grapple in certain life stages. For example, some young adults in the intimacy versus isolation stage may turn to religious institutions to find closeness to other like-minded people. They may use faith to help them establish intimacy. Conversely, some young adults may abandon their religious beliefs and practices because they cause conflict for their intimate relationships.

Still other theories specifically seek to explain faith and spirituality from a helping perspective. One of these theories is Fowler's theory of faith development.

Fowler's Theory of Faith Development One theory of spirituality, which was developed by James Fowler, a developmental psychologist, describes stages that people go through in finding spirituality. Fowler suggests that faith does not necessarily relate to organized religion or even God, but rather to ways in which people find meaning and connection with others. Fowler's theory observes that people begin developing their faith early in life and can continue doing so into old age (Fowler, 1981, 1996). Exhibit 10.1 describes the stages in this theory.

As you can see in Exhibit 10.1, this theory suggests that people move through consistent developmental stages. In the final stage, they experience a universalizing faith in which they are concerned with the well-being of all humankind. Although this theory suggests that, in general, people develop faith in a fairly straightforward, consistent manner as they age, Fowler acknowledges that only a small percentage of people actually reach Stage 6 or Stage 7. Moreover, people may vary with regard to the ages at which they reach certain stages and the extent to which they achieve developmental tasks in various stages.

According to Fowler (1981), young adults should be in Stage 5, in which they begin to think critically about their own personal beliefs, comparing them to the beliefs with which they were socialized. Assuming that many young adults reach this stage, Fowler's theory can help explain why many individuals are more tolerant of different religious beliefs in young adulthood than they were in younger years and why many young adults begin to develop their own definitions of spirituality.

Fowler's theory also helps explain why the spirituality of young adults, as a group, is relatively weak as compared to the spirituality of older adults. A longitudinal study found that spirituality tended to increase as individuals got older; it was at its lowest point in early adulthood and increased beginning in their thirties, reaching a peak at older adulthood (Wink & Dillon, 2002). Perhaps the tendency to question faith, spirituality, and religious beliefs in adolescence and early adulthood is just another manifestation of the developmental tasks of increasing experience and exposure to others (Paloutzian, 2000).

Spirituality in Social Work Practice Spirituality and participation in religious services can have a significant impact on people's worldviews, and religious affiliations provide social and other support networks for individuals. Thus social workers need to incorporate elements of spirituality and religious participation in their

STAGE	DESCRIPTION	
Stage 1: Primal or Undifferentiated Faith (birth to 2 years)	All infants begin life determining whether the world is safe and their needs are met. Children begin to use language to articulate their relationships with others.	**EXHIBIT 10.1** *Fowler's Theory of Faith Development*
Stage 2: Intuitive-Projective Faith (2 to 6 years)	Children take in information from their environments. They are unable to rationally think through what is spiritual, but they subscribe to what they are told.	
Stage 3: Mythic-Literal Faith (6 to 12 years)	Children relate to stories and symbolism and use these elements to represent their faith. They still cannot think critically about facets of beliefs.	
Stage 4: Synthetic-Conventional Faith (12+ years)	People are exposed to information through their interactions with others. They find meaning in symbols and traditions, but they still adhere to conventional ways of thinking about faith.	
Stage 5: Individuative-Reflective Faith (Early adulthood+)	People think critically about the meaning of faith and what their personal beliefs are. People are able to compare their beliefs with those they were taught.	
Stage 6: Conjunctive Faith (Midlife+)	People accept that conflicts exist between their beliefs and those of conventional religions. Spirituality takes on deeper meaning.	
Stage 7: Universalizing Faith (Midlife+)	People integrate conflicts in beliefs and work toward ensuring the well-being of humankind. They recognize injustice and find meaning in self-sacrifice for the greater good.	

Source: Adapted from Fowler, 1981

assessments and interventions when working with clients. Often, clients' religious beliefs and views on spirituality provide insights into the ways in which clients view problems and solutions, and they can be sources of strength in helping clients to overcome obstacles. Understanding a client's level of spirituality can help a social worker facilitate development and well-being, but it is important for the social worker to avoid imposing her or his own beliefs on the client.

Fowler's model of spiritual development is helpful to social workers, as are other theories. However, keep in mind that theories of faith development are difficult to form and articulate, and like so many other theories, they may not capture the rich cultural and spiritual context in which clients live.

In Gudrun's case, you will want to find out if she has any religious affiliations in the community. A church or other organization may be able to provide needed support as she works to maintain her independence. Further, depending on her views, Gudrun's spirituality may be a strength that you can use in your work with her. You could also explore Gudrun's moral and spiritual development if she agrees that it might be useful. In terms of morality, you may not need to know which stage Gudrun has reached, but discussing with Gudrun her overall worldview and perspective on life might be helpful.

Gudrun seems to be at a crisis point in her life, so exploring issues of faith may be useful to her in making sense of her situation. You might want to explore whether her beliefs and her views on faith are consistent with those espoused by her religious leaders. In doing so, you may be able to help Gudrun come to terms with how her symptoms are impacting her life.

THE FAMILY AND IMMEDIATE ENVIRONMENT IN EARLY ADULTHOOD

Young adulthood tends to be a time when many individuals begin to redefine their relationships with others. Many young adults find themselves exploring their roles and relationships in the family, with peers, in the workplace, and in intimate relationships. This section includes a discussion on a couple of issues that may impact the well-being of young adults on this level: alternative relationships and living arrangements, as well as domestic violence.

Alternative Relationships and Living Arrangements

Since the 1950s, young adults increasingly have been choosing to remain single. Instead of marrying, many are either remaining in their parents' homes, living by themselves, or living with friends or significant others. The U.S. Census Bureau (2013a) reports that the overall percentage of adults who were married declined to 50.5 percent in 2013 from 54.1 percent in 2010. As Exhibit 10.2 shows, roughly half of the men interviewed for one Centers for Disease Control and Prevention study (Copen, Daniels, Vespa, & Mosher, 2012) were single, and the percentage of single women has not been far behind.

Cohabitation before marriage has become a common arrangement between couples. Indeed, two-thirds of recently married individuals have cohabited (Schoen, Landale, & Daniels, 2007). Exhibit 10.2 also shows that men and especially women are far more likely to be cohabiting now than they were in the early 1980s, while rates of marriage have decreased.

As we saw in the discussion on emerging adulthood, another living arrangement that is increasingly common is young adults living with their parents. Between 2005 and 2012, the proportion of young adults living in their parents' homes increased, according to the U.S. Census Bureau (2013a). The percentage of men aged 25 to 34 living in their parents' homes rose from 14 percent in 2005 to 16 percent in 2013; women living with parents rose from 8 percent to 10 percent over the same period.

Trends in delaying marriage are likely due to increasing numbers of women participating in the labor force, leaving them economically able to delay marriage or to choose other relationship and living options. Still, many women who are single express a desire to marry in the future.

Percentages in each type of relationship at time of interview								
	1982		1995		2002		2006–2010	
	Men	Women	Men	Women	Men	Women	Men	Women
First marriage		44.1		39.9	35.0	37.5	32.8	36.4
Second or higher marriage		8.1		9.3	7.2	8.5	4.8	5.1
Cohabiting		3.0		7.0	9.2	9.0	12.2	11.2
Single, never married		33.5		33.4	41.6	35.0	45.0	38.2
Single, formerly married		11.3		10.3	7.0	9.9	5.2	9.2

EXHIBIT 10.2

Changes in Relationship Status for Men and Women Ages 15–44

Source : Adapted from Copen, Casey E., Kimberly Daniels, Jonathan Vespa, and William D. Mosher, "First Marriages in the United States: Data from the 2006–2010 National Survey of Family Growth," National Health Statistics Reports, Number 49, March 22, 2012, National Center for Health Statistics, Centers for Disease Control and Prevention, U.S. Department of Health and Human Services. Accessed 8/5/12 at www.cdc.gov/nchs/data/nhsr/nhsr049.pdf

Because of the persistent pay gap between men and women, as well as other economic factors, marriage often improves the financial status of women. Furthermore, marriage allows some women to quit their paid jobs to raise children. In 2010, 23 percent of married couples with children under 15 had a stay-at-home mother, up from 21 percent in 2000. In 2007, before the recession of 2008, stay-at-home mothers were found among 24 percent of married couples with children under 15 (U.S. Census Bureau, 2010b).

One study of over 500 undergraduate students captured this attitude about marriage and family (O'Laughlin, 2001). Results indicated that 80 percent of respondents had a desire to have a family of their own, although those who expressed ambivalence seemed to have realistic worries about the difficulties of balancing family with work, school, and other responsibilities. Realistic expectations about starting a family also increased as age increased: Those aged 18 to 30 held more unrealistic ideas about marriage and family than those aged 30 and older. For example, younger people thought it would be relatively easy to balance work with family and to support a family financially. In this study, men seemed to have more unrealistic expectations about parenting than women, which may reflect the reality that parenting often impacts women more negatively in all realms of life than it does men. This effect may be why so many women are waiting longer before they marry and have children.

Increased acceptance of gay and lesbian relationships may be another reason why some young people are remaining single and cohabiting. Many gay and lesbian people may now be choosing to remain true to their sexual identity rather than succumbing to pressure to marry opposite-sex partners. Many do not have the option to marry their same-sex partners, which also affects marriage statistics.

Though gay and lesbian couples still face many legal and social obstacles in maintaining committed relationships, they may also enjoy stronger relationships than heterosexual couples. Some research indicates that gay and lesbian couples may possess stronger problem-solving skills and have more favorable opinions about their partners than heterosexual couples. Gay and lesbian couples may also be more autonomous and open-minded than their heterosexual counterparts. However, gay and lesbian couples tend to report fewer social supports than heterosexual couples, which may reflect societal opinions about homosexuality. The exception is that lesbian women do report more support from their friends and higher relationship satisfaction than either gay men or heterosexual couples, which may be indicative of the way in which females tend to be socialized (Gotta *et al.*, 2011; Kurdek, 2001).

As relationship and living arrangement patterns change in Western society, social workers must stay abreast of the social implications that these changes can have for individuals and communities. Finances, communication, family dynamics, and family and gender roles may all be affected. Attachment theory, psychodynamic theories, and other models of human development can be useful when working with young adults dealing with relationship issues. In addition, social workers can benefit from applying models such as systems and ecological theories when conceptualizing and intervening with the issues that some couples face.

Gudrun, because of her problems with mental health and family dynamics, will likely need extra support in developing and maintaining relationships. She has shown the ability to form relationships in the past, which is a strength; however, other problems related to her mental health and family relationships may pose problems for future relationships. You can apply systems or ecological theories in Gudrun's case to help guide assessment and intervention and to ensure that various factors affecting her well-being are considered.

Domestic Violence

Young adulthood is a time when many people experience their first intimate relationships. It is also a time when they learn to negotiate conflict and to compromise with an intimate partner. Sometimes, however, normal conflict escalates to domestic violence, also known as intimate violence. Young adults may not yet have the confidence and knowledge to deal with this sort of serious issue. Also, because young adults often live somewhere other than the family home, domestic violence may be more difficult to identify. The problem is exacerbated by the victim's desire to maintain newly won independence, which the abuser may exploit in an effort to keep the partner isolated from friends and family. In either case, intervention with victims of domestic violence becomes more difficult.

In 1995–1996, the National Institute of Justice and the Centers for Disease Control and Prevention jointly sponsored the National Violence Against Women survey. The results, which were published in 2000, indicate that each year 1.3 million women and 835,000 men are victims of physical violence committed by an intimate partner (Tjaden & Thoennes, 2000). Although both men and women may have to deal with domestic violence, women are at significantly greater risk. According to the Bureau of Justice Statistics (2013), approximately one-third of female homicide victims were likely killed by an intimate partner. Indeed, females are more likely than males to be victimized by someone they know, and seven in 10 female sexual assault victims stated that the perpetrator was known to them (Bureau of Justice Statistics, 2009).

The effects of domestic violence on children are well documented (e.g., Heugten & Wilson, 2008; Humphreys, Lowe, & Williams, 2009; Perloff & Buckner, 1996; Shepard, 1992) and are similar to those found for abused children (see the discussion in Chapter 7). Children who witness domestic violence are at risk for developing into young adults who either perpetrate violence against their partners or become targets for abuse (Evans, Davies, & DiLillo, 2008; Tutty & Wagar, 1994). They are also more likely to engage in bullying behavior, do poorly in school, and abuse drugs and alcohol (Centers for Disease Control and Prevention, 2011a). In young and later adulthood, victims of domestic violence can be exposed to myriad problems that include mental illness, physical injury, loss of employment, PTSD, and of course, death (Evans, Davies, & DiLillo, 2008).

Many of the issues discussed here are evident in Gudrun's case. The description indicates that Gudrun has witnessed domestic violence with her parents. This situation may have put her at risk for being abused in her relationships, which may be part of the reason for her problems with her boyfriend. You may choose to assess this situation, as Gudrun could be at risk for being abused by significant others, which will impact her future relationships and her overall well-being.

Theories of Domestic Violence A number of theories have been used to explain the causes of domestic violence:

- *Social learning and family systems theories:* Maintain that violence is cyclical and that the tendency to use violence in intimate relationships can be passed from generation to generation. For example, some research suggests that factors such as child abuse, poor family cohesion, familial substance abuse, domestic violence, and exposure to violence in the media are associated with domestic violence problems in adulthood (Bevan & Higgins, 2002). Children who are abused and exposed to violence and substance abuse are more likely to carry out these behaviors as adults.

- *Ecological theory:* Includes the aforementioned factors in explaining domestic violence as well as other factors, such as a genetic disposition to violent behavior and other problems such as poverty, unemployment, and shifting gender roles.

- *Feminist theory:* Argues that patriarchal society, which gives power to men, perpetuates the problem of violence against women and children. Accepting the power of men coincides with accepting the subjugation and second-class status of women.

For social workers, poverty and welfare reform are particularly salient issues connected to domestic violence. The 1996 welfare reforms impacted victims of domestic violence who rely on public assistance, particularly those who have left their abusers:

- It often takes many years to successfully end abusive relationships, and often women leave and return to the abuser multiple times. Each time they leave and try to live on their own, they may have to rely on public assistance. However, the 60-month lifetime limit on public assistance that was included in the reform package makes valuable resources inaccessible to many women.

- Abusers often isolate their victims from employment to control them. Thus, many women who have been abused may be unable to work or do not have the skills and experience necessary to find and keep stable, well-paying employment (Chanley & Alozie, 2001). The mandatory work requirements included in the reform can work against these women.

- Child support and paternity identification requirements included in the reform can actually increase the likelihood of violence against women, particularly for women who are still living with their abusers or who are hiding from them.

- Women who need medical attention due to abuse are harmed by limits to medical benefits that were imposed in the reform.

- Immigrant women are cut off from benefits altogether.

- Because states control welfare programs, benefits and eligibility requirements can vary drastically from state to state. Thus, women may find it difficult to relocate if they need to move away from their abusers. Of course, states have the option to consider domestic violence circumstances when designing programs, but the treatment of this issue is by no means consistent, and there is no guarantee that requirements will be flexible for victims (Chanley & Alozie, 2001).

Domestic Violence and Social Work Practice   Though social workers frequently deal with policies and interventions surrounding domestic violence, the profession has been accused of not responding adequately to this particular issue. Some critics have accused social workers of not giving domestic violence priority and for allowing harmful policies, such as welfare reform, to be developed and implemented. Because so many social workers work in agencies that serve children and families, many critics argue that they should be on the front lines, fighting for policies and programs that will support persons who are victims of domestic violence. Instead, social workers are often seen as bureaucrats who perpetuate the problem by blaming victims, not using comprehensive theories to guide assessment and intervention, and hindering the development and implementation of programs that allow these individuals to gain independence (Danis, 2003).

In fact, many social workers have been involved in developing policies and programs that advocate for persons who are victims of domestic violence. For example, many social workers have trained law enforcement officers in methods for dealing with domestic violence situations. They also have worked to make the court system more accessible to victims of domestic violence and more effective in supporting efforts by these individuals to move out of abusive relationships.

THE LARGER SOCIAL ENVIRONMENT IN EARLY ADULTHOOD

As young adults move out into the world to assert themselves and find their place in the larger community, they are increasingly likely to encounter issues on the macro level that will impact their lives. Politics, the economy, workplace policies, and educational issues are just a few of the factors with which young adults may find themselves grappling. We look next at some of the areas in the larger social environment that may impact the lives of young adults.

Higher Education

After graduating from high school, many young adults struggle with the decision of whether to go to college or to work. Some young adults cannot afford to go to college, while others are not aware of their choices because of, among other things, poor guidance in high school, from counselors or parents. This is particularly true for schools in low-income areas that have few resources. Students are often not well informed about their options, and they have fewer opportunities to prepare for college admission exams like the SATs than students from wealthier school districts (Hollenshead & Miller, 2001). Moreover, these students often have few role models who encourage or expect them to continue with their education. For students who are the first generation to pursue higher education, the process of getting to college and actually graduating can be difficult.

Further, young adults who come from low-income households often have many disadvantages before they ever graduate from high school. They usually receive a less than adequate high school education, which makes them less competitive in the college admission process. They often do not have the life experiences, such as travel and volunteer experiences, that can make their applications look positive. In addition, they frequently lack the financial or social support to pursue higher education, and they often do not understand how to research schools to choose one that will meet their needs and goals. Compounding these problems, parents in low-income situations tend to be less optimistic about their children's chances of succeeding in college because they either did not go to college themselves or they were not successful because they faced their own barriers. Consequently, these parents are not likely to encourage their children to pursue higher education (Crosnoe, Mistry, & Elder, 2002).

Social learning theory is useful in explaining this phenomenon. If parents have low self-efficacy because of their lack of experience with higher education, they are unlikely to act as positive role models for their children. These young adults are also not likely to be socialized around individuals who have attended college, and they are unlikely to be reared in an environment that values higher education.

The issue of self-efficacy can be an important one for women who are pursuing higher education. Historically, women have been underrepresented in colleges and universities. However, that trend has changed significantly. Indeed, some people argue that men are now at risk for becoming underrepresented among college graduates, at least at the bachelor's level. Currently, women are outperforming men in high school and are entering colleges and universities in larger numbers than men (Conlin, 2003).

Others argue that although women are more likely to enroll in college than men, men's overall enrollment patterns have increased over the years, particularly among men in high-income brackets. Moreover, men still outnumber women in earning professional degrees and PhDs, especially in male-dominated fields such as engineering and physical sciences. Men also outnumber women in faculty and educational administrative positions in colleges and universities, particularly in more prestigious institutions (Hollenshead & Miller, 2001). These patterns have economic and other ramifications on the power and status of women.

Social workers can be of great support to those students who may want to go to college but who face multiple barriers in achieving their goals. Social workers can also assist young adults who are in college but are struggling with academic or other problems.

As Gudrun's social worker, you may want to suggest that she pursue a college degree to help increase her employment skills. If she is dealing with a mental illness, she may fare better enrolling in school to develop skills that will help her obtain and maintain steady employment.

Sexism

The fact that women are underrepresented in some degree programs and in some occupational fields leads to a discussion of sexism. Chapter 5 discusses racism, prejudice, and oppression. Sexism is similar to these issues in definition and in the ways in which it tends to occur and affect individuals and society. Like other isms, **sexism** involves stereotyping and generalizing about women and men and treating them in particular ways based on these stereotypes.

Most often, social workers deal with sexism when it has negative impacts on their clients or some aspect of society. As men and women move into young adulthood, they will be expanding their contacts with areas of society, such as employment and education, where sexism is likely to be found. Though people may experience sexism in younger years, young adulthood is when they begin to understand its ramifications for their lives and for society in general.

Though sexism has negative consequences for men (for example, men are expected to be unemotional, which can have ramifications for their health), it tends to be a more pervasive problem for women. Women tend to have more negative stereotypes attributed to them than men do, and as feminists would argue, women have less power than men. This disparity makes stereotypes more damaging and more effective at keeping women from gaining power and equality. Sexism, particularly institutional sexism and the discrimination that results, can create and maintain a cycle of poverty for many women. Poverty can contribute to many problems, including mental illness, reduced life expectancy, and poor physical health (Belle & Doucet, 2003).

To help prevent some of the damage created by sexism, social workers who work with young women need to educate them about the issues surrounding sexism. Social workers also need to pinpoint ways in which sexism can be combated in young adulthood to help ward off problems in middle and older adulthood.

The Wage Gap   One area in which sexism continues to be a problem is in the workforce. Even though a higher percentage of employed women (38 percent) have college degrees than employed men (31 percent), women's pay is still only around

84 percent of men's pay, even when factors such as education, seniority, and type of job are held constant (Pew Research Center, 2014a). In 2014, the median weekly income for men was $872, and for women it was $722 (Bureau of Labor Statistics, 2014).

Wage discrepancies between the sexes can be seen in almost all professions. For example, male computer analysts make approximately 26 percent more than their female counterparts. Male lawyers earn 44 percent more than female lawyers, and male accountants earn 39 percent more than female accountants (U.S. Bureau of Labor Statistics, 2009). The median weekly income for women in management, professional, and related occupations is $975. For men, it is $1,130 (Bureau of Labor Statistics, 2014). For most women of color and older women, the wage gap is even wider (U.S. Census Bureau, 2013b).

Moreover, professions that are dominated by women are paid less than those dominated by men. To illustrate this situation, Exhibit 10.3 displays the correlation between the percentages of women in various occupations and the average salary of persons employed in those occupations. As you can see, there is a clear inverse relationship between the percentage of female employees and the average salary.

While women are making advances into male-dominated occupations and more males are moving into female-dominated occupations, the wage gap persists. For example, women still make up 91 percent of the nursing profession where the average salary is $51,100. The average pay of men who now make up the other nine percent of the nursing workforce is $60,700. More women are becoming truck drivers, but their median weekly income is $542 compared to $709 for men (U.S. Census Bureau, 2013c).

These discrepancies are particularly troublesome for women in young adulthood because they begin their careers at a disadvantage. That disadvantage will follow them throughout the remainder of their work years and into retirement. Although experience and career advancement that come with age do raise women's wages, the disadvantage continues and compounds throughout women's careers. For example, women may leave the workforce temporarily to have children, and women are still more likely than men to take days off or leave the workforce to care for children or aging parents (Pew Research Center, 2014a). When these young women reach old age, they will have less money than men for living, medical, and other expenses. The amount they receive from Social Security and other pensions will be less than men receive because the women earned less and thus contributed less while they were working. They will also have earned less money to invest in savings and other sources that could generate interest and wealth on which they could rely in older age. Many young women today feel discouraged by their prospects of equal pay later on in their careers and feel it is much easier for men to advance to high-paying, high-level jobs than women (Pew Research Center, 2014a).

Causes of the Wage Gap   The reasons for the persistence of the wage gap have been extensively researched. One common explanation is women's responsibilities

Occupation	Percentage of Workers Who Are Female	Average Annual Salary	
Engineer	10.8	$92,260	**EXHIBIT 10.3**
Architect	20.7	$79,300	
Chief executive officer	24.2	$176,550	*Relationship between Dominance of*
Lawyer	24.2	$130,490	
Physician or surgeon	24.2	$184,650	*Women in an Occupation*
Cashier	73.6	$20,230	*and the Occupation's*
Elementary school teacher	81.7	$55,270	*Average Salary*
Librarian	86.2	$57,020	
Child care worker	94.5	$21,320	

Sources: From Mismatch: *The Growing Gulf Between Women and Men*, by Andrew Hacker. Copyright © 2003 by Andrew Hacker. Adapted with the permission of Scribner, an imprint of Simon & Schuster Adult Publishing Group

for childbearing and childrearing. Women who have started families often have less time to spend at work, and they are less mobile geographically when opportunities for promotion arise (Hacker, 2003).

Evidence also suggests that, all other things being equal, women who are mothers (or who are thought to be mothers) are discriminated against in hiring decisions—a phenomenon known as the "motherhood penalty." One study compared the work experiences of two groups of women (Correll, Benard, & Paik, 2007). Both groups had identical sets of top-notch resumes and work histories, but one set of resumes included experience with a parent–teacher organization, which could suggest that the women were mothers. The study showed that the women who were perceived to be "moms" were viewed as less competent and committed to work, were offered $11,000 less in starting salary than the "non-moms," and were judged more harshly for lateness after they were hired.

Many people argue that unequal pay is rooted in institutional sexism; that is, opportunities for high-paying jobs and positions of power still elude women. And because relatively few women are in high-level positions, policy and other changes that will open more opportunities for women tend not to be initiated. Many critics of institutional sexism also argue that laws and policies do not go far enough to guard against discrimination. For example, the **Civil Rights Act of 1964** prohibited discrimination in hiring practices for institutions receiving federal dollars and established the Equal Employment Opportunity Commission. However, laws related to this Act passed afterward, such as the Equal Employment Opportunity Act of 1972, have not addressed the wage gap between men and women, nor do they address inequities that this gap creates for women across the life span.

To alleviate gender-based wage disparities, many feminist advocates have fought for **comparable worth** legislation, in which compensation is based on the calculated value of the work rather than on the sex of the worker. In addition, comparable worth legislation would specify that uncompensated work such as preparing meals, rearing children, and attending to housework should be paid just like comparable jobs that are compensated (for example, taxi services, food preparation, and child care services). However, efforts to pass such legislation have failed, primarily because of opposition by business and prevailing values in society that place more value on work outside of the home than in it (Gibelman, 2003).

Theories of Sexism   Feminists argue that sexism persists in U.S. society for a variety of reasons linked to stereotypes in a male-dominated society:

- Many women, particularly young women, generally lack power and public leadership positions in most venues. Women continue to be perceived as less competent than men, particularly where leadership is concerned.

- When women do hold positions of power, those positions tend to be devalued. Or if it is impossible to deny the importance of the position, a woman's success in that position is seen as luck or caused by outside forces, such as the help of colleagues or special treatment.

- If it is impossible to deny the competence of the woman in the position, then she tends to be resented for her ability and for violating gender stereotypes and norms. These women tend to be labeled "bitches," "selfish," and "bitter." Interestingly, this phenomenon tends to transcend cultural boundaries (Carli & Eagly, 2001).

- The media tend to perpetuate sexism and negative stereotypes about women. For example, ads in fashion magazines that target professional women show them as being competent but still being dressed in feminine clothing and maintaining their "soft" side. Presumably, this makes women less threatening and ensures that they conform to expected gender norms. Some argue that the negative images of women that are portrayed in the media aggravate the situation by reinforcing ideas about the roles, norms, and abilities of women (Fouts & Burggraf, 2000).

- Women's success may be attributed to their looks, sexuality, reliance on a male colleague, or affirmative action. Young women are especially susceptible to these stereotypes and prejudices because of their age: Supervisors and coworkers may think they could not possibly be skilled because they are too young and naïve. Young women are more likely than young men to have their ideas and skills disregarded and their success attributed to some other factor.

Skillful management is often described in masculine terms; thus, many administrators and other workers presume that women do not have the inherent skills. Even when a woman's work is identical to that of a man, hers is viewed as inferior. For example, if women work in teams, they are less likely to get credit for good work whereas men in the same teams will have success credited to their own abilities. Some scholars argue that being a woman and competent in the workplace may actually hinder women and keep them from advancing in their occupations.

Theories of racism, prejudice, and oppression discussed in Chapter 5 can help to elucidate the causes and effects of sexism. Processes that take place through history and socialization, for example, can explain how sexism is perpetuated as well as why it can be so difficult to eradicate. Feminist theory also provides a lens through which to view sexism, as you have seen throughout this section. From this perspective, sexism is maintained through structures of patriarchy and power that invalidate women's attempts to gain power, and maintain gendered norms and stereotypes that undermine the value of women's work.

Sexism and Social Work   Even the social work profession is guilty of perpetuating sexism. A content analysis conducted on the *Journal of Social Work Education* found sexist language and a general lack of attention to gender issues in its publications (Grise-Owens, 2002). The author of this study argued that it is exactly this type of inattention to gender issues that helps to maintain institutional sexism.

The *Code of Ethics* (NASW, approved 1996, revised 2008) stands in contrast to this bias. Social workers have an ethical responsibility to challenge discrimination and social injustices, such as those caused by sexism. Because of these charges, social workers need to take the lead in advocating for laws and policies that work toward ending sexism. Social workers can educate lawmakers and policy-makers about the sources and effects of sexism as well as ways in which to design laws and policies to help end it. Further, the ways in which social workers conduct practice and scholarship must be a model for others. Ensuring that sexism does not take place in agencies, classrooms, and research is one avenue through which social workers can help to eradicate sexism.

Though Gudrun's case scenario does not give any information regarding issues of sexism, she could have problems related to sexism as she attempts to establish and maintain employment. Potential employers may have stereotypical expectations about Gudrun's capabilities based on her gender, which may decrease her chances of getting fair treatment in her job. Specifically, an employer could assume that because she is a woman, she is not capable of performing well at her job or that she does not possess the skills needed to advance in the workplace. If Gudrun's mental health issues or lack of job skills in a particular area keep her from performing as needed, her performance problems may be blamed on her gender, which may impede her ability to get the help she needs to improve her performance. You can assist Gudrun in this area by helping her advocate for herself to secure needed resources and to ensure that her employers are aware and supportive of her needs and situation.

Sexual Harassment

As discussed in the previous section, sexism is still pervasive in U.S. society, and one way it is played out is through sexual harassment. Young adults entering the workforce may experience or recognize harassment for the first time; they may also become aware of how the media and other social forces reinforce sexist attitudes that lead to harassment.

Sexual Harassment and Popular Culture   Many feminists argue that society continues to condone sexual harassment and that this support of sexist attitudes is reflected in popular culture. For instance, the media tend to reinforce sexist attitudes through advertisements and situation comedies that make light of degrading comments and circumstances. For example, office humor that objectifies women is still prevalent on many sitcoms—in essence, trivializing the devaluing of women. Feminists posit that popular culture is actually representing an underlying hostility toward women (Montemurro, 2003), especially as women make advances in the workplace, politics, athletics, and other arenas. To be fair, though, some programs, including *The Office* and *South Park,* have used humor to draw attention to sexual harassment as a social and workplace issue.

Sexual harassment is also widespread on college campuses. Results from one study indicated that approximately 33 percent of the 158 college students sampled had sexually harassed a professor (DeSouza and Fansler, 2003). Over half of the 209 professors sampled reported having been harassed by students. Interestingly, men and women reported similar rates of harassment, but women reported more negative psychological ramifications of that harassment than did men. Given the high rate of sexual harassment perpetrated by college students in this study, it seems that many young adults may not fully understand what sexual harassment is or the effects that it can have on others.

Many college campuses have instituted programs to increase awareness of sexual harassment and its effects. Social workers can help to educate young adults on the subject in other venues as these young adults move into the workforce and other situations where they can perpetuate harassment.

Theories of Sexual Harassment   Both the conflict and the feminist perspectives are useful in conceptualizing harassment and reasons why it occurs. For instance, these perspectives might view harassment as a strategy to perpetuate men's power. Harassment can intimidate victims, and thus many victims hesitate to report the behavior. The perpetrator of the harassment remains in power by using it to keep the victim in a vulnerable position. If the person being harassed is a woman and she complains, she is likely to be viewed as a troublemaker, which will likely hurt her chances for advancement and keep her from positions of power from which she can challenge the behavior of others.

Social learning theory also provides a lens through which to view sexual harassment. Jokes, comments, and harassing behaviors portrayed by the media and other people in a child's environment are ways in which a child learns what is valued by society. Children who are exposed to sexual harassment, and who see that this behavior is often positively reinforced, learn that this type of behavior is acceptable. Once these children reach young adulthood, they are in positions where their learned behaviors of harassment can be acted out in ways that can harm others. For example, young adults may harass their co-workers or their college professors, as mentioned in the earlier study.

Strategies to Prevent Sexual Harassment   Persons who are victims of harassment are often afraid to come forward. They are often blamed for the harassment, or they are not believed when they make a complaint, especially if they wait to do so. These individuals' motives may be questioned, particularly if they are young women. Some people may speculate that the woman has something to gain from bringing attention to sexual harassment (for example, money or publicity), or they may accuse her of being too sensitive or of being a troublemaker (Balogh, Kite, Pickel, Canel, & Schroeder, 2003). Young women are especially vulnerable to these types of reactions because they may be viewed as having "asked for" the harassment through their style of dress or behavior.

One problem that may contribute to these reactions to charges of sexual harassment is the lack of consensus on definitions of concepts such as discrimination and harassment. Although most people would agree that acts such as rape are not tolerable, disagreement abounds about whether behaviors such as joking, touching, compliments, and other "friendly" comments and gestures are appropriate or whether they constitute harassment. Various federal policies and laws make it unlawful for employers to discriminate against individuals based on sex, and harassment is included as a form of discrimination. However, these policies and laws are troublesome because the essential concepts are difficult to define.

Although definitions can be produced through lawsuits and court cases, some social workers agree that prevention is a better approach. Social workers are in a position to educate young adults about sexual harassment. They can also model respect, leadership, and good communication, which is considered an effective strategy (American Academy of Pediatrics, 2000). Finally, social workers are in a position to help to shape definitions and boundaries of harassing behavior.

Depending on the particular perspective from which social workers conceptualize sexual harassment, they can do much to help prevent it and intervene when it occurs. Social workers can provide education and a safe environment for open communication when problems arise. From the conflict and feminist perspectives, social workers can strive to alter the power structure in various institutions to help change the environment. Women need to be in positions of power to assist in developing policies and laws that will combat sexual harassment. From the social learning perspective, social workers can act as models for clients and others to demonstrate appropriate ways to interact and treat others.

Civil Rights Laws and Affirmative Action

As young adults move into employment, education, and other realms, discrimination may become a salient issue. For some young adults, discrimination may prevent them from attending their preferred college or from receiving a job promotion. For other young adults, they may be in decision-making positions where they can discriminate against others. In this section, we look specifically at some of the laws and policies in place to help avoid discriminatory actions based on race or ethnicity. However, the discussion also applies to discrimination based on gender.

Civil rights laws of the 1960s were developed and enacted to help ensure that everyone was assured the basic rights stated in the U.S. Constitution. **Affirmative action** efforts stem from civil rights laws and require that employers and other institutions actively recruit women and other minority group members (Gibelman, 2000).

The Affirmative Action Debate   Affirmative action is one area that brings out many strong opinions. Most people in the United States believe in equality, but only for the "worthy." This line of thinking supports the notion that affirmative action serves only to promote the well-being of those who are not qualified or willing to work, which makes them "unworthy." Others think that inequality is a result of years of injustice and discrimination, and while laws can help to ensure some level of equality, individuals are responsible for changing society. Many feel that policies like affirmative action make matters worse by disempowering the minority groups they are intended to help and even leading to **reverse discrimination**—a condition in which whites are discriminated against in favor of less qualified or deserving minorities. This line of thinking posits that giving special privileges to minority groups through policies like affirmative action only makes those in the majority hostile toward minority group members and does not allow minority group members to "make it on their own" or to demonstrate their inherent worth and capability (Gibelman, 2000).

The following two positions on affirmative action tend to predominate in the debate about the policy:

- Liberal individualism argues that individuals are responsible for their behavior, so they do not need any special protections from the government to ensure that their rights are protected or that they will not become victims of discrimination. Those who take this stance would not view institutional sexism or racism as problems; rather, they likely would view these problems as a result of individual behavior. From this perspective, therefore, affirmative action policies go too far because they actively seek to recruit people from minority groups, seemingly regardless of their capabilities and at the expense of individuals who might be more qualified (Pierce, 2003). From this viewpoint comes the argument that affirmative action is simply a form of reverse discrimination.

- At the other end of the spectrum are people who argue that because of institutionalized discrimination, we need more minority representation in positions of power to "level the playing field." This viewpoint takes the stance that people from minority groups are not necessarily less qualified than whites, but that minority individuals often have difficulty getting good positions because they lack the power and connections that whites have. Thus, affirmative action policies ensure that people from minority groups can compete for good jobs by taking power and connections out of the hiring process. Further, this point of view posits that society benefits from minority representation in business, education, and other settings because it ensures diversity and exposes others to different cultures and worldviews.

This debate is frequently played out in various private and public venues. For example, in 2003 the U.S. Supreme Court upheld the University of Michigan Law School's use of race as a variable in its admission policy (*Lancet,* 2003). To some extent, that decision supported affirmative action policies at other universities. However, in 2014, with a substantially different and more conservative court in place, the University of Michigan decision was negated. The Supreme Court also heard a new case involving a challenge to affirmative action policies at the University of Texas, however this resulted in an ambiguous ruling that sent the case back to a lower court.

Evidence to suggest that any one group is at a disadvantage because of affirmative action policies has been scarce. Rather, there is evidence that discrimination remains a problem in many businesses and social institutions, and methods to eradicate it, such as affirmative action, are still needed. For example, one study found that white men had an advantage over black men and women in areas such as job training and over black women in education (Caputo, 2002).

Theoretical Bases of Affirmative Action   Many of the arguments for dismantling affirmative action policies can be explained by theories of discrimination discussed in Chapter 5. Explanations that include history, frustration-aggression, and competition and exploitation all provide reasons why some people may be hostile toward affirmative action policies. For example, when a member of a minority group is hired for a job instead of a white applicant, it is easy for the white person to complain that affirmative action was the reason why the minority applicant got the job.

Thus, the minority person becomes the scapegoat for the frustration that the white person feels for not being hired. Blaming affirmative action may be preferable to the person's acknowledging that she or he was not as qualified as the person who got the job, or perhaps to blaming the economy for not supporting enough jobs to employ everyone.

The utilitarian approach would argue that affirmative action benefits society because it allows everyone who can contribute to participate. That outcome is worthwhile, even at the expense of a few who may suffer because others are receiving preferential treatment.

Social justice theories also offer frameworks from which to view policies like affirmative action. Distributive justice, as discussed in Chapter 5, is concerned with ensuring that everyone in society has equal rights and resources—everyone is deserving. From this perspective, then, affirmative action could be considered an appropriate response to institutional discrimination.

On the other hand, the concept of distributive justice and the social justice perspective could also be used to argue that affirmative action is not fair. After all, it gives special consideration to some members in society. A libertarian perspective on justice, which posits that government should have a very limited role in the lives of individuals, would support the idea of dismantling affirmative action. From this perspective, affirmative action gives too much power to the government to dictate how businesses and other institutions operate.

Affirmative Action and Social Work   Historically, the social work profession has not been active in the debate over affirmative action. As with other social issues and problems, however, social workers need to be leaders in the debate and in the applications of affirmative action policies. Fighting discrimination is a basic tenet of the *Code of Ethics,* and this policy can have dramatic effects on clients. Furthermore, social work has much to contribute with regard to research and education on discrimination and the strengths and limitations of interventions, such as affirmative action, to eradicate it. Social workers can be especially effective by applying social planning and policy development theory and knowledge to guide reform and by addressing institutional racism (Gibelman, 2000). Thus, they need to remain informed about the debate over affirmative action and play an active role in any reformations of the policy that may take place.

In Gudrun's situation, because of potential sexism, she could benefit from policies like affirmative action. Because she is a member of a minority group, she could take advantage of affirmative action policies as she looks for work. Any barriers that she may face due to her gender would be related to discrimination in general, and you could rely on specific policies such as affirmative action to help advocate for Gudrun's rights.

CONCLUSION

Young adulthood is a time of great change. Many individuals undergo changing roles, achieve independence, and embark on new experiences. Although there are no definitive events in Western culture that mark the movement from adolescence to young adulthood, many observers would consider actions such as establishing intimate relationships, going off to college, taking a job, and moving away from home to be sure signs that the individual has reached this stage in life.

For many individuals, young adulthood and the changes associated with it are exciting; however, these changes can also cause stress, confusion, and ambivalence. And because many individuals experience increasing responsibility during this time of life, their problems are more likely to interfere with their functioning and well-being than when they were younger. Often, these problems bring young adults to the attention of social workers.

Social workers may work with young adults in many capacities to assist in increasing independence, self-assurance, decision-making capacities, and function-ing as responsible adults. Whether it is in an educational, mental health, workplace, or other setting, social workers can help not only in solving problems that may occur for some young adults, but also in preventing problems that may develop as they move into middle and later adulthood.

MAIN POINTS

- Physical and cognitive growth begins to stabilize during young adulthood, while continued development occurs emotionally, intellectually, and interpersonally.

- Emerging adulthood is a newly conceptualized life stage that helps to explain the shifts in the developmental processes between adolescence and the mid-twenties that have begun to occur.

- Mental illness and disability can arise at any time in the life span, with symptoms affecting well-being and functioning. Social workers frequently use the medical model to guide assessment and intervention in these cases, but they can also draw on systems and ecological theories and consider factors on the micro, mezzo, and macro levels.

- Spirituality and religious participation, for some young adults, are a source of stability. Fowler's theory of faith development consists of seven stages that describe how people develop faith and meaning in their lives.

- Mindfulness is an evidence-based technique that helps clients learn to focus on goals by attending to the present moment and approaching problems with an attitude of openness and acceptance.

- Increasingly, young adults are choosing lifestyles that include cohabiting, delaying marriage, and remaining single. However, for some individuals, living with a partner, regardless of the arrangements, also brings with it issues of domestic violence. Social workers can use the lenses of social learning, family systems, and feminist theories to help understand domestic violence and intervene effectively with clients.

- Choosing whether or not to attend college can be a struggle for some young adults; still others do not have the opportunity to pursue a college education because of financial and other constraints. Social workers can use social learning theory to understand clients' situations and help them overcome barriers to achieving their goals—whether they involve getting into the college of their choice or succeeding in school.

- Young adults—especially women—are likely to face sexism and sexual harassment as they enter the workforce, begin college, and take on other new roles. Women do not receive equal pay for equal work, and they are frequently discriminated against on the job; these are issues with which social workers must contend.

- Some think that affirmative action does nothing but create reverse discrimination, while others think that it is needed to help eradicate institutional discrimination. Social workers need to be informed about this debate and play an active role in policy-making.

EXERCISES

1. *Hudson City interactive case at* www.routledgesw.com/cases. Review the issues in the case and answer the following questions:
   a. How might issues faced by the community impact development in early adulthood, particularly with regard to "emerging adulthood"?
   b. How could community issues interact and interface with problems around mental illness, particularly PTSD, contributing to problems for both the individual and the community?
   c. What particular issues might residents with disabilities face in this community?
   d. How might residents' faith development be impacted by circumstances of this community?
2. Riverton *interactive case at* www.routledgesw.com/cases. Review the case, paying particular attention to Mary Stark and John Washington. Then answer the following questions:
   a. What issues discussed in this chapter might apply to the individual situations of Mary and John?
   b. Keeping in mind the issues you picked above, what theoretical perspective(s) might you choose to work with Mary and John?

c. In what ways might the issues presented in this chapter apply to the community as a whole?

3. *RAINN interactive case at* www.routledgesw.com/cases. Review Sarah's situation and then answer these questions:

   a. Attending church is the only social activity Sarah had in the weeks following the rape by her uncle. How do you think her spirituality has been impacted by the sexual assault?

   b. Where is she in her faith development, according to Fowler?

   c. What is spirituality? How can Sarah's faith be used to help her recover from the sexual assault?

4. *RAINN interactive case at* www.routledgesw.com/cases. A social worker at RAINN is aware that gender norms and stereotypes can have a big impact on male victims of sexual assault, such as Alan.

   a. What are some ways in which gender norms and stereotypes may have hurt Alan?

   b. How can the social worker use elements of social learning theory to help Alan develop a more positive self-image?

5. *Sanchez Family interactive case at* www.routledgesw.com/cases. Review the major issues involving the Sanchez family, focusing on Vicki and Gloria. Then answer the following questions:

   a. Given our discussion in this chapter, what issues might be pertinent in working with Vicki and Gloria? Are there other issues not discussed in this chapter that might be relevant in working with these two family members?

   b. Imagine that you are a social worker assigned to work with Vicki and her symptoms of autism. Using the case study on the Sanchez family, conduct an assessment for Vicki using ecological theory to guide it. What issues on different levels might impact Vicki and her functioning? What interventions might be warranted based on this assessment?

   c. Using ecological theory, conduct an assessment regarding Gloria and her domestic violence situation. Articulate what your intervention(s) would look like based on your assessment.

   d. What strengths and limitations can you see in using ecological theory in your work with these family members? Are there any ethical dilemmas that you might need to work through?

CHAPTER 11

Development in Middle Adulthood

Tina is a 48-year-old married Caucasian woman with two children who are both in their early twenties and live near Tina and her husband. This is Tina's second marriage, and it has lasted 10 years. Tina and her husband own a small business and spend long hours working to keep it successful. Tina's first husband, the father of her children, has had no contact with her or her children since the children were very young.

Since Tina's children were very young, they have exhibited numerous behavioral problems, and recently her oldest son was arrested for assault in a bar fight. Tina admits that the hours she puts into the business as well as her children's problems cause her a great deal of stress. She is moody, has frequent migraine headaches, and spends most of her free time drinking or sleeping. Tina has smoked most of her life and does not exercise. She tends to have a negative outlook on life and has few friends or positive relationships with family members. Recently, Tina consulted a social worker to help her manage stress, and she is complaining of moodiness and restless sleep.

MIDDLE ADULTHOOD CAN BE A VERY ENJOYABLE, SATISFYING time for many people. By the time they enter their forties, many people have successfully moved through the challenges of early adulthood and have achieved many of their educational, vocational, and interpersonal goals. During their time, most people maintain a relatively stable period of productiveness. Nevertheless, for others, middle adulthood can be a time of great stress resulting from problems such as illness, divorce, and employment difficulties.

In the following sections we will look at some of the issues relevant to middle adulthood and ways in which social workers might assist people in improving their quality of life.

DEVELOPMENTAL MILESTONES IN MIDDLE AGE

Middle adulthood, in general, can be a time when people enjoy all of the hard work their bodies have put into physical development through puberty and young

QUICK GUIDE 16 Developmental Milestones in Middle Adulthood	
PHYSICAL	**COGNITIVE**
• Some declines in metabolism, energy level, eyesight, hearing, muscle tone.	• Some declines in memory, reaction time if not cognitively active.
• Increase in appearance of wrinkles, gray hair, thinning hair.	• Increases in cognitive performance can occur because new information is linked with past experiences.
• Increased weight gain.	• Increased problem-solving skills.
• Increased prevalence of chronic illnesses such as cancer, diabetes, and heart disease.	• Increased creativity.
• Women undergo menopause, and men may experience a male climacteric.	
• Problems in sexual functioning may occur.	

adulthood and the hard work of their brains in developing cognitively. Although middle age is a time when energy, eyesight, hearing, metabolism, memory, and reaction time begin to decline, many people usually do not notice a marked difference from when they were younger. At the same time, they can enjoy better problem-solving skills and creativity. For an overview of the developmental milestones in middle age, see Quick Guide 16.

Physical Developments in Middle Adulthood

Many of the physical issues that may arise during middle age can be treated, and even prevented, so this becomes a time when people need to get regular checkups and pay attention to their lifestyles. However, among the most troublesome changes that occur with middle age, at least in U.S. culture, are those involving the person's physical appearance. Though for many people these changes are gradual, for others, depending on their lifestyles and genetic makeup, the changes can be rapid and dramatic. For example, many men and women begin to see small wrinkles appear on their faces, they may get more and more gray hairs, and their hair may begin to thin. Many men lose their hair and gain weight that produces a "spare tire" around their middle, while women typically gain weight around their hips and find that their breasts have begun to sag. Because of these changes, some people in middle age opt for cosmetic surgery to retain their youthful appearances.

Most women (and many men) in the United States would agree that there is a double standard with regard to aging. Specifically, women argue that they are treated more negatively than men when it comes to the consequences of aging. For example, men's graying hair and wrinkles are considered "distinguished," while the same processes in women put them "over the hill." Older men are viewed as more attractive and desirable than older women, a perception that can affect women in many realms, including the workplace. Hollywood and the media are especially guilty of perpetuating these attitudes. Consider, for example, how many aging male actors such as George Clooney, Denzel Washington, and Jeff Bridges are paired with young women in movies and sometimes in real life. In contrast, seeing older women in major roles in the movies is less common, let alone seeing them romantically paired with younger men. Even when older female actors such as Meryl Streep, Diane Keaton, and Helen Mirren are in romantic roles, their relationships are often played comedically. In reality, some older women do have younger men as partners, but this arrangement is not as common as seeing older men with younger women.

Obviously, many of the physical changes that occur in middle adulthood can be explained through the medical model. Biological explanations abound that attempt to describe processes that slow us down as we age. Certainly, having a working knowledge of the physical problems that can develop as a person ages is useful in working with clients.

Similarly, feminist theory and various sociological theories may help social workers understand how problems such as the double standard in aging occur and how they may impact the lives of middle-aged women and men. For example, feminists and conflict theorists might argue that patriarchal society perpetuates this type of discrimination because men have power over media and other sources that put out messages about what is attractive and desirable. Social workers relying on these perspectives to inform their work with clients would need to find ways to empower clients and change the social structure that invalidates processes of aging.

Cognitive Developments in Middle Adulthood

In contrast to their physical appearance, the cognitive capacities of most healthy, intellectually active middle-aged adults do not show much decline. Declines in the speed of processing information have been documented in middle age, but these are generally so small that they are not noticeable outside the laboratory (Salthouse, 2006). Otherwise, middle-aged people can match—and often exceed—the cognitive abilities of younger people.

For example, people who engage in mental activity through work, continued education, or reading show increases in mental capacities such as vocabulary. Moreover, people in middle age tend to be at their best creatively, and they are better at integrating new knowledge with what they already know because their rich experiences have created many neural connections. As a result, middle-aged adults tend to be better problem solvers than young adults. People in middle age also tend to be better at reflecting on information and judging it for its value and worth both personally and practically (Papalia, Olds, & Feldman, 2003).

Such theories as Erik Erikson's theory on psychosocial development, various sociological theories, and feminist theory can help social workers make sense of the psychological and social ramifications of physical aging. For example, according to Erikson, middle adulthood is a time when people are investing in their work, families, and community. Stage 7 of Erikson's theory states that people in middle adulthood are facing the conflict of Generativity vs. Stagnation:

- *Generativity:* The willingness to care about the people and things one has produced as well as a commitment to protecting and enhancing the conditions of one's society. Adults in this stage are working to establish continuity between generations and are continuing to grow and expand in emotional depth and social roles (Wood, 2006).

- *Stagnation:* The lack of psychological growth, which includes being self-centered, seeking pleasure at the expense of others, and having difficulty seeing beyond one's own needs. Adults in middle adulthood who cannot look beyond their own emotional needs may be in stagnation, which can affect their development into older age and Erikson's final stage of Integrity vs. Despair.

Many middle-aged adults are performing well creatively and intellectually; they have much to contribute to different realms of their lives. However, if people have stopped learning or have a physical problem that keeps them from engaging in work or relationships, they may feel stagnant or be less productive than they would like. Using this theory, social workers can help middle-aged clients to identify ways in which they may not feel fulfilled and can then concentrate their efforts on helping clients move toward productive, more meaningful lives.

Tina's situation may have physical causes that you can assess, but you may also want to explore how aging has affected Tina psychologically. Perhaps some of the characteristics described in the opening scenario—for example, moodiness and a negative outlook on life—are associated to some degree with changes brought on by aging. Understanding the powerful interplay between aging and women's status in society is helpful in working with female clients, and it might be worth your time to assess Tina's attitudes and feelings about aging-related physical changes and how they might impact her continued development.

Levinson's Theory of Adult Development

Although Erikson and others offer insights into challenges that take place across the life span, including middle age, psychologist Daniel Levinson offers a more detailed approach to development during middle and late adulthood. Levinson's theory is built around the idea of **life structures**, or patterns of behavior that, in combination with the environment, are shaping forces in people's lives. Life structures consist of events, people, culture, religion, and other aspects of life that people find important at different stages of their lives. As people move through life, these life structures often shift and adjust as people gain new experiences and reevaluate what is important to them (Levinson, 1978). Exhibit 11.1 displays the stages in Levinson's theory in the form of a timeline.

Within each stage, people must master various developmental tasks:

- *Early adulthood:* As they make the transition from adolescence into adulthood, people must begin dealing with the tasks of establishing an adult identity. They face decisions about work, education, relationships, and independence. By the time they reach the transition into their early thirties, these decisions should be made and serve as the foundation for an adult identity. The culminating life structure for early adulthood is determining their goals for adulthood—for instance, whether to start a family and what type of a career to pursue.

- *Middle adulthood:* By the middle adult transition, people have established themselves in their families and careers (or they have achieved some success with whatever goals they set in their thirties). During this transition, people question what lies ahead for them in middle adulthood. The life structures

EXHIBIT 11.1	AGE		
Levinson's Theory of Adult Development	17–22	Early adult transition	Early adulthood
	22–28	Entry life structure for early adulthood	
	28–33	Age 30 transition	
	33–40	Culminating life structure for early adulthood	
	40–45	Middle adult transition	Middle adulthood
	45–50	Entry life structure for middle adulthood	
	50–55	Age 50 transition	
	55–60	Culminating life structure for middle adulthood	
	60–65	Late adult transition	Late adulthood
	60+	Late adulthood	

Source: Adapted from Levinson, 1978

and transitions that take place during the forties and fifties consist of questioning what it means to grow old, assessing whether choices made previously are satisfying, and making changes that will lead to greater satisfaction. These changes might include divorcing, remarrying, starting a new family, or changing careers.

- *Late adulthood:* The late adult transition involves changes such as retirement, becoming a grandparent, and increased likelihood of health problems and impairments. These are times when people reflect on their lives and approach an old age whose contours are based on personal and societal expectations.

One major criticism of Levinson's theory is that its tenets were developed to describe the life course of men. Levinson developed this theory by observing 40 men in prestigious occupations. Thus, some critics contend that his theory cannot be generalized to women or to other culturally and economically diverse populations. However, Levinson later developed a similar theory for women (Levinson & Levinson, 1996), and other behavioral scientists have developed theories that address limitations to Levinson's theory. Women's development tends to differ from men's in that women are much less likely to have a mentor than men and their "dream" tends to be more focused on the needs of others, especially the well-being of family. In contrast, Levinson describes men's "dream" as focused on personal goals and career attainment.

You could apply Levinson's theory to Tina's case by assessing which stage she is in and which tasks she should be mastering. Based on her age, 48, she should be in the entry life structure for middle adulthood. Therefore, she may be reflecting on her life and the choices she has made thus far regarding her career, education, and family. If she believes that she has made some poor choices or has not achieved the goals she set in young adulthood, she may be feeling regret or despair. In turn, these feelings could be manifesting themselves through symptoms of stress, depression, fatigue, and heavy drinking. You could help Tina by exploring the areas of her life with which she feels disappointment or regret and helping her to contemplate what she would like to do differently in future stages to achieve greater satisfaction as she ages.

Motivational Interviewing

In working with clients in middle adulthood who may be struggling with developmental tasks, social workers may choose to employ **Motivational Interviewing** (MI), a person-centered therapeutic technique and clinical style based in Cognitive Behavioral Theory and Carl Rogers' Person-Centered Therapy. Research has suggested that MI is very effective in working with a wide range of problems from weight loss, smoking cessation, and substance abuse and addictions to serious and chronic mental health issues. Through this research, a theory of MI is emerging (Miller & Rose, 2009).

MI promotes behavior change by creating an environment of empathy, developing cognitive dissonance in the client, and exploring client ambivalence so that the client can begin to argue for change. In the use of MI, the therapist is not the "expert" on the client's experience, trying to impose her or his views onto the client. Rather, the therapist works to develop trust and a partnership with the client to draw out the client's thoughts on issues. In this sense, the therapist does not try to convince the client that change is needed. Rather, the therapist helps the client develop and articulate arguments for and against change. This approach helps to build client self-efficacy and helps the client explore ambivalence and resistance to change (Miller & Rose, 2009; Motivational Interviewing, 2011).

As Tina's social worker, you might want to employ MI to help her explore the pros and cons of remaining in her current situation, which is causing stress, sleeplessness, and moodiness. You could follow with an exploration of the pros and cons of making changes. You might want to draw out Tina's feelings of ambivalence to change and use cognitive dissonance to help strengthen the contrast between Tina's wish to change and the behaviors, such as overworking and drinking, that keep her in her current situation.

THE INDIVIDUAL IN MIDDLE ADULTHOOD

Physical changes in middle adulthood are not necessarily as bad as U.S. society makes them out to be. Although there are some declines in certain areas, the rate and extent to which people show signs of aging vary a great deal from person to person. Further, not everyone responds to these changes in the same way, and not everyone perceives these changes as negative.

This section deals with specific issues on an individual level that tend to occur in middle age: menopause, the male climacteric, midlife crisis, and chronic illness and disease. Although these issues do not affect all middle-aged adults, social workers need to have basic knowledge of them and understand how they create problems for some people.

Menopause

Menopause is the cessation of a woman's menstrual cycle. Some women say that they welcome the changes that menopause brings, while others view menopause as a negative sign that they are aging. These disparate views underscore the fact that no two women react or adjust to menopause in quite the same way.

The timing of the onset of menopause, as well as its course, vary greatly among women. The average age of onset is approximately age 51, but it can begin in one's early thirties or as late as the sixties. The average course of menopause is approximately two to five years, during which time women's bodies go through many physiological changes (North American Menopause Society, 2006).

Menopause begins when a woman's periods start to become irregular. Patterns of irregularity include skipped periods, decreased blood flow, and the cessation of periods. During this time, the ovaries stop releasing eggs, levels of estrogen and progesterone drop, the fallopian tubes become shorter and smaller, the uterus becomes smaller and harder, and the vagina becomes shorter and less elastic. Women may also experience decreased lubrication of the vagina, making intercourse uncomfortable or painful. Other symptoms that some women experience include headaches, insomnia, hot flashes, thinning hair, weight gain, skin changes, mood fluctuations, and growth of hair in unwanted places, including increased facial hair (North American Menopause Society, 2006).

Hormone replacement therapy (HRT) is one option for women to help ease the symptoms of menopause and prevent problems that can be brought on by menopause. This therapy helps to shore up declining levels of reproductive hormones in a woman's body. Seen from the medical model, HRT is a way to replace the hormones that women lose through the process of menopause and to alleviate some of its symptoms and negative effects—including bone loss, hot flashes, and sleep problems—that women may experience (North American Menopause Society, 2006; Sommer, 2001).

However, some evidence suggests that HRT may do as much harm as good. It increases the risk of stroke, breast cancer, and heart disease for some women, particularly with long-term use. Hormone treatment may also make cancers that do develop more advanced and deadly (Chlebowski *et al.*, 2010). Indeed, recent declines in breast cancer in the U.S. have been linked to decreases in women's use of HRT, which began after research made the link between breast cancer and HRT (Ravdin *et al.*, 2007). Other research, however, suggests that the use of estrogen-only therapy actually reduces risk of breast cancer and heart attack (Writing Group for the Women's Health Initiative Investigators, 2002). The National Institutes of Health and other health experts recommend that women who are considering HRT talk with their health providers to determine whether the benefits of HRT outweigh the risks in their particular situations (North American Menopause Society, 2006; Stephens, Budge, & Carryer, 2002).

The Psychological Dimension of Menopause Psychological reactions to menopause vary significantly among women, depending on their personalities, coping skills, support systems, and general attitudes about life and aging. Some women welcome the changes that occur with menopause: They value their new-found freedom from the hassle and expense of regular periods, and they no longer have to worry about becoming pregnant. Conversely, other women experience anxiety, depression, and lowered self-esteem because they identify menopause with a loss of fertility and attractiveness. Research indicates that women who are well adjusted emotionally before menopause tend to be well adjusted during and after menopause. Specifically, these women are unlikely to experience any negative psychological reactions to menopause (Strong, DeVault, Sayad, & Yarber, 2002).

One study using data from 1,572 women indicated that women tend to place as much importance on the sociocultural aspects of menopause as they do on its health implications (Ballard, Kuh, & Wadsworth, 2001). Many respondents discussed menopause and its effects in relation to their family and work relationships. With increasing life expectancies and volatile economic circumstances, many women find that they want, or need, to work longer to care for aging parents and children who are young adults and still living at home. Thus, many women viewed menopause as a developmental milestone, which indicated to them that new possibilities in family and work life lay ahead. In other words, menopause may be a time when a woman is able to reevaluate her life choices and to perceive these choices as new opportunities rather than negative life events. Moreover, because more women have attained higher educational levels than in the past, they have more career and other options to consider as they make a transition into a new chapter of their lives (Ballard *et al.*, 2001).

The Cultural Dimension of Menopause Reactions to menopause also have a cultural component. For example, U.S. culture, which values youth, might view menopause negatively, identifying it with aging, the loss of vitality and attractiveness, and the end of the reproductive years. From this perspective, the symptoms are something that need to be "cured." However, other cultures perceive menopause as a natural progression of lifelong development or even as a rite of passage. Cultures that value the elderly, for example, define menopause as a hallmark or milestone in the life course (Starck, 1993).

In one study on rural African–American women's perceptions of menopause, religion and internal strength were important for dealing with symptoms. These women turned to prayer and other religious supports to increase their sense of self-efficacy during the onset of menopause, and they were unlikely to use physicians or therapies such as HRT. Indeed, these women were much more likely than white women to view menopause as a natural event in the course of life. These women viewed symptoms as something to be mastered, much as they mastered other events and circumstances in their lives, such as poverty and oppression (Nixon, Mansfield, Kittell, & Faulkner, 2001).

In line with feminist and similar theories, some theorists speculate that Western culture views menopause negatively because we have "medicalized" or "pathologized" it. That is, we define menopause as a set of symptoms that can be cured or at least reduced. In addition, because we consider reproduction to be one of women's primary functions, we interpret menopause to mean that women's bodies are ceasing to perform their biological "duties." Thus, much of the psychological stress that many women feel as they go through menopause might arise from the negative messages they receive about their changing roles. Conversely, other experts argue that at least some of the psychological stress that women encounter during this time can be attributed to biological changes in the body rather than to social pressures (Chornesky, 1998).

In sum, then, regardless of a person's views on the implications of menopause for a woman's psychological and emotional health, a combination of social, cultural, emotional, biological, cognitive, and psychological processes influence the outcome.

> *Given Tina's age and the headaches and moodiness she has described, it would be worthwhile to assess whether Tina is going through menopause. It could be that she is experiencing some hormonal changes that may be affecting her mood and other aspects of her well-being. You may want to spend some time talking with Tina about her perceptions of menopause and whether she is noticing any other symptoms that might indicate that she is undergoing this process. If Tina is concerned about experiencing menopause or feels that she would benefit from treatment, you would be able to explore Tina's options with her and refer her to the appropriate resources.*
>
> *Further, because Tina is a smoker and leads a sedentary lifestyle, she may be at risk for osteoporosis or other diseases associated with menopause. You will want to discuss with Tina some of the health implications related to her age and lifestyle habits.*

The Male Climacteric

Evidence suggests that males also experience a climacteric, or a change in life, that corresponds with female menopause. Indeed, this change has been referred to as the "male menopause" or "andropause," though no evidence exists to suggest that it is equivalent to the physiological changes that women experience (Sommer, 2001).

The **male climacteric** refers to the period between ages 35 and 60 when many men reevaluate their careers, familial relationships, and other major life decisions. Some men experience physical symptoms of anxiety and depression while going through this assessment process. Moreover, many men experience physical symptoms of aging such as hair loss, weight gain, diminished energy, decreased muscle strength, decreased hormone production, a slowed sexual response cycle, and sexual dysfunction, which may aggravate these feelings of anxiety and depression (Matsumoto, 2002; Vermeulen, 1994; Vermeulen & Kaufman, 1995; Wespes & Schulman, 2002). Other men, however, do not experience a need to reevaluate their situations, nor do they experience any symptoms of distress.

Evidence suggests that some men may benefit from testosterone replacement therapy to alleviate symptoms associated with andropause, though as in HRT for women, there are side effects that need to be evaluated. Indeed, many of the long-term implications of testosterone replacement therapy are unknown (Asthana *et al.*, 2004; Isidori, 2008; Matsumoto, 2002; Wespes & Schulman, 2002).

One way to approach the male climacteric is through Levinson's theory of adult development. Recall that according to Levinson (1978), men in their forties and fifties are in their middle adult transition. During this time, men go through many changes, including reevaluating their choices in careers and relationships and taking advantage of new opportunities to help them find fulfillment. Levinson argues that although this process may be stressful for some men, reevaluation is a natural part of reaching certain milestones in a person's life that can lead to greater satisfaction and fulfillment.

Midlife Crisis

The various processes associated with the male climacteric, especially the psychological processes, also have been referred to as the *midlife crisis*. Popular opinion supports the notion that middle adulthood is a time when many people, particularly men, undergo a crisis in which they reevaluate their lives and often take drastic measures to recapture their youth. Stereotypical behaviors associated with midlife crises include buying an expensive sports car, divorcing and then finding romance with someone younger, engaging in risky behaviors such as skydiving, and undergoing plastic surgery.

Psychological Adjustment in Midlife   There is some question about whether the phenomenon of a midlife crisis actually exists. It may be that many people, particularly men, do experience a great deal of anxiety about growing older, which can set into motion various behaviors that appear to be attempts at recapturing or hanging onto youth. As people reevaluate their lives—their careers, relationships, and other life choices—they may experience panic or distress about not achieving their goals, as well as dissatisfaction about their current progress. Consequently, some people may develop feelings of depression or other negative responses to their life review. Further, because U.S. culture tends to place great value on youth, any loss of vitality or attractiveness may be enough to cause psychological distress in some people. Recent data from the Centers for Disease Control and Prevention (2013f) indicate that suicide rates among Americans aged 35 to 64 rose by nearly 30 percent between 1999 and 2010, a jump that particularly affected men in their fifties (they saw a 50 percent increase in suicides in that same time frame). There are varied explanations for this rise in suicide rates, which range from easier access to prescription medications to higher suicidality rates for this cohort when they were adolescents.

In addition, some people might develop psychological symptoms in response to the physiological changes of middle age. It is also possible that psychological symptoms of anxiety and depression could have physiological bases in and of themselves. For instance, menopause brings with it hormonal changes that can bring about symptoms such as hot flashes, which could be mistaken by some as anxiety. In other words, psychological distress that occurs in midlife could be a natural reaction to, or consequence of, physiological changes that also occur during this time.

However, at the same time, some people move through middle age without experiencing any psychological distress, regardless of the physiological or other changes that happen to them. Therefore, the notion that there is, indeed, a well-defined, specific crisis that occurs during this time is difficult to support. It is more likely that reactions to aging that can look like crises are individualistic in nature, varying in degree and frequency from person to person, depending on many factors such as coping skills, personality structures, and attitudes about life and aging.

Theories and Perspectives on Midlife Crisis   Various research studies and theoretical perspectives have yielded diverging viewpoints on midlife crises. Levinson's theory of adult development, for example, would describe various points in midlife as crises that people must experience at different phases in life to complete tasks, put closure on past events, and move on to the next phase. According to this perspective, the behaviors associated with the midlife crisis might actually reflect the "normal tasks" of adult development rather than responses to the aging process.

Other research suggests that most people do not experience crises at specific points in middle adulthood. Rather, most participants express increased feelings of stability, security, autonomy, confidence, and competence in midlife compared to their younger years. These studies support the notion that factors such as maturity and emotional stability, as well as a sense of responsibility, remain relatively stable from young adulthood into later life (Brim, 1999; Keyes & Ryff, 1999; McCrae & Costa, 1990; Röcke & Lachman, 2008).

Another perspective on midlife adjustment is **Peck's theory** of psychological development in "the second half of life." According to Robert C. Peck (1955, 1968), people have four adjustments to make during middle adulthood:

* *Valuing wisdom over physical powers:* Occurs when people recognize that physical strength is no longer the only or primary way to create action and change. Middle adults are recognized to have superior problem-solving skills over their younger counterparts even when they may lose some physical strength.

* *Socializing versus sexualizing:* Describes the transition away from younger adulthood, when finding a mate and creating a family were key tasks. People reorder their social priorities and emphasize the importance of companionship.

* *Emotional flexibility versus emotional impoverishment:* Occurs when middle adults shift emotional investment outside of the immediate family, which allows people to absorb and adjust to losses they will face as they age.

- *Mental flexibility versus mental rigidity:* Describes the challenge of maintaining open mindedness and emphasizing problem solving. People in middle adulthood need to adjust to change in family situations as well as societal changes (Wood, 2006).

Some of Tina's complaints, such as moodiness, drinking, headaches, and a general negative outlook on life, could be attributed to problems of adjustment to midlife changes. Of course, other issues—quite possibly a combination of factors—could be contributing to her symptoms. You need to conduct a thorough assessment of Tina and her symptoms to better understand which forces may be influencing her well-being. Because numerous issues on the individual, familial, and social levels could be stressors for Tina, you can help her to examine each one separately and determine which ones merit further attention.

Chronic Illness and Disease

The longer we live, the longer we are exposed to internal and external agents that can cause damage and, ultimately, disease. Some of this damage is caused by genetic factors, and some of it can be caused by time, lifestyle, and other factors such as poverty, discrimination, and exposure to environmental toxins. For example, evidence suggests that substances we are exposed to on a daily basis—such as BPA, a chemical widely used in plastics, including food and beverage containers—contribute to diabetes and obesity (Nadal, 2012).

While some factors associated with poor health are difficult to control and change, many diseases can be avoided or tempered by lifestyle habits and changes. For example, many common diseases that develop in middle age are related to inactivity or obesity. Many people decrease their level of activity as they age, which can result in weight gain and, in turn, can contribute to other diseases such as diabetes, hypertension, and breast cancer (Endogenous Hormones and Breast Cancer Collaborative Group, 2011).

In addition, poor diet, smoking, and overexposure to the sun or certain chemicals—hazards associated with some occupations—can lead to various forms of cancer. Further, various health problems and medications taken for different illnesses, such as blood pressure medication, can cause other problems such as sexual dysfunction (Westheimer & Lopater, 2004).

Common Diseases Emerging in Middle Age   Some of the more common diseases that occur in middle adulthood include arthritis, diabetes, heart disease, and hypertension. The rates of these diseases, for both men and women, increase with age.

- *Diabetes.* Approximately 16 percent of people between the ages of 40 and 64 have diabetes, both diagnosed and undiagnosed. There were 892,000

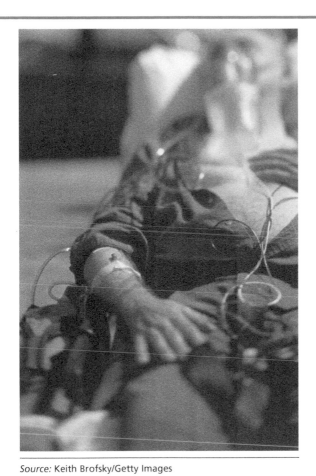

PHOTO 11-A

Chronic illness is a major issue for many people in middle adulthood

ETHNIC GROUP	PERCENTAGE WITH DIABETES
Non-Hispanic Whites	7.6
Asian Americans	9.0
Non-Hispanic Blacks	13.2
Hispanics	12.8
Native Americans/Alaskan Natives	15.9

Source: Adapted from National Diabetes Information Clearinghouse, 2014

EXHIBIT 11.2

Prevalence of Diagnosed and Undiagnosed Diabetes among Adult Americans of Different Ethnic Groups

new cases diagnosed among people in the 40 to 64 age range in 2012, the most for any age group (National Diabetes Information Clearinghouse, 2014). Diabetes rates vary by ethnicity, however. Exhibit 11.2 compares the prevalence rates for diabetes between different ethnic groups in the U.S. As the table indicates, diabetes rates are highest for Native American/Alaskan Native groups followed by certain Hispanic populations, with the highest rates among Puerto Ricans (14.8 percent) and Mexican Americans (13.9 percent). These higher rates are likely caused by a combination of biological and social factors, including genetic predisposition and lack of access to fresh food in isolated communities (American Heart Association, 2001; Mitchell, Kammerer, Reinhart, & Stern, 1994; Ramirez, 1996; National Diabetes Information Clearinghouse, 2014).

- *Heart disease.* The risk of developing heart disease after age 40 is almost 50 percent for men and 32 percent for women, and it accounts for more than 50 percent of all heart problems for people under age 75. After suffering a heart attack, the chances of further illness and death increase for people aged 40 to 69: The risk increases 8 percent for white men, 12 percent for white women, 14 percent for black men, and 11 percent for black women (American Heart Association, 2009).

- *Hypertension.* 13.4 percent of men between ages 20 and 34 are diagnosed with hypertension; the prevalence increases to 64.1 percent of men after age 75. For women, rates go from 6.2 percent to 76.4 for the same age categories (American Heart Association, 2009).

Health Disparities   In Chapters 6 and 7, we touched on problems associated with a lack of access to health care and being uninsured or underinsured. The effects on health are particularly noticeable for people in ethnic minority groups. Health disparities for ethnic minority groups in the United States are rooted in an historical context that promoted the systematic discrimination and exploitation of people in these groups. Health disparities are also well documented and are reflected in many of the statistics on chronic illness and disease just presented. For example, health disparities are reflected in the fact that African Americans have an infant mortality rate that is more than double that of Caucasians and that African–American males have a life expectancy of 71.1 years compared to 76.4 years for Caucasian men (Centers for Disease Control and Prevention, 2014l). And, 20 years ago, white and black women had similar mortality risk rates from breast cancer; beginning in the 1990s, white women's mortality risk began to fall, while black women's risk only fell slightly. Currently, there is a strong correlation between race and breast cancer morality rates. On average, black women are 40 percent more likely to die of breast cancer than white women. In some areas like Los Angeles, black women are 70 percent more likely to die than white women (Hunt, Whitman, & Hurlbert, 2014).

The exact reasons why those in ethnic minority groups experience poorer health outcomes than their white counterparts are difficult to pinpoint. Certainly, the historical exploitation of African Americans and other groups, such as forced sterilization, involuntary medical experimentation, and the view that individuals in ethnic minority groups are genetically inferior to whites laid the foundation for institutional discrimination leading to the health disparities we see today (Golash-Boza, 2015). Further, many of the issues we have discussed thus far likely contribute to health disparities: poverty; discrimination; environmental issues; unequal access to education, employment, and other opportunities; and barriers to health care and other resources that promote good health. For example, people in ethnic minority groups are more likely to live in poverty without access to recreational opportunities, high-paying jobs, safe neighborhoods, quality health clinics, and stores that sell fresh, quality food. Because of violence, poverty, discrimination, and other related socioeconomic factors, they are more likely to suffer from stress that, in and of itself, can lead to disease. Stress can also lead to poor health habits such as smoking, substance abuse, and overeating, which can lead to disease (Kaiser Family Foundation, 2005; U.S. Department of Health and Human Services, 2004).

Health disparities are also an issue for people identifying as transgender. Research indicates that people in transgender communities experience an array of issues that can have negative impacts on health, mental health, and social functioning throughout their lives. These issues include suicidality; substance abuse; exposure to abuse, violence, and harassment; and discrimination in employment, education, health care, and other arenas (Bradford, Reisner, Honnold, & Xavier, 2013; Clements-Nolle, Marx, & Katz, 2006; Hotton, Garofalo, Kuhns, & Johnson, 2013; Nuttbrock et al., 2010). Further, needs of people in this community often are not tracked in health and other systems or well researched, so the extent of the needs and disparities between transgender communities and cisgender communities are not well established. This lack of knowledge compounds the difficulties some in this community face in accessing services (Reisner, White, Bradford, & Mimiaga, 2014). Social workers can be effective allies for transgender communities in advocating for research, access to health care and other services, changes in discriminatory policies that create barriers to services, and public education on issues those in these communities face.

Habits that Tina reports, such as smoking and inactivity, will likely cause health problems later in life, if they have not done so already. You will want to stress the need for a comprehensive physical exam to determine whether Tina's symptoms are physiologically based. Even if Tina is not currently suffering from any physical disorders, you should still assess Tina's need for education about her risks for developing various diseases and strategies for preventing these diseases from occurring later in life.

THE FAMILY AND IMMEDIATE ENVIRONMENT IN MIDDLE ADULTHOOD

Although some physical changes are inevitable in the aging process, there are still other areas of life in which people are just hitting their stride. With increased experiences come more opportunities for change, growth, and continued development. Although these opportunities are often experienced as positive, they can create problems. Thus, in middle age people often need to adjust, rely on coping skills, and reevaluate their goals and priorities. In this section, we look at issues surrounding middle adulthood that involve family, relationships, and changing social and other roles.

Love and Marriage in Middle Age

By the time people reach middle adulthood, they have likely experienced at least one significant love relationship. Some of these relationships will have resulted in marriage, cohabitation, civil union, or divorce. Many of these relationships may have produced children, others not.

An increasing number of middle-aged people are single, however. Approximately 33 percent of people aged 46 to 64 were divorced, separated, or had never been married in 2010, compared to about 13 percent in 1970. However, many of them form alternative relationships instead of marrying. To many of these people, being single means freedom, independence, and liberation. However, unmarried people in this age group are five times more likely than their married counterparts to live in poverty and face other challenges (Lin & Brown, 2012).

Understanding why couples make a commitment and why they do or do not stay together is useful knowledge for social workers. The following sections examine love, marriage, divorce, and remarriage.

Sternberg's Theory of Love   Many researchers have been interested in the construct of love, and this interest has led to various studies and theories on types of love and which types are likely to lead to successful relationships. One theoretical approach to love, developed by Robert Sternberg (1988), is illustrated in Exhibit 11.3. There are three core types of love, denoted at the corners of the triangle:

- *Passionate love, or infatuation:* The "head over heels" kind of love in which an individual is preoccupied with thoughts of the other person. People feel a strong attraction to, and tend to idealize, each other.

- *Intimate love, or liking:* The type of love that results in feeling close to each other. Couples have a sense of rapport, a sense of "we," and they respect and look out for each other. Couples who experience intimate love enjoy spending time together.

- *Commitment, or empty love:* The kind of love that has no elements of closeness. Rather, couples have a steady, enduring, and predictable relationship in which partners trust and are devoted to each other, but they do not necessarily share some of the deeper, intimate feelings associated with passionate love. Relationships based on commitment might best describe **empty shell marriages,** in which couples stay together for various reasons that are based on practicality rather than intimate feelings. For example, some couples stay together to keep up outward appearances or for financial reasons.

Sternberg's theory also describes the types of love that can result when different elements of the theory are combined. These also are highlighted in Exhibit 11.3, along the legs of the triangle:

• *Romantic love:* A combination of intimate and passionate love; describes people who are drawn to each other with feelings of closeness and intense attraction. Romantic love often begins as infatuation.

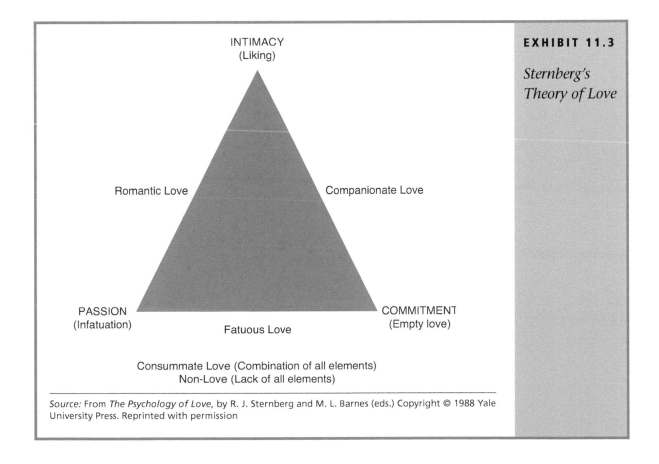

EXHIBIT 11.3

Sternberg's Theory of Love

Source: From *The Psychology of Love*, by R. J. Sternberg and M. L. Barnes (eds.) Copyright © 1988 Yale University Press. Reprinted with permission

- *Companionate love:* A combination of intimate and commitment love; describes people who feel close to each other and are committed, but whose relationship lacks an element of passion. Most romantic relationships eventually become companionate love when passion fades. Not surprisingly, then, companionate love is common in long-term marriages.

- *Fatuous love:* A combination of passionate and commitment love. This is the "silly" love in which people become quickly and intensely involved and might even rush into marriage or move in together right away.

Sternberg's theory identifies two additional types of love, listed below the triangle in the exhibit:

- *Consummate love:* A combination of all three components. It is an ideal love, but it is difficult to achieve and maintain.

- *Non-love:* Void of any of the three components. Non-love would describe casual relationships and interactions with others.

Although Sternberg's theory, in and of itself, cannot predict which couples will stay together and which ones will separate, it does offer valuable insights into the qualities that are present or absent in couple relationships. These insights can help social workers understand people's expectations about love and intimate relationships as well as their motives for continuing some relationships and not others.

Perils of Romantic Love   Another way to understand love and marriage is to look at why couples commit to each other in the first place. One theory posits that many people, particularly in U.S. culture, adhere to the notion of romantic love: We just need to find that one, right person for us, and we will live happily ever after. Many critics argue that this notion alone is responsible for many marriages in the United States ending in divorce (Kornblum & Julian, 2001). People who look only for romantic love and expect it to last become disappointed in their partners when the romance dies down.

Whether or not this argument is valid, the idea that romantic love, in and of itself, is a reasonable basis for long-term relationships is questionable. Particularly as people live longer and longer, the notion of "until death do you part" can mean many years of hard work that may or may not result in a lasting relationship. The length of time that people may spend together now that our life spans have increased is such that couples will almost assuredly change and many potentially grow apart. This is particularly true if a couple marries at a young age. Further, the cultural emphasis on individualism may make it more difficult for some people to sacrifice certain things, such as careers, for a relationship. Even though plenty of couples succeed in managing very long-term relationships that are based on romantic love, social workers still see many who do not.

Marital Satisfaction   Though there are many ways in which people form meaning-ful relationships, marriage still tends to be a popular choice for most people, particu-larly for people in middle age. Indeed, many married middle-aged people express a great deal of satisfaction with their spousal relationship, particularly when there is a great deal of communication and shared activities in the marriage (Orbuch, House, Mero, & Webster, 1996; Schmitt, Kliegal, & Shapiro, 2007; Ward, 1993).

Which factors help to predict successful and long-lasting marital relationships? Research indicates that one key factor is the nature of the couple's relationship when it began. For instance, couples who start out with a lack of trust, love, and liking for one another showed high rates of separation and problems later in their marriages. Further, married individuals who were struggling with psychological problems or other distress when the relationships began also showed high rates of marital discord later as well as overall dissatisfaction with life (Kurdek, 2002).

Conversely, some couples who start out with a great deal of conflict and distress are able to overcome their problems and establish more stable, loving relationships by midlife. The reason may be that many of the stressors straining the relationship early on decreased over time, leaving the couple with more time and energy to focus on the relationship. Specifically, some middle-aged couples may find themselves more financially stable and freer to pursue other things as their children move out. Some couples are able to direct their energies toward working on the relationship and spending more time together (Brim, 1999).

Although a rocky start to a marriage may contribute to the separation and divorce of many couples, some couples will overcome these problems and enjoy long-lasting, fulfilling marriages. Social workers may be able to help struggling couples work on trust, conflict, and related issues that put a strain on marriage and lead to its demise.

Some studies have found a link between companionship and marital satisfac-tion. Another study found that marital satisfaction was associated with particular patterns of leisure time that couples spend together (Crawford, Houts, Huston, & George, 2002). Specifically, husbands in this study did not enjoy participating in activities without their wives if the activity was something that both partners enjoyed. For example, if both partners enjoyed traveling, husbands were unhappy if they traveled alone. Wives in this study were dissatisfied when their husbands were off pursuing their own interests or when, as a couple, they participated in activities in which only the husbands were interested. Presumably, these couples valued activi-ties that they both could enjoy together, and women resented making sacrifices so that they could spend time with their husbands.

These findings have important implications for social workers who work with couples. They may need to attend to the quality of leisure time and not assume that the important thing for couples' well-being in the relationship is that they simply spend time together (Crawford *et al.*, 2002).

Divorce   Couples separate or divorce for many reasons, including issues surround-ing feelings of love, liking, respect, and commitment. Evidence suggests that, before divorcing, couples tend to feel distant from each other and no longer feel much love toward or interest in each other (Gottman & Levenson, 2000).

There are diverse opinions about the effects of divorce on the couple. In fact, research indicates that the effects can be positive or negative, depending on the people involved and the circumstances surrounding the divorce. For example, a divorce that takes place during middle adulthood may be less intense than a divorce that occurs in younger years. This difference may occur because older couples have more time, money, maturity, and resources to deal with the divorce than young adults do. In addition, they are less likely to have to worry about the effects of the breakup on young children, which can be very stressful (Corley & Woods, 1991; Tucker, Kressin, Spiro, & Ruscio, 1998; Wrosch & Heckhausen, 1999).

Nevertheless, divorce in middle age can present difficulties. For instance, some couples who have been together for a long time may find themselves socially, emotionally, and financially tied to the relationship. In addition, some couples may have trouble dividing possessions, property, and finances. Moreover, divorce can cause problems at work as well as with relationships with friends and family members, particularly if the couple is experiencing great emotional difficulty and brings negativity into other realms of their lives (Papalia *et al.*, 2003). Divorce can have other deleterious effects as well. In general, divorced people have shorter life spans than married people, and divorced men exhibit higher suicide rates than married men. Significantly, women generally are the ones who suffer financially after a divorce (Wauterickx, Gouwy, & Bracke, 2006).

Regardless of the consequences, divorce today does not carry the stigma that it once did, and women have more financial and other choices that allow them to leave relationships that are unfulfilling or abusive. Especially when there is considerable conflict in a marriage, divorce may be a good choice for all involved, and it can lead to more satisfying lives and greater well-being for both parties.

Remarriage By the time they reach middle age, many people have been married, divorced, and remarried. Indeed, after a divorce, people typically remarry within five years (Kreider, 2006). Increasingly, remarriage is a viable option for people, particularly as they age.

Though remarriage is often a positive experience, it can present many challenges. Remarriage at any age can mean a great deal of adjustment for the couple. This is particularly true if one or both of the individuals have children from a previous marriage and they are bringing them into the new family. Depending on the ages of the children, this process can generate a variety of problems that the couple must overcome. In general, most newly formed families must contend with figuring out new roles, rules, expectations, adjustments, and relationships. New family members may be accustomed to the way life used to be before remarriage occurred, and they need time to adjust to the dynamics of the new family and to develop feelings for one another.

Gay Marriage   Gay marriage, or more precisely same-sex marriage, has been a topic for public debate in recent years. More than 30 states and the District of Columbia allow marriage for same-sex couples, and others have established civil unions for same-sex couples as an alternative to marriage. In Massachusetts, Connecticut, and Iowa, the states' highest courts ruled that the states' constitutions required that same-sex couples be accorded the same marriage rights as opposite-sex couples. In Vermont, New Hampshire, the District of Columbia, and New York, legislative bodies have passed statutory changes that allow same-sex marriages (National Conference of State Legislatures, 2012). And, in June of 2013, the Supreme Court struck down as unconstitutional the 1996 Defense of Marriage Act, which allowed states to deny recognition of a same-sex marriage from another state.

Like heterosexual couples, many gay and lesbian couples want the right to legally marry. They want not only to symbolize their commitment to their relationships but also to enjoy the many social and financial benefits that come along with it. There are over 1,000 federal benefits attached with marriage.

Family Patterns in Middle Age

Middle adulthood is a time when the pattern of family life often shifts. Most couples in their forties and fifties have already finished the stage of family life in which they are rearing small children. Their children are likely to be in their teens or older and therefore do not require as much attention as when they were young. At the same time, the parents of middle-aged people are entering old age and may be becoming more dependent. Here are some of the family situations that social workers may encounter with middle-aged clients:

- *"Empty nest":* Most middle-aged parents experience their children leaving home to make their own way in the world. The **empty nest syndrome** refers to the supposedly negative effects on parents of their last child leaving. Some experts have blamed the empty nest syndrome for decreased marital satisfaction. Some research suggests that if parents have based their marital satisfaction in parenting, they may experience dissatisfaction when their children leave home. At that point couples need to find other interests and sources of fulfillment to remain satisfied in their marriage. However, other evidence suggests that the marital satisfaction of many couples actually increases when their children leave home. These couples can now enjoy time together and invest resources into the marital relationship that were once devoted to child rearing. They may find that they are more emotionally available to each other and can spend more time together pursuing mutual interests (Crowley, Hayslip, & Hobdy, 2003; Kausler, Kausler, & Krupsaw, 2007; Ward & Spitze, 2004). Because of these contradictory findings, social workers need to explore the individual perceptions of clients whose children are leaving home. Some clients may be distressed by "losing" their children and their role of caregiver, while others may be excited about the prospect of freedom and independence from their caregiving responsibilities.

- *Adult children living at home:* Parents who look forward to their children leaving home may be dismayed by adult children who do not leave home when expected. Increasingly, children are leaving home at older ages, and some children who have left return to live with their parents. Circumstances such as divorce, unemployment, and additional schooling lead some adult children to live with their parents rather than independently (Kausler *et al.*, 2007). Obviously, some parents may not be prepared for their adult children to live with them, particularly after the children have been living on their own. Often, these arrangements require that family members readjust to their new living arrangements. Problems with roles, rules, communication, and relationships can develop among family members.

- *Childless by choice or other circumstances:* Although much depends on the circumstances, there is little evidence to suggest that couples suffer psychologically if they did not have children. However, women who regret not having children are at higher risk for psychological problems such as loneliness and depression than women who do not hold negative attitudes about their childlessness. These same patterns do not necessarily hold true for men. Rather, socialization processes regarding gender roles may place more pressure on women to bear children. Being a parent does not necessarily guarantee psychological well-being either. Evidence suggests that parents who have poor relationships with their children are at risk for psychological problems such as depression (Koropeckyj-Cox, 2002).

- *Caregiving for elderly parents:* Some middle-aged people may find themselves a part of the **sandwich generation**, which is what occurs when they find themselves caring for their parents as well as their children (Uhlenberg, 1996). In middle adulthood, people's parents are likely to be of an age when chronic illness and disability require extra care. This situation can be extremely stressful for people who find themselves spending a great deal of time, money, and energy caring for their families. Without appropriate resources and social support, these caregivers may find themselves at risk for various physical and mental health problems.

Social Work with Couples and Families

Social workers who are working with couples and families have a lot to think about with regard to family systems and relationships. Because various issues such as living and relationship arrangements, as well as situations regarding children and other family members, can be problematic for some families, social workers need to be skilled at assessing these issues and determining how they affect particular family members.

Systems theory, along with genograms and ecomaps, can be useful in helping social workers organize the mass of information about families and conduct a comprehensive assessment on the issues that may affect them. Social workers can rely on concepts such as roles, rules, boundaries, and homeostasis to help a family better understand how these concepts play out in their particular situation. For example, if a couple has remarried and brought children into the new family from previous marriages, these concepts can help family members to better understand how they are interacting with one another and where problems may occur. The social worker may point out to individual family members that homeostasis for the new family system needs to be developed and maintained; each member has been used to a certain way of functioning in the old system that was probably comfortable for her or him. In this new family system, members will need to find their places and define their relationships to allow the new family to function smoothly. In working toward this goal, the social worker can help new family members identify their roles and boundaries within the system, establish relationships with one another, and articulate new family rules.

Other developmental models could also be useful for clients who may be dealing with issues surrounding not having children or having adult children who move back home, for example. Because these issues potentially can cause psychological problems for some individuals, using developmental models such as Erik Erikson's or Levinson's can help social workers conceptualize the developmental tasks that might be important for clients and how certain issues may pose problems for their developmental progress. For instance, middle-aged people who do not have children, for whatever reason, may struggle with feeling stagnant, according to Erikson. If they have not had a "traditional" family in which to invest, and their careers or other areas of their lives have not allowed them to feel productive, they may need to work through these feelings to successfully move through this particular stage.

You may want to assess Tina's family situation to see if specific areas may be contributing to her complaints. Trouble with her children may be placing stress on her relationships with both her children and her husband, especially in view of her son's recent arrest. If her relationship with her children deteriorates, it may put her at risk for additional stress and even psychological problems later on.

You could also help Tina explore her relationship with her husband. To help improve their marriage or to help maintain its quality if it is already strong, the couple might need to find leisure activities that they both enjoy and that allow them to spend time together. You may find valuable information by exploring how Tina and her husband felt toward each other when they first married. If there was a lack of trust or positive feelings, Tina and her husband could be headed for marital conflict.

Conversely, if Tina states that she has a strong marriage, you could help her maintain it and take advantage of this strength as she works on other issues.

Retirement

Retirement, as it is perceived by most people, is a relatively new phenomenon in the United States. Until the past half century or so, most people did not conceive of leaving the workforce at a designated time in life to pursue recreation or other interests.

The traditional retirement age in the United States is 65. Thus U.S. workers spend, on average, approximately 10 to 15 percent of their lives in retirement. With life expectancy rates rising, older adults can potentially spend, on average, 18 to 20 years in retirement if they retire at age 65 (Atchley & Barusch, 2004).

The retirement age in the United States has increased in the face of Social Security solvency issues and will probably continue to increase. Nevertheless, many people still opt for early retirement. Many businesses and organizations offer people incentives to retire early to open up jobs to younger workers, who can generally be paid less than their older counterparts (though this practice is illegal). Older workers may also be encouraged to retire during poor economic times when unemployment is high (Quadagno, 2008).

Retirement Patterns   A popular view of retirement is that it is a single event that occurs after a lifetime of education and work. However, this view is not completely accurate. Sociologists and other researchers have discovered many definitions and patterns of retirement. For example, the number of older, male part-time workers has increased over the past several decades (Piasna, 2010). Women's participation in the workforce has also increased since the 1960s, particularly for women in their fifties. Though some people, particularly men, drop out of the workforce in their fifties because of health and other reasons, the majority of people remain working until later life (Quadagno, 2008).

Older people experience varied patterns of employment and retirement, which are affected by socioeconomic issues, including the effects of the "great recession" of 2007–2008, which drastically reduced many workers' retirement savings at the same time as it forced many businesses to lay off workers, including many nearing retirement age (Johnson, 2012). Another factor in retirement decisions is discrimination. For example, African–Americans face high unemployment rates early on in life, which have ramifications for later employment and financial security, including their ability to retire. Particularly in midlife, African–American men also face health disparities, which often lead to high rates of disability, affecting their ability to work. Lifelong physical and psychosocial stressors caused by poverty, discrimination, and employment in stressful, blue-collar jobs that lack supportive health care and other benefits also contribute to disabilities that can affect these men's ability to accumulate wealth and participate in the workforce later on in life. This same pattern holds true for men and women in other ethnic minority groups (Brown & Warner, 2008; U.S. Department of Labor, 2007).

Actual retirement patterns for both men and women vary a great deal:

- Many middle-aged adults decide to begin new careers after retiring from old ones. They may decide to return to school, volunteer, or take a job in a different field.

- Some people may decide to partially retire by reducing the number of hours they work or by finding new jobs that require fewer hours (Moen & Wethington, 1999). With regard to this last pattern, many people take **bridge jobs,** or jobs that fill the gap between full-time employment and full retirement; this trend has been steadily increasing over the past several decades (Cahill, Giandrea, & Quinn, 2006; Quinn & Kozy, 1996).

- Many people have to continue working because they cannot afford to retire.

These particular patterns can be positive, however: Continued activity in work and related activities may help people to stay cognitively healthy as they move into older adulthood. For example, research indicates that engaging in volunteer activities, which many people do before and after retirement, has many social and health-related benefits. Volunteerism is associated with lower rates of mortality, depression, and heart disease and higher rates of life satisfaction and functional mobility (Grimm, Spring, & Dietz, 2007).

Preparation for Retirement   Some people begin financial and other planning for retirement early in adulthood, while others find that retirement sneaks up on them before they have thought about their financial, career, or life goals. Particularly when people are working in low-wage jobs that only allow them to live paycheck to paycheck, it can be difficult to save money or imagine a day when they can retire.

The employment choices that women make throughout adulthood can have profound economic and other impacts on their retirement plans and later life. For instance, some women begin careers and then put them on hold to rear children, reentering the workforce after their children have grown. Other women work part time or full time while taking care of their family, while still others choose not to have families and devote themselves to full-time work. Generally speaking, women's employment patterns tend to be more varied than men's throughout the life course. We consider the issues related to women's work and retirement in greater detail in Chapter 12.

Some research has compared the patterns of retirement planning among different groups of people in U.S. society. For example, one study found that same-sex and opposite-sex couples were similar in terms of determining the age of retirement, beginning the planning process, and anticipating health and housing needs (Mock, 2001). However, married couples reported higher rates of implementing their plans than gay, lesbian, and cohabiting, unmarried heterosexual couples. Of all the groups, lesbian couples reported the lowest level of financial readiness for retirement. In addition, only the married couples reported plans to spend time volunteering during retirement, which has been associated with high levels of well-being in old age. In general, then, gay, lesbian, and unmarried heterosexual couples may be on a road toward lower levels of financial and psychological well-being in older age than married couples are.

Theoretical Perspectives on Retirement Adjustment to retirement is a rather complex issue, and positive or negative adjustment depends on many constructs, including individual personalities, situations, and attitudes. Though these complexities must be kept in mind, research suggests that factors such as financial stability, good physical health, a positive social and living environment, and voluntary retirement are associated with positive adjustment to retirement (Lowis, Edwards, & Burton, 2009; Quick & Moen, 1998; Reitzes, Mutran, & Pope, 1991).

Several theories discussed in more detail in Chapter 12 help to explain a person's adjustment to retirement:

- Continuity theory: Some research on retirement adjustment seems to be supported by this theory. It posits that as we age, we maintain continuity in our roles, personality, relationships, and activities (Atchley, 1989). This consistency helps us adjust to the aging process. So, during retirement, the more we can maintain the sense of satisfaction and well-being that we might have had during our working years, the better we will adjust to our new circumstances.

- Disengagement theory: Retirement can be viewed as a natural process of older people "removing" themselves from the workforce to make way for younger people. People who do not want to disengage from employment will likely experience problems in adjusting to retirement.

- Activity theory: Retirement can also be viewed as a transition in which people invest their energies into something other than work. People who do not have other meaningful activities in which they can engage are also likely to experience problems in retirement.

Regardless of the theoretical lens through which social workers view retirement, they need to consider the potential impacts that retirement can have on clients. Social workers can attend to the consequences that retirement might have on their clients' economic and psychosocial well-being to prevent problems that might occur at this time in life.

Although retirement issues may not be a priority for Tina now, you may still want to explore Tina's feelings about it. She may have thought about retirement, which may be part of why she has been experiencing some of the troubling symptoms. By asking about it, you can either rule out the association between Tina's current problems and retirement-related issues or pursue it, if Tina does want to explore this issue. If it is not an issue now, you can pursue it later on in the working relationship.

THE LARGER SOCIAL ENVIRONMENT IN MIDDLE ADULTHOOD

Biological, psychological, emotional, social, and vocational issues can cause problems for people as they reach middle age. The two addressed here—ageism and immigration issues—make this time of life more challenging for individuals and threaten their well-being in a wide variety of ways.

Ageism

A negative attitude toward aging and older people based on beliefs that older people cannot function as well as younger people is called **ageism.** Ageist beliefs assert that middle-aged and elderly people are not sexual, intelligent, or capable (Atchley & Barusch, 2004). Ageism, and the prejudiced attitudes and beliefs about older people that underlie it, often lead to discrimination or treating people differently, usually in negative ways, because of their age. Though it can affect people at any age, ageism probably becomes more noticeable to many people during middle adulthood.

Attitudes about aging have been slowly changing, but many myths and stereotypes still exist. With the aging of the baby boom generation, some of these attitudes will continue to change. However, given the cultural emphasis on youth, ageist attitudes are hard to avoid.

Some theories and perspectives that describe aging can perpetuate ageist attitudes. For example, disengagement theory may reinforce beliefs that people lose their usefulness as they age. People who view aging from this lens may expect aging individuals to naturally step aside from their roles, thereby devaluing their contributions to society.

As with other isms that exist in society, social workers can be effective agents of change with regard to ageism. On a social scale, social workers can help to eradicate myths and stereotypes of aging through education and by modeling behaviors that support the uniqueness and worth of the aging process. This education can also be conducted on an individual level: Social workers can help clients who may be struggling with the aging process to better understand how their own ageist attitudes may be thwarting their well-being as they move through middle adulthood and into older age.

Though it is not evident in the case study, Tina is likely experiencing ageism in her life. Social forces, attitudes of her friends and family, and even her own perceptions of aging may all have a negative influence on the way Tina views herself and her worth. As part of a biopsychosocial assessment, you can explore how ageism may be impacting Tina. Any intervention that is conducted with Tina can incorporate aspects of societal and personal beliefs about aging to reconstruct them into more positive perspectives that will support her healthy aging process.

Ageism in the Workplace   One area in which ageism tends to be prevalent is the workplace. Misconceptions that older workers cannot learn new tasks, are incapable of producing good work, and are resistant to change are just a few that exist among employers as well as the general public. In fact, research on older workers indicates that they tend to be better and more effective workers than younger people. Research suggests that compared to younger workers, older workers take fewer sick days, are more punctual and reliable, are less likely to be injured on the job, are more loyal to their employers, are less likely to leave a job, express higher job satisfaction, and exhibit better attitudes toward work (Atchley & Barusch, 2004; U.S. Department of Labor, 2008).

In an effort to guard against discrimination in the workplace, Congress passed the **Age Discrimination in Employment Act** in 1967. This law prohibits employers from firing or reducing the wages or positions of people based on age, specifically between 40 and 65 years of age. At that time many employers required workers to retire at 65. However, in 1978 the federal government raised the mandatory retirement age from 65 to 70 in both private business and the federal government, which extended the protection against discrimination. Then, in 1986, Congress banned mandatory retirement altogether except in certain industries, including law enforcement and aviation, where the age of the worker might put others at risk (Quadagno, 2008).

Because there are now no federal requirements for mandatory retirement, except in certain industries, age discrimination may be more of an issue for workers as they reach ages that are beyond the norms for retirement. Specifically, people who wish to work into their seventies, eighties, and even nineties may be at high risk for discrimination.

Ageism in Popular Culture   As people move through middle age, and especially as they reach late adulthood, they may increasingly find themselves being patronized and infantilized. For example, younger people often assume that middle-aged adults are not sexual, cannot perform certain tasks, or should be given special treatment because they are perceived to be less physically capable than younger adults.

Unfortunately, Western culture tends to perpetuate ageist myths and stereotypes. Though this happens in many ways, one of the most visible forms of ageism is transmitted through the media. Until recently, middle-aged and elderly adults were not frequently cast in television shows. More recently, television shows have included middle-aged and older adults as major characters who are confident and competent (Bell, 1992). However, there is still a dearth of serious roles for middle-aged and older adults, particularly for women over the age of 40 (Media Report to Women, 1999, 2001, 2009). Ageism extends to other media as well: One cross-cultural comparison study of older adults' portrayal in magazines in the U.S. and India found that older women in both countries were underrepresented, while younger women were over-represented (Raman, Harwood, Weis, Anderson, & Miller, 2008).

Even when middle-aged and older adults are portrayed, the media still tend to portray them negatively, reinforcing harmful stereotypes. For example, one study found that by the time children enter elementary school, many have already developed negative stereotypes of older adults through their exposure to media representations of older people, particularly through Disney films and other children's programming (Robinson & Anderson, 2006; Robinson, Callister, Magoffin, & Moore, 2007). And advertisements still tend to portray middle-aged and older people in a negative light. Although a small percentage of advertisements on major network channels now show people over the age of 50, they generally sell food, health, or hygiene-related products or products only associated with stereotypically age-related concerns (Atkins, Jenkins, & Perkins, 1990–1991; Raman *et al.*, 2008).

Immigration

Many immigrants who come to the U.S. arrive as young adults and remain in the country as they age. Consequently, many social workers work with immigrants who are in middle and older age and who face specific issues relating to poverty, social support, the legal system, and other challenges. Further, many immigrants face issues around discrimination and an increasingly hostile political climate, in which many states are passing restrictive immigration policies that limit employment and other opportunities.

The terms **foreign born** and **immigrant** are often used interchangeably and refer to anyone in the U.S. who does not have citizenship at birth. Foreign-born individuals can be any of the following:

- refugees;
- people granted asylum;
- unauthorized immigrants;
- naturalized citizens;
- lawful permanent residents;
- persons on temporary visas.

In 2012 there were 41 million foreign-born people in the U.S., and about half of those (51 percent) were women. Approximately 18.7 million immigrants in the U.S.

were naturalized citizens, with the remaining 54 percent being lawful permanent residents, unauthorized immigrants, and legal residents on temporary visas.

Mexican-born immigrants make up the majority of the foreign born population in the U.S. at 28 percent. (The next largest group of immigrants is from China at 5 percent.) Almost half (47 percent) of immigrants in the U.S. reported having Hispanic or Latino origins, and over half (52 percent) had limited English proficiency. Most Mexican-born immigrants live in the West and Southwest, with more than half (58 percent) living in Texas and California. The largest proportion of immigrants (80 percent) are between the ages of 18 and 64, and another 12 percent are 65+ (Migration Policy Institute, 2014).

Although all immigrants are subject to discrimination, it is the unauthorized immigrants who have the most tenuous situation. In 2012 there were an estimated 11.5 million unauthorized immigrants in the U.S., and most of these (around 8.9 million) were from North and Central American areas including Mexico, Central America, and Canada. California has the biggest share of unauthorized immigrants at 25 percent, followed by Texas at 16 percent and Florida at 6 percent. Arizona and Georgia, two states that passed onerous immigration enforcement laws, also have a large number of unauthorized immigrants (Migration Policy Institute, 2014).

Immigrants from Mexico are a special case, perhaps because they are more numerous and more visible than immigrants from other areas. About 70 percent of Mexican-born immigrants are in the U.S. workforce. Many immigrants from Mexico work in the U.S. to help support their families who still live in Mexico. Indeed, estimates are that about one in 10 Mexican families relies on money sent home from U.S. immigrants. Some immigrants may be supporting a family in Mexico as well as a new family created in the U.S., further straining their financial resources as well as sometimes creating stress in their personal relationships (Migration Policy Institute, 2014). In addition, many Mexican-born immigrants lack a high level of education, are uninsured, and face poverty (Camarota, 2001).

All immigrants face limitations on access to quality education, opportunities to learn and master English, and access to secure jobs that pay a living wage. Further, many immigrants suffer from social isolation; poor-quality, overcrowded housing; problems with incorporation into a new culture; problems associated with loss of status, identity, and community; mental health issues resulting from stress; and discrimination and oppression both from people in their communities as well as from social policies that further isolate them from services and opportunities to improve their lives and well-being (Garrett, 2006).

Social workers can be a strong source of support for immigrants facing these and other issues, on all three levels:

- *Micro level:* Help individuals access services; adjust to life in a new culture, sometimes without family or social supports; and improve the quality of their lives and well-being.

- *Mezzo level:* Empower families and communities to build networks and infrastructures that will help support immigrant communities.

- *Macro level:* Educate the public and law makers on the challenges that immigrants face; create services that are accessible to and specialized for immigrants; and challenge oppressive policies that create barriers for immigrants.

Social workers can be of particular help and support to immigrants who intend to remain in the U.S. as they age. These immigrants often face a specific set of challenges, including issues around health, family, employment, social support, and incorporation into a new culture.

CONCLUSION

Middle adulthood can be a time for continued growth and development in many ways, including emotionally, spiritually, socially, and vocationally. Although physical decline does occur and some people may notice themselves slowing down in some ways, for many people most changes are not significant enough to cause serious problems.

For many people, middle adulthood is a time to enjoy the fruits of their labor in many areas. With the insecurities, struggles, and hard work of young adulthood behind them, many middle-aged adults find themselves freer to be themselves and enjoy their successes. However, some people find changes in middle adulthood to be troublesome. Adjusting to aging, experiencing illness, changing careers, ending relationships, and beginning new ones can create stress or other psychological and emotional problems.

One role that social workers can fill is to help people who have trouble coping with issues that may present themselves in middle age. Assessing areas that might be troublesome for people during this time, or that might create barriers to well-being in older age, is an important goal for social workers working with middle-aged adults.

MAIN POINTS

- For many, physical aspects such as energy, eyesight, hearing, and metabolism begin to decline in adulthood, but most people usually do not notice a marked difference from when they were younger, especially with cognitive abilities. In U.S. culture with its emphasis on youth, many people are most troubled by changes in physical appearance involving such things as wrinkles, gray hair, and weight gain.

- Levinson proposed a theory of adult development for men that focuses on transitions and life structures, or patterns of behavior that shape experiences. The life structures and transitions that take place during the forties and fifties consist of questioning what it means to grow old, assessing whether choices made previously are satisfying, and making changes that will lead to greater satisfaction.

- The experience of menopause, or the cessation of a woman's menstrual cycle, varies greatly from woman to woman and from culture to culture. Some women welcome the changes, and others experience anxiety; some cultures regard the process as natural, and others—especially Western culture—regard it as a loss of vitality and attractiveness.

- Many men experience a male climacteric in midlife during which they may reevaluate their careers, familial relationships, and other life decisions they have made. This climacteric includes physical changes that many men experience such as hair loss, weight gain, and a decrease in sexual vitality.

- Middle adulthood is a time when genetics and unhealthy lifestyle habits such as smoking and poor diet can catch up to individuals, causing chronic illnesses such as cancer, diabetes, and heart disease.

- During middle adulthood, many people may be dealing with issues related to marriage, divorce, and remarriage that can affect their well-being. Social workers can help clients explore their expectations about intimate relationships as well as their motives for continuing some relationships and not others.

- Familial patterns often change in middle age and may include blended families, empty nests, and responsibility for both children and aging parents.

- Retirement patterns for both men and women vary greatly; many people begin second or even third careers in middle age and continue working into old age. Planning for and adjusting to retirement are two areas in which social workers can be helpful to clients.

- Ageism, or discriminating against people because of their age, may begin to be noticeable to people in middle age. Social workers need to be at the forefront of eradicating myths and stereotypes of aging.

- Immigration is an issue that many social workers may encounter when working with clients in middle age. Foreign-born clients may bring problems associated with finances, social isolation, mental health, family dynamics, access to services, and loss of status and identity among other problems.

EXERCISES

1. *Sanchez Family interactive case at* www.routledgesw.com/cases. Review the major issues involving the family, particularly for Hector and Celia Sanchez. Then answer the following questions:
   a. Developmentally, what issues might Hector be facing at this time in his life? How might these issues impact his current work and family situation and his well-being in older adulthood?
   b. What issues might Celia be facing? How might they impact her current situation and her well-being?
   c. How might ageist and racist attitudes and other social forces affect Hector and Celia's well-being emotionally, psychologically, interpersonally, spiritually, socially, and economically?
   d. What issues might affect Hector's and Celia's marital satisfaction?
   e. What are the immigration issues facing Hector and Celia?
   f. Which theory or theories do you think would be helpful to employ in working with Hector and Celia? Why? What would be some limitations?
2. *Carla Washburn interactive case at* www.routledgesw.com/cases. Review the information presented in this chapter on Levinson's Theory of Adult Development, including Exhibit 11.1. Then answer the following questions:
   a. Based on the information you have on Carla now, what hunches do you have about her early and middle adult development based on Levinson's theory?
   b. What issues from her earlier development might be creating problems for her now, in later adulthood?
   c. What other issues presented in this chapter might be, or might have been, issues for Carla, impacting the problems she is experiencing now?
3. *RAINN interactive case at* www.routledgesw.com/cases. As RAINN gets more established, the staff is looking to reach out to parts of the population who may not otherwise receive services following a sexual assault. How might ageism affect potential clients?
4. *Hudson City interactive case at* www.routledgesw.com/cases. Review the issues in the case and answer the following questions:
   a. With reference to Levinson's theory, what might be some areas of concern for middle-aged clients, particularly in light of problems faced by the community?
   b. In what ways might illness and chronic disease affect middle-aged residents, given some of the problems facing the Hudson community?
   c. How might problems in Hudson City impact familial and work patterns for residents in middle adulthood, particularly residents who are immigrants?

CHAPTER 12

Development in Late Adulthood

Judy is an 80-year-old woman who has been living at Sunset Homes, a residential care facility, for the past three years. She has problems dressing, bathing, and managing her medications, and she needs assistance with grocery shopping and making it to her doctor's appointments. With only a modest income from Social Security, Judy relies on Medicaid to fund her care at Sunset Homes.

Recently, budget cuts in social services have necessitated decreases in Medicaid funding to elders living in these types of facilities. The state where Judy lives has mandated that all elders not meeting a specified level of physical care be evicted from their facilities. Judy does not currently meet the new criteria for funding and has received a notice from the state saying that she has two weeks to vacate the facility. Judy has a daughter, but she lives in another state and is unable to provide the care Judy needs. Judy cannot afford to pay the monthly rates of the facility on her income, and there are no other facilities in her city that provide housing for low-income elders who need assistance. Judy can appeal the state's decision, but she will need help from a social worker who understands Medicaid policy, state bureaucracy, and ways to advocate for older people like Judy with special care needs.

UNFORTUNATELY, JUDY'S SITUATION IS NOT UNUSUAL. Worldwide, the population is growing older, and all societies will face special challenges in caring for their elders. As health care improves and new technologies become available, individuals, families, and communities will face a plethora of issues surrounding needs and services for the elderly. Because of these challenges, there is an increasing need for social workers who are trained in gerontology and who can negotiate the complex individual, relational, and societal needs facing older populations.

In this chapter, we explore some of the issues surrounding **senescence,** or the process of aging. In most cases we will examine these issues from the perspective of the medical model because they tend to be biological in nature. However, many factors relating to processes of physical and cognitive aging have implications for adjustment to growing older and the level of functioning that the older individual maintains. Thus, other theories of development can be useful in helping to understand how biological changes can affect an individual's reactions to the aging process. Also keep in mind that although these changes commonly tend to be associated with aging, not everyone goes through these changes at the same rate, just as some expected changes do not necessarily happen to all people or to the same degree.

DEVELOPMENTAL MILESTONES IN OLDER ADULTS

The aging process can be measured in many different ways. In U.S. culture, we tend to rely on **chronological age**, or a person's age in years, to determine whether a person is considered an older adult. This measure is often used to determine a person's eligibility for programs such as Medicare or a senior citizen discount at restaurants. However, this particular measure tends to be somewhat arbitrary. Certainly chronological age can help to guide service provision, but it does not tell you much about how old the person feels subjectively or how well the person is functioning physically or psychologically.

A related way to discuss aging is to place people into subcategories based on their chronological age:

- **Young-old:** People aged from 65 to 74 years.
- **Middle-old:** People aged from 75 to 84 years.
- **Oldest-old:** People aged 85 years or older.

An alternative to the chronological age measure is **functional age**, which focuses on how well people perform their usual roles in their daily lives. For example, a 50-year-old person who has severe arthritis and is not very mobile without assistance would have an older functional age than a 75-year-old person who runs two marathons a year and needs no assistance with daily tasks.

To measure the level of functioning, social workers generally assess the types of activities that older people are able to complete on their own. These activities fall into two general categories (Centers for Medicare and Medicaid Services, 2011):

- **Activities of daily living (ADLs):** Tasks related to personal care such as eating, walking, dressing, bathing, toileting, and getting in and out of bed.
- **Instrumental activities in daily living (IADLs):** Tasks related to independent living such as performing housework, shopping, preparing meals, managing money, and using a telephone.

Social workers often use these assessments to reliably measure the level of functioning a person is able to manage in daily life. These measures are also used by various social service agencies to determine eligibility for certain services, such as Medicaid.

Level of functioning relates to the many physical and cognitive/psychological changes that are common in late adulthood. Quick Guide 17 summarizes those changes, which are discussed in greater depth in the following sections.

Physical Changes in Late Adulthood

When we think of aging, we often think of developing wrinkles and gray hair and slowing down physically. Though some of these changes do occur, the amount of change that individuals go through varies a great deal and reflects the interaction of genetics, lifestyle, and societal expectations. Probably one of the most obvious changes that we go through as we age is bodily changes. Though individuals vary greatly, certain bodily changes are relatively consistent.

Osteoporosis Our skeletal system develops throughout our twenties and reaches its peak mass during our thirties. As we age past our thirties, bone is broken down faster than our bodies can reproduce it, leaving us with bone loss. When optimal bone mass is not achieved in adolescence or when bone loss in older age is severe, it can lead to **osteoporosis**, which leaves the bones weak and vulnerable to fractures. In older age, hip and spine breaks are particularly worrisome because they often require surgery, hospitalization, and rehabilitation. Fractures of the spine can result in chronic back pain and loss of height.

Though both men and women can develop osteoporosis, women tend to be at higher risk for the disease. This higher risk occurs for two reasons: (1) Women tend to have smaller and lighter bones than men, and (2) after menopause, women's ovaries stop producing estrogen, which appears to protect against bone loss (National Institutes of Health, 2011; Nguyen *et al.*, 1994).

QUICK GUIDE 17 Developmental Milestones in Later Adulthood

PHYSICAL	COGNITIVE
• Declines in bone and muscle mass. • Increased prevalence of diseases such as arthritis and osteoporosis. • Increased appearance of wrinkles, gray hair, loose skin, age spots. • Loss of teeth and dental problems. • Increased vision and hearing problems. • Declines in central nervous system functioning affecting reaction time, coordination.	• Increased prevalence of dementias. • Some declines in memory and functioning if not cognitively active.

Older Caucasian and Asian women appear to be at higher risk for osteoporosis than African–American or Hispanic/Latino women. Approximately 20 percent of Caucasian and Asian women aged 50+ are estimated to have osteoporosis, and another 52 percent are estimated to be at risk for osteoporosis because of low bone mass. This is compared to estimates that 5 percent of older African–American women and 10 percent of older Hispanic women have the disease, though the risk for Hispanic women is increasing rapidly when compared to other ethnic groups. Although older men have a lower risk of developing the disease, it is estimated that osteoporosis affects approximately 7 percent of Asian men, 4 percent of African–American men, and 3 percent of Hispanic men.

Though the factors contributing to ethnic differences in osteoporosis are unclear, research indicates that, in general, higher peak bone mass and diets rich in calcium may mediate the development of the disease for women in some ethnic groups. Other risk factors for the disease include smoking, a family history of osteoporosis, and a history of bone fractures. Alcohol abuse and excessive caffeine intake may increase the risk for osteoporosis (National Institutes of Health, 2001, 2009a; National Osteoporosis Foundation, 2008).

Osteoporosis can have profound personal, financial, and social consequences. Hip fractures often lead to permanent disabilities, which can create fear, anxiety, and depression in people who are at risk. In the United States, the financial costs for treatment of fractures were estimated at $19 billion in 2005 because of hospitalization, community-based care services, and lost wages and productivity; it is predicted that these costs will rise to $25.3 billion by the year 2025 (National Osteoporosis Foundation, 2008).

Much can be done to prevent and treat osteoporosis, including exercise, a balanced diet, and hormone replacement therapy (HRT). However, although evidence suggests that HRT can be effective for the prevention and management of osteoporosis for high-risk women, particularly for women younger than 60, it may put some older women at higher risk for breast cancer, myocardial infarction (heart attacks), and other diseases (Rymer, Wilson, & Ballard, 2003; Studd, 2009).

Loss of Muscle Mass Another concern as people age is loss of muscle mass. Typically, people experience a gradual loss of muscle strength in their thirties, but these changes often are not noticeable until their fifties. However, much of the muscle strength that people lose results from inactivity rather than a normal decline in functioning or loss of tissue. Indeed, older individuals who practice regular strength training can actually slow down the losses that often occur with age as well as regain or increase their muscle strength (Campbell & Leidy, 2007; Fielding, 1995).

Arthritis Another problem that is typically associated with old age is arthritis. Broadly, **arthritis** is inflammation or degeneration within the joints. These changes can make movement in the affected joints very painful. Although arthritis can occur in younger people, it occurs more frequently in older people.

There are more than 100 types of arthritis. Two of the most common types are:

- **Osteoarthritis:** Causes the cartilage that covers the joints to deteriorate with "wear and tear" over time. This deterioration is caused when enzymes break down cartilage during normal use of the joints. In younger people, this cartilage is usually replaced; however, as we age, our bodies are not as efficient in replacing cartilage, resulting in gradual exposure of the joint. Osteoarthritis affects approximately 30 million people in the United States (Centers for Disease Control and Prevention, 2014f; Lawrence *et al.*, 2008; Spence, 1999).

- **Rheumatoid arthritis:** An autoimmune disease that causes inflammation of membranes that surround the joints, resulting in scarring of the surrounding tissue. This scarring can cause severe pain and disability. Rheumatoid arthritis frequently occurs among older people, but it is also seen in younger adults. Symptoms generally appear before age 50, and they gradually become worse as a person ages. Rheumatoid arthritis tends to attack smaller bones such as those in the hands, feet, and wrists, and it is more common among women than men. Several theories exist about the causes of rheumatoid arthritis: a genetic predisposition to the disease, an autoimmune response that attacks the tissues around the joints, and a bacterial or viral infection (Hewagama & Richardson, 2009; Spence, 1999).

Hearing-Related Problems Hearing acuity tends to reach its peak in the twenties and then decline as people age. Normal hearing loss that occurs from declines associated with aging, called **presbycusis,** can produce numerous types of problems. For example, some people lose sensitivity to sound and require increased volume; some lose the ability to hear high-pitched sounds (which enable us to differentiate between consonants like *p* and *t* or *f* and *s*); some hear sounds that are distorted, particularly when people talk quickly or slur their words; and some experience chronic tinnitus, or ringing in the ears (Spence, 1999). Hearing loss is more common among men than women, probably due in part to men having more exposure, on average, to noisy work environments such as construction sites and factory floors.

Environmental factors can accelerate the loss of hearing. Attending loud rock concerts, listening to music with the volume turned up high, and being exposed to loud noises in the street such as car horns and jackhammers can all cause cumulative damage to hearing and add to troubles that people may experience with older age (Digiovanna, 1994).

Hearing loss often leaves the hearing-impaired person feeling isolated because she or he has trouble engaging in conversations and social activities. In addition, people may interpret a person's difficulties in hearing as "not paying attention" or showing a lack of interest in interactions; this in turn may cause people to disengage from the hearing-impaired person or to respond with annoyance (Takahashi, Okhravi, Lim, & Kasten, 2004).

Vision-Related Problems   Like hearing, vision tends to decline with age, usually beginning in young adulthood. By the time most people reach 60, they need glasses or contact lenses. Different parts of the eye, such as the lens, retina, and optic nerve, deteriorate over time, causing various problems. For example, with age the vitreous humor, or fluid behind the lens, becomes more opaque, and the lens loses elasticity, creating the need for additional light or more time to adjust to distance changes to see objects accurately. Depth perception can also deteriorate, increasing the risks for tripping or falling. **Presbyopia,** or the inability to focus on nearby objects, can cause problems for people trying to read the fine print on medication bottles or the dials on the stove. Because of these conditions, many older people cannot drive at night, or have difficulty negotiating road signs or traffic signals. These conditions can also lead to problems such as taking the wrong medications in the wrong doses or leaving the stove burners on (Digiovanna, 1994).

Disorders such as **glaucoma** and **cataracts** are not necessarily a normal part of aging, but with time many people develop problems that can lead to these disorders:

- **Glaucoma:** Results from a buildup of fluid and pressure in the eye, which damages the eye and can result in blindness. Unfortunately, many people experience no symptoms to warn of developing glaucoma, but routine eye exams can detect the disease before it progresses.

- **Cataracts:** Caused by clouding of the lens, which decreases the amount of light that can pass through. The person with developing cataracts may notice glare and may find colors looking less bright than they once did. Though cataracts can severely limit sight if untreated, they can be removed through laser surgery.

- **Macular degeneration:** Is age related and causes a loss of detail in vision. Because the brain can compensate for partially missing data in the images we see, many people are not diagnosed with the disorder until it is advanced. It is estimated that one in four people between the ages of 64 and 74 and one in three people aged 75+ are affected by macular degeneration. Lifestyle factors such as a high-fat diet and smoking as well as genetics have been linked to the disease (Macular Degeneration Foundation, 2002). As of yet there is no cure for macular degeneration, but some treatments are available that can slow its progress in some cases (Macular Degeneration Foundation, 2002)

Changes within the environment can help older individuals with vision problems negotiate their homes and other places. For example, changing the color and size of the typeface on signs and altering the lighting in rooms can greatly enhance an older person's ability to see objects. Often, older adults must make adjustments in their lives to accommodate for failing eyesight, such as purchasing phones with larger numbers and driving only in the day and only on routes with which they are familiar (Stevens-Ratchford & Krause, 2004).

Slower Reaction Time and Decreased Coordination   As people age, their central nervous system tends to slow down, which can slow down their reaction time as well. It may take people longer to attend to all the cues in their environment and to react to those cues. Sensorimotor coordination can also become less efficient in old age. The use of certain medications can intensify this decline in coordination.

This issue becomes particularly important for older people who want to keep driving. For many elders, driving is a necessary part of maintaining independence, which is why the issue of driving for the elderly can be a touchy subject. One study summarized the top frustrations for 148 older adults about not being able to drive: loss of spontaneity, loss of independence, loss of social connections and social activities, and difficulties with emotions associated with not driving, such as frustration and being a "non-person" because so much of U.S. identity is associated with driving (Rosenblum & Corn, 2002).

Although older drivers can pose certain risks, some researchers argue that older drivers can compensate sufficiently to drive safely and maintain their independence. Indeed, some studies suggest that older drivers are safer than younger drivers because they avoid risky and dangerous driving situations (Langford, Bohensky, Koppel, & Newstead, 2008; Loughran, Seabury, & Zakaras, 2007; McKnight, 2000). Trying to strike a balance, some states have enacted legislation that requires drivers older than a certain age to show proof of passing an eye exam, take an on-road driving exam, or provide some other standard of being fit to drive.

Changes in Appearance   The changes in physical appearance that begin in middle adulthood continue to increase in late adulthood. Few things in U.S. culture seem to cause as much anxiety as the physical changes associated with aging. You need only to pay attention to television commercials to get a feel for the latest products that promise to fight wrinkles, whiten teeth, get rid of gray hair, and soften rough spots in the skin. Of course, cosmetic surgery and related procedures are also options to fight the signs of aging. Specifically, botox treatments, chemical peels, and face-lifts are increasingly popular choices for people who want to turn back the hands of time.

Although many changes in appearance associated with age cannot be completely prevented, some can be minimized by changes in lifestyle:

- *Wrinkled and sagging skin:* With time and use, skin loses elasticity, leading to wrinkles and sags. However, wrinkles are also caused by excessive exposure to the sun, smoking, dehydration, poor diet, and lack of exercise. Therefore, modifying these behaviors could diminish the extent or severity of wrinkling.

- *Age spots:* Some people experience age spots, or discolored skin on the face or hands. This spotting is caused by an accumulation of pigment in the skin, which, like wrinkled skin, can be made worse by excessive sun exposure. Although age spots are harmless, they can be a source of embarrassment for some people.

- *Graying hair:* When hair follicles in the scalp lose their pigment-producing function, the result is a loss of color in the hair. This graying process occurs at varying ages. Some people discover their first gray hair at age 25; others do not notice any gray hairs until their seventies. One study suggests that stress damages our DNA, depleting the pigment-making cells within our hair follicles, turning our hair gray (Inomata *et al.*, 2009).

- *Hair loss and hair growth:* Many men and women experience thinning hair or hair loss on their scalp. However, hair growth may occur more frequently in unwanted places such as the ears, nostrils, and for women, along the upper lip.

- *Loss of teeth:* As we age, our gums naturally recede, and the development of gum disease leading to tooth loss becomes an increasing problem (Digiovanna, 1994). Many people keep their teeth throughout their entire life, but others must rely on dentures. Dentures can be cost prohibitive for many older people, and if they do not fit correctly or comfortably, they can be very painful. Denture pain can lead to malnutrition in some older people because eating becomes too much of a burden (Semba *et al.*, 2006; Takahashi, Okhravi, Lim, & Kasten, 2004).

- *Weight gain:* As discussed in Chapter 11, weight gain is a common complaint among aging individuals (Digiovanna, 1994).

Social Workers and the Physical Changes of Late Adulthood Social workers can do much to support clients who experience negative effects as they age or to promote optimal well-being for aging clients. For example, social workers can educate clients about prevention and management of diseases such as arthritis, osteoporosis, and macular degeneration. They can also assist clients in becoming more active to mediate the effects of muscle loss, which may help to prevent more serious problems later on. Social workers can also encourage clients to modify their environment to maximize safety and functionality as well as help clients to access resources that will allow them to maintain independence as long as possible.

Judy is displaying some of the typical changes that take place as people age. In Judy's case, her chronological age is 80, so that would place her in the middle-old group. However, because she has some problems with functioning, her functional age may be viewed as slightly older, depending on how you view the normal functionality of

80-year-old people in general. With regard to functioning, Judy needs some assistance with ADLs and IADLs. You will need to be familiar with physical issues that affect the elderly as well as how various agencies measure ability to best help Judy secure the services she needs.

Cognitive and Psychological Changes in Late Adulthood

Unfortunately, popular stereotypes associate growing older with senility, forgetfulness, and loneliness and promote visions of the disagreeable little old lady or little old man. Fortunately, as with most stereotypes, these ideas are highly oversimplified and often inaccurate. However, some of the psychological changes (which can include cognitive changes such as dementia) that occur in late adulthood pose special challenges for aging individuals and their support systems.

Dementia   Perhaps one of the main concerns that most people have about aging, beyond changes in appearance, is cognitive changes—especially dementia, the most common form of which is Alzheimer's disease. As with physical changes, cognitive changes vary a great deal among individuals. Dementia in and of itself should not be considered a part of the "normal" aging process. Rather, dementias occur as part of specific disease processes, which may or may not occur as people age.

Dementias are defined as syndromes or mental disorders caused by deterioration of the brain, and many forms of dementia can occur in both young and old age. **Alzheimer's disease** causes the type of dementia that occurs most frequently and seems to strike the most fear in people (American Psychiatric Association, 2000). The disease causes a generally slow and gradual cognitive decline through the accumulation of twisted protein fragments inside nerve cells, called *tangles,* and the abnormal buildup of dead nerve cells and protein, called *plaques.*

One of the first signs of Alzheimer's disease is a permanent loss of short-term memory, or more precisely, episodic memory. People with the disease may quickly forget a name or an address after having heard it, or lose the ability to perform a simple task like making a sandwich. Although many people, both young and old, forget these things from time to time, people who are not afflicted with the disease will usually remember them eventually. Unfortunately, people with Alzheimer's disease will not. Other signs of the disease include confusion, disorientation, loss of language skills, and difficulty learning.

As the disease progresses, memory loss worsens, and personality changes can emerge. Some people may become more aggressive or withdrawn, or they might develop problems with delusions or hallucinations. Eventually, people with the disease lose their long-term memory. They die from complications such as pneumonia and infections or from the loss of brain function (Alzheimer's Association, 2012a).

Most cases of Alzheimer's disease are found among people age 65+, with the incidence increasing with age. It is estimated that as many as 13 percent of people age 65+ and 50 percent of people age 85+ suffer from Alzheimer's disease (Alzheimer's Association, 2012a, 2014). Early onset Alzheimer's disease is not as prevalent. This form of the disease occurs in people younger than 65, with a few cases developing before age 50 (American Psychiatric Association, 2000). However, evidence suggests that Alzheimer's deaths are underreported. One study indicated that 500,000 people die from the disease each year, which is more than five times the number reported by the Centers for Disease Control and Prevention. This change in numbers makes Alzheimer's disease the third leading cause of death; currently it is ranked sixth by the Centers for Disease Control and Prevention (James *et al.*, 2014).

Until recently, Alzheimer's disease used to be diagnosed well after dementia symptoms were present, and the only way to confirm a diagnosis was through autopsy after death. However, recent diagnostic advancements now allow doctors to detect changes in the body, blood, and brain decades before symptoms are present. These advancements have led to a new categorization of the progression of Alzheimer's disease into three stages: preclinical disease, mild cognitive impairment due to Alzheimer's disease, and Alzheimer's dementia (Alzheimer's Association, 2012b; Mapstone *et al.*, 2014).

Many of the Alzheimer's drugs that are now being formulated and tested are targeted at treating the disease in its early stages, before any permanent damage is done to the brain. Thus new tests and procedures are being developed to help detect Alzheimer's disease early and to predict who may be high risk for developing the disease. For example, MRI and PET scans can be used to image the brain and look for plaques and other brain changes that are characteristic of the disease. Spinal taps can be used to detect the accumulation of certain proteins that are present among those who are likely to develop the disease. Research is also focusing on treatments that may stop the disease from developing, such as insulin administered intranasally, from where it travels to the brain to provide glucose for brain cells; drugs that help the body clear amyloid plaques; promotion of antibodies that stop cell-to-cell transmission of the disease; and tests for a lack of protein that is thought to protect the aging brain from stress, inflammation, and development of disease (De Meyer *et al.*, 2010; Lu *et al.*, 2014; Perneczky *et al.*, 2012).

Interestingly, many physicians refuse to offer these new diagnostic tools to patients, citing ethical concerns. For example, since there is no cure for the disease, and most of the treatments to halt the disease are still being developed and tested, and their true efficacy is not yet known, what purpose does early diagnosis serve? Further, many of the new diagnostic tests are not completely accurate in predicting who will eventually develop the disease. Some argue that even limited diagnostic information could be used to plan for future care and other issues; others argue it just causes unnecessary anxiety among those who get an early diagnosis, particularly when the tests are not 100 percent accurate. This will be an ongoing debate as the research on Alzheimer's disease continues. Social workers can be a part of this debate, helping to shape thinking around the positive and negative effects of early testing on individuals, families, organizations, and systems.

Another issue related to Alzheimer's disease with which social workers are concerned is caregiving. Caregiving for people with Alzheimer's disease is a serious issue. Research indicates that caregivers who care for a partner with Alzheimer's disease have a six-fold increase in the risk of developing Alzheimer's disease themselves, because of the physical and psychological stress associated with caregiving (Norton *et al.*, 2010). Many social service policies and programs have been developed in the past several decades to address this issue. Services such as respite care, adult day care, in-home care, and skilled nursing facilities have assumed the responsibility to research and develop effective ways to care for people with Alzheimer's disease. We will explore issues of caregiving more thoroughly later in the chapter.

Cognitive Changes   Despite the widespread occurrence of dementias, many people do not lose significant cognitive functioning as they age, and they find great satisfaction in lifelong activity and learning. People may decide to change careers in their sixties or to earn a second or third degree in their seventies. Memory and learning do not necessarily decline because of age. Indeed, many researchers posit that the "use it or lose it" adage is true: The more we use our memories, stimulate our thinking, and expose ourselves to new learning, the more we can maintain the mental capacities we enjoyed in younger years. Conversely, some research indicates that as we age, our prefrontal cortex loses volume, affecting sleep quality, which in turn affects our long-term memory. To slow memory decline, we need to improve sleep, particularly the slow-wave phase of sleep (Mander *et al.*, 2013).

Although people may experience some slowing in cognitive processes as they age, research indicates that many barriers that older people may face in learning are caused by environmental factors or poor instruction rather than deficits in memory or learning capacity. For example, some of the eyesight and hearing changes that take place as people age can be a barrier to learning; however, if modifications are made, many older adults learn just as well as younger adults. Moreover, if new material can be linked with the older learner's existing experiences, learning can be just as effective for older adults as it is for younger adults (Dunlosky *et al.*, 2007; Moore & Piland, 1994).

We used to believe that brain activity would slow down as we aged, so that older brains would show less activity overall than younger ones. New neuroimaging studies, however, show that this is not the case at all. Researchers now have evidence that older adults use both sides of their brain for decision making and accomplishing tasks, whereas younger adults only use one side, possibly making older adults more efficient or less prone to error (Phillips, 2011).

Continued cognitive activity such as crossword puzzles and simple memory quizzes can help keep the brain healthy and functioning, particularly when people are suffering from dementia. In cases of dementia, these memory techniques can help people cope and feel more in control of their lives. One particularly effective technique is the use of a memory notebook to help compensate for memory changes. The use of the notebook can lead to increased confidence and decreased anxiety among those with memory problems (Greenaway, Hanna, Lepore, & Smith, 2008).

Personality and Aging   Many studies have examined how various personality traits play out over time. This research has addressed such issues as whether personality traits remain stable, why some people seem to have a "good attitude" about aging while others are negative about the experience, and why some people are better able than others to cope with loss and change.

There appear to be two major arguments about how personality affects aging:

- *An individual's personality tends to remain stable over time.* For example, a person who is easygoing and copes well with change when younger is likely to be easygoing and to cope well as she or he ages. According to this line of thinking, you can tell a lot about how a person will cope in older age based on her or his responses to events in younger age (Bleidorn, Kandler, Riemann, Angleitner, & Spinath, 2009; Ruth & Coleman, 1996; Tickle, Heatherton, & Wittenberg, 2001).

- *Universal personality traits are activated at different times of life.* Personality traits serve certain purposes at different points of our lives. The traits that we express at any given time ensure that our needs are met at different developmental stages. Thus, we will express various traits more actively at some points in our lives than at others, depending on the needs that these traits are fulfilling.

This second idea is summarized in a cross-cultural study that explored age differences in personality in five different countries (Germany, Italy, Portugal, Croatia, and South Korea) (McCrae, *et al.* 1999). Respondents in this study showed a consistent set of personality traits based on age across cultures, regardless of different political, cultural, or historical contexts. Respondents younger than 30 tended to display more extroversion, more adventurousness, and less conscientiousness than respondents older than 30. As respondents aged, they tended to show characteristics of increased trust, self-control, self-consciousness, and dutifulness. Older respondents also tended to show less hostility, activity, anxiety, depression, and assertiveness than younger respondents. The authors argue that traits seen in younger respondents may serve them well in tasks appropriate to that developmental stage, such as finding a mate or a job. Conversely, traits seen in older respondents may be advantageous in fulfilling familial and community responsibilities.

Depression and Suicide   Another major concern related to growing older is depression. The prevalence of depression among older populations is difficult to determine, mostly because of the different ways in which depression is defined. Estimates range from 2.5 to 45 percent, with an average of 20 percent—dramatically higher than estimates for younger populations, which range from 0.7 to 2.7 percent (McCullough, 1991). However, more conservative estimates suggest that rates of major depression among the elderly range from 1 to 5 percent, though this does not include older adults who exhibit symptoms of mild depression and fall short of the full diagnostic criteria of major depression (Alexopoulos, 2000; Hybels & Blazer, 2003).

Do higher rates of depression among the elderly mean that depression is a by-product of the aging process? Not necessarily. There is no evidence to suggest that depression is a normal part of aging. Depression can be partially related to personality characteristics such as the ability to cope with change. Situational factors can also influence the chances of an older person's developing this condition. Illness, disability, discrimination, changing roles, and loss of financial, social, and other supports are often an inevitable part of living a long life. It is much more likely that a combination of socioeconomic factors and a person's ability to cope and adapt to changing circumstances plays a role in the development of depression (George, 1993). This is particularly true for older women, who live longer than men and are more likely than men to be living in poverty.

Several studies have suggested that physical illness may play a significant role in an older person's risk of developing depression (Barusch, Rogers, & Abu-Bader, 1999; Hybels & Blazer, 2003; Rogers, 1999). Some estimates suggest that depression and physical illness coexist in as many as 45 percent of older adults (Gerety & Farnett,

PHOTO 12-A

Depression in later life is a major concern for many older individuals and their families

Source: Mel Curtis/Getty Images

1995). Though these statistics do not prove that poor health directly causes depression, they suggest that a serious illness, whether physical or mental, may seriously compromise an older adult's ability to cope with the challenges of growing older, thus making the person more vulnerable to developing an additional illness. For example, an older person who is suffering from an illness that causes a disability may be more vulnerable to developing depression if she or he must rely on family members for care, or if she or he experiences financial problems because of the costs of care.

Conversely, compared to those who do not have depressive symptoms, an older person who is suffering from depression may be at higher risk for developing a physical illness because of poor eating habits, lack of activity and interest in daily activities, and neglect of self-care in general. Poor eating habits and neglect in self-care may lead to poor nutrition and other issues that can contribute to feelings of depression and hopelessness.

Thus, social workers should not only assess the emotional well-being of older adults but also ask questions about what they are eating and how often. Some medications make people feel less hungry, or people may forget to eat. Other older adults may find themselves having such a tight budget that they have to choose between eating and taking medications.

One of the biggest concerns about depression among the elderly is a tendency toward suicide. Often when we think about suicide, we think of younger adults. However, suicide is a leading cause of death among elderly people. Suicide risk increases with age, particularly among white American men age 85+, who have the highest rates of suicide in almost all the industrialized nations (Boyd, 2007; National Institute of Mental Health, 2009; Pearson & Conwell, 1995). Elderly people are also more likely than younger people to complete suicide. This is because elderly individuals tend to plan their deaths and give fewer indications of their suicidal thoughts or previous attempts than do younger people (Conwell *et al.*, 1998). Further, suicide rates among older adults may be underestimated. Some elderly people may deliberately stop taking medications, overdose on medications, become self-neglectful, or have accidents that cause death but that are deemed "natural causes" (Osgood, 1991).

Social Workers and the Psychological Changes of Late Adulthood   Social workers are an important part of the service network for people with dementia and other health and mental health problems. Social workers play crucial roles in developing effective interventions and programs for people with dementia as well as support services for caregivers.

Social workers also work with older clients who may be having trouble coping with changes associated with aging. They can help older clients maximize their functioning and well-being. Many social workers are also involved in researching biopsychosocial issues that affect the health and well-being of older adults, helping to improve the services that are provided to clients.

Given the research that suggests a link between depression and poor physical health, as Judy's social worker, you may want to focus on her mental and physical health in your assessment and intervention. Because Judy is coping with issues of functioning, she may be at risk for developing depression or other mental health problems, especially if she is unable to maintain supportive and other services to help with her care. You could help Judy get support through programs such as Meals On Wheels, Senior Backpack programs, or other senior nutrition programs that can help ensure she gets the nutrition she needs.

THE INDIVIDUAL IN LATE ADULTHOOD

In the following sections, we examine some of the issues on an individual level that can affect development in older age. Many of these issues are inextricably linked with interpersonal and social development, which must be considered when working with older adults.

Psychosocial Theories of Aging

The medical model helps to organize information on disease processes that may occur in later life, but other theories can help social workers to explain psychosocial issues that may impact the well-being of older adults. Although the list of theories is too exhaustive to discuss all of them here, we will take a look at several that are often used in the literature and in work with older adults.

Disengagement Theory   The first theory proposed to describe social processes of aging was disengagement theory (Cumming & Henry, 1961; Henry, 1963). Disengagement theorists argue that to expect older people to be fully active in societal roles is unrealistic. Rather, people naturally disengage from formal roles and responsibilities as they age. For example, it is normal for people to retire from the workplace. At the same time, the larger society pulls away from older people because they are viewed as disruptive to the system. This disengagement, then, is a mutual "agreement" between an aging person and society. The process is viewed as positive, because both the older person and society view this disengagement as necessary for the well-being of both parties.

Disengagement theory can be viewed as very negative and pessimistic. Particularly in a time when technology is enabling people to live longer, this theory may seem outdated. Some critics argue that disengagement theory is simply a reflection of society's views on older people: Ours is a youth-oriented culture that tends to devalue the experiences of elderly people.

Despite this criticism, proponents of disengagement theory point out that it is the first theory that attended to the interaction between the older person and society. Some proponents also argue that disengagement theory is more realistic than activity-focused theories of aging. Specifically, some theories suggest that we should all remain active as we age, and this may be an overly optimistic expectation.

Activity Theory   A second popular theory is activity theory, which states that it is not necessarily normal or natural for people to "drop out" of life as they age (Havighurst, Neugarten, & Tobin, 1968). Rather, the needs and wishes of people as they age are similar to those at any point of life. If people do disengage from their roles, it is usually because of factors outside of their control such as economics, discrimination, and poor health.

Activity theory takes a much more positive view on aging than disengagement theory does. It holds societal expectations of aging responsible for "forcing" people out of various roles as they age.

However, some people feel that this view places undue pressure on people to remain active as they age: If older adults are not happy, productive seniors, then there is something "wrong" with them. However, activity theorists acknowledge that some people prefer to disengage in their later years.

PHOTO 12-B

Many individuals maintain active lives as they age

Source: Ryan McVay/Getty Images

Continuity Theory   This theory, based on activity theory, uses a life span perspective to describe processes of aging (Atchley, 1989). Continuity theory emphasizes the role of personality in determining the outcomes of older age. As people age, they establish life structures, or patterns of being, that result from interacting with others and the world and that connect them with their past experiences. These structures not only offer people a foundation on which they continue to develop, but also determine how people will cope and function in the future. People maintain continuity in roles, personality, relationships, and activities; the continuity in these areas can help them adjust (or not) to aging.

As with the other theories on aging, continuity theory does not account for profound changes that can occur as people age. For example, chronic illness and disability can seriously alter an older person's activities and attitude about life. It may be unreasonable to expect people to maintain continuity when such changes occur.

Nevertheless, continuity theory may describe what actually happens to many people as they age, particularly if they are lucky enough to escape a serious illness or other events that compromise their well-being. Even if such events do occur, some people cope and adjust in such a way that continuity is not radically disturbed.

Peck's Theory of Ego Integrity   Robert Peck's (1955, 1968) theory of emotional and social development in late adulthood focuses on attaining ego integrity and, consequently, well-being, in older age. He specifies three distinct **tasks of ego integrity** during late adulthood:

- *Ego differentiation versus work and role preoccupation:* Affirming self-worth through family, friendship, and community life rather than using past career success and physical ability as a measuring stick for worth. These tasks include negotiating family changes such as the "empty nest" and acquiring new interests.

- *Body transcendence versus body preoccupation:* Surmounting physical limitations by emphasizing the compensating rewards of cognitive, emotional, and social powers. Tasks here include developing the capacity to enjoy life instead of focusing on bodily functions and "aches and pains."

- *Ego transcendence versus ego preoccupation:* Facing the reality of death constructively through efforts to make life more secure, meaningful, and gratifying for younger generations.

In Peck's theory, ego integrity requires older adults to move beyond their life's work, their bodies, and their separate identities. Other tasks include reflecting on one's life, focusing on spiritual matters, and developing the ability to see life in larger context (Berk, 2011; Wood, 2006).

Aging Well   Another perspective that helps to explain the dynamics of aging, particularly individual variation in aging, examines the art of aging well or successfully. Various theories explain how some people remain relatively free from disease and maintain optimal cognitive, physical, and social functioning as they age. Some research suggests that older adults report greater happiness than younger adults, reinforcing the notion that successful aging or aging well is not only possible but common (Sorrell, 2009).

People who age "successfully" are engaged in life, are emotionally and instrumentally supportive of others, and are proactive with regard to their health, finances, environment, and interpersonal relationships. Conversely, people who age "unsuccessfully" do not possess these qualities and thus show the physical and psychosocial declines that many people associate with aging (Kahana & Kahana, 1996, 2003; Kahana, Kahana, & Kercher, 2003; Rowe & Kahn, 1987, 1997).

How might Judy's situation be viewed from these theories and perspectives? This probably depends on your views as the social worker. For example, if you adopt the perspective of disengagement theory, you might view Judy's situation as normal. That is, you might interpret the problems that Judy is having with physical and housing issues as a natural part of aging and the disengagement process.

If you were to look at Judy's situation through the lens of continuity theory, you would want to know how Judy functioned in the past to help her function as she ages. You might explore characteristics of her roles, personality, relationships, and so on to help her connect with her past and plan for her future. You would also advocate for appropriate housing and care for Judy so that she can maintain her current level of functioning and remain as independent as possible.

In contrast, if you use activity theory, Peck's theory of ego integrity, or the "aging well" perspective, you might characterize Judy's current state of functioning and her housing problems as "abnormal." Though Judy does have some physical problems, activity theory would dictate that she maintain her normal roles and activities as she ages, as much as her health permits. The other perspectives would prompt you to assess her feelings about her life at this point and to encourage her to seek more social support from family.

Judy's current problem with losing her housing would be viewed as a dysfunctional societal response to the care of elderly individuals. You would thus intervene to improve this care.

Spirituality and Aging

There is a strong movement in social work to incorporate spirituality into the overall understanding of the human development process. That interest extends to researchers who study aging: There also has been a call to pay more attention to how spirituality affects the aging process (Kimble, 2001; MacKinlay, 2001; Nelson-Becker & Canda, 2008; Watkins, 2009; Yoon & Lee, 2007). Some researchers argue that in a society that emphasizes individuality and independence, many older adults may feel increased spiritual isolation and loneliness. This condition may be particularly relevant because many older adults live alone.

Much of the research conducted on religion, spirituality, and aging has focused on the general meaning of religious belief and specific faiths (Atchley & Barusch, 2004). However, little research explores the role of faith and spirituality, in general, on overall life satisfaction of the elderly, especially with regard to issues of loss and disability related to age (Koenig, 1995). Nonetheless, research that explores this area suggests that spirituality may enhance emotional and psychological well-being in the face of loss (Wink, Dillon, & Prettyman, 2007).

Many older adults participate in organized religion, and those who have an affiliation with a particular institution report more subjective feelings of religiosity and spirituality than those who do not identify with a religious institution. Membership in a formal religious organization can have many benefits. Many churches offer programs and services that can support older adults who live in the community. This is particularly true for African–American groups. Religious organizations appear to be the foundations for many African–American communities (Billingsley & Morrison-Rodriguez, 2007; Chatters & Taylor, 1994). Regular attendance at religious services can keep elders active in their communities, offer resources for recreation and socialization, and provide additional caregiving support to elders and their families. However, more research needs to be conducted on the effects of regular church attendance for older adults.

Models of faith and spiritual development can be useful in guiding your understanding of the impacts of spirituality on older adults. Recall James Fowler's stages of faith development discussed in Chapter 10 (Fowler, 1981). According to Fowler, older adults are in the last stage of faith development, universalizing faith. During this time, older adults resolve conflicts in their beliefs and work toward ensuring the well-being of humankind. Using this theory, social workers can help older clients to explore the meaning of their faith and come to terms with unresolved conflicts that may still be creating barriers to achieving a sense of peace and life satisfaction. In doing so, many older adults may find a sense of purpose in helping others and contributing to the well-being of their communities, which may in turn help them achieve an individual sense of health, well-being, and spirituality that will support their overall development in older adulthood.

In working with Judy, you may want to explore her sense of faith and spirituality. It may be that, if cultivated, this can be a source of strength for Judy as she works through some of her physical and other problems. Moreover, if Judy is affiliated with a specific religious organization, you could help her access the resources that it might provide.

Sexuality in Late Adulthood

One stereotype of aging is that older adults lose their sexuality and thus no longer enjoy sexual intimacy. This stereotype could not be further from the truth. It may be entrenched in U.S. society because sexuality of older adults tends to be invisible in the media and elsewhere and because people tend to define aging as a lonely stage in life that is filled with disability and illness. In addition, people tend to view older adults as unattractive and past their need for romance and intimate companionship.

Although sexual functioning does decrease somewhat with age, many people find effective ways to compensate for such decreases. For example, a variety of creams and gels are available to supplement vaginal lubrication in older women, and men who experience erectile dysfunction may benefit from one of several available drugs that aid in attaining and sustaining an erection. Some older people do report a decrease in the frequency of sex, but a majority of older people maintain an active sex life and report an increase in their interest in, quality of, and satisfaction with sex as they age (Lindau *et al.*, 2007; Westheimer & Lopater, 2004).

Sexual changes that occur as people age are closely associated with other psychosocial changes that occur with aging (Segraves & Segraves, 1995). Sexual functioning in older age has much to do with health status, the availability of a partner, and the relationship with a partner. Moreover, sexuality among older adults is inextricably linked with biopsychosocial and cultural factors.

Social workers need to be leaders in correcting myths and stereotypes about sexuality in old age and educating clients and others about the importance of continued sexual intimacy as they age. Because sexual intimacy can be a source of great pleasure and satisfaction in relationships, social workers need to pay attention to this area in assessing and intervening with older adults.

Gay, Lesbian, Bisexual, and Transgendered Older Adults

In regard to aging and sexuality, gay, lesbian, bisexual, and transgendered (GLBT) older adults face a double stereotype: They are gay and old. Fortunately, however, many older GLBT adults lead happy and satisfying lives, sexually and otherwise. GLBT couples who are in long-term, committed relationships can offer the same type of support and companionship to each other as they age as heterosexual couples. These relationships provide intimacy, caregiving, and social and financial support.

Of course, older GLBT adults face similar obstacles to those that younger GLBT people face, such as discrimination, social disapproval, familial strife, and laws prohibiting marriage. These laws can cause additional problems with regard to benefits, housing, property, parenting, and guardianship rights. Some older couples may find that their family members disapprove of their relationship and refuse to acknowledge it. This can pose emotional and other problems for older adults, especially if they find themselves reliant in any way on family members for caregiving. Further, older GLBT people may face homophobia and discrimination in care facilities, forcing them back in the closet. In the United States and in other countries, some care facilities cater to GLBT elders or at least provide services geared toward supporting people in this population (Gulli, 2009).

There are also considerations with regard to how GLBT people perceive their own aging and how their aging plays out in their communities. For example, results from one study that examined perceptions of aging among 183 gay and lesbian respondents found that young and old gay men felt that gay society viewed aging very negatively; a significantly smaller percentage of lesbian women thought that lesbian society viewed aging negatively. Gay men also perceived aging as occurring at significantly younger years than lesbian women did. This finding has implications for gay men's attitudes about being "dateable" and their abilities to secure partners, especially partners who can serve as caregivers in old age. Gay men did not necessarily define their own aging in very negative terms, but they still perceived the gay community as ageist. Conversely, lesbian women held more positive attitudes about aging and their prospects for intimate relationships as they aged. These relationships, in combination with access to more formal social supports organized by older lesbian women, make it more likely that lesbian women will have more support in old age than gay men will have (Schope, 2005).

Social workers need to be aware of the various issues that can create potential problems for older GLBT clients. On an individual level, social workers can help older GLBT clients work through personal beliefs and attitudes about aging that might inhibit personal growth. On an interpersonal level, social workers can be of great assistance in helping clients to work on meaningful relationships that will provide support and fulfillment in older years. They can also help clients deal with the effects of ageism in their community. Finally, on a societal level, social workers can work to overcome barriers created by institutional ageism, heterosexism, and discrimination, which can put older GLBT clients at risk for poor psychosocial health and well-being.

Grief and Loss

Throughout this chapter, many issues have surfaced that could create the potential for grief. Loss of health, abilities, supports, possessions, independence, relationships, friendships, and various roles leave people vulnerable to developing grief. With the passage of time, everyone will inevitably face losses in one form or another. Ultimately they will face their own death, which is their final loss.

As you have seen, people react very differently to loss, depending on many factors such as their personalities, coping skills, and personal resources. Research suggests that there are also many factors that impact the way a person experiences or expresses grief (Worden, 2009). Exhibit 12.1 lists some of the important factors that social workers should consider when working with clients who are experiencing these and related issues. Many of these characteristics can influence the outcomes of

- Personality (sense of identity, maturity, self-esteem)
- Social and gender roles
- Perceived relationship with the deceased (importance and nature of the relationship; roles within the relationship)
- Values and beliefs (views on life and death; importance person places on events)
- Coping patterns (how survivor copes with events, expresses feelings, adapts)
- Mode of death (anticipated vs. sudden death; violent vs. nonviolent death; natural vs. non-natural death)
- Availability of support
- Number of losses (experiencing multiple losses at once or over short period of time vs. every once in a while)

EXHIBIT 12.1

Factors Influencing the Grief Process

the grief process and the ways in which people adjust to loss or the finality of death. Indeed, social workers need to be mindful of problems that can occur in grieving or barriers that may prevent clients from working through grief in ways that promote well-being.

Normal Grief and Complicated Grief Successful grief outcomes are often referred to as "normal grief," and unsuccessful outcomes, "complicated grief" (Rando, 1993):

- **Normal grief** refers to the idea that there is a wide range of emotional, cognitive, and behavioral responses to loss and these are all "normal." People tend to work through loss and grief successfully on their own or with the help of informal support networks such as friends and family or with the help of a therapist or counselor. Research suggests that people generally just need the reassurance that the wide range of emotions they may feel are normal and okay, though they can be frightening and overwhelming at times.

- **Complicated grief** refers to people who might have difficulties coping with loss and who might experience prolonged periods of distress and adjustment problems, long after a loss occurs. This is characterized by symptoms such as a persistent sense of disbelief and anger regarding the loss; recurring painful emotions; and preoccupation with thoughts of the deceased years after the loss. Research suggests there are several factors that can put people at risk for complicated grief including a lack of social support; death of a child; circumstances surrounding the loss (e.g., expected vs. unexpected); being denied the opportunity to grieve; high-profile losses (e.g., those that are covered in the media); and losses accompanied by multiple stressors (e.g., losing a partner in a fire that also destroys the home, pets, and belongings and that brings financial hardships) (Rando, 1993).

One issue that can complicate grief is when people are denied the opportunity to grieve. **Disenfranchised grief** (Doka, 2002) refers to situations when people's reactions to loss are unacknowledged by others around them or by larger society. Each culture has its own rules and traditions that govern which losses can be grieved, who can grieve them, and in what ways. Only the losses that are socially sanctioned can be grieved, and those grieving in socially sanctioned ways will receive sympathy and support, both informally through support networks and formally through laws and policies. Disenfranchised grief occurs when people experience losses or process grief in ways that are not socially acceptable. It often results in empathic failure—the failure of one part of the system to understand the meaning and experience of another.

In the United States, for example, rules emphasize that family members have a right to grieve the deaths of other family members, usually defined as biological relations or families created through marriage. Family members get time off work, social support, financial benefits, and diminished social responsibilities when they experience a loss of another family member. However, when people experience loss in a relationship that is not socially sanctioned or in a family system that is not legally recognized, their grief might not be acknowledged or supported. For example, the loss may occur among partners who choose not to marry; gay, lesbian, bisexual, or transgender partners; or partners who are estranged, divorced, or no longer together. Similarly, people may lose pets, close friends, co-workers, foster children, children of significant others, or even possessions such as a home. They may not get any sympathy, financial benefits, time off work to attend the funeral, or control over decision-making processes about the deceased after the loss.

Grief can also be disenfranchised when the loss occurs under socially unacceptable circumstances, such as a death from suicide, an act of violence, or self-neglect or self-abuse. A chronic smoker's death from cancer might be looked upon very differently from a non-smoker's death from lung cancer.

Even our grief process is socially sanctioned. If our grief extends past a socially acceptable time frame, or if we exhibit socially unacceptable behaviors in response to loss, we may be diagnosed with a mental illness or lose social support. For example, culturally suspect behaviors might include the ideas that some people do not cry, do not grieve long enough, grieve too long, or cry too much.

Although researchers and helping professionals are still debating what constitutes normal grief and complicated grief, because grief is so individualistic, these are still helpful concepts to keep in mind while working with clients. Different people cope with and adjust to loss in very different ways and over very different time frames. Thus it is difficult to determine exactly what constitutes complicated grief or when or if intervention would be helpful. However, debates aside, it is important to remember that individual clients may *perceive* their grief as normal or complicated, which may be even more important than an actual diagnosis for better understanding and supporting a client who is grieving.

Other Theories of Grief   There are many other models that attempt to more fully describe and explain how we process grief:

- **Working through grief** model: Suggests that the focus of grief work is withdrawing our energy from the person or thing we lost (DeSpelder & Strickland, 2011). Grief is an active and adaptive response to loss. Over time, it allows us to confront and accept our loss so that we can move on with our lives.

- **Continuing bonds** model: Describes grief as a process whereby people create enduring connections to the person or thing they lost (Klass & Goss, 1999). We might create symbols or memories or use objects to link us to the person or thing, which allows us to establish a new kind of relationship with that person or thing.

- **Dual-process of coping** model: Suggests that people express both "letting go" and "holding on" types of behavior in response to loss (Stroebe & Schut, 1999).

- **Loss-oriented coping** model: Suggests that people process death or loss through such behaviors as crying, looking at photos, or thinking about the deceased person.

- **Restoration-oriented coping** model: Suggests that people adjust to a new life without the person or object through behaviors such as moving, changing jobs, or taking on new roles.

- **Tasks of mourning** model: Focuses on the tasks that people engage in to adjust to loss. Tasks that are important for adjustment according to this model include accepting the reality of the loss, processing pain, adjusting to life without the person or object, and establishing an enduring connection with the person or object (Worden, 2009).

Kübler-Ross's Theory of Death and Dying   One well-known approach to conceptualizing clients' grief is Elisabeth Kübler-Ross's theory of death and dying (1969). Kübler-Ross, a psychiatrist, conducted extensive interviews with hundreds of dying patients. Through talking with them about their feelings, thoughts, and experiences, she developed a model of the stages of dying that were typical among those she interviewed. Although the model is built around those who are experiencing the death process, it can be applied to people who have experienced any major loss, such as divorce or unemployment.

Exhibit 12.2 describes the stages in Kübler-Ross's model. She found that many people went through stages in a predictable manner, though the exact process varied from person to person. For example, some people may get "stuck" in a stage, unable to move on to the next. Others may skip a stage or two altogether. Still others may find themselves moving backward into a previous stage, even though it seemed they had done the work necessary in that stage. Note also that not all people will make it successfully to the final stage; that is, some people may never be able to accept their impending death or their loss (Kübler-Ross, 1969, 1971). So, while there may be some general pattern to the way some people deal with death and dying, there are circumstances where people do not deal with death or other loss in such a predictable manner.

The Kübler-Ross model provides a straightforward approach to reactions to death and dying, and the stages are fairly easy to apply in cases where clients are dealing with loss. Also, in a "death-denying" culture such as the United States, the ideas behind this model are useful to help understand, tolerate, and work with the variety of reactions that can occur with loss. However, the Kübler-Ross model may not account for cultural or spiritual variations that different people bring to their

---

EXHIBIT 12.2

Kübler-Ross's Model of Death and Dying

STAGE ONE: DENIAL

This is the initial stage in which people first learn the news that they or someone they know is dying. Denial can be useful in that it helps to protect the person against the shock of receiving such news. People in the denial stage might respond with, "No, not me," or, "There must be a mistake," or, "Why my child?"

STAGE TWO: ANGER

Once a person has worked through denial, a typical reaction to surface is anger. People often respond with anger as a way to work through their intense feelings. People may lash out at their care providers, family members, or even God. Some anger-based responses might include, "Why me?" or "Why would God do this?" or "What did I do to deserve this?"

STAGE THREE: BARGAINING

Once the anger has dissipated, people may try to bargain with health care professionals or God to restore their health. Typical responses include, "If I could just get healthy again, I'll go to church"; or, "If you'll just give me more time, I'll . . ."; or, "I promise I'll do better if you'll just let me live." Kübler-Ross found that even people who did not believe in God would often engage in bargaining with a higher power.

STAGE FOUR: DEPRESSION

Once people realize that bargaining is not working, they frequently become depressed. Sometimes the depression is active: People actively grieve their losses or potential losses. Sometimes depression is passive: People become silent and turn inward.

STAGE FIVE: ACCEPTANCE

This stage occurs after people have worked through the preceding stages and have attained a sense of peace with the realization that they (or a loved one) will die. If people reach this stage, they are often able to resolve unfinished business and bring closure to their relationships and lives.

Source: Kübler-Ross, 1971

experience. There is the danger that if clients do not adhere to these particular stages, for whatever reason, they may be viewed as deviant or somehow disordered for not dealing with their loss in the expected way. Further, many helping professionals feel that this model is much too prescriptive—that is, many would argue that the process of working through grief, loss, and end-of-life issues is much more complex and nuanced than components of this model can capture.

Terror Management Theory   A more recent model examines how we cope with the awareness of our own deaths using concepts from Freud's Psychodynamic Theory. **Terror management theory** (Greenberg, Solomon, & Pyszczynski, 1997) posits that, because humans have the capacity for self-awareness and contemplation of the past and future, we know that we will die one day. This death awareness has the potential to cause paralyzing fear and anxiety. To manage these emotions and keep death thoughts at bay, we use defense mechanisms:

- **Proximal defenses:** Mechanisms we use to keep thoughts of death out of our awareness. They include suppressing death thoughts and denying personal vulnerability to disease and premature death. For example, someone using proximal defenses might start exercising more, switch to a healthier diet, or start wearing sunscreen. All of these behaviors give a person a sense of control over health, thereby decreasing feelings of vulnerability and anxiety over premature death.

- **Distal defenses:** Mechanisms that are used after a person has suppressed death thoughts. These defenses have to do with the cultural world view (a system of beliefs and practices) and self-esteem a person develops and maintains to make sense of and give meaning to life and death. For example, a person may believe that her life has particular meaning because she is contributing something valuable to the world and will leave a legacy (perhaps through her work, her children, or a foundation that she supports). These beliefs decrease feelings of anxiety about death, because life has meaning attached to it. A person may also believe that death has meaning—for example, by living a good life, a person will "go to a better place" after death—which also helps to decrease anxiety about death.

According to terror management theory, without these defenses to reduce anxiety about death and dying, our terror would paralyze us and we would not be able to function in our daily lives.

Life Review and Narrative Therapies   These two interventions can be effective in work with older adults and others who are facing end-of-life or grief issues:

- **Life review therapy,** sometimes referred to as reminiscence therapy: Helps facilitate the process of reflecting on and reviewing one's life. It involves mentally taking stock of one's life, addressing unresolved conflicts or issues, and elucidating positive past events and accomplishments (Butler, 1963; Westerhof, Bohlmeijer, & Webster, 2010).

- **Narrative therapy,** based in the strengths perspective: Helps clients recount dominant life stories that have shaped and formed their identities as well as the problems with which they have struggled. Narrative therapy can help clients reconstruct meanings to promote a more positive self-identity and different perspectives on problems (Cooper & Lesser, 2011; Crocket, 2013). Keep in mind that culture impacts how these meanings are shaped and contributes to how a person views her or his identity.

Life review and narrative therapies can be used in combination to help clients at the end of life or who are dealing with grief to develop alternative life stories. They allow clients to take responsibility for the way they want to live and to redefine themselves in the wake of loss or impending death (Bohlmeijer, Kramer, Smit, Onrust, & van Marwijk, 2009).

Social Work with the Grieving and Dying   All of the models presented here can be used either by themselves or in some combination to help work with and support people who are experiencing grief and loss. People might respond to loss in different ways, so having a variety of models and therapies is likely to be useful. It is also important to understand how clients' grieving processes affect them and those around them. In addition, because older adults often experience losses in various biopsychosocial areas (for example, physically, financially, socially), social workers also need to be aware of the complexity of the relationship between physical factors and other psychosocial and environmental factors that can affect well-being.

Further, social workers need to be aware of emerging movements and trends in dealing with death, grief, and dying to help connect clients with resources and alternative ways of viewing their options and situations. For example, one resource that many people are finding helpful are Death Cafés, where people get to gather to eat, drink, and discuss death. The objective of these gatherings is to help increase awareness of death while helping people make the most of their lives. These gatherings offer an alternative for people who may find our death-denying culture a less than welcoming place to discuss life, death, and issues related to the dying process (Death Café, 2014). Other movements are also emerging for funeral services and memorials such as "fun funerals" and services during which the bodies of the deceased are posed and staged in roles they had or wished they had in life. While some may find these concepts strange, others feel that our traditional way of dealing with death needs to change.

In Judy's case, she has already experienced losses in the form of disability and moving into a care facility. With the notice that she will need to vacate Sunset Homes, she faces the prospect of more loss. These potential losses could affect her physical health if the issues surrounding them are not addressed. For example, extensive loss could lead to depression, which could compromise her physical health. However, the fact that she seems settled in the care facility speaks well to her ability to adjust to change.

You can assess Judy's strengths to ensure available resources are used to help her deal with the need to move. How Judy deals with this loss will depend on many factors, including her personality, coping skills, cultural background, and personal philosophy on life. You might examine how Judy is approaching her grief work and in what ways she may be holding on to or letting go of the losses she is experiencing.

You may want to consider that Judy is experiencing disenfranchised grief. Many people around her might not recognize or validate the impact that her losses are having on her. It may be that Judy is at risk for complicated grief given the circumstances surrounding her situation.

Though Judy is not faced with imminent death, you could also make use of Kübler-Ross's theory as well as other models that help to explain loss and grief. You may want to explore her thoughts and feelings about her physical changes. These are areas that you could explore to evaluate in which stage Judy is currently situated as well as how she can be helped to progress into the final stage of grief, which is acceptance. According to Kübler-Ross, the goal in working with Judy is to help her to accept her physical losses and limitations and to come to terms with the changes that she will inevitably experience in the future.

Life review and narrative therapies might be good treatment modalities in Judy's case. They could help her to reconstruct the narrative of her life and her current situation as well as recall her past accomplishments and successes. Those processes could help facilitate adaptation to her circumstances now and in the future.

THE FAMILY AND IMMEDIATE ENVIRONMENT IN LATE ADULTHOOD

So far, we have explored issues that pertain to the individual. In this section, we will look at ways in which older adults are influenced by their immediate environment. While considering issues that can occur at this level, keep in mind how physical factors can influence the dynamics of familial and other functioning.

Families can be a rich source of physical, emotional, financial, and psychological support as people age. Family dynamics are continually changing: New family members are added and old ones lost, roles and relationships change, and events occur to change the way people view themselves in the context of their families. The "empty nest" transition typically occurs in middle to late adulthood as children grow up and move out to establish their own families. Moreover, advances in technology and changes in values, culture, and attitudes leave families facing new challenges, which in turn affect family dynamics and roles for family members. For aging individuals, these changes can be positive and negative.

Grandparenting

Traditionally, grandparenting is viewed as an important role in U.S. society. The general perception of grandparents is as older, supportive, secondary caregivers to grandchildren. Grandparents usually leave the primary rearing and disciplining responsibilities to the parents. These patterns reflect the fun seeker, distant figure, and formal figure styles of grandparenting discussed in Chapter 7.

However, with changing economic and social times, more families are finding it necessary to have two breadwinners, leaving them with child care needs. Many families have difficulties affording good day care or after-school programs for their children. With increasing alternative family situations such as single-parent households, families need to be creative and resourceful with regard to finding ways to rear their children. Additionally, issues such as AIDS/HIV, criminal activity, drug abuse, and other problems are leaving families without their primary caregivers. Finally, many people would agree that child rearing today is more challenging and complex than it has ever been.

In response to these developments, more primary caregivers are turning to **kinship care,** which is care given to children by relatives when parents are unable to do so. Often, grandparents are the ones to help (Davitt, 2006). Indeed, increasing numbers of grandparents are assuming the primary caregiver or surrogate parent role for children. Consider these facts:

- According to census data from 2010, 5.4 million children are living with a grandparent. Further, 2.7 million grandparents were responsible for most of the basic needs (i.e., food, shelter, clothing) of one or more grandchildren who lived with them in 2010 (U.S. Census Bureau, 2012).

- Most grandparents raising grandchildren are in the 55 to 64 age range; however, approximately 25 percent of primary caregiving grandparents are age 65+.

- Grandparents from all ethnic groups are taking responsibility for their grandchildren, with Caucasians being almost half (47 percent) of all grandparent caregivers.

- Grandparents who are primary caregivers are more likely than noncaregivers to be living in poverty—approximately 19 percent are considered poor (American Association of Retired Persons, 2003; U.S. Census Bureau, 2001). Grandparents who are primary caregivers are likely to be female and living on a fixed income, so the additional expense of raising children may hit them hard.

Grandparents face many legal issues when taking on primary-care responsibilities for their grandchildren. Some of these issues include legal guardianship and financial and other supports (Kruk, 1994). For example, many grandparents may be eligible for support through Temporary Assistance for Needy Families (TANF), which is the program commonly thought of as "welfare." However, if the grandparent is the one receiving the grant, she or he is required to meet the work requirements mandated by the program. Grandparents can apply for a grant for their grandchildren, but these grants are limited in the amount of money awarded and the amount of time for which the grandparent can receive aid.

Some grandparents may also face challenges because they do not have legal custody of their grandchildren. In addition to the emotional issues that can surface when grandparents assume responsibility for their grandchildren, their authority and child-rearing efforts can be undermined when adult children reenter the picture. In some cases, grandparents are also grieving for their own children's situations when these children are overcome by drug, criminal, or health problems (Burnette, 1998). Many grandparents find that they are emotionally and physically overwhelmed by the complex challenges they face trying to balance relationships between their adult children and their grandchildren.

Social workers can assist clients who are providing care for their grandchildren to secure social services or other resources. Social workers may also need to help older clients cope with the challenges that often come with caregiving. For example, though parenting a grandchild can bring joy and satisfaction, it can also strain finances and relationships. It may also bring a wide range of feelings such as fear, anger, sadness, and resentment. And, though a caregiving relationship between a grandparent and grandchild might be positive for those involved, it may still take time for all those in the relationship to adjust. Social workers can help facilitate this adjustment and help clients to establish positive relationships.

Older Adults and their Caregivers

Increasingly, adult children and other family members are becoming the caregivers of their parents and older relatives. It is estimated that in 2009, over 42 million Americans were caring for an elderly or disabled loved one, and that number continues to grow (Feinberg, Reinhard, Houser, & Choula, 2011). Caregiving arrangements vary widely from family to family; but regardless of the situation, caregiving can take a large physical, financial, emotional, and psychological toll on adult children and other family members.

The majority of care for older adults is given by a spouse or an adult child, both of whom are usually female. Of adult children who are caring for elderly parents, approximately 75 to 90 percent are daughters who, on average, are married and working full time (Family Caregiver Alliance, 2003; Mellor, 2000). Adult children who are caring for their aging parents as well as their own children are said to be part of the sandwich generation, discussed in Chapter 11. Many of these caregivers find themselves pulling double duty as they struggle to care for an aging parent while raising their children and tending to other familial and work responsibilities. And, because many older GLBT adults do not have children or because of family issues, caregiving in the GLBT community is often done through non-traditional means such as friends or other non-legal relations like members of chosen families (Croghan, Moone, & Olson, 2014).

Unique caregiving issues are emerging for those in different ethnic groups, and these issues are changing the way children view caregiving for their elders. For example, a child caring for parents among Asian-American and Hispanic communities has been viewed as a tradition. However, the growing numbers of older adults in these groups as well as increasing numbers of families that are geographically dispersed are eroding this tradition. Families are struggling to find appropriate long-term care for their elders, particularly care that meets diverse cultural and language needs. These issues are not only arising in the U.S. but in other countries like China, and they are resulting in rising poverty and suicide rates among ethnically diverse elders. In 2012, for example, the suicide rate for Asian-American women aged 75+ was almost twice that of other women the same age (Department of Health and Human Services, 2014).

Effects of Caregiving on Caregivers A great deal of research has focused on the effects that caregiving can have on caregivers. Much of this research has pointed to feelings of fear, grief, anger, guilt, worry, sadness, fatigue, and isolation in the caregiver. These feelings can be even more pronounced among caregivers who are not employed outside of the home or who do not have a good support system on which to rely (Scharlach, 1994). A caregiver who is not able to address the stress of caregiving may experience more severe physical and mental health problems.

There are also financial consequences for caregivers, who are mostly women. They are more likely than noncaregivers to earn low wages, have jobs that offer few benefits, and experience many interruptions in steady employment—all of which have long-term ramifications and contribute to the poverty of women (Family Caregiver Alliance, 2003). Indeed, caregivers spend, on average, about 10 percent of their income on caregiving expenses. Many end up taking out loans, spending savings, and forgoing their own health care to help cover caregiving costs (National Alliance for Caregiving, 2007).

Caregiving for an older family member can bring many benefits to the caregiver and the family, however (Plowfield, Raymond, & Blevins, 2000). It can:

- enable family members to express love and commitment to other members;
- provide financial and emotional stability to the older adult and the family members;
- strengthen the bonds among family members;
- bring a sense of satisfaction and accomplishment to the caregiver.

Various services have been developed to help support caregivers and to provide respite for them—particularly those who are providing care for a victim of Alzheimer's disease—so that they can take care of themselves and address their other responsibilities. Services provided by professionals or financed by the government are referred to as **formal caregiving**. Caregiving that occurs within a person's environment, such as that given by family, friends, and church members, is considered **informal caregiving** (Pickens, 1998). Many formal caregiving services are described later in the chapter.

One way of viewing caregiving is through **exchange theory**, which examines the extent to which participants in a particular relationship are satisfied. Specifically, the more that people in a relationship feel overbenefited (they are getting more from a partnership than they are giving) or underbenefited (they are getting less from a partnership than they are giving), the more dissatisfied they will be (Berkowitz & Walster, 1976; Dowd, 1975, 1980). In a caregiving relationship, an older person who needs care may feel overbenefited because she or he is physically, cognitively, or emotionally unable to contribute. The caregiver may feel underbenefited because she or he constantly gives care but receives little in return. This dynamic may leave both parties feeling angry, resentful, and unhappy with the relationship.

Caregiving and Social Work   In working with caregiving situations, social workers can help clients to explore their feelings about the amount of effort and commitment they are contributing to a caregiving relationship and help clients to resolve negative feelings that may result from unequal contributions.

On a broader scale, social workers have assumed leadership in many areas of caregiving and services for older adults and their caregivers. Because of the potentially negative consequences of caregiving for older adults and their families, social workers need to focus on issues such as physical health, mental health, and access to resources. This leadership will become increasingly important as the older population grows. More and more people will be living in the community as they age, relying on family members for some form of care.

Judy's care needs provide a good example of how caregiving issues can create problems for older adults. Judy's daughter seems like a natural choice to provide care for Judy, but it appears that there are barriers—logistical ones, given that her daughter lives in another state—if not other, more personal factors keeping her daughter from being more involved in Judy's life. In addition, the level of care that Judy needs might be too advanced for her daughter to assume entirely on her own. However, there could be some roles that Judy's daughter could play to improve Judy's situation or at least to improve familial interactions. As the social worker, you may want to learn more about Judy's family dynamics to better understand how these relations are affecting Judy's physical and psychosocial health and whether any intervention could take place.

Elder Abuse and Neglect

One of the unfortunate side effects of caregiver stress can be elder abuse and neglect. Family members are the perpetrators of much of the mistreatment of older adults. Neglect, abandonment, physical abuse, sexual abuse, financial exploitation, and emotional or psychological abuse are all forms of maltreatment of older adults. Because many cases of abuse and neglect are not reported to authorities, only estimates exist on how many elders are abused or neglected each year.

A survey of state Adult Protective Services agencies showed that in 2004 approximately 566,000 cases of people aged 60+ being abused or neglected had been reported (National Committee for the Prevention of Elder Abuse and National Adult Protective Services Association, 2006). This was an increase of 19.6 percent over the 2000 survey. Exhibit 12.3 shows the breakdown of forms of abuse that were reported. Self-neglect—in other words, older adults reported by family, neighbors, and others for neglecting their own care—was the largest category, but 20 percent of cases were due to neglect or abuse by others. A more recent study of over 3,000 older adults found that approximately 13 percent had experienced some kind of abuse, and few had reported abuse by family members to authorities (Laumann, Leitsch, & Waite, 2008).

Most victims of abuse and neglect are age 80+. However, abandonment victims tend to be younger than 80. Over half of victims are women, and most are Caucasian. Most victims of abuse and neglect, about 75 percent, are frail and dependent on a caregiver (Administration on Aging, 1998).

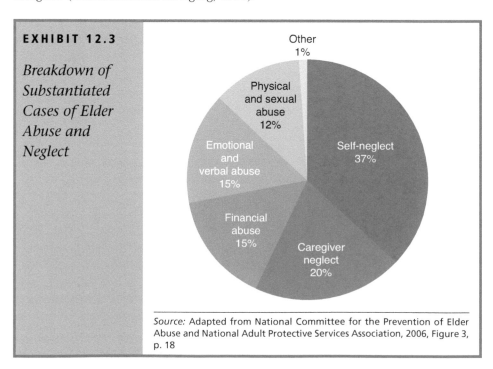

EXHIBIT 12.3

Breakdown of Substantiated Cases of Elder Abuse and Neglect

Other
1%

Physical and sexual abuse
12%

Emotional and verbal abuse
15%

Self-neglect
37%

Financial abuse
15%

Caregiver neglect
20%

Source: Adapted from National Committee for the Prevention of Elder Abuse and National Adult Protective Services Association, 2006, Figure 3, p. 18

Men tend to commit most acts of abuse, while women are responsible for the majority of neglect. Overall, about two-thirds of perpetrators of abuse and neglect are in the age range of 40 to 59 years old, and about three-quarters of them are Caucasian. Finally, nearly half of the perpetrators of abuse and neglect are adult children of the victims. The second most frequent perpetrators of abuse and neglect are spouses. When the adult child was financially dependent on the victim, the risk of abuse and neglect increased.

Exchange theory, discussed in the previous section, can help to explain how elder abuse and neglect occur. If caregivers feel that they are overextended with the amount of time and energy that they are putting into caregiving, they can experience feelings of anger and resentment, which in turn can lead to abuse or neglect.

Similarly, family systems theory can be used to help understand how family dynamics in a caregiving situation may lead to problems. A lack of homeostasis, changing roles and boundaries, and the need for adaptation can all pose problems for people struggling to adjust to a relationship in which caregiving and dependence are permanent defining characteristics.

Given the stress that caregiving can bring, as well as changes in the structures and responsibilities of contemporary families, social workers need to be cognizant of the potential for abuse and neglect of elderly individuals. When working with an older adult, social workers must include the caregiver and other familial support systems in the assessment. Assessment of the family situation can offer insights into potential risks to clients in late adulthood. However, because caregivers provide such crucial services to older adults, social workers also need to ensure that caregivers are getting the supports and services that they need to be effective care providers as well as healthy, happy individuals. Moreover, the caregiver's overall health is as important as that of the person receiving care.

THE LARGER SOCIAL ENVIRONMENT IN LATE ADULTHOOD

This section discusses broader issues that affect people as they age. Many of these issues have to do with policies and services that impact individuals and that influence the choices people make and the ways in which people live.

Long-Term and Alternative Care

Because people are living longer, an emerging issue in elder care is long-term care alternatives. The phrase "long-term care" often invokes images of nursing homes and other institutionalized care. However, those are costly options, and elders generally prefer to stay in their own community as long as possible. Thus **long-term care (LTC)** is really much more than institutionalized housing. It involves any set of services provided to people who need sustained help with ADLs and IADLs (National Association of Social Workers, 1987). Some people in the field are calling for LTC to be renamed "long-term living" to help alleviate negative and ageist assumptions about LTC (along with other language changes such as from "senior citizen" to "honored citizen").

This broad definition of LTC implies that care can be classified along a continuum (see Exhibit 12.4). This continuum is helpful in describing the levels of care that people might need at different points in their lives as well as the array of services that might be provided within each level. The services provided along the continuum can be given either in the home or in an institutional setting. They

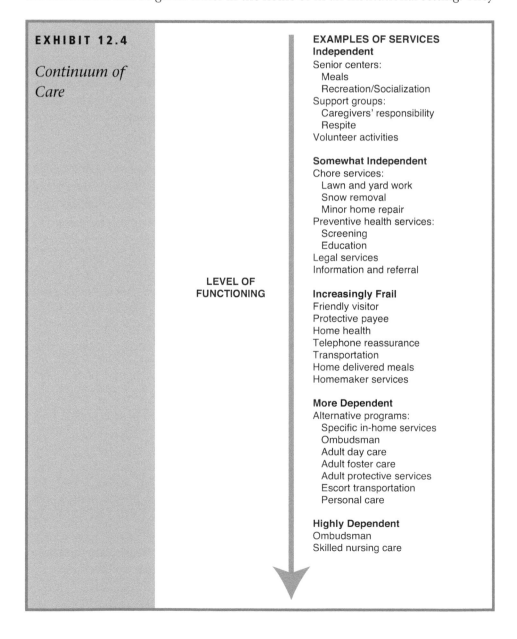

EXHIBIT 12.4

Continuum of Care

LEVEL OF FUNCTIONING

EXAMPLES OF SERVICES
Independent
Senior centers:
    Meals
    Recreation/Socialization
Support groups:
    Caregivers' responsibility
    Respite
Volunteer activities

Somewhat Independent
Chore services:
    Lawn and yard work
    Snow removal
    Minor home repair
Preventive health services:
    Screening
    Education
Legal services
Information and referral

Increasingly Frail
Friendly visitor
Protective payee
Home health
Telephone reassurance
Transportation
Home delivered meals
Homemaker services

More Dependent
Alternative programs:
    Specific in-home services
    Ombudsman
    Adult day care
    Adult foster care
    Adult protective services
    Escort transportation
    Personal care

Highly Dependent
Ombudsman
Skilled nursing care

are usually provided by skilled employees from various social service agencies and funded by a variety of sources. Some services are offered to all seniors, while others are targeted specifically to low-income seniors.

Often, agencies will employ social workers or other professionals to provide care management services. Care managers ensure that services are appropriate for the level of care needed and that services are not duplicated. Especially when services are tied to eligibility criteria, care managers are needed to assess individuals' level of functioning and economic status and to ensure that regulations are being followed.

Managed Care and LTC Insurance   With health care costs soaring, and older adults living longer and experiencing more chronic illness, long-term care options can be especially cost effective. The goal is to prevent more serious problems such as disability and institutionalization.

Managed care companies have entered the mix to try to cap spending on health care services. Many senior advocates fear that older adults will be harmed by this type of system. For example, managed care programs can dictate the number of days a person may be hospitalized based on the reasons for hospitalization (Atchley & Barusch, 2004). Unfortunately, many older adults who suffer from multiple health problems and whose recovery is longer than that for younger adults are discharged before they have fully recuperated. This premature discharge may place them at risk for developing other illnesses or becoming dependent on other caregivers for assistance while they recover.

LTC insurance was designed as a solution to financing care. Several private insurance companies now offer LTC policies that people can purchase in younger years to pay for care in older age. However, people who are struggling to afford health and other insurance that will cover their current needs are reluctant to buy a policy that will serve them only when they are older. Though these policies vary a great deal, they are mostly designed to pay for medical and other costs that occur when people need an ongoing high level of care such as that offered in skilled nursing facilities.

Because Medicare and many private insurance policies are limited in the coverage they offer for LTC services, many people find themselves spending all of their assets to pay for care when they get older. Once that happens, they become eligible for Medicaid, which will cover many LTC costs. However, many people do not want to use all of their savings and other resources for care, which makes LTC insurance a viable option for many seniors if they can afford it.

Housing Options   An issue related to LTC is housing for the elderly. Over the past few decades, various innovative housing options have become available for older adults. Housing options run the gamut from totally independent living to skilled nursing facilities (also known as nursing homes or transitional care units), where people can recover after being discharged from the hospital. These facilities offer intensive medical care for people who need extensive services and equipment, and they tend to be the most expensive option for care.

Between these ends of the continuum, there are several options:

- Boarding homes and group homes: For fully independent older adults. Residents usually share chores such as house and yard work, meals, shopping, and running errands.

- Congregate housing: For people who need minimal support. They live in one community of individual apartments or shared housing.

- Retirement or residential living options: For older adults who want their own apartments within a larger community of older adults. Generally, these communities offer services such as on-call health professionals, organized activities and recreation, transportation, and congregate meals.

- Assisted living facilities: For those who want private living quarters with more advanced services such as on-site medical and personal care. These facilities offer a bridge between living at home or in a retirement complex and living in a skilled nursing facility.

- Life care communities, or **continuing care retirement communities (CCRCs)**: For older adults who want to remain in the same facility regardless of their needs, which minimizes the disruption of moving. An older adult can initially move into an independent apartment and subsequently move to accommodations that offer higher levels of care as the need arises. Residents can maintain their friendships and their link to a community even as their care needs change. This arrangement is particularly helpful for couples in which each partner may be at a different level of functioning from the other and need different types of facilities. Couples can remain on the same grounds, which can greatly enhance the quality of life for both partners.

Be aware that gay and lesbian couples may not be permitted to share housing in many traditional facilities. However, housing communities for gay and lesbian adults are being developed nationwide to address this issue.

Sunset Homes, where Judy has been living, is a type of CCRC. Because Judy needs a fairly high level of care, she resides in a unit that provides some skilled care. However, this arrangement is quite expensive, so she has to rely on Medicaid to fund it. Medicaid eligibility requirements are becoming stricter in Judy's state, however, so as her social worker, you will have to find ways to continue funding her care.

One approach would be to have Judy's ADLs and IADLs reassessed. Because Judy has been living in Sunset Homes for three years, her activity levels may not have been assessed in a while and her care needs may have increased. A new assessment may more accurately reflect her current abilities, which could meet the new Medicaid criteria.

Another approach you could take is to appeal Medicaid's decision to cut funding for Judy. You could advocate on Judy's behalf to try to restore funding, even if Judy's needs do not meet new eligibility standards.

Finally, you could help Judy find housing elsewhere—possibly with her daughter—and contract with other agencies for in-home care. However, given Judy's situation, it is likely that Judy needs a variety of services and that her daughter would need extra support to prevent the problems that caregiving can create.

Poverty and Older Adults

Contrary to commonly held stereotypes of older adults being wealthy misers, many older adults, particularly women and seniors from ethnic minority groups, live on fixed incomes that barely provide basic necessities. The U.S. Census Bureau estimates that in 2012, nearly 9 percent of people age 65+ lived in poverty. When medical out-of-pocket expenses were deducted from the total income of people age 65+, the poverty rate jumped to 16 percent (DeNavas-Walt, Proctor, & Smith, 2013). Widowhood, disability, retirement, unemployment, chronic illness, medication costs, age discrimination, and increased costs of living can all contribute to poverty among older adults.

The poverty rate for some ethnic minorities is higher than the average. For example, in the 2012 Census Bureau study, the poverty rate for African Americans age 65+ was 27 percent; for Hispanics it was 25 percent; and for Asian/Pacific Islanders it was 11.7 percent. For Caucasians, the poverty rate was 12.7 percent. Poverty rates also differed by gender: The average poverty rates in 2012 were 13.6 percent for men and 16.3 percent for women (DeNavas-Walt, Proctor, & Smith, 2013).

Women and ethnic minorities are more vulnerable than Caucasian men to poverty in old age because they are also vulnerable to discrimination during their working lives. For example, many women and ethnic minorities earn less than Caucasian men over their lifetime, which means that they will have accumulated less in Social Security, pensions, and 401k accounts. Thus, payments they might receive from these sources are less than Caucasian men receive. The term **triple jeopardy** has been used to describe "female ethnic-minority elderly." Members of this particular group face discrimination in three ways—being a woman, elderly, and a member of an ethnic minority group—putting them even more at risk for poverty than other older adults.

Poverty can be a transitory problem for many younger adults, but it can be a permanent aspect of life for older adults (Hillier & Barrow, 2006; Quadagno, 2008). They have little opportunity to increase their income, and their expenses for medication and care tend to rise over time.

Living in poverty can lead to other problems for older adults such as stress, prolonged illness and disability, reduced access to health care, and poor living conditions. Poverty, then, becomes inextricably linked with other issues we have discussed, potentially decreasing the life satisfaction and well-being of many older adults.

Judy's case is a good example of how poverty can cause added stress in the lives of elderly people, especially when poverty is tied to health and other problems.

Policies Linked to Services for Older Adults

Many social service and other policies have been developed and enacted over the centuries to address the needs of the elderly population. Some of the largest and most successful pieces of legislation ever enacted in the United States have been those for the elderly.

Social Security   Many people use the term Social Security to describe the payments that older and disabled U.S. citizens receive. In reality, Social Security is a little more complicated. The Social Security Act, passed in 1935, provides Old-Age, Survivors, and Disability Insurance (OASDI). OASDI provides cash payments to retired workers and survivors of insured workers. Thus spouses of workers and their children younger than age 18 are also entitled to the worker's benefit should that worker die. In 1956, the Act was amended to provide payments to disabled workers and their families, known as Disability Insurance (National Association of Social Workers, 1987). Workers who suffer long-term (12 months or more) health or mental health disabilities are also entitled to Social Security.

The Social Security Act represents the first intergenerational contract to provide financial support to older adults. In order for it to pass, younger generations had to agree to pay taxes to support the current cohort of older adults, with the promise that the younger workers in turn would be supported once they turned 65. Social Security provides benefits to workers as an entitlement without any means tests or income tests. In other words, people are entitled to Social Security if they are able to work.

Social Security benefits are calculated through a complex formula that includes the total earnings of workers and the amount of time worked. As discussed previously, women and ethnic minorities tend to receive lower benefits than Caucasian men because they tend to earn lower wages. Further, their work is often interrupted due to childbirth, child care, and adult care. In addition, women and ethnic minorities tend to be overrepresented in part-time, contingent, and seasonal work, which means that they are often the first to be laid off in times of recession.

Older Americans Act   Congress passed the **Older Americans Act (OAA)** in 1965, at a time when concern over the poor and disenfranchised was fueling a sense of social responsibility to provide services for those who could not provide for themselves. It is a comprehensive piece of legislation that seeks to improve the well-being of older adults. The OAA consists of several "titles" that articulate the overall charge of the legislation (Administration on Aging, 2006). Exhibit 12.5 lists the titles and describes the basic functions of each.

TITLE I: DECLARATION OF OBJECTIVES AND DEFINITIONS

Objectives include aspects such as achievement of an adequate income in retirement, achievement of good health and mental health, access to affordable housing and services, opportunities for employment, benefits from continued research, and protection from abuse and neglect.

TITLE II: ADMINISTRATION ON AGING (AOA)

The AoA, housed in the Department of Health and Human Services, is charged with administering the OAA. It serves to administer funds and grants to social service agencies for the elderly, provide consultation and guidance to states, and manage resources allocated by the legislation. Title II articulates the responsibilities on which to base policies and services for older adults to ensure their well-being.

TITLE III: GRANTS FOR STATE AND COMMUNITY PROGRAMS ON AGING

This is the largest title under the OAA. This title articulates the responsibilities of the states and their respective State Units on Aging (SUA) and Area Agencies on Aging (AAA). SUAs are responsible for dividing states into service areas governed by AAA, which are entities that administer and manage local social service agencies. This title has several parts that describe particular services and programs that must be administered. These include access services such as transportation and case management, in-home services, legal services, supportive services, senior centers, congregate and home-delivered meals, disease prevention and health promotion services, and a national family caregiver support program.

TITLE IV: ACTIVITIES FOR HEALTH, INDEPENDENCE AND LONGEVITY

This title administers competitive grants to social service agencies and other organizations and institutions to carry out research and to develop programs.

TITLE V: COMMUNITY SERVICE SENIOR OPPORTUNITIES ACT

This title is charged with promoting part-time employment opportunities for unemployed, low-income older adults.

TITLE VI: GRANTS FOR NATIVE AMERICANS

This title provides advocacy for older Indians, Alaskan Natives, and Native Hawaiians. This includes culturally competent supportive and nutrition services. In 2002, a Native American caregiver support program was added to this title.

TITLE VII: VULNERABLE ELDER RIGHTS PROTECTION

This title establishes protective programs such as the ombudsman program; prevention of elder abuse, neglect, and exploitation; and legal assistance.

Source: Administration on Aging, 2006

EXHIBIT 12.5

The Older Americans Act (OAA)

The OAA has established a broad network of administrative bodies that assist in disseminating funding and services from the federal to local levels. The **Administration for Community Living (ACL)** was created in 2012 to help older adults remain in their communities. To this end, the ACL brings together the efforts of several organizations including the Office on Disability; the Administration on Aging; and the Administration on Intellectual and Developmental Disabilities to focus attention and resources on the needs of older adults and people with disabilities across the lifespan. Here, we focus on the structure and programs of the Administration on Aging:

- **Administration on Aging (AoA):** Federal body that oversees the administration of the OAA.

- State Units on Aging (SUAs): Responsible for organizing states into smaller service areas based on populations of older adults.

- **Area Agencies on Aging (AAA):** Entities in charge of each service area in each state and responsible for administering funds to local service agencies in various communities in each service area.

- Local service agencies: Provide services to older adults in their respective communities. Many services described earlier under "Long-Term and Alternative Care" are funded through the OAA and are provided by local agencies that contract with their AAAs to respond to the needs of older adults.

Exhibit 12.6 offers a visual overview of this administrative structure.

Many programs and services found in state and local governments are authorized through the OAA. Programs such as Adult Protective Services and mental health and health services are often provided through state, city, or county governments, or they are contracted out to local agencies through governmental agencies. For example, **ombudsman programs**, which offer advocacy for older adults who are residing in skilled nursing facilities, generally are offered through governmental organizations. Ombudsmen ensure that the rights of residents are being respected, and they intervene on behalf of residents if a skilled nursing facility is suspected of violating those rights.

Medicare A federal program enacted in 1965 under the Social Security Act, Medicare has two parts:

- **Medicare Part A:** Hospital insurance to cover hospital stays.

- **Medicare Part B:** Supplemental insurance that older adults purchase to pay for some costs not covered by Part A.

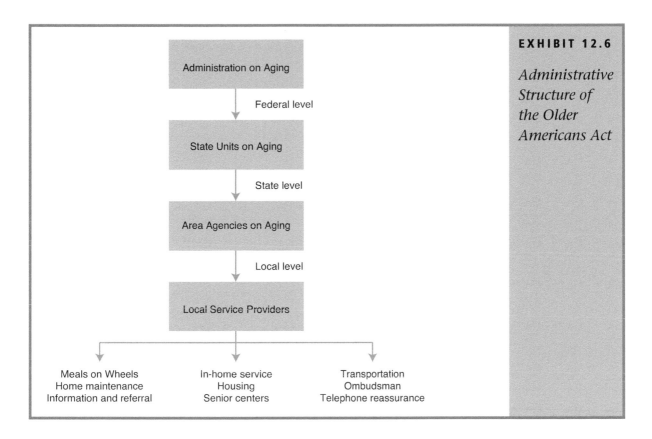

EXHIBIT 12.6

Administrative Structure of the Older Americans Act

Older adults age 65+ who are eligible for Social Security are eligible for Medicare Part A. Also eligible are disabled workers, disabled widows and widowers age 50+, workers who have disabled adult children (age 18+) who became disabled before age 22, and workers and family members who need kidney dialysis or transplants (Centers for Medicare and Medicaid Services, 2000).

Part A insurance provides limited coverage for costs incurred through hospitalization, skilled nursing facility care, and home health and hospice care. Coverage under Part A tends to be limited to basic services and has time limits on any one hospital or skilled nursing facility stay as well as lifetime limits on total care that people can receive. Further, insured older adults must pay deductibles, depending on the amount of time hospitalized. In May of 2014, the exclusion of coverage for sex reassignment surgery was eliminated because the procedure is no longer considered experimental. Medicare can now cover people seeking this surgery, and they can receive necessary hormone therapy through Medicare Part D, which covers prescription costs (National Center for Transgender Equality, 2014).

Because Medicare Part A coverage is limited, older adults are encouraged to purchase Part B or supplemental insurance. Part B insurance is designed to cover costs of services not offered through Part A, such as outpatient office visits, laboratory tests, and medical equipment. Although Part B can be useful in curbing health care costs, it too is limited as to which services it will cover. Moreover, premiums and deductibles may be cost prohibitive for low-income seniors. For example, the minimum premium for Part B in 2012 was just under $100 a month, which does not include the costs of deductibles for other services that older adults must pay (Centers for Medicare and Medicaid Services, 2012).

Another option available to older adults to defray the costs of health care are **Medigap** policies. These policies are designed to cover health services not covered by standard Medicare. Medigap offers an array of different policy choices, which are sold through private insurance companies that set the regulations and costs for each plan. Thus, costs for plans can vary a great deal from company to company. Depending on the policy, Medigap can cover such things as deductibles for Medicare, outpatient copayments, mental health treatment, prescription drugs, and other services such as preventive care.

Because of the complexity of Medicare and Medigap programs, seniors often need assistance in understanding the programs and wading through the policies, rules, and regulations for each one. Social workers can be very useful in helping older clients and their families to understand Medicare and Medigap programs and to help them choose plans that will meet their needs.

Although Judy has Medicare Part A, it is unlikely she has Part B or any Medigap policy. Even if she did, these policies would do little to help her in her current situation. Part A will help her should she need hospitalization or other types of rehabilitation, but it will not fund her long-term care needs. For those, she has been depending on Medicaid.

Medicaid   A health care program for the poor that is administered jointly by federal and state entities, Medicaid was also enacted in 1965. Older adults who are poor can become eligible for Medicaid even though they are already receiving Medicare benefits.

Many older adults cannot afford to purchase extra coverage through Medicare Part B or Medigap policies; thus, they often find that their assets are depleted rapidly when they experience a lengthy or expensive illness. For many seniors, the cost of prescription drugs alone forces them to spend far beyond their means. Thus, many older adults rely on Medicaid to cover their health care costs.

Many elders find that they need Medicaid when they suffer a debilitating illness that requires them to spend time in a skilled nursing facility. Medicare covers only a limited number of days in skilled nursing care, and many older adults cannot afford to pay for the care on their own. Thus, many older adults find themselves "spending down" their assets, or impoverishing themselves, until they become poor enough to become eligible for Medicaid. Medicaid offers more liberal coverage than Medicare, and many older adults come to rely on it to pay for the expensive care that can come with chronic illness and disability. Some of the services covered by Medicaid that are excluded by Medicare include homemaker services, eye and hearing care, and prescription drugs.

Social workers can be instrumental in helping clients to understand the Medicaid program and navigate the application process. Debates on Medicaid, Medicare, and Social Security reform are also ever present. Changes in these programs have a direct impact on elderly clients. Because laws and legislation can change rapidly, social workers need up-to-date information on these issues to support clients who might depend on these programs.

Because Judy's care has been funded through Medicaid, she will not have any substantial income or assets to help her purchase alternative care. As mentioned earlier, you will need to help Judy find other ways to tap into Medicaid funds for her care needs.

End-of-Life Considerations

Many people would like to have some control over end-of-life decisions such as pain management and the use of technology to extend life. They would like the right to live with dignity and the right to end life when pain and suffering outweigh the quality of life.

Many older adults who are terminally ill are able to exert considerable control over the dying process. However, more and more means are available to keep people alive. The availability of life-sustaining technology raises ethical questions concerning how far modern medicine should go in prolonging the dying process. Should we be keeping people alive at all costs just because we have the capability to do so? It also raises questions for people as they age such as how much control they will have over illness and health and whether family members and health care professionals will respect their wishes regarding these issues. Social workers, particularly those working in health care settings, need to be aware of local and national laws and policies that impact older adults as they approach the end of life.

Assisted Suicide   One of the most hotly debated end-of-life issues involves **euthanasia,** or assisted suicide. Euthanasia can be placed in two categories:

- **Active euthanasia,** also known as mercy killing or assisted suicide, involves a physician, friend, or family member assisting someone in terminating her or his life. An example of active euthanasia is administering lethal doses of drugs to the dying person.

- **Passive euthanasia** is the omission of acts that prolong life, such as withholding medications or nutrition or respecting a Do Not Resuscitate (DNR) order (Gorman, 1999). The omission of these interventions ultimately leads to death.

Much of the current debate over assisted suicide involves active euthanasia. Task forces of physicians, scholars, ethicists, and other professionals are discussing definitions of euthanasia and physician-assisted suicide and the ethical issues associated with them (Materstvedt *et al.*, 2003). For the most part, people in the United States have a right to refuse treatment if they are competent to make decisions. The courts agree that this right is constitutionally guaranteed (Pence, 1995). Indeed, for years, health care professionals have been allowing people to die through omission of treatment. However, active euthanasia is illegal in most states.

The debate over assisted suicide in the United States was brought to the forefront by people such as Dr. Jack Kevorkian, who helped several people end their lives in the 1990s. At the crux of his actions is the question of whether physicians have a duty to end patients' suffering or to preserve life.

Throughout the past couple of decades, several landmark laws and court decisions have pushed this debate even further. In 1994, Oregon became the first state to legalize physician-assisted suicide. Opponents of this law have since attempted to challenge it in court but have been unsuccessful. Washington became the second state to support such legislation, passing their Death With Dignity Act in 2008. Other states have also pressed the issue. Courts have responded with the argument that determining whether a terminally ill individual is competent to make this decision is questionable at best. There is a risk that people who are incompetent to make a life-and-death decision will be granted the right. Thus, through misuse of the law or through error, people who are not competent to make a decision on their own could die.

Other countries allow assisted suicide and have elaborate procedures for determining whether or not a dying person is a candidate. For example, the Netherlands requires that a request to die be voluntary, that the patient be informed, that the patient consistently expresses the desire to die, and that at least two physicians agree that the person is competent to make the decision. In addition, several national and international organizations support assisted suicide and offer supports and referrals to people wishing to die. For example, the Hemlock Society, which is active in some states, and Compassion and Choices, a national organization, advocate for the rights of people to make end-of-life decisions and campaigns for assisted suicide laws.

Advance Directives and Living Wills   One way in which people can become active in planning for issues that may surface during an illness or hospital stay is through **advance directives.** All states have legislation that allows patients to articulate in advance their wishes about the type of care they desire should they be admitted into a hospital. The Patient Self-Determination Act requires all health providers who receive government funding to offer patients the opportunity to complete advance directives (Cartwright & Steinberg, 1995).

These directives can be written into a **living will,** which provides detailed instructions about such things as the use of respirators or other artificial means of life support. Living wills can also appoint someone to advocate on the patient's behalf.

Palliative Care and Hospices   People who have life-limiting illnesses or injuries are increasingly making use of **palliative care** and **hospice care,** which seek to control pain and discomfort at the end of life. The goal of both is to manage pain and symptoms, not to cure disease. Both types of care are provided by interdisciplinary teams consisting of nurses; clergy; physicians; social workers; trained volunteers; home health aides; and speech, physical, and occupational therapists. Generally, hospice care is available to people whose life expectancy is six months or less, while palliative care is generally available to people who are in earlier stages of a terminal illness or injury.

Services, provided either in the patient's home or in a care facility, focus on giving medical, psychological, and spiritual support to people so that they may live as fully and comfortably as possible. Services include pain management; medical supplies; spiritual counseling; speech and physical therapy; care education for the patient's family; emotional support for the patient and family; and bereavement counseling for the family after the patient's death.

Many people have the misconception that choosing hospice or palliative care means that people are "giving up" on life. However, advocates point out that, by maximizing the dying person's comfort in multiple dimensions—physical, emotional, relational, spiritual—these services are an empowerment for focusing on life and living it to the fullest (National Hospice and Palliative Care Organization, 2012).

CONCLUSION

As you have seen, older age is a period in human development that can bring about many changes—although the amount and type of change vary widely from individual to individual. And, like any phase in human development, the aging process can be filled with rewards and challenges.

During late adulthood, the interplay of the physical, psychological, familial, and social can affect individuals personally and politically. In addition, cultural expectations of aging can impact the way individuals interpret the changes they are experiencing and how they react to them. The ways in which people develop throughout the life span also influence how they perceive and react to growing old.

As technological advances allow people to live longer, we will all face ethical and other challenges related to physical, spiritual, economical, psychological, and interpersonal well-being. Social workers need to be at the forefront of these challenges to help older adults work through issues that may impede development and to help them attain an acceptable quality of life.

MAIN POINTS

- Many physical, psychological, and social changes occur during the aging process; however, social workers need to be aware that these changes are different for each individual. Typical physical changes that occur as we age affect bone and muscle mass, hearing, eyesight, and reaction time.

- Some changes such as dementia and depression can be severe, but they can be mitigated by good health, spirituality, and social support.

- Some psychosocial theories on aging emphasize positive responses to the many changes that take place during late adulthood—for instance, finding self-worth through other means than work and physical abilities and staying as active and engaged as possible.

- A variety of theories and models attempt to explain grief and reactions to loss. The best-known is Kübler-Ross's five stages of death and dying: denial, anger, bargaining, depression, and acceptance. People may also go through these processes in coping with loss.

- Increasingly, families are relying on grandparents as child-rearing resources. Many grandparents who are rearing their grandchildren are 65+ years of age and are living in poverty.

- Adult children caring for aging parents is a major issue for many families. Caregiving stress can lead to serious problems such as depression and health decline for the caregiver.

- Some of the most serious issues facing older adults raise legal, ethical, and financial questions about their long-term health care and personal care. Poverty, which is inextricably linked with these issues, can be a permanent aspect of life for many older adults.

- Major government policies affecting older adults and their well-being are the Older Americans Act, Social Security, Medicare, and Medicaid. Social workers can be instrumental in helping clients understand and navigate these programs.

EXERCISES

1. *Carla Washburn interactive case at* www.routledgesw.com/cases. Review the case and answer the following questions:
   a. What physical and cognitive aspects might you want to assess with Carla and why?
   b. Given what you know about Carla and her situation, which theory of aging would you say best represents Carla's progression into older adulthood? Why?
   c. What information presented in this chapter might be useful in your work with Carla and why?
   d. In what ways could you work with Carla to help her move toward aging well?
2. *RAINN interactive case at* www.routledgesw.com/cases. RAINN staff are applying for a grant to use technology to reach out to an underserved population. RAINN is partnering with the Area Agency on Aging, which recently concluded through survey research that an increasing number of older adults are victims of sexual assault. What are some possible reasons why older adults are becoming more at risk for sexual assault (or at least that agencies are hearing about it) than in the past?
3. *Sanchez Family interactive case at* www.routledgesw.com/cases. Review the major micro, mezzo, and macro issues involving the Sanchez parents. After giving this information thorough review, answer the following questions:
   a. What biological and psychological factors might influence the Sanchez parents' aging process and how?
   b. What familial and community factors might impact their aging process and how?
   c. What theories or theoretical concepts might help in conceptualizing the aging process for the Sanchez parents?
   d. What policies might the parents need to rely on as they grow into older age? What barriers might they face in accessing resources offered by these policies?
4. *Hudson City interactive case at* www.routledgesw.com/cases. Review the case and answer the following questions:
   a. In what ways might the situation in Hudson City create problems for older adults?
   b. What theoretical or other perspectives could you use in working with older residents of Hudson City? How might these approaches be particularly useful for older adults?
   c. What strengths might older adults bring to the situation that could be useful in solving both personal and community problems?

Looking Forward: Challenges and Opportunities for the Social Work Profession

IN THIS TEXT, WE HAVE EXPLORED many issues that affect people and their well-being throughout the life span. We have examined how the relationship between human development and behavior and the environment interact to cause problems for people and bring opportunity for growth. And, of course, the relationship between human behavior and the environment is complex and ever changing. This is one reason why it is so important for social workers to consider the broader social environment when working with individuals, groups, and communities in the helping process. Similarly, because the interaction between human development and behavior and the social environment is so complex and dynamic, and the changes we see in these contexts are so fluid, it is imperative that social workers keep abreast of research and new developments in health, science, politics, education, environment, and a whole host of other realms.

In this final chapter, we will discuss some of the changes occurring in our world that will affect our development, behavior, environment, and the social work profession. Change brings ethical, practice, and other challenges as well as opportunities to reconceptualize theories and the ways in which we view and approach problems. Change also brings opportunities to improve circumstances and ways of doing things that can potentially maximize the growth and development of the people, organizations, and communities with which we work.

Here, we will first explore some of the major issues facing the profession in terms of human behavior and the environment, the ways in which social workers are responding to these issues, and opportunities these issues offer to the profession now and in the future. We will end by exploring potential future directions of the social work profession.

ENVIRONMENTAL ISSUES AND SUSTAINABILITY

In social work, we often think of the concept of "environment" as it relates to our immediate and larger social environment. Indeed, many theories we've covered in this text, such as systems and ecological theory, look at environment from this perspective. However, given climate change and other environmental concerns, many social workers are calling for our conceptualization of environment to increasingly include the physical, natural aspects of our environment and how the physical and social environment interact to affect people and their behavior.

Social work is concerned with social and economic justice, and this can be linked to environmental justice. It is important to think about how the social and physical environment impact environmental justice—such as equal access to natural resources, safe and healthy living environments, environmental health and sustainability, and other issues that impact the spaces in which people live. And because a primary concern for social work is the interaction between human beings and the social environment, we can see the importance of the physical environment in our well-being and survival. Our ecosystems depend not only on human beings' interdependence on one another and our social systems, but also on the physical ecosystems that impact aspects of our survival such as nutritious food, clean water and air, and healthy systems among animal and other species that help keep the environment in balance (Dominelli, 2011; McKinnon, 2008).

Social and Environmental Sustainability

Climate change and the social, economic, geographic, environmental, and other issues it brings will have profound effects on human behavior and development and how humans interact with the environment. It will bring many new challenges as well as opportunities related to how we live, interact with one another, use and conserve resources, and approach problems. When we think of climate change, we often think of global warming, extreme weather, and natural disasters. But climate change encompasses much more than changes in the weather. Viewed through systems theory, for instance, we as human beings and all other living creatures are connected to our environment and ecosystem, working together to maintain homeostasis for survival. Once part of the system is altered, in this case the environment, other parts of the system are affected and must adapt to find a new way of functioning (negative entropy) or they will die (entropy). We see humans attempting to adapt to these changes, while other parts of the ecosystem, such as certain species of plants and animals, are becoming extinct.

Climate Change and the Larger System

In thinking about a larger system, you can imagine the many ways in which humans and animals are impacted by climate change. For example, climate change affects our health, food supply, living conditions, and use of resources such as water, land, and fossil fuels. It affects the structure of communities, local and global economies, migration of global populations, and the ecosystem on which we rely to survive. Climate change has the potential to impact almost every aspect of our lives and the world in which we live (Natural Resources Defense Council, 2014).

Let us look at a few examples of how climate change has already affected our health, behavior, environment, and welfare. Degradation of agricultural soil among rural farms is not only impacting the food supply, but it is affecting social factors that keep rural communities alive such as declining populations; degradation of health, retail, transportation, and other services; and reduced governmental supports to invest in communities (Cheers & Taylor, 2005). Lack of fresh water and rainfall has been strongly associated with outbreaks of violence and war (Levy, Thorkelson, Vörösmarty, Douglas, & Humphreys, 2006). Young children, older adults, and others with compromised health and immune systems are ill equipped to deal with rising temperatures and other environmental changes, resulting in increased cases of asthma, malnutrition, infectious disease, mental health issues, and other chronic health conditions (Lam, 2007; McMichael, Woodruff, & Hales, 2006). Degradation of land, coastal ecosystems, and fisheries can be expected to result in increased and more severe natural disasters as well as loss of livelihood and displacement, leading to poverty, adverse health outcomes, and increased migration or "climate migrants" (Levy *et al.*, 2006; United Nations Environment Program, 2007; United Nations Development Programme, 2008). Increasingly, it is evident that our physical and social systems can and do reach critical tipping points that bring abrupt and irreversible changes affecting our health and livelihood (United Nations Environment Program, 2007).

Social Work's Role in Climate Change

Though climate change and its potential implications to our way of living seem particularly dire, the social work profession is in a unique position to intervene with the challenges caused by our changing ecosystem. Social workers already have been involved in the conversation about social and environmental change to help reconceptualize our views around climate change and the ways in which we approach problems stemming from environmental degradation.

Social work's comprehensive view of the interaction between person and environment provides a solid foundation on which to build conceptualizations of the natural and physical environment and its role in human behavior. In this way, our physical environment becomes part of the assessment process when looking at problems, and it becomes a crucial consideration when we conceptualize all that impacts our well-being. This makes it more likely that we will not only foster respect and care for our environment, but that we will focus on the ways in which the physical environment and climate change help or hinder the welfare of humans and other ecosystems that rely on it for life.

The social work profession is also well positioned to educate about and inter-vene with climate change from this comprehensive view of person-in-environment. For example, efforts could focus on promoting actions and policies that cut carbon emissions and increase our use of clean, renewable energy. Social workers can work on policy changes that help with community planning and preparing for flooding, drought, storms, and other consequences of climate change. Social workers already have the expertise to focus on capacity building for communities that will help build long-term environmental and social sustainability. These efforts can also focus on the ways in which climate change impacts human behavior and welfare through health and other implications, on micro, mezzo, and macro levels, and perpetuates social and environmental injustice by impacting poor, disenfranchised communi-ties and populations more severely.

Another way that the social work profession has been and could be address-ing climate change and impacts on human behavior is by emphasizing in its code of ethics the important link between the health of the physical environ-ment and the health of human beings. For example, the Australian Association of Social Workers includes "promot[ing] the protection of the natural environment as inherent to social wellbeing" in their code of ethics (Australian Association of Social Workers, 2010, p. 13). Social work values around social justice and anti-dis-crimination and oppression also can be used to guide future practices and poli-cies related to climate change. For example, social workers can advocate for green energy and technology that is accessible to all; work against practices that con-tribute to the degradation of our environment; advocate for fair immigration poli-cies that don't marginalize people as migration occurs due to climate change; and provide services and supports on the micro, mezzo, and macro levels for those affected by climate change, from individual needs to community, organizational, national, and global challenges brought on by climate change (Moth & Morton, 2009).

Given climate change and the unique issues it brings, the social work profes-sion has an unparalleled opportunity to renew and enhance its commitment to social and environmental sustainability and help to secure the long-term health and viability of our social and natural environment. This commitment takes vision and planning, not only short-term action. For instance, part of this work involves ensuring equitable access to services and resources among populations, genera-tions, and cultures; respecting diverse values and perspectives; increasing awareness of the issues and opportunities we face with climate change; understanding the importance of widespread political and community engagement; and empowering communities to identify its needs, strengths, resources, and capabilities in creating healthy, sustainable communities that support all its members (McKenzie, 2004; McKinnon, 2008).

ECONOMIC DISPARITIES

Social work has always been concerned with income and wealth inequality and poverty. This focus is one of the hallmarks of the profession, and working toward social and economic justice and equality is one of the values on which the profession is grounded. The emphasis on economic inequality has never been more important. Indeed, in 2013, President Obama remarked that income inequality is the "defining challenge of our time" (The White House, Office of the Press Secretary, 2013).

The Widening Gap between the Rich and the Poor

Worldwide, the gap between the wealthiest individuals and the poor is widening. Many factors are driving this gap, including economic philosophies and practices entrenched in the United States. For example, many economists and others posit that free-market capitalism has contributed to this gap, which is guided by the philosophy that income inequality will stabilize on its own if we leave the economic system unfettered by government intervention and regulation (Harvey, 2005). Economic policies during the Reagan era, supporting "trickle down economics," posited that tax cuts for corporations and wealthy individuals would encourage savings to be spent on goods and services, benefiting everyone (Parenti, 1999). And, many Americans believe that wealth and success are the direct result of hard work. However, in spite of these types of beliefs and practices, we have been experiencing increasing numbers of people living in poverty (Golash-Boza, 2015).

Over the past several decades, a small percentage of Americans have been able to amass huge fortunes from profits and salaries, which can be reinvested, resulting in even larger fortunes. Corporate profits are growing, while workers' salaries are stalling, and inherited wealth is growing faster than the economy, concentrated mostly among a small percentage of people (McCall & Percheski, 2010).

This phenomenon, along with others such as the economic downturn in 2008, poses a threat to the survival of the middle class, and it has many health, social, political, and other implications. Indeed, writers and theorists such as Karl Marx, discussed in Chapter 4, and Michael Harrington (1981), who wrote *The Other America: Poverty in the United States,* focus on the unequal distribution of wealth in the United States and its effects on individuals, communities, and our sociopolitical systems. Data from the United States Census Bureau (2013a) indicate that in the year 2013, the average household income was $51,017, roughly the same as it was a quarter of a century earlier. The proportion of the U.S. income that goes to corporate profits is higher than it has been since the 1920s; in contrast, workers' wages are the lowest since the mid-1960s when adjusted for inflation. The wealthiest 10 percent of Americans possess over half of the nation's income (Feller & Stone, 2009; Reich, 2010), and Thomas Piketty (2014), an economist at the Paris School of Economics, predicted that the richest 1 percent of the population might hold about half of the nation's income in the not-too-distant future. Economic disparities are also stark when viewed from the perspective of race and ethnicity: Black and Latino families possess only five cents of wealth for every dollar possessed by white families (Kochhar, Taylor, & Fry, 2011).

The technological and other advances made in recent decades have been astounding, and many Americans can benefit from these advances—but the American middle class has not gained greater economic security in the same time span, and its standard of living has actually decreased. Higher tuition, housing, and health care costs; student debt; housing bubbles; predatory lending practices; and increasing income inequality mentioned previously are all contributing to the erosion of the middle class. A study by the U.S. Department of Commerce (2010) suggests that dual-earner families making $81,000 in 2008—far above the median income reported by the Census Bureau—would have a more difficult time living a middle-class lifestyle (e.g., owning a home, taking a vacation, paying for college and retirement) than a middle-class family in 1990.

Wealth inequality also leads to profound deleterious effects in our political and other systems. For example, court decisions such as the Supreme Court's ruling in *Citizens United v. Federal Election Commission* have given the wealthiest individuals and their hired lobbyists unprecedented access to politicians and the political process, enabling them to funnel large amounts of money into campaigns to support specific candidates and special interests (Edgar, 2010). This phenomenon has the potential to continuously erode our democratic system and harm individuals and communities by focusing on the wishes of the wealthiest few (Gilens, 2005; Reich, 2010).

Outsourcing, Underemployment, and Livable Wages

About the same time as the country experienced the economic policies of the Reagan administration, we also saw increasing outsourcing of manufacturing jobs overseas and cuts to the social welfare safety net. This outsourcing has continued to decimate individual lives as well as whole communities, plunging people into poverty, near-poverty, and underemployed conditions (Golash-Boza, 2015). More recently, an increasing shift to an information-based economy caused by globalization has placed strain on global economies, displaced workers, deflated wages, and contributed to the increasing wealth of a small percentage of individuals (American Academy of Social Work and Social Welfare, 2013).

While unemployment continues to be an issue, underemployment is a particularly insidious problem that continues to disproportionately affect black and Latino workers. In 2013, 22 percent of black workers and 19 percent of Latino workers were considered underemployed, compared to 12 percent of white workers (Shierholz & Mishel, 2013). And, while nonwhites have a higher risk of being economically insecure than whites, the biggest increases in poverty rates are seen among whites. In a 2013 survey conducted by the Associated Press, more than 76 percent of whites reported experiencing joblessness or living at or close to poverty at some point in their working lives. For the first time in decades, the number of impoverished female-headed households surpassed other categories of impoverished households such as black family and Hispanic single mother households. Further, we are seeing an increase in the numbers of children living in impoverished neighborhoods (Agiesta, Junius, & McCown, 2013). Indeed, the U.S. has one of the highest rates of children living in poverty compared to other developed countries. In 2012, the overall poverty rate for children was 22.6 percent; for children in urban and rural areas, the rates of poverty were almost 30 percent and 26 percent respectively (Mattingly, Carson, & Schaefer, 2013).

Overall, approximately four of every five adults struggle with unemployment, near-poverty conditions, or reliance on welfare services for at least part of their lives, partly because of the loss of jobs in the U.S., the globalization of the U.S. economy, and the deterioration of the livable wage (Agiesta, Junius, & McCown, 2013). It is estimated that by 2030, almost 85 percent of all working-age adults in the U.S. will experience situational economic insecurity, especially as it becomes increasingly easier for individuals to become impoverished through situational factors such as illness, accident, mental illness, job loss, or death of a partner (Coleman, 2012).

Social Work and Responses to the Wealth Gap

It is possible that, eventually, economic disparity and wealth inequality will lead to public anger and outrage, resulting in broad socioeconomic change and reform. The social work profession can be at the forefront of helping communities move beyond outrage to organization and mobilization that leads to action. Using theories around social change and action and community organization discussed in Chapter 5, social workers can provide a great deal of leadership in mobilizing action leading to economic restructuring and change.

Given its value base, the social work profession has a responsibility to renew efforts to address issues of economic inequity and its impacts on individuals, families, and communities. Some social workers argue that the profession, in honing its focus on issues of diversity (e.g., with regard to race, ethnicity, and sexual orientation), has all but forgotten issues of socioeconomic class, particularly the middle class, and the socioeconomic problems that have contributed to the widening economic gap and resulting increased inequality (Coleman, 2012).

Social workers should guide efforts to not only curb the effects of current policies and practices that contribute to economic disparities, but they also need to be leading the development of innovative policies, advocacy, and interventions that turn the tide on harmful practices impacting the economic well-being of individuals, families, and communities. For example, social workers can advocate for federal minimum wage laws that provide livable wages. As of July 1, 2015, 29 states and the District of Columbia have minimum wages higher than the federal minimum wage of $7.25 per hour. However, five states do not have an established minimum wage.

Seattle will have a citywide minimum wage of $15.00 per hour by 2018, and several states including Connecticut, Maryland, Hawaii, and others have set or scheduled to phase in a minimum wage floor at $10.10 an hour (U.S. Department of Labor, 2014b). Social workers can have considerable impact on minimum wage legislation at local and state levels to increasingly set rates that support individuals, families, and communities.

Social workers also can be active in legislative and policy efforts that call for tax reform and regulation of financial institutions. Further, social workers can become involved in financial services and asset building consultations that give poor and middle-class individuals and families access to resources that help them build credit, secure mortgages, and save and invest money—avenues that can help people move out of poverty and build wealth that is sustainable over generations (American Academy of Social Work and Social Welfare, 2013).

HEALTH DISPARITIES

In previous chapters, we explored health disparities and their effects on individuals, families, and communities. While the Affordable Care Act has strengthened the health care safety net for many Americans, more effort is needed to reform our health care system, including improving access to care and reducing discrimination that contributes to health disparities. Given that health disparities persist and are becoming even worse for many minority groups, it is imperative that the social work profession becomes more engaged in creating systematic change in the health and mental health arenas.

Health Issues in Our Environment

We have not yet discussed in this text one issue that contributes to health disparities, increased health care costs, and increases in chronic disease. That issue is related to the toxins and chemicals in our environment as well as in food growing and production practices that affect our food supply. For example, research indicates that practices such as fish farming and antibiotics and growth hormones given to cattle and poultry are not only compromising the land and water used to grow our food but are disrupting the hormonal and other systems in our bodies (Centers for Disease Control and Prevention, 2013a; Food and Water Watch, 2014; U.S. Food and Drug Administration, 2014). Increases in cancer, endocrine disruption, and neurological problems have been linked to these practices. Factories and other industries that dump toxic waste into canals, rivers, and streams have been linked to severe health problems such as miscarriage, birth deformities, chronic illnesses of various kinds, cancer, and premature death. Chemically processed foods are generally high in salt, sugar, transfats, high fructose corn syrup, and other chemicals that are contributing to unprecedented rates of obesity, diabetes, and other health issues, particularly in the U.S. (Kenny, 2011; Schulze *et al.*, 2004). Many of these food processing practices disproportionately affect minority and low-income individuals and communities, as "junk food" is less expensive and more widely available in such communities. Historically, racial segregation has left many communities without grocery stores that sell healthy food. The same communities also lack access to affordable health care resources—which contributes to the increase in illness, disease, and poverty— and political and economic power to fight industries that pollute the environment (Williams & Collins, 2001).

Globally, decimation of natural resources and increased pollution are linked to increased health problems, and those in poorer countries, with few resources and political and economic power, are affected most (Donohoe, 2003; Rabinowitz & Conti, 2013). Further, when epidemics occur, such as the 2014 Ebola outbreak in West Africa, poorer communities with a lack of infrastructure to contain these diseases and lack of medical and other supplies to treat those who contract them suffer huge losses. Many people in these communities die, endure illness, lose their livelihoods, and leave children orphaned. Whole communities can be devastated by an outbreak of disease or natural disaster that taxes the community's abilities and resources to protect the health of its members.

Access to Health Care

Limited access to affordable health care and increasing health care costs continue to be pressing issues in the U.S. and many countries. Particularly in the United States, we see a widening gap between wealthy and poor individuals in the incidence of chronic illness and lack of treatment, particularly for those in minority groups. Earlier in the text, we discussed the deleterious effects that lack of health care has for minority populations. While some advances are being made to decrease disparities for some minority groups, many health issues persist for those in minority communities. For example, African–Americans, who disproportionately experience poverty, segregation, discrimination, and lack of access to resources also disproportionately experience poor health outcomes associated with situational and institutional racism and the lifetime of stress it causes (Golash-Boza, 2015). Those in the GLBT community, particularly transgender individuals, continue to experience discrimination, culturally incompetent care, and poorer health outcomes than those in other populations (Mayer *et al.*, 2008).

Social Work's Role in Reducing Health Disparities

Social workers can play vital roles in health and mental health arenas to help reduce health disparities and increase equal access to services and healthy environments. One area in which social workers make an important difference is in health research, legislation, and public policy. Social workers help inform and shape health care policy, educating legislators and administrators about the impact of health, environmental, and other policy on individual lives and communities. Social workers can also focus on legislation to help improve and support aspects of health care and resources that create equity and challenge dubious practices by employers, insurance companies, and health and mental health care providers. For example, the Affordable Care Act ensures people cannot be denied insurance due to preexisting conditions, increases the age that dependent children can be covered under parents' insurance policies, and does not allow most employers to deny benefits to certain groups (e.g., contraceptives for women). Further, Medicaid and Medicare now cover sex reassignment surgery, though often patients still need to advocate for themselves to take advantage of that coverage; and the Veterans Benefits Administration now covers certain treatments like hormone therapy, preoperative evaluations, and post-operative and long-term care for transgender individuals (National Center for Transgender Equality, 2014; U.S. Department of Veterans Affairs, 2014). Social workers can work to maintain and improve upon policies such as these. Social workers can also advocate for increased research funding that is inclusive of minority groups to ensure that health practices are representative of the needs of diverse groups and take into consideration geographical segregation that perpetuates inequalities.

The social work profession is also in a position to increase efforts in the health care arena to provide culturally appropriate and competent care and practices, particularly since many minority groups, historically, have experienced unethical and discriminatory treatment, often with deadly consequences. Because of this, there has been an erosion of trust among diverse groups toward mainstream health care institutions and health providers, which further contributes to disparity issues. Social workers can help build trust among communities and health providers as well as promote health care that is inclusive of the views and practices of diverse groups and empower communities to provide culturally appropriate care for their members. This can include supporting programs and policies that offer equal coverage, particularly for vulnerable populations, and working toward parity for health and mental health coverage.

More work is also needed to shape health policies that better support individuals, families, communities, and the environment in which we live. For example, social workers can work toward implementing and improving policies around paid leave for events such as birth, illness, caregiving, and the death of loved ones. And, social workers can lead environmental justice movements in communities to improve conditions and the right to live in healthy, toxin-free, sustainable environments.

DEMOGRAPHIC SHIFTS

Many global and national demographic shifts are occurring that will have long-term social, political, economic, and other effects on our well-being. More than ever before, social workers are facing great challenges and opportunities brought on by changes in the make-up of community, particularly with regard to age and ethnicity.

Global Aging

The aging of the population is a worldwide trend. Since the mid-20th century, not only have medical advances enabled people to live longer, but access to family planning has increased and cultural norms have increasingly valued smaller families. The resulting decline in birth rates has left a "bump" in the proportion of older people in the population. In the United States, there were a little over 43.1 million (13.7 percent) people aged 65 and older in 2012. By the year 2020, that number will rise to 54 million, and by 2050, 20 percent of our population will be over the age of 65. Further, the oldest-old, those 85 and older, are the fastest growing cohort, predicted to increase by 350 percent by 2050 (Administration for Community Living, 2014). Other countries are experiencing similar trends in the aging of their populations.

This population aging will have long-lasting, significant impacts on our economic, health care, and other systems. Advances in technology and health care mean that people are living longer, but often with chronic health care issues and needs around transportation, caregiving, and living arrangements. And while older adults increasingly will be better educated and enjoy more socioeconomic resources than past generations, many older adults continue to live in poverty and rely on federal programs like Medicaid, Medicare, and Social Security. Benefits from these programs are not sufficient to meet the needs of many older adults, and because of the growth of the older population, the ability for these programs to remain solvent in the near future is in question (DeNavas-Walt, Proctor, & Smith, 2013; National Center for Health Workforce Analysis, 2006; Weiner & Tilly, 2002).

Another major challenge that comes with the aging population revolves around service provision. Aging often brings with it chronic illness and disability that necessitates more and different types of care than is needed by younger populations. A growing older population means a greater demand for these services; however, our service system is not necessarily prepared to meet this demand. Many service providers and systems are not adequately trained to work with diverse older populations and their unique needs, particularly for the growing populations of older ethnic minority individuals (National Center for Health Workforce Analysis, 2006).

As was discussed in Chapter 12, the aging population will bring challenges to informal and formal caregiving. Families will continue to struggle with caregiving responsibilities, and communities will need to find inventive ways to adapt to changing demographics and needs of older residents. New ways of thinking about supportive services for families, older adults, transportation, and living environments are necessary. Changes in technology that help prolong life bring with them ethical dilemmas about end-of-life decisions and other health issues, but they also bring opportunities to help older adults remain independent in their own homes longer. More on technology will be discussed in the next section.

Changing Ethnic Demographics

Many demographic changes with regard to ethnicity are taking place worldwide, due to aging, immigration, and other factors. According to the Pew Research Center (Passel & Cohn, 2008), by the year 2050, non-Hispanic whites will no longer be the majority group in the U.S.; they will make up only 47 percent of the U.S. population. Hispanics will account for 29 percent of the U.S. population, blacks 13 percent, and Asian Americans 9 percent. Indeed, ethnic minorities account for almost 92 percent of the U.S. population growth over the past decade (Pew Research Center, 2011). Part of this trend in diversification of the population includes older adults, a group that will become more ethnically diverse than in the past (National Center for Health Workforce Analysis, 2006); people living in rural areas (Lichter, 2012); and mixed-race populations (Kotkin, 2010).

These demographic changes will come to bear on many areas including politics, economics, education, caregiving, health care, the workforce, voting patterns, family structure, living arrangements, community infrastructure, the nature of service delivery, and interracial relationships and communication. There is evidence to suggest that increased ethnic diversity has economic and other advantages that can improve the lives of individuals and communities. For example, in the past decade, even during the recession, we have seen increased numbers of minority-owned businesses. Further, studies suggest that diversity in business, schools, and other working groups increases financial and organizational performance because a diverse workforce tends to bring different perspectives, creativity, and skills to learning, planning, and problem solving. All of this contributes to healthier and stronger social, educational, economic, and other institutions (Page, 2007; Slater, Weigand, & Zwirlein, 2008).

Racism and Prejudice

Throughout the text, we have discussed issues of racism and prejudice and how they play out on micro, mezzo, and macro levels. While social work as a profession has helped to promote equality and work toward social and economic justice for minority populations, there is still much work to be done. Individual, institutional, cultural, structural, and systemic racism and prejudice are still entrenched and widespread in U.S. society. And, with the increasing diversity of the U.S. population, racism and prejudice will continue to be an important focus of the social work profession.

According to a Pew Research Center survey (2013), fewer than half (45 percent) of people in the U.S. feel that gains in racial equality have been made over the past 50 years. In the same survey, almost a third of black respondents (35 percent), 20 percent of Hispanic respondents, and 10 percent of white respondents said they had been treated unfairly because of their race in the past year. Persistent and widening gaps can be found between blacks and whites with regard to income, wealth, poverty, incarceration, marriage rates, single parenthood, and home ownership. And, segregation in our communities and institutions continues to persist, creating socioeconomic inequality for minority groups (Golash-Boza, 2015). Conversely, gaps have narrowed between blacks and whites in the areas of educational attainment, life expectancy, and voter turnout (Pew Research Center, 2013), suggesting that positive change is possible.

Unlike racism and prejudice in our history, when bigotry, hatred, discrimination, and oppression were much more overt and socially acceptable, racism and prejudice have become more covert, subtle, and ambiguous, making them, in some ways, more difficult to identify and address (Sue, 2010). Racist attitudes and prejudices tend to remain embedded in our cultural values and beliefs, which then become part of our institutional infrastructure, playing themselves out in policies and practices (Sue, Capodilupo, Nadal, & Torino, 2008). Sometimes these racist practices come to a boiling point, sometimes violently, where they are exposed and can be examined—for example, the racist practices that led to the 2014 police shooting of unarmed black teenager Michael Brown and resulting riots in Ferguson, Missouri. But more often than not, racism and prejudice are nebulous, almost unconscious, and allowed to play out "under the radar." Thus, it can be much more difficult to pinpoint the source of racist practices and to intervene against them. Some of the names for these more recent manifestations of racism include modern racism (McConahay, 1986), symbolic racism (Sears, 1988), and aversive racism (Dovidio & Gaertner, 1996). Microaggressions, discussed in Chapter 5, are another way that racism is played out in more subtle ways than it was in the past. These different forms of racism highlight that even the most well-intentioned individuals cannot be immune from inheriting racial biases that are embedded in our culture, which often lead to discriminatory actions.

Social Work and Demographic Shifts

As we have discussed, the social work profession adheres to values and ethics that promote cultural competence and social and economic justice. These values can help guide social workers as we face existing and new challenges around changing demographics and forms of racism and prejudice. Using some of our existing theoretical perspectives, social workers can respond to these challenges in many ways including providing education, advocacy, community development and empowerment, and support of policies and legislation that create equity in areas such as jobs, education, service access, and more humane handling of immigration.

As we experience demographic shifts, social workers can work with institutions and communities to adapt to population changes and the opportunities and challenges they bring. Both rural and urban areas will need to address unique needs, and social workers can bring organization and practice perspectives and skills to help communities meet challenges and needs and capitalize on opportunities, helping communities thrive.

Part of this work involves a continued commitment to cultural competence and agility as we interface with diverse individuals and communities. Social workers need to develop a comprehensive view of cultural competence, which is not just limited to attending to facets of difference like culture, religion, and labels. It also includes critical thinking about and reflection on the roles race and ethnicity play in power dynamics and personal and professional relationships, and how race and ethnicity are impacted by historical, political, socioeconomic, and multiple other forces (Garran & Rozas, 2013; Seipel & Way, 2006).

Some of this work can take the form of changing our language and understanding of race as socially constructed for the purposes of discrimination and oppression based on skin color and other physical characteristics to maintain socioeconomic and political power. Attending to language usage is one way to highlight the significant role it has in maintaining power imbalance and discriminatory treatment of certain groups. It also calls for social workers to become even more self-reflective of their views and biases and to better understand their own history and its impact on their beliefs about different groups. This can be accomplished, in part, by reflecting on their own privilege and how they have perpetuated and continue to perpetuate oppression, discrimination, microaggressions, and other subtle forms of racism through attitudes, beliefs, and everyday actions, which play out in their practice. Committing to and using approaches that call for cultural humility and agility such as critical practice theory, discussed in Chapter 4, and anti-oppression practice, discussed in Chapter 5, can help social workers embark on this self-reflection by examining larger, macro forces that may be reinforcing racist and prejudiced attitudes and beliefs. In turn, social workers can change their own practice and help to dismantle prejudice and discrimination in larger institutions and culture.

TECHNOLOGY AND TECHNOLOGICAL ADVANCES

Advances in technology, health care, and medical and other sciences are bringing sweeping changes to the way we view a whole host of issues affecting every aspect of our everyday lives. Areas such as aging, caregiving, relationships, health care, living arrangements, service provision, and beginning and end-of-life care are being transformed by emerging technology. This transformation also brings with it ethical considerations and controversial debates about how to use technology in our lives as well as whether or not certain technologies should even be developed.

Aging, Caregiving, and Aging in Place

Earlier in this chapter, we discussed issues around global aging. In the face of these changing demographics have come technological advances to address the unique needs of older adults. For example, one major challenge to our aging society is related to living arrangements and caregiving. Many older adults prefer to age in place, and remaining independent for as long as possible is not only desirable for many people, but it is a cost-effective alternative to assisted living or skilled nursing facility placements (National Care Planning Council, 2014). To help facilitate and support independent living arrangements, in-home technology is being developed that tracks the movements and behaviors of older adults. The goal of this technology is to predict health-related and other problems that can compromise independence, leading to preventive interventions before these problems cause immobility or other health problems that require full-time care (Oregon Health Sciences University, 2014).

Living and community designs are being reconceived not only to maximize the health and social benefits of older adults, but to enrich the health and welfare of entire communities by promoting healthy intergenerational relationships and support. For example, models of intergenerational community living that have existed for decades are being revived and reinvented to encourage mutually beneficial intergenerational relationships. One such model is Generations of Hope, in which older adults provide childcare for working parents who adopt foster children (Eheart, Hopping, Power, Mitchell, & Racine, 2009), all of whom live in the same housing community. Viewed through the lens of Erikson's theory, this living arrangement allows individuals in each generation to work on developmental tasks in a supportive environment that may not have existed otherwise. Children receive care and guidance from several adults who can help them develop independence, identity, and intimacy; parents receive support and child care while working full time, allowing them to invest in work, family, and community; and older adults have the opportunity to work on integrity as they provide an invaluable service to families and the community. These older adults not only help with child care duties, but they provide mentorship to younger children and their parents. Older adults are able to maintain social roles, and in turn, a sense of self-worth and purpose.

Technological advances are also being made in caregiving. Applications that track medications, health care appointments, and other logistics provide much needed support to independent-living older adults as well as informal caregivers, who often find these tasks overwhelming. In several countries, including Japan, social companion robots are being designed to provide reminders about medications and appointments and encourage exercise, healthy eating, and social activity. Other approaches that allow for remote caregiving are becoming increasingly popular. These include computer and video technologies, such as telehomecare, that facilitate remote communication and monitoring. Through these methods, health care providers and other caregivers can monitor such things as older adults' vital signs, mobility, and medications as well as communicate about test results, nutrition, and pain management. These methods allow caregivers to collect a whole host of data on older adults to track health and other issues that might compromise independence. It also allows for care to be given even when older adults and their caregivers are geographically far apart (National Care Planning Council, 2014).

Health, Mental Health, and Social Well-Being

Huge strides are being made in the health and mental health arenas with regard to technology. Advances in the medical sciences are transforming the ways we view health and mental health issues as well as the ways we treat them. For example, through technology, we can now perform womb, retina, and face transplants; grow bodily organs from stem cells; print bodily organs and other items from 3D printers; use mobile phone apps and technology to help children with autism interact with others; freeze eggs to implant later in life; and even have technology implanted into our bodies to facilitate internet searches, purchase products, or see color in the case of colorblindness. We also have the capability to genetically modify food and use pesticides and other chemicals to make our food supply more robust—though, as discussed earlier, the long-term impacts on our health and environment from such engineering and practices can be deleterious. The implications technology has for addressing problems such as food insecurity, reproductive issues, cognitive and physical disabilities, and social interactions are endless.

Social and other media make it possible to remain constantly connected to others, find sexual and relationship partners, provide health care and caregiving (as discussed earlier), and provide remote mental health therapy and other supports. For example, location-based social network apps like Tinder and Grindr allow people to find and get together with others who are in close geographical proximity; avatars can be used remotely by therapists to help people with agoraphobia by having clients assume an identity via computer that can be exposed to social situations without the client ever having to leave the house; and social workers and other helping professionals can provide therapy and outreach via Skype and other social media. And, increasingly we are pushing the boundaries of life and death through the use of technology at both the beginning and end of life.

Probably more than in any other area, technological advances are raising many ethical issues with which social workers need to grapple. Privacy, confidentiality, and efficacy issues have been key concerns for social workers with the increase of online and remote technologies to provide services, including mental health therapy. Further, there are serious privacy and confidentiality concerns related to the use of small, unobtrusive mobile devices that record or communicate remotely; wearable technology such as Google Glass, "smart" neckties and wristwatches, and other "fashion electronics"; and technological implants such as recording-communicating microchips and even "smart" tattoos. These issues are important not just for helping professionals, but also for the general public who use such technologies or associate with others who do (Tehrani & Michael, 2014). Indeed, a novel set in the not-too-distant future, *Super Sad True Love Story* (Shteyngart, 2010), bases its premise on a social world in which we all wear electronic devices that track every piece of personal data, including others' assessments of our attractiveness, which is then broadcast publicly. Imagine a world where our demographic information, economic situation, and health and mental health status are made public on a daily basis. Perhaps this scenario is not too far off in the future.

The corporate employers Facebook and Apple announced in 2014 that they would offer egg freezing to delay motherhood as a benefit to their female employees (CNN Money, 2014), and other employers may not be far behind. While egg freezing was a technique initially developed for women undergoing cancer treatment, it is quickly becoming a workplace commodity to attract female workers who can now choose to postpone pregnancy to focus on their careers. However, some argue it is a way to exploit women, sending mixed messages about the worth of women and motherhood and relieving companies from addressing reasonable work–life balance.

And debates rage on about how and when technology should be used in beginning- and end-of-life care. Should we use technology to allow a severely premature infant to live, even if the baby will suffer significant cognitive and physical disabilities throughout life? Should we use technology to keep someone alive who likely will remain in a vegetative state? Do we want to develop technology that will allow us to live beyond the age of 130, even if quality of life suffers? Can technology give us extended quality of life? Advances in technology have spurred the passage of laws such as Death with Dignity and policies around advanced directives to help ensure people have choices about end-of-life care. For example, in a well-publicized case in 2014, 29-year-old Brittany Maynard moved from California to Oregon to take advantage of Oregon's Death with Dignity law after being diagnosed with a terminal brain tumor. Much debate surfaced after she made her situation and choice public.

Social networking also has raised issues about how these platforms are transforming sexual and other relationships and communication. Many argue that social media has made it easier for people to connect to others and communities, while others argue that this media has promoted more superficial sexual and other relationships, destroying our ability to communicate in meaningful ways and form deep connections with others. We have seen that social networking can be extremely successful in promoting causes and fundraising, but it also can be highly destructive when it is used to malign or attack individuals or groups. Social workers are and will continue to be at the forefront of helping to shape debate on these and other issues and tackling the ethical issues technological advances bring.

Social Work and Technological Advances

There are many ways in which social workers can respond to technological advances. From biopsychosocial and ecosystems approaches, for instance, social workers can think about how technology affects people on micro, mezzo, and macro levels and the benefits, challenges, and ethical dilemmas it might pose. From these perspectives, social workers can ensure that people have equal access to technology that is helpful and improves well-being; be critical thinkers about how technology affects relationships and our everyday lives; advocate for legislation and policies that promote as well as regulate technology; and be leaders in discourse on the ethics of various technologies and how they are and will be used, for example in reproduction, end-of-life care, online counseling, use of green technology, and decision making about how technology is allocated to different groups. Social workers already help individuals think about end-of-life planning such as advanced directives and use of services like hospice and palliative care. But social workers can go further in helping people think about options like physician-assisted suicide, and they can help shape the debate about how and when technology should be used at the beginning and end of life and the implications on individuals, families, communities, and institutions as we develop new technologies that extend life.

As the world's population continues to age, social workers are taking leading roles in community and service development to help support older adults and their families and communities. The opportunities are endless in the realm of independent and community living for older adults as well as other social, familial, and health services aimed at supporting caregivers and keeping older adults independent for longer periods of time. And, in thinking about aging according to Erikson's theory, for example, there are many opportunities to help support integrity as we age—from new thinking on retirement and activity to innovations on health care and end-of-life support.

GLOBAL TENSION AND VIOLENCE

The social work profession has long been concerned with international issues and the ways in which we are all connected and impacted by global events and interconnections. And with advances in technology, the global landscape is shrinking and becoming even more accessible to everyone, bringing us closer together in a global community.

Increasingly, specific global issues are becoming even more important and impactful to our well-being, and social workers in the U.S., even if they never leave their hometowns, are interacting with others in ways that highlight our growing global interdependence. One devastating example of this is the terrorist attacks in New York on September 11, 2001. This event had and still has far-reaching, complex impacts on individuals, communities, and systems with which many social workers interact. And, this event has brought needed awareness of the global issues and tensions leading to such a tragedy. It is critical that social workers better understand cultural, historical, religious, economic, political, geographical, and philosophical issues and differences of our communities, both locally and globally, as they will continue to impact our world.

As globalization increases, so does our contact with one another, bringing opportunities and challenges to our efforts to respect differences, capitalize on similarities, and live together harmoniously. Globalization has offered great opportunities for individuals, communities, and organizations to develop creative intercultural collaborations that help to solve problems and promote community development and health. It also has brought increased religious and cultural tensions resulting in war, terrorism, violent conflict, and increased threats of biological and nuclear warfare. These issues have serious impacts not only on the people directly involved in the conflicts, but on all of us around the world. For example, social workers often work with people returning from war, emigrating from conflict-ridden areas, or suffering from posttraumatic stress disorder after experiencing a traumatic event. Social workers, for instance, might be asked to help with hundreds of parentless children fleeing South America being held in U.S. detention centers. Or social workers might work with families impacted by international kidnappings or terror attacks. Global issues change the way we view our world and live within it.

Social Work and Global Conflict

The social work profession has a responsibility to engage in a global worldview, examining how global issues impact individuals, families, communities, and institutions globally and locally. Cultural competence plays a key role in understanding and working with global issues like terrorism and violence. Much of what we have talked about in this chapter—climate change, shifting demographics, economic and health disparities, among others—plays a role in global conflict. Advocating for policies and legislation that are sensitive to global conflict and tension and how they impact the welfare of people is an important part of international social work. Working toward economic, environmental, and social justice is also an important aspect of international social work. Social workers can be leaders in terms of educating policy makers and others about these issues, helping to shape the way we see the world and work to solve problems.

SHIFTING CULTURAL VIEWS ON SOCIAL ISSUES

In addition to globalization, and perhaps, in some ways, in response to it, we are seeing many shifts in our cultural views and attitudes on social and related issues. One area where this is apparent is views on homosexuality. For example, just in the past decade, we have seen sweeping changes on attitudes around same-sex marriage, culminating in the 2015 Supreme Court ruling that such marriages must be recognized nationwide. In addition, we are seeing other changes in attitudes around marriage in general, with approximately 42 million (about 20 percent) U.S. residents age 25 and above who have never been married. These shifts have ramifications not only for family structure, but also for policies dealing with taxes, entitlements, and child guardianship (Pew Research Center, 2014b).

Other cultural shifts that have been occurring include changes in attitudes about legalized drugs like marijuana for both recreational and medicinal use; innovative ideas around sustainable community living; shifting ideas about the meaning of higher education and its costs; and changing attitudes about end-of-life care, how we die, and even burial practices. For example, many are challenging the meaning of college degrees and whether or not the cost for higher education is worth it. The emergence of massive online open courses and distance education is changing the way we view and even value higher education as well as how marginalized populations (e.g., people living in poverty or in rural areas) access it.

Earlier, we talked about technology prolonging life, which has spurred debate about the ethics of using it to extend life, particularly in dire situations, and the autonomy people have in making end-of-life decisions. Movements in hospice and palliative care have helped shaped this conversation, bringing attention to the quality of life during chronic illness or after sustaining life-threatening trauma. Further, death and burial practices are being re-examined, with people questioning established practices of dying in hospitals, families incurring the costs of expensive funerals, and the environmental sustainability of traditional burials. For instance, we are seeing an increase in the use of green burials in which bodies are not infused with chemicals and are buried in designated green spaces without caskets or markers. More people are opting for "fun" funerals in which their bodies are dressed and posed in situations they enjoyed when living. A recent *New York Times* article featured several funeral homes in Puerto Rico and New Orleans that have staged bodies on the wishes of the deceased or family. Examples given include a boxer who was posed in the corner of a boxing ring for his wake, a grandmother who was propped up in her rocking chair, and a paramedic staged behind the wheel of his ambulance (*New York Times*, 2014).

Social Work's Role in Cultural Change

Social workers can be leaders in thinking about cultural and philosophical shifts in our views on various issues. We can be advocates for new, inventive ways of thinking and problem solving that improve our well-being and promote equity. By serving as leaders in this regard, we have opportunities to shape the conversation about change to ensure that change and our reactions to it are not based in fear, stereotypes, or lack of information. Rather, social workers can bring empirical evidence, practice experience, theoretical perspectives, and information based in the profession's values to help support cultural change in ways that promote fairness, equity, and sustainability for individuals, communities, and institutions. And, social workers can help elucidate the possibilities and opportunities that change can bring without further marginalizing vulnerable groups.

THE FUTURE OF THE SOCIAL WORK PROFESSION

As you probably have gathered by the discussion above, it is both an exciting and challenging time to be a social worker and for the profession as a whole. So much in our world is changing very rapidly, which raises many problems and obstacles but also presents great opportunity. Change not only requires the social work profession to reconsider its purpose, perspectives, and methods but also paves the way for social workers to be more creative and expansive in the way we think about, approach, and intervene with problems. It is a time when social workers have a great deal of potential to influence lives and our environment on every level.

Given the changes we are seeing in our world, various social work organizations have been developing strategic plans for the profession to address these changes as they impact individuals and the environment, and to anticipate problems and opportunities they will create. For example, in 2010, several hundred social work leaders convened to discuss issues facing the social work profession and our role and purpose in light of local and global shifts. The themes that emerged from this discussion included the need for leadership development, management skills, and educational support among social workers. Specifically, participants saw the need within the profession for training in use of technology that ethically and practically serves clients and consumers, business and management practices that support services, recruitment and retention practices to build the profession and highlight the value of social work education, practices that increase social work's influence in government and industry, and strategies that identify emerging leaders in the profession (National Association of Social Workers, 2010).

Another group of social work educators and professionals has been working on a document outlining the current and future "grand challenges" of the profession. In this document, the core values of the profession along with its philosophical base and purpose are articulated to highlight how the profession is already poised to provide leadership in the years ahead. This includes the profession's emphasis on the person in environment as well as on worth, dignity, agency, capability, and difference of individuals. It also includes the profession's emphasis on the "social" in a world that has been increasingly placing importance on individuality. The changing context in which social workers will be practicing necessitates a plan for the profession to proactively meet the challenges we face as well as to participate in creative, innovative efforts that build on the work of the profession. This innovation and proactive stance requires that the profession continue to lead in interdisciplinary organizational collaborations to identify opportunities and develop interventions that capitalize on our changing world and its needs (American Academy of Social Work and Social Welfare, 2013). Related to this, social workers need to be thinking about the changing landscape of service provision and ensuring social workers are leaders in service provision to ensure quality care. This includes attending to policy shifts on the larger level that dictate changes in service provision, philosophies, and approaches—for example, recall the shift to person-centered, participant-directed approaches driven by the Affordable Care Act discussed earlier in the book. Social workers must be ready to respond to these changes, and we must be able and willing to anticipate and initiate change if we are to be leaders in shaping the future of society.

To this end, many social workers are calling for changes in the way we conceptualize and intervene with problems. Some of these shifts are profound and very different from the ways in which the profession has functioned in the past. For example, with climate change and other threats, social workers will need to become more proficient in larger macro theories that have not necessarily been foundational in social work education and training. Many social workers feel we need more comprehensive, green theories and values. For example, social workers could expand their understanding of systems and how they impact individuals and our physical environment by incorporating deep ecology (Naess, 1973). Deep ecology puts emphasis on the earth and its highly complex, interrelated systems and functions. When humans interfere with these complex systems, such as when we pollute our environment, we disrupt the natural balance of the environment and its interactions with human and animal life.

Ecological, green theoretical philosophies can push the profession further in its thinking by reinforcing and underscoring values similar to those that are foundational for the profession. These theoretical perspectives call for renewed efforts in striving for equality; respect for difference; social, economic, and environmental justice; and empowerment for individuals and communities. They go further than we have in the past in calling for personal and global responsibility for sustainable communities that also respect the natural environment and its role in human welfare (Shaw, 2008). These ways of thinking can help social workers better incorporate the physical environment into their conceptualization of how human behavior affects and is affected by the social environment. Approaches such as these help us to expand our thinking about problems and solutions to emerging issues as well as promote innovative thinking to change our approaches to working with these issues.

Still, other shifts can be viewed as a move back to the methods on which the profession was founded, as many social workers argue that the profession has drifted too far from its social change roots. For example, many social work educators are calling for more macro content in social work curricula to better prepare students to become leaders in policy and legislative change. To meet future challenges, we need social workers who are well prepared to tackle institutional and systemic issues that cause problems for individuals, families, communities, and our physical and social environment. This is in contrast to the seemingly current favored approach to social work on the micro level and therapeutic interventions focused on the individual. Many social workers are calling for social work that brings attention to issues on every level and for social workers who are competent to bring change to every level.

CONCLUSION

Social work is a dynamic, expansive field, filled with opportunities to influence social and environmental dynamics. We are experiencing exciting changes in our world that challenge the profession to bring new ideas and thinking to our approaches in a changing world. The social work profession is well positioned to be the social and environmental change leaders of the future, if we are willing to take on that challenge!

MAIN POINTS

- Social work as a profession is concerned with social and economic justice, so climate change and sustainability are issues that social workers must address. Climate change and the social, economic, geographic, environmental, and other issues it brings will have profound effects on human behavior and development and how humans interact with the environment.

- Social work's use of the person-in-environment perspective makes it well suited to intervene with climate change and the challenges it will bring.

- Globally, the economic gap between the rich and poor has been widening due to economic philosophies and policies that benefit a small percentage of people.

- Factors such as outsourcing, underemployment, unemployment, and a lack of livable wages contribute to economic disparities.

- Social workers can be involved in many arenas such as policy, advocacy, and legislation to help address economic disparities, particularly as they affect the poorest and most vulnerable populations.

- Increasing health care costs, chronic illness, and environmental hazards as well as unequal access to health care are contributing to health disparities. Social workers have a role to play with regard to addressing issues related to health disparities including education, advocacy, and structural change.

- Demographic changes such as the aging of the population, increasing ethnic diversity, and complex issues around racism and prejudice bring issues that social workers will increasingly face in their work with clients. Because of these shifts, the profession's interface with communities and institutions will become increasingly important.

- Advances in technology, health care, and medical and other sciences are bringing sweeping changes to the way we view a whole host of issues affecting every aspect of our everyday lives. These areas include aging, caregiving, relationships, health care, living arrangements, service provision, and beginning- and end-of-life care. Social workers need to be leaders in shaping and using technology so that it benefits everyone and ethical issues surrounding its use are addressed.

- Globalization, and the conflict and opportunities it can bring, affects all of us, even if we never travel outside our physical communities. Increasingly, social workers are faced with clients who bring problems associated with global violence and struggles associated with globalization.

- Cultural views on many social issues are changing, including recreational drug use, same-sex marriage, end-of-life issues, and others. Social workers can be leaders in thinking about shifting views and how to advocate for inventive ways to address conflict and problems they may bring.

- Social workers are responding to changing times, including providing leadership in education and micro and macro practice to address issues these changes bring. Social work, along with other helping professions, must also think about how its methods and approaches must change and adapt to changing social views and attitudes about social problems.

EXERCISES

1. *RAINN interactive case* at www.routledgesw.com/cases. Review information on the RAINN case and answer the following questions:
   a. Describe how technology is being used by this organization in ways that may not have been possible even ten years ago.
   b. In what ways might the use of technology be helpful to its clients?
   c. What potential problems or ethical issues might the use of technology cause?
2. *Hudson City interactive case* at www.routledgesw.com/cases. Take some time to explore the Hudson City case and the environmental context in which this case is situated. Then answer the following:
   a. In what ways might this community's situation be similar to other areas around the globe faced by climate change?
   b. What are some of the needs and barriers faced by the community's residents?
   c. What are some ways that the social work profession might better respond to climate change and the needs of those affected by it?
3. *Carla Washburn interactive case* at www.routledgesw.com/cases. Explore Carla's case and her community. Then respond to the following:
   a. How does Carla's situation exemplify the issues faced by the global aging of the population?
   b. How will communities need to change and adapt to these issues?
   c. What are some ways in which the social work profession can help to address these issues?

References

AASECT. (2004). Subject of John/Joan twins case dies. *Contemporary Sexuality, 38*(6), 8–9.

AbouZahr, C., & Wardlaw, T. (2001). Maternal mortality at the end of a decade: Signs of progress? *Bulletin of the World Health Organization, 79*(6), 561–573.

Adlard, P. A., Parncutt, J. M., Finkelstein, D. I., & Bush, A. I. (2010). Cognitive loss in zinc transporter-3 knock-out mice: A phenocopy for the synaptic and memory deficits of Alzheimer's disease? *Journal of Neuroscience, 30*(5), 1631–1636.

Administration for Children and Families. (2013). Head Start fact sheet. [Online.] Washington, DC: Author. Retrieved July 11, 2013, from https://eclkc.ohs.acf.hhs.gov/hslc/data/factsheets/docs/hs-program-fact-sheet-2013.pdf

Administration for Community Living. (2014). [Online.] Retrieved on October 27, 2014, from http://www.aoa.gov/Aging_Statistics/Profile/2013/3.aspx.

Administration on Aging. (1998). *The national elder abuse incidence study; final report.* National Center on Elder Abuse, American Public Human Services Association. [Online.] Retrieved March 13, 2003, from http://www.aoa.gov/AoARoot/AoA_Programs/Elder_Rights/Elder_Abuse/Index.aspx.

Administration on Aging. (2006). *A layman's guide to the Older Americans Act.* [Online.] Retrieved June 24, 2009, from http://www.aoa.gov/AoARoot/site_utilities/Search.aspx?cx=012624277387271114612:pl-yugpymdgq&cof=FORID:11&q=guide%20wto%20older%20americans%20act.

Adolphs, R. (2009). The social brain: Neural basis of social knowledge. *Annual Review of Psychology, 60,* 693–716.

Adorno, T. W., Frenkel-Brunswik, E., Levinson, D. J., & Sanford, R. N. (1950). *The authoritarian personality.* Oxford: Harpers.

Affordable Care Act for Americans with Disabilities. (2012). [Online.] Retrieved May 16, 2012, from http://www.healthcare.gov/news/releases/index.html.

Agiesta, J., Junius, D., & McCown, D. (2013). Four in five Americans face near-poverty, no work under Obama. [Online.] Retrieved October 20, 2014, from http://www.newsmax.com/Newsfront/Poverty-Struggling-Whites/2013/07/28/id/517420/?s=al&promo_code=9898-1?s=al&promo_code=1452A-1.

Ahmad, K. (2000, September 23). Women suffer first from lack of health-care services. *Lancet, 356*(9235), 1085.

Ainsworth, M. D. S. (1979). Infant-mother attachment. *American Psychologist, 34,* 932–937.

Alegria, M., Woo, M., Cao, Z., Torres, M., Meng, X. L., Striegel-Moore, R. (2007). Prevalence and correlates of eating disorders in Latinos in the United States. *International Journal of Eating Disorders, 40,* S15–S21.

Alexopoulos, G. S. (2000). Mood disorders. In B. J. Sadock & V. A. Sadock (Eds.), *Comprehensive textbook of psychiatry* (7th ed., pp. 1284–1440). Baltimore, MD: Williams and Wilkins.

Almeida, J., Johnson, R., Corliss, H., Molnar, B., & Azrael, D. (2009). Emotional distress among LGBT youth: The influence of perceived discrimination on sexual orientation. *Journal of Youth & Adolescence, 38*(7), 1001–1014.

Alzheimer's Association. (2012a). *Alzheimer's disease: Facts and figures.* New York: Alzheimer's Association.

Alzheimer's Association. (2012b). *New diagnostic criteria and guidelines for Alzheimer's disease.* [Online.]

Retrieved May 31, 2012, from http://www.alz.org/research/diagnostic_criteria/#overview.

Alzheimer's Association. (2014). *Alzheimer's disease: facts and figures.* [Online.] Retrieved July 11, 2014, from http://www.alz.org/alzheimers_disease_facts_and_figures.asp#cost.

Amato, P. (2000). The consequences of divorce for adults and children. *Journal of Marriage and the Family, 62*(4), 1269–1287.

Amato, P. (2001). Children of divorce in the 1990s: An update of the Amato and Keith (1991) meta-analysis. *Journal of Family Psychology, 15*(3), 355–370.

Amato, P. R., & Sobolewski, J. M. (2001). The effects of divorce and marital discord on adult children's psychological well-being. *American Sociological Review, 66,* 900–921.

American Academy of Child & Adolescent Psychiatry. (2011a). Reactive attachment disorder. *Facts for Families* (85). Retrieved February 26, 2012, from http://www.aacap.org/cs/root/facts_for_families/reactive_attachment_disorder.

American Academy of Child & Adolescent Psychiatry. (2011b). *The Impact of Media Violence on Children and Adolescents: Opportunities for Clinical Interventions.* [Online.] Retrieved July 11, 2014, from http://www.aacap.org/aacap/Medical_Students_and_Residents/Mentorship_Matters/DevelopMentor/The_Impact_of_Media_Violence_on_Children_and_Adolescents_Opportunities_for_Clinical_Interventions.aspx.

American Academy of Pediatrics. (2000). Prevention of sexual harassment in the workplace and educational settings. *Pediatrics, 106,* 1498–1499.

American Academy of Pediatrics. (2001, November). Media violence. *Pediatrics, 108*(5), 1222–1226.

American Academy of Pediatrics. (2002, February). Coparent or second-parent adoption by same-sex parents. *Pediatrics, 109*(2), 339–341.

American Academy of Social Work and Social Welfare. (2013, November). Introduction and Context for Grand Challenges for Social Work (Grand Challenges for Social Work Initiative, Working Paper No. 1). Baltimore, MD: Author.

American Association of Retired Persons. (2003). *Facts about grandparents raising grandchildren.* [Online.] Retrieved March 13, 2003, from http://search.aarp.org/browse?Ntt=facts%20about%20grandparents%20raising%20grandchildren.

American College of Obstetricians and Gynecologists. (1996). Maternal serum screening. *ACOG Technical Bulletin, 228.* Washington, DC: Author.

American Heart Association. (2001). *Statistical fact sheet—populations.* [Online.] Retrieved February 6, 2004, from http://www.heart.org/HEARTORG/Advocate/PolicyResources/FactSheets/Fact-Sheets_UCM_304921_TabbedPage.

American Heart Association. (2009). *Heart disease and stroke statistics.* Dallas, TX: American Heart Association.

American Psychiatric Association. (2000). *Diagnostic and statistical manual of mental disorders* (4th ed., text revision). Washington, DC: American Psychiatric Association.

American Psychiatric Association. (2013). *Diagnostic and statistical manual of mental disorders* (5th ed.). Washington, DC: American Psychiatric Association.

American Social Health Association. (2010). *STI statistics and young people.* [Online.] Retrieved August 4, 2012, from http://www.iwannaknow.org/educators/statistics.html.

Anderson, G. M. (2004). Making sense of rising caesarean section rates. *British Medical Journal, 329*(7468), 696–697.

Anderson, H. D., Pace, W., Libby, A. M., West, D. R., & Valuck, R. J. (2012). Rates of 5 common antidepressant side effects among new adult and adolescent cases of depression: A retrospective US claims study. *Clinical Therapeutics, 34*(1), 113–123.

Anderson, L. M., Shinn, C., Charles, J., Scrimshaw, S. C., Fielding, J. E., Normand, J., *et al.* (2002, February 1). Community interventions to promote healthy social environments: Early childhood development and family housing. *Morbidity & Mortality Weekly Report, 51*(4), 1–7.

Anderssen, N., Amlie, C., & Ytteroy, E. A. (2002). Outcomes for children with lesbian or gay parents. A review of studies from 1978 to 2000. *Scandinavian Journal of Psychology, 43,* 335–351.

Andreasen, N. C. (2001). *Brave new brain: Conquering mental illness in the era of the genome.* New York: Oxford University Press.

Ängarne-Lindberg, T., & Wadsby, M. (2009). Fifteen years after parental divorce: Mental health and experienced life-events. *Nordic Journal of Psychiatry, 63*(1), 32–43.

Angold, A., Costello, E. J., & Worthman, C. M. (1998). Puberty and depression: The roles of age, pubertal status and pubertal timing. *Psychological Medicine, 28*, 51–61.

Anxiety Disorders Association of America. (2010). *Childhood anxiety disorders.* [Online.] Retrieved February 27, 2012 from http://www.adaa.org/living-with-anxiety/children/childhood-anxiety-disorders.

Apolloni, A., Lin, M. H., Sivakumaran, H., Li, D., Kershaw, M. H. R., & Harrich, D. (2013). A mutant Tat protein provides strong protection from HIV-1 infection in human CD4+ T cells. *Human Gene Therapy, 24*(3), 270–282. DOI: 10.1089/hum.2012.176.

Appleby, G. A., & Anastas, J. W. (1998). *Not just a passing phase: Social work with gay, lesbian, and bisexual people.* New York: Columbia University Press.

Arcizet, F., Mirpour, K., & Bisley, J. W. (2011). A pure salience response in posterior parietal cortex. *Cerebral Cortex, 21*(11), 2498–2505.

Arendt, R., Angelopoulos, J., Salvator, A., & Singer, L. (1999). Motor development of cocaine-exposed children at age two years. *Pediatrics, 103*, 86–92.

Arnedo, J., Svrakic, D. M., del Val, C., Romero-Zaliz, R., Hernández-Cuervo, H., Fanous, A. H., *et al.* (2014). Uncovering the hidden risk architecture of the schizophrenias: Confirmation in three independent genome-wide association studies. *American Journal of Psychiatry, 172*(2), 139–153. DOI: 10.1176/appi.ajp.2014.14040435.

Arnett, J. J. (2000). Emerging adulthood: A theory of development from the late teens through the twenties. *American Psychologist, 55*(5), 469–480.

Arnett, J. J. (2010). Oh, grow up!: Generational grumbling and the new life stage of emerging adulthood—commentary on Trzesniewski & Donnellan. *Perspectives on Psychological Science, 5*(1), 89–92.

Arnett, J. J. (2011). Emerging adulthood: The cultural psychology of a new life stage. In *Bridging Cultural and Developmental Approaches to Psychology.* New York: Oxford University Press.

Aseltine, R. H., & Gore, S. L. (2000). The variable effects of stress on alcohol use from adolescence to early adulthood. *Substance Use and Misuse, 35*(5), 643–668.

Ashing-Giwa, K. T., & Lim, J. W. (2011). Examining emotional outcomes among a multiethnic cohort of breast cancer survivors. *Oncology Nursing Forum, 38*(3), 279–288.

Asthana, S., Bhasin, S., Butler, R. N., Fillit, H., Finkelstein, J., Harman, S. M., *et al.* (2004). Masculine vitality: Pros and cons of testosterone in treating andropause. *Journals of Gerontology Series A: Biological Sciences & Medical Sciences, 59A*(5), 461–465.

Atchley, R. C. (1989). A continuity theory of normal aging. *The Gerontologist, 29,* 183–190.

Atchley, R. C., & Barusch, A. (2004). *Social forces and aging* (10th ed.). Belmont, CA: Wadsworth.

Atkins, T. V., Jenkins, M. C., & Perkins, M. H. (1990–1991). Portrayal of persons in television commercials age 50 and older. *Psychology: A Journal of Human Behavior, 27*(4)–*28*(1), 30–37.

Australian Association of Social Workers. (2010). *Code of Ethics.* Canberra: AASW

Autism Consortium. (2009). *Autism genome scan.* [Online.] Retrieved June 17, 2009, from http://www.autismconsortium.org/research-collaborations/autism-genome-scan-2.html.

Auyeung, B., Baron-Cohen, S., Ashwin, E., Knickmeyer, R., Taylor, K., & Hackett, G. (2009). Fetal testosterone and autistic traits. *British Journal of Psychology, 100*, 1–22.

Auyeung, B., Lombardo, M.V., & Baron-Cohen, S. (2013). Prenatal and postnatal hormone effects on the human brain and cognition. *Pflügers Archiv European Journal of Physiology, 465*, 557–571.

Baillargeon, R. (1987). Object permanence in 3½–4½-month-old infants. *Developmental Psychology, 23*(5), 655–664.

Baldwin, S. A., & Hoffmann, J. P. (2002). The dynamics of self-esteem: A growth-curve analysis. *Journal of Youth and Adolescence, 31*(2), 101–113.

Ballard, K. D., Kuh, D. J., & Wadsworth, M. E. J. (2001). The role of the menopause in women's experiences of the "change of life." *Sociology of Health and Illness, 23*(4), 397–424.

Balogh, D. W., Kite, M. E., Pickel, K. L., Canel, D., & Schroeder, J. (2003). The effects of delayed report and motive for reporting on perceptions of sexual harassment. *Sex Roles, 48*(7/8), 337–348.

Bandura, A. (1965). Influence of models' reinforcement contingencies in the acquisition of imitative responses. *Journal of Personality and Social Psychology, 1,* 589–595.

Bandura, A. (1977). *Social learning theory.* Englewood Cliffs, NJ: Prentice Hall.

Bandura, A. (1997). *Self-efficacy.* New York: W. H. Freeman.

Barker, D. (2008). *Nutrition in the womb.* Portland, OR: The Barker Foundation.

Barker, D. J. (2001). The malnourished baby and infant: Relationship with type 2 diabetes. *British Medical Bulletin, 60*(1), 69–88.

Barker, R. L. (2003). *The social work dictionary.* Washington, DC: NASW.

Barkley, R. A. (2002). Psychosocial treatments for attention-deficit/hyperactivity disorder in children. *Journal of Clinical Psychiatry, 63*(12), 36–43.

Barr, H. M., & Streissguth, A. P. (2001). Identifying maternal self-reported alcohol use associated with fetal alcohol spectrum disorders. *Alcoholism: Clinical and Experimental Research, 25,* 283–287.

Barrett, A. E., & White, H. R. (2002, December). Trajectories of gender role orientations in adolescence and early adulthood: A prospective study of the mental health effects of masculinity and femininity. *Journal of Health and Social Behavior, 43,* 451–468.

Barry, R. A., Kochanska, G., & Philibert, R. A. (2008). G {mult} E interaction in the organization of attachment: Mothers' responsiveness as a moderator of children's genotypes. *Journal of Child Psychology and Psychiatry, 49*(12), 1313–1320.

Barusch, A. S., Rogers, A., & Abu-Bader, S. (1999). Depressive symptoms in the frail elderly: Physical and psycho-social correlates. *The International Journal of Aging and Human Development, 49*(2), 107–125.

Bateson, G. (1972). *Steps to an ecology of mind.* New York: Ballantine.

Bateson, G. (1978, April 21). The double-bind theory—misunderstood? *Psychiatry News,* p. 40.

Bauer, C. R., Langer, J. C., Shankaran, S., Bada, H. A., Lester, B., Wright, L. L., *et al.* (2005). Acute neonatal effects of cocaine exposure during pregnancy. *Archives of Pediatrics and Adolescent Medicine, 159*(9), 824–834.

Baumrind, D. (1968). Authoritarian vs. authoritative parental control. *Adolescence, 3*(11), 255–272.

Baumrind, D. (1971). Current patterns of parental authority. *Developmental Psychology Monographs, 4*(1, Pt. 2), 1–103.

Baumrind, D. (1994). The social context of child maltreatment. *Family Relations, 43*(4), 360–368.

Beauvoir, Simone de. (1949). *The second sex.* New York: Knopf.

Beavan, V. & Read, J. (2010). Hearing voices and listening to what they say: The importance of voice content in understanding and working with distressing voices. *Journal of Nervous and Mental Disease, 198*(3), 201–205.

Becker, S. P., Marshall, S. A., & McBurnett, K. (2014). Sluggish cognitive tempo in abnormal child psychology: An historical overview and introduction to the special section. *Journal of Abnormal Child Psychology, 42*(1), 1–6.

Beckett, J. O., & Johnson, H. C. (1995). Human development. In R. L. Edwards (Ed.), *Encyclopedia of social work* (19th ed., Vol. 2, pp. 1385–1405). Washington, DC: NASW Press.

Behavioral Health Treatment. (1997). APA passes resolution on homosexuality conversion therapy. *Behavioral Health Treatment, 2*(9), 5.

Bell, J. (1992). In search of a discourse on aging: The elderly on television. *The Gerontologist, 32,* 305–311.

Belle, D., & Doucet, J. (2003). Poverty, inequality, and discrimination as sources of depression among U.S. women. *Psychology of Women Quarterly, 27*(2), 101–113.

Belsky, J. (2009). Classroom composition, child-care history and social development: Are childcare effects disappearing or spreading? *Social Development, 18*(1), 230–238.

Belsky, J., & Braungart, J. M. (1991). Are insecure avoidant infants with extensive daycare experience less stressed by and more independent in the strange situation? *Child Development, 62*(3), 567–571.

Bengtson, V., Horlacher, G., Putney, N., & Silverstein, M. (2008). *Growth and decline of religiosity across time and age.* Conference Papers—American Sociological Association, 2008 Annual Meeting.

Benjet, C., & Kazdin, A. E. (2003). Spanking children: The controversies, findings, and new directions. *Clinical Psychology Review, 23,* 197–224.

Bergin, D. (1988). Stages of play development. In D. Bergin (Ed.), *Play as a medium for learning and development.* Portsmouth, NH: Heinemann.

Berk, L. E. (2011). *Exploring lifespan development* (2nd ed.). New York: Pearson.

Berkman, C. S., & Zinberg, G. (1997). Homophobia and heterosexism in social workers. *Social Work, 42,* 319–332.

Berkowitz, L., & Walster, E. (1976). Equity theory: Toward a general theory of social interaction. In L. Berkowitz & E. Walster (Eds.), *Advances in experimental social psychology* (Vol. 9, pp. 1–261). New York: Academic Press.

Berlin, L. J. (2001). Promoting early childhood development through comprehensive community initiatives. *Children's Services: Social Policy, Research, & Practice 4*(1), 1–23.

Berne, E. (1961). *Transactional analysis in psychotherapy.* New York: Grove Press.

Berry, M., Cavazos Dylla, D. J., Barth, R. P., & Needell, B. (1998). The role of open adoption in the adjustment of adopted children and their families. *Children and Youth Services Review, 20*(1–2), 151–171.

Bertalanffy, L. von. (1972). The history of general systems theory. In G. J. Klir (Ed.), *Trends in general systems theory* (pp. 21–41). New York: Wiley-Interscience.

Bertram, R., Helena, C. V., Gonzales-Iglesias, A. E., Tabak, J., & Freeman, M. E. (2010). A tale of two rhythms: The emerging roles of oxytocin in rhythmic prolactin release. *Journal of Neuroendocrinology, 22*(7), 778–784.

Berwick, R. C. (2009). What genes can't learn about language. *Proceedings of the National Academy of Sciences, 106*(6), 1685–1686.

Bevan, E., & Higgins, D. J. (2002). Is domestic violence learned? The contribution of five forms of child maltreatment to men's violence and adjustment. *Journal of Family Violence, 17*(3), 223–243.

Bifulco, A., Moran, P. M., Ball, C., Jacobs, C., Baines, R., Bunn, A., & Cavagin, J. (2002). Childhood adversity, parental vulnerability and disorder: Examining intergenerational transmission of risk. *Journal of Child Psychology and Psychiatry, 43*(8), 1075–1086.

Billingsley, A., & Morrison-Rodriguez, B. (2007). The black family in the twenty-first century and the church as an action system. In L. A. Lee (Ed.), *Human behavior in the social environment from an African-American perspective* (2nd ed., pp. 31–48). New York: Haworth Press.

Bing, N. M., Nelson, W. M., & Wesolowski, K. L. (2009). Comparing the effects of amount of conflict on children's adjustment following parental divorce. *Journal of Divorce & Remarriage, 50*(3), 159–171.

Bishop, A. (1994). *Becoming an ally: Breaking the cycle of oppression.* Halifax, Canada: Fernwood.

Bitto, A., & Gray, R. H. (1997). Adverse outcomes of planned and unplanned pregnancies among users of natural family planning: A prospective study. *American Journal of Public Health, 87*(3), 338–343.

Bjerkedal, T., Kristensen, P., Skjeret, G. A., & Brevik, J. I. (2007). Intelligence test scores and birth order among young Norwegian men (conscripts) analyzed within and between families. *Intelligence, 35*(5), 503–514.

Blake, S. M., Kiely, M., Gard, C. C., El-Mohandes, A. A. E., & El-Khorazaty, N. (2007). Pregnancy intentions and happiness among pregnant black women at high risk for adverse infant health outcomes. *Perspectives on Sexual & Reproductive Health, 39*(4), 194–205.

Blakemore, J. E. O., Berenbaum, S. A., & Liben, L. S. (2009). *Gender development.* New York: Psychology Press.

Blasi, A., Mercure, E., Lloyd-Fox, S., Thomson, A., Brammer, M., Sauter, D., *et al.* (2011). Early specialization for voice and emotion processing in the infant brain. *Current Biology, 21,* 1220–1224.

Bleidorn, W., Kandler, C., Riemann, R., Angleitner, A., & Spinath, F. M. (2009). Patterns and sources of adult personality development: Growth curve analyses of the NEO PI-R scales in a longitudinal twin study. *Journal of Personality & Social Psychology, 97*(1), 142–155.

Blom, B. (2009). Knowing or un-knowing? That is the question: In the era of evidence-based social work practice. *Journal of Social Work, 9*(2), 158–177.

Bloom, B., Cohen, R. A., & Freeman, G. (2010). Summary health statistics for U.S. children: National Health Interview Survey, 2010. National Center for Health Statistics. *Vital and Health Statistics, 10*(250).

Blumer, H. (1969). *Symbolic interaction: Perspective and method.* Englewood Cliffs, NJ: Prentice-Hall.

Bohlmeijer, E. T., Kramer, J., Smit, F., Onrust, S., & van Marwijk, H. (2009). The effects of integrative reminiscence on depressive symptomatology and mastery of older adults. *Community Mental Health Journal, 45,* 476–484.

Bolognini, M., Laget, J., Plancherel, B., Stephan, P., Corcos, M., & Halfon, O. (2002). Drug use and suicide attempts: The role of personality factors. *Substance Use and Misuse, 37*(3), 337–356.

Bonilla-Silva, E., & Dietrich, D. R. (2009). The Latin Americanization of US race relations: A new pigmentocracy. In E. Glenn (Ed.), *Shades of difference: Why skin color matters* (pp. 40–60). Stanford, CA: Stanford University Press.

Bostwick, J., & Martin, K. (2007). A man's brain in an ambiguous body: A case of mistaken gender identity. *American Journal of Psychiatry, 164,* 1499–1505.

Bowlby, J. (1969). *Attachment and loss* (Vol. I). London: Hogarth Press.

Bowlby, R. (2007). Babies and toddlers in non-parental daycare can avoid stress and anxiety if they develop a lasting secondary attachment bond with one carer who is consistently accessible to them. *Attachment & Human Development, 9*(4), 307–319.

Boyd, M. A. (2007). *Psychiatric nursing* (4th ed.). Baltimore, MD: Lippincott, Williams, & Wilkins.

Boye, B., Bentsen, H., & Malt, V. F. (2002). Does guilt proneness predict acute and long-term distress in relatives of patients with schizophrenia? *Acta Psychiatrica Scandinavica, 106*(5), 351–357.

Bradford, J., Reisner, S., Honnold, J., & Xavier, J. (2013). Experiences of transgender-related discrimination and implications for health: Results from the Virginia Transgender Health Initiative Study. *American Journal of Public Health, 103,* 1820–1829.

Bradley, R. H., & Corwyn, R. F. (2002). Socioeconomic status and child development. *Annual Review of Psychology, 53,* 371–399.

Brandell, J. R. (Ed.). (1997). *Theory and practice in clinical social work.* New York: The Free Press.

Brandtjen, H., & Thomas, V. (2001). Short and long term effects on infants and toddlers in full time daycare centers. *Journal of Prenatal & Perinatal Psychology & Health, 15*(4), 239–286.

Bray, J., & Kelly, J. (1998). *Stepfamilies: Love, marriage, and parenting in the first decade.* New York: Broadway Books.

Brewis, A. A., Meyer, M. C., & Schmidt, K. L. (2002). Does school, compared to home, provide a unique adaptive context for children's ADHD-associated behaviors? A cross-cultural test. *Cross-Cultural Research, 36*(4), 303–320.

Brim, O. (1999). *The MacArthur Foundation study of midlife development.* Vero Beach, FL: MacArthur Foundation.

Brittan, A., & Maynard, M. (1984). *Sexism, racism, and oppression.* New York: Basil Blackwell Publisher.

Bronfenbrenner, U. (1979). *The ecology of human development.* Cambridge, MA: Harvard University Press.

Bronstein, P., & Clauson, J. (1993). Parenting behavior and children's social, psychological, and academic adjustment in diverse family structures. *Family Relations, 42,* 268–276.

Brooks, D., & Goldberg, S. (2001). Gay and lesbian adoptive and foster care placements: Can they meet the needs of waiting children? *Social Work, 46*(2), 147–157.

Brooks-Gunn, J., & Warren, M. P. (1989). The psychological significance of secondary sexual characteristics in 9- to 11-year-old girls. *Child Development, 59,* 161–169.

Brown, J. (1977). *Mind, brain, and consciousness.* New York: Academic Press.

Brown, T. H., & Warner, D. F. (2008). Divergent pathways? Racial/ethnic differences in older women's labor force withdrawal. *Journals of Gerontology Series B: Psychological Sciences & Social Sciences, 36B*(3), S122–S134.

Bryan, A., & Stallings, M. C. (2002). A case control study of adolescent risky sexual behavior and its relationship to personality dimensions, conduct disorder, and substance use. *Journal of Youth and Adolescence, 31*(5), 387–396.

Buhrmester, D., & Furman, W. (1987). The development of companionship and intimacy. *Child Development, 58,* 1101–1113.

Bulik, C. M., Baucom, D. H., Kirby, J. S., & Pisetsky, E. (2011). Uniting couples (in the treatment of) anorexia nervosa. *International Journal of Eating Disorders, 44*(1), 19–28.

Bureau of Justice Statistics. (2009). *Crime characteristics.* [Online.] Retrieved June 24, 2009, from http://www.ojp.usdoj.gov/bjs/cvict_c.htm#relate.

Bureau of Justice Statistics. (2013). *Intimate partner violence: Attributes of victimization, 1993–2011.* [Online.] Retrieved July 11, 2014, from http://www.bjs.gov/index.cfm?ty=pbdetail&iid=4801.

Bureau of Labor Statistics. (2012a). *Economic News Release.* [Online.] Table 1: National Employment and Wage Date from the Occupational Employment Statistics Survey by Occupation, May 2011. Retrieved August 5, 2012, from http://www.bls.gov/news.release/ocwage.t01.htm.

Bureau of Labor Statistics. (2012b). *Labor force statistics from the current population survey.* Table 11: Employed Persons by Detailed Occupation, Sex, Race, and Hispanic or Latino Ethnicity (in Thousands). [Online.] Retrieved August 5, 2012, from http://www.bls.gov/cps/cpsaat11.htm.

Bureau of Labor Statistics. (2014). *2014 Usual Weekly Earnings of Wage and Salary Workers.* [Online.] Retrieved July 11, 2014, from http://www.bls.gov/schedule/archives/wkyeng_nr.htm#current.

Burnette, D. (1998). Grandparents rearing grandchildren: A school-based small group intervention. *Research on Social Work Practice, 8*(1), 10–27.

Butler, R. (1963). The life review: An interpretation of reminiscence in the aged. *Psychiatry, 26,* 65–76.

Buzwell, S., & Rosenthal, D. (1996). Constructing a sexual self: Adolescents' sexual self-perceptions and sexual risk-taking. *Journal of Research on Adolescence, 6,* 489–513.

Cahill, K., Giandrea, M., & Quinn, J. (2006). Retirement patterns from career employment. *Gerontologist, 46*(4), 514–532.

Caldwell, K., & Claxton, C. (2010). Teaching family systems theory: A developmental-constructivist perspective. *Contemporary Family Therapy: An International Journal, 32,* 3–21. DOI: 10.1007/s10591–009–9106–6.

California Department of Public Health. (2011). *The California pregnancy-associated mortality review.* California: Publisher.

Camarota, S. A. (2001). *Immigration from Mexico: Study examines costs and benefits to the United States.* [Online.] Retrieved May 17, 2012, from http://cis.org/CostBenefitsMexicanImmigration.

Campbell, C. (2003). Anti-oppressive theory and practice as the organizing theme for social work education: The case in favour. *Canadian Social Work Review, 20,* 121–125.

Campbell, W. W., & Leidy, H. J. (2007). Dietary protein and resistance training effects on muscle and body composition in older persons. *Journal of the American College of Nutrition, 26*(6), 696S–703S.

Canda, E. R. (2008). Spiritual connections in social work: Boundary violations and transcendence. *Journal of Religion & Spirituality in Social Work, 27*(1–2), 25–40.

Cantor, J. (2000). Media violence. *Journal of Adolescent Health, 27*(2), 30–34.

Caputo, R. K. (2002). Discrimination and human capital: A challenge to economic theory and social justice. *Journal of Sociology and Social Welfare, 24*(2), 105–124.

Caputo, R. K. (2003). Head Start, other preschool programs, and life success in a youth cohort. *Journal of Sociology and Social Welfare, 30*(2), 105–126.

Carli, L. L., & Eagly, A. H. (2001). Gender, hierarchy, and leadership: An introduction. *Journal of Social Issues, 57*(4), 629–636.

Carroli, G., & Mignini, L. (2009). Episiotomy for vaginal birth. *PubMed, 21*(1). Retrieved June 17, 2009, from http://www.cochrane.org/reviews/en/ab000081.html.

Carter, C. S. (2002). Perinatal care for women who are addicted: Implications for empowerment. *Health and Social Work, 27*(3), 166–174.

Cartwright, C., & Steinberg, M. (1995). Decision-making in terminal care: Older people seek more involvement. *Social Alternatives, 14*(2), 7–10.

Centers for Disease Control and Prevention. (1995). Chorionic villus sampling and amniocentesis: Recommendations for prenatal counseling. *Morbidity and Mortality Weekly Report, 44*(R-9). Atlanta, GA: Author.

Centers for Disease Control and Prevention. (1998). Trends in sexual risk behaviors among high school students—United States, 1991–1997. *Morbidity and Mortality Weekly Report, 47*(36), 749–752.

Centers for Disease Control and Prevention. (2000a). *Tracking the hidden epidemics: Trends in STDs in the United States.* [Online.] Retrieved November 5, 2003, from http://www.cdc.gov/nchstp/dstd/Stats_Trends/Trends2000.pdf.

Centers for Disease Control and Prevention. (2000b). Youth risk behavior surveillance—United States 1999. *Morbidity and Mortality Weekly Report, 49(SS-5).*

Centers for Disease Control and Prevention. (2001). *Data and statistics: Adolescent pregnancy.* Atlanta: Author.

Centers for Disease Control and Prevention. (2005). National Center for Health Statistics. Births: Final Data for 2005. National Vital Statistics Reports. *56*(6).

Centers for Disease Control and Prevention. (2009). *Preventing teen pregnancy: An update in 2009.* [Online.] Retrieved June 23, 2009, from http://www.cdc.gov/reproductivehealth/AdolescentReproHealth/AboutTP.htm.

Centers for Disease Control and Prevention. (2010). *Facts about traumatic brain injury.* [Online.] Retrieved May 10, 2010, from http://www.brainline.org/content/2008/07/facts-about-traumatic-brain-injury.html.

Centers for Disease Control and Prevention. (2011a). *Bullying among middle school and high school students—Massachusetts, 2009.* [Online.] Retrieved November, 23, 2011, from http://nces.ed.gov/programs/crimeindicators2010.

Centers for Disease Control and Prevention. (2011b). *National lead poisoning prevention week 2011.* [Online.] Retrieved February 10, 2012, from http://www.cdc.gov/Features/LeadPoisoning/.

Centers for Disease Control and Prevention. (2011c). *STDs in adolescents and young adults. Table 10, in 2010 Sexually transmitted diseases surveillance.* [Online.] Retrieved 4 August, 2012, from http://www.cdc.gov/std/stats10/adol.htm.

Centers for Disease Control and Prevention. (2011d). *Youth risk behavior surveillance—United States, 2011.* U.S. Department of Health and Human Services, June 8, 2012, pp. 26–27.

Centers for Disease Control and Prevention. (2012a, June 7). *Trends in the prevalence of behaviors that contribute to violence on school property: National YRBS, 1991–2011.* In Health topics: Injury & violence (including suicide). [Online.] Retrieved August 4, 2012, from http://www.cdc.gov/healthyyouth/injury/.

Centers for Disease Control and Prevention (2012b). *Update on Blood Lead Levels in Children.* [Online.] Retrieved May 23, 2014 from http://www.cdc.gov/nceh/lead/ACCLPP/blood_lead_levels.htm.

Centers for Disease Control and Prevention (2012c). *U.S. Totals Blood Lead Surveillance Report 1997–2012.* CDC's National Surveillance Data (1997–2012). Retrieved May 23, 2014, from http://www.cdc.gov/nceh/lead/data/national.htm.

Centers for Disease Control and Prevention. (2013a). Antibiotic resistance threats in the United States, 2013. [Online.] Retrieved October 27, 2014, from http://www.cdc.gov/drugresistance/threat-report-2013/pdf/ar-threats-2013-508.pdf#page=11.

Centers for Disease Control and Prevention. (2013b). Birth defects. [Online.] Retrieved September 18, 2014, from http://www.cdc.gov/ncbddd/birthdefects/data.html.

Centers for Disease Control and Prevention. (2013c). Births: Final data for 2012. [Online.] Retrieved July 11, 2014, from http://www.cdc.gov/nchs/data/nvsr/nvsr62/nvsr62_09.pdf#table16.

Centers for Disease Control and Prevention (2013d). CDC health disparities and inequality report. *Morbidity and Mortality Weekly Report, 62*(3), 61–64.

Centers for Disease Control and Prevention. (2013e). National survey of children's health. [Online.] Retrieved July 12, 2014, from http://www.cdc.gov/nchs/slaits/nsch.htm.

Centers for Disease Control and Prevention. (2013f). Suicide among adults aged 35–64 Years—United States, 1999–2010. [Online.] Retrieved July 17, 2014, from http://www.cdc.gov/mmwr/preview/mmwrhtml/mm6217a1.htm?s_cid=mm6217a1_w.

Centers for Disease Control and Prevention. (2014a). Autism Spectrum Disorder. [Online.] Retrieved July 10, 2014, from http://www.cdc.gov/ncbddd/autism/data.html.

Centers for Disease Control and Prevention. (2014b). Chlamydia fact sheet. [Online.] Retrieved July 11, 2014, from http://www.cdc.gov/std/chlamydia/STDFact-chlamydia-detailed.htm.

Centers for Disease Control and Prevention. (2014c). *Fetal Alcohol Spectrum Disorders (FASDs).* [Online.] Retrieved May 21, 2014 from http://www.cdc.gov/ncbddd/fasd/faqs.html.

Centers for Disease Control and Prevention. (2014d). Herpes fact sheet. [Online.] Retrieved July 11, 2014, from http://www.cdc.gov/std/Herpes/STDFact-Herpes.htm.

Centers for Disease Control and Prevention. (2014e). HIV among youth. [Online.] Retrieved July 11, 2014, from http://www.cdc.gov/hiv/risk/age/youth/index.html?s_cid=tw_drmermin-00186.

Centers for Disease Control and Prevention. (2014f). *Osteoarthritis.* [Online.] Retrieved July 11, 2014, from http://www.cdc.gov/arthritis/basics/osteoarthritis.htm.

Centers for Disease Control and Prevention. (2014g). Racial disparities in breastfeeding. [Online.] Retrieved September 18, 2014, from http://www.nlm.nih.gov/medlineplus/news/fullstory_147986.html.

Center for Disease Control and Prevention. (2014h). Reported STDs in the United States. [Online.] Retrieved July 11, 2014 from http://www.cdc.gov/nchhstp/newsroom/docs/STD-Trends-508.pdf.

Centers for Disease Control and Prevention. (2014i). Sexual Risk Behavior: HIV, STD, & Teen Pregnancy Prevention. [Online.] Retrieved July 14, 2014, from http://www.cdc.gov/healthyyouth/sexualbehaviors/index.htm.

Centers for Disease Control and Prevention. (2014j). Suicide: Facts at a Glance. [Online.] Retrieved July 11, 2014, from http://www.cdc.gov/violenceprevention/pub/suicide_datasheet.html.

Centers for Disease Control and Prevention. (2014k). Syphilis fact sheet. [Online.] Retrieved July 11, 2014, from http://www.cdc.gov/std/syphilis/STDFact-Syphilis.htm.

Centers for Disease Control and Prevention. (2014l). United States Life Tables, 2009. *National Vital Statistics Reports, 62*(7). Retrieved July 11, 2014, from http://www.cdc.gov/nchs/data/nvsr/nvsr62/nvsr62_07.pdf.

Centers for Disease Control and Prevention. (2014m). *Youth Risk Behavior Surveillance - United States, 2013.* [Online.] Retrieved July 11, 2014, from http://www.cdc.gov/mmwr/pdf/ss/ss6304.pdf.

Centers for Medicare and Medicaid Services. (2000). *Health and Human Services announces Medicare premium and deductible rates for 2001.* Press release, October 18, 2000. U.S. Department of Health and Human Services.

Centers for Medicare and Medicaid Services. (2002, August). *Medicare current beneficiary survey.* [Online.] Retrieved March 10, 2003, from http://www.cms.hhs.gov/mcbs/CMSsrc/1996/cp96appb.pdf.

Centers for Medicare and Medicaid Services. (2011). *State Operations Manual, §483.25(a)(1).* Retrieved March 5, 2012, from www.cms.gov/manuals/Downloads/som107ap_pp_guidelines_ltcf.pdf.

Centers for Medicare and Medicaid Services. (2012). *Health and Human Services announces Medicare premium and deductible rates for 2012.* Washington, DC: U.S. Department of Health and Human Services.

Chanley, S. A., & Alozie, N. O. (2001). Policy for the "deserving," but politically weak: The 1996 welfare reform act and battered women. *Policy Studies Review, 18*(2), 1–25.

Chatters, L. M., & Taylor, R. J. (1994). Religious involvement among older African-Americans. In J. S. Levin (Ed.), *Religion in aging and health* (pp. 196–230). Thousand Oaks, CA: Sage.

Chau, K. L. (Ed.). (1991). *Ethnicity and biculturalism.* New York: Haworth.

Cheers, B., & Taylor, J. (2005). Social work in rural and remote Australia. In M. Alston & J. McKinnon (Eds.), *Social work: Fields of practice* (pp. 237–248). Melbourne: Oxford University Press.

Cheslack-Postava, K., Liu, K., & Bearman, P. S. (2011). Closely spaced pregnancies are associated with increased odds of autism in California sibling births. *Pediatrics, 127,* 246–253.

Chess, S., & Thomas, A. (1977). Temperamental individuality from childhood to adolescence. *Journal of Child Psychiatry, 16,* 218–226.

Chesson, H. W., Blandford, J. M., Gift, T. L., Tao, G., & Irwin, K. L. (2004). The estimated direct medical costs of sexually transmitted diseases among American youth, 2000. *Perspectives on Sexual and Reproductive Health, 36*(1), 11–19.

Chickering, A. W., & Reisser, L. (1993). *Education and identity* (2nd ed.). San Francisco: Jossey-Bass.

Child Sexual Abuse Task Force and Research & Practice Core, National Child Traumatic Stress Network. (2004). *How to implement trauma-focused cognitive behavioral therapy.* Durham, NC, and Los Angeles: National Center for Child Traumatic Stress.

Child Trends. (2001). *Trends among Hispanic children, youth, and families.* Washington, DC: Author.

Child Trends Databank. (2014). Learning disabilities. [Online.] Retrieved September 22, 2014, from http://www.childtrends.org/?indicators=learning-disabilities.

Child Welfare Information Gateway. (2008). *Long-term consequences of child abuse and neglect. U.S. Department of Health and Human Services.* [Online.] Retrieved June 17, 2009, from http://www.childwelfare.gov/pubs/factsheets/long_term_consequences.cfm.

Children's Defense Fund. (2008). *The state of American's children: 2008 report of child health and health coverage.* Washington, DC: Author.

Children's Defense Fund. (2012). *Portrait of inequality: Black children in America.* Washington, DC: Author.

Children's Institute International. (1999). *Breaking the habit.* [Online.] Retrieved September 5, 2003, from http://www.childrensinstitute.org/press/spanking.html.

Chiriboga, C. A. (2003). Fetal alcohol and drug effects. *The Neurologist, 9*(6), 267–279.

Chiriboga, C. A., Burst, J. C. M., Bateman, D., & Hauser, W. A. (1999). Dose-response effect of fetal cocaine exposure on newborn neurologic function. *Pediatrics, 103,* 79–85.

Chlebowski, R. T., Anderson, G. L., Gass, M., Lane, D. S., Aragaki, A. K., Kuller, L. H., *et al.* (2010). Estrogen plus progestin and breast cancer incidence and mortality in postmenopausal women. *JAMA, 304*(15), 1684–1692.

Choi, J. (2010). Nonresident fathers' parenting, family processes, and children's development in urban, poor, single-mother families. *Social Service Review, 84*(4), 655–677.

Choi, J., & Jackson, A. P. (2011). Fathers' involvement and child behavior in poor African American single-mother families. *Children & Youth Services Review, 33*(5), 698–704.

Chomsky, N. (1975). *Reflections on language.* New York: Pantheon.

Chornesky, A. (1998). Multicultural perspectives on menopause and the climacteric. *Affilia, 13*(1), 31–46.

Christakis, D. A., & Zimmerman, F. J. (2005). Violent television viewing during preschool is associated with antisocial behavior during school age. *Pediatrics, 120*(5), 993–999.

Christian, K. M., Miracle, A. D., Wellman, C. L., & Nakazawa, K. (2011). Chronic stress-induced hippocampal dendritic retraction requires CA3 NMDA receptors. *Neuroscience, 174,* 26–36.

Chumlea, W. E., Schubert, C. M., Roche, A. F., Kulin, H. E., Lee, P. E., Himes, J. H., *et al.* (2003). Age at menarche and racial comparisons in US girls. *Pediatrics, 111,* 110–113.

Cianciotto, J., & Cahill, S. (2006). *Youth in the cross hairs: The third wave of ex-gay activism.* Washington,

DC: National Gay and Lesbian Task Force Policy Institute.

Cicchetti, D., & Toth, S. L. (2005). Child maltreatment. *Annual Review of Clinical Psychology, 1,* 409–438.

Cicirelli, V. G. (1994). Sibling relationships in cross-cultural perspective. *Journal of Marriage and the Family, 56*(1), 14–20.

Clark, A. (2011). Falling through the cracks: Queer theory, same-sex marriage, Lawrence v. Texas and luminal bodies. *Disclosure,* 20. Retrieved on May 14, 2012, from http://web.ebscohost.com/ehost/detail?sid=e531069f-503e-40d9-8ffa-9cb24ca7d6b d%40sessionmgr13&vid=4&hid=7&bdata=JmxvZ2luLmFzcD9jdXN0aWQ9czg0NzQxNTQmc2l0ZT1laG9zdC1saXZlJnNjb3BlPXNpdGU%3d#db=aph&AN=61047391.

Clark, E. (2000). Language acquisition. In A. Kazdin (Ed.), *Encyclopedia of psychology.* Washington, DC: American Psychological Association.

Clarkberg, M. (1999). The price of partnering: The role of economic well-being in young adults' first union experiences. *Social Forces, 77*(3), 945–968.

Clements-Nolle, K., Marx, R., & Katz, M. (2006). Attempted suicide among transgender persons: The influence of gender-based discrimination and victimization. *Journal of Homosexuality, 51*(3), 53–69.

Clocksin, B. D., Watson, D. L., & Ransdell, L. (2002). Understanding youth obesity and media use: Implications for future intervention programs. *Quest, 54,* 259–275.

CNN Money. (2014). Facebook, Apple pay to freeze employees' eggs. [Online.] Retrieved July 21, 2015, from http://money.cnn.com/2014/10/14/news/companies/facebook-apple-egg-freeze/.

Cohen, S. A. (2008). Abortion and women of color: The bigger picture. *Guttmacher Policy Review, 11*(3), 2–12.

Coleman, P. K., & Karraker, K. H. (2003). Maternal self-efficacy beliefs, competence in parenting, and toddlers' behavior and developmental status. *Infant Mental Health Journal, 24*(2), 126–148.

Coleman, R. A. (2002). A mediated model of social adjustment: Exploring the links between attachment security, social information processing, and prosocial behavior. *Dissertation Abstracts International: Section B: The Sciences and Engineering, 63*(6–B), 3039.

Coleman, S. (2012). The decimation of America's middle class and its meaning for social work. *Journal of Progressive Human Services, 23*(1), 76–93. DOI: 10.1080/10428232.

Conlin, M. (2003, May 26). The new gender gap. *Business Week, 3834,* 74–80.

Conwell, Y., Duberstein, P. R., Cox, C., Herrman, J., Forbes, N., & Caine, E. (1998). Age differences in behaviors leading to completed suicide. *American Journal of Geriatric Psychiatry, 6*(2), 122–126.

Cooley, C. H. (1902). *Human nature and the social order.* New York: Scribner.

Cooper, M. G., & Lesser, J. G. (2011). *Clinical social work practice: An integrated approach* (4th ed.). Boston: Allyn & Bacon.

Copen, C. E., Daniels, K., Vespa, J., & Mosher, W. D. (2012, March 22). First marriages in the United States: Data from the 2006–2010 National Survey of Family Growth. *National Health Statistics Reports, 49.* National Center for Health Statistics, Centers for Disease Control and Prevention, U.S. Department of Health and Human Services. Retrieved August 5, 2012, from http://www.cdc.gov/nchs/data/nhsr/nhsr049.pdf.

Corley, C. J., & Woods, A. Y. (1991). Socioeconomic, sociodemographic and attitudinal correlates of the tempo of divorce. *Journal of Divorce & Remarriage, 16*(1–2), 47–68.

Correll, S. J., Benard, S., & Paik, I. (2007). Getting a job: Is there a motherhood penalty? *American Journal of Sociology, 112*(5), 1297–1338.

Corstens, D., Longden, E., & May, R. (2012). Talking with voices: Exploring what is expressed by the voices people hear. *Psychosis: Social and Integrative Approaches, 4*(2), 95–104.

Côté, S., DeCelles, K. A., McCarthy, J. M., VanKleef, G. A., & Hideg, I. (2011). The Jekyll and Hyde of emotional intelligence: Emotion-regulation knowledge facilitates both prosocial and interpersonally deviant behavior. *Psychological Science, 22*(8), 1073–1080. DOI: 10.1177/095679761141625.

Council on Social Work Education. (2008). *Educational policy and accreditation standards.* Alexandria, VA: Author.

Craig, A. P., & Beishuizen, J. J. (2002). Psychological testing in a multicultural society: Universal or particular competencies? *Intercultural Education, 13*(2), 201–213.

Crawford, D. W., Houts, R. M., Huston, T. L., & George, L. J. (2002). Compatibility, leisure, and satisfaction in marital relationships. *Journal of Marriage and the Family, 64*(2), 433–449.

Creasey, G. L. (1993). The association between divorce and late adolescent grandchildren's relations with grandparents. *Journal of Youth and Adolescence, 22*(5), 513–529.

Crocket, L. (2013). Narrative therapy. In J. Frew & M. D. Spiegler (Eds.), *Contemporary psychotherapies for a diverse world* (pp. 459–500). New York: Routledge.

Crockett, J. B., & Kauffman, J. M. (1999). *The least restrictive environment.* Mahwah, NJ: Erlbaum.

Croghan, C. F., Moone, R. P., & Olson, A. M. (2014). Friends, family, and caregiving among midlife and older lesbian, gay, bisexual, and transgender adults. *Journal of Homosexuality, 61*, 79–102.

Crosnoe, R., & Elder, G. H. (2002). Life course transitions, the generational stake, and grandparent-grandchild relationships. *Journal of Marriage and Family, 64*(4), 1089–1096.

Crosnoe, R., Mistry, R. S., & Elder, G. H. (2002). Economic disadvantage, family dynamics, and adolescent enrollment in higher education. *Journal of Marriage and the Family, 64*(3), 690–702.

Crowley, B. J., Hayslip, B., & Hobdy, J. (2003). Psychological hardiness and adjustment to life events in adulthood. *Journal of Adult Development, 10*(4), 237–248.

Cumming, E., & Henry, W. (1961). *Growing old: The process of disengagement.* New York: Basic Books.

Curtis, G. B., & Schuler, J. (2004). *Your pregnancy week by week.* Cambridge, MA: Da Capo Press.

Dahrendorf, R. (1958). Toward a theory of social conflict. *Journal of Conflict Resolution, 2*(June), 170–183.

Daniel, S. S., Grzywacz, J. G., Leerkes, E., Tucker, J., & Han, W. J. (2009). Nonstandard maternal work schedules during infancy: Implications for children's early behavior problems. *Infant Behavior & Development, 32*(2), 195–207.

Danis, F. (2003). Social work response to domestic violence: Encouraging news from a new look. *Affilia, 18*(2), 177–191.

Darmasseelane, K., Hyde, M. J., Santhakumaran, S., Gale, C., & Modi, N. (2014). Mode of delivery and offspring body mass index, overweight and obesity in adult life: A systematic review and meta-analysis. *PLoS ONE, 9*(2): e87896. DOI: 10.1371/journal.pone.0087896.

Davidovici, B. B., Orion, E., & Wolf, R. (2008). Cutaneous manifestations of pituitary gland diseases. *Clinics in Dermatology, 26*(3), 288–295.

Davidson, H. (1997). The legal aspects of corporal punishment in the home: When does physical discipline cross the line to become child abuse? *Children's Legal Rights Journal, 17,* 18–29.

Davis, J. M., & Watson, N. (2001). Where are the children's experiences? Analysing social and cultural exclusion in "special" and "mainstream" schools. *Disability & Society, 16*(5), 671–687.

Davitt, J. (2006). Policy to protect the rights of older adults. In B. Berkman (Ed.), *Handbook of social work in health and aging* (pp. 923–936). New York: Oxford University Press.

de Anda, D. (1984). Bicultural socialization: Factors affecting the minority experience. *Social Work, 29*(2), 101–107.

Death Café. (2014). Welcome to Death Café. [Online.] Retrieved July 18, 2014, from deathcafe.com.

Dehlendorf, C., Rodriguez, M. I., Levy, K., Borrero, S., & Steinauer, J. (2010). Disparities in family planning. *American Journal of Obstetrical Gynecology, 202*(3), 214–220.

DeJong, P., & Berg, I. K. (2012). *Interviewing for solutions* (4th ed.). Pacific Grove: Cengage.

De Meyer, G., Shapiro, F., Vanderstichele, H., Vanmechelen, E., Engelborghs, S., De Deyn, P., *et al.* (2010). Diagnosis-independent Alzheimer disease biomarker signature in cognitively normal elderly people. *Archives of Neurology, 67*(8), 949–956.

DeNavas-Walt, C., Proctor, B. D., & Smith, J. C. (2013). Income, poverty, and health insurance coverage in the United States: 2012. *Current Population Reports,* P60-245. Washington, DC: U.S. Government Printing Office.

Denham, S. A. (1998). *Emotional development in young children.* New York: Guilford.

Department of Health and Human Services. (2014). A statistical profile of Asian older Americans aged 65+. [Online.] Retrieved July 18, 2014, from http://www.aoa.gov/AoARoot/Aging_Statistics/minority_aging/Facts-on-API-Elderly2008-plain_format.aspx.

DeSouza, E., & Fansler, A. G. (2003). Contrapower sexual harassment: A survey of students and faculty members. *Sex Roles, 48*(11/12), 529–542.

DeSpelder, L. A., & Strickland, A. L. (2011). *The last dance* (9th ed.). New York: McGraw-Hill.

Devaney, S. A., Palomaki, G. E., Scott, J. A., & Bianchi, D. W. (2011). Noninvasive fetal sex determination using cell-free fetal DNA. *JAMA, 306*(6), 627–636.

DeVoe, J. E., Graham, A. S., Angier, H., Baez, A., & Krois, L. (2008). Obtaining health care services for low-income children: A hierarchy of needs. *Journal of Health Care for the Poor and Underserved, 19*(4), 1192–1211.

Digiovanna, A. G. (1994). *Human aging: Biological perspectives.* New York: McGraw-Hill.

Dodd, B., & Carr, A. (2003). Young children's letter-sound knowledge. *Language, Speech, and Hearing Services in Schools, 34,* 128–137.

Doka, K. J. (2002). *Disenfranchised grief: New directions, challenges, and strategies for practice.* Champaign, IL: Research Press.

Dominelli, L. (2002). Anti-oppressive practice in context. In R. Adams, L. Dominelli, & M. Payne (Eds.), *Social work: Themes, issues, and critical debates* (2nd ed., pp. 3–19). Houndmills, Basingstoke, UK: Palgrave Macmillan.

Dominelli, L. (2011). Climate change: Social workers' roles and contributions to policy debates and interventions. *International Journal of Social Welfare, 20*(4), 430–438.

Donohoe, M. (2003). Causes and health consequences of environmental degradation and social injustice. *Social Science & Medicine, 56*(3), 573–587.

Donovan, J. (1994). *Feminist theory: The intellectual traditions of American feminism.* New York: Continuum.

Dorn, L. D., Kolko, D. J., Susman, E. J., Huang, B., Stein, H., Music, E., et al. (2009). Salivary gonadal and adrenal hormone differences in boys and girls with and without disruptive behavior disorders: Contextual variants. *Biological Psychology, 81*(1), 31–39.

Dott, M., Rasmussen, S. A., Hogue, C. J., Reefhuis, J. (2010). Association between pregnancy intention and reproductive-health related behaviors before and after pregnancy recognition, National Birth Defects Prevention Study, 1997–2002. *Journal of Maternal Child Health, 1,* 373–381.

Dovidio, J. F., & Gaertner, S. L. (1996). Affirmative action, unintentional racial biases, and intergroup relations. *Journal of Social Issues, 52,* 51–75.

Dowd, J. J. (1975). Aging as exchange: A preface to theory. *Journal of Gerontology, 30*(5), 584–594.

Dowd, J. J. (1980). Exchange rates and old people. *Journal of Gerontology, 35,* 596–602.

Du Bois, W. E. B. (1911). The girl nobody loved. *Social News, 2*(November), 3.

Du Bois, W. E. B. (1970). *The negro American family.* Cambridge, MA: MIT Press.

Dunifon, R., & Bajracharya, A. (2012). The role of grandparents in the lives of youth. *Journal of Family Issues, 33*(9), 1168–1194.

Dunlosky, J., Cavallini, E., Roth, H., McGuire, C. L., Vecchi, T., & Hertzog, C. (2007). Do self-monitoring interventions improve older adult learning? *Journals of Gerontology Series B: Psychological Sciences & Social Sciences, 62B,* 70–76.

Durkheim, E. (1933). *The division of labor in society.* New York: Free Press.

Durkheim, E. (1938). *The rules of the sociological method.* Chicago: The University of Chicago Press.

Early, T. J., & GlenMaye, L. F. (2000). Valuing families: Social work practice with families from a strengths perspective. *Social Work, 45*(2), 118–130.

Easter, A., Treasure, J., & Micali, N. (2011). Fertility and prenatal attitudes towards pregnancy in women with eating disorders: Results from the Avon Longitudinal Study of Parents and Children.

International Journal of Obstetrics and Gynaecology, 118(12), 1491–1498.

Eckstein, D. (2000). Empirical studies indicating significant birth-order-related personality differences. *Journal of Individual Psychology, 56*(4), 481–494.

Ecojustice. (2008). Aamjiwnaang Bucket Brigade discovers alarming levels of toxic chemicals in Sarnia. Retrieved June 14, 2009, from http://www.ecojustice.ca/media-centre/press-releases/aamjiwnaang-bucketbrigade-discovers-alarming-levels-of-toxicchemicals-in-sarnia.

Edgar, B. (2010). Supreme court's campaign ruling: A bad day for democracy. [Online.] Retrieved July 21, 2015, from http://www.csmonitor.com/Commentary/Opinion/2010/0122/Supreme-Court-s-campaign-ruling-a-bad-day-for-democracy.

Eheart, B. K., Hopping, D., Power, M. B., Mitchell, E. T., & Racine, D. (2009). *Generations of hope communities.* Champaign, IL: Generations of Hope Development Corporation.

Eisenberg, N., Chang, L., Ma, Y., & Huang, X. (2009). Relations of parenting style to Chinese children's effortful control, ego resilience, and maladjustment. *Development and Psychopathology, 21*(2), 455–477.

Eldar-Avidan, D., Haj-Yahia, M. M., & Greenbaum, C. W. (2009). Divorce is a part of my life . . . resilience, survival, and vulnerability: Young adults' perception of the implications of parental divorce. *Journal of Marital and Family Therapy, 35*(1), 30–46.

Encyclopedia of Mental Disorders. (2014). Reactive attachment disorders of infancy or early childhood. Retrieved May 30, 2014 from http://www.minddisorders.com/Py-Z/Reactive-attachment-disorder-of-infancy-or-early-childhood.html.

Endogenous Hormones and Breast Cancer Collaborative Group. (2011). Circulating sex hormones and breast cancer risk factors in postmenopausal women: Reanalysis of 13 studies. *British Journal of Cancer, 105,* 709–722.

Eriksen, J., Jorgensen, T. N., & Gether, U. (2010). Regulation of dopamine transporter function by protein-protein interactions: new discoveries and Methodological challenges. *Journal of Neurochemistry, 113*(1), 27–41.

Erikson, E. (1950). *Childhood and society.* New York: W. W. Norton.

Ersche, K. D., Jones, S., Williams, G. B., Turton, A. J., Robbins, T. W., & Bullmore, E. T. (2012). Abnormal brain structure implicated in stimulant drug addiction. *Science, 335*(6068), 601–604.

Esposito, N. W. (1999). Marginalized women's comparisons of their hospital and freestanding birth center experiences: A contrast of inner-city birthing systems. *Health Care for Women International, 20*(2), 111–126.

Evans, J. L. (2001). Eight is too late: Investment in early childhood development. *Journal of International Affairs, 55*(1), 91–109.

Evans, S. E., Davies, C., & DiLillo, D. (2008). Exposure to domestic violence: A meta-analysis of child and adolescent outcomes. *Aggression & Violent Behavior, 13*(2), 131–140.

Facts for special edition. Retrieved March 5, 2012, from http://www.census.gov/newsroom/releases/archives/facts_for_features_special_editions/cb11-ff17.html.

Fairburn, C. G., & Harrison, P. J. (2003, February 1). Eating disorders. *Lancet, 361,* 407–416.

Family Caregiver Alliance. (2003). *Women and care-giving: Facts and figures.* San Francisco: Author.

Faraone, S. V., Brown, C. H., Glatt, S. J., & Ming, T. T. (2002). Preventing schizophrenia and psychotic behavior: Definitions and methodological issues. *Canadian Journal of Psychiatry, 47*(6), 527–537.

Feinberg, L., Reinhard, S. C., Houser, A., & Choula, R. (2011). *Valuing the invaluable: 2011 update, the growing contributions and costs of family caregiving.* [Online.] Retrieved May 31, 2012, from http://www.aarp.org/relationships/caregiving/info-07-2011/valuing-the-invaluable.html.

Felitti, V. R. (1998). The relationship of adult health status to childhood abuse and household dysfunction. *American Journal of Preventive Medicine, 14*(4), 245–258.

Feller, A., & Stone, C. (2009, September 9). Top 1 percent of Americans reaped two-thirds of income gains in last economic expansion. Washington,

DC: Center on Budget and Policy Priorities. [Online.] Retrieved October 20, 2014, from http://www.cbpp.org/cms/index. cfm?fa=view&id=2908.

Fellin, P. (2000, Spring/Summer). Revisiting multi-culturalism in social work. *Journal of Social Work Education, 36*(2), 261–278.

Fielding, R. A. (1995). The role of progressive resistance training and nutrition in the preservation of lean body mass in the elderly. *Journal of the American College of Nutrition, 14*(December), 87–94.

Finer, L. B., & Henshaw, S. K. (2006). Disparities in rates of unintended pregnancy in the United States, 1994 and 2001. *Perspectives in Sexual Reproductive Health, 38*(2), 90–96.

Finer, L. B., & Zolna, M. R. (2011). Unintended pregnancy in the United States: Incidence and disparities, 2006. *Contraception, 84*(5), 478–485.

Fischer, J. (1981). The social work revolution. *Social Work, 26*(3), 199–207.

Fisher, J., Cabral de Mello, M., Patel, V., Rahman, A., Tran, T., Holton, S., *et al.* (2012). Prevalence and determinants of common perinatal mental disorders in women in low- and lower-middle-income countries: A systematic review. *Bulletin of the World Health Organization, 90,* 139–149. DOI: 10.2471/BLT.11.091850.

Fong, R., Spickard, P. R., & Ewalt, P. L. (1995). A multiracial reality: Issues for social work. *Social Work, 40*(6), 725–727.

Food and Water Watch. (2014). Top 10 problems. [Online.] Retrieved October 27, 2014, from http://www.foodandwaterwatch.org/common-resources/fish/fish-farming/offshore/problems/.

Forness, S. R., & Kavale, K. A. (2001). ADHD and a return to the medical model of special education. *Education and Treatment of Children, 24*(3), 224–247.

Fouts, G., & Burggraf, K. (2000). Television situation comedies: Female weight, male negative comments, and audience reactions. *Sex Roles, 42*(9/10), 925–932.

Fowler, J. (1981). *Stages of faith: The psychology of human development and the quest for meaning.* San Francisco: Harper & Row.

Fowler, J. (1996). *Faithful change: The personal and public challenges of postmodern life.* Nashville, TN: Abingdon Press.

Fox, M., Berzuini, C., & Knapp, L. A. (2013). Maternal breastfeeding history and Alzheimer's disease risk. *Journal of Alzheimer's Disease, 37*(4), 809–821. DOI: 10.3233/JAD-130152.

Frances, A. (2013). The new somatic symptom disorder in DSM-5 risks mislabeling many people as mentally ill. *BMJ, 346,* f1580. DOI: 10.1136/bmj.f1580.

Frank, D. A., Augustyn, M., Knight, W. G., Pell, T., & Zuckerman, B. (2001). Growth, development, and behavior in early childhood following prenatal cocaine exposure. *The Journal of the American Medical Association, 285*(12), 1613–1625.

Freedle, R. (2006). How and why standardized tests systematically underestimate African-Americans' true verbal ability and what to do about it: Towards the promotion of two new theories with practical applications. *St. John's Law Review, 80*(1), 183–226.

Freire, P. (1972). *Pedagogy of the oppressed.* London: Penguin.

Freud, S. (1909). *Selected papers on hysteria and other psychoneuroses.* New York: The Journal of Nervous and Mental Disease Publishing Company.

Freud, S. (1914). *The psychopathology of everyday life.* London: Adelphi Terrace.

Freud, S. (1920a). *A general introduction to psychoanalysis.* New York: Washington Square Press.

Freud, S. (1920b). *Three contributions to the theory of sex* (2nd ed.). New York: The Journal of Nervous and Mental Disease Publishing Company.

Freud, S. (1955). The psychogenesis of a case of homosexuality in a woman. In J. Strachey (Ed. & Trans.) *The standard edition of the complete psychological works of Sigmund Freud.* (Vol. 28, pp. 145–172). London, UK: Hogarth Press. (Original work published 1920.)

Freud, S. (1961). Female Sexuality. In J. Strachey (Ed. & Trans.) *The standard edition of the complete psychological works of Sigmund Freud.* (Vol. 21, pp. 225–245). London, UK: Hogarth Press. (Original work published 1931.)

Fried, P. A., & Smith, A. M. (2001). A literature review of the consequences of prenatal marijuana exposure: An emerging theme of a deficiency in executive function. *Neurotoxicology and Teratology, 23,* 1–11.

Fried, P. A., & Watkinson, B. (1990). Thirty-six and forty-eight month neurobehavioral follow-up of children prenatally exposed to marijuana, cigarettes, and alcohol. *Developmental and Behavioral Pediatrics, 11,* 49–58.

Funk, J. B., Buchman, D. D., Jenks, J., & Bechtoldt, H. (2002, November). An evidence-based approach to examining the impact of playing violent video and computer games. *Simile, 2*(4), 1–11.

Gallup Organization. (1995). *Disciplining children in America: A Gallup poll report.* Princeton, NJ: Gallup Organization.

Gardella, J. R., & Hill, J. A. (2000). Environmental toxins associated with recurrent pregnancy loss. *Seminars in Reproductive Medicine, 18,* 407–424.

Gardner, H. (1983). *Frames of mind.* New York: Basic Books.

Garety, P. (1991). Reasoning and delusions. *British Journal of Psychiatry, 159*(suppl. 14), 14–18.

Garner, D. M., & Desai, J. J. (2001). Eating disorders in children and adolescents. In J. N. Stevenson, J. N. Hughes, A. M. La Greca, & J. C. Conoley (Eds.), *Handbook of psychological services for children and adolescents* (pp. 399–420). New York: Oxford University Press.

Garran, A., & Rozas, L. (2013). Cultural competence revisited. *Journal of Ethnic and Cultural Diversity in Social Work, 22* (2), 1–10.

Garreau, J. (1992). *Edge city: Life on the new frontier.* New York: Anchor Books.

Garrett, K. E. (2006). *Living in America: Challenges facing new immigrants and refugees.* Robert Wood Johnson Foundation: Publisher.

Gaten, D. R. (2009). Elementary school principals' perceptions of corporal punishment. *Dissertation Abstracts International Section A: Humanities and Social Sciences, 69*(7-A), 2542.

Gazzaniga, M. S. (2010). *The cognitive neurosciences* (4th ed.). New York: Cambridge University Press.

Gender Spectrum. (2014). *Understanding gender.* [Online.] Retrieved June 25, 2014, from http://www.genderspectrum.org/child-family/understanding-gender.

George, L. K. (1993). Depressive disorders and symptoms in later life. *Generations,* Winter/Spring, 35–38.

Gerety, M. B., & Farnett, L. (1995). Management of depression in the elderly. *Strategies in Geriatrics, 2*(6), 137–143.

Gershoff, E. T. (2002). Parental corporal punishment and associated child behaviors and experiences: A meta-analytic and theoretical review. *Psychological Bulletin, 128,* 539–579.

Gibelman, M. (2000). Affirmative action at the crossroads: A social justice perspective. *Journal of Sociology and Social Welfare, 27*(1), 153–174.

Gibelman, M. (2003). So how far have we come? Pestilent and persistent gender gap in pay. *Social Work, 48*(1), 22–32.

Gilead Sciences. (2014). How is Truvada used to treat HIV-1 infection? [Online.] Retrieved July 14, 2014, from http://www.truvada.com/.

Gilens, M. (2005). Inequality and democratic responsiveness. *Public Opinion Quarterly, 69*(5), 778–796.

Gilligan, C. (1982). *In a different voice: Psychological theory and women's development.* Cambridge, MA: Harvard University Press.

Gilligan, C., & Attanucci, J. (1988). Two moral orientations. In C. Gilligan, J. V. Ward, J. M. Taylor, & B. Bardige (Eds.), *Mapping the moral domain* (pp. 73–86). Cambridge, MA: Harvard University Press.

Glazer, S. (1993, November 26). *Do current policies punish kids awaiting adoption?* The CQ Researcher [Online.] Available at http://0-library.cqpress.com.clark.up.edu/cqresearcher/document.php?id=cqresrre1993112607.

Global Community Monitor. (2007). *Canada: Aamjiwnaang First Nation: Toxic cocktail being tracked with buckets.* Retrieved June 14, 2009, from http://www.shellfacts.com/article.php?id=580.

Goffman, E. (1959). *The presentation of self in everyday life.* Garden City, NY: Anchor Books.

Gogtay, N., Giedd, J. N., Lusk, L., Hayashi, K. M., Greenstein, D., Vaituzis, A. C., *et al.* (2004). Dynamic mapping of human cortical development during childhood through early adulthood. *Proceedings of the National Academy of Sciences of the United States of America, 101*(21), 8174–8179.

Gokcay, G. (2009). Breastfeeding for the sake of Europe and the world: European society for social pediatrics and child health position statement. *Child: Care, Health, and Development, 35*(3), 293–297.

Golash-Boza, T. M. (2015). *Race and racisms: A critical perspective*. New York: Oxford University Press.

Goldberg, J., Holtz, D., Hyslop, T., & Tolosa, J. E. (2002). Has the use of routine episiotomy decreased? Examination of episiotomy rates from 1983 to 2000. *Obstetrics and Gynecology, 99*(3), 395–400.

Goldenberg, I., & Goldenberg, H. (2004). *Family therapy: An overview*. Belmont, CA: Brooks/Cole.

Goldsmith, H. H., Buss, K. A., & Lemery, K. S. (1997). Toddler and childhood temperament: Expanded content, stronger genetic evidence, new evidence for the importance of environment. *Developmental Psychology, 33*(6), 891–905.

Goldsmith, H. H., Lemery, K. S., Buss, K. A., & Campos, J. J. (1999). Genetic analyses of focal aspects of infant temperament. *Developmental Psychology, 35*(4), 972–985.

Goleman, D. (2006). *Emotional intelligence*. New York: Bantam Books.

Golombok, S. (2002). Adoption by lesbian couples. *British Medical Journal, 324*(7351), 1407–1409.

Gonzales, J. (2009). Prefamily counseling: Working with blended families. *Journal of Divorce & Remarriage, 50*(2), 148–157.

Goodman, A. H. (2000). Why genes don't count (for racial differences in health). *American Journal of Public Health, 90*(11), 1699–1702.

Gordon, W. (1969). Basic constructs for an integrative and generative conception of social work. In G. Hearn (Ed.), *The general systems approach: Contributions toward an holistic conception of social work*. New York: Council on Social Work Education.

Gorman, D. (1999). Active and passive euthanasia: The cases of Drs. Claudio Alberto de la Rocha and Nancy Morrison. *Canadian Medical Association Journal, 160*(6), 857–860.

Gotta, G., Green, R. J., Rothblum, E., Solomon, S., Balsam, K., & Schwartz, P. (2011). Heterosexual, lesbian, and gay male relationships: A comparison of couples in 1975 and 2000. *Family Process, 50*(3), 353–376.DOI:10.1111/j.1545–5300.2011.01365.x.

Gottman, J. M., & Levenson, R. W. (2000). The timing of divorce: Predicting when a couple will divorce over a 14-year period. *Journal of Marriage and the Family, 62*, 737–745.

Gould, J. (2008). Non-standard assessment practices in the evaluation of communication in Australian Aboriginal children. *Clinical Linguistics & Phonetics, 22*(8), 643–657.

Gould, S. J. (1996). *The mismeasure of man*. New York: W. W. Norton & Company.

Grace, S. L., Evindar, A., & Stewart, D. E. (2003). The effect of postpartum depression on child cognitive development and behavior: A review and critical analysis of the literature. *Archives of Women's Mental Health, 6*(4): 263–274.

Grauerholz, E., & King, A. (1997). Prime time sexual harassment. *Violence Against Women, 3*, 129–148.

Gray, M. (2011). Back to basics: A critique of the strengths perspective in social work. *Families in Society, 92*(1), 5–11.

Greenaway, M. C., Hanna, S. M., Lepore, S. W., & Smith, G. E. (2008). A behavioral rehabilitation intervention for amnestic mild cognitive impairment. *American Journal of Alzheimer's Disease & Other Dementias, 23*(5), 451–461.

Greenberg, J., Pyszczynski, T., & Solomon, S. (1986). The causes and consequences of a need for self-esteem: A terror management theory. In R. F. Baumeister (Ed.), *Public self and private self* (pp. 189–212). New York: Springer-Verlag.

Greenberg, J., Solomon, S., & Pyszczynski, T. (1997). Terror management theory of self-esteem and social behavior: Empirical assessments and conceptual refinements. In M. P. Zanna (Ed.), *Advances in experimental social psychology* (Vol. 29, pp. 61–139). San Diego, CA: Academic Press.

Greene, R. W., & Ablon, J.S. (2006). *Treating explosive kids: The collaborative problem solving approach*. New York: Guilford Press.

Greene, R. W., & Doyle, A. E. (1999). Toward a transactional conceptualization of oppositional defiant disorder: Implications for assessment and treatment. *Clinical Child and Family Psychology Review, 2*(3), 129–148.

Grigorenko, E. L. (2001). Developmental dyslexia: An update on genes, brains, and environments. *Journal of Child Psychology and Psychiatry, 42*(1), 91–125.

Grimm, R., Spring, K., & Dietz, N. (2007). *The health benefits of volunteering: A review of recent research.* New York: Corporation for National and Community Service.

Grise-Owens, E. (2002). Sexism and the social work curriculum: A content analysis of the *Journal of Social Work Education. Affilia, 17*(2), 147–166.

Gross, H. E. (1993, May/June). Open adoption: A research-based literature review and new data. *Child Welfare, 72*(3), 269–285.

Gulli, C. (2009). Gay seniors get a place to call home. *Maclean's, 122*(14), 23.

Gurman, A. S. (1977). The patient's perception of the therapeutic relationship. In A. S. Gurman & A. M. Razin (Eds.), *Effective psychotherapy: A handbook of research* (pp. 503–543). Oxford: Pergamon.

Guthrie, M. L., & Bates, L. W. (2003). Sex education sources and attitudes toward sexual precautions across a decade. *Psychological Reports, 92*, 581–592.

Guttery, E. G., Friday, G. A., Field, S. S., Riggs, S. C., & Hagan, J. F. (2002, June). Coparent or second-parent adoption by same-sex parents. *Pediatrics, 109*(6), 1192–1194.

Guttmacher Institute. (2012). *Facts on American Teens' Sources of Information About Sex.* [Online.] Retrieved July 14, 2014, from http://www.guttmacher.org/pubs/FB-Teen-Sex-Ed.html.

Habermas, T., & Bluck, S. (2000). Getting a life: The emergence of the life story in adolescence. *Psychological Bulletin, 126*, 748–769.

Habermas, T., Ehlert-Lerche, S., & de Silveira, C. (2009). The development of the temporal macrostructure of life narratives across adolescence: Beginnings, linear narrative form, and endings. *Journal of Personality, 77*(2), 527–560. DOI: 10.1111/j.1467–6494.2008.00557.x.

Habicht, J. P., Davanzo, J., & Butz, W. P. (1986). Does breastfeeding really save lives, or are apparent benefits due to biases? *American Journal of Epidemiology, 123*, 279–290.

Hacker, A. (2003). *Mismatch: The growing gulf between women and men.* New York: Scribner.

Hagan, J. F. (2002, August). It's about their children. *Pediatrics, 110*(2), 408–410.

Hagg, T. (2009). From neurotransmitters to neurotrophic factors to neurogenesis. *The Neuroscientist, 15*(10), 20–27.

Haight, W. L., Kagle, J. D., & Black, J. E. (2003). Understanding and supporting parent–child relationships during foster care visits: Attachment theory and research. *Social Work, 48*(2), 195–209.

Haines, J. D., Inglese, M., & Casaccia, P. (2011). Axonal damage in multiple sclerosis. *The Mount Sinai Journal of Medicine, 78*(2), 231–243.

Håkansson, K. (1982) *Ovetande och Vetande* [Un-knowing and knowing]. Göteborg: Korpen.

Haksoon, A. (2012). Child care subsidy, child care costs, and employment of low-income single mothers. *Children & Youth Service Review, 34*(2), 379–387.

Hallahan, D. P., & Kauffman, J. M. (2000). *Exceptional learners: Introduction to special education* (8th ed.). Boston: Allyn & Bacon.

Hallmayer, J., Cleveland, S., Torres, A., Phillips, J., Cohen, B., Torigoe, T., *et al.* (2011). Genetic heritability and shared environmental factors among twin pairs with autism. *Archives of General Psychiatry, 68*(11), 1095–1102.

Hamilton, B. E., Martin, J. A., Osterman, M. J. K., & Curtin, S. C. (2014). Births: Preliminary data for 2013. *National Vital Statistics Reports, 63*(2), 1–20.

Hamilton, B. E., Martin, J. A., & Ventura, S. J. (2011). Births: Preliminary data for 2010. *National Vital Statistics Reports, 60*(2), 16, Table 8.

Hamilton, L., Cheng, S., & Powell, B. (2007). Adoptive parents, adaptive parents: Evaluating the importance of biological ties for parental investment. *American Sociological Review, 72*(1), 95–116.

Hammock, E. A. D., & Levitt, P. (2006). The discipline of neurobehavioral development: The emerging interface of processes that build circuits and skills. *Human Development, 49*(5), 294–309.

Hanna, F. J., Talley, W. B., & Guindon, M. H. (2000). The power of perception: Toward a model of cultural oppression and liberation. *Journal of Counseling & Development, 78,* 430–441.

Harkness, S. (1990). A cultural model for the acquisition of language: Implications for the innateness debate. *Developmental Psychobiology, 23,* 727–739.

Harlow, H. F., & Zimmerman, R. R. (1959). Affectional responses in the infant monkey. *Science, 130,* 421–432.

Harrington, M. (1981). *The other America: Poverty in the United States.* New York: Simon & Schuster, Inc.

Harris, D. R., & Sim, J. J. (2002). Who is multiracial? Assessing the complexity of lived race. *American Sociological Review, 67,* 614–627.

Hart, B., & Risley, T. R. (1995). *Meaningful differences in the everyday experience of young American children.* Baltimore, MD: P. H. Brookes.

Harter, S. (1999). *The construction of self.* New York: Guilford.

Harvard Mental Health Letter. (2002, November). The spanking debate. *Harvard Mental Health Letter, 19*(5), 1–3.

Harvey, D. (2005). *A brief history of neoliberalism.* New York: Oxford University Press.

Hashimoto-Torii, K., Kawasawa, Y. I., Kuhn, A., & Rakic, P. (2011). Combined transcriptome analysis of fetal human and mouse cerebral cortex exposed to alcohol. *Proceedings of the National Academy of Science, 108*(10), 4212–4217.

Hassold, T., & Patterson, D. (Eds.). (1998). *Down syndrome: A promising future together.* New York: Wiley Liss.

Hatzenbuehler, M. L. (2011). The social environment and suicide attempts in lesbian, gay, and bisexual youth. *Pediatrics, 127,* 896–903.

Havighurst, R. J., Neugarten, B. L., & Tobin, S. S. (1968). Disengagement and patterns of aging. In B. Neugarten (Ed.), *Middle age and aging: A reader in social psychology* (pp. 161–172). Chicago: University of Chicago Press.

Haws, W. A., & Mallinckrodt, B. (1998). Separation individuation from family of origin and marital adjustment of recently married couples. *American Journal of Family Therapy, 26*(4), 293–306.

Hay, D. F., Pawlby, S., Angold, A., Harold, G. T., & Sharp, D. (2003). Pathways to violence in the children of mothers who were depressed postpartum. *Developmental Psychology, 39*(6): 1083–1094.

Healey, J. F. (1997). *Race, ethnicity and gender in the United States.* Thousand Oaks, CA: Pine Forge Press.

Healey, M., & Jenkins, A. (2000). Kolb's experiential learning theory and its application in geography in higher education. *Journal of Geography, 99,* 185–195.

Heider, F. (1958). *The psychology of interpersonal relations.* New York: Wiley.

Heikkiia, K., Sacker, A., Kelly, Y., Renfrew, M. J., & Quigley, M. A. (2011). Breastfeeding and child behavior in the millennium cohort study. *Archives of Disorders in Childhood, 96,* 635–642.

Heilman, M. E. (2001). Description and prescription: How gender stereotypes prevent women's ascent up the organizational ladder. *Journal of Social Issues, 57*(4), 657–674.

Held, D. (1980). *Introduction to critical theory: Horkheimer to Habermas.* Los Angeles: University of California Press.

Helsen, M., Vollebergh, W., & Meeus, W. (2000). Social support from parents and friends and emotional problems in adolescence. *Journal of Youth and Adolescence, 29*(3), 319–335.

Henry, W. (1963). The theory of intrinsic disengagement. In P. F. Hansen (Ed.), *Age with a future.* Copenhagen: Monksgaard.

Herek, G. M. (2001). On heterosexual masculinity: Some psychical consequences of the social construction of gender and sexuality. *American Behavioral Scientist, 29*(5), 563–577.

Herrera, N. C., Zajonc, R. B., Wieczorkowska, G., & Cichomski, B. (2003). Beliefs about birth rank and their reflection in reality. *Journal of Personality and Social Psychology, 85*(1), 142–150.

Hetherington, E. M. (2000). Divorce. In A. Kazdin (Ed.), *Encyclopedia of psychology* (pp. 61–65). Washington, DC: American Psychological Association.

Hetherington, E. M. (2003). Social support and the adjustment of children in divorced and remarried families. *Childhood, 10*(2), 217–236.

Heugten, K., & Wilson, E. (2008). Witnessing intimate partner violence: Review of the literature on coping in young persons. *Social Work Review, 20*(3), 52–62.

Hewagama, A., & Richardson, B. (2009). The genetics and epigenetics of autoimmune diseases. *Journal of Autoimmunity, 33*(1), 3–11.

Hibel, J., Farkas, G., & Morgan, P. L. (2010). Who is placed into special education? *Sociology of Education, 83*(4), 312–332. DOI: 10.1177/0038040710383518.

Hildyard, K. L., & Wolfe, D. A. (2002). Child neglect: Developmental issues and outcomes. *Child Abuse and Neglect, 26*, 679–695.

Hillier, S., & Barrow, G. M. (2006). *Aging, the individual, and society* (8th ed.). Belmont, CA: Wadsworth.

Himmelstein, K. E. W., & Bruckner, H. (2011). Criminal-justice and school sanctions against nonheterosexual youth: A national longitudinal study. *Pediatrics, 127*(1), 49–57.

Hirata, A., & Castro-Alamancos, M. A. (2010). Neocortex network activation and deactivation states controlled by the thalamus. *Journal of Neurophysiology, 103*(3), 1147–1157.

Hirsch, B. J., Mickus, M., Boerger, R. (2002). Ties to influential adults among black and white adolescents: Culture, social class, and family networks. *American Journal of Community Psychology, 30*(2), 289–303.

Hobbins, J. C. (1997). Alpha-fetoprotein screening for neural tube defects. *Contemporary Ob/Gyn*, 160–161.

Hodges, E. V. E., & Card, N. A. (Eds.). (2003). *Enemies and the darker side of peer relations*. San Francisco: Jossey-Bass.

Hoek, H. W. (2006). Incidence, prevalence, and mortality of anorexia nervosa and other eating disorders. *Current Opinion in Psychiatry, 19*(4), 389–394.

Hoff, E. (2003). The specificity of environmental influence: Socioeconomic status affects early vocabulary development via maternal speech. *Child Development, 74*(5), 1368–1378.

Hoffman, L. (1981). *Foundations of family therapy*. New York: Basic Books.

Hollenshead, C. S., & Miller, J. E. (2001). *Diversity workshops: Gender equity—a closer look*. [Online.] Retrieved January 21, 2004, from http//www.diversityweb.org/Digest/Sp01/research2.html.

Holzel, B. K., Carmody, J., Vangel, M., Congleton, C., Yerramsetti, S. M., Gard, T., & Lazar, S. W. (2011). Mindfulness practice leads to increases in regional brain gray matter density. *Psychiatry Research: Neuroimaging, 191*, 36–43.

Homan, M. S. (1999). *Promoting community change: Making it happen* (2nd ed.). Pacific Grove, CA: Brooks/Cole.

Homans, G. C. (1967). *The nature of social science*. New York: Harcourt, Brace & World.

Hopper, R., & Naremore, R. (1978). *Children's speech: A practical introduction to communication development*. New York: Harper & Row.

Hotton, A. L., Garofalo, R., Kuhns, L. M., & Johnson, A. K. (2013). Substance use as a mediator of the relationship between life stress and sexual risk among young transgender women. *AIDS Education and Prevention, 25*(1), 62–71.

Howie, P. W., Forsyth, J. S., Ogston, S. A., Clark, A., Du, V., & Florey, C. (1990). Protective effect of breast feeding against infection. *British Journal of Medicine, 300*, 1–11.

Huang, C. C., & Chang, Y. C. (2009). The long-term effects of febrile seizures on the hippocampal neuronal plasticity—clinical and experimental evidence. *Brain and Development, 31*, 383–387.

Huang, Z. J., Yu, S. M., Liu, X. W., Young, D., & Wong, F. Y. (2009). Beyond medical insurance: Delayed or forgone care among children in Chinese immigrant families. *Journal of Health Care for the Poor and Underserved, 20*(2), 364–377.

Hudson, J. I., Hiripi, E., Pope, H. G., & Kessler, R. C. (2007). The prevalence and correlates of eating disorders in the National Comorbidity Survey Replication. *Biological Psychiatry, 61*(3), 348–358.

Huesmann, L. R., Moise-Titus, J., Podolski, C., & Eron, L. D. (2003). Longitudinal relations between children's exposure to TV violence and their aggressive and violent behavior in young adulthood:

1977–1992. *Developmental Psychology, 39*(2), 201–221.

Hulsey, T. M., Laken, M., Miller, V., & Ager, J. (2000). The influence of attitudes about unintended pregnancy on use of prenatal and postpartum care. *Journal of Perinatology, 20,* 513–519.

Humphreys, C., Lowe, P., & Williams, S. (2009). Sleep disruption and domestic violence: Exploring the interconnections between mothers and children. *Child & Family Social Work, 14*(1), 6–14.

Hunt, B. R., Whitman, S., & Hurlbert, M. S. (2014). Increasing Black:White disparities in breast cancer mortality in the 50 largest cities in the United States. *Cancer Epidemiology, 38*(2), 118–123. DOI: 10.1016/j.canep.2013.09.009.

Hunter College Women's Studies Collective (1995). *Women's realities, women's choices: An introduction to women's studies.* New York: Oxford University Press.

Hybels, C. F., & Blazer, D. G. (2003). Epidemiology of late-life mental disorders. *Clinics in Geriatric Medicine, 19,* 663–696.

Ibrahim, A., Tran, T., Pierce, D., Johnston, J., Richmond, N., & Berry, S. (2014). Racial disparity in birth defects: Who has higher risk? *Online Journal of Public Health Informatics, 6*(1), e62.

Inomata, K., Aoto, T., Binh, N. T., Okamoto, N., Tanimura, S., Wakayama, T., *et al.* (2009). Genotoxic stress abrogates renewal of melanocyte stem cells by triggering their differentiation. *Cell, 137*(6), 1088–1099.

Institute of Medicine. (1997). *The hidden epidemic.* Washington, DC: National Academy Press.

International Women's Health Coalition. (1997, May 21). *A women's lens on foreign policy: A symposium.* [Online.] Conference proceedings retrieved July 15, 2003, from http://www.iwhc.org/uploads/womenslens.pdf.

Intersex Society of North America. (2012). *What is intersex?* [Online.] Retrieved May 15, 2012, from http://www.isna.org/faq/what_is_intersex.

Isidori, A. (2008). Myths and reality of male andropause. *Sexologies, 17*(1), S24–S25.

Izard, C. E. (1982). *Measuring emotions in infants and young children.* New York: Cambridge University Press.

Izard, C. E. (1991). *The psychology of emotions.* New York: Plenum Press.

Jackson, D. D. (1957). The question of family homeostasis. *Psychiatric Quarterly Supplement, 31,* 79–90.

Jacobsen, S. W., Jacobson, J. L., Sokol, R. J., Martier, S. S., & Ager, J. W. (1993). Prenatal alcohol exposure and infant information processing ability. *Child Development, 64,* 1706–1721.

Jacobson, L. (2003, May 28). Head Start bill jump-starts debate on program's future. *Education Week, 22*(38), 20.

Jakupcak, M., Wagner, A., Paulson, A., Varra, A., & McFall, M. (2010). Behavioral activation as a primary care-based treatment for PTSD and depression among returning veterans. *Journal of Traumatic Stress, 23*(4), 491–495.

James, B. D., Leurgans, S. E., Hebert, L. E., Scherr, P. A., Yaffe, K., & Bennett, D. A. (2014). Contribution of Alzheimer disease to mortality in the United States. *Neurology, 82*(12), 1045–1050. DOI: 10.1212/WNL.0000000000000240.

Jensen, R., & Burgess, H. (1997). Mythmaking: How introductory psychology texts present B. F. Skinner's analysis of cognition. *Psychological Record, 47*(2), 221–231.

Johnson, C. C., & Johnson, K. A. (2000). High-risk behavior among gay adolescents: Implications for treatment and support. *Adolescence, 35*(140), 619–637.

Johnson, H. C., Atkins, S. P., Battle, S. F., Hernandez-Arata, L., Hesselbrock, M., Libassi, M. F., *et al.* (1990). Strengthening the "bio" in the biopsychosocial paradigm. *Journal of Social Work Education, 26*(2), 109–123.

Johnson, R. W. (2012). *Older workers, retirement, and the great recession.* Stanford, CA: Stanford Center on Poverty and Inequality.

Johnston, L. D., O'Malley, P. M., & Bachman, J. G. (2001). *Monitoring the future: 2001.* Ann Arbor, MI: Institute for Social Research.

Jones, M. C. (1965). Psychological correlates of somatic development. *Child Development, 36,* 899–911.

Jones, M. C., & Bayley, N. (1950). Physical maturing among boys as related to behavior. *Journal of Educational Psychology, 41,* 129–148.

Jones, R. K., & Jerman, J. (2014). Abortion incidence and service availability in the United States, 2011. *Perspectives on Sexual and Reproductive Health, 46*(1), 3–14.

Jones, T. (2007). Examining potential determinants of parental self-efficacy. *Dissertation Abstracts International: Section B: The Sciences and Engineering, 67*(9-B), 5383.

Jones, W., & Klin, A. (2013). Attention to eyes is present but in decline in 2–6-month-old infants later diagnosed with autism. *Nature, 504*, 427–431.

Jordan, B. (2008). Social work and world poverty. *International Social Work, 51*(4), 440–452.

Joyce, T., & Kaestner, R. (2000). The effect of pregnancy intention on child development. *Demography, 37*(1), 83–94.

Joyce, T., Kaestner, R., & Korenman, S. (2000). The stability of pregnancy intentions and pregnancy-related maternal behaviors. *Maternal & Child Health Journal, 4*(3), 171–178.

Jung, C. G. (1961). The theory of psychoanalysis. In R. F. C. Hull (Trans.) *The collected works of C. G. Jung* (Vol. 4, pp. 83–228). Princeton, NJ: Princeton University Press. (Original work published in 1913 and 1955.)

Kabat-Zinn, J. (1994). *Mindfulness meditation for everyday life.* New York: Hyperion.

Kahana, E., & Kahana, B. (1996). Conceptual and empirical advances in understanding aging well through proactive adaptation. In V. Bengtson (Ed.), *Adulthood and aging: Research on continuities and discontinuities* (pp. 124–145). New York: Springer Publishing.

Kahana, E., & Kahana, B. (2003). Contextualizing successful aging: New directions in an age-old search. In R. Settersten, Jr. (Ed.), *Invitation to the life course: A new look at old age.* Amityville, NY: Baywood Publishing.

Kahana, E., Kahana, B., & Kercher, K. (2003). Emerging lifestyles and proactive options for successful aging. *Ageing International, 28*(2), 155–180.

Kaiser Family Foundation. (2005). *Inaugural health education research disparities summit: Health disparities and social inequities: Plenary II—Framing solutions for the elimination of health disparities.* August 8, 2005.

Kaiser Family Foundation. (2010). Generation M2: Media in the lives of 8- to 18-year-olds. [Online.] Retrieved July 11, 2014, from http://kaiserfamilyfoundation.files.wordpress.com/2013/04/8010.pdf.

Kaliman, P., Álvarez-López, M., Cosín-Tomás, M., Rosenkranz, M. A., Lutz, A., & Davidson, R. J. (2014). Rapid changes in histone deacetylases and inflammatory gene expression in expert meditators. *Psychoneuroendocrinology, 40*, 96–107. DOI: 10.1016/j.psyneuen.2013.11.004.

Katz, A. H. (1983). Deficiencies in the status quo. *Social Work, 28*(1), 71.

Kauffman, J. M., & Hallahan, D. P. (2005). *The illusion of full inclusion* (2nd ed.). Austin, TX: Pro-Ed Publishers.

Kausler, D. H., Kausler, B. C., & Krupsaw, J. A. (2007). *The essential guide to aging in the twenty-first century.* Columbia: University of Missouri Press.

Keating, D. P. (1990). Adolescent thinking. In S. S. Feldman & R. Elliott (Eds.), *At the threshold: The developing adolescent* (pp. 54–92). Cambridge, MA: Harvard University Press.

Kelley, B. T., Thornberry, T. P., & Smith, C. A. (1997). *In the wake of childhood violence.* Washington, DC: National Institute of Justice.

Kendall, K. (2003, Summer). Lesbian and gay parents in child custody and visitation disputes. *Human Rights: Journal of the Section of Individual Rights and Responsibilities, 30*(3), 8–10.

Kendall, T., Bird, V., Cantwell, R., & Taylor, C. (2012). To meta-analyse or not to meta-analyse: Abortion, birth, and mental health. *The British Journal of Psychiatry, 200*(1), 12–14.

Kenny, P. J. (2011). Common cellular and molecular mechanisms in obesity and drug addiction. *National Review of Neuroscience, 12*(11), 638–651.

Keyes, C., & Ryff, C. (1999). Psychological well-being in midlife. In S. L. Willis & J. D. Reid (Eds.), *Life in the middle* (pp. 161–178). San Diego, CA: Academic Press.

Kilduff, M., Chiaburu, D. S., & Menges, J. I. (2010). Strategic use of emotional intelligence in organizational settings: Exploring the dark side. *Research in Organizational Behavior, 30,* 12–152. DOI: 10.1016/j.riob.2010.10.002.

Kim, C. J. (2004, September 1). Unyielding positions: A critique of the "race" debate. *Ethnicities, 337*–355.

Kim, P., Evans, G. W., Angstadt, M., Ho, S. S., Sripada, C. S., Swain, J. E., Liberzon, I., & Phan, K. L. (2013). Effects of childhood poverty and chronic stress on emotion regulatory brain function in adulthood. *Proceedings of the National Academy of Sciences.* DOI: 10.1073/pnas.1308240110.

Kimble, M. A. (2001). Beyond the biomedical paradigm: Generating a spiritual vision of ageing. *Journal of Religious Gerontology, 12*(3/4), 31–41.

Kinsley, M. (1995). The spoils of victimhood: The case against the case against affirmative action. *New Yorker,* 62–69.

Klass, D., & Goss, R. (1999). Spiritual bonds to the dead in cross-cultural and historical perspective: Comparative religion and modern grief. *Death Studies, 23*(6), 547–567.

Klaus, M. H., & Fanaroff, A. A. (Eds.) (2001). *Care of the high-risk neonate.* Philadelphia: Saunders.

Kling, K. C., Hyde, J. S., Showers, C. J., & Buswell, B. N. (1999). Gender differences in self-esteem: A meta-analysis. *Psychological Bulletin, 125*(4), 470–500.

Klump, K. L., Keel, P. K., Culbert, K. M., & Edler, C. (2008). Ovarian hormones and binge eating: Exploring associations in community samples. *Psychological Medicine, 38*(12), 1749–1757.

Kochhar, R., Taylor, P., & Fry, R. (2011). *Wealth gaps rise to record highs between whites, blacks, and hispanics.* Washington, DC.: Pew Research Center.

Koenig, H. G. (1995). *Aging and God: Spiritual pathways to mental health in midlife and later years.* New York: Haworth Pastoral Press.

Kohlberg, L. (1969). *Stages in the development of moral thought and action.* New York: Holt, Rinehart, & Winston.

Kohlberg, L. (1976). Moral stages and moralization: The cognitive-developmental approach. In T. Lickona (Ed.), *Moral development and behavior.* New York: Holt, Rinehart, & Winston.

Kohlberg, L. (1978). Revisions in the theory and practice of moral development. *New Directions for Child and Adolescent Development, 1978*(2), 83–87.

Kohlberg, L. (1981). *The philosophy of moral development.* New York: Harper & Row.

Kolb, D. A. (1984). *Experiential learning: Experience as the source of learning and development.* Englewood Cliffs, NJ: Prentice Hall.

Kools, S. M. (1997). Adolescent identity development in foster care. *Family Relations, 46*(3), 263.

Kornblum, W., & Julian, J. (2001). *Social problems* (10th ed.). Upper Saddle River, NJ: Prentice-Hall.

Koropeckyj-Cox, T. (2002). Beyond parental status: Psychological well-being in middle and old age. *Journal of Marriage and the Family, 64*(4), 957–971.

Korvatska, E., Van de Water, J., Anders, T. F., & Gershwin, M. E. (2002). Genetic and immunologic considerations in autism. *Neurobiology of Disease, 9*(2), 107–125.

Kost, K., Landry, D. J., & Darroch, J. (1998). The effects of pregnancy planning status on birth outcomes and infant care. *Family Planning Perspectives, 30*(5), 223–230.

Kosterman, R., Graham, J. W., Hawkins, J. D., Catalano, R. F., & Herrenkohl, T. I. (2001). Childhood risk factors for persistence of violence in the transition to adulthood: A social development perspective. *Violence and Victims, 16*(4), 355–369.

Kotkin, J. (2010). Millennial surprise. [Online.] Retrieved on October 28, 2014, from http://www.newgeography.com/content/001631-millennial-surprise.

Kozhimannil, K., Law, M. R., & Virnig, B. A. (2013). Cesarean delivery rates vary tenfold among U.S. hospitals; reducing variation may address quality and cost issues. *Health Affairs, 32*(3), 527–535.

Krakowiak, P., Walker, C. K., Bremer, A. A., Baker, A. S., Ozonoff, S., Hansen, R. L., *et al.* (2012). Maternal metabolic conditions and risk for autism and other neurodevelopmental disorders. *Pediatrics, 129*(5), 2011–2583.

Kreider, R. (2006). Remarriage in the United States. Presented at the American Sociological Association, Montreal, CA. August 10–14.

Krisberg, K. (2003, Dec/Jan). Deaths due to unintended pregnancies on the rise. *Nation's Health, 32*(10), 12.

Kristjansson, K. (2007). *Aristotle, emotions, and education.* Aldershot, UK: Ashgate.

Kruk, E. (1994). Grandparent visitation disputes: Multi-generational approaches to family mediation. *Mediation Quarterly, 12*(1), 37–53.

Kuan, T. S. (2009). Current studies on myofacial pain syndrome. *Current Pain and Headache Reports, 3,* 365–369.

Kübler-Ross, E. (1969). *On death and dying.* New York: Macmillan.

Kübler-Ross, E. (1971). Stages of dying. In R. H. Davis (Ed.), *Confrontation with dying.* Los Angeles: Gerontology Center, University of Southern California.

Kuhl, P. (1993). Infant speech perception: A window on psycholinguistic development. *International Journal of Psycholinguistics, 9,* 33–56.

Kuhn, D. (2008). Formal operations from a twenty-first century perspective. *Human Development, 51,* 48–55.

Kuhn, D., & Pease, M. (2006). Do children and adults learn differently? *Journal of Cognition and Development, 7,* 279–293.

Kurdek, L. A. (2001). Differences between heterosexual-nonparent couples and gay, lesbian, and heterosexual-parent couples. *Journal of Family Issues, 22*(6), 728–755.

Kurdek, L. A. (2002). Predicting the timing of separation and marital satisfaction: An eight-year prospective longitudinal study. *Journal of Marriage and the Family, 64*(1), 163–179.

Kwalombota, M. (2002). The effect of pregnancy in HIV-infected women. *AIDS Care, 14*(3), 431–433.

LaGasse, L. L., Derauf, C., Smith, L. M., Newman, E., Shah, R., Neal, C., *et al.* (2012). Prenatal meth-amphetamine exposure and childhood behavior problems at 3 and 5 years of age. *Pediatrics, 129*(4), 681–688.

Lam, L. T. (2007). The association between climatic factors and childhood illnesses presented to hospital emergency among young children. *International Journal of Environmental Health Research, 17*(1), 1–8.

Lambon Ralph, M. A., Ehsan, S., Baker, G. A., Rogers, T. T. (2012). Semantic memory is impaired in patients with unilateral anterior temporal lobe resection for temporal lobe epilepsy. *Brain: A Journal of Neurology, 135*(1), 242–258.

Lancet. (2003, July 5). A victory for afirmative action. *Lancet, 362*(9377), 1.

Langford, J., Bohensky, M., Koppel, S., & Newstead, S. (2008). Do older drivers pose a risk to other road users? *Traffic Injury Prevention, 9*(3), 181–189.

Lanphear, B. P., Vorhees, C. V., & Bellinger, D. C. (2005). Protecting children from environmental toxins. *PLoS Medicine, 2*(3), e61.

Lansford, J. E., & Dodge, K. A. (2008). Cultural norms for adult corporal punishment of children and societal rates of endorsement and use of violence. *Parenting: Science and Practice, 8*(3), 257–270.

Larkin, G. L., & Beautrais, A. L. (2011). A preliminary naturalistic study of low-dose ketamine for depression and suicide ideation in the emergency department. *International Journal of Neuropsychopharmacology, 14*(8), 1127–1131.

LaRochebrochard, E., & Thonneau, P. (2002). Paternal age and maternal age are risk factors for miscarriage: Results of a multicentre European study. *Human Reproduction, 17*(6), 1649–1656.

Laumann, E. O., Leitsch, S. A., & Waite, L. J. (2008). Elder mistreatment in the United States: Prevalence estimates from a nationally representative study. *Journals of Gerontology Series B: Psychological Sciences & Social Sciences, 63B*(4), S248–S254.

Lawrence, R. C., Felson, D. T., Helmick, C. G., Arnold, L. M., Choi, H., Deyo, R. A., *et al.* (2008). Estimates of the prevalence of arthritis and other rheumatic conditions in the United States. Part II. *Arthritis and Rheumatism, 58*(1), 26–35.

Lee, D. J. (2010). Adrenal fatigue syndrome, Part 2: Adrenal function and overtraining. *Athletic Therapy Today, 15*(2), 28–31.

Lee, S. A., & Kushner, J. (2008). Single-parent families: The role of parent's and child's gender on academic achievement. *Gender & Education, 20*(6), 607–621.

Lefebvre, H. (1968). *The sociology of Marx.* New York: Columbia University Press.

Lemery, K. S., Goldsmith, H. H., Klinnert, M. D., & Mrazek, D. A. (1999). Developmental models of infant and childhood temperament. *Developmental Psychology, 35*(1), 189–204.

Lenski, G. (1988). Rethinking macrosociological theory. *American Sociological Review, 53,* 163–171.

Leon, K. (2003). Risk and protective factors in young children's adjustment to parental divorce: A review of the research. *Family Relations, 52,* 258–270.

Lepage, J. F., & Theoret, H. (2010). Brain connectivity: Finding a cause. *Current Biology, 20,* R66–R67.

Levinson, D. J. (1978). *The seasons of a man's life.* New York: Knopf.

Levinson, D. J., & Levinson, J. D. (1996). *The seasons of a woman's life.* New York: Knopf.

Levy, M. A., Thorkelson, C., Vörösmarty, C., Douglas, E., & Humphreys, M. (2006). Freshwater availability anomalies and outbreak of internal war: Results from a global spatial time series analysis. Paper presented at the International Studies Association annual meeting. San Diego, CA.

Lewiecki, E. M. (2009). Current and emerging pharmacologic therapies for the management of postmenopausal osteoporosis. *Journal of Women's Health, 18*(10), 1615–1626.

Lichter, D. T. (2012). Immigration and the new racial diversity in rural America. *Rural Sociology, 77*(1), 3–35.

Lichtman, J. W., Livet, J., & Sanes, J. R. (2008). A technicolour approach to the connectome. *Nature, 9*(6), 417–422.

Lin, I.-F., & Brown, S. L. (2012). Unmarried boomers confront old age: A national portrait. *The Gerontologist, 52*(2), 153–165.

Lindau, S. T., Schumm, L. P., Laumann, E. O., Levinson, W., O'Muircheartaigh, C. A., & Waite, L. J. (2007). A study of sexuality and health among older adults in the United States. *New England Journal of Medicine, 357*(8), 762–774.

Lindberg, L. D., Boggs, S., Porter, L., & Williams, S. (2000). *Teen risk-taking: A statistical report.* Washington, DC: Urban Institute.

Litz, B. T., & Schlenger, W. E. (2009). PTSD in service members and new veterans of the Iraq and Afghanistan wars: A bibliography and critique. *PTSD Research Quarterly, 20*(1). Retrieved March 1, 2012, from http://www.ptsd.va.gov/professional/newsletters/research-quarterly/V20N1.pdf.

Liu, C. H., & Tronick, E. (2013). Rates and predictors of postpartum depression by race and ethnicity: Results from the 2004 to 2007 New York City PRAMS survey (Pregnancy Risk Assessment Monitoring System). *Maternal Child Health Journal, 17,* 1599–1610.

Liu, H. M., Kuhl, P. K., & Tsao, F. M. (2003). An association between mothers' speech clarity and infants' speech discrimination skills. *Developmental Science, 6*(3), 1–9.

Lorenz, K. Z. (1965). *Evolution and the modification of behavior.* Chicago: University of Chicago Press.

Loughran, D. S., Seabury, S. A., & Zakaras, L. (2007). *Regulating older drivers. Are new policies needed?* [Online.] Retrieved July 1, 2009, from http://www.rand.org/pubs/occasional_papers/2007/RAND_OP189.pdf.

Lowis, M. J., Edwards, A. C., & Burton, M. (2009). Coping with retirement: Well-being, health, and religion. *Journal of Psychology, 143*(4), 427–448.

Lu, T., Aron, L., Zullo, J., Pan, Y., Kim, H., Chen, Y., et al. (2014). REST and stress resistance in ageing and Alzheimer's disease. *Nature, 507,* 448–454. DOI: 10.1038/nature13163.

Luhrmann, T. T. (2007). Social defeat and the culture of chronicity: Or, why schizophrenia does so well over there and so badly here. *Culture, Medicine & Psychiatry, 31*(2), 135–172. DOI: 10.1007/s11013-007-9049-z.

Lum, D. (1995). Cultural values and minority people of color. *Journal of Sociology and Social Welfare, 22*(1), 59–74.

Lupton, C. (2003). *The financial impact of fetal alcohol syndrome.* SAMHSA Fetal Alcohol Spectrum Disorders Center for Excellence. [Online.] Retrieved June 14, 2009, from http://www.fasdcenter.samhsa.gov/publications/cost.cfm.

Luxton, D. D. (2008). The effects of inconsistent parenting on the development of uncertain self-esteem and depression vulnerability. *Dissertation Abstracts International: Section B: The Sciences and Engineering, 69*(4-B), 2631.

Mackelprang, R. W., & Salsgiver, R. O. (2009). *Disability: A diversity model approach in human service practice* (2nd ed.). Chicago: Lyceum Books Inc.

MacKinlay, E. (2001). Ageing and isolation: Is the issue social isolation or is it lack of meaning in life? *Journal of Religious Gerontology, 12*(3/4), 89–99.

Macular Degeneration Foundation. (2002). *Adult macular degeneration.* [Online.] Retrieved March 11, 2003, from http://www.eyesight.org/Adult/adult.html.

Magnuson, K. A., Meyers, M. K., & Waldfogel, J. (2007). Public funding and enrollment in formal child care in the 1990s. *Social Service Review, 81,* 47–83. DOI: 10.1086/511628.

Maier, W., Gansicke, M., Freyberger, H. J., Linz, M., Heun, R., & Lecrubier, Y. (2000). Generalized anxiety disorder (ICD-10) in primary care from a cross-cultural perspective: A valid diagnostic entity? *Acta Psychiatrica Scandinavica, 101*(1), 29–36.

Malinosky-Rummell, R., & Hansen, D. J. (1993). Long-term consequences of childhood physical abuse. *Psychological Bulletin, 114,* 68–79.

Malpas, J. (2011). Between pink and blue: A multi-dimensional family approach to gender non-conforming children and their families. *Family Process, 50*(4), 453–470.

Mander, B. A., Rao, V., Lu, B., Saletin, J. M., Lindquist, J. R., Ancoli-Israel, S., *et al.* (2013). Prefrontal atrophy, disrupted NREM slow waves and impaired hippocampal-dependent memory in aging. *Nature Neuroscience, 16,* 357–364.

Mangione-Smith, R., DeCristofaro, A. H., Setodji, C. M., Keesey, J., Klein, D. J., Adams, J. L., *et al.* (2007). The quality of ambulatory care delivered to children in the United States. *New England Journal of Medicine, 357*(15), 1515–1523.

Mapstone, M., Cheema, A. K., Flandaca, M. S., Zhong, X., Mhyre, T. R., MacArthur, L. H., *et al.* (2014). Plasma phospholipids identify antecedent memory impairment in older adults. *Nature Medicine, 20,* 415–418. DOI: 10.1038/nm.3466.

March of Dimes. (2006). *Global report on birth defects.* [Online.] Retrieved May 23, 2014, from http://www.marchofdimes.com/materials/global-report-on-birth-defects-the-hidden-toll-of-dying-and-disabled-children-full-report.pdf.

March of Dimes. (2009). *Quick references and fact sheets.* [Online.] Retrieved June 14, 2009, from http://search.marchofdimes.com/cgi-bin/MsmGo.exe?grab_id=6&page_id=10027264&query=birth+defects&hiword=BIRTHED+BIRTHING+BIRTHS+DEFECT+DEFECTIVE+DEFECTOS+birth+defects+.

March of Dimes. (2010). *Hospital rates of early scheduled deliveries.* [Online.] Retrieved April 6, 2012, from http://www.marchofdimes.com/baby/premature_indepth.html.

March of Dimes. (2013). *Long term health effects of premature birth.* [Online.] Retrieved May 21, 2014, from http://www.marchofdimes.com/baby/long-term-health-effects-of-premature-birth.aspx.

March of Dimes. (2014). *Facts about birth defects.* [Online.] Retrieved May 23, 2014, from http://www.cdc.gov/ncbddd/birthdefects/facts.html.

Marriage Equality USA. (2004). *1,138 Federal rights.* [Online.] Retrieved May 14, 2012, from http://www.marriageequality.org/1-138-federal-rights.

Martin, K. P., & Wellman, C. L. (2011). NMDA receptor blockade alters stress-induced dendritic remodeling in medial prefrontal cortex. *Cerebral Cortex, 21*(10), 2366–2373.

Martin, M. A. (2012). Family structure and the inter-generational transmission of educational advantage. *Social Science Research, 41*(1), 33–47.

Martin, S. K., & Lindsey, D. (2003). The impact of welfare reform on children: An introduction. *Children and Youth Services Review, 25*(1/2), 1–15.

Martin, S. L., Kupper, L. L., Mackie, L., Clark, K. A., Buescher, P. A., & Halpern, C. (2001). Are abused women more or less likely to use health care services during pregnancy? *Paediatric and Perinatal Epidemiology, 15,* A1–A38.

Martorell, R., Mendoza, F., & Castillo, F. (1988). Poverty and stature in children. In J. C. Waterlow (Ed.), *Linear growth retardation in less developed countries.* New York: Raven.

Marx, K. (1973). *On society and social change.* Chicago: University of Chicago Press.

Marx, K. (1987). *Das Kapital*. Washington, DC: Regnery Gateway.

Marx, K. (1994). Classes in capitalism and pre-capitalism. In D. B. Grusky (Ed.), *Social stratification: Class, race, and gender in sociological perspective* (pp. 69–78). San Francisco: Westview Press.

Marx, K., & Engels, F. (1977). *The communist manifesto*. Mattituck, NY: Amereon House.

Maslow, A. H. (1954). *Motivation and personality*. New York: Harper & Brothers.

Massachusetts General Hospital, School Psychiatry Program and Mood & Anxiety Disorders Institute Resource Center. (2010). Anxiety: Generalized anxiety disorders. Retrieved February 27, 2012, from http://www2.massgeneral.org/schoolpsychiatry/anxiety_print.asp.

Materstvedt, L. J., Clark, D., Ellershaw, J., Forde, R., Gravgaard, A. B., Muller-Busch, H. C., *et al.* (2003). Euthanasia and physician-assisted suicide: A view from an EAPC ethics task force. *Palliative Medicine, 17*, 97–101.

Mather, J. H., & Lager, P. B. (2000). *Child welfare: A unifying model of practice*. Belmont, CA: Wadsworth.

Mathers, C. D., & Loncar, D. (2006). Projections of global mortality and burden of disease from 2002 to 2030. *PLoS Medicine, 3*(11), 2011–2203.

Matsumoto, A. M. (2002). Clinical implications of the decline in serum testosterone levels with aging in men. *The Journals of Gerontology, 57A*(2), M76–M99.

Mattingly, M. J., Carson, J. A., & Schaefer, A. (2013). 2012 National child poverty rate stagnates at 22.6 percent. The Carsey Institute at the Scholars' Repository. Paper 201, 1–9.

Maxson, P., & Miranda, M. L. (2011). Pregnancy intention, demographic differences, and psycho-social health. *Journal of Women's Health, 20*(8). DOI: 10.1089/jwh.2010.2379.

Mayer, K. H., Bradford, J. B., Makadon, H. J., Stall, R., Goldhammer, H., & Landers, S. (2008). Sexual and minority health: What we know and what needs to be done. *American Journal of Public Health, 98*(6), 989–995.

Maynard, R. (1996). *Kids having kids: Robin Hood Foundation special report on the costs of adolescent childbearing*. New York: Robin Hood Foundation.

McAdam, D., McCarthy, J., & Zald, M. (Eds.). (1996). *Comparative perspectives on social movements*. New York: Cambridge University Press.

McCall, L., & Percheski, C. (2010). Income inequality: New trends and research directions. *Annual Review of Sociology, 36*, 329–347.

McCluskey, C. P., Krohn, M. D., Lizotte, A. J., & Rodriguez, M. L. (2002). Early substance use and school achievement: An examination of Latino, White, and African American youth. *Journal of Drug Issues, 32*(3), 921–943.

McConahay, J. B. (1986). Modern racism, ambivalence, and the modern racism scale. In J. F. Dovidio & S. L. Gaertner (Eds.), *Prejudice, discrimination, and racism* (pp. 91–126). Orlando, FL: Academic Press.

McCrae, R. R., & Costa, P. T. (1990). *Personality in adulthood*. New York: Guilford.

McCrae, R. R., Costa, P. T., Pederoso de Lima, M., Simões, A., Ostendorf, F., Angleitner, A., *et al.* (1999). Age differences in personality across the adult life span: Parallels in five cultures. *Developmental Psychology, 35*(2), 466–477.

McCullough, P. K. (1991, October). Geriatric depression: Atypical presentations, hidden meanings. *Geriatrics, 46*, 72–76.

McElwain, N. L., & Booth-LaForce, C. (2006). Maternal sensitivity to infant distress and nondistress as predictors of infant–mother attachment security. *Journal of Family Psychology, 20*(2), 247–255.

McElwain, N. L., Booth-LaForce, C., Lansford, J. E., Wu, X., & Dyer, W. J. (2008). A process model of attachment-friend linkages: Hostile attribution biases, language ability, and mother–child affective mutuality as intervening mechanisms. *Child Development, 79*(6), 1891–1906.

McIntosh, P. (2008). White privilege: Unpacking the invisible knapsack. In Alexandra Miletta & Maureen McCann Miletta (eds.), *Classroom conversations: A collection of classics for parents and teachers* (pp. 169–170). New York: The New Press.

McKenzie, S. (2004). Social sustainability: Towards some definitions. Hawke Research Institute Working Paper Series, no. 27. Magill: University of South Australia.

McKerrow, R. E. (1989). Critical rhetoric: Theory and praxis. *Communication Monographs, 56*(2), 91–111.

McKinnon, J. (2008). Exploring the nexus between social work and the environment. *Australian Social Work, 61*(3), 256–268.

McKnight, A. J. (2000, Winter). Too old to drive? *Issues in Science and Technology, 17*(2), 1–11.

Mcleod, S. A. (2009). *Simply Psychology.* Retrieved February 17, 2012, from http://www.simplypsychology.org/authoritarian-personality.html.

McMichael, A., Woodruff, R., & Hales, S. (2006). Climate change and human health: Present and future risks. *The Lancet, 367*(9513), 859–869.

Mead, G. H. (1934). *Mind, self, and society from the standpoint of a social behaviorist.* Chicago: University of Chicago Press.

Mead, G. H. (1956). *On social psychology.* Chicago: University of Chicago Press.

Media Report to Women. (1999). Women 40 and older underrepresented in acting jobs, Screen Actors Guild says. *Media Report to Women, 27*(2), 3.

Media Report to Women. (2001). SAG: Women still underrepresented on screen: Ageism, role prominence factors. *Media Report to Women, 29*(1), 1.

Media Report to Women. (2009). *Industry statistics.* [Online.] Retrieved June 25, 2009, from http://www.mediareporttowomen.com/statistics.htm.

Mellor, J. (2000). Filling the gaps in long-term care insurance. In M. H. Meyer (Ed.), *Care work* (pp. 202–216). New York: Routledge.

Menkes, J. H., & Till, K. (1995). Malformations of the central nervous system. In J. H. Menkes (Ed.), *Textbook of child neurology* (5th ed.). Baltimore, MD: Williams & Wilkins.

Merton, R. K. (1968). *Social theory and social structure.* New York: Free Press.

Migration Policy Institute. (2014). *Frequently Requested Statistics on Immigrants and Immigration in the United States.* [Online.] Retrieved July 11, 2013, from http://www.migrationpolicy.org/article/frequently-requested-statistics-immigrants-and-immigration-united-states#1.

Miller, W. R., & Rose, G. S. (2009). Toward a theory of motivational interviewing. *American Psychologist, 64*(6), 527–537.

Mills, C. W. (1959). *The sociological imagination.* London: Oxford University Press.

Mills, C. W. (1994). The power elite. In D. B. Grusky (Ed.), *Social stratification: Class, race, and gender in sociological perspective* (pp. 161–170). San Francisco: Westview Press.

Minuchin, P. (1985). Families and individual development: Provocations from the field of family therapy. *Child Development, 56,* 289–302.

Minuchin, S. (1974). *Families and family therapy.* Cambridge, MA: Harvard University Press.

Mitchell, B. D., Kammerer, C. M., Reinhart, L. J., & Stern, M. P. (1994, June). NIDDM in Mexican American families: Heterogeneity by age of onset. *Diabetes Care, 17*(6), 567–573.

MMWR. (2005). *Mental health in the United States: Prevalence of diagnosis and medication treatment for attention-deficit/hyperactivity disorder—United States, 2003.* [Online.] Retrieved June 21, 2009, from http://www.cdc.gov/mmwr/preview/mmwrhtml/mm5434a2.htm.

Mock, S. (2001). Retirement intentions of same-sex couples. *Journal of Gay and Lesbian Social Services, 13*(4), 81–86.

Moen, P., & Wethington, E. (1999). Midlife development in a life course context. In S. L. Willis & J. D. Reid (Eds.), *Life in the middle: Psychological and social development in middle age* (pp. 1–18). San Diego, CA: Academic Press.

Moffitt, T. E., Arseneault, L., Belsky, D., Dickson, N., Hancox, R. J., Harrington, H., *et al.* (2011). A gradient of childhood self-control predicts health, wealth, and public safety. *Proceedings of the National Academy of Sciences of the United States of America, 108*(7), 2693–2698.

Möhler, H. (2012). The GABA system in anxiety and depression and its therapeutic potential. *Neuropharmacology, 62*(1), 42–53.

Mokrue, K., Chen, Y. Y., & Elias, M. (2012). The interaction between family structure and child gender on behavior problems in urban ethnic minority children. *International Journal of Behavioral Development, 36*(2), 130–136.

Molino, A. C. (2007). Characteristics of help-seeking street youth and non-street youth. In D. Dennis,

G. Locke, & J. Khadduri (Eds.), *National Symposium on Homelessness Research*. Retrieved July 20, 2008, from http://aspe.hhs.gov/hsp/homelessness/symposium07/molino/index.htm.

Montague, A. (1964). *Man's most dangerous myth: The fallacy of race* (4th ed.). Cleveland, OH: World.

Montemurro, B. (2003). Not a laughing matter: Sexual harassment as "material" on workplace-based situation comedies. *Sex Roles, 48*(9/10), 433–445.

Montgomery, K. S. (2001). Planned adolescent pregnancy: What they needed. *Issues in Comprehensive Pediatric Nursing, 24,* 19–29.

Montgomery, S. M., Ehlin, A., & Sacker, A. (2006). Breastfeeding and resilience against psychosocial stress. *Archives of Disease in Childhood, 91*(12), 990–994.

Moodie-Dyer, A. (2011). A policy analysis of child care subsidies: Increasing quality, access, and affordability. *Children & Schools, 33*(1), 37–45.

Moolchan, E. T., & Mermelstein, R. (2002). Research on tobacco use among teenagers: Ethical challenges. *Journal of Adolescent Health, 30,* 409–417.

Moore, K. L., & Persaud, T. V. N. (1998). *The developing human*. Philadelphia: W. B. Saunders.

Moore, M. L., & Piland, W. E. (1994). Impact of the campus physical environment on older adult learners. *Educational Gerontology, 20*(2), 129–138.

Morén, S. (1994). Social work is beautiful. On the characteristics of social work. *Scandinavian Journal of Social Welfare, 3*(3), 158–66.

Morris, L. A., Ulmer, C., & Chimnani, J. (2003). A role for community healthcorps members in youth HIV/AIDS prevention education. *Journal of School Health, 73*(4), 138–142.

Moster, D., Lie, R. T., & Markestad, T. (2008). Long-term medical and social consequences of preterm birth. *New England Journal of Medicine, 359*(3), 262–273.

Moth, R., & Morton, D. (2009). Social work and climate change: A call to action. [Online.] Retrieved October 15, 2014, from http://www.socialworkfuture.org/articles-and-analysis/articles/55-social-work-and-climate-change-a-call-to-action-rich-moth-a-dan-morton.

Motivational Interviewing. (2011). *An overview of motivational interviewing.* [Online.] Retrieved May 16, 2012, from http://www.motivationalinterview.org/quick_links/about_mi.html.

Moxnes, K. (2003). Risk factors in divorce. *Childhood, 10*(2), 131–146.

Mullaly, B. (1997). *Structural social work: Ideology, theory and practice* (2nd ed.). Toronto, Canada: Oxford University Press.

Mumme, D. L., Fernald, A., & Herrera, C. (1996). Infants' responses to facial and vocal emotional signals in a social referencing paradigm. *Child Development, 67*(6), 2319–2337.

Murkoff, H., & Mazel, S. (2008). *What to expect when you're expecting* (4th ed.). New York: Workman Publishing.

Murphy, D. (2007). Theory of mind functioning in mentally disordered offenders detained in high security psychiatric care: Its relationship to clinical outcome, need and risk. *Criminal Behaviour and Mental Health, 17,* 300–311.

Muth, J. L., & Cash, T. F. (1997). Body-image attitudes: What difference does gender make? *Journal of Applied Social Psychology, 27,* 1438–1452.

Nadal, A. (2012). *New study strengthens link between obesity, diabetes, and BPA.* [Online.] Retrieved May 16, 2012, from http://www.treehugger.com/health/new-study-strengthens-link-between-obesity-diabetes-and-bpa.html.

Naess, A. (1973). The shallow and the deep, long-range ecology movement. A summary. *Inquiry: An Interdisciplinary Journal of Philosophy, 16* (1–4), 95–100, DOI: 10.1080/00201747308601682.

Narang, A., & Jain, N. (2001). Haemolytic disease of newborns. *Indian Journal of Pediatrics, 58,* 167–172.

Nash, R. (2001). Class, ability, and attainment: A problem for the sociology of education. *British Journal of Sociology of Education, 22*(2), 189–202.

National Alliance for Caregiving. (2007). *Evercare study of family caregivers: What they spend, what they sacrifice.* Bethesda, MD: Author.

National Association for Down Syndrome. (2012). *Facts about Down syndrome.* Retrieved May 28, 2014, from http://www.nads.org/pages_new/facts.html.

National Association of Social Workers. (1987). *Encyclopedia of social work* (18th ed., 2 vols.). Silver Spring, MD: Author.

National Association of Social Workers. (approved 1996, revised 2008). *Code of ethics.* Washington, DC: NASW.

National Association of Social Workers. (2001). *NASW standards for cultural competence in social work practice.* Washington, DC: NASW.

National Association of Social Workers. (2010). Social work leaders adopt 10 imperatives to shape profession's future. [Online.] Retrieved November 8, 2014, from http://www.socialworkers.org/pressroom/2010/050510Congress.asp.

National Autism Association. (2009). *Autism is treatable.* [Online.] Retrieved June 17, 2009, from http://www.nationalautismassociation.org/psa.php.

National Care Planning Council. (2014). About caregiving. [Online.] Retrieved November 3, 2014, from http://www.longtermcarelink.net/eldercare/caregiving.htm.

National Center for Health Statistics (2000). *Health United States, 2000, with adolescent health chartbook.* Bethesda, MD: Department of Health and Human Services.

National Center for Health Statistics. (2008a). *Health, United States, 2008.* Hyattsville, MD: Author.

National Center for Health Statistics (2008b). *Understanding school violence.* [Online.] Retrieved June 23, 2009, from http://www.cdc.gov/ViolencePrevention/pdf/SchoolViolence_FactSheet-a.pdf.

National Center for Health Workforce Analysis. (2006). *The impact of the aging population on the health workforce in the United States: Summary of key findings.* Albany, NY: Center for Health Workforce Studies, University at Albany.

National Center for Transgender Equality. (2014). Medicare and transgender people. [Online.] Retrieved July 18, 2014, from http://transequality.org/PDFs/MedicareAndTransPeople.pdf.

National Coalition for the Homeless. (2008). *Homeless youth: NCH Fact sheet #13.* [Online.] Retrieved June 23, 2009, from http://www.nationalhomeless.org/factsheets/youth.html.

National Committee for the Prevention of Elder Abuse and National Adult Protective Services Association. (2006). The 2004 Survey of State Adult Protective Services: Abuse of Adults 60 Years of Age and Older.

National Conference of State Legislatures. (2012). *Defining marriage: Defense of marriage acts and same-sex marriage laws.* [Online.] Retrieved February 27, 2012, from http://www.ncsl.org/issues-research/human-services/same-sex-marriage-overview.aspx.

National Diabetes Information Clearinghouse. (2011). [Online.] Retrieved on January 16, 2016 from http://www.cdc.gov/diabetes/pubs/pdf/ndfs_2011.pdf.

National Diabetes Information Clearinghouse. (2014). *National Diabetes Statistics Report, 2014.* [Online.] Retrieved July 11, 2014, from http://www.cdc.gov/diabetes/pubs/statsreport14/national-diabetes-report-web.pdf.

National Down Syndrome Society. (2009). *About Down syndrome.* New York: Author.

National Hospice and Palliative Care Organization. (2012). *About hospice and palliative care.* [Online.] Retrieved May 31, 2012, from http://www.nhpco.org/i4a/pages/index.cfm?pageid=4648&openpage=4648.

National Institute of Child Health and Human Development. (2008). *Autism spectrum disorders.* National Institutes of Health. [Online.] Retrieved June 17, 2009, from http://www.nichd.nih.gov/health/topics/asd.cfm.

National Institute of Child Health and Human Development. (2013). *Infertility and Fertility.* [Online.] Retrieved May 23, 2014, from http://www.nichd.nih.gov/health/topics/infertility/conditioninfo/Pages/common.asp.

National Institute of Environmental Health. (2008). *Smoking.* Washington, DC: National Institutes of Health.

National Institute of Mental Health. (2009). *Older adults: Depression and suicide facts.* [Online.] Retrieved June 30, 2009, from http://www.nimh.nih.gov/health/publications/older-adultsdepression-and-suicide-facts-fact-sheet/index.shtml.

National Institute of Mental Health. (2011). *Anxiety disorders in children and adolescents* (Fact Sheet).

[Online.] Retrieved February 15, 2012, from http://www.nimh.nih.gov/health/publications/anxietydisorders-in-children-and-adolescents/index.shtml.

National Institute of Mental Health. (2014). Anxiety disorders in children and adolescents (Fact Sheet). [Online.] Retrieved July 11, 2014, from http://www.nimh.nih.gov/health/publications/anxiety-disorders-in-children-and-adolescents/index.shtml.

National Institute on Drug Abuse. (2001). *Marijuana*. Washington, DC: National Institutes of Health.

National Institute on Drug Abuse. (2008). Behavioral problems related to maternal smoking during pregnancy manifest early in childhood. *NIDA Notes, 21*(6). [Online.] Retrieved June 14, 2009, from http://www.drugabuse.gov/news-events/nida-notes/2008/06/behavioral-problems-related-to-maternal-smoking-during-pregnancy-manifest-early-in-childhood.

National Institutes of Health. (2001). NIH consensus statement: Osteoporosis prevention, diagnosis, and therapy. *JAMA, 285*(6), 785–795.

National Institutes of Health. (2009a). *Bone health and osteoporosis: A guide for Asian women age 50 and older.* [Online.] Retrieved June 30, 2009, from http://www.niams.nih.gov/health_info/bone/osteoporosis/background/asian_women_guide.asp.

National Institutes of Health. (2009b). *What is post-traumatic stress disorder, or PTSD?* Retrieved on March 1, 2012, from http://www.nimh.nih.gov/health/publications/post-traumatic-stress-disorderptsd/what-is-post-traumatic-stress-disorder-or-ptsd.shtml.

National Institutes of Health. (2011). *Osteoporosis overview.* [Online.] Retrieved March 5, 2012, from http://www.niams.nih.gov/Health_Info/Bone/Osteoporosis/overview.asp.

National Institutes of Health. (2012). *Traumatic brain injury: Hope through research.* [Online.] Retrieved April 19, 2012, from http://www.ninds.nih.gov/disorders/tbi/detail_tbi.htm.

National Osteoporosis Foundation. (2008). *Fast facts on osteoporosis.* [Online.] Retrieved June 29, 2009, from http://www.nof.org/osteoporosis/disease facts.htm.

National Vital Statistics Reports. (2005). *Trends in cesarean rates for first births and repeat cesarean rates for low-risk women: United States, 1990–2003.* [Online.] Retrieved June 23, 2009, from http://www.cdc.gov/search.do?queryText=trends+in+cesarean+rates&searchButton.x=0&searchButton.y=0&action=search.

National Women's Health Information Center. (2013). *Infertility.* [Online.] Retrieved May 23, 2014, from http://www.cdc.gov/reproductivehealth/infertility/.

National Women's Law Center. (2012). *Turning to fairness.* Washington, DC: Author.

Natural Resources Defense Council. (2014). *Priority issues.* [Online.] Retrieved October 15, 2014, from http://www.nrdc.org/issues/.

Neiss, M. B., Stevenson, J., Legrand, L. N., Iacono, W. G., & Sedikides, C. (2009). Self-esteem, negative emotionality, and depression as a common temperamental core: A study of mid-adolescent twin girls. *Journal of Personality, 77*(2), 327–346.

Neisser, U., Boodoo, G., Bouchard, T. J., Boykin, A. W., Brody, N., Ceci, S. J., *et al.* (1996). Intelligence: Knowns and unknowns. *American Psychologist, 51,* 77–101.

Nelson-Becker, H., & Canda, E. R. (2008). Spirituality, religion, and aging research in social work: State of the art and future possibilities. *Journal of Religion, Spirituality, and Aging, 20*(3), 177–193.

Neugarten, B., & Weinstein, K. (1964). The changing American grandparent. *Journal of Marriage and the Family, 26,* 199–205.

Newacheck, P., Hung, Y., Hochstein, M., & Halfon, N. (2002). Access to health care for disadvantaged young children. *Journal of Early Intervention, 25*(1), 1–11.

Newman, B., & Newman, B. (2009). *Development through life: A psychosocial approach* (10th ed.). Belmont, CA: Thomson.

Newman, W. (1973). *American pluralism: A study of minority groups and social theory.* New York: Harper & Row.

Newport Academy. (2014). Teen Bulimia Statistics. [Online.] Retrieved July 11, 2014, from http://www.newportacademy.com/bulimia-treatment/statistics/.

New York Times. (2014). Rite of the sitting dead: Funeral poses mimic life. [Online.] Retrieved on November 3, 2014, from http://www.nytimes.com/2014/06/22/us/its-not-the-living-dead-just-a-funeral-with-flair.html?emc=edit_th_20140622&nl=todaysheadlines&nlid=55116972.

Nguyen, J., & Brown, B. (2010). Making meanings, meaning identity: Hmong adolescent perceptions and use of language and style as identity symbols. *Journal of Research on Adolescence (Blackwell Publishing Limited)*, *20*(4), 849–868.

Nguyen, T. V., Kelly, P. J., Sambrook, C., Gilbert, N. A., Pocock, N. A., & Eisman, J. A. (1994). Lifestyle factors and bone density in the elderly: Implications for osteoporosis prevention. *Journal of Bone Mineral Research*, *9*, 1339–1346.

Nixon, E., Mansfield, P. K., Kittell, L. A., & Faulkner, S. L. (2001). "Staying strong": How low-income rural African American women manage their menopausal changes. *Women & Health*, *34*(2), 81–95.

Nordqvist, C. (2011, February 28). Hepatitis B rates drop among kids due to effective vaccination programs, more efforts needed for adults. *Medical News Today*. [Online.] Retrieved August 4, 2012, from http://www.medicalnewstoday.com/articles/217713.php.

North American Menopause Society. (2006). *Menopause guidebook: Helping women make informed healthcare decisions through perimenopause and beyond.* Cleveland, OH: Author.

Norton, D. (1978). *The dual perspective: Inclusion of ethnic minority content in the social work curriculum.* Washington, DC: Council on Social Work Education.

Norton, M. C., Smith, K. R., Ostbye, T., Tschanz, J. T., Corcoran, C., Schwartz, S., *et al.* (2010). Greater risk of dementia when spouse has dementia? The Cache County study. *Journal of the American Geriatrics Society*, *58*(5), 895–900.

NUA Internet Surveys. (2002). *IM programs draw US kids and teens online.* [Online.] Retrieved September 9, 2003, from http://www.nua.ie/surveys/index.cgi.

Nuba, H., Searson, M., & Sheiman, D. L. (Eds.). (1994). *Resources for early childhood: A handbook.* New York: Garland Publishers.

Nuttbrock, L., Hwahng, S., Bockting, W., Rosenblum, A., Mason, M., Macri, M., *et al.* (2010). Psychiatric impact of gender-related abuse across the life course of male-to-female transgender persons. *Journal of Sex Research*, *47*(1), 12–23.

Nybo Andersen, A. M., Hansen, K. D., Andersen, P. K., & Smith, D. (2004). Advanced paternal age and risk of fetal death: A cohort study. *American Journal of Epidemiology*, *160*, 1214–1222.

O'Connor, M. J., Kogan, N., & Findlay, R. (2002). Prenatal alcohol exposure and attachment behavior in children. *Alcoholism: Clinical and Experimental Research*, *26*(10), 1592–1602.

O'Connor, T. P., Hoge, D. R., & Alexander, E. (2002). The relative influence of youth and adult experiences on personal spirituality and church involvement. *Journal for the Scientific Study of Religion*, *41*(4), 723–733.

Oddy, W. H. (2002). The impact of breastmilk on infant and child health. *Breastfeeding Review*, *10*(3), 5–18.

O'Donohue, W., & Caselles, C. E. (1993). Homophobia: Conceptual, definitional, and value issues. *Journal of Psychopathology and Behavioral Assessment*, *15*(3), 177–195.

O'Hara, M. W. (2009). Postpartum depression: What we know. *Journal of Clinical Psychology*, *65*(12), 1258–1269.

O'Laughlin, E. M. (2001). Perceptions of parenthood among young adults: Implications for career and family planning. *American Journal of Family Therapy*, *29*(2), 95–108.

Olfson, M., Gameroff, M. J., Marcus, S. C., & Jensen, P. S. (2003). National trends in the treatment of attention deficit hyperactivity disorder. *American Journal of Psychiatry*, *160*(6), 1071–1077.

Omar, H. A., Fowler, A., & McClanahan, K. K. (2008). Significant reduction of repeat teen pregnancy in a comprehensive young parent program. *Journal of Pediatric & Adolescent Gynecology*, *21*(5), 283–287.

Orbuch, T. L., House, J. S., Mero, R. P., & Webster, P. S. (1996). Marital quality over the life course. *Social Psychology Quarterly*, *59*, 162–171.

Oregon Health Sciences University. (2014). ORCHATECH: Sensing life kinetics. [Online.] Retrieved October 20, 2014, from http://www.ohsu.edu/xd/research/centers-institutes/orcatech/about/welcome.cfm.

Orlinsky, D. E., & Howard, K. I. (1986). Process and outcome in psychotherapy. In S. L. Garfield & A. E. Bergin (Eds.), *Handbook of psychotherapy and behavior change* (3rd ed., pp. 311–381). New York: John Wiley.

Osgood, N. J. (1991). Prevention of suicide in the elderly. *Journal of Geriatric Psychiatry, 24*(2), 293–306.

Osmani, S., & Sen, A. (2003). The hidden penalties of gender inequality: Fetal origins of ill-health. *Economics and Human Biology, 1,* 105–121.

Osmond, J., & O'Connor, I. (2006). Use of research and theory in social work practice: Implications for knowledge-based practice. *Australian Social Work, 59*(1), 5–19.

Owen, M. T. (2002). NICHD study of early child care. In J. G. Borkowski, S. L. Ramey, & M. Bristol-Power (Eds.), *Parenting and the child's world: Influences on academic, intellectual, and social-emotional development* (pp. 99–124). Mahwah, NJ: Lawrence Erlbaum Associates.

Pagani, L. S., Fitzpatrick, C., Barnett, T. A., & Dubow, E. (2010). Prospective associations between early childhood television exposure and academic, psychosocial, and physical well-being by middle childhood. *Archives of Pediatrics & Adolescent Medicine, 164*(5), 425–431.

Page, S. E. (2007). *The difference: How the power of diversity creates better groups, firms, schools, and societies.* Princeton, NJ: Princeton University of Press.

Paloutzian, R. (2000). *Invitation to the psychology of religion* (3rd ed.). Boston: Allyn & Bacon.

Papalia, D. E., Olds, S. W., & Feldman, R. D. (2001). *Human development* (8th ed.). Boston: McGraw-Hill.

Papalia, D. E., Olds, S. W., & Feldman, R. D. (2003). *Human development* (9th ed.). Boston: McGraw-Hill.

Parenti, C. (1999). *Lockdown America: Police and prisons in the age of crisis.* New York: Verso.

Parfitt, Y., & Ayers, S. (2009). The effect of post-natal symptoms of post-traumatic stress and depression on the couple's relationship and parent–baby bond. *Journal of Reproductive & Infant Psychology, 27*(2), 127–142.

Parker, J. G., Rubin, K. H., Erath, S., Wojslawowicz, J. C., & Buskirk, A. (2006). Peer relationships, child development, and adjustment: A developmental psychopathology perspective. In D. Cicchetti (Ed.), *Developmental psychopathology:* Vol. 2: *Risk, disorder, and adaptation.* New York: Wiley.

Parry, D. C. (2008). "We wanted a birth experience, not a medical experience": Exploring Canadian women's use of midwifery. *Health Care for Women International, 29*(8/9), 784–806. DOI: 10.1080/07399330802269451.

Parsons, T. (1951). *The social system.* New York: Free Press.

Parsons, T. (1994). Equality and inequality in modern society, or social stratification revisited. In D. B. Grusky (Ed.), *Social stratification: Class, race, and gender in sociological perspective* (pp. 670–685). San Francisco: Westview Press.

Partamian, C. M. (2009). The impact of child adjustment to preschool on maternal separation anxiety. *Dissertation Abstracts International: Section B: The Sciences and Engineering, 69*(8-B), 5046.

Parten, M. (1932). Social play among preschool children. *Journal of Abnormal and Social Psychology, 27,* 243–269.

Parton, N. (2000). Some thoughts on the relationship between theory and practice in and for social work. *British Journal of Social Work, 30*(4), 449–464.

Passel, J., & Cohn, D. (2008). *U.S. population projections: 2005–2050.* Washington, DC: Pew Research Center.

Pasterski, V., Hindmarsh, P., Geffner, M., Brook, C., Brain, C., & Hines, M. (2007). Increased aggression and activity level in 3- to 11-year-old girls with congenital adrenal hyperplasia (CAH). *Hormones & Behavior, 52*(3), 368–374.

Pastor, P. N., & Reuben, C. A. (2005). Racial and ethnic differences in ADHD and LD in young school-age children: Parental reports in the National Health Interview Survey. *Public Health Report, 120*(4), 383–392.

Pastor, P. N., & Reuben, C. A. (2008). Diagnosed attention deficit hyperactivity disorder and learning disability: United States, 2004–2006. National Center for Health Statistics. *Vital and Health Statistics, 10*(237), 1–13.

Patterson, C. H. (1984). Empathy, warmth, and genuineness in psychotherapy: A review of reviews. *Psychotherapy, 21,* 431–438.

Patterson, W. M., Dohn, H. H., Bird, J., & Patterson, G. A. (1983). Evaluation of suicidal patients: The SAD PERSONS scale. *Psychosomatics, 24*(4), 343–345.

Paul, J. P., Catania, J., Pollack, L., Moskowitz, J., Canchola, J., Binson, D., et al. (2002). Suicide attempts among gay and bisexual men: Lifetime prevalence and antecedents. *American Journal of Public Health, 92*(8), 1338–1345.

Pauls, B. S., & Daniels, T. (2000). Relationship among family, peer networks, and bulimic symptomatology in college women. *Canadian Journal of Counseling, 34,* 260–272.

Paus, T. (2010). Growth of white matter in the adolescent brain: Myelin or axon? *Brain & Cognition, 72*(1), 26–35.

Pavlov, I. P. (1927). *Conditioned reflexes: An investigation of the physiological activity of the cerebral cortex.* New York: Dover Publications.

Payne, M. S. (1997). *Modern social work theory* (2nd ed.). Chicago: Lyceum Books.

Pearson, J. L., & Conwell, Y. (1995). Suicide in late life: Challenges and opportunities for research. *International Psychogeriatrics, 7,* 131–135.

Peck, R. (1955). Psychological developments in the second half of life. In J. E. Anderson (Ed.), *Psychological aspects of aging.* Washington, DC: American Psychological Association.

Peck, R. (1968). Psychological developments in the second half of life. In B. L. Neugarten (Ed.), *Middle age and aging* (pp. 88–92). Chicago: University of Chicago Press.

Pelkonen, M., Marttunen, M., Kaprio, J., Huurre, T., & Aro, H. (2008). Adolescent risk factors for episodic and persistent depression in adulthood. A 16-year prospective follow-up study of adolescents. *Journal of Affective Disorders, 106*(1/2), 123–131.

Pence, G. E. (1995). *Classical cases in medical ethics.* New York: McGraw-Hill.

Penner, J., Rupsingh, R., Smith, M., Wells, J. L., Borrie, M.J., & Bartha, R. (2010). Increased glutamate in the hippocampus after galantamine treatment for Alzheimer's Disease. *Progress in NeuroPsychopharmacology and Biological Psychiatry, 34,* 104–110.

Perkins, D. F., & Hartless, G. (2002). An ecological risk factor examination of suicide ideation and behavior of adolescents. *Journal of Adolescent Research, 17*(1), 3–26.

Perloff, J., & Buckner, J. (1996). Fathers of children on welfare: Their impact on child well-being. *American Journal of Orthopsychiatry, 66,* 557–571.

Perls, F., Hefferline, R. F., & Goodman, P. (1973). *Gestalt therapy: Excitement and growth in the human personality.* Harmondsworth, Middlesex: Penguin Books.

Perneczky, R., Tsolakidou, A., Arnold, A., Diehl-Schmid, J., Grimmer, T., Forstl, H., et al. (2012). CSF soluble amyloid precursor proteins in the diagnosis of incipient Alzheimer disease. *Neurology, 77*(1), 35–38.

Perrin, E. C. (2002, February). Technical report: Co-parent or second-parent adoption by same-sex parents. *Pediatrics, 109*(2), 341–344.

Pettigrew, T. (1980). Prejudice. In Stephen Thornstrom (Ed.), *Harvard Encyclopedia of Ethnic Groups* (pp. 820–829). Cambridge, MA: Harvard University Press.

Pew Research Center. (2011). Minorities account for nearly all U.S. population growth. [Online.] Retrieved October 28, 2014, from http://www.pewresearch.org/daily-number/minorities-account-for-nearly-all-u-s-population-growth/.

Pew Research Center. (2012, January 11). *Rising share of Americans see conflict between rich and poor.* [Online.] http://pewresearch.org/pubs/2167/rich-poor-social-conflict-class.

Pew Research Center. (2013). King's dream remains an elusive goal; many Americans see racial disparities. [Online.] Retrieved October 28, 2014, from http://www.pewsocialtrends.org/2013/08/22/kings-dream-remains-an-elusive-goal-many-americans-see-racial-disparities/.

Pew Research Center. (2014a). *On pay gap, millennial women near parity—for now.* [Online.] Retrieved July 15, 2014, from http://www.pewsocialtrends.org/2013/12/11/on-pay-gap-millennial-women-near-parity-for-now/.

Pew Research Center. (2014b). *Record share of Americans have never married.* [Online.] Retrieved on November 3, 2014, from http://www.

pewsocialtrends.org/2014/09/24/record-share-of-americans-have-never-married/.

Philliber, S., Kaye, J. W., Herrling, S., & West, E. (2002). Preventing pregnancy and improving health care access among teenagers: An evaluation of the children's aid society-Carrera program. *Perspectives on Sexual and Reproductive Health, 34*(5), 244–251.

Phillips, M. L. (2011). The mind at midlife. *Monitor on Psychology, 42*(4), 38. [Online.] Retrieved March 5, 2012, from www.apa.org/monitor/2011/04/mind-midlife.aspx.

Piaget, J. (1952). *The origins of intelligence in children.* New York: International Universities Press.

Piaget, J. (1972). Intellectual evolution from adolescence to adulthood. *Human Development, 15*(1), 1–12.

Piaget, J., & Inhelder, B. (1969). *The psychology of the child.* New York: Basic Books.

Piasna, A. A. (2010). Changing images of retirement and the "flexicurity" policy: Labour market flexibility, mobility and security in social dialogue on retirement in Poland. *International Journal of Interdisciplinary Social Science, 5*(5), 121–133.

Pickens, J. (1998). Formal and informal care of people with psychiatric disorders: Historical perspectives and current trends. *Journal of Psychosocial Nursing, 36*(1), 37–43.

Pierce, J. L. (2003). Racing for innocence: Whiteness, corporate culture, and the backlash against affirmative action. *Qualitative Sociology, 26*(1), 53–70.

Piketty, T. (2014). *Capital in the twenty-first century.* Cambridge, MA: Harvard University.

Pinto-Martin, J. A., Levy, S. E., Feldman, J. F., Lorenz, J. M., Paneth, N., & Whitaker, A. H. (2011). Prevalence of autism spectrum disorder in adolescents born weighing <2000 grams. *Pediatrics.* DOI: 10.1542/peds.2010-2846.

Plaitakis, A., Latsoudis, H., & Spanaki, C. (2011). The human GLUD2 glutamate dehydrogenase and its regulation in health and disease. *Neurochemistry International, 59*(4), 495–509.

Plöderl, M., & Fartacek, R. (2009). Childhood gender nonconformity and harassment as predictors of suicidality among gay, lesbian, bisexual, and heterosexual Austrians. *Archives of Sexual Behavior, 38*(3), 400–410.

Plowfield, L. A., Raymond, J. E., & Blevins, C. (2000). Holism for aging families: Meeting needs of caregivers. *Holistic Nursing Practice, 14*(4), 51–59.

Pluess, M., & Belsky, J. (2009). Differential susceptibility to rearing experience: The case of childcare. *Journal of Child Psychology and Psychiatry, 50*(4), 396–404.

Polce-Lynch, M., Myers, B. J., Kliewer, W., & Kilmartin, C. (2001). Adolescent self-esteem and gender: Exploring relations to sexual harassment, body image, media influence, and emotional expression. *Journal of Youth and Adolescence, 30*(2), 225–243.

Polenski, T. A. (2002). Child characteristics and relations in the family as predictors of peer relationships. *Dissertation Abstracts International: Section B: The Sciences and Engineering, 63*(5-B), 2624.

Polivka, L. (2000). The ethical and empirical basis for consumer-directed care for the frail elderly. *Contemporary Gerontology, 7*(2), 50–52.

Polivka, L, & Salmon, J. R. (2001). *Consumer-directed care: An ethical, empirical, and practical guide for state policymakers.* Tampa, FL: Florida Policy Exchange Center on Aging.

Pollastri, A. R., Epstein, L. D., Heath, G. H., & Ablon, J. S. (2013). The collaborative problem solving approach: Outcomes across settings. *Harvard Review of Psychiatry, 21*(4), 188–199.

Popenoe, D. (2008). *Cohabitation, marriage, and child wellbeing. NJ: The National Marriage Project.* [Online.] Retrieved February 16, 2012, from http://lists101.his.com/pipermail/smartmarriages/1999-February/001982.html.

Popper, K. R. (1959). *The logic of scientific discovery.* London: Hutchinson.

Potera, C. (2008). Comprehensive sex education reduces teen pregnancies. *American Journal of Nursing, 108*(7), 18.

Presser, H. B., & Ward, B. W. (2011). Nonstandard work schedules over the life course: A first look. *Monthly Labor Review, 134*(7), 3–16.

Prigoff, A. W. (2003). Social justice framework. In J. Anderson & R. W. Carter (Eds.), *Diversity perspectives for social work practice.* Boston: Allyn & Bacon.

Pruger, R., & Specht, H. (1969). Assessing theoretical models of community organization practice: Alinsky as a case in point. *The Social Service Review, 43*(2), 123–135.

Pungello, E. P., Iruka, I. U., Dotterer, A. M., Mills-Koonce, R., & Reznick, J. S. (2009). The effects of socioeconomic status, race, and parenting on language development in early childhood. *Developmental Psychology, 45*(2), 544–557.

Quadagno, J. (2008). *Aging and the life course* (4th ed.). Boston: McGraw-Hill.

Quick, H., & Moen, P. (1998). Gender employment and retirement quality: A life course approach to the differential experiences of men and women. *Journal of Occupational Health Psychology, 3*(1), 44–64.

Quinn, J., & Kozy, M. (1996). The role of bridge jobs in the retirement transition: Gender, race and ethnicity. *The Gerontologist, 36,* 363–372.

Quiroz, P. (2007). Color-blind individualism, inter-country adoption and public policy. *Journal of Sociology & Social Welfare, 34*(2), 57–68.

Rabinowitz, P., & Conti, L. (2013). Links among human health, animal health, and ecosystem health. *Annual Review of Public Health, 34,* 189–204.

Radtke, K. M., Ruf, M., Gunter, H. M., Dohrmann, K., Schauer, M., Meyer, A., *et al.* (2011). Transgenerational impact of intimate partner violence on methylation in the promoter of the glucocorticoid receptor. *Translational Psychiatry, 1,* 2011–2021.

Rahnev, D., Lau, H., & de Lange, F. P. (2011). Prior expectation modulates the interaction between sensory and prefrontal regions in the human brain. *Journal of Neuroscience, 31*(29), 10741–10748.

Rajkumar, R., & Mahesh, R. (2010). The auspicious role of the 5-HT 3 receptor in depression: a probable neuronal target? *Journal of Psychopharmacology, 24*(4), 455–469.

Raman, P., Harwood, J., Weis, D., Anderson, J. L., & Miller, G. (2008). Portrayals of older adults in U.S. and Indian magazine advertisements: A cross-cultural comparison. *Howard Journal of Communications, 19*(3), 221–240.

Ramchand, R., Schell, T. L., Karney, B. R., Osilla, K. C., Burns, R. M., & Caldarone, L. B. (2010). Disparate prevalence estimates of PTSD among service members who served in Iraq and Afghanistan: Possible explanations. *Journal of Traumatic Stress, 23*(1), 59–68. DOI: 10.1002/jts.20486.

Ramirez, A. G. (1996). Hypertension in Hispanic Americans: Overview of the population. *Public Health Report, 111*(2), 25–26.

Rando, T. A. (1993). *The treatment of complicated grief.* Champaign, IL: Research Press.

Rapport, M. D., Bolden, J., Kofler, M. J., Sarver, D. E., Raiker, J. S., & Alderson, R. M. (2009). Hyperactivity in boys with attention-deficit/hyperactivity disorder (ADHD): A ubiquitous core symptom or manifestation of working memory deficits? *Journal of Abnormal Child Psychology, 37*(4), 521–534.

Ravdin, P. M., Cronin, K. A., Howlader, N., Berg, C. D., Chlebowski, R. T., Feuer, E. J., *et al.* (2007). The decrease in breast cancer incidence in 2003 in the United States. *New England Journal of Medicine, 356*(16), 1670–1674.

Rawls, J. (1971). *A theory of justice.* Cambridge, MA: Harvard University Press.

Reardon, L. E., Leen-Feldner, E. W., & Hayward, C. (2009). A critical review of the empirical literature on the relation between anxiety and puberty. *Clinical Psychology Review, 29*(1), 1–23.

Reich, R. (2010). *Aftershock: The next economy and America's future.* New York: Alfred A. Knopf/Random House.

Reinharz, S. (1992). *Feminist methods in social research.* New York: Oxford University Press.

Reinisch, J. M. (1990). *The Kinsey Institute new report on sex.* New York: St. Martin's Press.

Reisner, S. L., White, J. M., Bradford, J. B., & Mimiaga, M. J. (2014). Transgender health disparities: Comparing full cohort and nested matched-pair study designs in a community health center. *LGBT Health, 1*(3), 177–184. DOI: 10.1089/lgbt.2014.0009.

Reitzes, D. C., Mutran, E., & Pope, H. (1991). Location and well-being among retired men. *Journal of Gerontology, 46,* 195–203.

Remafedi, G., French, S., Story, M., Resnick, M. D., & Blum, R. (1998). The relationship between suicide risk and sexual orientation: Results of a population-based study. *American Journal of Public Health, 88,* 57–60.

Rende, R. (2000). Emotion and behavior genetics. In M. Lewis & J. M. Haviland-Jones (Eds.), *Handbook of emotions* (2nd ed.). New York: Guilford Press.

Riaza Bermudo-Soriano, C., Perez-Rodriguez, M. M., Vaquero-Lorenzo, C., & Baca-Garcia, E. (2012). New perspectives in glutamate and anxiety. *Pharmacology, Biochemistry, & Behavior, 100*(4), 752–774.

Rich, J., Corbin, T., Bloom, S., Rich, L., Evans, S., & Wilson, A. (2009). *Healing the hurt: Trauma-informed approaches to the health of boys and young men of color.* Philadelphia, PA: Drexel University College of Medicine.

Richardson, G. A., Ryan, C., Willford, J., Day, N. L., & Goldschmidt, L. (2002). Prenatal alcohol and marijuana exposure: Effects on neuropsychological outcomes at 10 years. *Neurotoxicology and Teratology, 24*(3), 309–320.

Richmond, M. (1920). *Social diagnosis.* New York: Russell Sage Foundation.

Rickman, J. (1957). *A general selection from the works of Sigmund Freud.* New York: Doubleday & Company.

Ritter, J., Stewart, M., Bernet, C., Coe, M., & Brown, S. A. (2002). Effects of childhood exposure to familial alcoholism and family violence on adolescent substance use, conduct problems, and self-esteem. *Journal of Traumatic Stress, 15*(2), 113–122.

Robbins, J. M., Bird, T. M., Tilford, J. M., Cleves, M. A., Hobbs, C. A., Grosse, S. D., *et al.* (2007). Hospital stays, hospital charges, and in-hospital deaths among infants with selected birth defects—United States, 2003. *Journal of the American Medical Association, 297*(8), 802–803.

Robbins, S. P. (1984). Anglo concepts and Indian reality: A study of juvenile delinquency. *Social Casework, 65*(4), 235–241.

Roberts, A. L., Gilman, S. E., Breslau, J., Breslau, N., Koenen, K. C. (2011). Race/ethnic differences in exposure to traumatic events, development of post-traumatic stress disorder, and treatment-seeking for post-traumatic stress disorder in the United States. *Psychological Medicine, 41*(1), 71–83.

Roberts, R. N. (2002). Stating the obvious: Why do we care about access to health care? *Journal of Early Intervention, 25*(1), 12–14.

Robertson, E., Grace, S., Wallington, T., & Stewart, D. E. (2004). Antenatal risk factors for postpartum depression: A synthesis of recent literature. *General Hospital Psychiatry, 26,* 289–295.

Robinson, T., & Anderson, C. (2006). Older characters in children's animated television programs: A content analysis of their portrayal. *Journal of Broadcasting & Electronic Media, 50*(2), 287–304.

Robinson, T., Callister, M., Magoffin, D., & Moore, J. (2007). The portrayal of older characters in Disney animated films. *Journal of Aging Studies, 21*(3), 203–213.

Röcke, C., & Lachman, M. E. (2008). Perceived trajectories of life satisfaction across past, present, and future: Profiles and correlates of subjective change in young, middle-aged, and older adults. *Psychology & Aging, 23*(4), 833–847.

Roediger, D. R. (1999). *The wages of whiteness: Race and the making of the American working class.* New York: Verso.

Rogers, A. T. (1999). Factors associated with depression and low life satisfaction in the low-income, frail elderly. *Journal of Gerontological Social Work, 31*(1/2), 167–194.

Rogers, C. R. (1951). *Client-centered therapy: Its current practice, implications, and theory.* Boston: Houghton Mifflin.

Rogers, S. J., Vismara, L., Wagner, A. L., McCormick, C., Young, G., & Ozonoff, S. (2014). Autism treatment in the first year of life: A pilot study of infant start, a parent-implemented intervention for symptomatic infants. *Journal of Autism and Developmental Disorders, 44*(12), 2981–2995.

Rosenbaum, J. E. (2009). Patient teenagers? A comparison of the sexual behavior of virginity pledgers and matched nonpledgers. *Pediatrics, 123*(1), 110–120.

Rosenblum, L. P., & Corn, A. L. (2002). Experiences of older adults who stopped driving because of their visual impairments: Part 3. *Journal of Visual Impairment & Blindness, 96*(10), 701–710.

Roth, L. M., & Henley, M. M. (2012). Unequal motherhood: Racial-ethnic and socioeconomic disparities in cesarean sections in the United States. *Social Problems, 59*(2), 207–227.

Rothenberg, A., & Weissman, A. (2002). The development of programs for pregnant and parenting teens. *Social Work in Health Care, 35*(3), 65–83.

Rothman, J. (1995). Approaches to community intervention. In J. Rothman, J. L. Erich, & J. E. Tropman (Eds.), *Strategies of community intervention* (5th ed.). Itasca, IL: F. E. Peacock Publishers.

Rowe, J. W., & Kahn, R. L. (1987). Human aging: Usual and successful. *Science, 237*(4811), 143–149.

Rowe, J. W., & Kahn, R. L. (1997). Successful aging. *Gerontologist, 37*(4), 433–440.

Ruschena, E., Prior, M., Sanson, A., & Smart, S. (2005). A longitudinal study of adolescent adjustment following family transitions. *Journal of Child Psychology and Psychiatry, 46*(4), 353–363.

Russell, S. T., & Joyner, K. (2001). Adolescent sexual orientation and suicide risk: Evidence from a national study. *American Journal of Public Health, 91,* 1276–1281.

Ruth, J. E., & Coleman, P. (1996). Personality and aging: Coping and management of the self in later life. In J. Birren and K. W. Schaie (Eds.), *Handbook of the psychology of aging* (pp. 308–322). San Diego, CA: Academic Press.

Ryan, C., Huebner, D., Diaz, R. M., & Sanchez, J. (2009). Family rejection as a predictor of negative health outcomes in White and Latino lesbian, gay, and bisexual young adults. *Pediatrics, 123*(1), 346–352.

Rymer, J., Wilson, R., & Ballard, K. (2003). Making decisions about hormone replacement therapy. *British Journal of Nursing, 326,* 322–326.

Saha, S., Barnett, A. G., Foldi, C., Burne, T. H., Eyles, D. W., Buka, S. L., et al. (2009). Advanced paternal age is associated with impaired neurocognitive outcomes during infancy and childhood. *PLoS Medicine, 6*(3), e1000040.

Saleebey, D. (1992). *The strengths perspective in social work practice.* New York: Longman.

Salter, M. D. (1940). *An evaluation of adjustment based upon the concept of security.* Toronto: University of Toronto Press.

Salthouse T. (2006). Mental exercise and mental aging: Evaluating the "use it or lose it" hypothesis. *Perspective on Psychological Sciences. 1,* 68–87.

Saltman, J. E. (2002). Theory and practice in social work: Two perspectives on reality. *Arete, 26*(part 2), 84–99.

Saltman, J. E., & Greene, R. R. (1993). Social workers' perceived knowledge and use of human behavior theory. *Journal of Social Work Education, 20*(1), 88–98.

Samuels, G. M. (2009). "Being raised by White people": Navigating racial difference among adopted multiracial adults. *Journal of Marriage and the Family, 71*(1), 80–94.

Sandin, S., Hultman, C. M., Kolevzon, A., Gross, R., MacCabe, J. H., & Reichenberg, A. (2012). Advancing maternal age is associated with increasing risk for autism: A review and meta-analysis. *Journal of the American Academy of Child & Adolescent Psychiatry, 51*(5), 477. DOI: 10.1016/j.jaac.2012.02.018.

Santos-Reboucas, C. B., Correa, J. C., Bonomo, A., Fintelman-Rodrigues, N., Moura, K. C. V., Rogrigues, C. S. C., et al. (2009). The impact of folate pathway polymorphisms combined to nutritional deficiency as a maternal predisposition factor for Down syndrome. *Disease Markers, 25*(3), 149–157.

Sarigiani, P. A., & Petersen, A. C. (2000). Adolescence: Puberty and biological maturation. In A. Kazdin (Ed.), *Encyclopedia of psychology* (pp. 39–46). Washington, DC: American Psychological Association.

Satcher, D., Fryer, G. E., McCann, J., Troutman, A., Woolf, S. H., & Rust, G. (2005). What if we were equal? A comparison of the Black-White mortality gap in 1960 and 2000. *Health Affairs, 24*(2), 459–464.

Sayer, D. (1989). *Readings from Karl Marx.* New York: Routledge.

Schaefer, R. T. (2001). *Sociology* (7th ed.). New York: McGraw-Hill Companies.

Schaie, K. W., & Willis, S. L. (2000). A stage theory model of adult development revisited. In R. Rubinstein, M. Moss, & M. Kleban (Eds.), *The many dimensions of aging: Essays in honor of M. Powell Lawton.* New York: Springer.

Scharlach, A. (1994). Caregiving and employment: Results of an employee survey. *The Gerontologist, 29,* 382–387.

Scher, A., & Mayseless, O. (2000). Mothers of anxious/ambivalent infants: Maternal characteristics and child-care context. *Child Development, 71*(6), 1629–1639.

Schiffman, J., Abrahamson, A., Cannon, T., LaBrie, J., Parnas, J., Schulsinger, F., *et al.* (2001). Early rearing factors in schizophrenia. *International Journal of Mental Health, 30*(1), 3–16.

Schiffman, J., LaBrie, J., Carter, J., Cannon, T., Schulsinger, F., Parnas, J., *et al.* (2002). Perception of parent–child relationships in high-risk families, and adult schizophrenic outcome of offspring. *Journal of Psychiatric Research, 36*(1), 41–47.

Schmitt, M., Kliegal, M., & Shapiro, A. (2007). Marital interaction in middle and old age: A predictor of marital satisfaction? *International Journal of Aging and Human Development, 65*(4), 283–300.

Schneider, B. H., Atkinson, L., & Tardif, C. (2001). Child–parent attachment and children's peer relations: A qualitative review. *Developmental Psychology, 37,* 86–100.

Schoen, J. (2000). Reconceiving abortion: Medical practice, women's access, and feminist politics before and after Roe v. Wade. *Feminist Studies, 26*(2), 349–376.

Schoen, R., Landale, N. S., & Daniels, K. (2007). Family transitions in young adulthood. *Demography, 44,* 807–820.

Schoendorf, K. C., & Kiely, J. L. (1992). Relationship of sudden infant death syndrome to maternal smoking during and after pregnancy. *Pediatrics, 90,* 905–908.

Schope, R. (2005). Who's afraid of growing older? Gay and lesbian perceptions of aging. *Journal of Gerontological Social Work, 45*(4), 23–38.

Schore, A. N. (2000). Attachment and the regulation of the right brain. *Attachment and Human Development, 2,* 23–47.

Schrag, S. G., & Dixon, R. L. (1985). Occupational exposure associated with male reproductive dysfunction. *Annual Review of Pharmacology and Toxicology, 25,* 467–592.

Schulze, M. B., Manson, J. E., Ludwig, D. S., Colditz, G. A., Stampfer, M. J., Willett, W. C., *et al.* (2004). Sugar-sweetened beverages, weight gain, and incidence of type 2 diabetes in young and middle-aged women. *JAMA, 292*(8), 927–934.

Scott, G., & Ni, H. (2004). Access to health care among Hispanic/Latino children: United States, 1998–2001. *Advance Data, 344,* 1–20.

Sears, D. O. (1988). Symbolic racism. In P. A. Katz & D. A. Taylor (Eds.), *Eliminating racism: Profiles in controversy* (pp. 53–84). New York: Putnam.

Sedgh, G., Henshaw, S., Singh, S., Ahman, E., & Shah, I. H. (2007). Induced abortion: Estimated rates and trends worldwide. *Lancet, 370*(9595), 1338–1345.

Sedgh, G., Singh, S., Shah, I. H., Ahman, E., Henshaw, S. K., & Bankole, A. (2012). Induced abortion: Incidence and trends worldwide from 1995 to 2008. *Lancet, 11,* 1–8.

Segraves, R. T., & Segraves, K. B. (1995). Human sexuality and aging. *Journal of Sex Education and Therapy, 21,* 88–102.

Seipel, A., & Way, I. (2006). Culturally competent social work: Practice with Latino clients. [Online.] Retrieved November 10, 2014, from http://www.socialworker.com/feature-articles/ethics-articles/Culturally_Competent_Social_Work_Practice_With_Latino_Clients/.

Semba, R. D., Blaum, C. S., Bartali, B., Xue, O. L., Ricks, M. O., Guralnik, J. M., *et al.* (2006). Denture use, malnutrition, frailty, and mortality among older women living in the community. *The Journal of Nutrition, Health, and Aging, 10*(2), 161–167.

Sexual Risk Behavior Data & Statistics 2013, Youth Risk Behavior Surveillance System. U.S. Centers for Disease Control and Prevention, 2014. Retrieved July 11, 2014, from http://www.cdc.gov/healthyyouth/sexualbehaviors/data.htm.

Shansky, J. (2002). Negative effects of divorce on child and adolescent psychosocial adjustment. *Journal of Pastoral Counseling, 37,* 73–87.

Shapiro, J., & Applegate, J. S. (2002). Child care as a relational context for early development: Research in neurobiology and emerging roles for social work. *Child and Adolescent Social Work Journal, 19*(2), 97–114.

Shargorodsky, J., Curhan, S. G., Curhan, G. C., & Eavey, R. (2010). Change in prevalence of hearing loss in U.S. adolescents. *Journal of the American Medical Association, 304*(7), 772–778.

Shaw, T. (2008). An ecological contribution to social welfare theory. *Social Development Issues, 30*(3), 13–26.

Shelton, J. F., Tancredi, D. J., & Hertz-Picciotto, I. (2010). Independent and dependent contributions of advanced maternal and paternal ages to autism risk. *Autism Research, 3*, 30–39.

Shepard, M. (1992). Child visiting and domestic abuse. *Child Welfare, 71*, 357–367.

Sheppard, M. (1998). Practice validity, reflexivity, and knowledge for social work. *British Journal of Social Work, 28*(5), 763–781.

Sherry, L., Murphy, B.S., Xu, J., & Kochanek, K. D. (2012). Deaths: Preliminary data for 2010. *National Vital Statistics Reports, 60*(4), Retrieved March 3, 2012, from http://www.cdc.gov/nchs/data/nvsr/nvsr60/nvsr60_04.pdf.

Shidlo, A., & Schroeder, M. (2002). Changing sexual orientation: A consumer's report. *Professional Psychology: Research and Practice, 33*(2), 249–259.

Shierholz, H., & Mishel, L. (2013). A decade of flat wages: The key barrier to shared prosperity and a rising middle class. [Online.] Retrieved October 20, 2014, from http://www.epi.org/publication/a-decade-of-flat-wages-the-key-barrier-to-shared-prosperity-and-a-rising-middle-class/.

Shih, M., & Sanchez, D. T. (2009). When race becomes more complex: Toward understanding the landscape of multiracial identity and experiences. *Journal of Social Issues, 65*(1), 1–11.

Shpancer, N., Bowden, J. M., Ferrell, M. A., Pavlik, S. F., Robinson, M. N., Schwind, J. L., *et al.* (2002). The gap: Parental knowledge about daycare. *Early Child Development and Care, 172*, 635–642.

Shteyngart, G. (2010). *Super sad true love story.* New York: Random House.

Siegel, D. J. (2007). *The mindful brain: Reflection and attunement in the cultivation of well-being.* New York: Norton.

Sigelman, C. K., & Rider, E. A. (2005). *Life-span human development* (5th ed.). Belmont, CA: Wadsworth Publishing.

Simmons, R. G., & Blyth, D. A. (1987). *Moving into adolescence.* Hawthorne, NY: Aldine.

Simon, B., & Thyer, B. (1994). Are theories for practice necessary? Yes/No! *Journal of Social Work Education, 30*(2), 144–153.

Simon, J. A. (2011). Identifying and treating sexual dysfunction in postmenopausal women: The role of estrogen. *Journal of Women's Health, 20*(10), 1453–1465.

Skinner, B. F. (1938). *The behavior of organisms: An experimental analysis.* New York: AppletonCentury-Crofts.

Skipworth, J. R. A., Szabadkai, G., Olde Damink, S. W. M., Leung, P. S., Humphries, S. E., & Montgomery, H. E. (2011). Review article: Pancreatic renin-angiotensin systems in health and disease. *Alimentary Pharmacology & Therapeutics, 34*(8), 840–852.

Slater, S. F., Weigand, R. A., & Zwirlein, T. J. (2008). The business case for commitment to diversity. *Business Horizons, 51*(3), 201–209.

Slicker, E. K. (1998). Relationship of parenting style to behavioral adjustment in graduating high school seniors. *Journal of Youth and Adolescence, 27*(3), 345–372.

Smith, L., Yonekura, M. L., Wallace, T., Berman, N., Kuo, J., & Berkowitz, C. (2003). Effects of prenatal methamphetamine exposure on fetal growth and drug withdrawal symptoms in infants born at term. *Journal of Developmental & Behavioral Pediatrics, 24*(1), 17–23.

Smith, R., Ashford, L., Gribble, J., & Clifton, D. (2009). *Family planning saves lives* (4th ed.). Washington, DC: Population Reference Bureau.

Snow, C. E. (1999). Social perspectives on the emergence of language. In B. MacWhinney (Ed.), *The emergence of language.* Mahwah, NJ: Lawrence Erlbaum Associates.

Solem, M. B., Christophersen, K. A., & Martinussen, M. (2011). Predicting parenting stress: Children's behavioural problems and parents' coping. *Infant & Child Development, 20*(2), 162–180.

Solomon, B. B. (1976). *Black empowerment: Social work in oppressed communities.* New York: Columbia University Press.

Sommer, B. (2001). Menopause. In J. Worell (Ed.), *Encyclopedia of women and gender* (pp. 729–738). San Diego, CA: Academic Press.

Sontag, L. M., Graber, J. A., Brooks-Gunn, J., & Warren, M. P. (2008). Coping with social stress: Implications for psychopathology in young adolescent girls. *Journal of Abnormal Child Psychology, 36*(8), 1159–1174.

Sorrell, J. M. (2009). Aging toward happiness. *Journal of Psychological Nursing, 47*(3), 23–26.

Spence, A. P. (1999). *Biology of human aging* (2nd ed.). Englewood Cliffs, NJ: Prentice Hall.

Spencer, K., Spencer, C. E., Power, M., Dawson, C., & Nicolaides, K. H. (2003). Screening for chromosomal abnormalities in the first trimester using ultrasound and maternal serum biochemistry in a one-stop clinic. *BJOG: An International Journal of Obstetrics & Gynaecology, 110*(3), 281–286.

Spina Bifida Association. (2014). *What is Spina Bifida?* [Online.] Retrieved May 28, 2014, from http://www.spinabifidaassociation.org/site/c.evKRI7OX-IoJ8H/b.8277225/k.5A79/What_is_Spina_Bifida.htm.

Squeglia, L. M., Schweinsburg, A. D., Pulido, C., & Tapert, S. F. (2011). Adolescent binge drinking linked to abnormal spatial working memory brain activation: Differential gender effects. *Alcoholism: Clinical and Experimental Research, 35*(10), 1831–1841.

Stafford, F. (2008). *Chore wars: Men, women, and housework.* [Online.] Retrieved on May 16, 2012, from http://www.nsf.gov/discoveries/disc_summ.jsp?org=NSF&cntn_id=111458&preview=false.

Stainsby, M., Sapochnik, M., Bledin, K. & Mason, O. J. (2010). Are attitudes and beliefs about symptoms more important than symptom severity in recovery from psychosis? *Psychosis: Psychological, Social and Integrative Approaches, 2*(1), 41–49.

Starck, M. (1993). *Women's medicine ways.* Freedom, CA: Crossing Press.

Stark, R. (1998). *Sociology* (7th ed.). Belmont, CA: Wadsworth.

Stattin, H., & Magnusson, D. (1990). *Pubertal maturation in female development: Paths through life* (Vol. 2). Hillsdale, NJ: Erlbaum.

Steelman, L. C., Powell, B., Werum, R., & Carter, S. (2002). Reconsidering the effects of sibling configuration: Recent advances and challenges. *Annual Review of Sociology, 28*, 243–269.

Stephens, C., Budge, R. C., & Carryer, J. (2002). What is this thing called hormone replacement therapy? Discursive construction of medication in situated practice. *Qualitative Health Research, 12*(3), 347–359.

Sternberg, R. J. (1977). *Intelligence, information processing, and analogical reasoning: The componential analysis of human abilities.* New York: John Wiley & Sons.

Sternberg, R. J. (1985). *Beyond IQ: A triarchic theory of human intelligence.* New York: Cambridge University Press.

Sternberg, R. J. (1988). Triangulating love. In R. J. Sternberg & M. L. Barnes (Eds.), *The psychology of love.* New Haven, CT: Yale University Press.

Stevens-Ratchford, R., & Krause, A. (2004). Visually impaired older adults and home-based leisure activities: The effects of person-environment congruence. *Journal of Visual Impairment & Blindness, 98*(1), 14–27.

Stolzenberg, R. M., Blair-Loy, M., & Waite, L. J. (1995). Religious participation in early adulthood: Age and family life cycle effects on church membership. *American Sociological Review, 60*, 84–103.

Strasburger, V., & Grossman, D. (2001). How many more Columbines? What can pediatricians do about school and media violence? *Pediatric Annals, 30*(2), 87–94.

Stratton, K., Howe, C., & Battaglia, F. (Eds.). (1996). *Fetal alcohol syndrome: Diagnosis, epidemiology, prevention, and treatment.* Washington, DC: National Academy Press.

Straus, M. A. (2001). *Beating the devil out of them: Corporal punishment in American families and its effects on children.* New Brunswick, NJ: Transaction Publishers.

Straus, M. A. (2008). The special issue on prevention of violence ignores the primordial violence. *Journal of Interpersonal Violence, 23*(9), 1314–1320.

Striegel-Moore, R. H., Rosselli, F., Perrin, N., DeBar, L., Wilson, G. T., May, A., *et al.* (2009). Gender difference in the prevalence of eating disorder symptoms. *International Journal of Eating Disorders, 42*(5), 471–474.

Striegel-Moore, R. H., Silberstein, L. R., & Rodin, J. (1993). The social self in bulimia nervosa: Public self-consciousness, social anxiety, and perceived fraudulence. *Journal of Abnormal Psychology, 102,* 297–303.

Striegel-Moore, R. H., Wilson, T. G., DeBar, L., Perrin, N., Lynch, F., Rosselli, F., *et al.* (2010). Cognitive-behavioral guided self-help for the treatment of recurrent binge eating. *Journal of Consulting and Clinical Psychology, 78*(3), 312–321.

Stroebe, M., & Schut, H. (1999). The dual process model of coping with bereavement: Rationale and description, *Death Studies, 23*(3), 197–224.

Strong, B., DeVault, C., Sayad, B. W., & Yarber, W. L. (2002). *Human sexuality: Diversity in contemporary America* (4th ed.). Boston: McGraw-Hill.

Studd, J. (2009). Estrogens as first-choice therapy for osteoporosis prevention and treatment in women under 60. *Climacteric, 12*(3), 206–209.

Sue, D. W. (2010). *Microaggressions in everyday life: Race, gender, and sexual orientation.* Hoboken, NJ: Wiley & Sons.

Sue, D. W., & Capodilupo, C. M. (2008). Racial, gender, and sexual orientation microaggressions: Implications for counseling and psychotherapy. In D. W. Sue & D. Sue (Eds.), *Counseling the culturally diverse. Theory and practice* (pp. 105–132). Hoboken, NJ: John Wiley & Sons.

Sue, D. W., Capodilupo, C. M., Nadal, K. L., & Torino, G. C. (2008). Racial microaggressions and the power to define reality. *American Psychologist, 63*(4), 277–279.

Sue, D. W., Capodilupo, C. M., Torino, G. C., Bucceri, J. M., Holder, A. M., Nadal, K. L., *et al.* (2007). Racial microaggressions in everyday life: Implications for clinical practice. *American Psychologist, 62*(4), 271–286.

Sullivan, M., & Wodarski, J. S. (2002). Social alienation in gay youth. *Journal of Human Behavior in the Social Environment, 5*(1), 1–17.

Sun, Y., & Li, Y. (2002, May). Children's well-being during parents' marital disruption process: A pooled time-series analysis. *Journal of Marriage and the Family, 64,* 472–488.

Sun, Y., & Li, Y. (2009). Parental divorce, sibship size, family resources, and children's academic performance. *Social Science Research, 38*(3), 622–634.

Swann, J. (2009). Learning: An evolutionary analysis. *Educational Philosophy & Theory, 41*(3), 256–269.

Swanson, L. M., Favorite, T. K., Horin, E., & Arnedt, J. T. (2009). A combined group treatment for nightmares and insomnia in combat veterans: A pilot study. *Journal of Traumatic Stress, 22*(6), 639–642. DOI: 10.1002/jts.20468.

Swenson, C. R. (1998). Clinical social work's contribution to a social justice perspective. *Social Work, 43*(6), 527–537.

Swisher, J. D., Gatenby, J. C., Gore, J. C., Wolfe, B. A., Moon, C. H., Kim, S. G., *et al.* (2010). Multiscale pattern analysis of orientation-selective activity in the primary visual cortex. *Journal of Neuroscience, 30,* 325–330.

Takahashi, P. Y., Okhravi, H. R., Lim, L. S., & Kasten, M. J. (2004). Preventive health care in the elderly population: A guide for practicing physicians. *Mayo Clinic Proceedings, 79,* 416–427.

Tanne, J. H. (2009). Obama diverts funds from abstinence-only sex education. *British Medical Journal, 338*(7705), 1232.

Tarhan, F., Faydaci, G., Gul, A. E., Kuyumcuoglu, U., & Eryldrirm, B. (2011). Oxytocin immunoreactivity in the corpus cavernosum of patients with erectile dysfunction. *Urologia Internationalis, 87*(2), 225–229.

Tarkan, L. (2011). An end to pain. *Prevention, 63*(6), 31–37.

Tarokh, L., Carskadon, M. A., & Achermann, P. (2011). Trait-like characteristics of the sleep EEG across adolescent development. *The Journal of Neuroscience, 31*(17), 6371–6378.

Tarrow, S. (1994). *Power in movement: Social movements, collective action, and politics.* New York: Cambridge University Press.

Tasker, F. (2005). Lesbian mothers, gay fathers, and their children: A review. *Journal of Developmental & Behavioral Pediatrics, 26*(3), 224–240.

Taylor, E. H. (2006). The weaknesses of the strengths model: Mental illness as a case in point. *Best Practices in Mental Health, 2*(1), 1–30.

Tehrani, K., & Michael, A. (2014). Wearable technology and wearable devices: Everything you need to know. [Online.] Retrieved on July 21, 2015, from http://www.wearabledevices.com/what-is-a-wearable-device/.

Teicher, M. H., Anderson, C. M., & Polcari, A. (2012). Childhood maltreatment is associated with reduced volume in the hippocampal subfields CA3. Dentate gyrus, and subiculum. *Proceedings of the National Academy of Sciences of the United States of America, 109*(9), E563–E572.

Tesser, A. (2000). Self-esteem. In A. Kazdin (Ed.), *Encyclopedia of psychology* (pp. 213–216). Washington, DC: American Psychological Association.

Thackray, H., & Tifft, C. (2001). Fetal alcohol syndrome. *Pediatric Review, 22*, 47–55.

The International Hearing Voices Network. (2014). About us. [Online.] Retrieved July 14, 2014, from http://www.intervoiceonline.org/about-intervoice.

The National Campaign to Prevent Teen and Unplanned Pregnancy. (2012). *Counting it up: The public costs of teen childbearing*. Retrieved February 28, 2012, from http://www.thenationalcampaign.org/costs/.

The National Center for Injury Prevention and Control. (2010). Traumatic brain injury. [Online.] Retrieved on October 25, 2015, from http://www.cdc.gov/traumaticbraininjury/pdf/blue_book.pdf.

The National Center for Participant-Directed Services. (2013). The National Center for Participant-Directed Services. Retrieved June 27, 2014, from https://www.caregiver.org/national-resource-center-participant-directed-services.

The White House. (2015). Expanding Medicaid. [Online.] Retrieved October 25, 2015, from https://www.whitehouse.gov/expanding-medicaid.

The White House, Office of the Press Secretary. (2013). Remarks by the President on economic mobility. [Online.] Retrieved October 20, 2014, from http://www.whitehouse.gov/the-press-office/2013/12/04/remarks-president-economic-mobility.

Thompson, R. A. (2000). Early experience and socialization. In A. Kazdin (Ed.), *Encyclopedia of psychology*. Washington, DC: American Psychological Association and Oxford University Press.

Thompson, S. J., Bender, K., Windsor, L., Cook, M. S., & Williams, T. (2010). Homeless youth: Characteristics, contributing factors, and service options. *Journal of Human Behavior in the Social Environment, 20*(2), 193–217. DOI: 10.1080/10911350903269831.

Tickle, J. J., Heatherton, T. F., & Wittenberg, L. G. (2001). Can personality change? In W. J. Livesley (Ed.), *Handbook of personality disorders* (pp. 242–258). New York: Guilford Press.

Tiggemann, M. (2001). The impact of adolescent girls' life concerns and leisure activities on body dissatisfaction, disordered eating, and self-esteem. *Journal of Genetic Psychology, 162*(2), 133–142.

Timins, J. K. (2001). Radiation during pregnancy. *New Jersey Medicine, 98*, 23–33.

Tjaden, P., & Thoennes, N. (1998). *Prevalence, incidence, and consequences of violence against women: Findings from the National Violence against Women Survey.* Washington, DC: National Institute for Justice and Centers for Disease Control and Prevention.

Tjaden, P., & Thoennes, N. (2000, November). *Full Report of the prevalence, incidence, and consequences of violence against women: Findings from the National Violence Against Women Survey.* National Institute of Justice. [Online.] Retrieved August 5, 2012, from http://www.nij.gov/pubs-sum/183781.htm.

Tokita, K., Yamaji, T., & Hashimoto, K. (2012). Roles of glutamate signaling in preclinical and/or mechanistic models of depression. *Pharmacology, Biochemistry, & Behavior, 100*(4), 6880704.

Tottenham, N., Hare, T. A., Millner, A., Gilhooly, T., Zevin, J. D., & Casey, B. J. (2011). Elevated amygdala response to faces following early deprivation. *Developmental Science, 14*(2), 190–204.

Trasande, L. & Liu, Y. (2011). Reducing the staggering costs of environmental disease in children, estimated at $76.6 billion in 2008. *Health Affairs, 30*(5), 863–870. DOI: 10.1377/hlthaff.2010.1239.

Tucker, C. J., & Updegraff, K. (2010). Who's the boss? Patterns of control in adolescents' sibling relationships. *Family Relations, 59*, 520–532. DOI: 10.1111/j.1741-3729.2010.00620.x.

Tucker, J. S., Kressin, N. R., Spiro, A., & Ruscio, J. (1998). Intrapersonal characteristics and the timing of divorce: A prospective investigation. *Journal of Social & Personal Relationships, 15*(2), 211–225.

Turner, J. H. (1998). *The structure of sociological theory.* New York: Wadsworth.

Turner, K. (2009). Mindfulness: The present moment in clinical social work. *Clinical Social Work, 37*, 95–103.

Tutty, L., & Wagar, J. (1994). The evolution of a group for young children who have witnessed family violence. *Social Work with Groups, 17*(1/2), 89–104.

Tylka, T., & Sabik, N. (2010). Integrating social comparison theory and self-esteem within objectification theory to predict women's disordered eating. *Sex Roles, 63*(1/2), 18–31. DOI: 10.1007/s11199-010 9785-3.

Uhlenberg, P. I. (1996). Mortality decline over the twentieth century and supply of kin over the life course. *Gerontologist, 36*, 681–685.

UNICEF. (2004). *Low birth weight: Country, regional, and global estimates.* New York: UNICEF.

UNICEF. (2007). *Progress for children: A world fit for children statistical review.* New York: UNICEF.

United Nations Development Programme. (2008). *Climate Change: Scaling Up to Meet the Challenge.* New York: United Nations Development Programme.

United Nations Environment Program. (2007). Global environment outlook: GEO4, summary for decision makers. Geneva: UNEP.

United Nations Millennium Development Goal Indicators. (2014). Adolescent birth rate, per 1,000 women. [Data file.] Retrieved May 23, 2014, from http://millenniumindicators.un.org/unsd/mdg/SeriesDetail.aspx?srid=761.

U.S. Bureau of Labor Statistics. (2002). *2002 National occupational employment and wage estimates.* Washington, DC: Author.

U.S. Bureau of Labor Statistics. (2009). *Usual weekly earnings of wage and salary workers news release.* Washington, DC: Author.

U.S. Census Bureau. (2001). *Households and families: 2000.* Washington, DC: U.S. Department of Commerce.

U.S. Census Bureau. (2003). *Marital status: 2000.* Washington, DC: U.S. Department of Commerce.

U.S. Census Bureau. (2006). *American community survey.* Washington, DC: U.S. Department of Commerce.

U.S. Census Bureau. (2008). *Household income rises, poverty rates unchanged, number of uninsured down.* Washington, DC: Department of Commerce.

U.S. Census Bureau. (2010a). *Population statistics.* Retrieved February 26, 2012, from http://www.census.gov/population/www/socdemo/hh-fam/cps2010.html.

U.S. Census Bureau. (2010b). *U.S. Census Bureau reports men and women wait longer to marry.* Retrieved on March 2, 2012, from http://www.census.gov/newsroom/releases/archives/families_households/cb10–174.html.

U.S. Census Bureau. (2011). *Health insurance: Highlights: 2010.* Retrieved August 1, 2012, from http://www.census.gov/hhes/www/hlthins/data/incpovhlth/2010/highlights.html.

U.S. Census Bureau. (2012). *Profile America: Facts for Features.* [Online.] Retrieved July 11, 2014, from https://www.census.gov/newsroom/releases/archives/facts_for_features_special_editions/cb12-ff17.html.

U.S. Census Bureau. (2013a). *America's Families and Living Arrangements: 2012.* [Online.] Retrieved July 11, 2014, from http://www.census.gov/prod/2013pubs/p20-570.pdf.

U.S. Census Bureau. (2013b). Income, poverty, and health insurance coverage: 2012. [Online.] Retrieved July 14, 2014, from http://www.census.gov/newsroom/releases/pdf/20130917_ipslides.pdf.

U.S. Census Bureau. (2013c). Male nurses becoming more commonplace, Census Bureau Reports.

[Online.] Retrieved July 14, 2014, from http://www.census.gov/newsroom/releases/archives/employment_occupations/cb13-32.html.

U.S. Department of Commerce. (2010). Middle class in America. [Online.] Retrieved October 20, 2014, from http://www.commerce.gov/sites/default/files/documents/migrated/Middle%20Class%20Report.pdf.

U.S. Department of Health and Human Services. (2001). *Women and Smoking: A Report of the Surgeon General.* Rockville: U.S. Department of Health and Human Services, Public Health Service, Office of the Surgeon General. Washington, DC: Government Printing Office.

U.S. Department of Health and Human Services. (2003). *Prevention pays: The costs of not preventing child abuse and neglect.* Washington, DC: Government Printing Office.

U.S. Department of Health and Human Services. (2004). *Literacy and health outcomes summary.* Washington, DC: U.S. Department of Health and Human Services, Agency for Healthcare Research and Quality.

U.S. Department of Health and Human Services. (2007a). *Child maltreatment 2007.* Washington, DC: Government Printing Office.

U.S. Department of Health and Human Services. (2007b). *Economic costs of injuries among children and adolescents.* Washington, DC: National Center for Injury Prevention and Control.

U.S. Department of Health and Human Services. (2009). *Child welfare outcomes 2006–2009:* Report to congress Administration for Children and Families, Administration on Children, Youth and Families, Children's Bureau. Retrieved February 26, 2012, from http://www.acf.hhs.gov/programs/cb/pubs/cwo06-09/cwo06-09.pdf.

U.S. Department of Health and Human Services. (2011). *Health Literacy Interventions and Outcomes: An Updated Systemic Review.* [Online.] Retrieved May 28, 2014, from http://www.ahrq.gov/research/findings/evidence-based-reports/litupsum.html.

U.S. Department of Health and Human Services. (2012). Preventive services covered under the Affordable Health Care Act. Retrieved July 8, 2014, from http://www.hhs.gov/healthcare/facts/factsheets/2010/07/preventive-services-list.html.

U.S. Department of Health and Human Services, Administration for Children and Families, Administration on Children, Youth and Families, Children's Bureau. (2011). *Child maltreatment 2010.* Retrieved February 26, 2012, from http://www.acf.hhs.gov/programs/cb/stats_research/index.htm#can.

U.S. Department of Health and Human Services, Administration for Children and Families, Administration on Children, Youth, and Families, Children's Bureau. (2013). *Child maltreatment 2012.* Retrieved July 2, 2014, from http://www.acf.hhs.gov/programs/cb/resource/child-maltreatment-2012.

U.S. Department of Labor. (2007). *Labor force characteristics by race and ethnicity.* [Online.] Retrieved June 25, 2009, from http://www.bls.gov/cps/cpsrace2007.pdf.

U.S. Department of Labor. (2008). *Report of the task-force on the aging of the American workforce.* [Online.] Retrieved June 25, 2009, from http://www.doleta.gov/reports/FINAL_Taskforce_Report_2_27_08.pdf.

U.S. Department of Labor. (2013). Beyond the numbers. [Online.] Retrieved July 8, 2014, from http://www.bls.gov/opub/btn/volume-2/paid-leave-in-private-industry-over-the-past-20-years.htm.

U.S. Department of Labor. (2014a). *Family and Medical Leave Act.* [Online.] Retrieved May 30, 2014, from http://www.dol.gov/whd/fmla/.

U.S. Department of Labor. (2014b). Minimum wage laws in the United States. [Online.] Retrieved October 24, 2014 from http://www.dol.gov/whd/minwage/america.htm#Oregon.

U.S. Department of Veterans Affairs. (2014). Federal benefits for veterans, dependents, and survivors. [Online.] Retrieved on November 10, 2014, from http://www.va.gov/opa/publications/benefits_book/benefits_chap01.asp.

U.S. Environmental Protection Agency. (2008). *Fast facts on children's environmental health.* Washington, DC. Available from http://yosemite.epa.gov/ochp/ochpweb.nsf/content/fastfacts.htm.

U.S. Food and Drug Administration. (2014). Report on the food and drug administration's review of the safety of recombinant bovine somatotropin. [Online.] Retrieved on October 27, 2014, from http://www.fda.gov/AnimalVeterinary/SafetyHealth/ProductSafetyInformation/ucm130321.htm.

U.S. Justice Department. (2005). *A guide to disability rights laws*. [Online.] Retrieved March 2, 2012, from http://www.ada.gov/cguide.htm.

U.S. Office of Personnel Management. (1993). *Federal employee entitlements under the Family and Medical Leave Act of 1993*. [Online.] Retrieved July 15, 2003, from http://www.opm.gov/compconf/Postconf00/leave/Herzbrg1.htm.

U.S. Office of Personnel Management (1997, April 11). *Memorandum for the heads of executive departments and agencies*. [Online.] Retrieved July 15, 2003, from http://www.opm.gov/oca/leave/html/fam pres.htm.

Uttal, L. & Han, C. (2011). Taiwanese immigrant mothers' childcare preferences: Socialization for bicultural competency. *Cultural Diversity and Ethnic Minority Psychology, 17*(4), 437–443. DOI: 10.1037/a0025435.

Vaish, A., & Striano, T. (2004). Is visual reference necessary? Contributions of facial versus vocal cues in 12-month-olds' social referencing behavior. *Developmental Science, 7*(3), 261–269.

Van Den Bergh, N., & Cooper, L. B. (Eds.). (1986). *Feminist visions for social work*. Silver Springs, MD: National Association of Social Workers.

Van der Kolk, B. (2005). Developmental trauma disorder. *Psychiatric Annals, 35*(4), 401.

Vanderplasschen, W., Wolf, J., Rapp, R. C., & Broekaert, E. (2007). Effectiveness of different models of case management for substance-abusing populations. *Journal of Psychoactive Drugs, 39*(1), 81–95.

Van Goozen, S. H. M., Matthys, W., Cohen-Kettenis, P. T., Thisjssen, J. H. H., & Van Engeland, H. (1998). Adrenal androgens and aggression in conduct disorder among prepubertal boys and normal controls. *Biological Psychiatry, 43*, 156–158.

Van Soest, D. (1994). Strange bedfellows: A call for reordering national priorities from three social justice perspectives. *Social Work, 39*(6), 710–717.

Van Soest, D. (1995). Peace and Social Justice. In *Encyclopedia of social work* (19th ed., Vol. 3, pp. 1810–1817). Washington, DC: National Association of Social Workers.

Vartanian, L. R., Giant, C. L., & Passino, R. M. (2001). "Ally McBeal vs. Arnold Schwarzenegger": Comparing mass media, interpersonal feedback and gender as predictors of satisfaction with body thinness and muscularity. *Social Behavior and Personality, 29*, 711–723.

Vermeulen, A. (1994). Andropause, fact or fiction? In G. Berg & M. Hammar (Eds.), *The modern management of the menopause* (pp. 567–577). New York: The Parthenon Publishing Group.

Vermeulen, A., & Kaufman, J. M. (1995). Ageing of the hypthalamo-pituitary-testicular axis in men. *Hormone Research, 43*, 25–28.

Vestergaard, M., Mork, A., Madsen, K. M., & Olsen, J. (2005). Paternal age and epilepsy in the offspring. *European Journal of Epidemiology, 20*, 1003–1005.

Viadero, D. (2003, June 18). Researcher insists NYC vouchers benefit black students. *Education Week, 22*(41), 16.

Vin-Raviv, N., Hillyer, G. C., Hershman, D. L., Galea, S., Leoce, N., Bovbjerg, D. H., et al. (2013). Racial disparities in posttraumatic stress after diagnosis of localized breast cancer: The BQUAL study. *Journal of the National Cancer Institute, 105*(8), 563–572.

Vogt, M. C., Paeger, L., Hess, S., Steculorum, S. M., Awazawa, M., Hampel, B., et al. (2014). Neonatal insulin action impairs hypothalamic neurocircuit formation in response to maternal high-fat feeding. *Cell, 156*(3), 495–509.

Waite, L. J., & Gallagher, M. (2000). *The case for marriage*. New York: Doubleday.

Waldfogel, J. (2001). *The future of child protection*. Cambridge, MA: Harvard University Press.

Waldman, M., Nicholson, S., Adilov, N., & Williams, J. (2008). Autism prevalence and precipitation rates in California, Oregon, and Washington Counties. *Archives of Pediatric and Adolescent Medicine, 162*(11), 1026–1034.

Walker, H. (1998, May 31). Youth violence: Society's problem. *Eugene Register Guard*, 1C.

Waller, M. R., & Bitler, M. P. (2008). The link between couples' pregnancy intentions and behavior: Does it matter who is asked? *Perspectives on Sexual & Reproductive Health, 40*(4), 194–201.

Wang, H., & Amato, P. (2000). Predictors of divorce adjustment: Stressors, resources, and definitions. *Journal of Marriage and the Family, 62*(3), 655–668.

Wang, S. H., & Morris, R. G. M. (2010). Hippocampal-neocritical interactions in memory formation, consolidation, and reconsolidation. *Annual Review of Psychology, 61,* 49–79.

Ward, R. A. (1993). Marital happiness and household equity in later life. *Journal of Marriage and the Family, 55,* 427–438.

Ward, R. A., & Spitze, G. D. (2004). Marital implications of parent–adult child coresidence: A longitudinal view. *Journals of Gerontology: Series B, 59B*(1), S2–S8.

Waters, S. F., Virmani, E. A., Thompson, R. A., Meyer, S., Raikes, H., & Jochem, R. (2010). Emotion regulation and attachment: Unpacking two constructs and their association. *Journal of Psychopathology & Behavioral Assessment, 32*(1), 37–47. DOI: 10.1007/s10862-009-9163-z.

Watkins, D. R. (2009). Spiritual formation of older persons. *Journal of Religion, Spirituality, and Aging, 21*(1–2), 7–16.

Watson, J. B. (1925). *Behaviorism.* New York: W. W. Norton.

Wauterickx, N., Gouwy, A., & Pracke, P. (2006). Parental divorce and depression: Long-term effects on adult children. *Journal of Divorce & Remarriage, 45*(3/4), 43–68.

Webb, M. B., & Harden, B. J. (2003). Beyond child protection: Promoting mental health for children and families in the child welfare system. *Journal of Emotional and Behavioral Disorders, 11*(1), 49–58.

Weber, M. (1957). *The theory of social and economic organization.* New York: The Free Press of Glencoe.

Weber, M. (1958). *The Protestant ethic and the spirit of capitalism.* Translated by Talcott Parsons. New York: Scribner.

Weber, M. (1968). *Economy and society.* Translated by Guenther Roth and Claus Wittich. New York: Bedminster Press.

Weber, M. (1994). Class, status, party. In D. B. Grusky (Ed.), *Social stratification: Class, race, and gender in sociological perspective* (pp. 113–122). San Francisco: Westview Press.

Weick, A., Rapp, C., Sullivan, W. P., & Kisthardt, W. (1989). A strengths perspective for social work practice. *Social Work, 34*(4), 350–354.

Weiner, J. M., & Tilly, J. (2002). Population ageing in the United States of America: Implications for public programmes. *International Journal of Epidemiology, 31*(4), 776–781.

Weinstein, L. B. (2000). Mothers and methadone. *American Journal of Nursing, 100,* 13–40.

Weitzman, M., Gortmaker, S., & Sobol, A. (1992). Maternal smoking and behavior problems of children. *Pediatrics, 90*(3), 342–349.

Werner, E. F., Savitz, D., Janevic, T., Thung, S. F., Funai, E. F., & Lipkind, H. (2012). *Method of delivery and neonatal outcomes in preterm, small for gestational age infants.* Paper presented at the Society for Maternal-Fetal Medicine conference, February 9, 2012, Dallas, TX.

Wespes, E., & Schulman, C. C. (2002). Male andropause: Myth, reality, and treatment. *International Journal of Impotence Research, 14*(1), 93–98.

Westerhof, G. J., Bohlmeijer, E. T., & Webster, J. D. (2010). Reminiscence and mental health: A review of recent progress in theory, research, and intervention. *Aging & Society, 30,* 697–721.

Westheimer, R. K., & Lopater, S. (2004). *Human sexuality.* Baltimore, MD: Lippincott Williams & Wilkins.

Whaley, A. L. (2000). Differential risk perceptions for unintended pregnancy, STDs, and HIV/AIDS among urban adolescents: Some preliminary findings. *Journal of Genetic Psychology, 161*(4), 435–452.

White, P. (2002). Access to health care: Health insurance considerations for young adults with special health care needs/disabilities. *Pediatrics, 110*(6), 1328–1335.

Whiting, B. B., & Edwards, C. P. (1988). *Children of different worlds.* Cambridge, MA: Harvard University Press.

Wilcox, S. (1997). Age and gender in relation to body attitudes: Is there a double standard of aging? *Psychology of Women Quarterly, 21,* 549–565.

Williams, D. R., & Collins, C. (2001). Racial residential segregation: A fundamental cause of racial disparities in health. *Public Health Reports, 116*(5), 404–416.

Williams, N. R., Lindsey, E. W., Kurtz, P. D., & Jarvis, S. (2001). From trauma to resiliency: Lessons from former runaway and homeless youth. *Journal of Youth Studies, 4*(2), 233–253.

Williams, W. I. (2006). Complex trauma: Approaches to theory and treatment. *Journal of Loss and Trauma, 11*, 321–335.

Wilson, B. (2010). *Proven sex-ed programs get a boost from Obama.* National Public Radio. Retrieved February 28, 2012, from http://www.npr.org/templates/story/story.php?storyId=127514185.

Wink, P., & Dillon, M. (2002). Spiritual development across the adult life course: Findings from a longitudinal study. *Journal of Adult Development, 9*, 79–94.

Wink, P., Dillon, M., & Prettyman, A. (2007). Religion as moderator of the sense of control—health connection: Gender differences. *Journal of Religion, Spirituality, and Aging, 19*(4), 21–41.

Winterbottom, J., Smyth, R., Jacoby, A., & Baker, G. (2009). The effectiveness of preconception counseling to reduce adverse pregnancy outcome in women with epilepsy: What's the evidence? *Epilepsy & Behavior, 14*(2), 273–279.

Wintre, M. G., & Vallance, D. D. (1994). A developmental sequence in the comprehension of emotions: Intensity, multiple emotions, and valence. *Developmental Psychology, 39*, 509–514.

Women's International Network. (1997). Teen pregnancy a major problem in the U.S. *Women's International Network News, 23*(3), 69–70.

Women's International Network. (1998). Making pregnancy and childbirth safer. *Women's International Network News, 24*(4), 19.

Wood, S. A. (2006). Developmental issues in older drinkers' decisions: To drink or not to drink. *Alcoholism Treatment Quarterly, 24*(4), 99–118. DOI: 10.1300/J020v24n04_07.

Worden, J. W. (2009). *Grief counseling and grief therapy: A handbook for the mental health practitioner* (4th ed.). New York: Springer.

World Bank. (2012). *World factbook.* [Online.] Retrieved May 21, 2014, from https://www.cia.gov/library/publications/the-world-factbook/rankorder/2091rank.html.

World Health Organization. (2000). *The World Health Report.* Geneva: Author.

World Health Organization. (2003). *Family planning.* [Online.] Retrieved July 15, 2003, from http://www.who.int/reproductive-health/family_planning.

World Health Organization. (2011). International classification of diseases (10th ed.). Geneva: World Health Organization.

World Health Organization. (2013). Disability and Health. [Online.] Retrieved July 11, 2014, from http://www.who.int/mediacentre/factsheets/fs352/en/.

Writing Group for the Women's Health Initiative Investigators. (2002). Risks and benefits of estrogen plus progestin in healthy postmenopausal women. *JAMA, 288*(3), 321–333.

Wrosch, C., & Heckhausen, J. (1999). Control processes before and after passing a developmental deadline: Activation and deactivation of intimate relationship goals. *Journal of Personality & Social Psychology, 77*(2), 415–427.

Xu, B., Roos, J. L., Dexheimer, P., Boone, B., Plummer, B., Levy, S., *et al.* (2011). Exome sequencing supports a de novo mutational paradigm for schizophrenia. *Nature Genetics, 43*, 864–868.

Yassin, A. A., Akhras, F., El-Sakka, A. I., & Saad, F. (2011). Cardiovascular diseases and erectile dysfunction: The two faces of the coin of androgen deficiency. *Andrologia, 43*(1), 1–8.

Yoon, D. P., & Lee, E. K. (2007). The impact of religiousness, spirituality, and social support on psychological well-being among older adults in rural areas. *Journal of Gerontological Social Work, 48*(3–4), 281–298.

Zabin, L., Hirsch, M. B., Smith, B. A., & Hardy, J. B. (1986). Evaluation of a pregnancy prevention program for urban teenagers. *Family Planning Perspectives, 18*(3), 119–126.

Zaider, T. I., Johnson, J. G., & Cockell, S. J. (2002). Psychiatric disorders associated with the onset and persistence of bulimia nervosa and binge eating disorder during adolescence. *Journal of Youth and Adolescence, 31*(5), 319–329.

Zald, M., & McCarthy, J. (1987). *Social movements in an organizational society.* New Brunswick, NJ: Transaction.

Ziegler, J. C., & Goswami, U. (2005). Reading acquisition, developmental dyslexia, and skilled reading across languages: A psycholinguistic brain size theory. *Psychological Bulletin, 131*(1), 3–29.

Zill, N., Morrison, D. R., & Coiro, M. J. (1993). Long-term effects of parental divorce on parent–child relationships, adjustment, and achievement in young adulthood. *Journal of Family Psychology, 7,* 91–103.

Zimmerman, P. (2004). Attachment representations and characteristics of friendship relations during adolescence. *Journal of Experimental Child Psychology, 88*(1), 83–101.

Glossary/Index

Page numbers in italics refer to figures. Page numbers in bold refer to tables.
Abbreviations used in index entries:

ADHD: attention deficit hyperactivity disorder
GLBT: gay, lesbian, bisexual, and transgendered
SES: socioeconomic status

178–9, 205; third trimester **173**; unwanted 176, 177; workplace policies on 199–200, 452

prejudice: The attitudes, beliefs, and stereotypes that one holds about others 146, 147, 168; ageism 381, 382; approach to 151, 152; attribution theory applied to 148–9; conflict theory applied to 149; demographic shifts 447–8, 458; discrimination *v.* 146, 147; heterosexism and 311–12; homosexual 150, 311–12; microaggressions 153–5, 168; origins 148–50; social learning theory applied to 149; theories 147–50

prenatal issues 171–208

prenatal testing 188–90; ethical dilemma 189–90, 191

preoperational stage: The stage in which from two to seven years of age, children show characteristics of egocentrism, animism, centration, classification, seriation, and irreversibility 79

presbycusis: A term for normal hearing loss 392

presbyopia: The inability to focus on nearby objects 393

"present oriented" approach (strengths perspective) 54

preterm: Babies born three weeks or more before the pregnancy has reached full term (35 weeks or less) 174, 184

primary oppression: The direct consequences of perceived group differences 151

primary sex characteristics: Aspects of development that are directly related to reproduction 279

privatization, health care 112

problem conceptualization 7, 31–3; strengths perspective and 50–1

problem solving 356

problem-focused approach 51; medical model critique of 77; strengths perspective *v.* 51, 53–4

Progressive Era 159

privilege: Refers to the advantages that a dominant group in society has 146–7

processed foods 443–4

projection: A defense mechanism described by Sigmund Freud (1914) that allows people to deny owning uncomfortable feelings or perceived negative characteristics by pointing out these same negative characteristics in others 84, **84**, 148, 150

proximal defenses: Mechanisms we use to keep thoughts of death out of our awareness. This would include suppressing death thoughts and denying personal vulnerability to disease and premature death 413

proximodistal development: Principle that

development of the trunk area occurs before development of the extremities 216

psychoanalysis: critique 86–7; goal 84 *see also* psychosexual development

psychoanalytic theory 82; defense mechanisms 84, **84**

psychodynamic theories 82–92; Erikson's psychosocial development 87–92; Freud's psychosexual 82–7; Gestalt therapy based on 99; transactional analysis based on 99

psychological changes, late adulthood 396–402

psychological disease *see* mental illnesses

psychological health, parents 180–2

psychological level, biopsychosocial approach 30, 31

psychological problems, childless couples 359

psychological stress: after trauma 323–4; health disparities and 369; menopause 363; midlife crisis 364–5

psychosexual development 60; application 85–6; characteristics **60;** child 83, 84–5; critique of 86–7; Freud's work 59, 82, 85, 103; key concepts **58;** sexual development in adolescents 295; stages **83**

psychosexual development theory 10, 82–7, 103; Erikson's theory integration 90–1

psychosocial development 61, 87–92, 103; adolescence **88,** 278, 287, 288, 295; aging theories of 89, 92, 357; application 89–90, 181–2, 206; characteristics **61;** children **88;** critique of 91–2; key concepts **61;** middle age, implications 357, 377; middle childhood **88,** 247; "normal," struggles in 92; Piaget's theory integration 90–1; religiosity and spirituality 331–2; sexual development in adolescents 295; stages 87, **88–9,** 90; young adults **88;** *see also* Erikson, Erik

psychosocial orientation 14–15

psychosocial theories of aging 402–5

PTSD *see* posttraumatic stress disorder (PTSD)

puberty: Time in life characterized by rapid physical and sexual growth, and it is often accompanied by hormonal, emotional, and other changes 279–80, 293, 315; blocking, intersex children 223

punishment: The application of something negative or the removal of something positive to weaken or reduce the frequency of a behavior 94, 261–4

Punnett squares 73, *74, 75*

"pure" behaviorist approach 92

"pure theorists" 13

purging 290

queer theory: A paradigm that examines socially constructed labels, categories, and relationships that

temperament styles 224

temporal lobes: Parts of the brain responsible for hearing, language, and memory 65

Temporary Assistance for Needy Families (TANF) 417

teratogens: Substances that can cause birth defects 182–6

terminal button: Little sacs containing neurotransmitters. When an electrical impulse travels down the axon of a neuron, it triggers the release of a neurotransmitter, which enters into the synaptic gap 68–9

terminal illness 431, 432

territorial community: Term used to describe the geographical boundaries that bind people together 164

terror management theory: Explains how we use defense mechanisms to deal with thoughts of death 87, 413

tertiary oppression: Perpetrated by members of an oppressed group when they seek acceptance by supporting the dominant group's oppressive acts 151

testes **72**, 221

testosterone 221, 227

testosterone replacement therapy 364

thalamus: Structure at the top of the brainstem that serves as a relay station for sensory information. It sorts information and sends it to other parts of the brain for interpretation. It also seems to be involved in sleep and wakefulness 64

theory: A set of ideas or concepts that when considered together help to explain certain phenomena and allow us to predict behavior and other events 5; application in social work 15–17; best "fit" 14–15; debate over 4–5, 7–9, 13–15; eclectic use of 12–15; evaluative criteria for 9, 10; interactions of 6–7; knowledge types and 7–9; multiple *v.* single, use 13–14; quality of 9–12; research pitfalls and 10–11; role 4–7; single use 13–14; single use, argument against 14–15; subcategories 5–6

therapeutic relationship 360

thinking, abstract 79

Thomas, Alexander 224, 244

tinnitus 392

toxoplasmosis 186

traditions 130

transactional analysis: A therapeutic technique that is based in psychodynamic theory and shares the notion that maladaptive behavioral patterns established in childhood often get in the way of well-being in later life 99, 102

transactions, in ecological theory 46, **46**

transgender: A term to describe when a person's gender identity is not congruent with her or his assigned sex at birth 220–1, 222

trauma: Any experience that is emotionally distressing enough to overwhelm an individual's ability to cope, often leaving the individual feeling powerless 323

trauma theory 323–5

trauma-focused cognitive behavioral therapy 229

traumatic brain injury (TBI) 65–6

triarchic theory of intelligence: Sternberg's theory that places emphasis on people's environmental context as well as how they adapt to their environment 250–2, 275

triple jeopardy: Used to describe "female ethnic-minority elderly." Members of this particular group face discrimination in three ways—being a woman, elderly, and a member of an ethnic minority group—putting them even more at risk for poverty than other older adults 425

trisomy *see* Down syndrome

trust **88**; toward a stranger 220

ultrasound: Procedure that uses sound waves to capture images of the fetus and can offer views of basic anatomy 188–9

unconditioned response: A response that occurs naturally or has not been learned 93

unconditioned stimulus: Something that occurs naturally that elicits a response 93

unconscious *see* defense mechanisms; id

underemployment 441–2, 458

unemployment 442, 458; ecological theory 43

unethical experiment 93

"unfinished business" 99

University of Michigan 349

unoccupied play **261**

unplanned pregnancy 176–9

utilitarian approach: A view of justice, which posits that justice is that which supports the "greatest good for the greatest number of people" 157, 350

value judgments 11

value process orientation, feminist theory and 129

verbal abuse, elders *420*

very low birth weight: Babies who weigh less than 3 pounds at birth 174